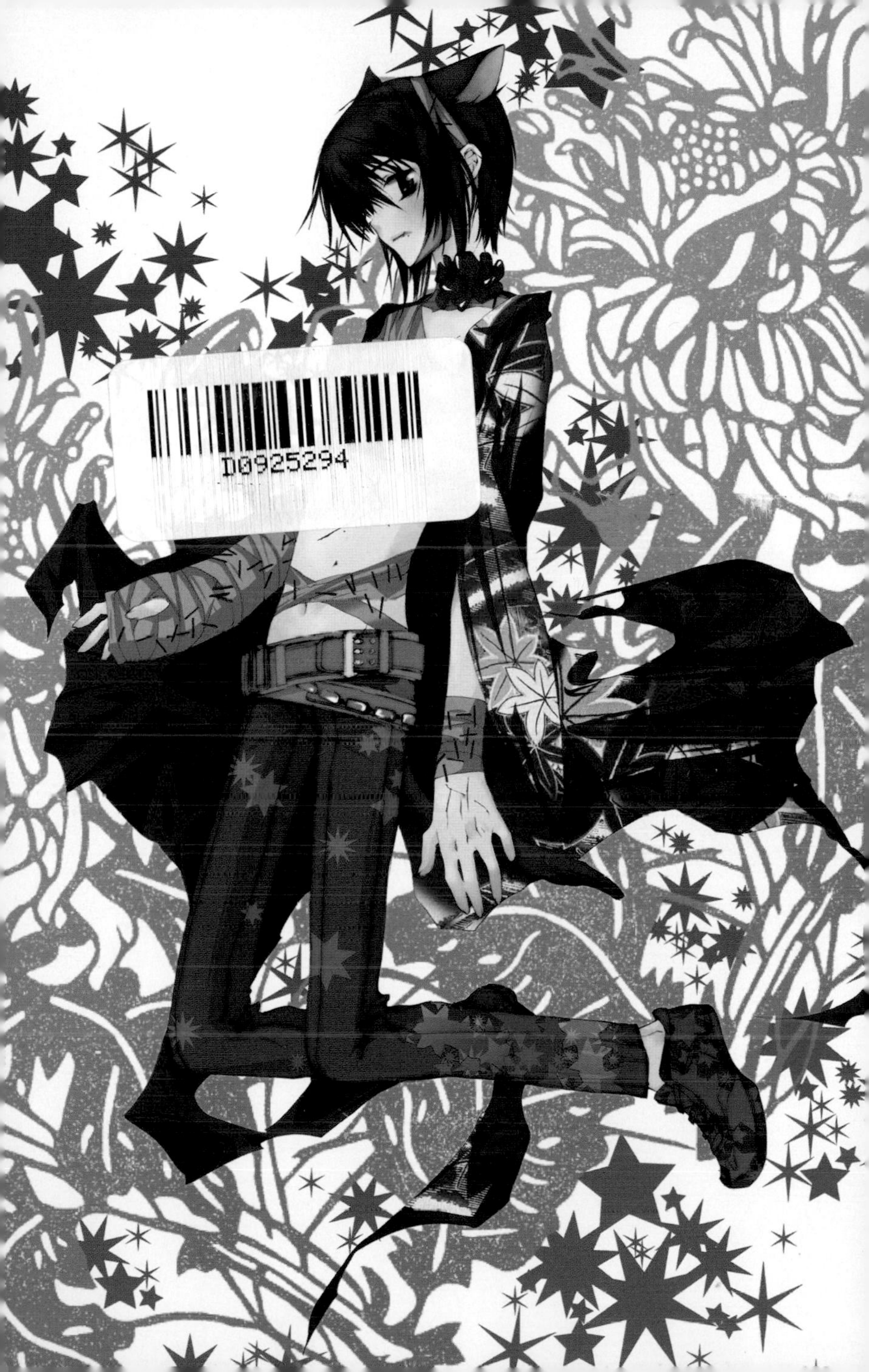

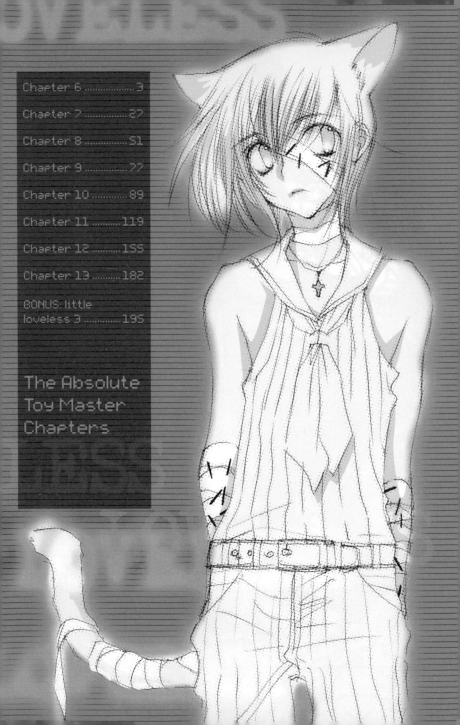

The Absolute
Toy Master
Chapters

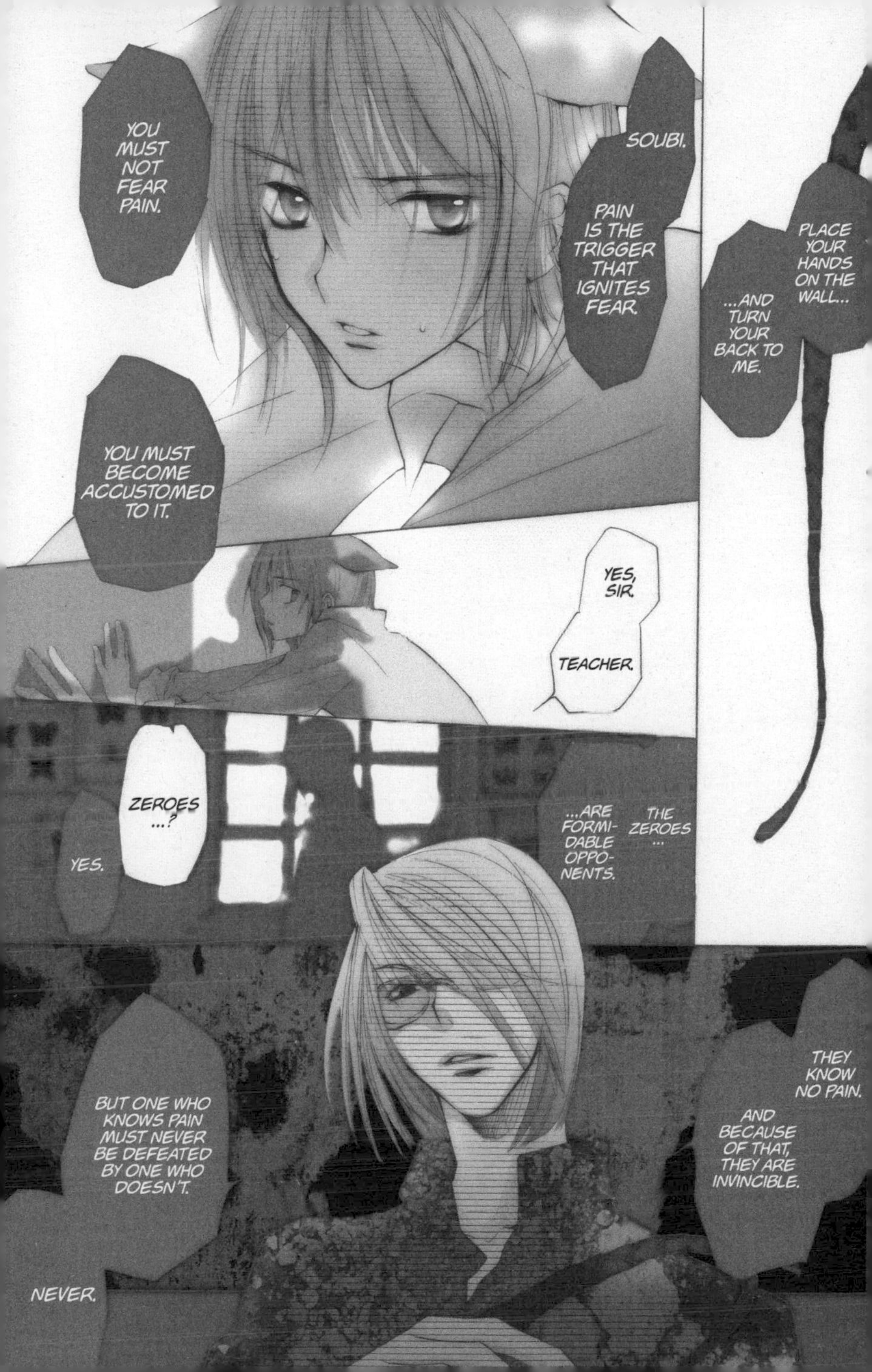
PLACE YOUR HANDS ON THE WALL...
...AND TURN YOUR BACK TO ME.
SOUBI.
PAIN IS THE TRIGGER THAT IGNITES FEAR.
YOU MUST NOT FEAR PAIN.
YOU MUST BECOME ACCUSTOMED TO IT.
YES, SIR.
TEACHER.
THE ZEROES...
...ARE FORMIDABLE OPPONENTS.
ZEROES...?
YES.
THEY KNOW NO PAIN.
AND BECAUSE OF THAT, THEY ARE INVINCIBLE.
BUT ONE WHO KNOWS PAIN MUST NEVER BE DEFEATED BY ONE WHO DOESN'T.
NEVER.

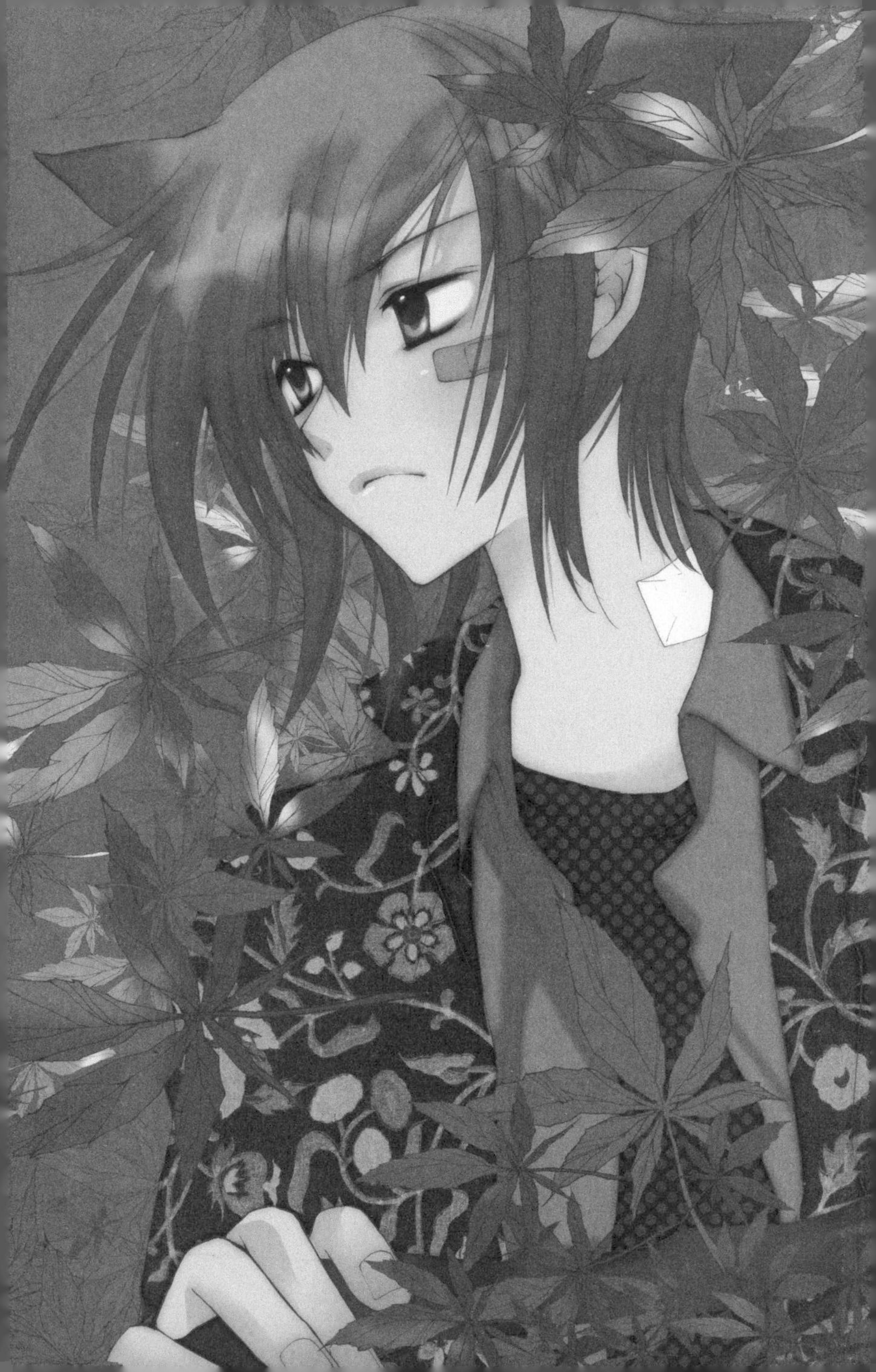

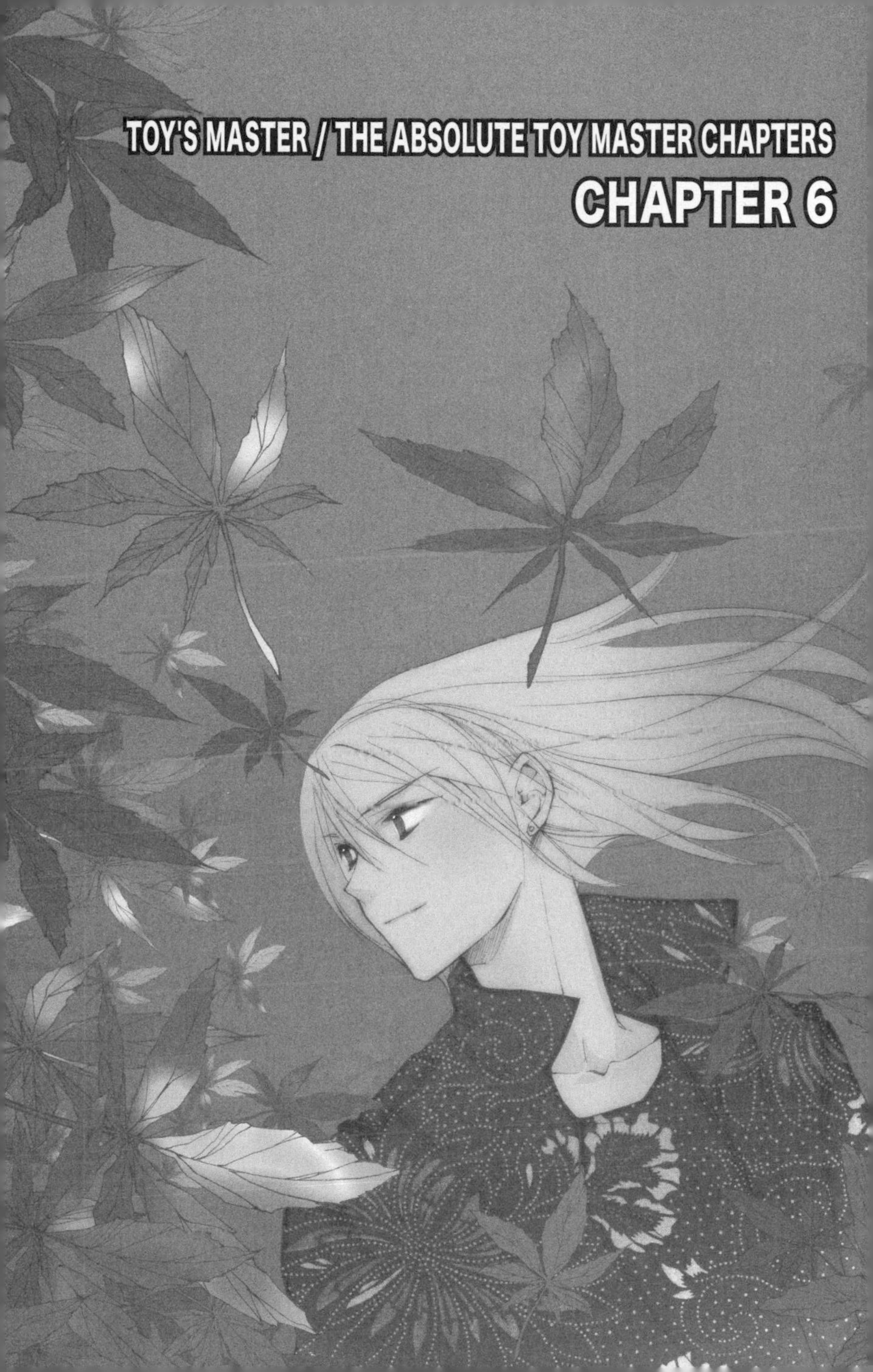
TOY'S MASTER // THE ABSOLUTE TOY MASTER CHAPTERS
CHAPTER 6

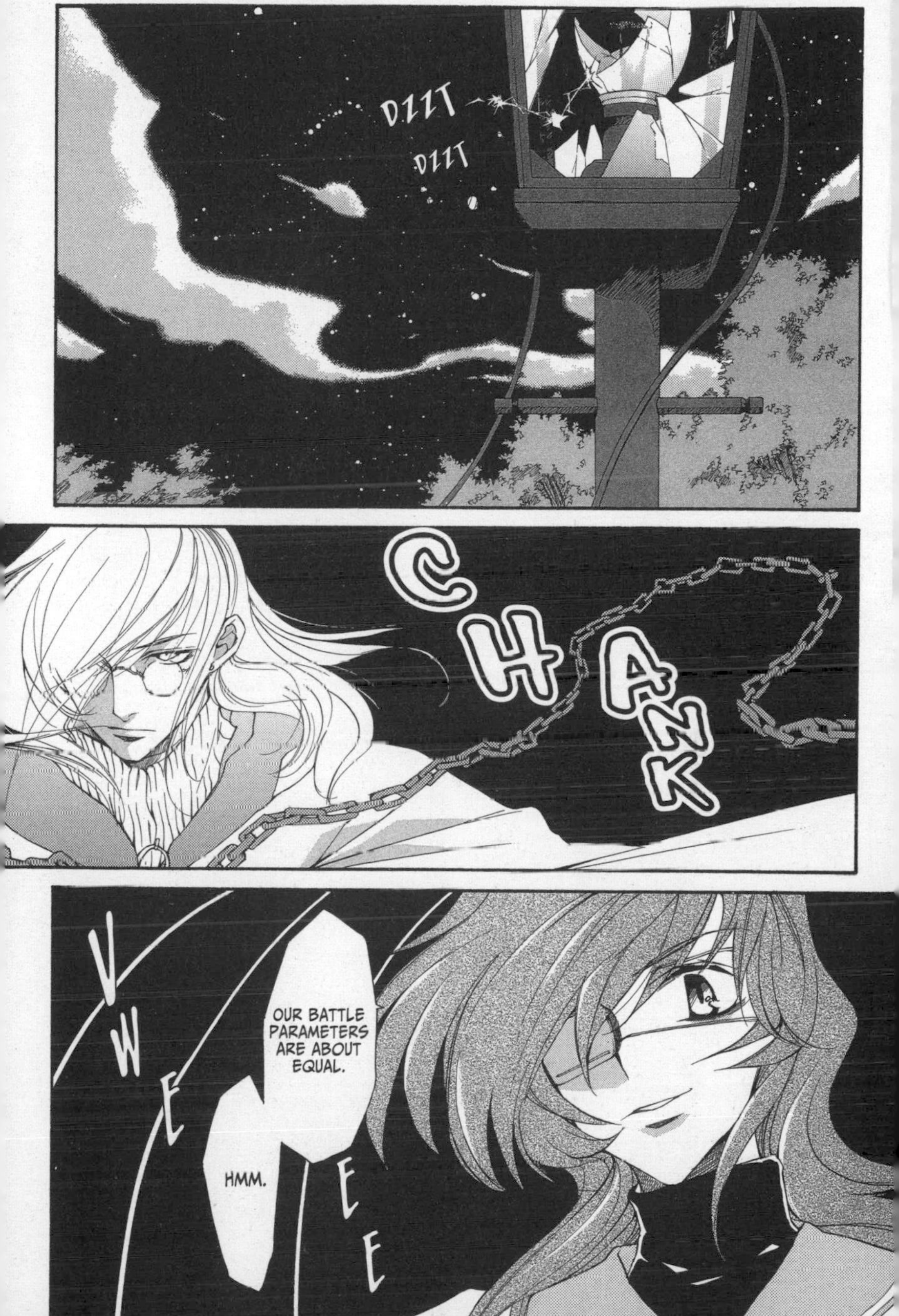
DZZT
DZZT
CHANK
OUR BATTLE PARAMETERS ARE ABOUT EQUAL.
HMM.
VWEEEE

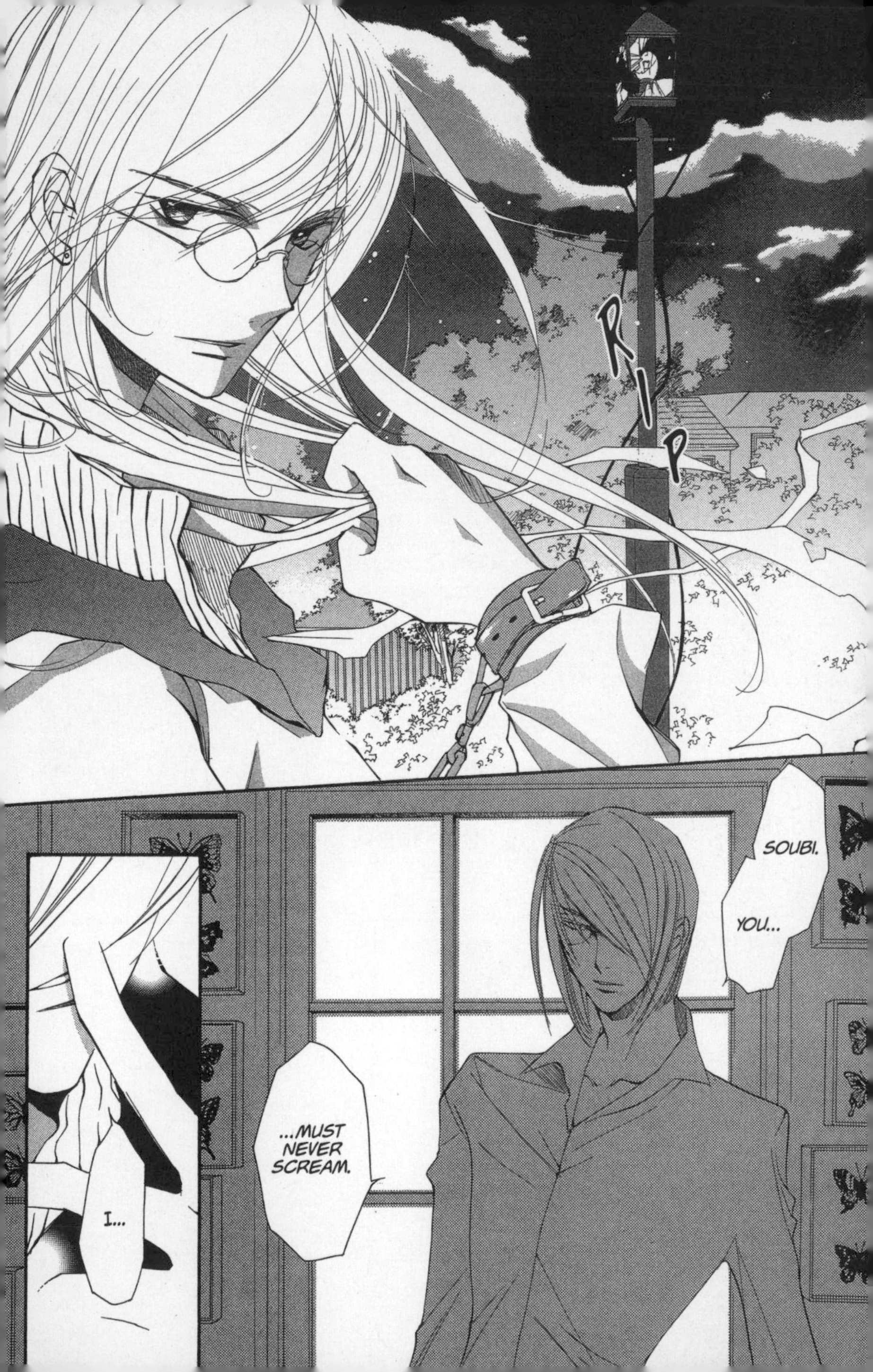
RIP
SOUBI.
YOU...
...MUST NEVER SCREAM.
I...

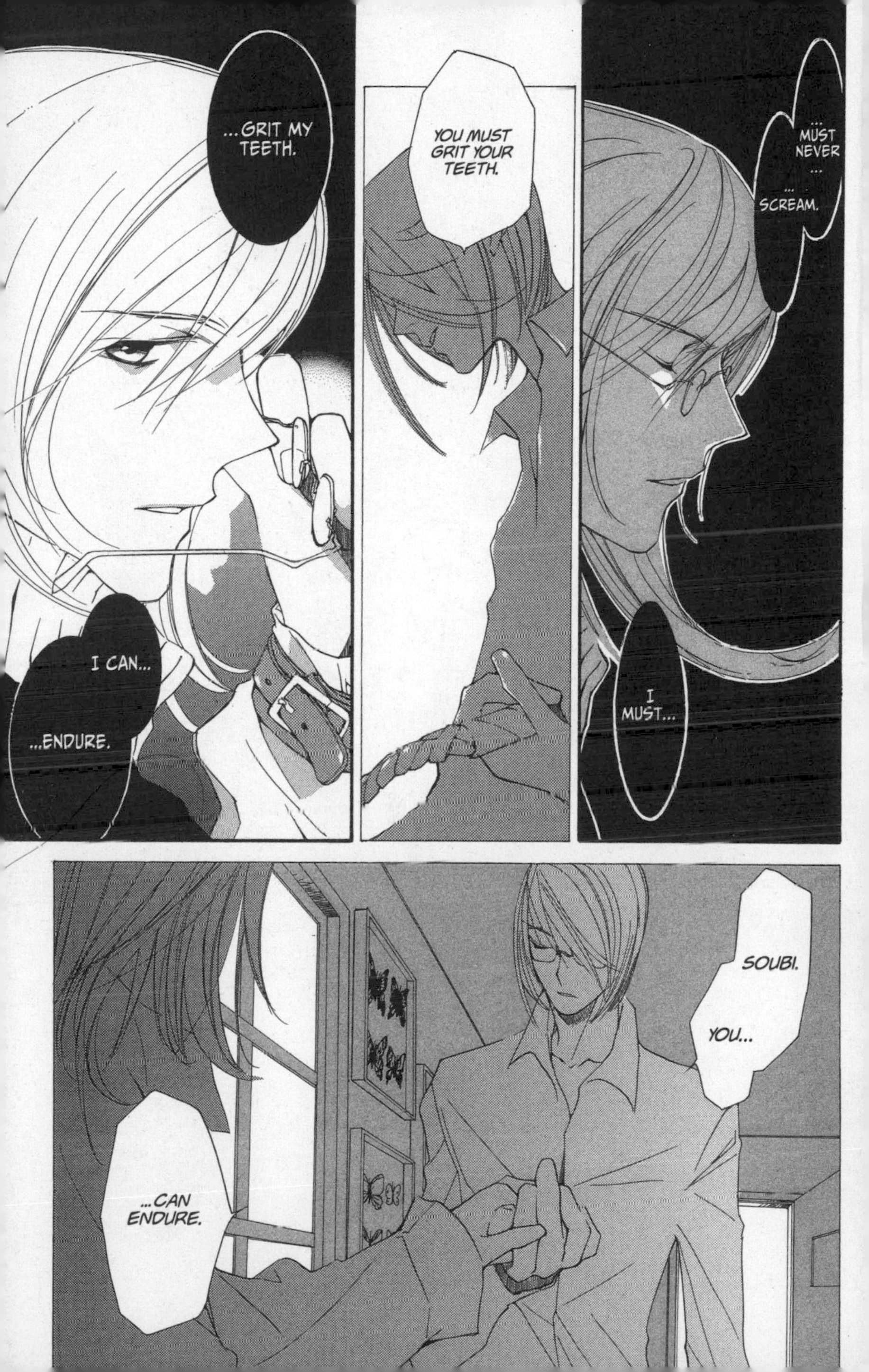
... MUST NEVER ... ... SCREAM.
I MUST...
YOU MUST GRIT YOUR TEETH.
...GRIT MY TEETH.
I CAN...
...ENDURE.
SOUBI.
YOU...
...CAN ENDURE.

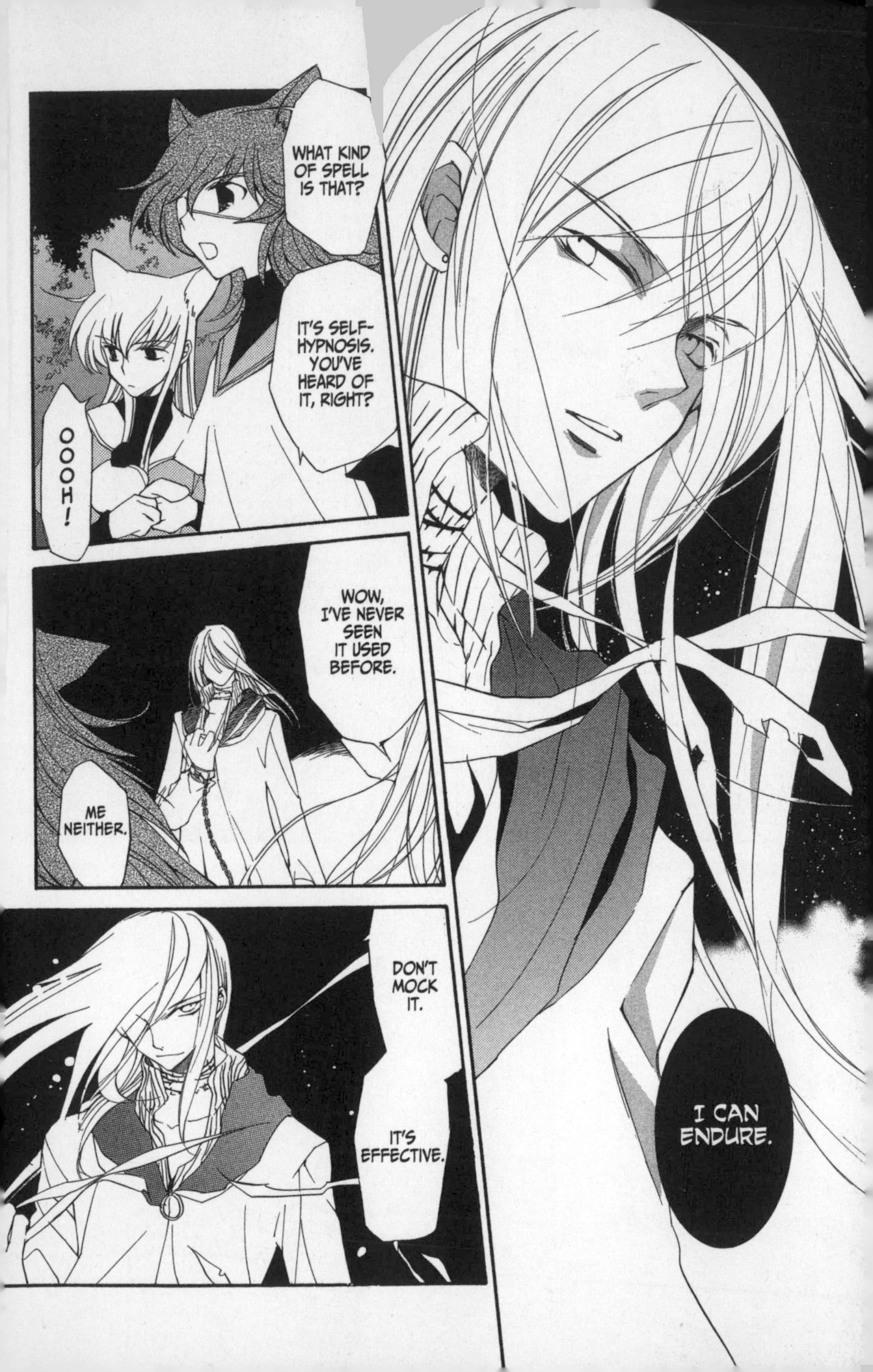
I CAN ENDURE.
WHAT KIND OF SPELL IS THAT?
IT'S SELF-HYPNOSIS. YOU'VE HEARD OF IT, RIGHT?
OOOH!
WOW, I'VE NEVER SEEN IT USED BEFORE.
ME NEITHER.
DON'T MOCK IT.
IT'S EFFECTIVE.

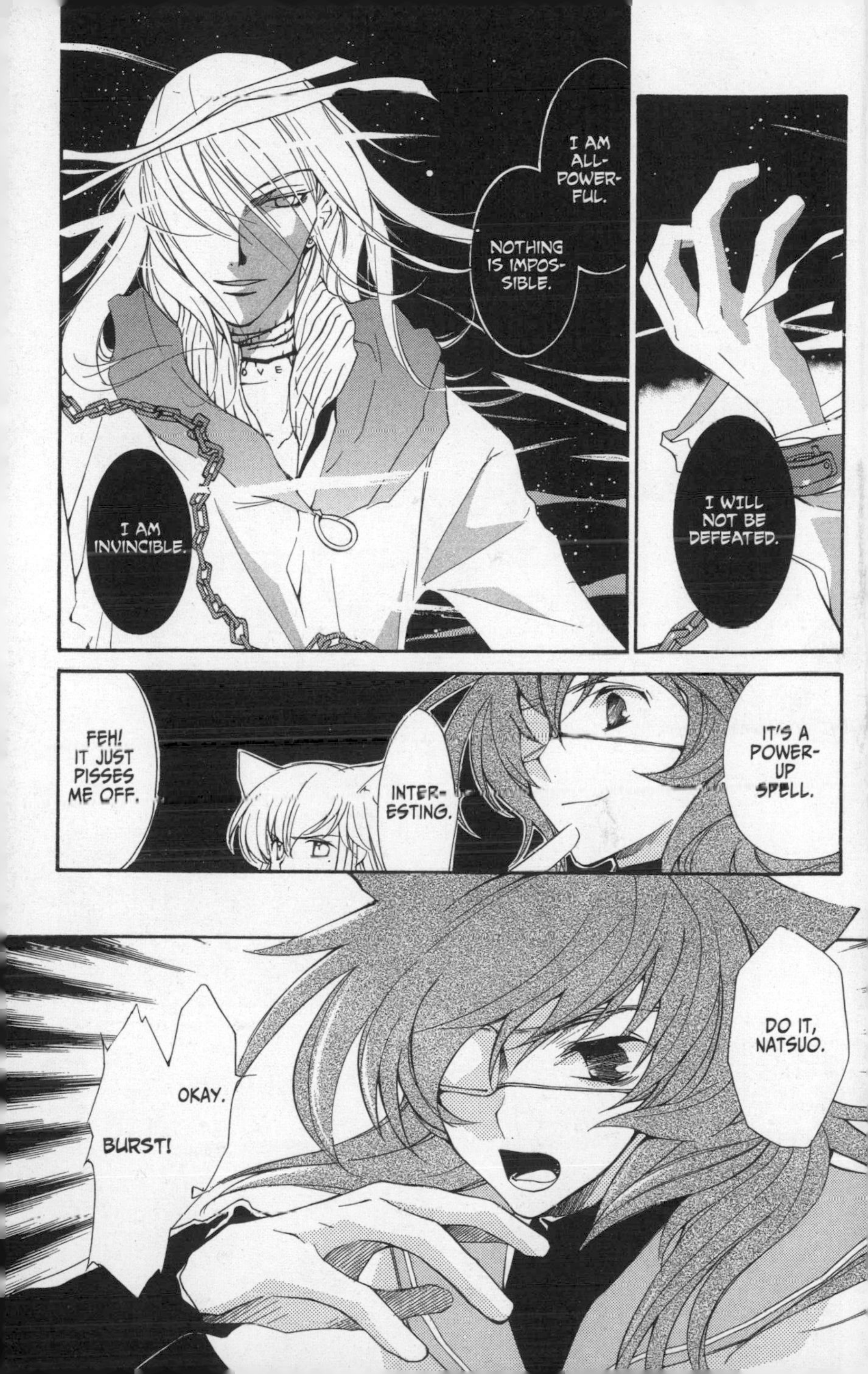
I WILL NOT BE DEFEATED.
I AM ALL-POWERFUL.
NOTHING IS IMPOSSIBLE.
I AM INVINCIBLE.
IT'S A POWER-UP SPELL.
INTERESTING.
FEH! IT JUST PISSES ME OFF.
DO IT, NATSUO.
OKAY.
BURST!

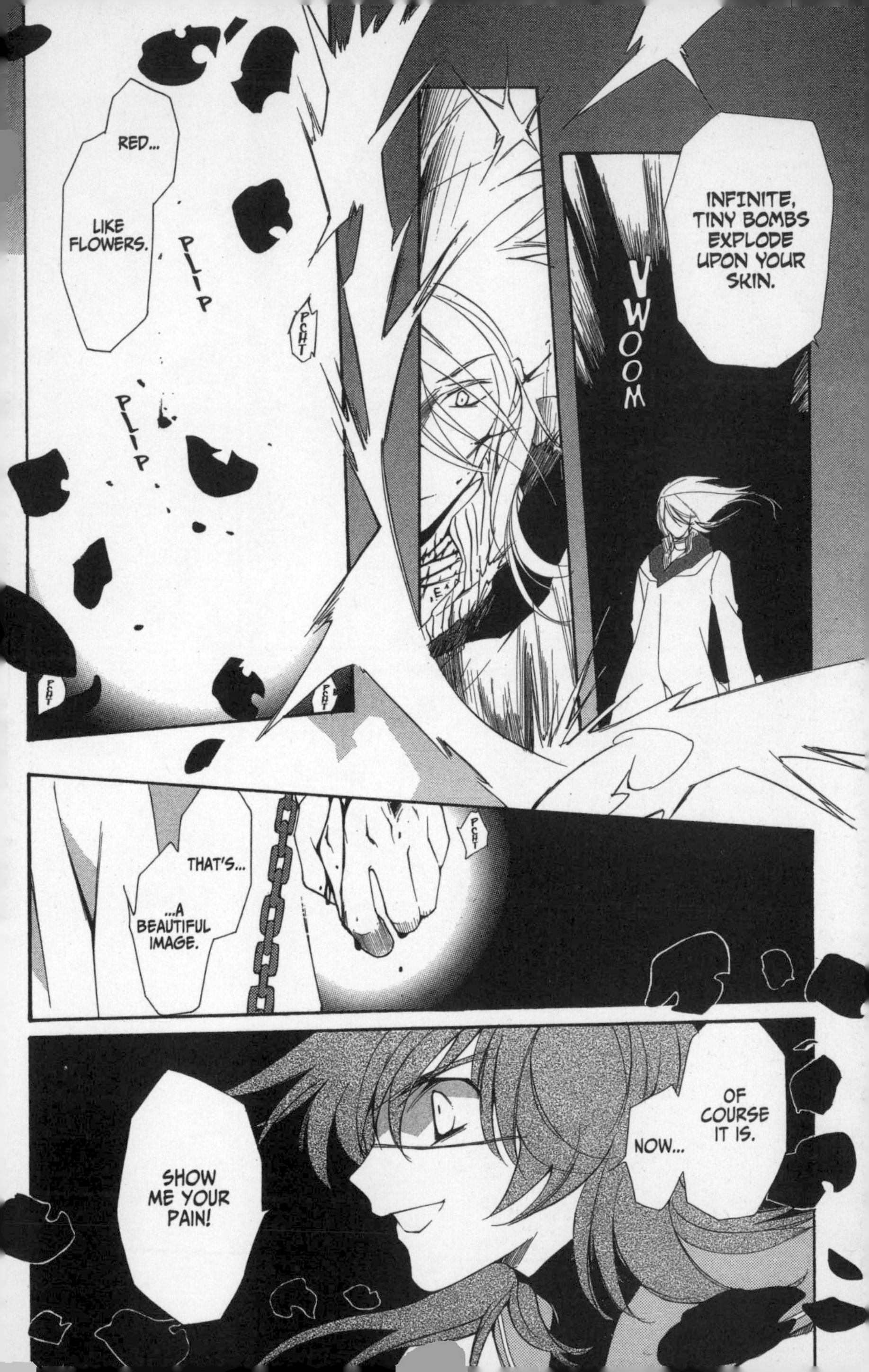

INFINITE, TINY BOMBS EXPLODE UPON YOUR SKIN.
VWOOM
RED...
LIKE FLOWERS.
PLIP
PCHT
PLIP
PCHT
PCHT
PCHT
THAT'S...
...A BEAUTIFUL IMAGE.
OF COURSE IT IS.
NOW...
SHOW ME YOUR PAIN!

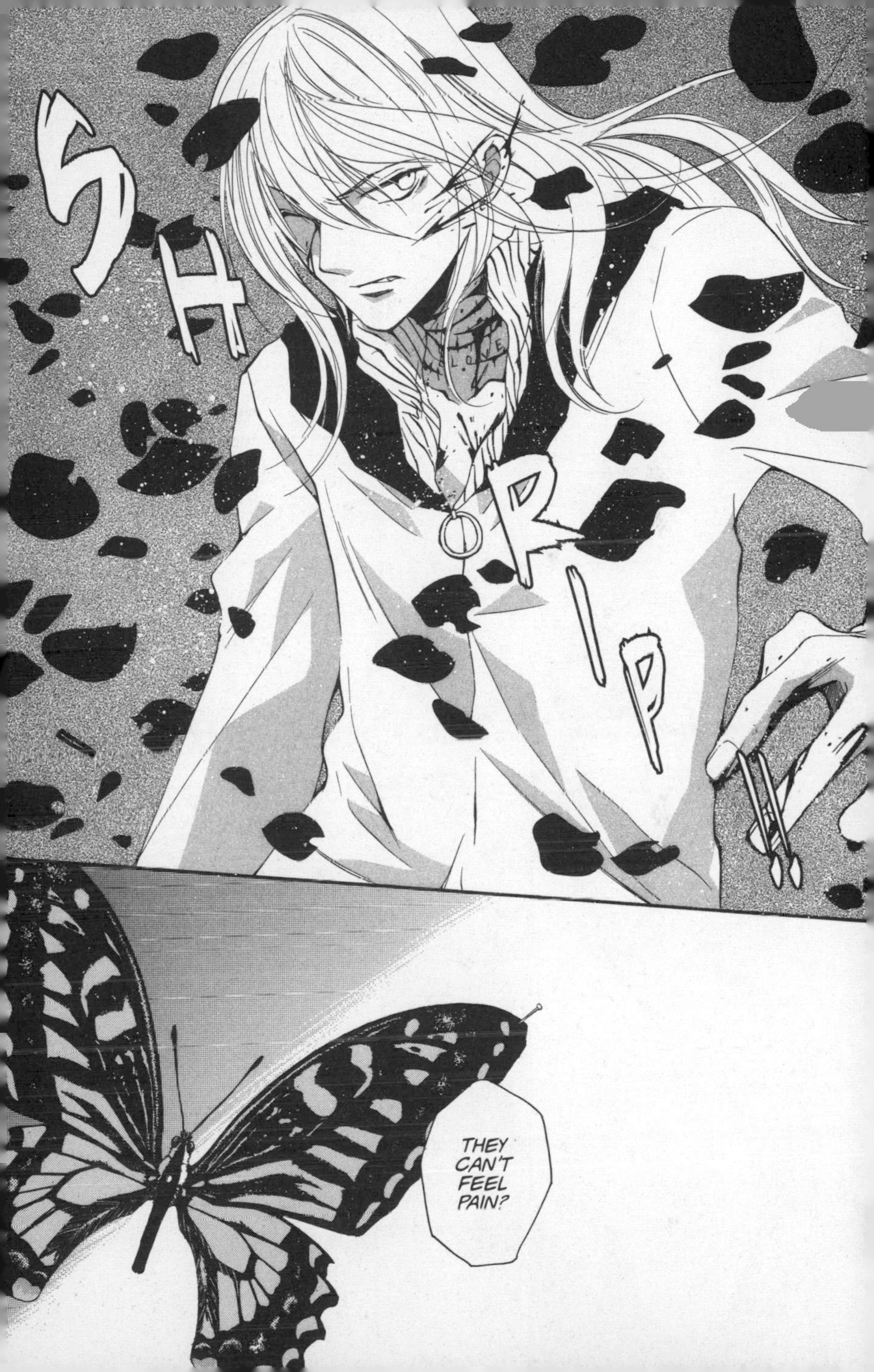
SH
LOVE
RIP
THEY CAN'T FEEL PAIN?

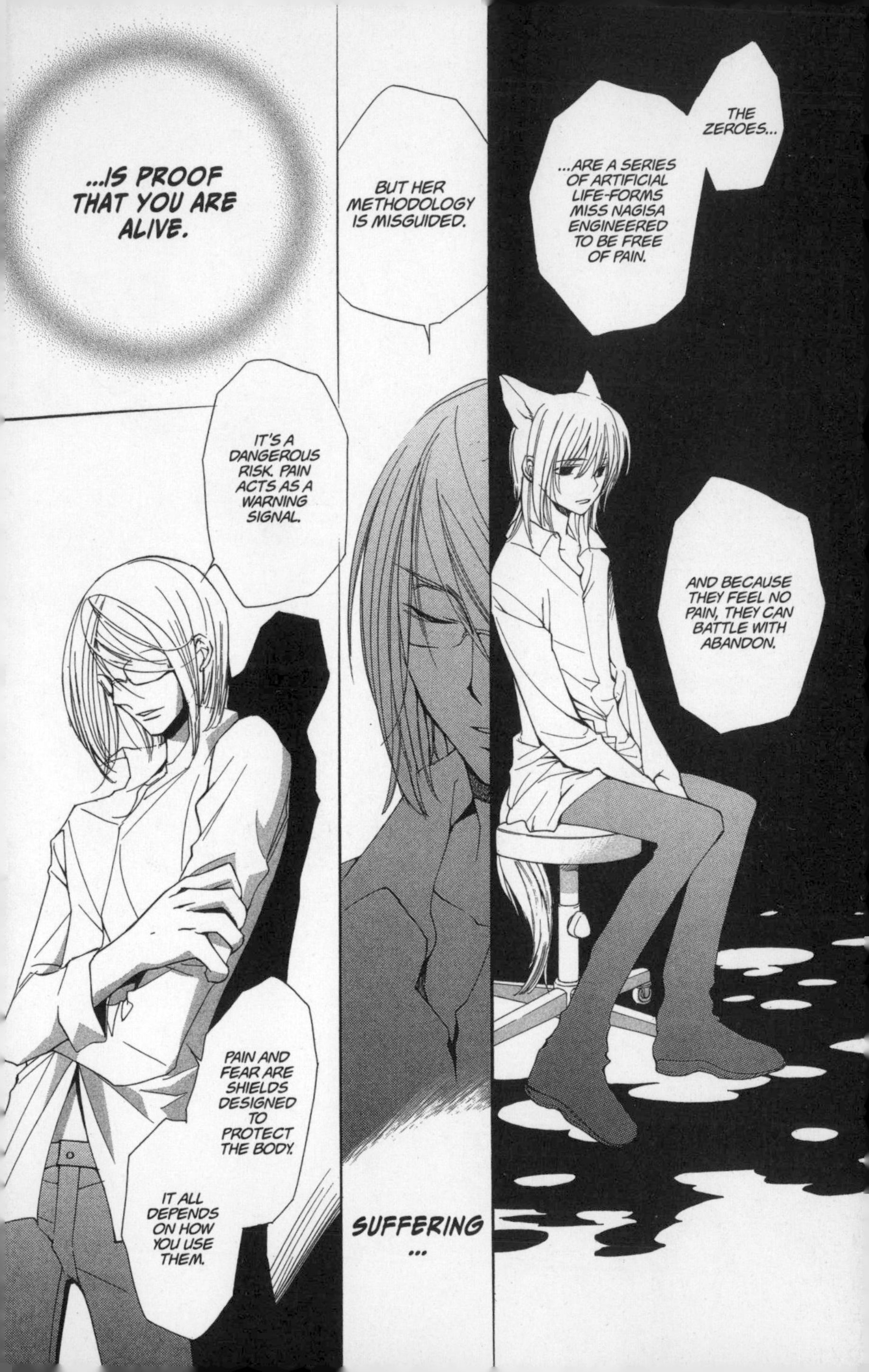
THE ZEROES...
...ARE A SERIES OF ARTIFICIAL LIFE-FORMS MISS NAGISA ENGINEERED TO BE FREE OF PAIN.
AND BECAUSE THEY FEEL NO PAIN, THEY CAN BATTLE WITH ABANDON.
BUT HER METHODOLOGY IS MISGUIDED.
SUFFERING ...
...IS PROOF THAT YOU ARE ALIVE.
IT'S A DANGEROUS RISK. PAIN ACTS AS A WARNING SIGNAL.
PAIN AND FEAR ARE SHIELDS DESIGNED TO PROTECT THE BODY.
IT ALL DEPENDS ON HOW YOU USE THEM.

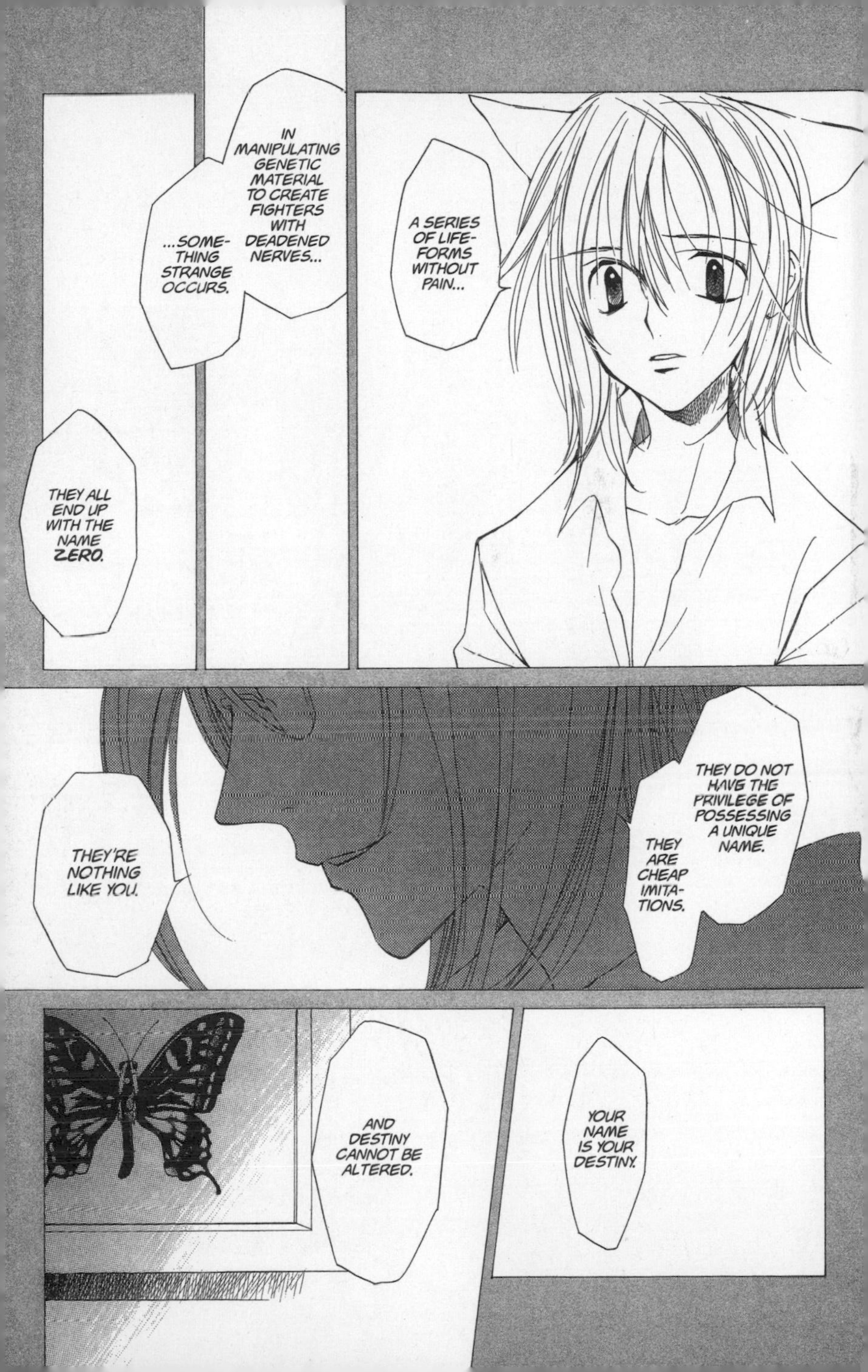
A SERIES OF LIFE-FORMS WITHOUT PAIN...
IN MANIPULATING GENETIC MATERIAL TO CREATE FIGHTERS WITH DEADENED NERVES...
...SOME-THING STRANGE OCCURS.
THEY ALL END UP WITH THE NAME ZERO.
THEY DO NOT HAVE THE PRIVILEGE OF POSSESSING A UNIQUE NAME.
THEY ARE CHEAP IMITA-TIONS.
THEY'RE NOTHING LIKE YOU.
YOUR NAME IS YOUR DESTINY.
AND DESTINY CANNOT BE ALTERED.

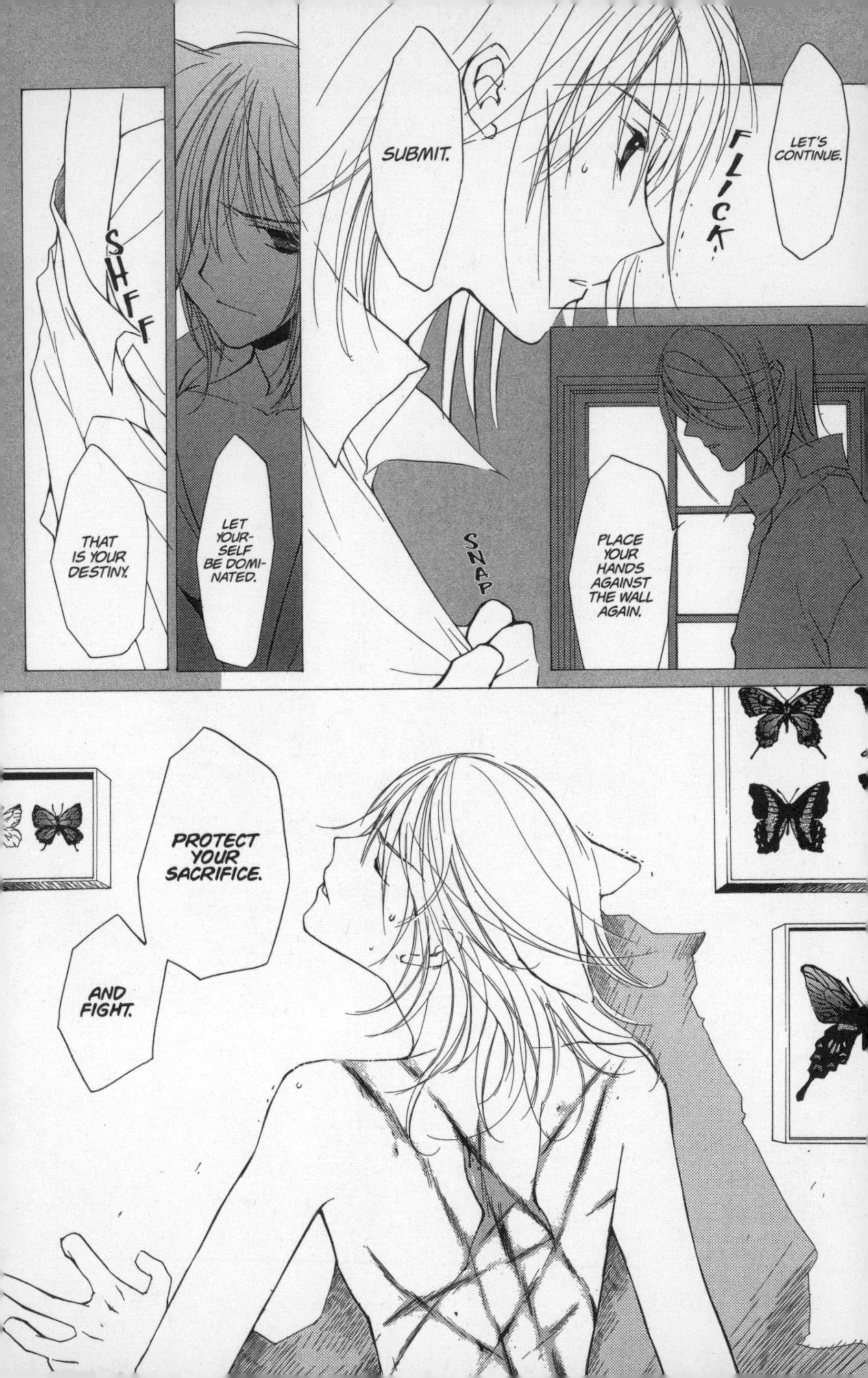
FLICK
LET'S CONTINUE.
PLACE YOUR HANDS AGAINST THE WALL AGAIN.
SUBMIT.
SNAP
LET YOURSELF BE DOMINATED.
SHFF
THAT IS YOUR DESTINY.
PROTECT YOUR SACRIFICE.
AND FIGHT.

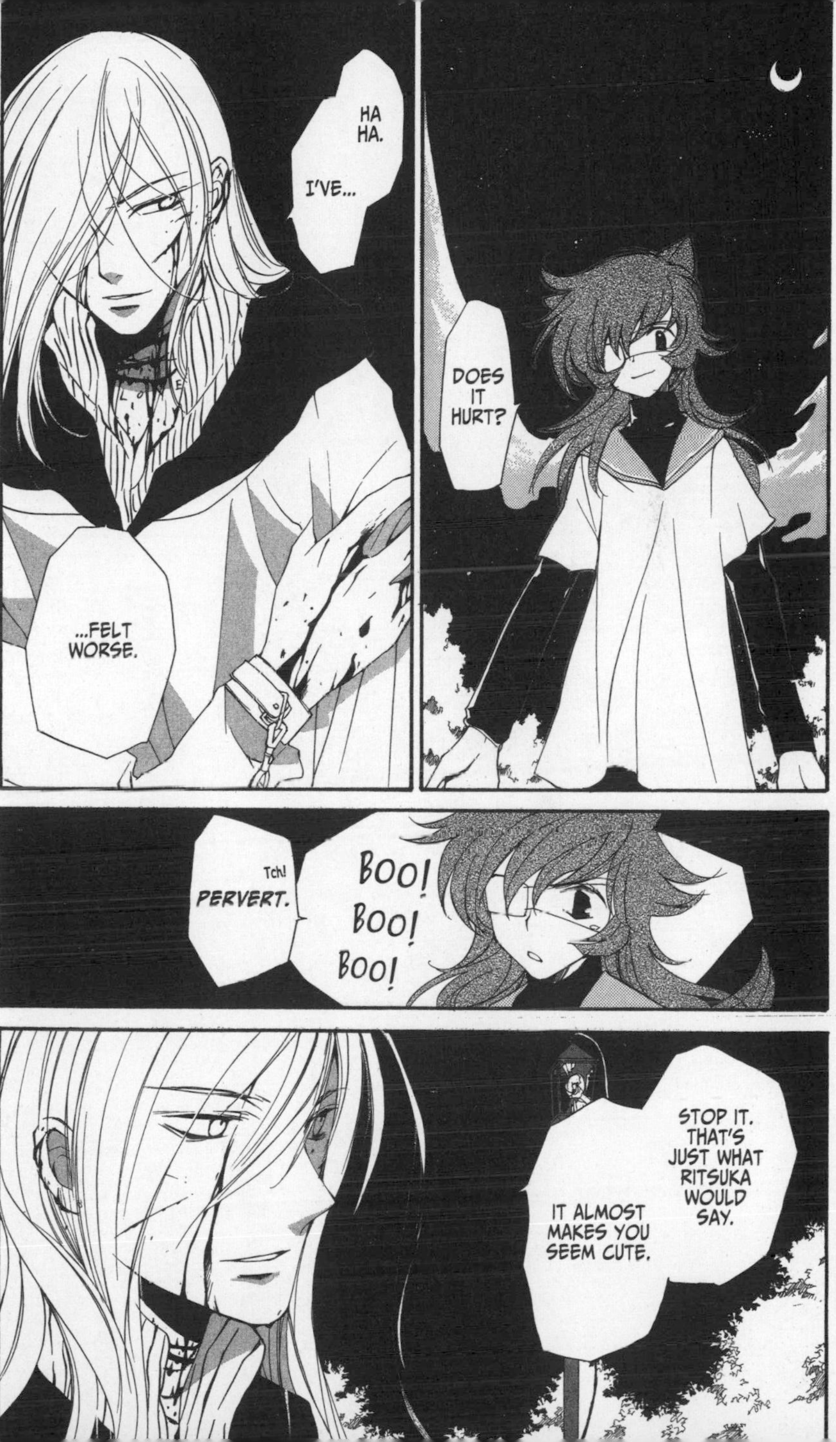
DOES IT HURT?
HA HA.
I'VE...
...FELT WORSE.
BOO! BOO! BOO!
Tch! PERVERT.
STOP IT. THAT'S JUST WHAT RITSUKA WOULD SAY.
IT ALMOST MAKES YOU SEEM CUTE.

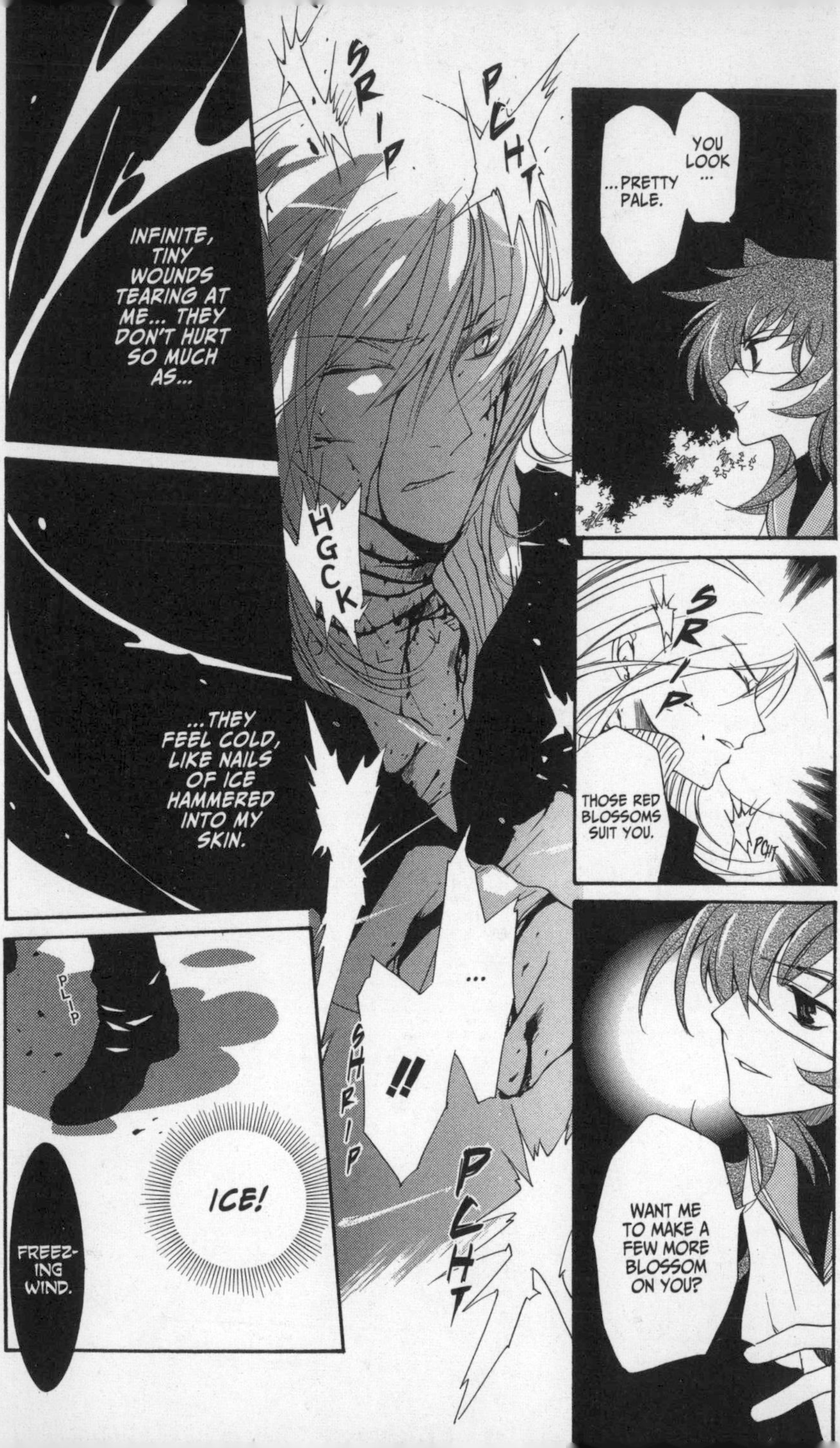
YOU LOOK ... ...PRETTY PALE.
SRIP
THOSE RED BLOSSOMS SUIT YOU.
PCHT
WANT ME TO MAKE A FEW MORE BLOSSOM ON YOU?
SRIP
PCHT
HGCK
...
!!
SHRIP
PCHT
INFINITE, TINY WOUNDS TEARING AT ME... THEY DON'T HURT SO MUCH AS...
...THEY FEEL COLD, LIKE NAILS OF ICE HAMMERED INTO MY SKIN.
PLIP
ICE!
FREEZ-ING WIND.

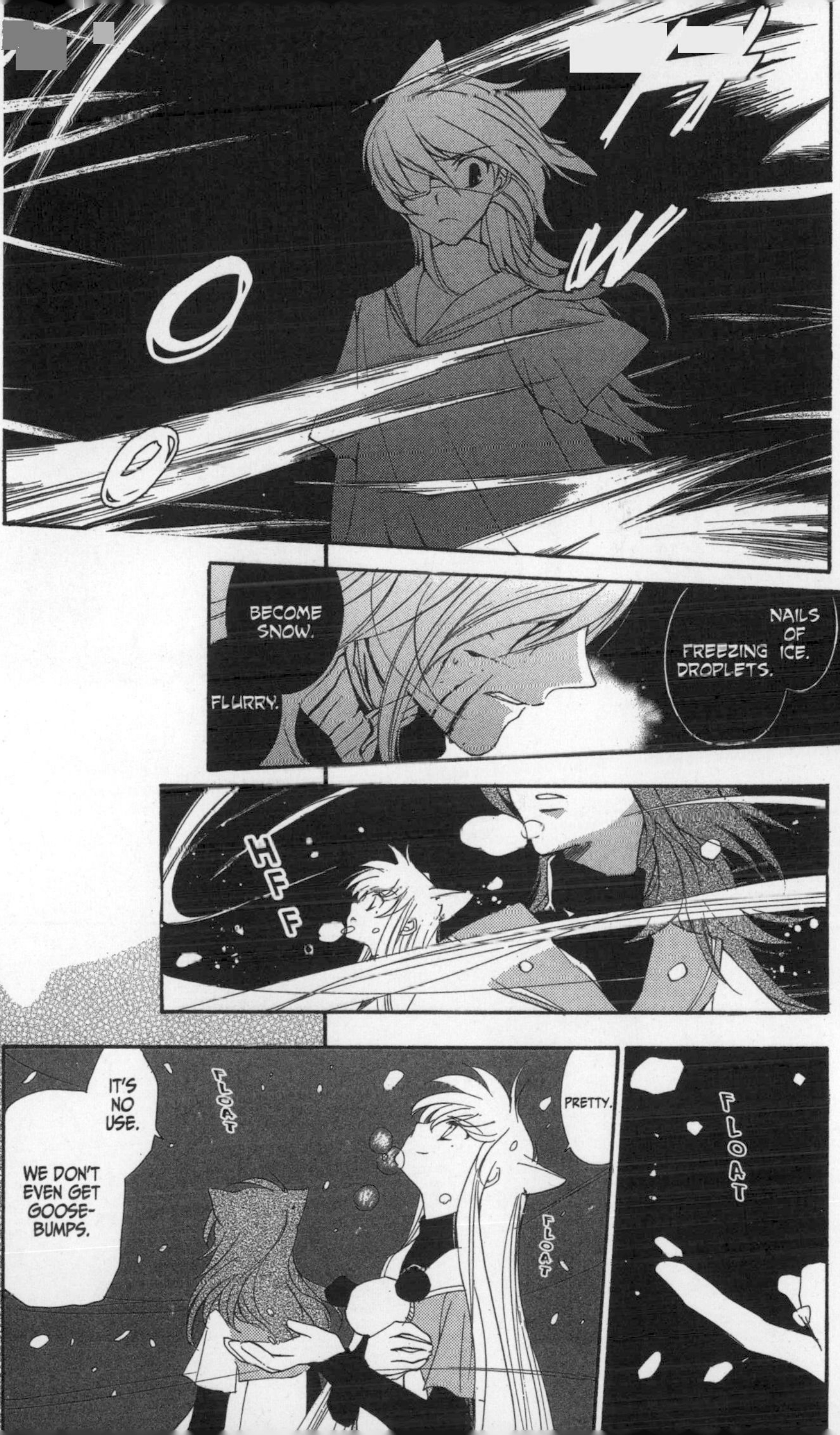
HFF
NAILS OF ICE. FREEZING DROPLETS.
BECOME SNOW.
FLURRY.
HFF
FLOAT
PRETTY.
FLOAT
IT'S NO USE.
WE DON'T EVEN GET GOOSE-BUMPS.
FLOAT

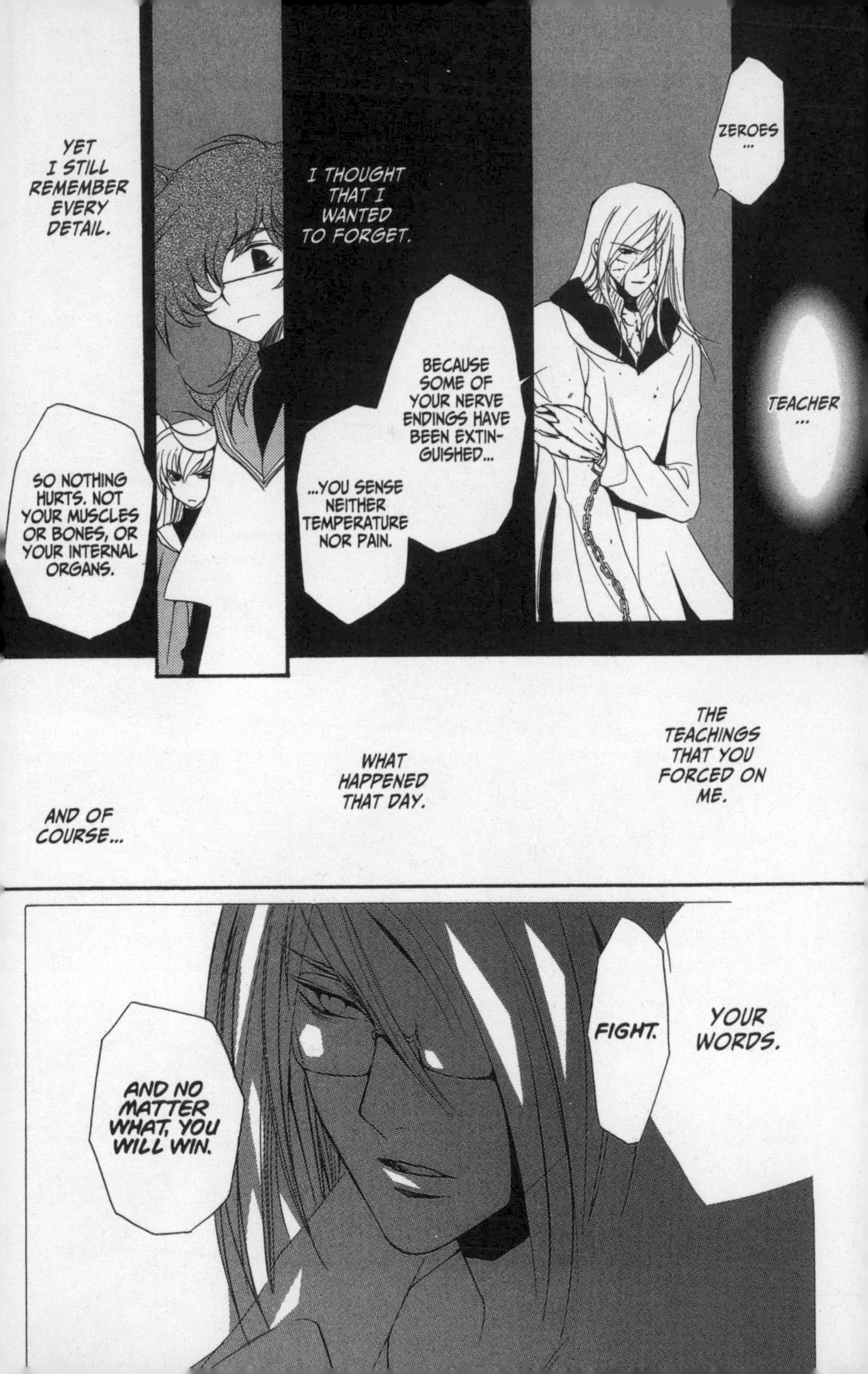
ZEROES ...
TEACHER ...
I THOUGHT THAT I WANTED TO FORGET.
BECAUSE SOME OF YOUR NERVE ENDINGS HAVE BEEN EXTIN-GUISHED...
...YOU SENSE NEITHER TEMPERATURE NOR PAIN.
YET I STILL REMEMBER EVERY DETAIL.
SO NOTHING HURTS. NOT YOUR MUSCLES OR BONES, OR YOUR INTERNAL ORGANS.
THE TEACHINGS THAT YOU FORCED ON ME.
WHAT HAPPENED THAT DAY.
AND OF COURSE...
YOUR WORDS.
FIGHT.
AND NO MATTER WHAT, YOU WILL WIN.

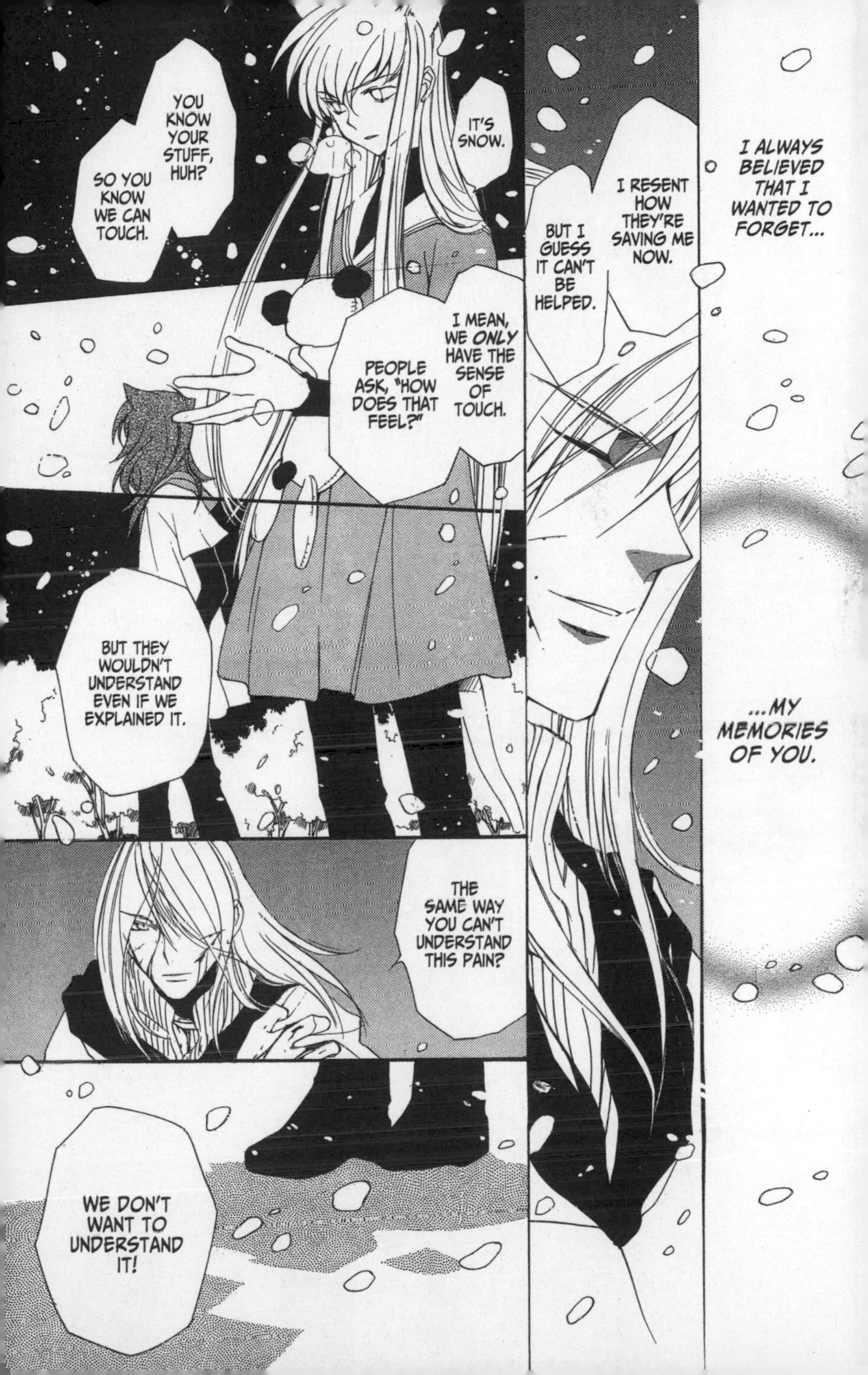
I ALWAYS BELIEVED THAT I WANTED TO FORGET...
...MY MEMORIES OF YOU.
I RESENT HOW THEY'RE SAVING ME NOW.
BUT I GUESS IT CAN'T BE HELPED.
IT'S SNOW.
YOU KNOW YOUR STUFF, HUH?
SO YOU KNOW WE CAN TOUCH.
I MEAN, WE *ONLY* HAVE THE SENSE OF TOUCH.
PEOPLE ASK, "HOW DOES THAT FEEL?"
BUT THEY WOULDN'T UNDERSTAND EVEN IF WE EXPLAINED IT.
THE SAME WAY YOU CAN'T UNDERSTAND THIS PAIN?
WE DON'T WANT TO UNDERSTAND IT!

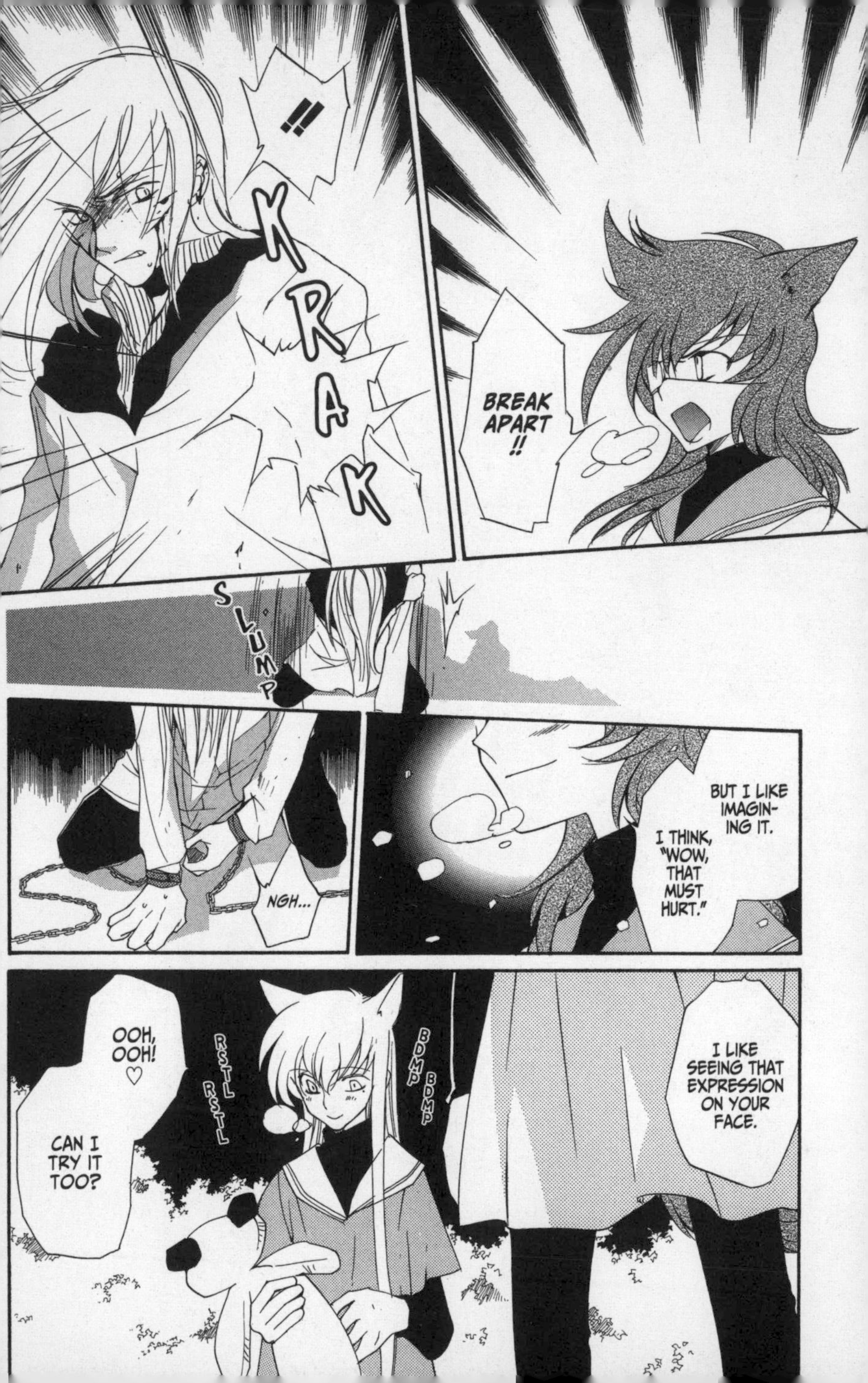
BREAK APART!!
!!
KRAK
SLUMP
BUT I LIKE IMAGINING IT.
I THINK, "WOW, THAT MUST HURT."
NGH...
I LIKE SEEING THAT EXPRESSION ON YOUR FACE.
BDMP BDMP
RSTL RSTL
OOH, OOH! ♡
CAN I TRY IT TOO?

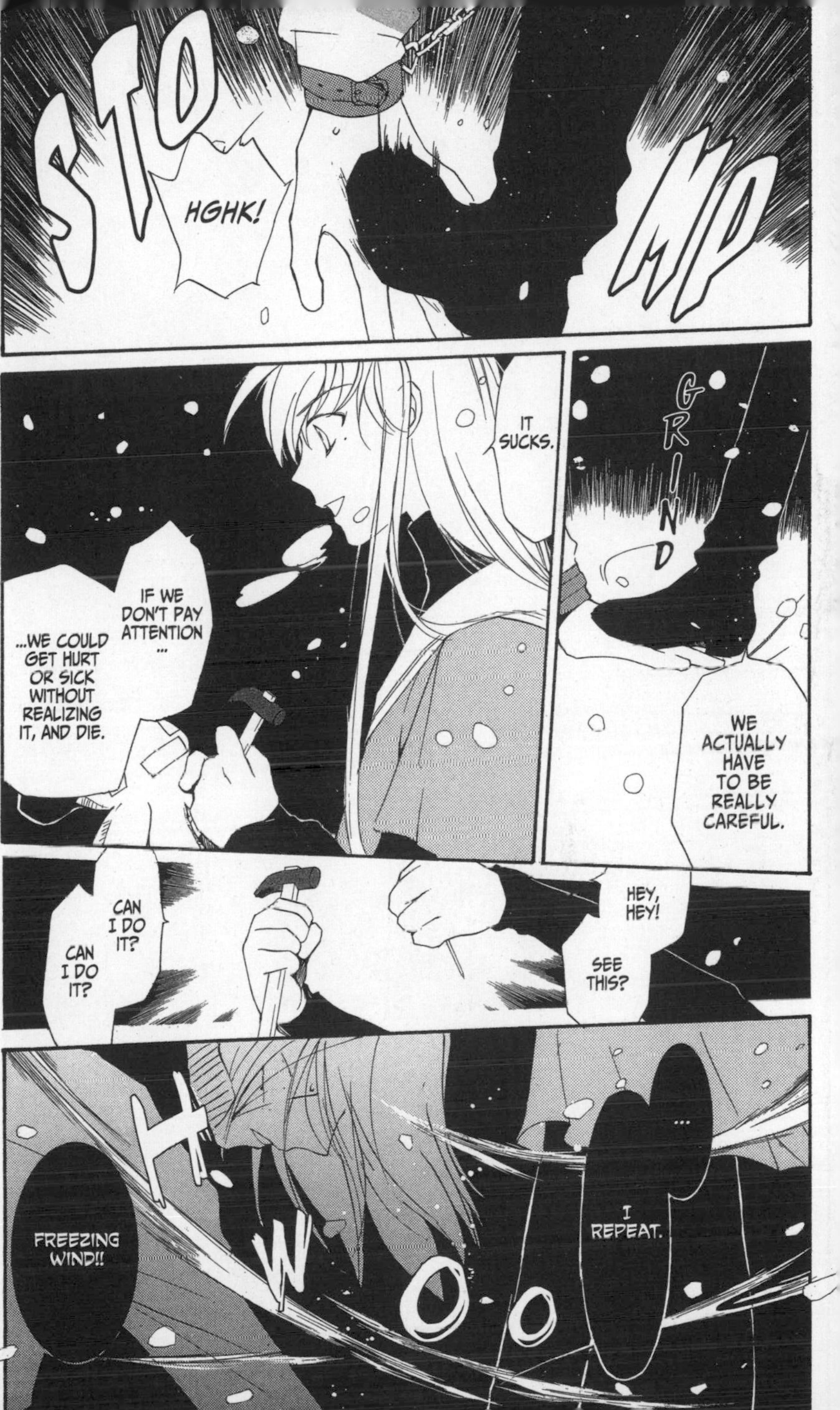
STOMP
HGHK!
GRIND
WE ACTUALLY HAVE TO BE REALLY CAREFUL.
IT SUCKS.
IF WE DON'T PAY ATTENTION...
...WE COULD GET HURT OR SICK WITHOUT REALIZING IT, AND DIE.
HEY, HEY!
SEE THIS?
CAN I DO IT?
CAN I DO IT?
...
I REPEAT.
HWOO
FREEZING WIND!!

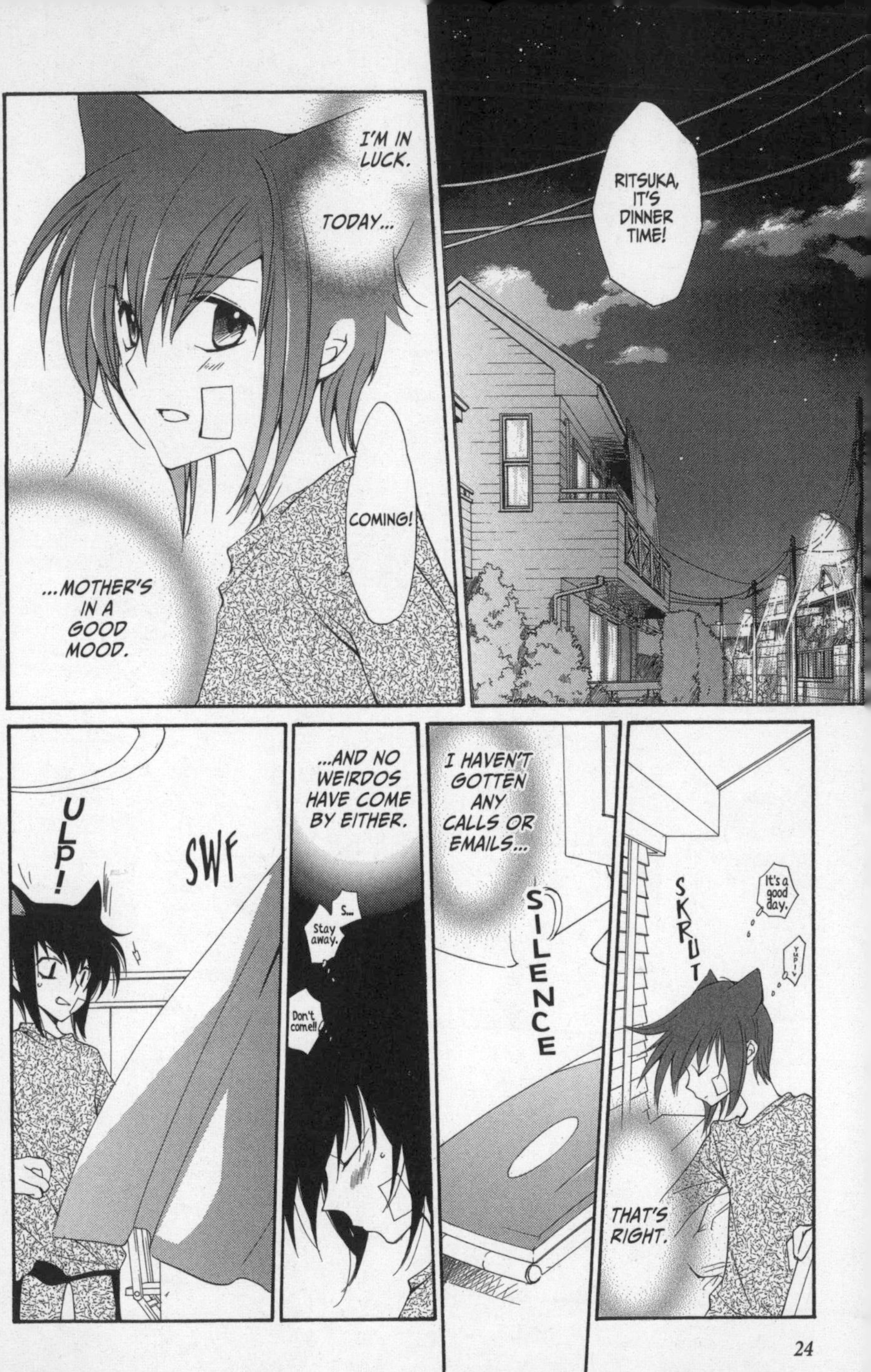
RITSUKA, IT'S DINNER TIME!
COMING!
I'M IN LUCK.
TODAY...
...MOTHER'S IN A GOOD MOOD.
SKRUT
It's a good day.
THAT'S RIGHT.
I HAVEN'T GOTTEN ANY CALLS OR EMAILS...
SILENCE
...AND NO WEIRDOS HAVE COME BY EITHER.
S...
Stay away.
Don't come!!
SWF
ULP!

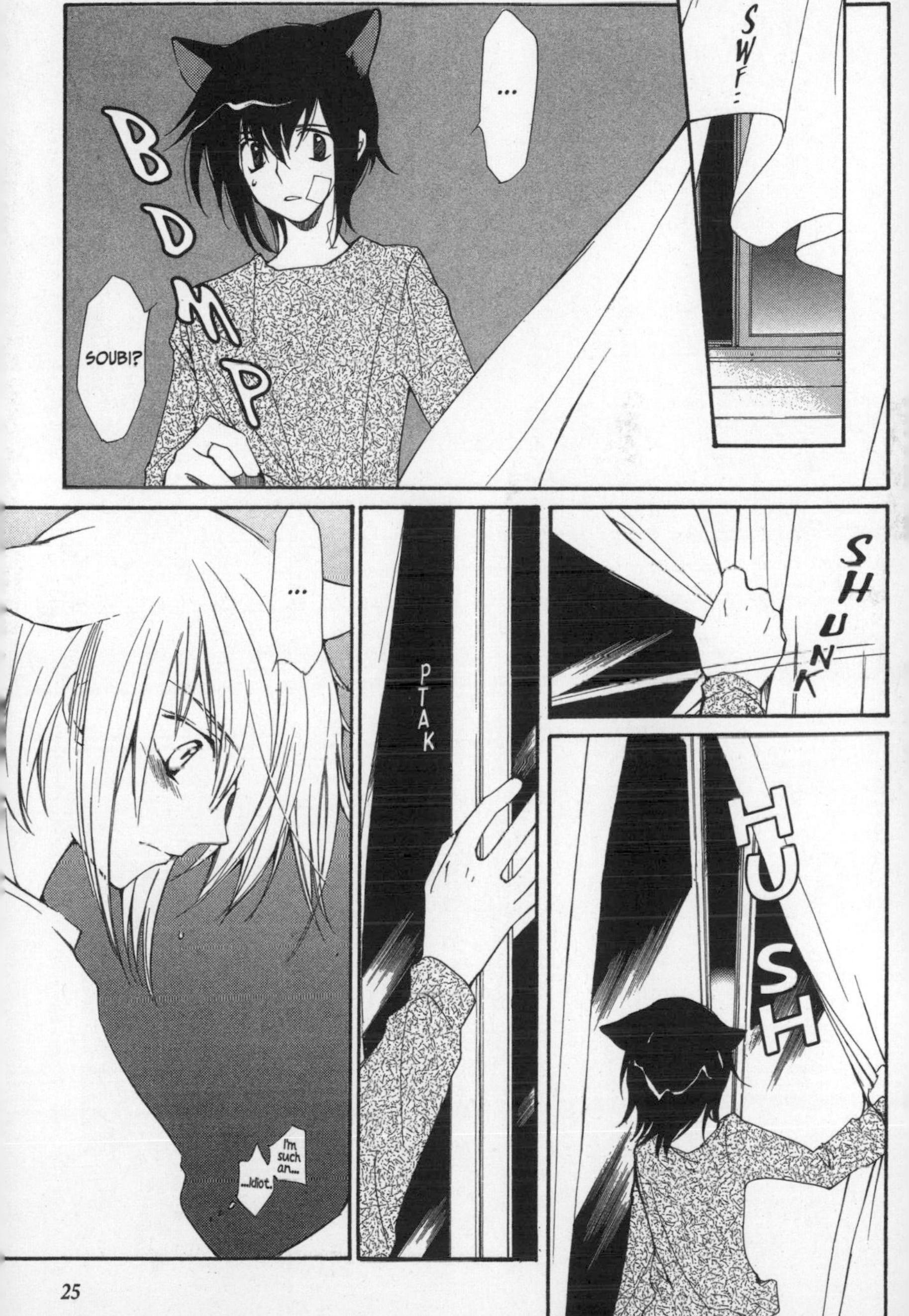
SWF!
...
BDMP
SOUBI?
SHUNK
HUSH
PTAK
...
I'm such an...
...idiot.

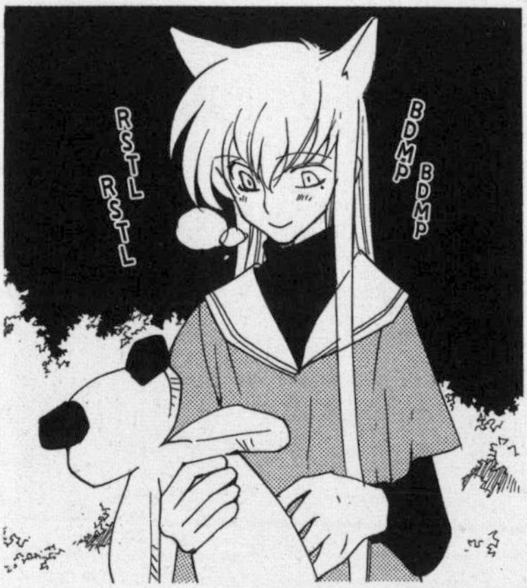
BDMP BDMP
RSTL RSTL

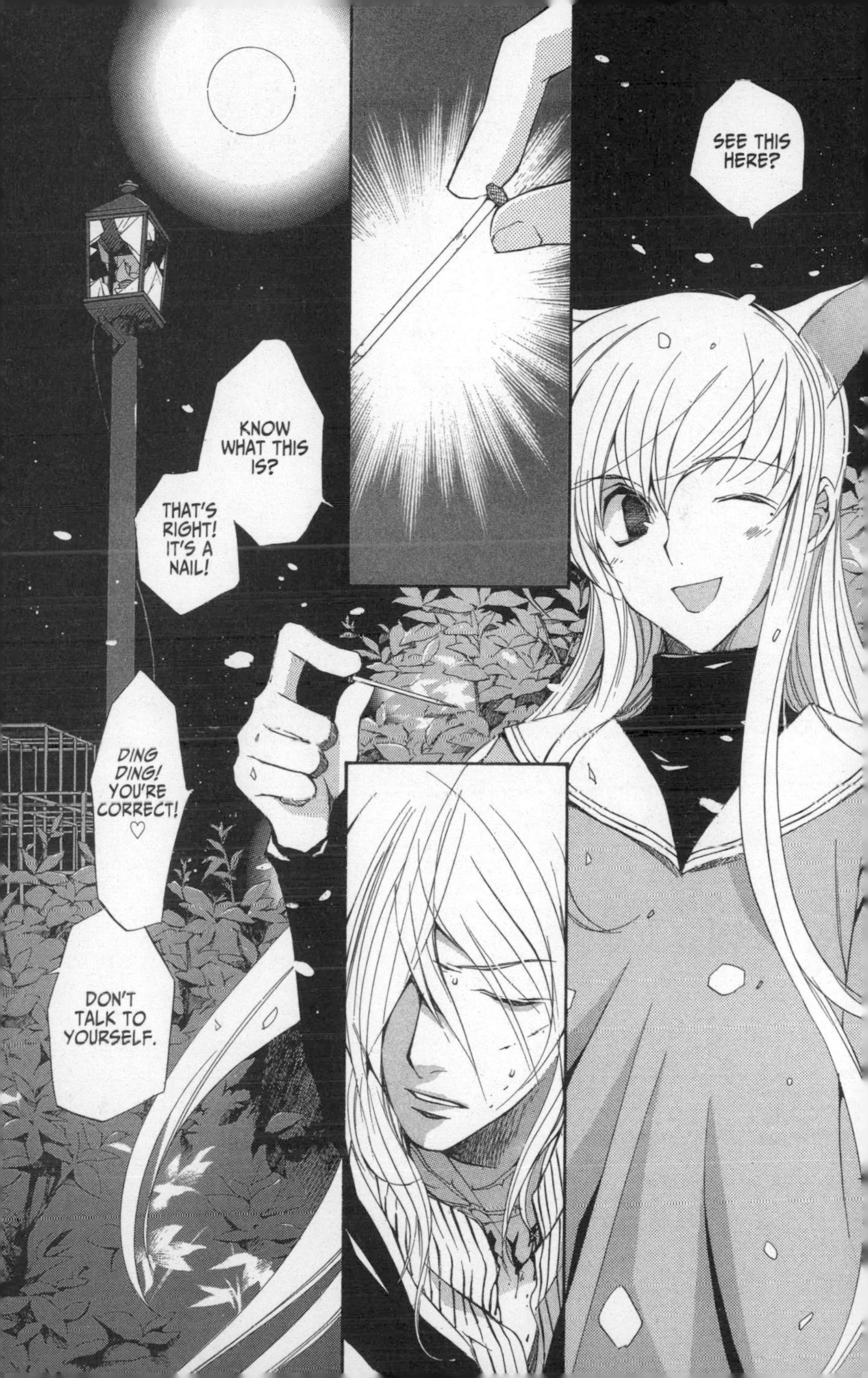
SEE THIS HERE?
KNOW WHAT THIS IS?
THAT'S RIGHT! IT'S A NAIL!
DING DING! YOU'RE CORRECT! ♡
DON'T TALK TO YOURSELF.

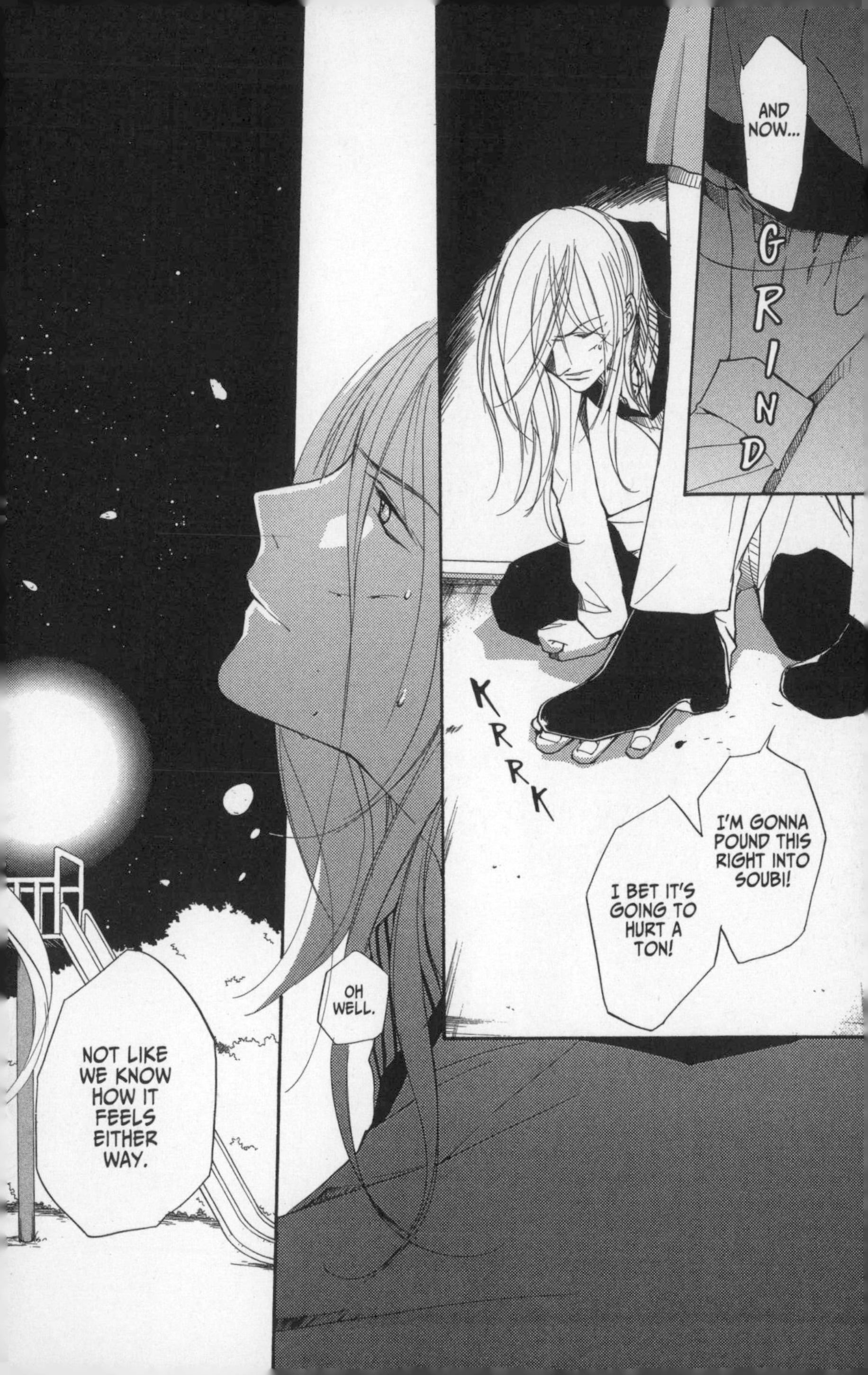
AND NOW...
GRIND
KRRK
I'M GONNA POUND THIS RIGHT INTO SOUBI!
I BET IT'S GOING TO HURT A TON!
OH WELL.
NOT LIKE WE KNOW HOW IT FEELS EITHER WAY.

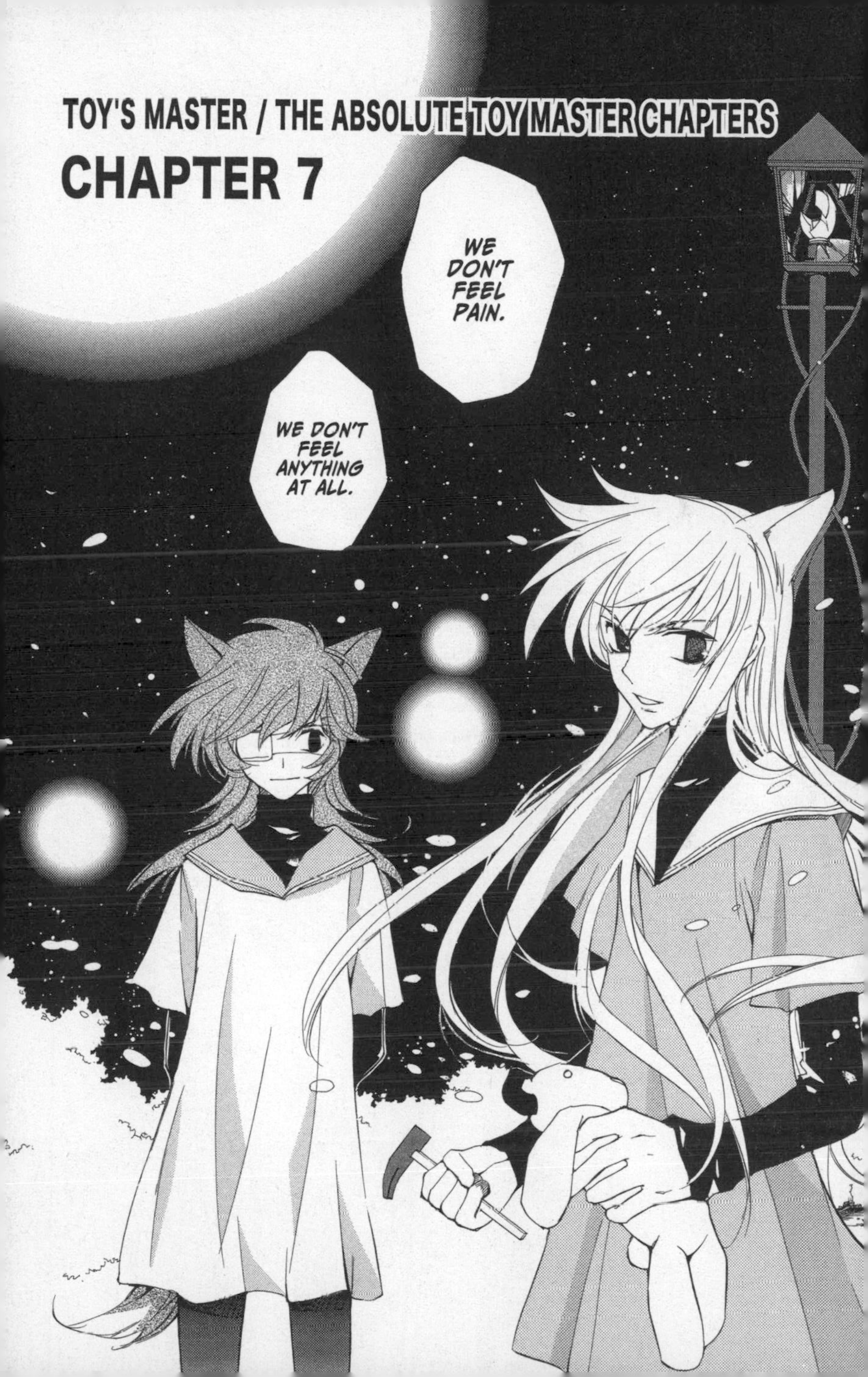
TOY'S MASTER / THE ABSOLUTE TOY MASTER CHAPTERS
CHAPTER 7
WE DON'T FEEL PAIN.
WE DON'T FEEL ANYTHING AT ALL.

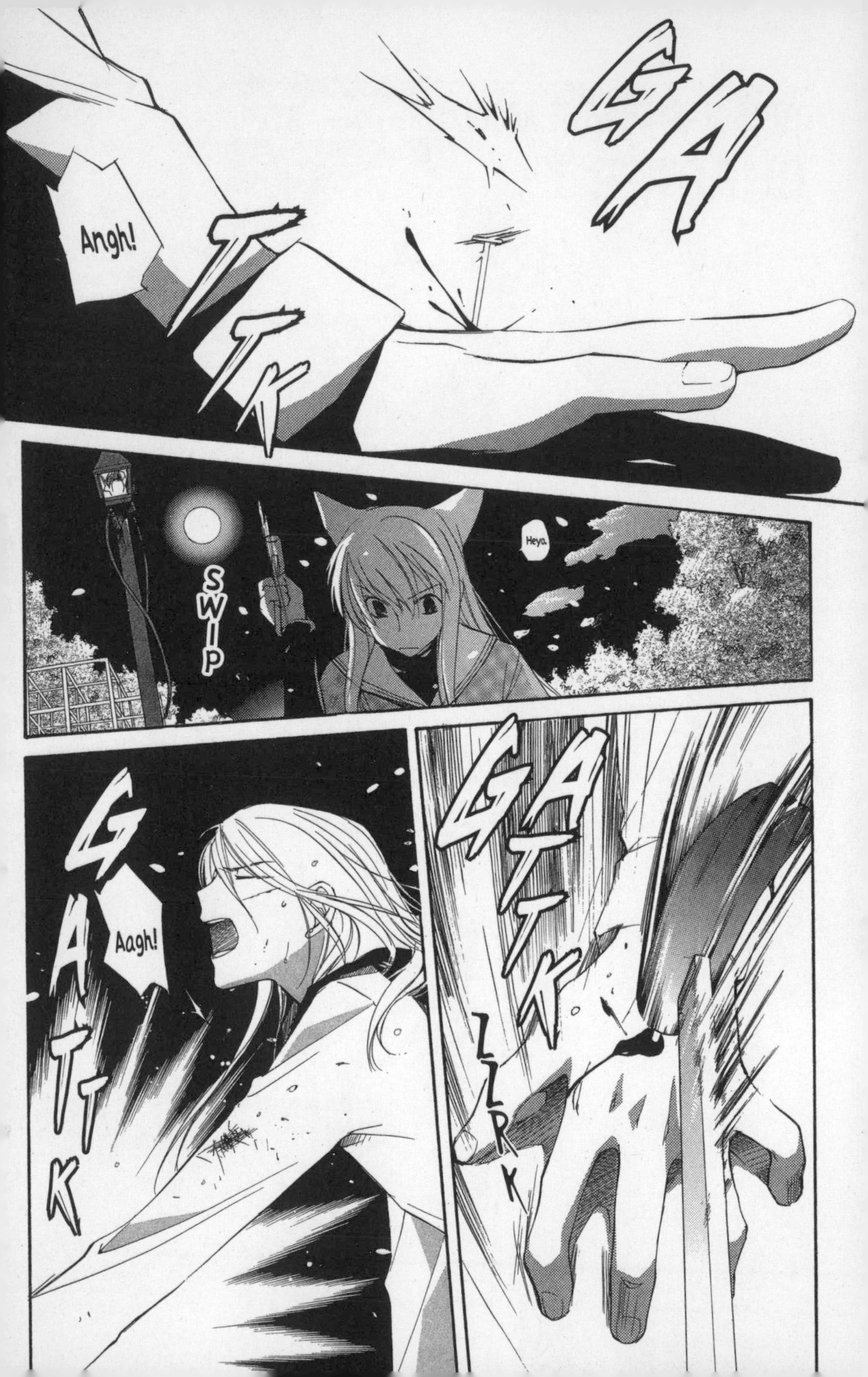
GA
Angh!
TTK
Heya.
SWIP
GATTK
ZZRK
Aagh!
GATTK

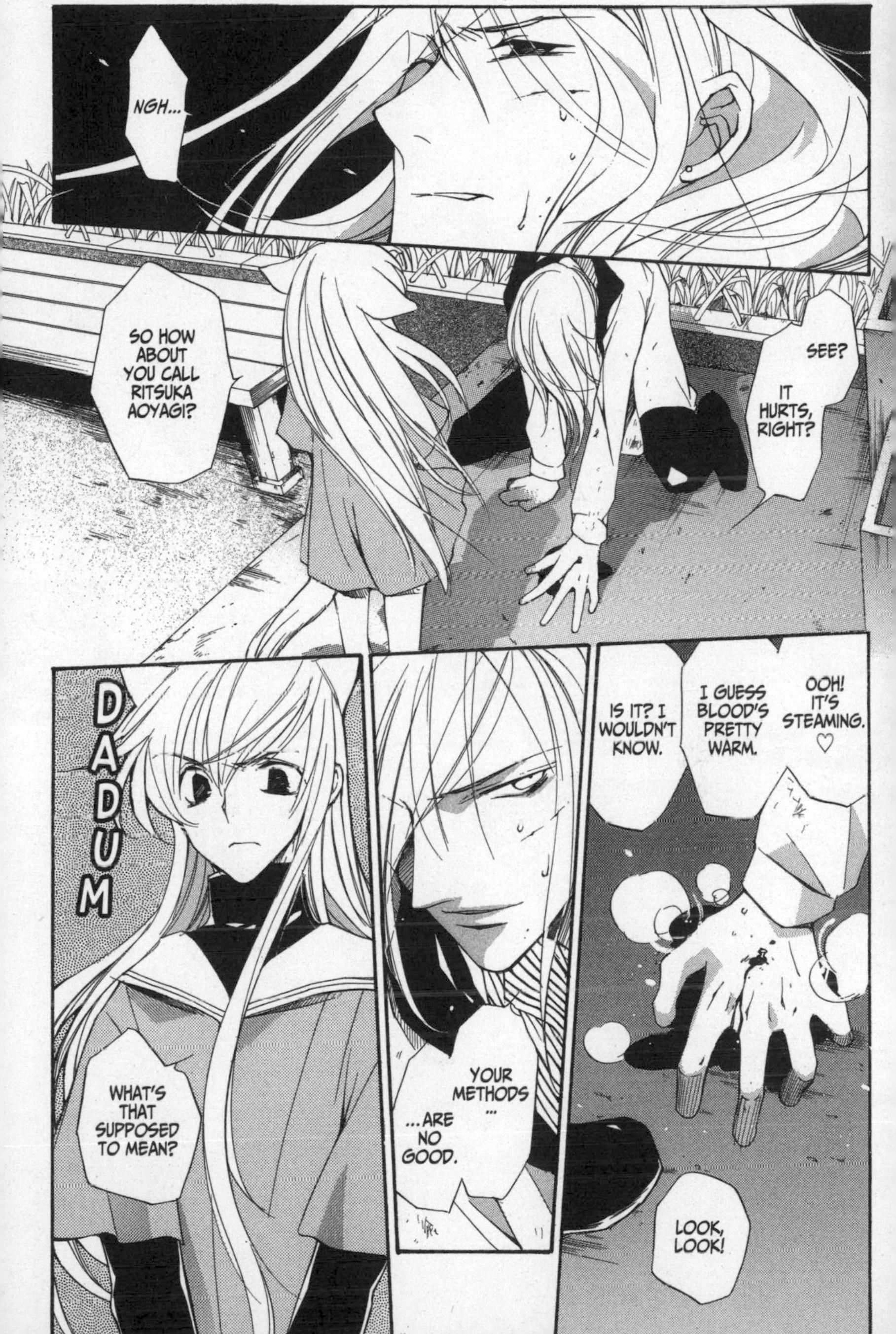
NGH...
SEE?
IT HURTS, RIGHT?
SO HOW ABOUT YOU CALL RITSUKA AOYAGI?
OOH! IT'S STEAMING. ♡
I GUESS BLOOD'S PRETTY WARM.
IS IT? I WOULDN'T KNOW.
LOOK, LOOK!
YOUR METHODS ...
...ARE NO GOOD.
DADUM
WHAT'S THAT SUPPOSED TO MEAN?

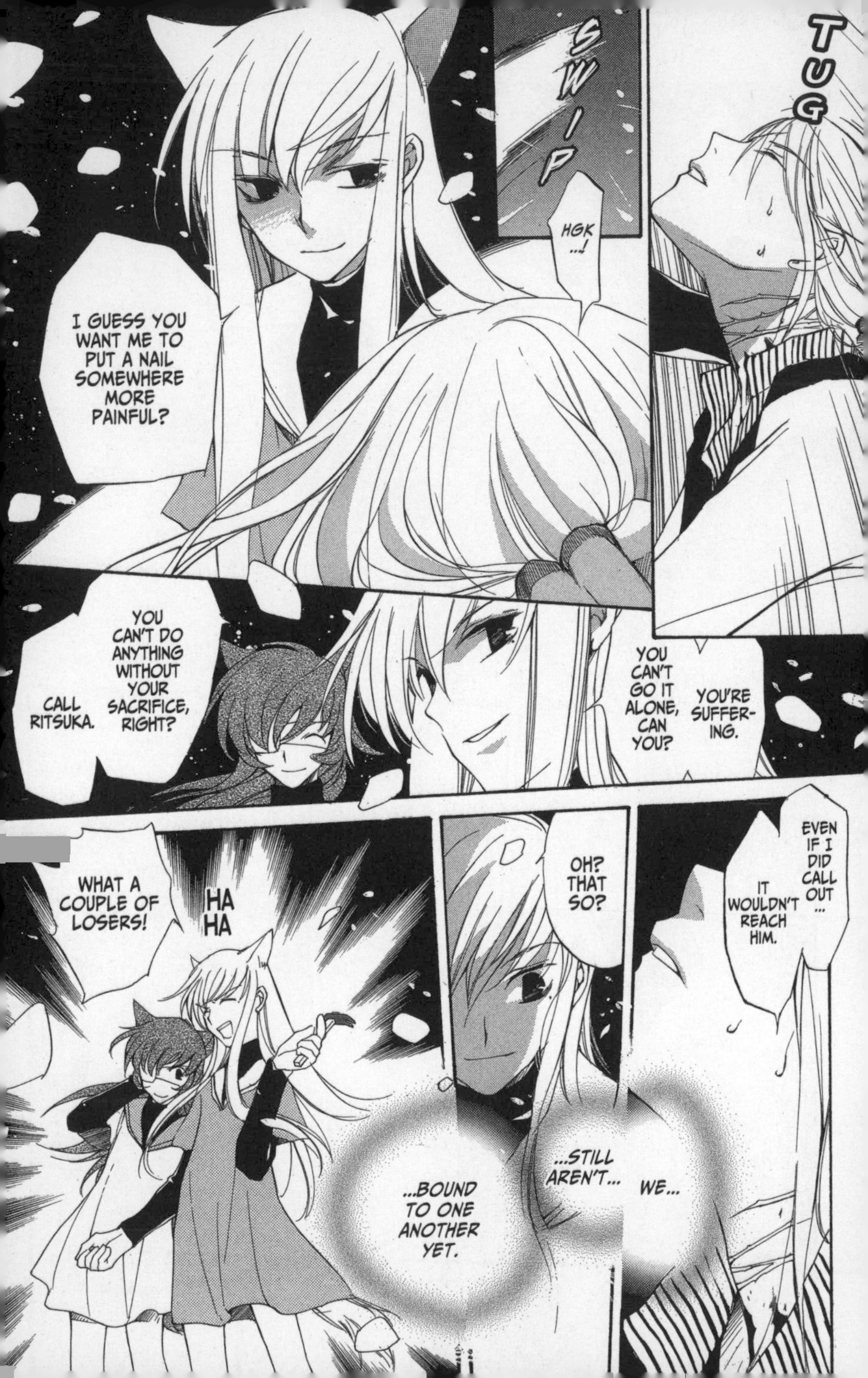
TUG
SWIP
HGK ...!
I GUESS YOU WANT ME TO PUT A NAIL SOMEWHERE MORE PAINFUL?
YOU'RE SUFFER-ING.
YOU CAN'T GO IT ALONE, CAN YOU?
YOU CAN'T DO ANYTHING WITHOUT YOUR SACRIFICE, RIGHT?
CALL RITSUKA.
EVEN IF I DID CALL OUT ...
IT WOULDN'T REACH HIM.
WE...
...STILL AREN'T...
...BOUND TO ONE ANOTHER YET.
OH? THAT SO?
WHAT A COUPLE OF LOSERS!
HA HA

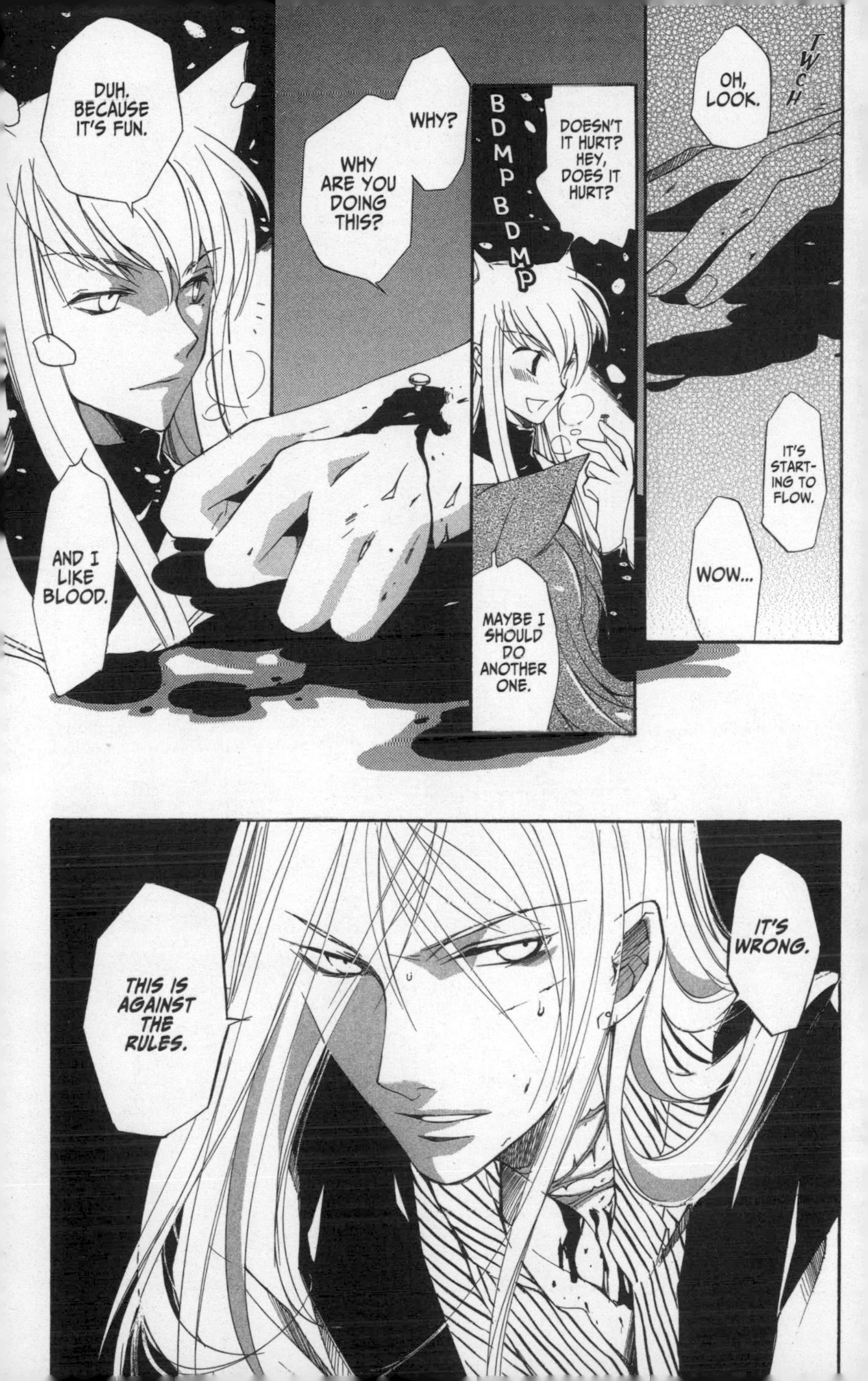
TWCH
OH, LOOK.
IT'S STARTING TO FLOW.
WOW...
DOESN'T IT HURT? HEY, DOES IT HURT?
BDMP BDMP
MAYBE I SHOULD DO ANOTHER ONE.
WHY?
WHY ARE YOU DOING THIS?
DUH. BECAUSE IT'S FUN.
AND I LIKE BLOOD.
IT'S WRONG.
THIS IS AGAINST THE RULES.

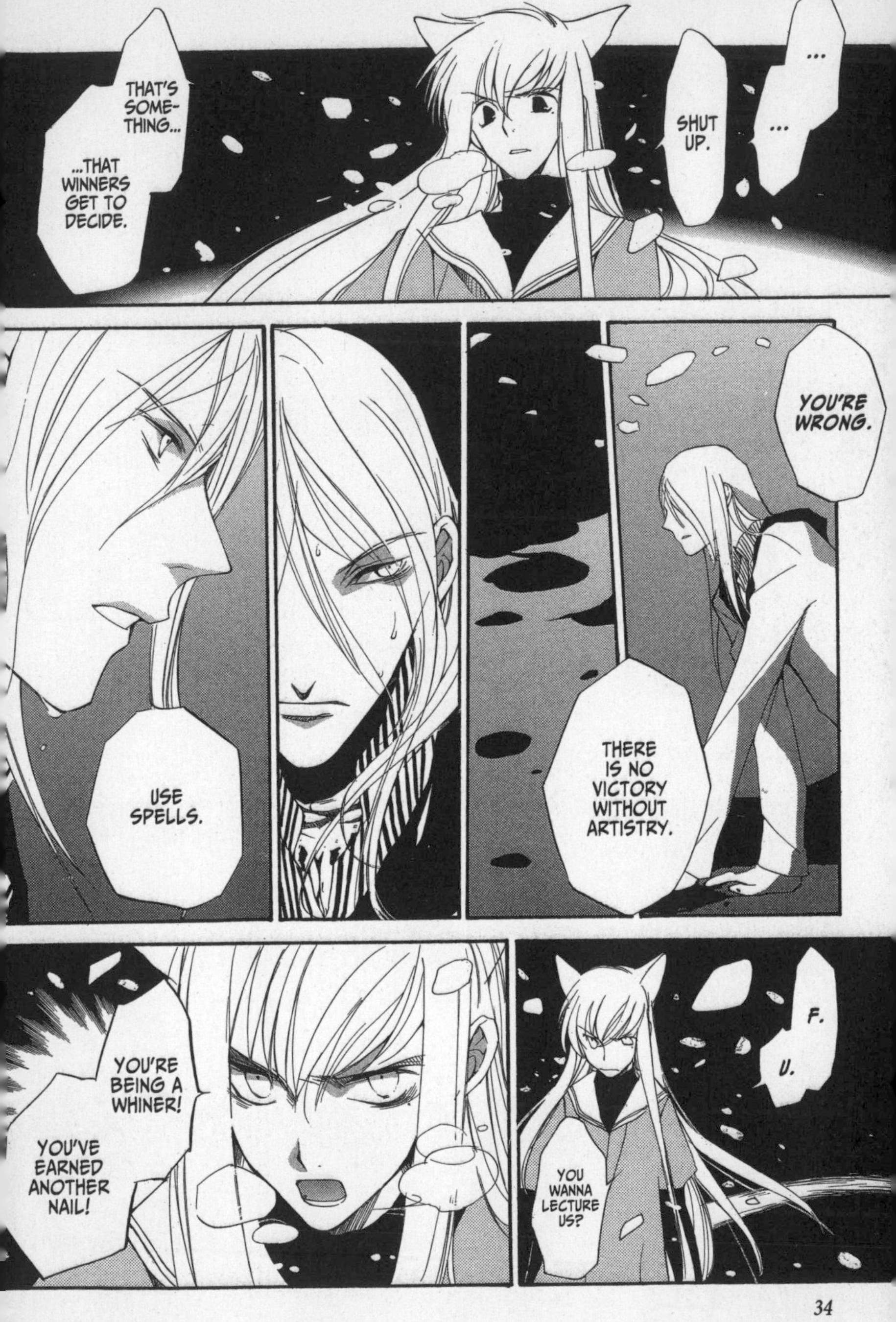
... ...
SHUT UP.
THAT'S SOMETHING...
...THAT WINNERS GET TO DECIDE.
YOU'RE WRONG.
THERE IS NO VICTORY WITHOUT ARTISTRY.
USE SPELLS.
F. U.
YOU WANNA LECTURE US?
YOU'RE BEING A WHINER!
YOU'VE EARNED ANOTHER NAIL!

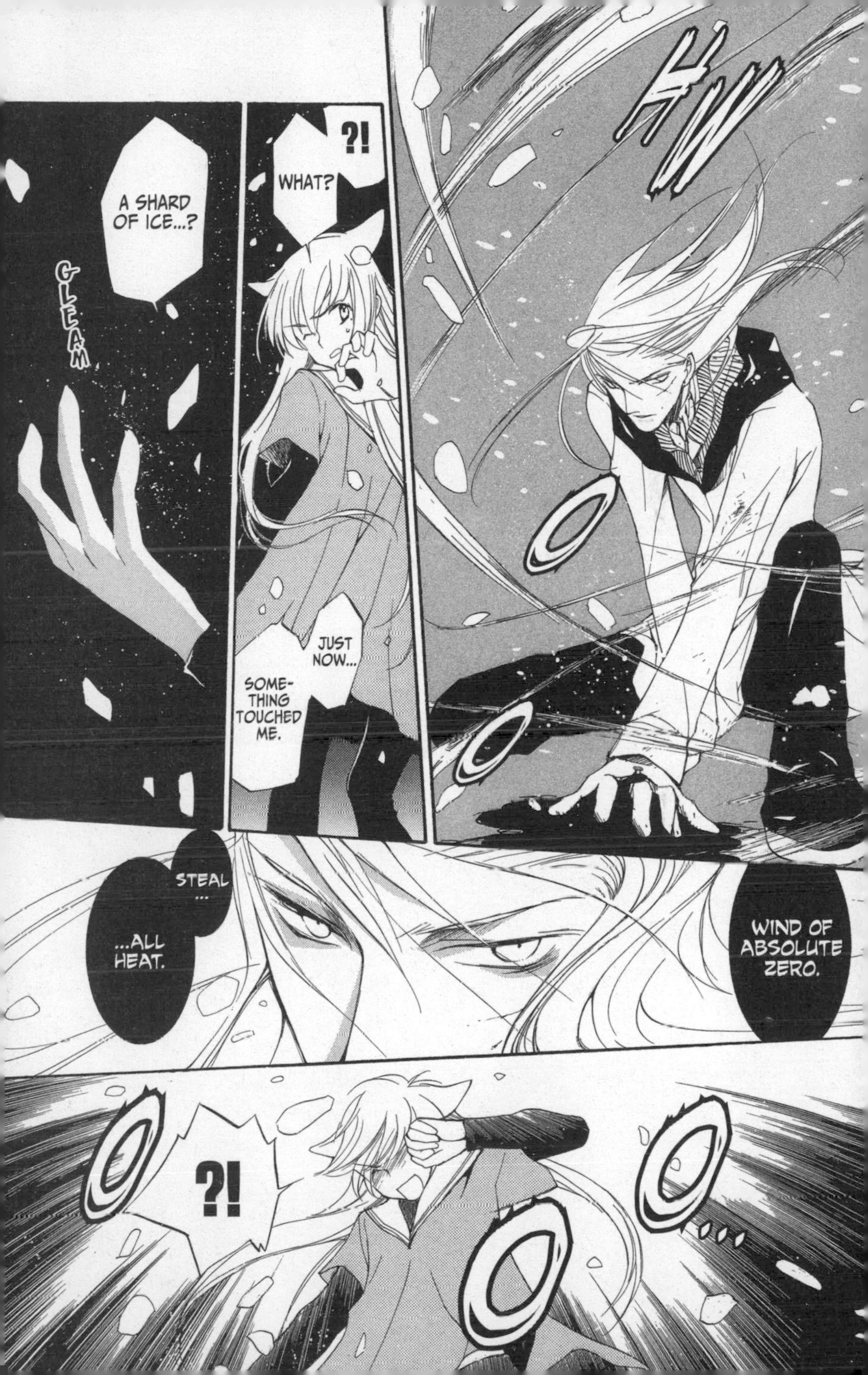
HW
?!
WHAT?
JUST NOW...
SOME-THING TOUCHED ME.
A SHARD OF ICE...?
GLEAM
WIND OF ABSOLUTE ZERO.
STEAL...
...ALL HEAT.
?!

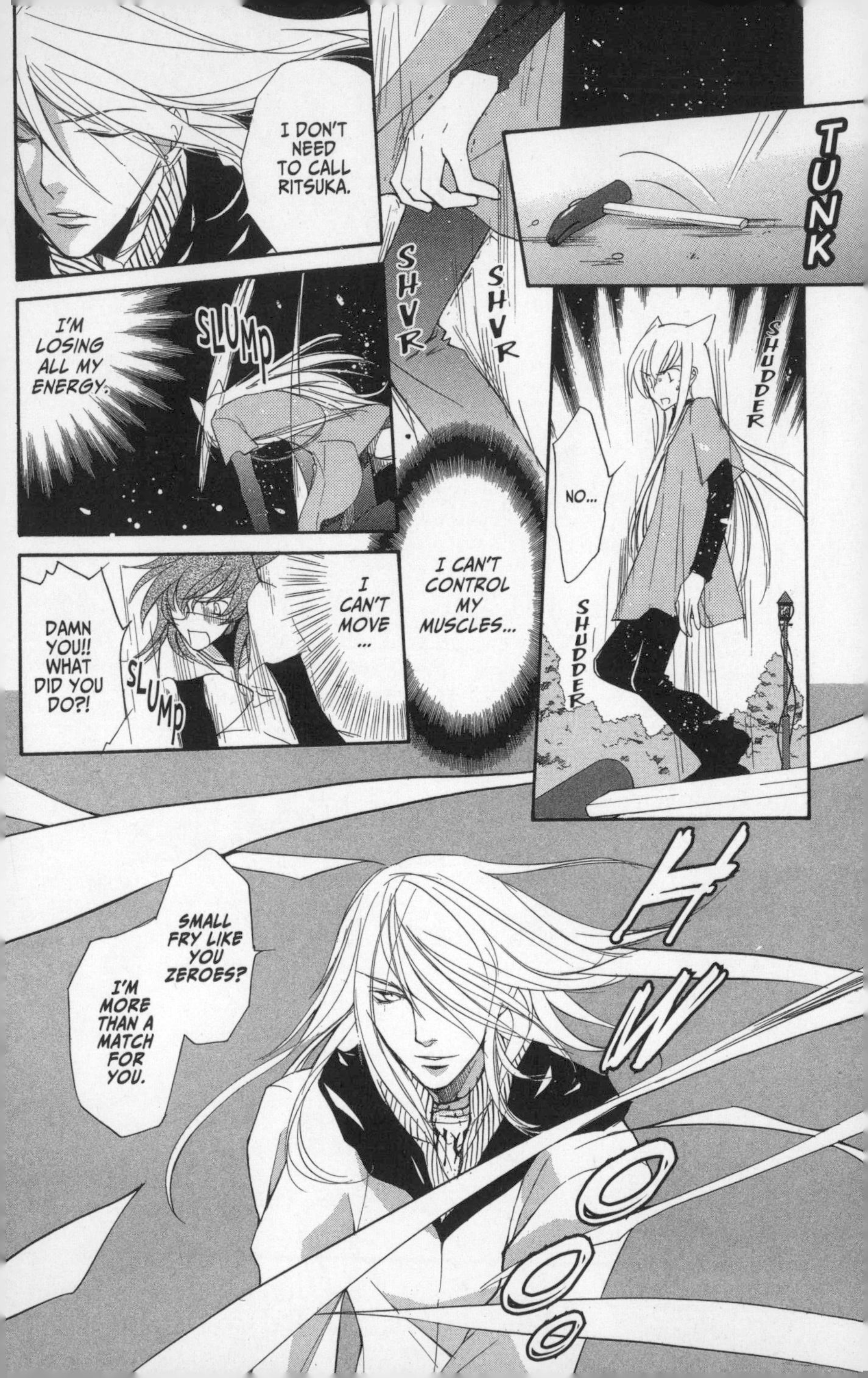
TUNK
SHUDDER
NO...
SHUDDER
SHVR
SHVR
I CAN'T CONTROL MY MUSCLES...
I CAN'T MOVE ...
I DON'T NEED TO CALL RITSUKA.
SLUMP
I'M LOSING ALL MY ENERGY.
DAMN YOU!! WHAT DID YOU DO?!
SLUMP
HWOOOO
SMALL FRY LIKE YOU ZEROES?
I'M MORE THAN A MATCH FOR YOU.

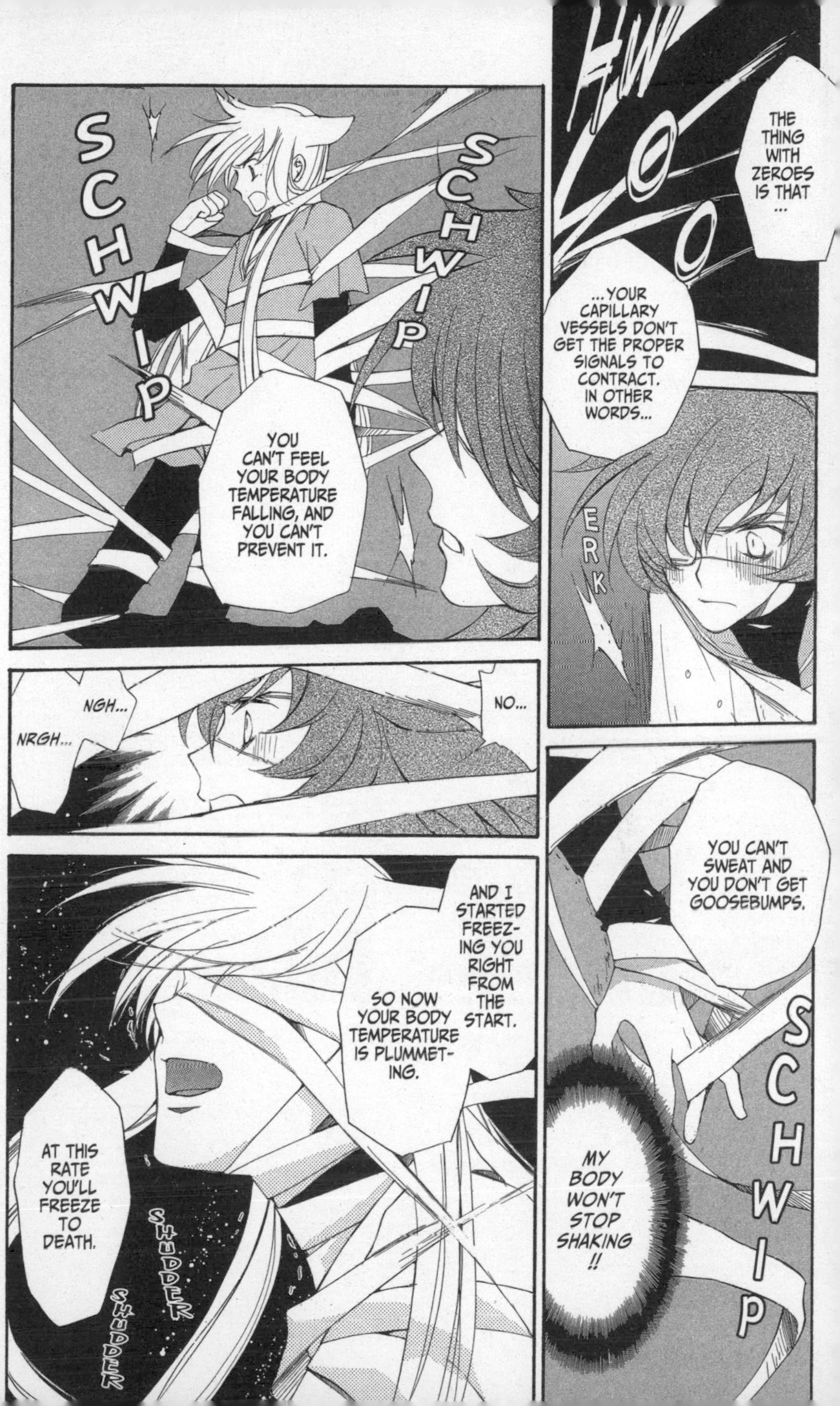
HWOOO
THE THING WITH ZEROES IS THAT...
...YOUR CAPILLARY VESSELS DON'T GET THE PROPER SIGNALS TO CONTRACT. IN OTHER WORDS...
SCHWIP
SCHWIP
YOU CAN'T FEEL YOUR BODY TEMPERATURE FALLING, AND YOU CAN'T PREVENT IT.
ERK
NO...
NGH...
NRGH...
YOU CAN'T SWEAT AND YOU DON'T GET GOOSEBUMPS.
SCHWIP
MY BODY WON'T STOP SHAKING!!
AND I STARTED FREEZ-ING YOU RIGHT FROM THE START.
SO NOW YOUR BODY TEMPERATURE IS PLUMMET-ING.
AT THIS RATE YOU'LL FREEZE TO DEATH.
SHUDDER
SHUDDER

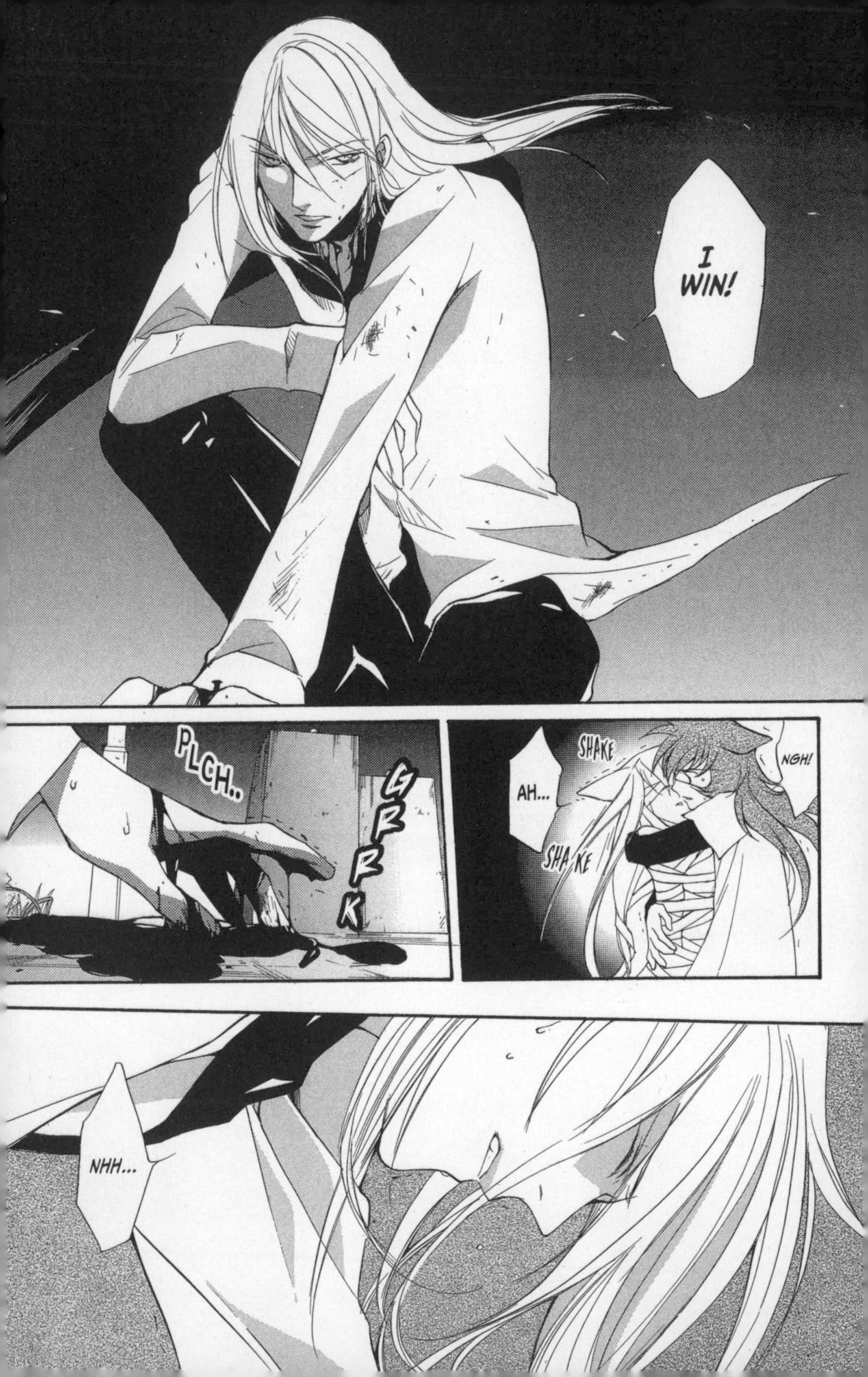
I WIN!
NGH!
SHAKE
AH...
SHAKE
PLCH..
GRRK
NHH...

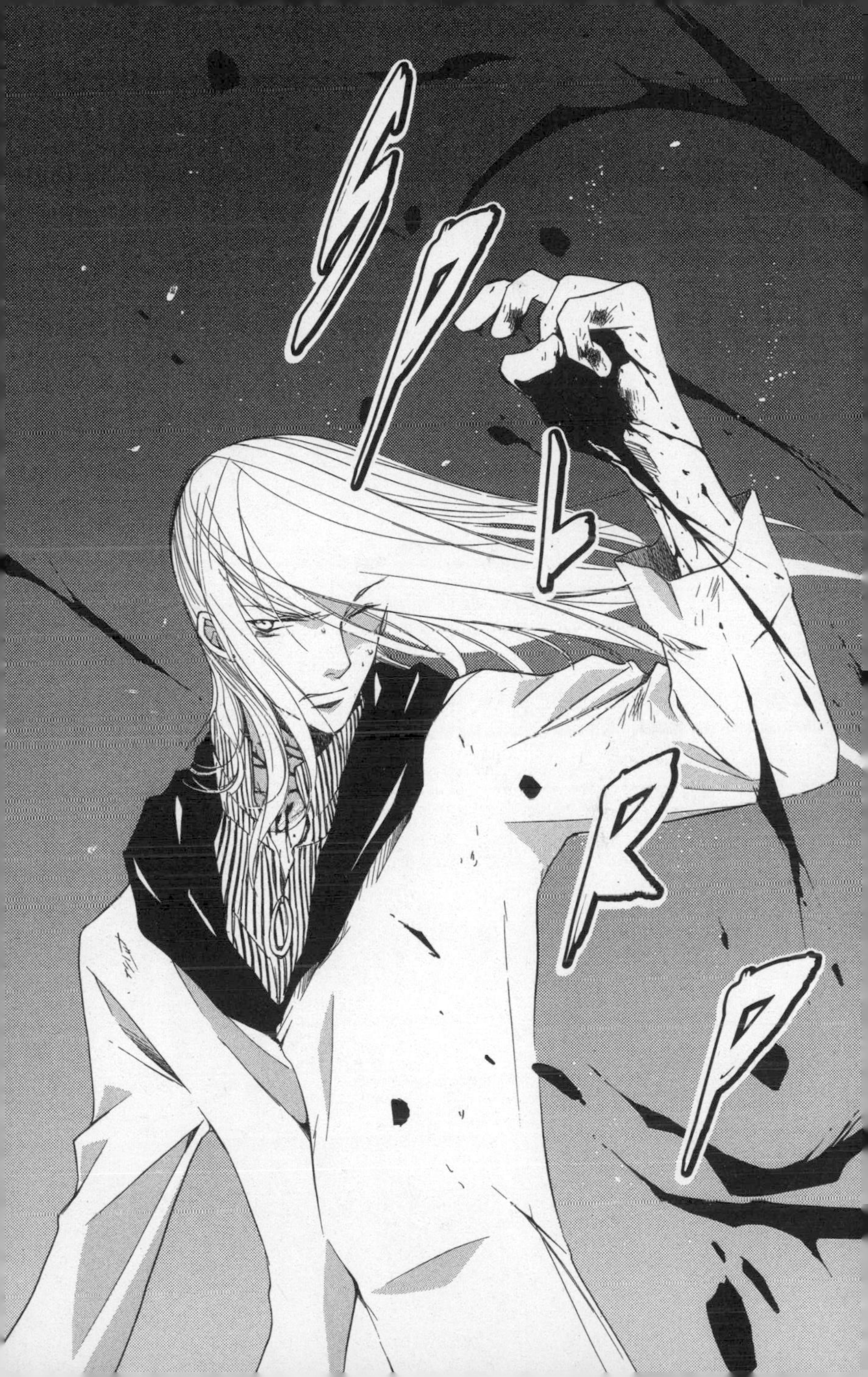
SPLRP

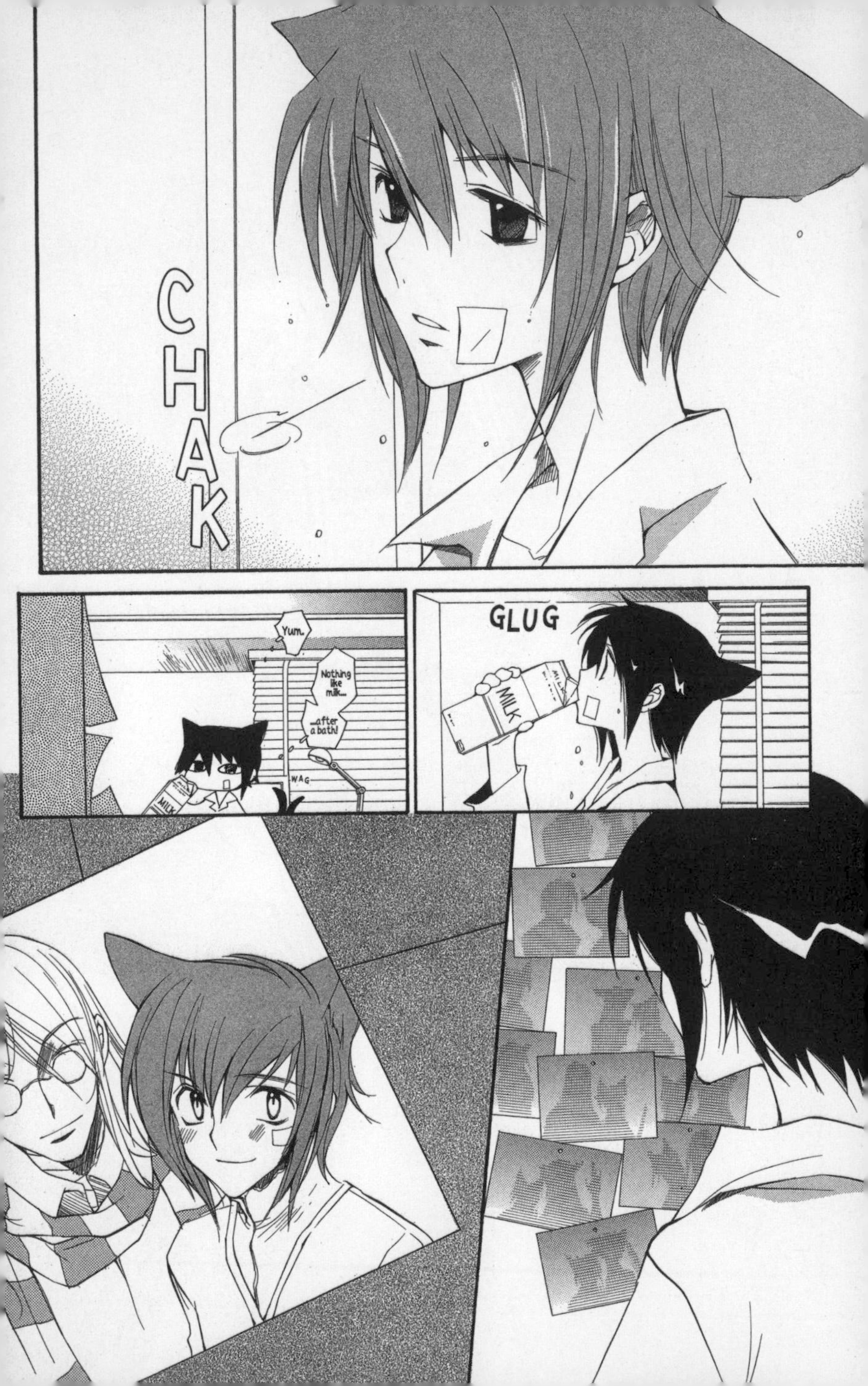
CHAK
GLUG
MILK
Yum.
Nothing like milk...
...after a bath!
WAG
MILK

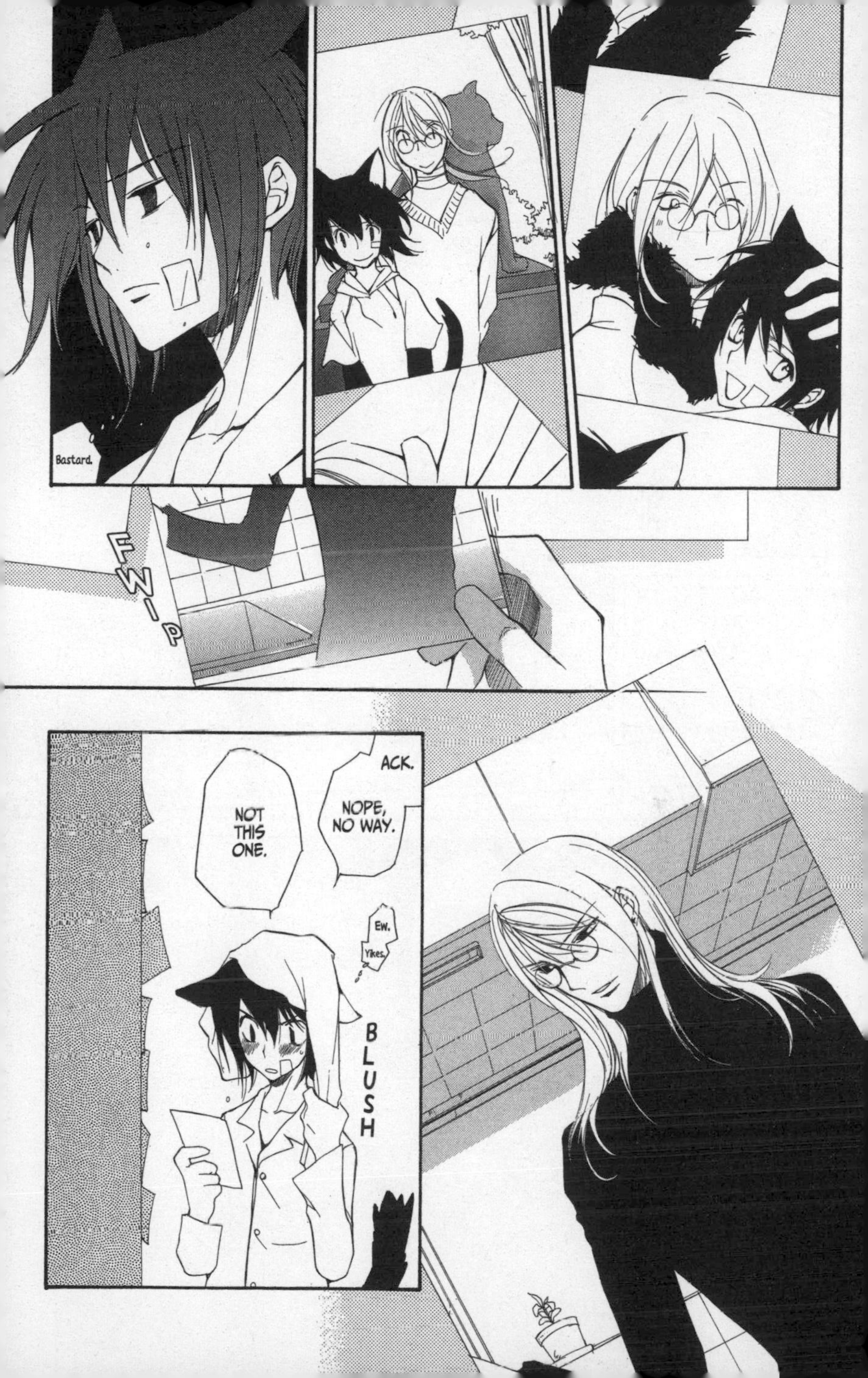
Bastard.
FWIP
ACK.
NOPE, NO WAY.
NOT THIS ONE.
Ew.
Yikes.
BLUSH

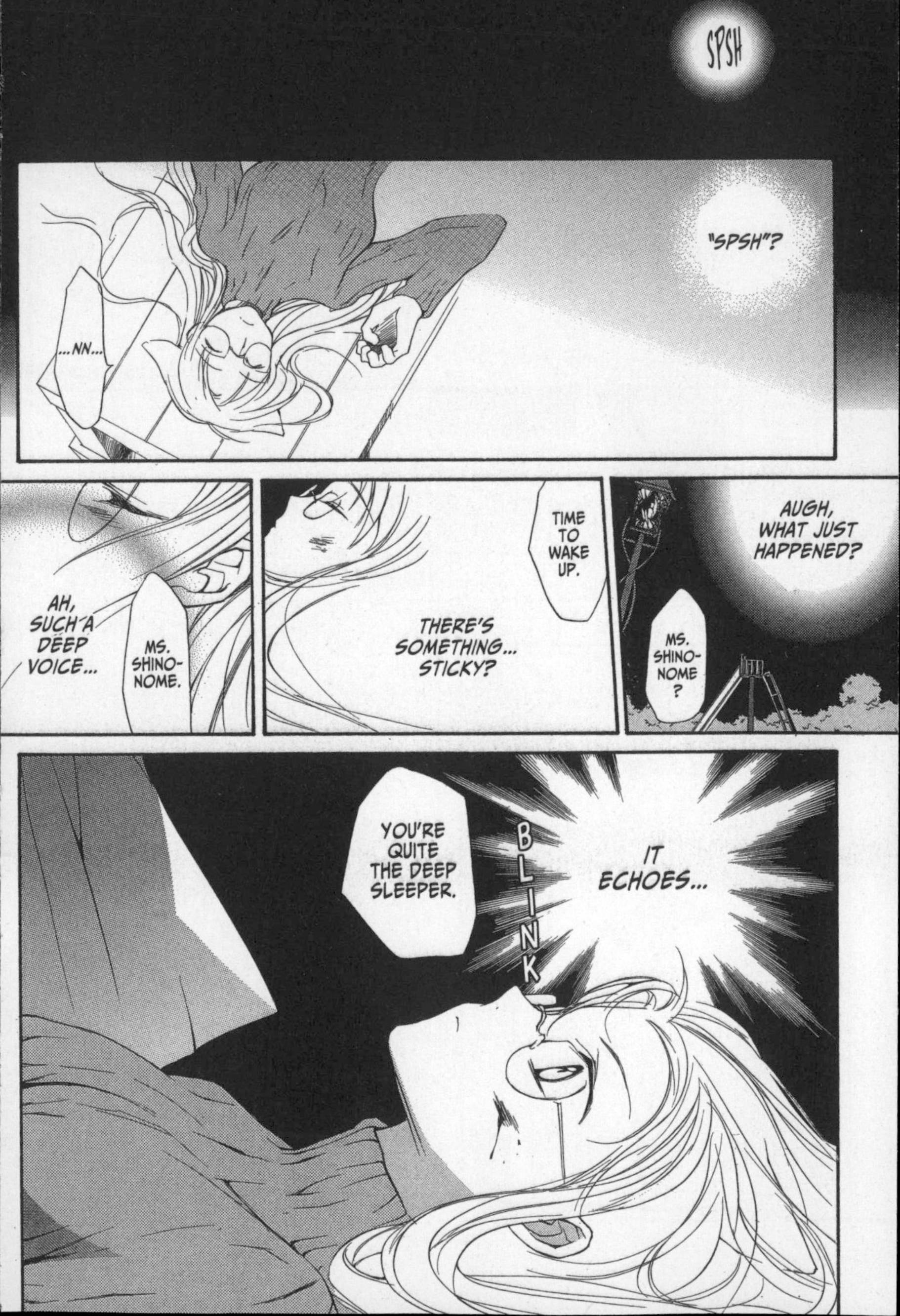
SPSH
"SPSH"?
...NN...
AUGH, WHAT JUST HAPPENED?
MS. SHINO-NOME?
TIME TO WAKE UP.
THERE'S SOMETHING... STICKY?
MS. SHINO-NOME.
AH, SUCH A DEEP VOICE...
IT ECHOES...
BLINK
YOU'RE QUITE THE DEEP SLEEPER.

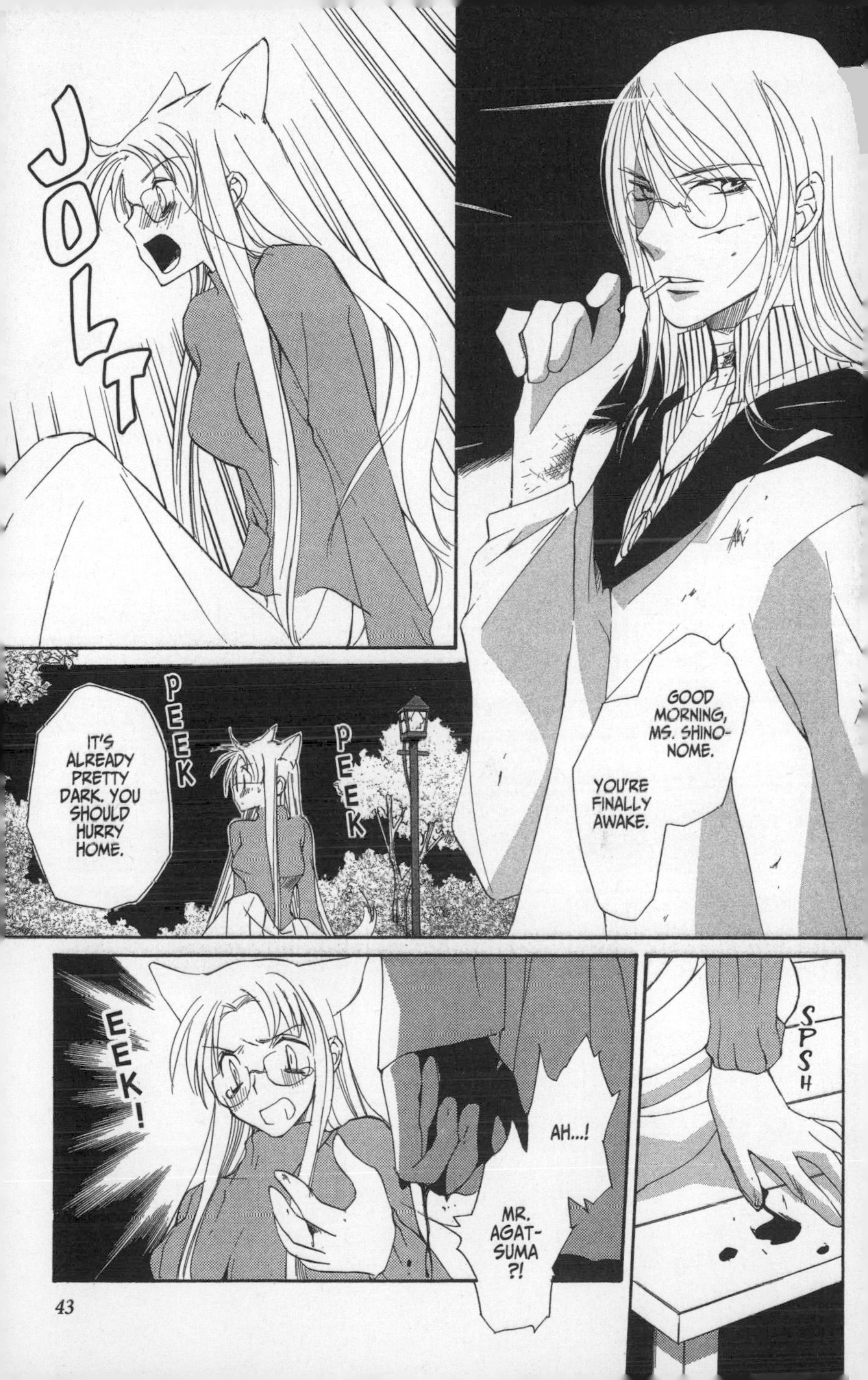
GOOD MORNING, MS. SHINONOME.
YOU'RE FINALLY AWAKE.
JOLT
PEEK
PEEK
IT'S ALREADY PRETTY DARK. YOU SHOULD HURRY HOME.
SPSH
AH...!
EEK!
MR. AGATSUMA?!

OH MY GOD!
WHAT HAPPENED?! HOW ON EARTH DID YOU GET HURT LIKE THAT?!
MS. SHINO-NOME!
OW!
DON'T TOUCH IT! THAT HURTS!
AWAH WAH WAH!
TMP
YEEP!
SPLCH
...
URK.
Is that...
...flesh?
IF IT GROSSES YOU OUT, THEN DON'T LOOK AT IT.
THIS IS AWFUL.
WE HAVE TO GET YOU TO A HOSPITAL.
TRMBL
WE SHOULD GO RIGHT NOW!
I'M FINE.
JUST LEAVE ME BE.
NO.
OH MY GOD... IS...

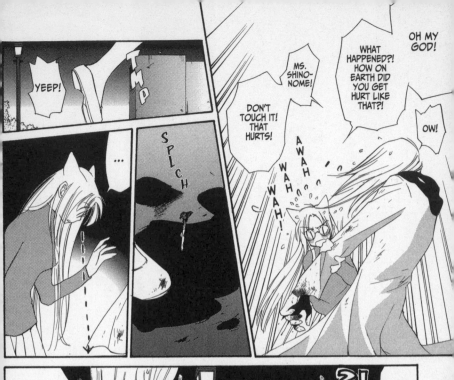

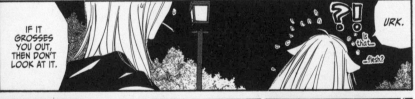

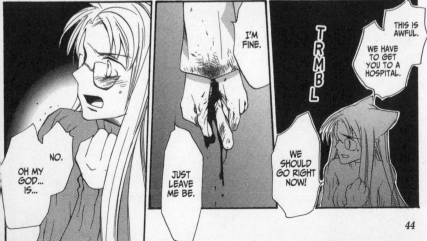

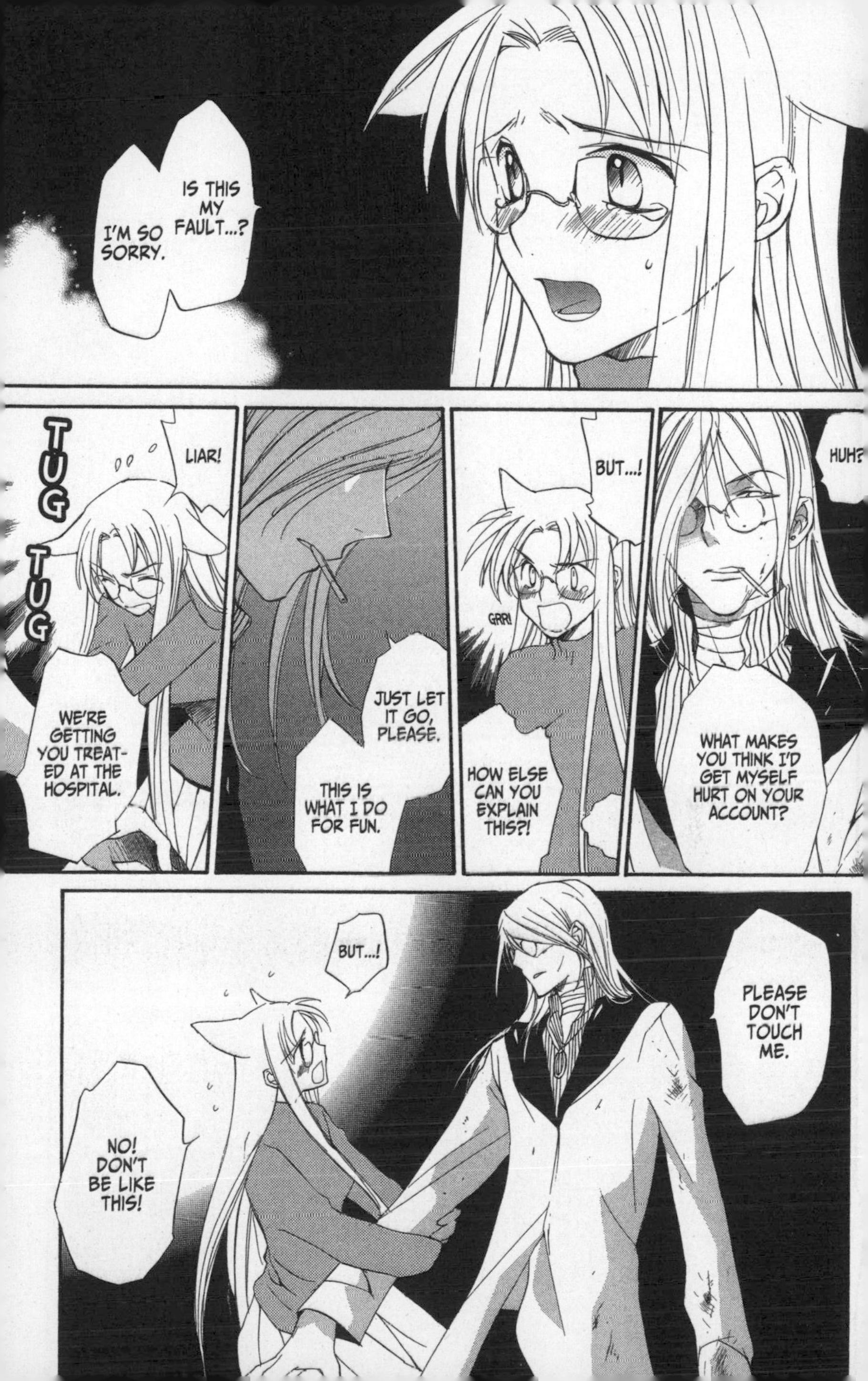
IS THIS MY FAULT...?
I'M SO SORRY.
HUH?
WHAT MAKES YOU THINK I'D GET MYSELF HURT ON YOUR ACCOUNT?
BUT...!
GRR!
HOW ELSE CAN YOU EXPLAIN THIS?!
JUST LET IT GO, PLEASE.
THIS IS WHAT I DO FOR FUN.
LIAR!
TUG TUG
WE'RE GETTING YOU TREAT-ED AT THE HOSPITAL.
PLEASE DON'T TOUCH ME.
BUT...!
NO! DON'T BE LIKE THIS!

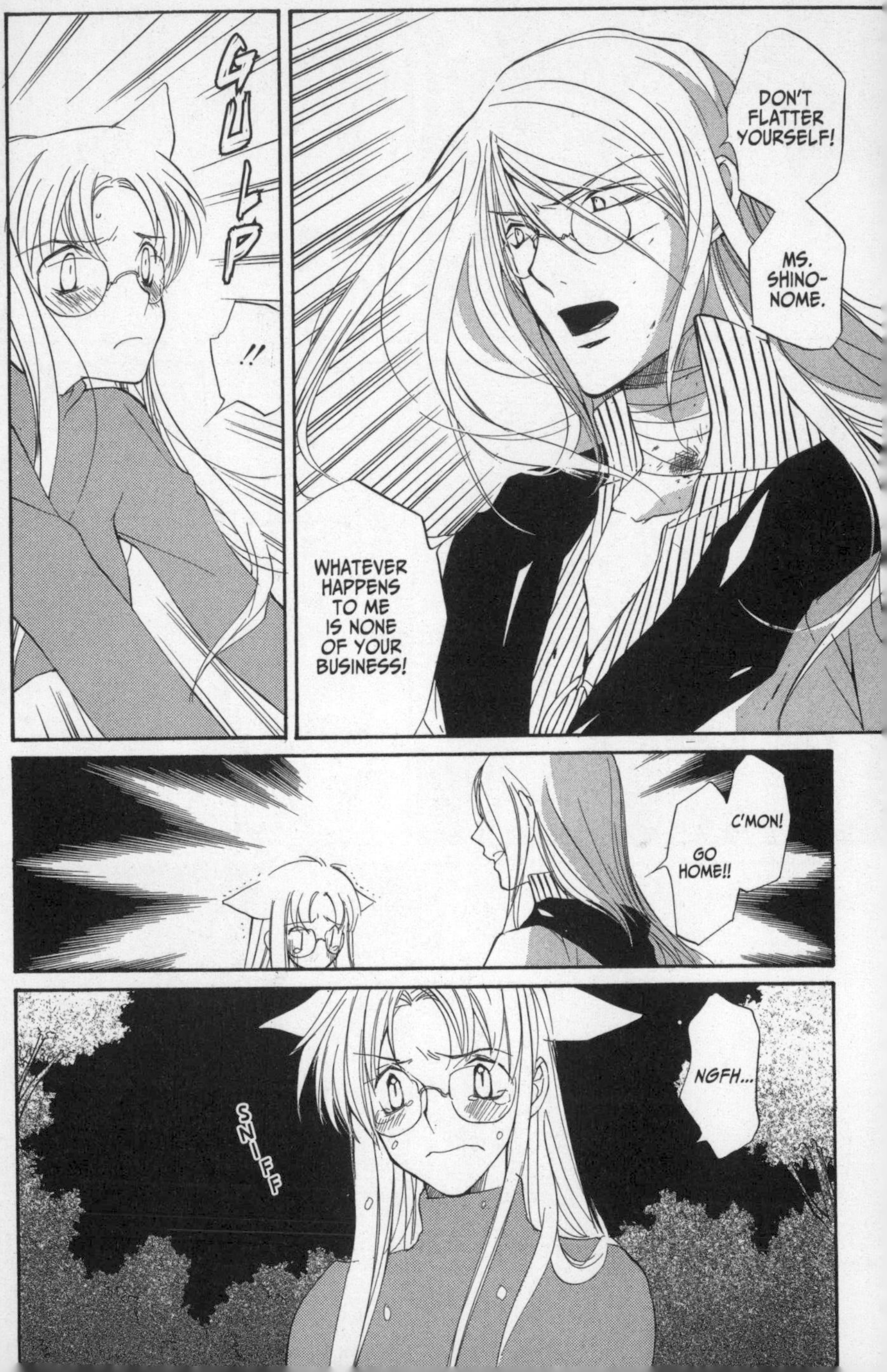
DON'T FLATTER YOURSELF!
MS. SHINO-NOME.
WHATEVER HAPPENS TO ME IS NONE OF YOUR BUSINESS!
GULP
!!
C'MON!
GO HOME!!
NGFH...
SNIFF

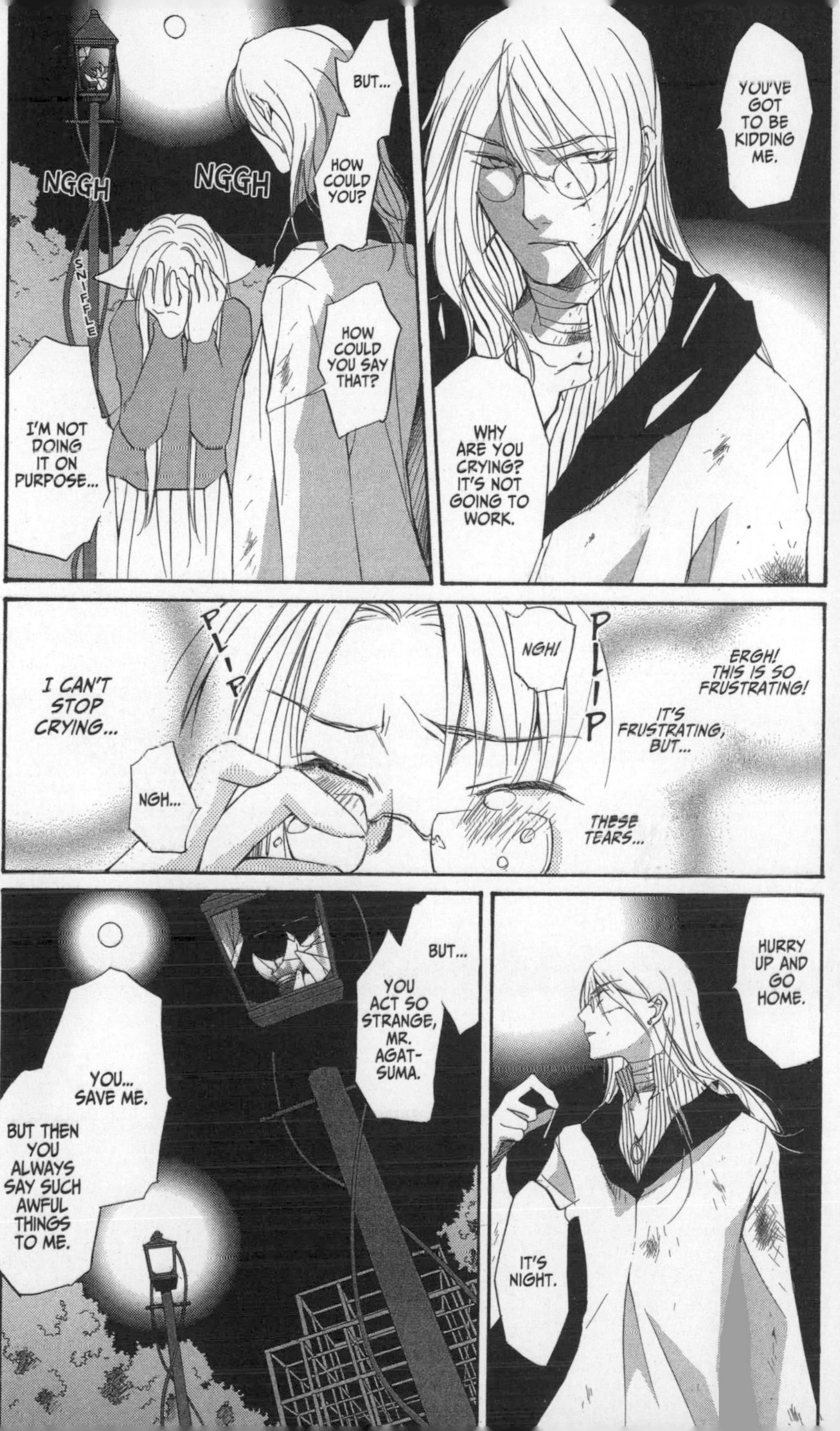
YOU'VE GOT TO BE KIDDING ME.
WHY ARE YOU CRYING? IT'S NOT GOING TO WORK.
BUT...
HOW COULD YOU?
NGGH
NGGH
SNIFFLE
HOW COULD YOU SAY THAT?
I'M NOT DOING IT ON PURPOSE...
ERGH! THIS IS SO FRUSTRATING!
IT'S FRUSTRATING, BUT...
PLIP
NGH!
PLIP
THESE TEARS...
I CAN'T STOP CRYING...
NGH...
HURRY UP AND GO HOME.
IT'S NIGHT.
BUT...
YOU ACT SO STRANGE, MR. AGAT-SUMA.
YOU... SAVE ME.
BUT THEN YOU ALWAYS SAY SUCH AWFUL THINGS TO ME.

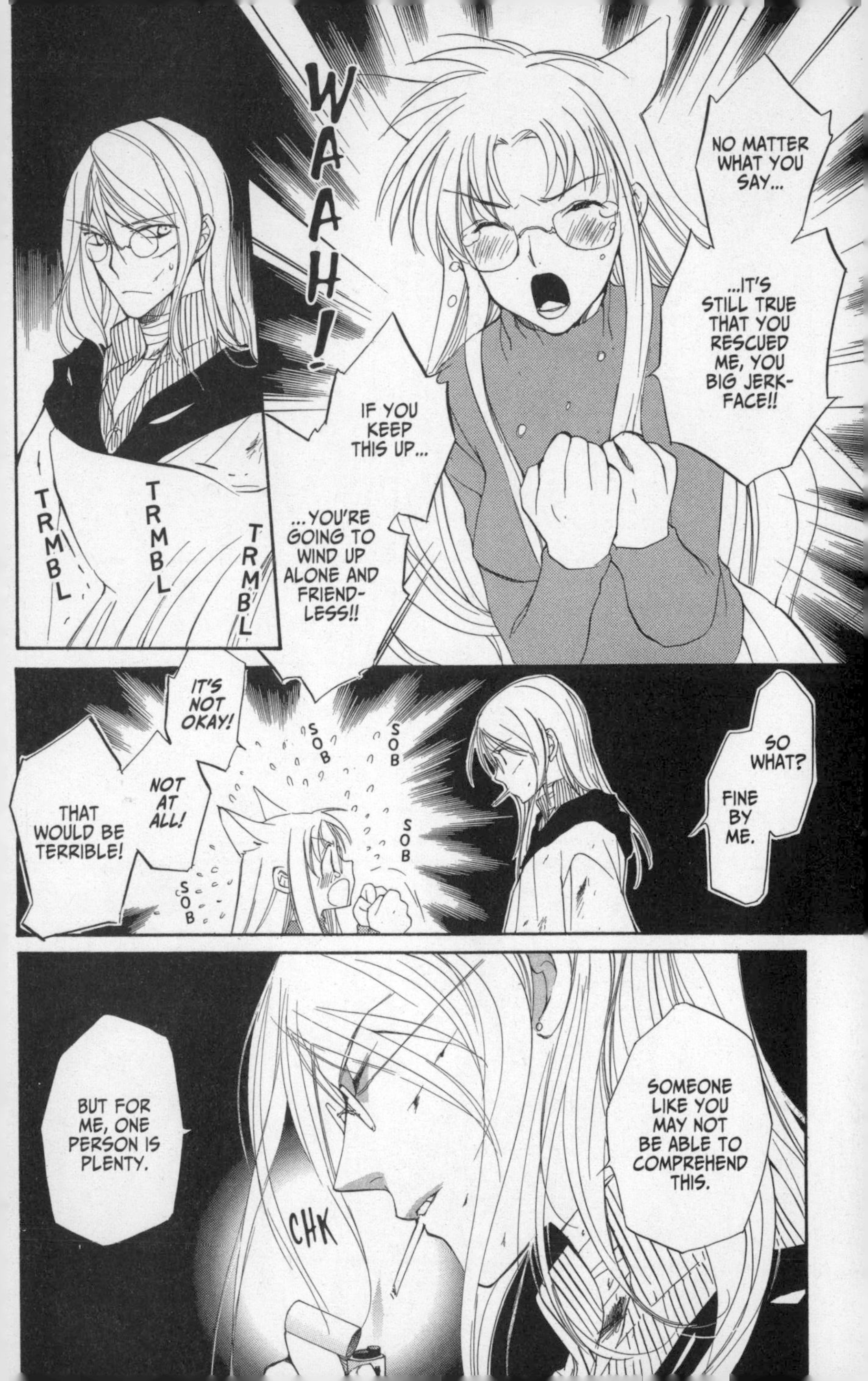
WAAH!
NO MATTER WHAT YOU SAY...
...IT'S STILL TRUE THAT YOU RESCUED ME, YOU BIG JERK-FACE!!
IF YOU KEEP THIS UP...
...YOU'RE GOING TO WIND UP ALONE AND FRIEND-LESS!!
TRMBL
TRMBL
TRMBL
SO WHAT?
FINE BY ME.
SOB
SOB
SOB
SOB
IT'S NOT OKAY!
NOT AT ALL!
THAT WOULD BE TERRIBLE!
SOMEONE LIKE YOU MAY NOT BE ABLE TO COMPREHEND THIS.
CHK
BUT FOR ME, ONE PERSON IS PLENTY.

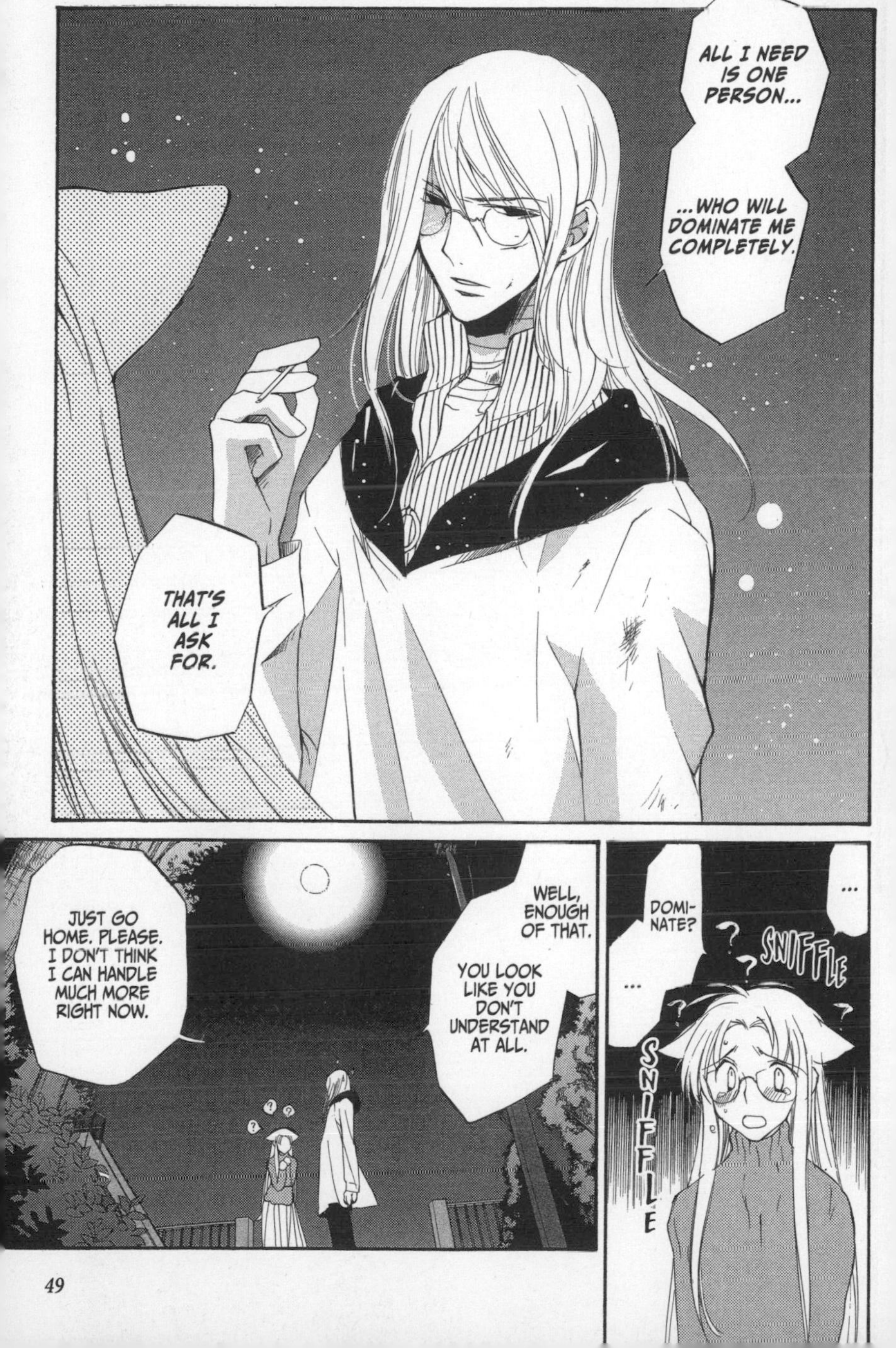
ALL I NEED IS ONE PERSON...
...WHO WILL DOMINATE ME COMPLETELY.
THAT'S ALL I ASK FOR.
...
DOMI-NATE?
...
SNIFFLE
SNIFFLE
WELL, ENOUGH OF THAT.
YOU LOOK LIKE YOU DON'T UNDERSTAND AT ALL.
JUST GO HOME. PLEASE. I DON'T THINK I CAN HANDLE MUCH MORE RIGHT NOW.

BLUSH

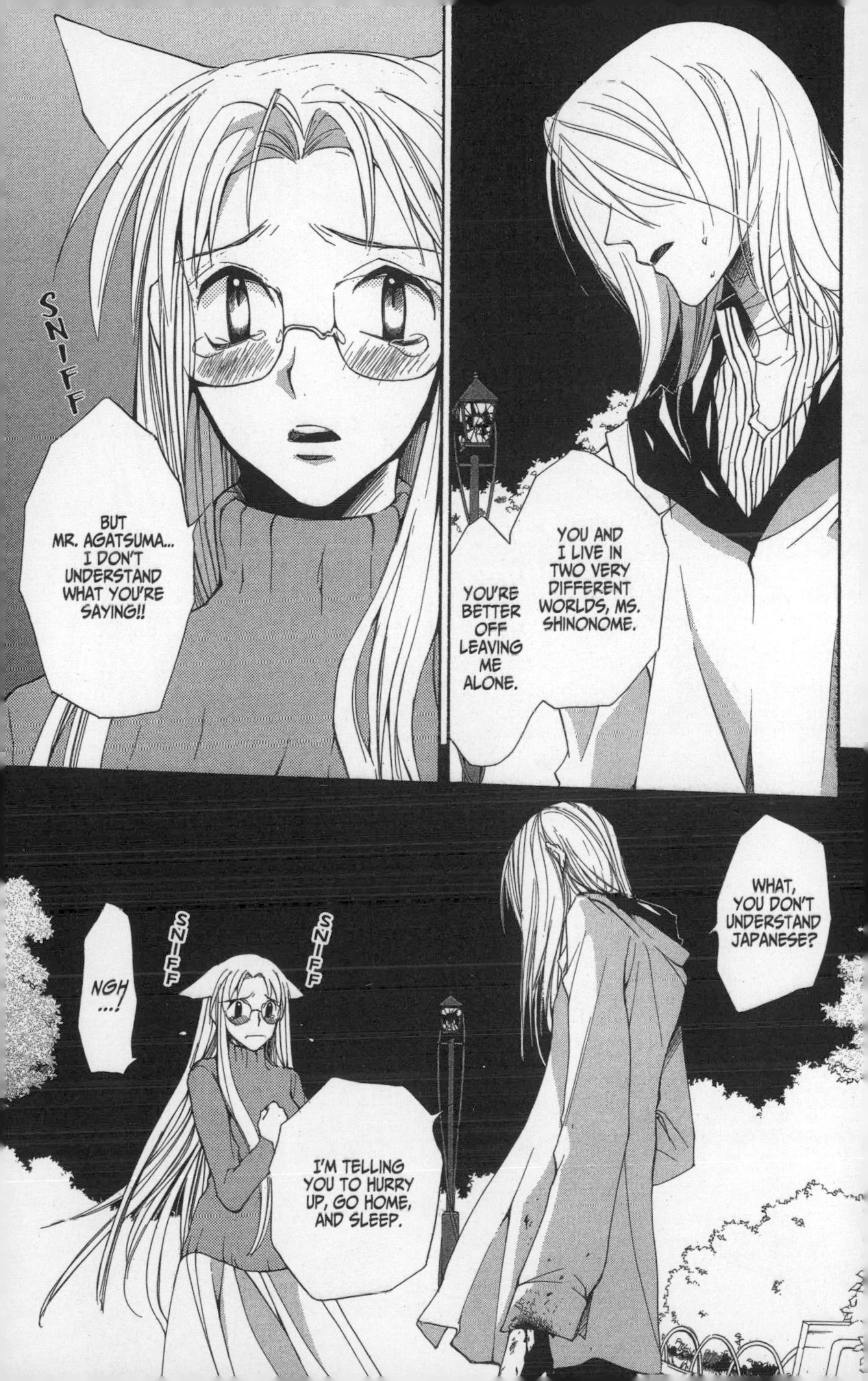
YOU AND I LIVE IN TWO VERY DIFFERENT WORLDS, MS. SHINONOME.
YOU'RE BETTER OFF LEAVING ME ALONE.
SNIFF
BUT MR. AGATSUMA... I DON'T UNDERSTAND WHAT YOU'RE SAYING!!
WHAT, YOU DON'T UNDERSTAND JAPANESE?
I'M TELLING YOU TO HURRY UP, GO HOME, AND SLEEP.
SNIFF
SNIFF
NGH...!

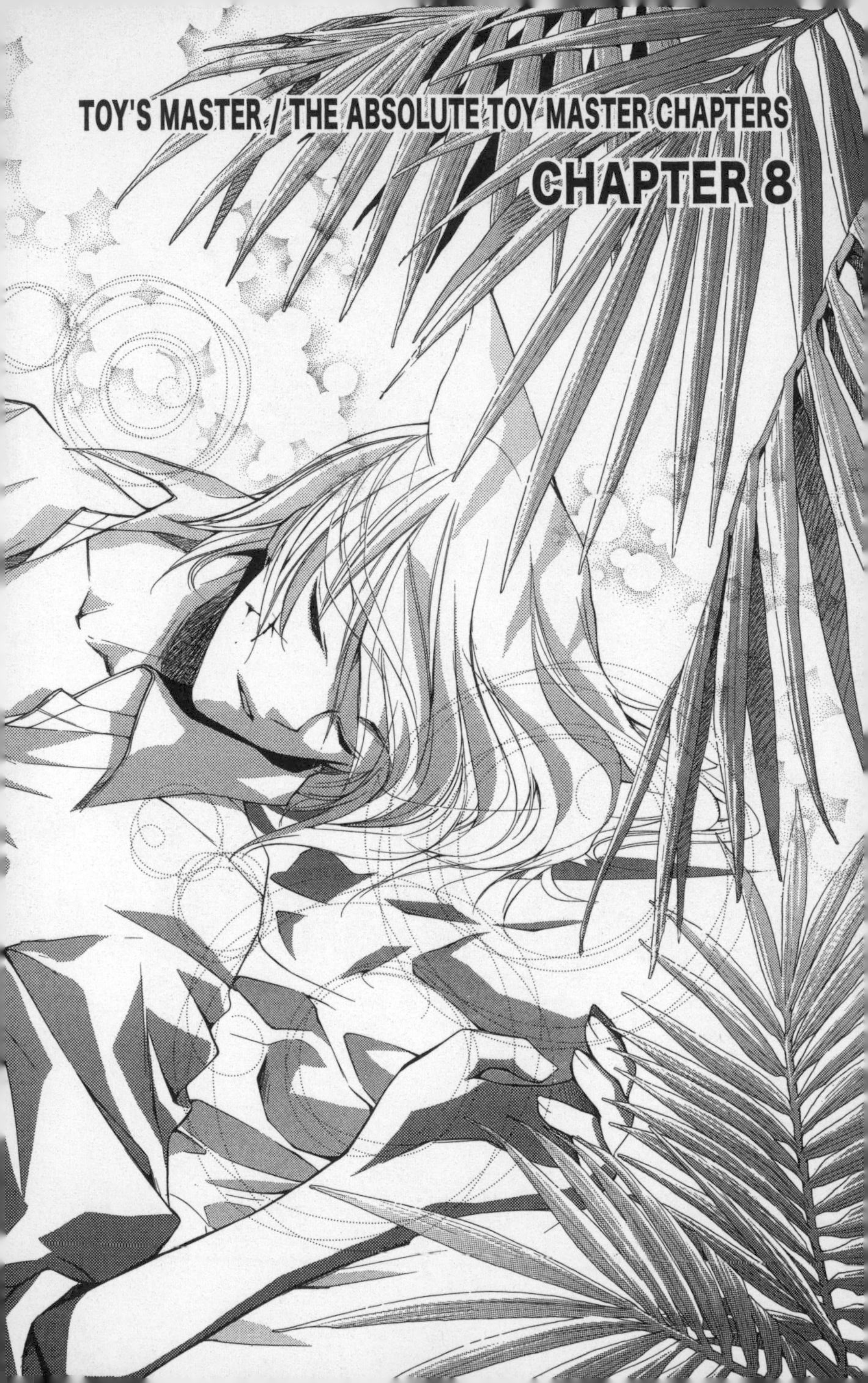

TOY'S MASTER / THE ABSOLUTE TOY MASTER CHAPTERS
CHAPTER 8

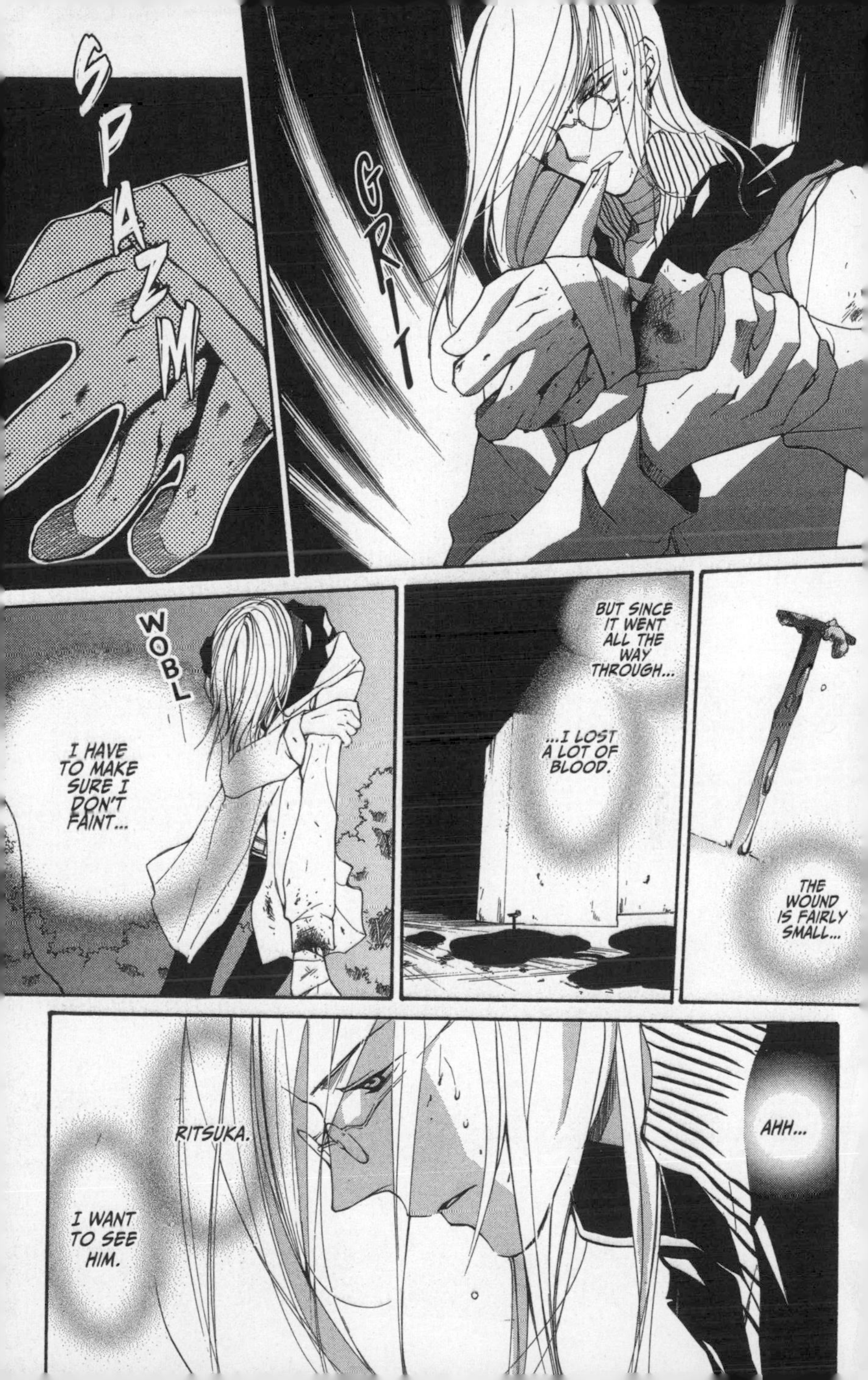
GRIT
SPAZM
THE WOUND IS FAIRLY SMALL...
BUT SINCE IT WENT ALL THE WAY THROUGH...
...I LOST A LOT OF BLOOD.
WOBL
I HAVE TO MAKE SURE I DON'T FAINT...
AHH...
RITSUKA.
I WANT TO SEE HIM.

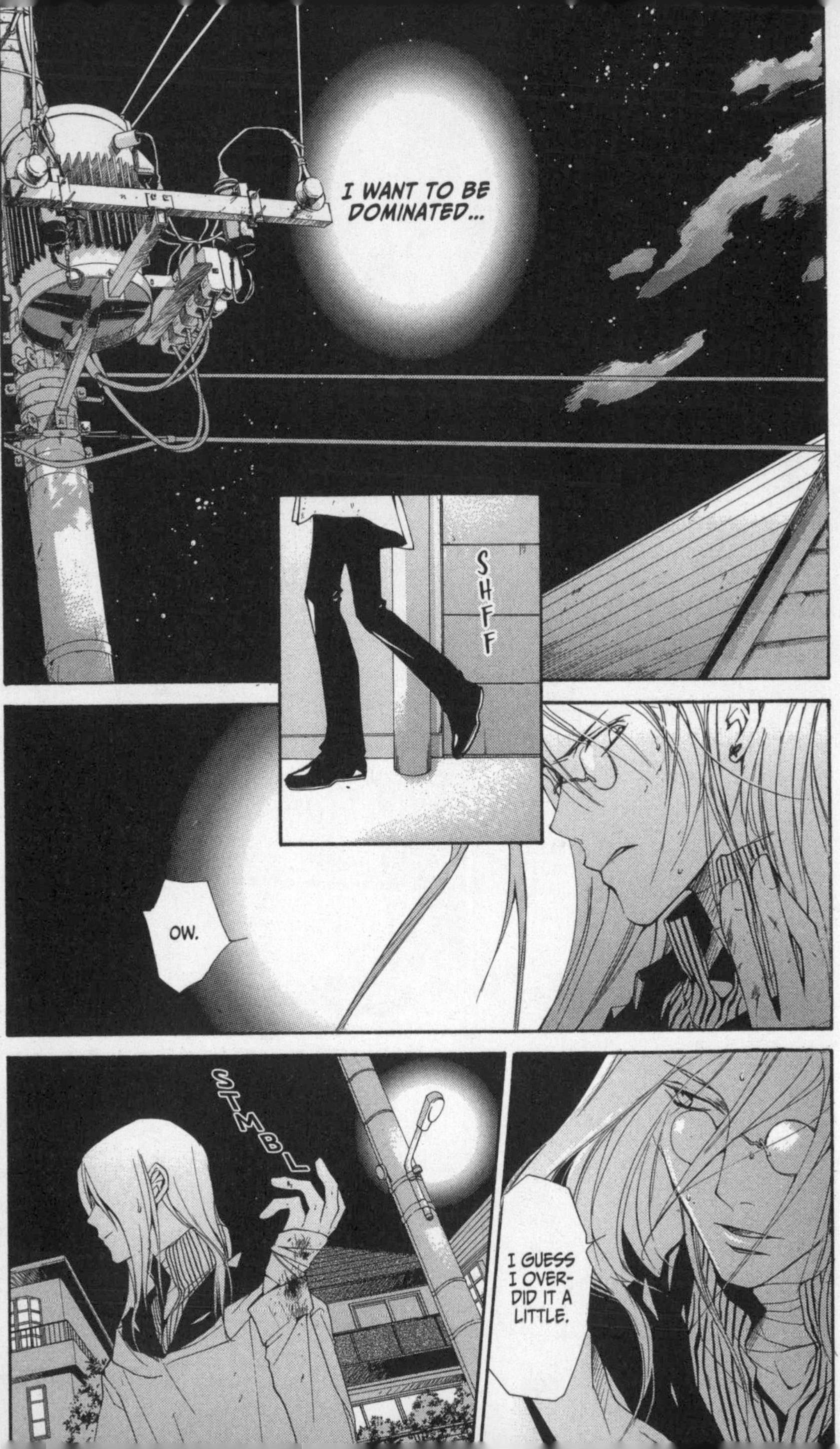
I WANT TO BE DOMINATED...
SHFF
OW.
I GUESS I OVER-DID IT A LITTLE.
STMBL

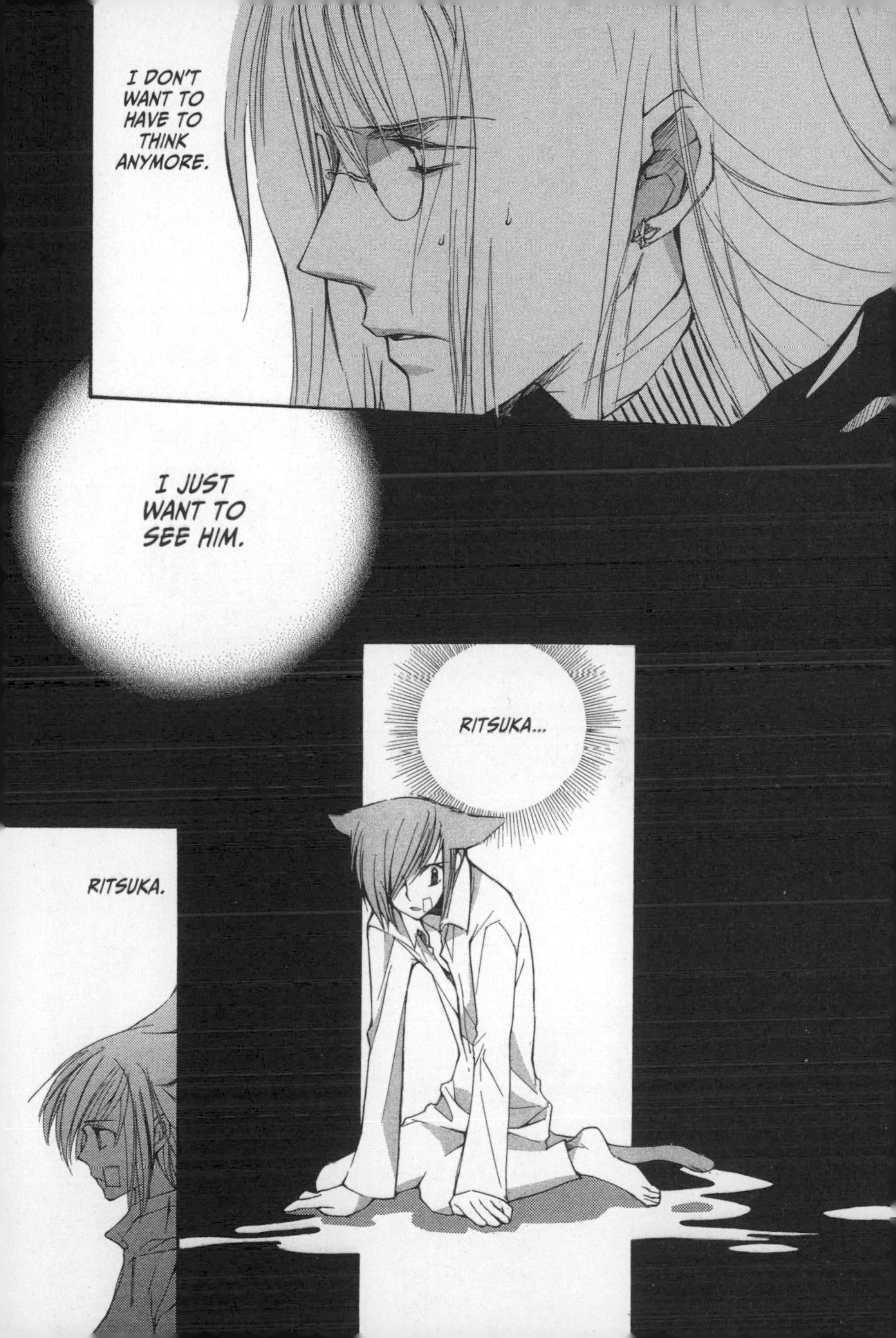
I DON'T WANT TO HAVE TO THINK ANYMORE.
I JUST WANT TO SEE HIM.
RITSUKA...
RITSUKA.

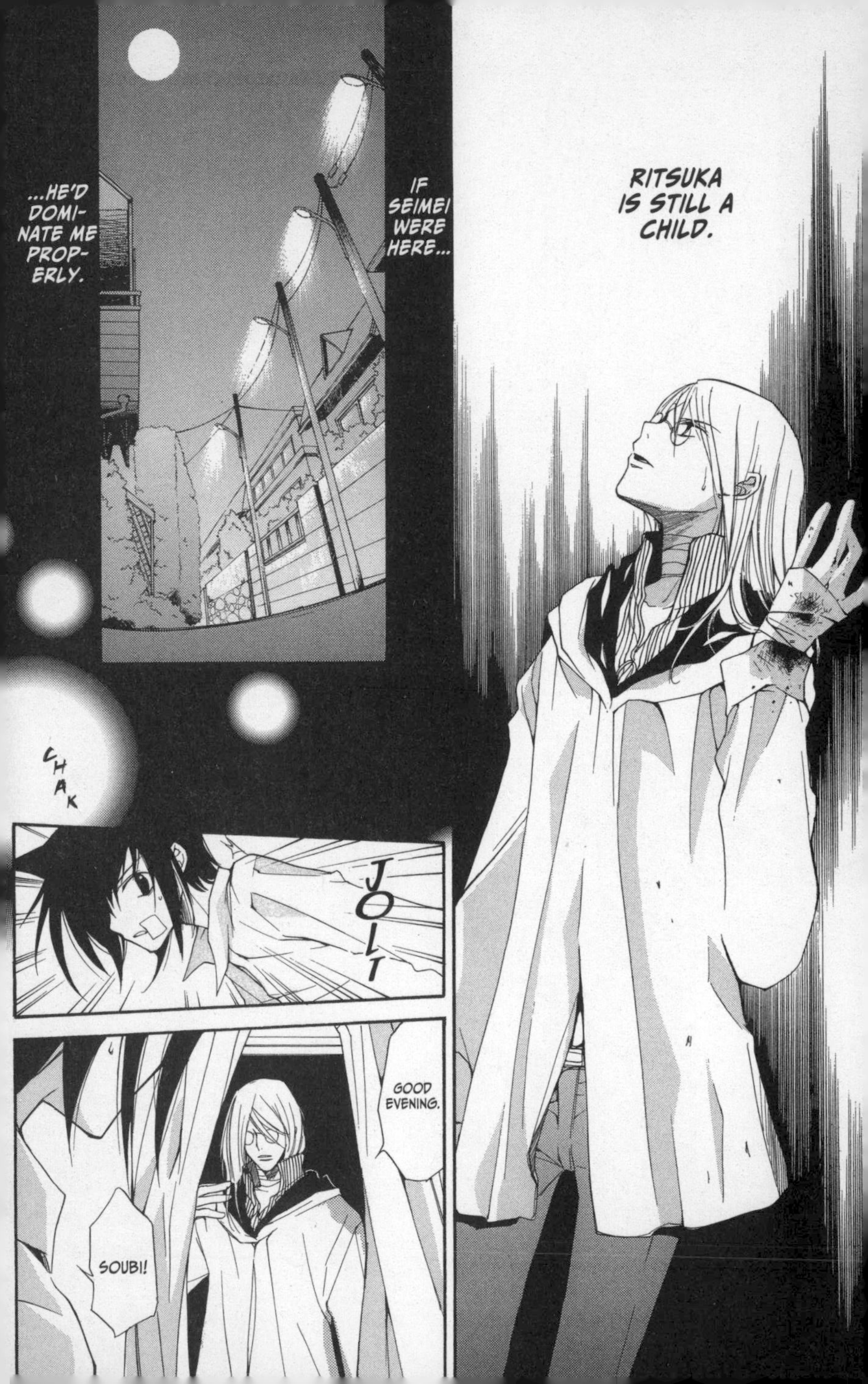
RITSUKA IS STILL A CHILD.
IF SEIMEI WERE HERE...
...HE'D DOMINATE ME PROPERLY.
CHAK
JOLT
GOOD EVENING.
SOUBI!

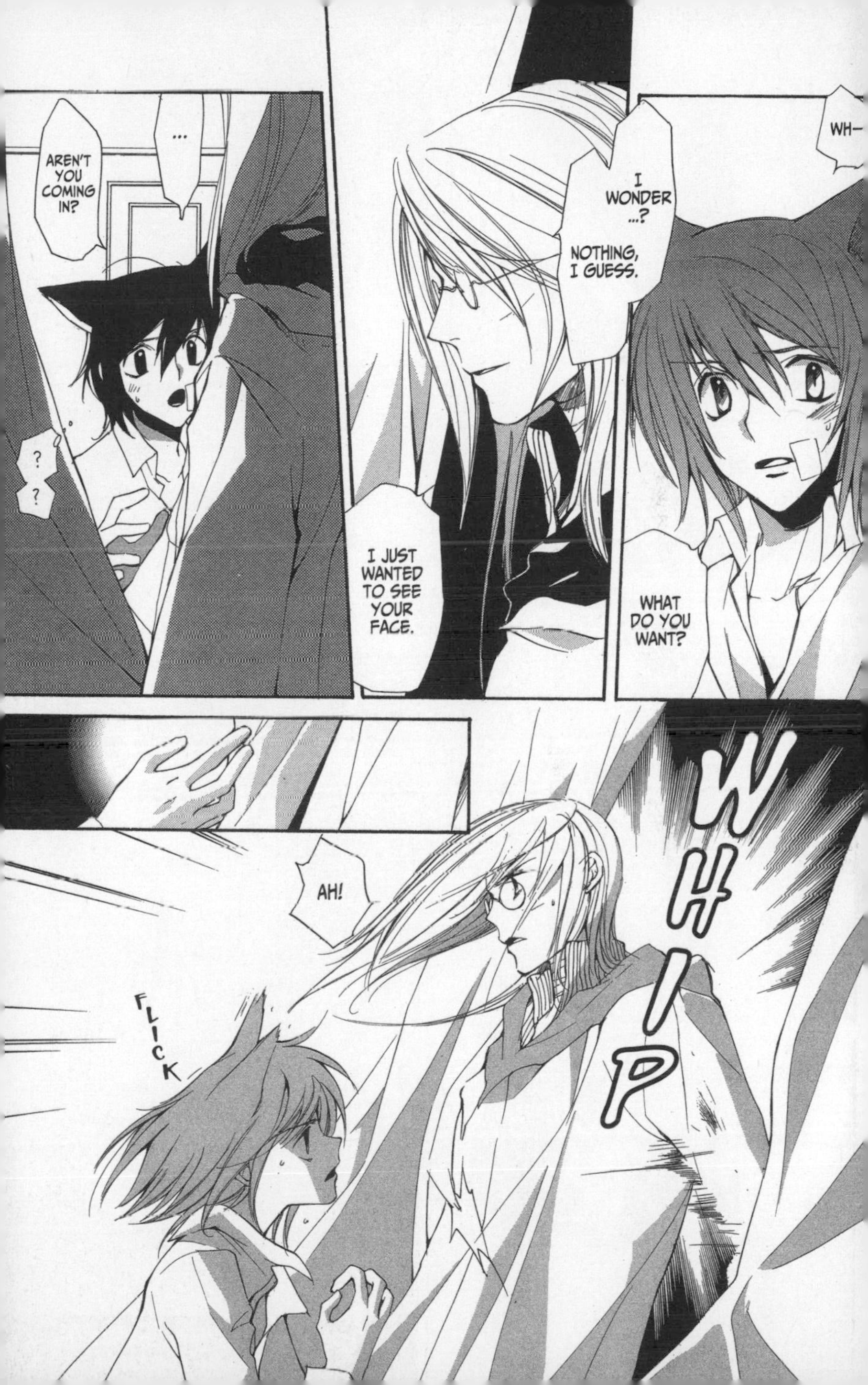
WH—
WHAT DO YOU WANT?
I WONDER ...?
NOTHING, I GUESS.
I JUST WANTED TO SEE YOUR FACE.
...
AREN'T YOU COMING IN?
?
?
WHIP
AH!
FLICK

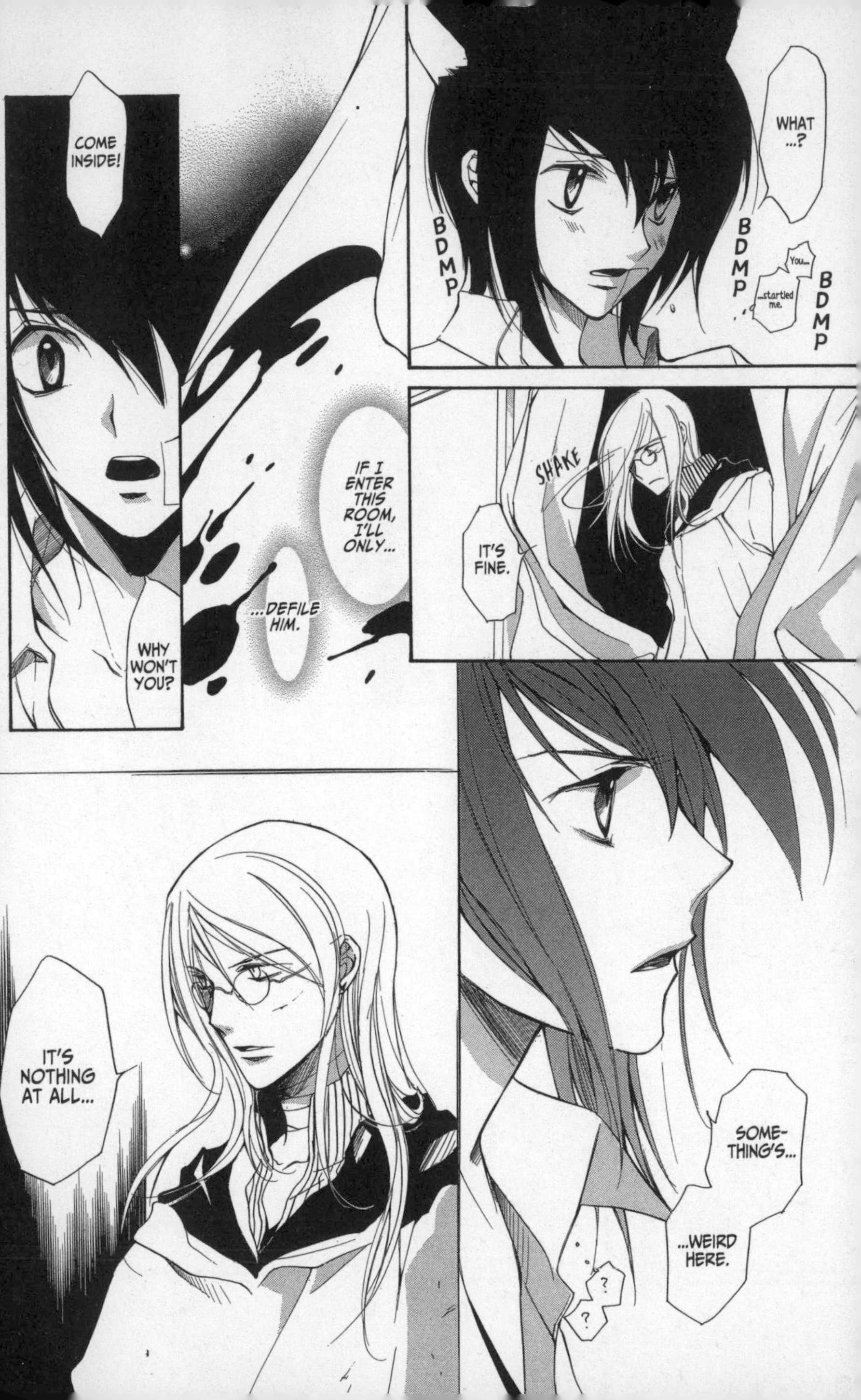
WHAT ...?
BDMP
BDMP
You... ...startled me.
BDMP
SHAKE
IT'S FINE.
COME INSIDE!
WHY WON'T YOU?
IF I ENTER THIS ROOM, I'LL ONLY...
...DEFILE HIM.
SOME-THING'S...
...WEIRD HERE.
?
?
IT'S NOTHING AT ALL...

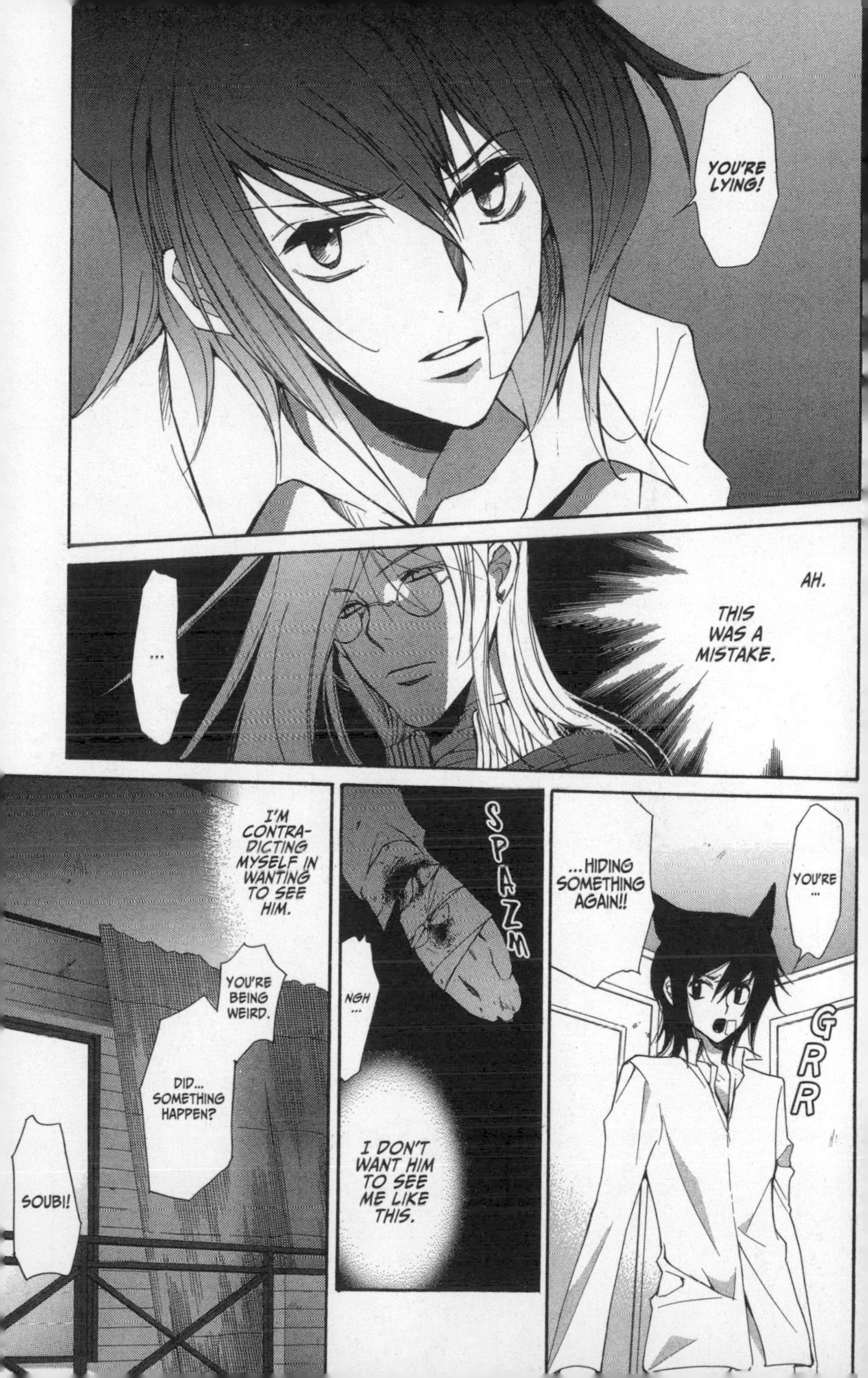
YOU'RE LYING!
AH.
THIS WAS A MISTAKE.
...
YOU'RE ...
...HIDING SOMETHING AGAIN!!
GRR
SPAZM
NGH ...
I DON'T WANT HIM TO SEE ME LIKE THIS.
I'M CONTRA-DICTING MYSELF IN WANTING TO SEE HIM.
YOU'RE BEING WEIRD.
DID... SOMETHING HAPPEN?
SOUBI!

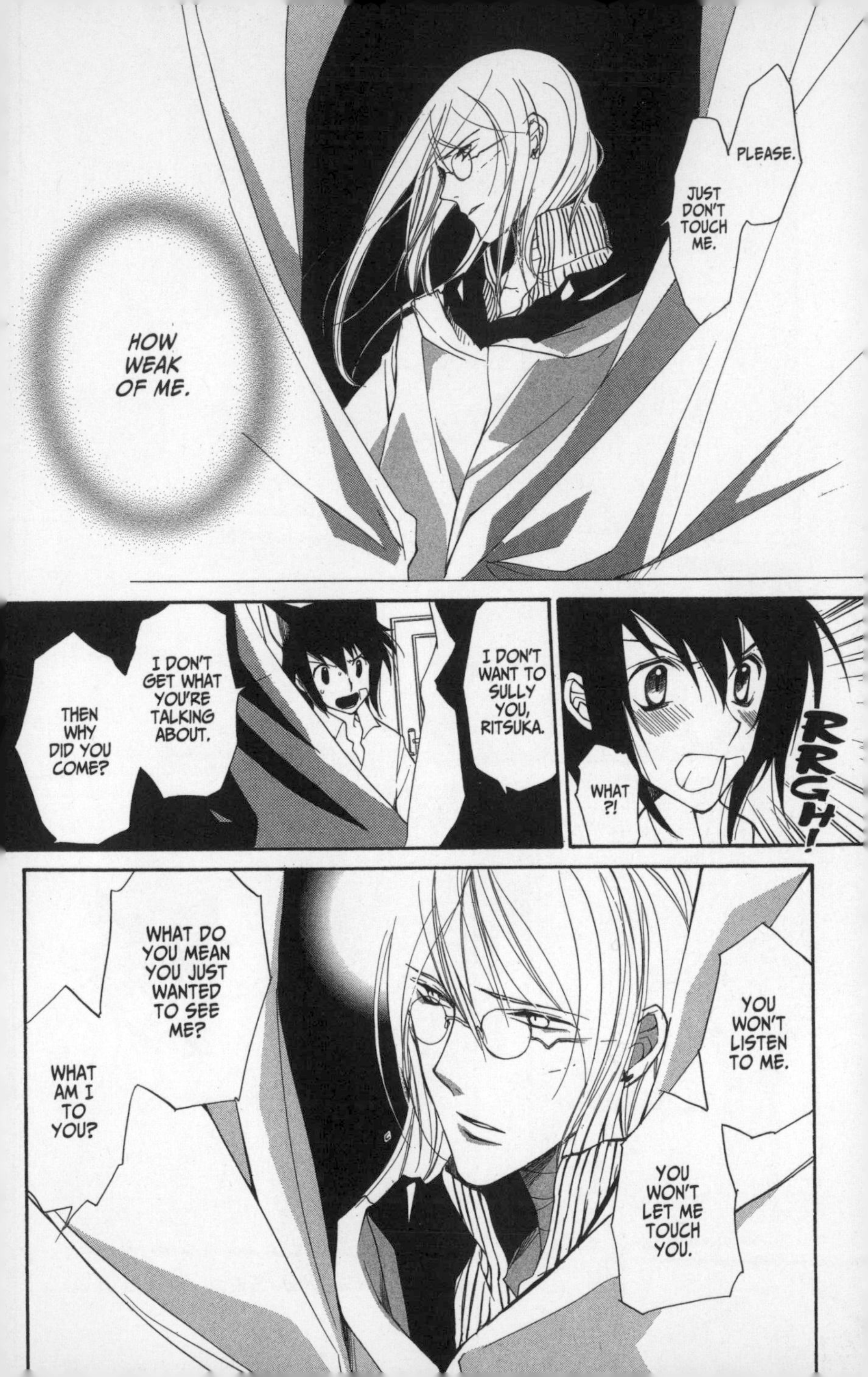
PLEASE.
JUST DON'T TOUCH ME.
HOW WEAK OF ME.
RRGH!
WHAT ?!
I DON'T WANT TO SULLY YOU, RITSUKA.
I DON'T GET WHAT YOU'RE TALKING ABOUT.
THEN WHY DID YOU COME?
YOU WON'T LISTEN TO ME.
YOU WON'T LET ME TOUCH YOU.
WHAT DO YOU MEAN YOU JUST WANTED TO SEE ME?
WHAT AM I TO YOU?

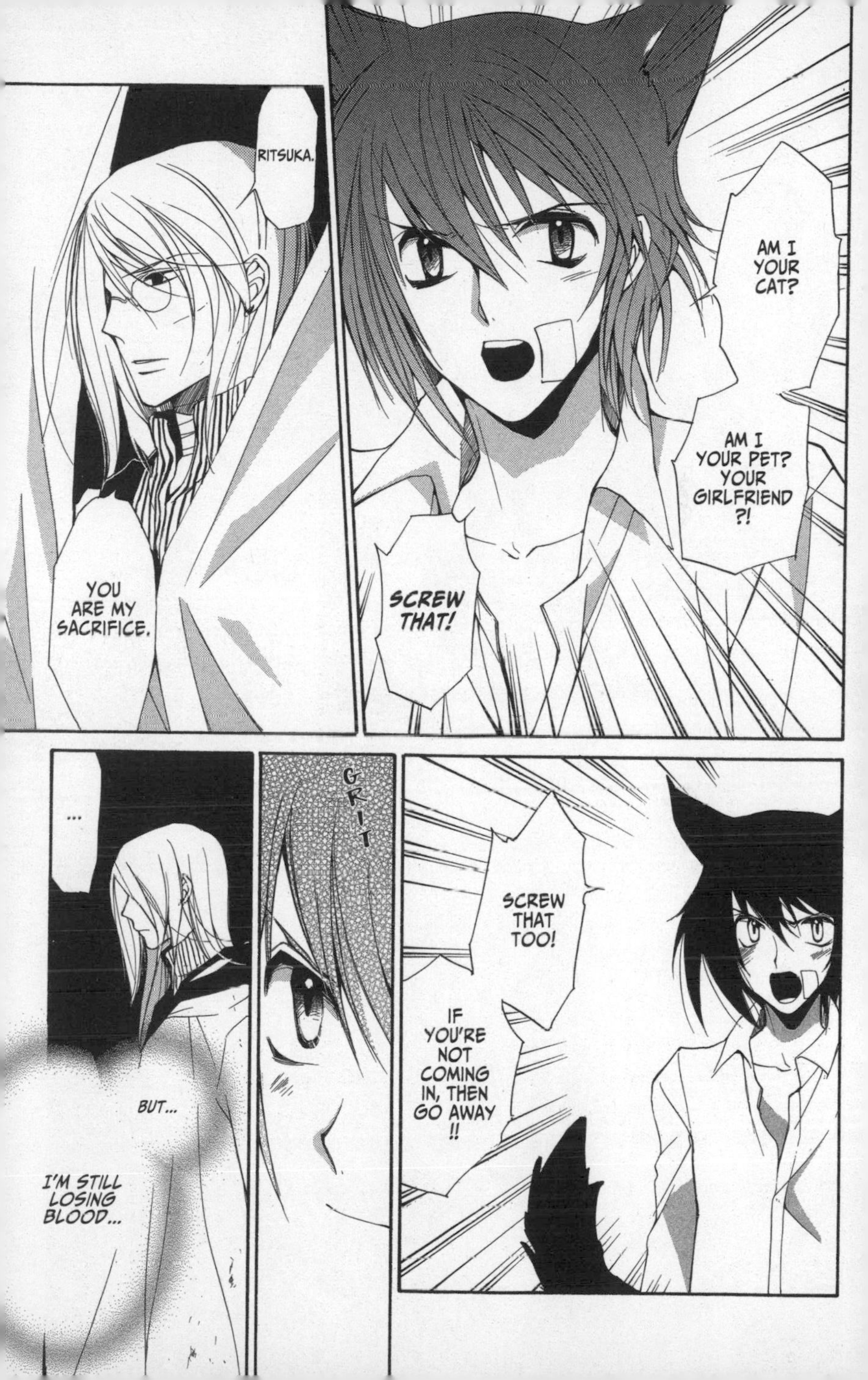
AM I YOUR CAT?
AM I YOUR PET? YOUR GIRLFRIEND ?!
SCREW THAT!
RITSUKA.
YOU ARE MY SACRIFICE.
SCREW THAT TOO!
IF YOU'RE NOT COMING IN, THEN GO AWAY !!
GRIT
...
BUT...
I'M STILL LOSING BLOOD...

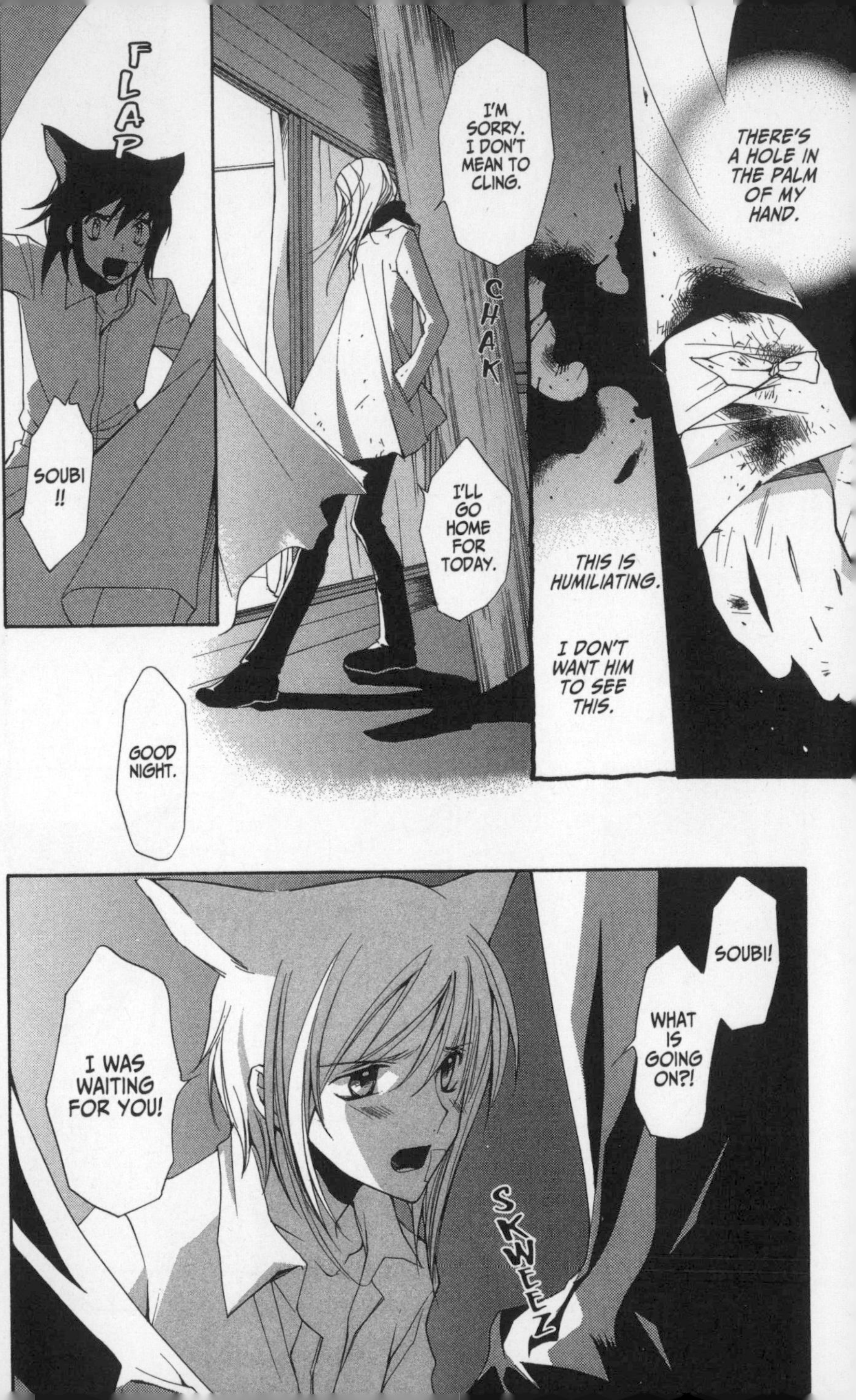
THERE'S A HOLE IN THE PALM OF MY HAND.
THIS IS HUMILIATING.
I DON'T WANT HIM TO SEE THIS.
I'M SORRY. I DON'T MEAN TO CLING.
CHAK
I'LL GO HOME FOR TODAY.
GOOD NIGHT.
FLAP
SOUBI !!
SOUBI!
WHAT IS GOING ON?!
SKWEEZ
I WAS WAITING FOR YOU!

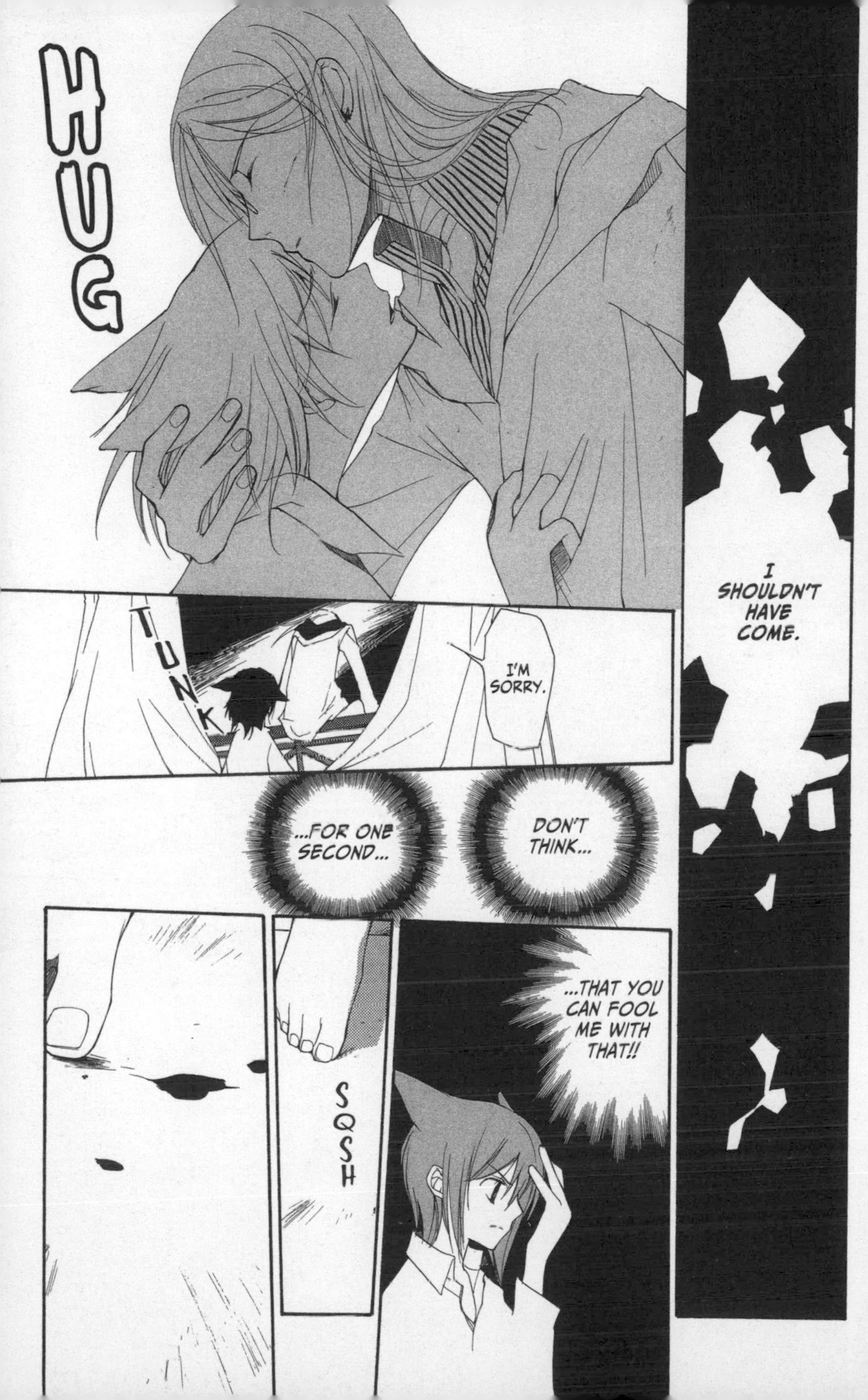
I SHOULDN'T HAVE COME.
HUG
I'M SORRY.
TUNK
DON'T THINK...
...FOR ONE SECOND...
...THAT YOU CAN FOOL ME WITH THAT!!
SQSH

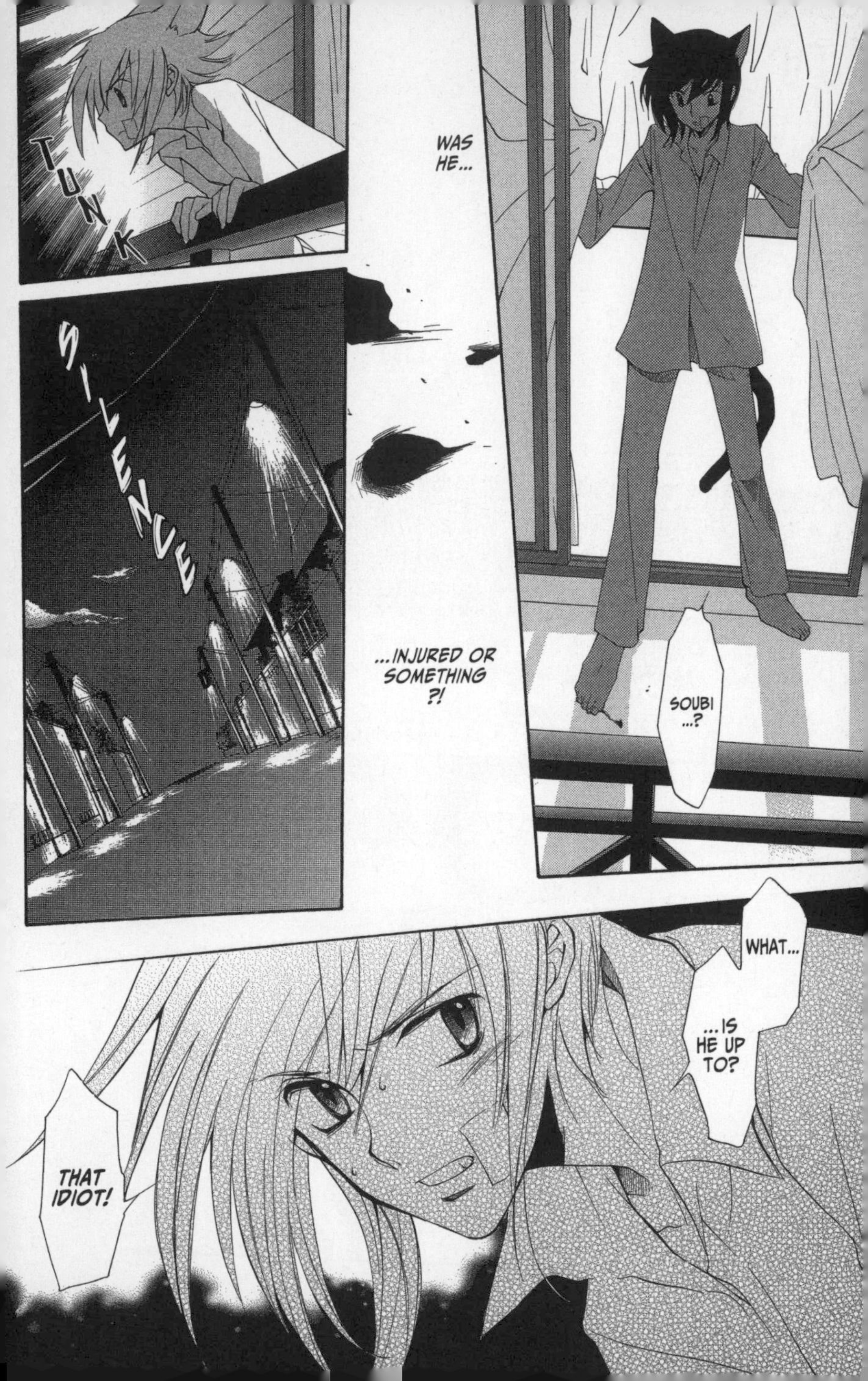

WAS HE...
...INJURED OR SOMETHING ?!
SOUBI ...?
TUNK
SILENCE
WHAT...
...IS HE UP TO?
THAT IDIOT!

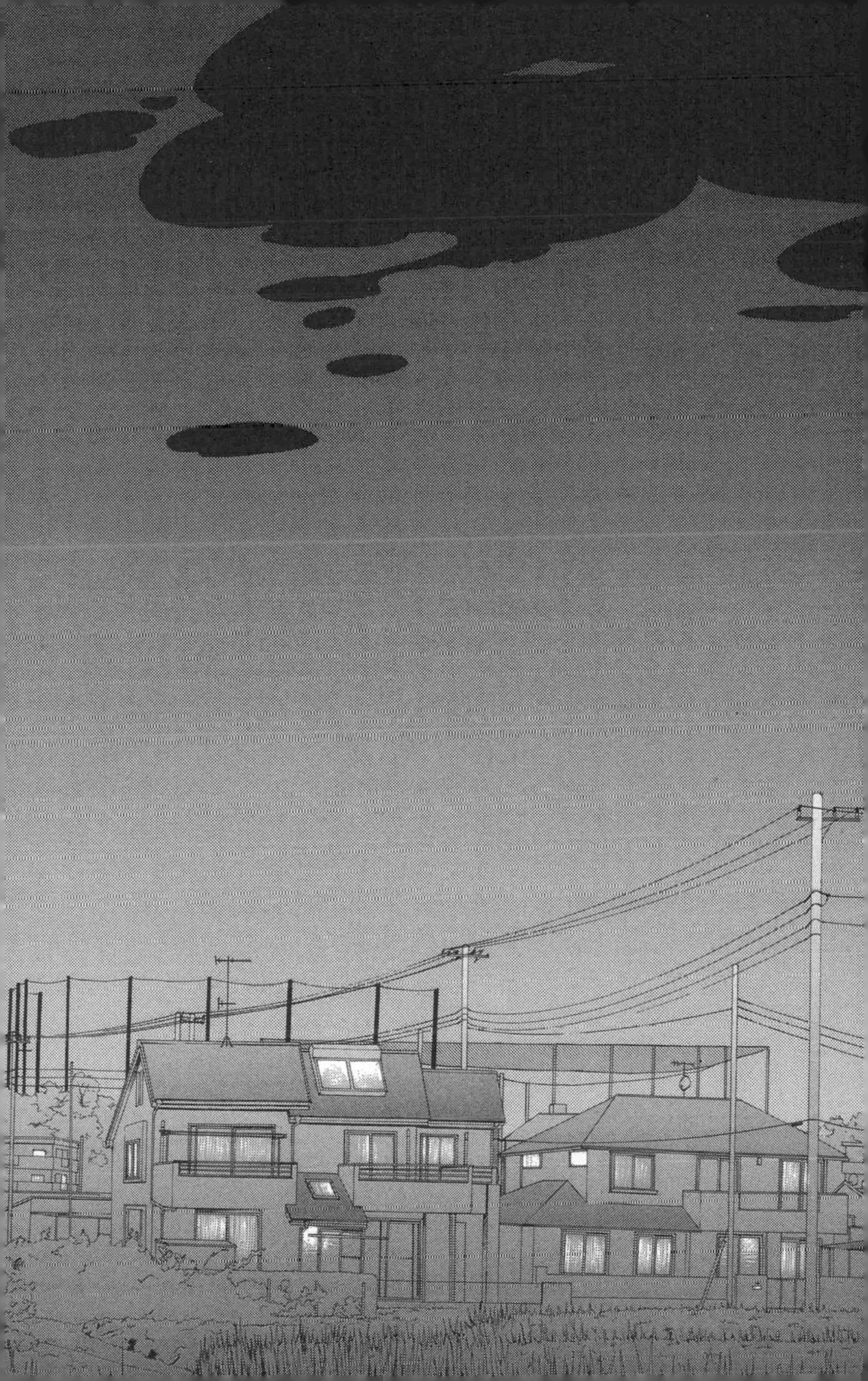

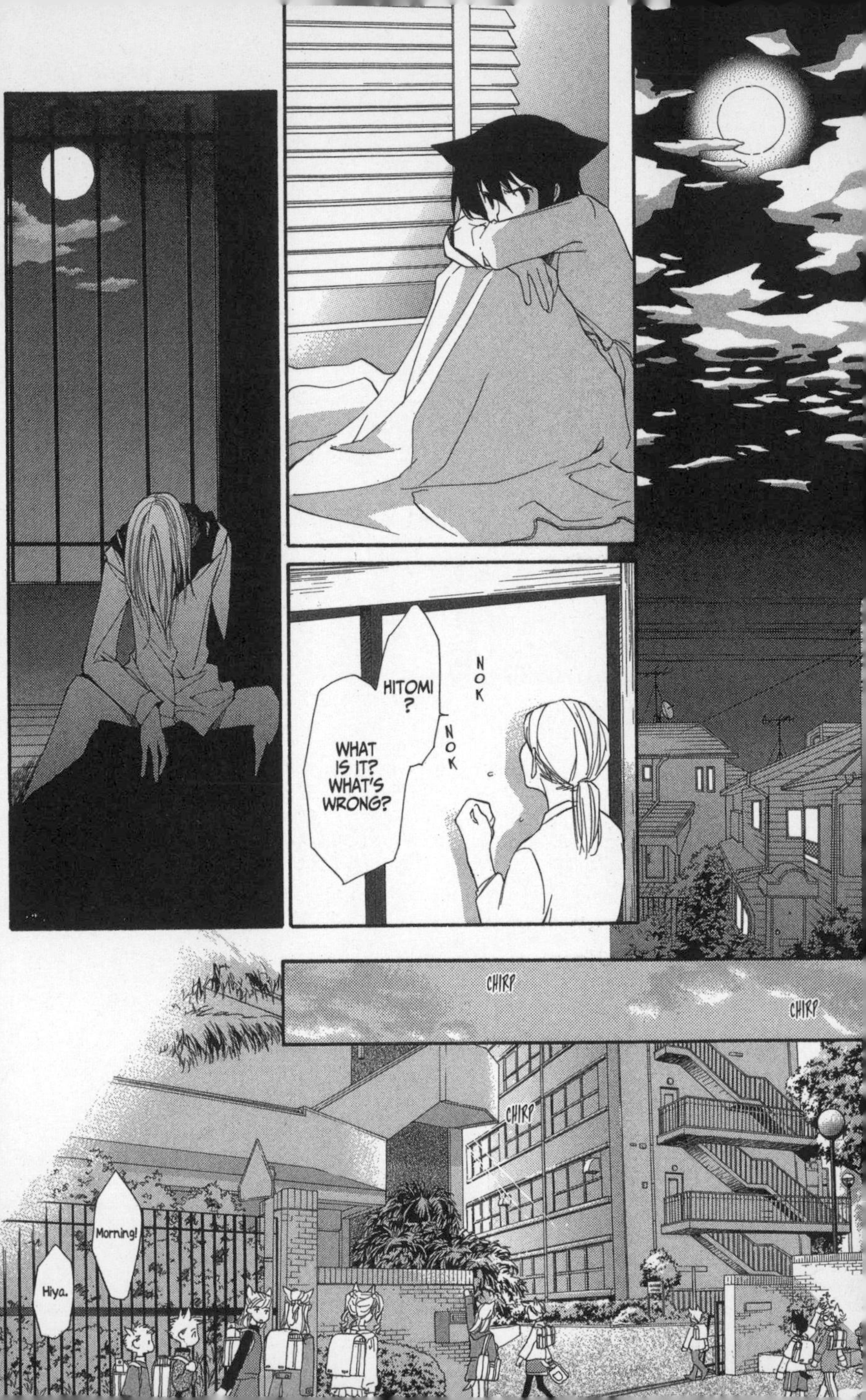
NOK
NOK
HITOMI?
WHAT IS IT? WHAT'S WRONG?
CHIRP
CHIRP
CHIRP
Morning!
Hiya.

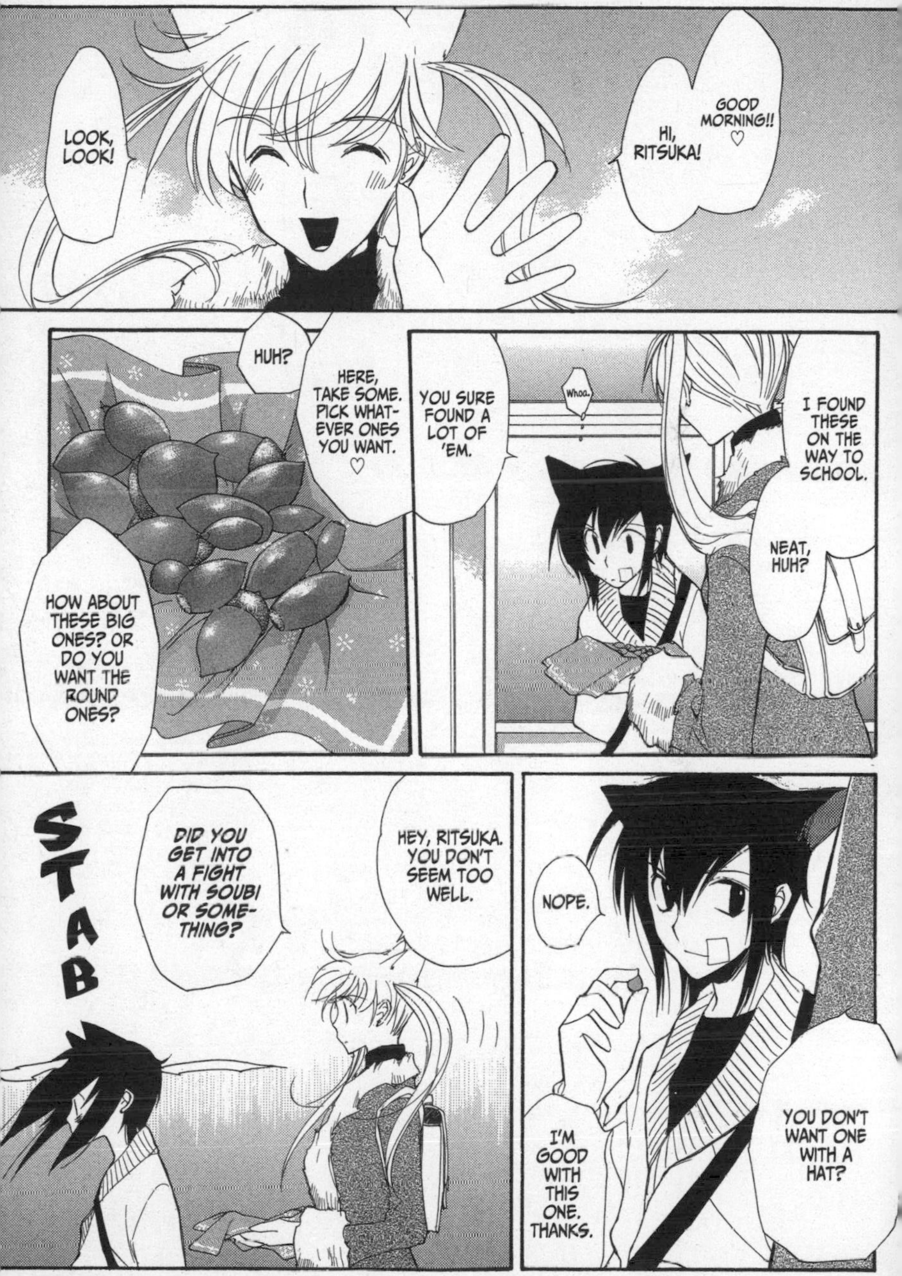
HI, RITSUKA!
GOOD MORNING!! ♡
LOOK, LOOK!
I FOUND THESE ON THE WAY TO SCHOOL.
Whoa.
NEAT, HUH?
YOU SURE FOUND A LOT OF 'EM.
HERE, TAKE SOME. PICK WHAT-EVER ONES YOU WANT. ♡
HUH?
HOW ABOUT THESE BIG ONES? OR DO YOU WANT THE ROUND ONES?
NOPE.
YOU DON'T WANT ONE WITH A HAT?
I'M GOOD WITH THIS ONE. THANKS.
HEY, RITSUKA. YOU DON'T SEEM TOO WELL.
DID YOU GET INTO A FIGHT WITH SOUBI OR SOME-THING?
STAB

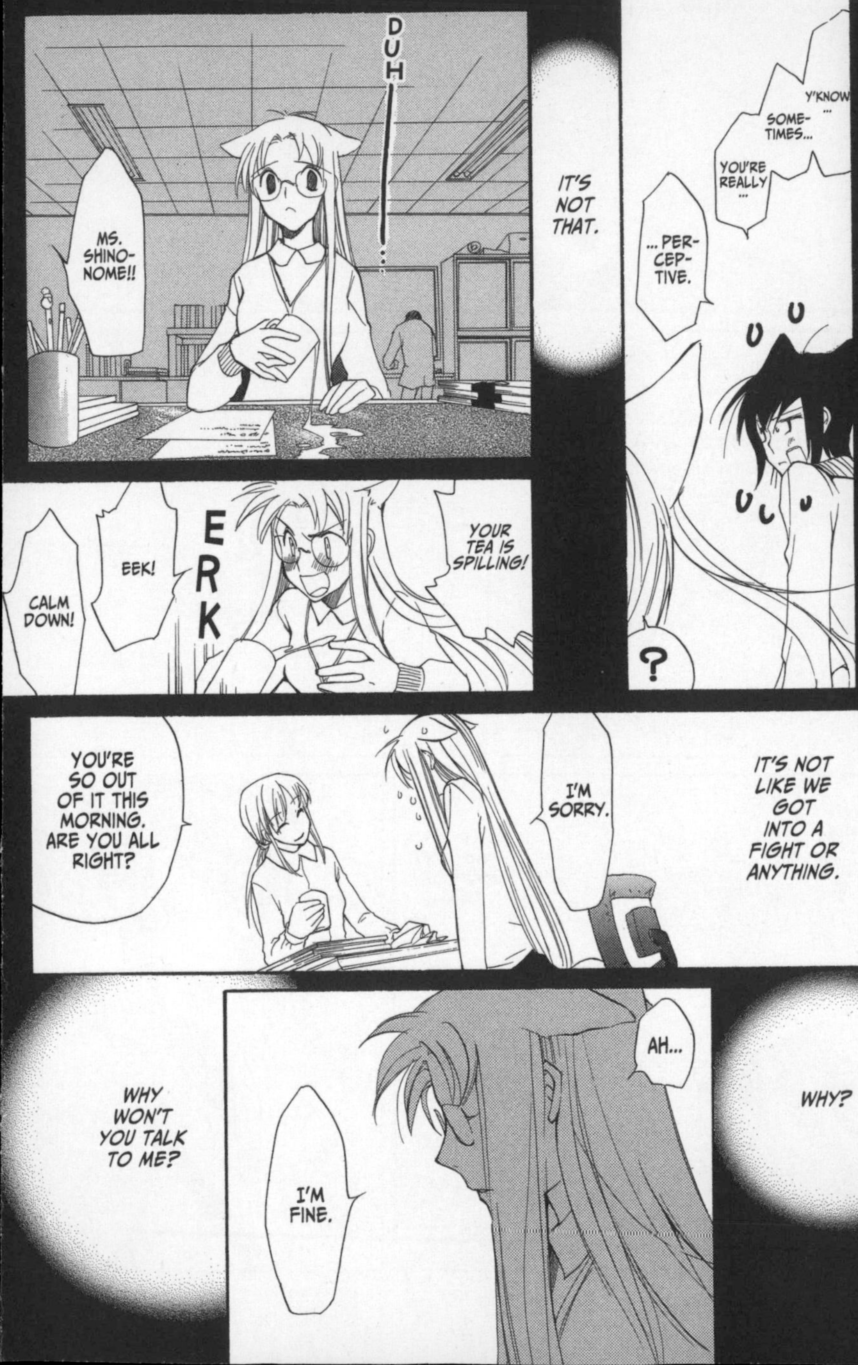
Y'KNOW...
SOME-TIMES...
YOU'RE REALLY...
...PER-CEP-TIVE.
?
IT'S NOT THAT.
DUH—...
MS. SHINO-NOME!!
YOUR TEA IS SPILLING!
ERK
EEK!
CALM DOWN!
IT'S NOT LIKE WE GOT INTO A FIGHT OR ANYTHING.
I'M SORRY.
YOU'RE SO OUT OF IT THIS MORNING. ARE YOU ALL RIGHT?
WHY?
AH...
I'M FINE.
WHY WON'T YOU TALK TO ME?

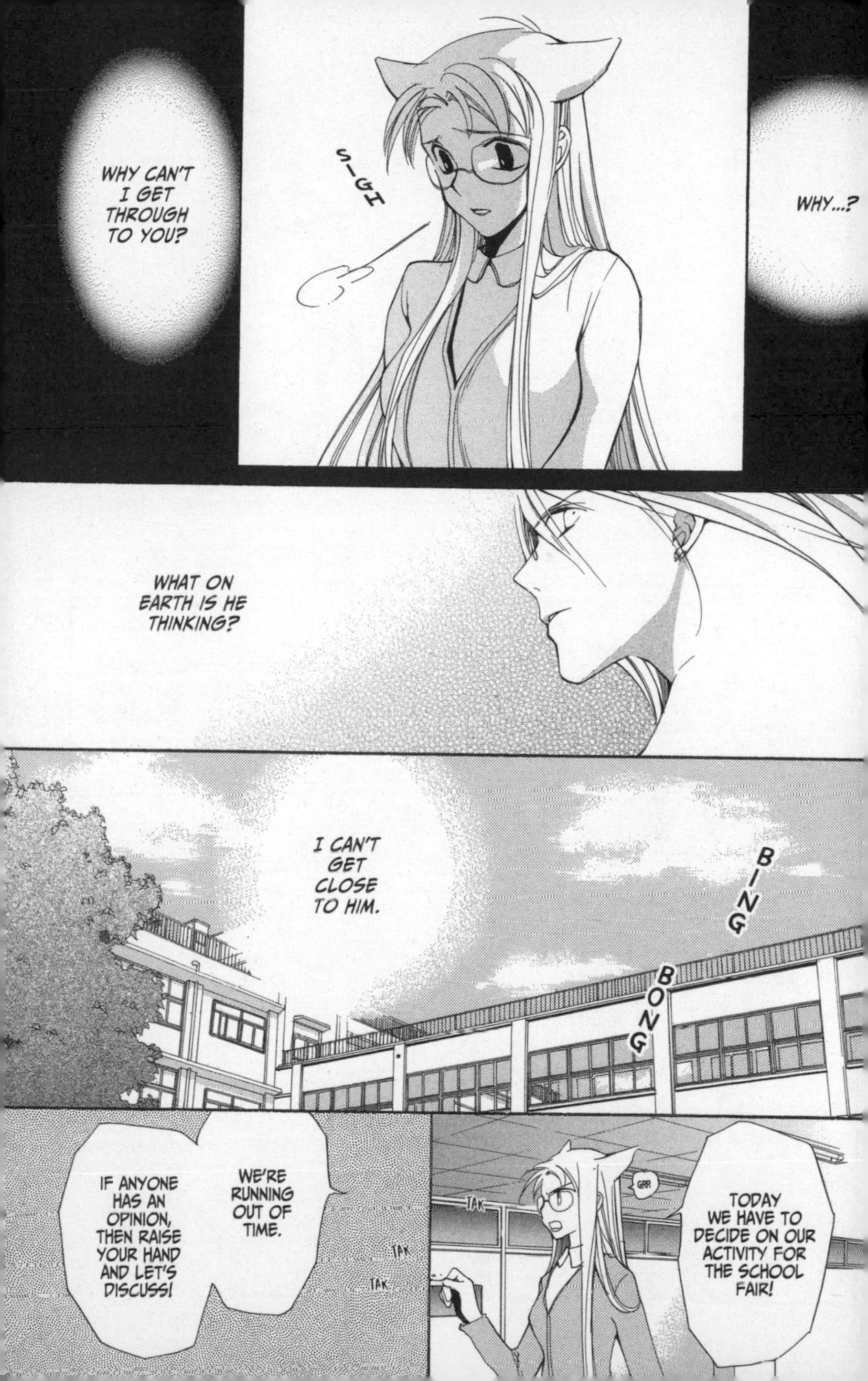
WHY...?
SIGH
WHY CAN'T I GET THROUGH TO YOU?
WHAT ON EARTH IS HE THINKING?
BING
BONG
I CAN'T GET CLOSE TO HIM.
TODAY WE HAVE TO DECIDE ON OUR ACTIVITY FOR THE SCHOOL FAIR!
GRR
TAK
WE'RE RUNNING OUT OF TIME.
IF ANYONE HAS AN OPINION, THEN RAISE YOUR HAND AND LET'S DISCUSS!
TAK
TAK

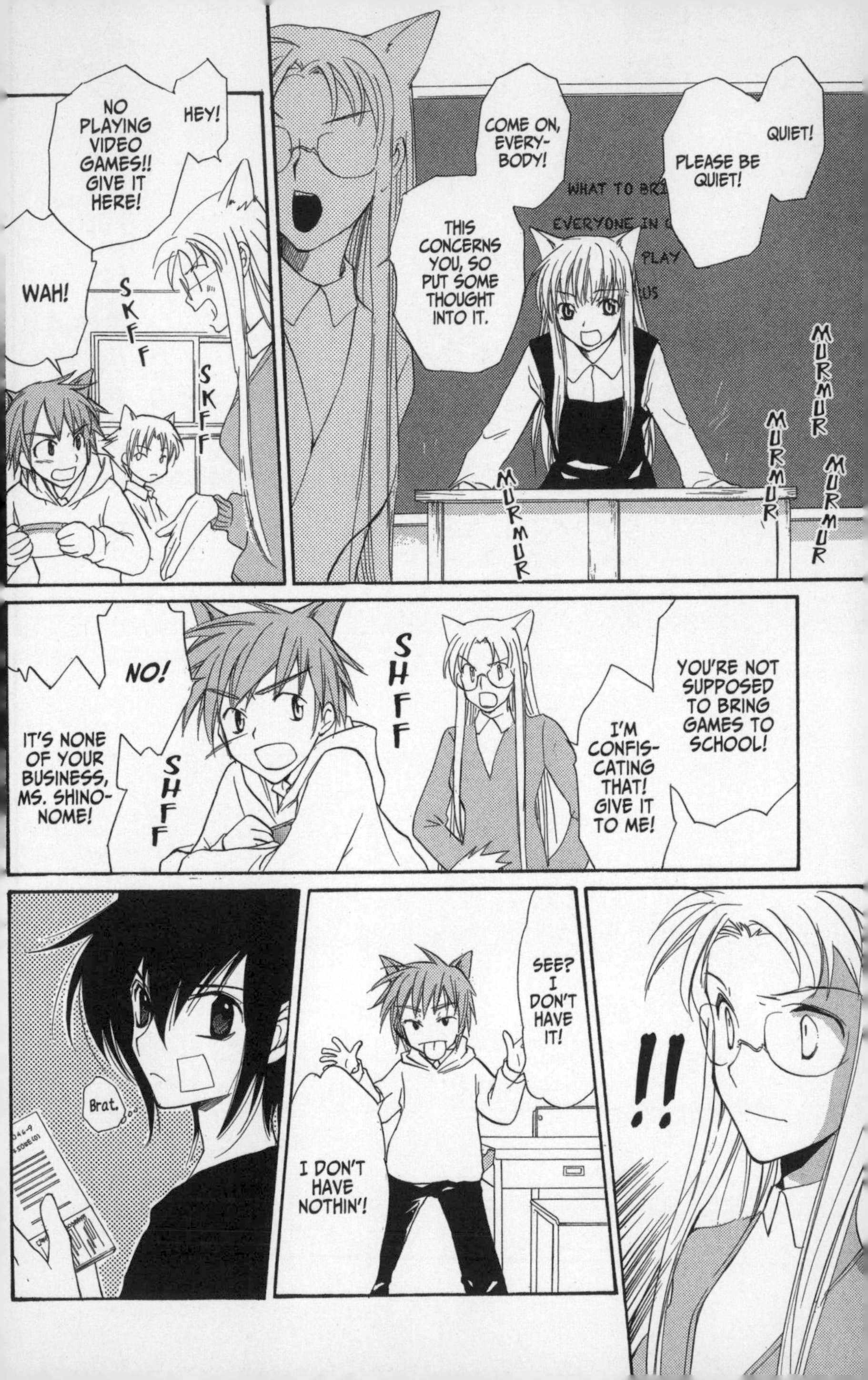
QUIET! PLEASE BE QUIET!
COME ON, EVERYBODY!
THIS CONCERNS YOU, SO PUT SOME THOUGHT INTO IT.
MURMUR
MURMUR
MURMUR
MURMUR
HEY! NO PLAYING VIDEO GAMES!! GIVE IT HERE!
SKFF
SKFF
WAH!
YOU'RE NOT SUPPOSED TO BRING GAMES TO SCHOOL!
I'M CONFISCATING THAT! GIVE IT TO ME!
SHFF
NO!
IT'S NONE OF YOUR BUSINESS, MS. SHINONOME!
SHFF
!!
SEE? I DON'T HAVE IT!
I DON'T HAVE NOTHIN'!
Brat.

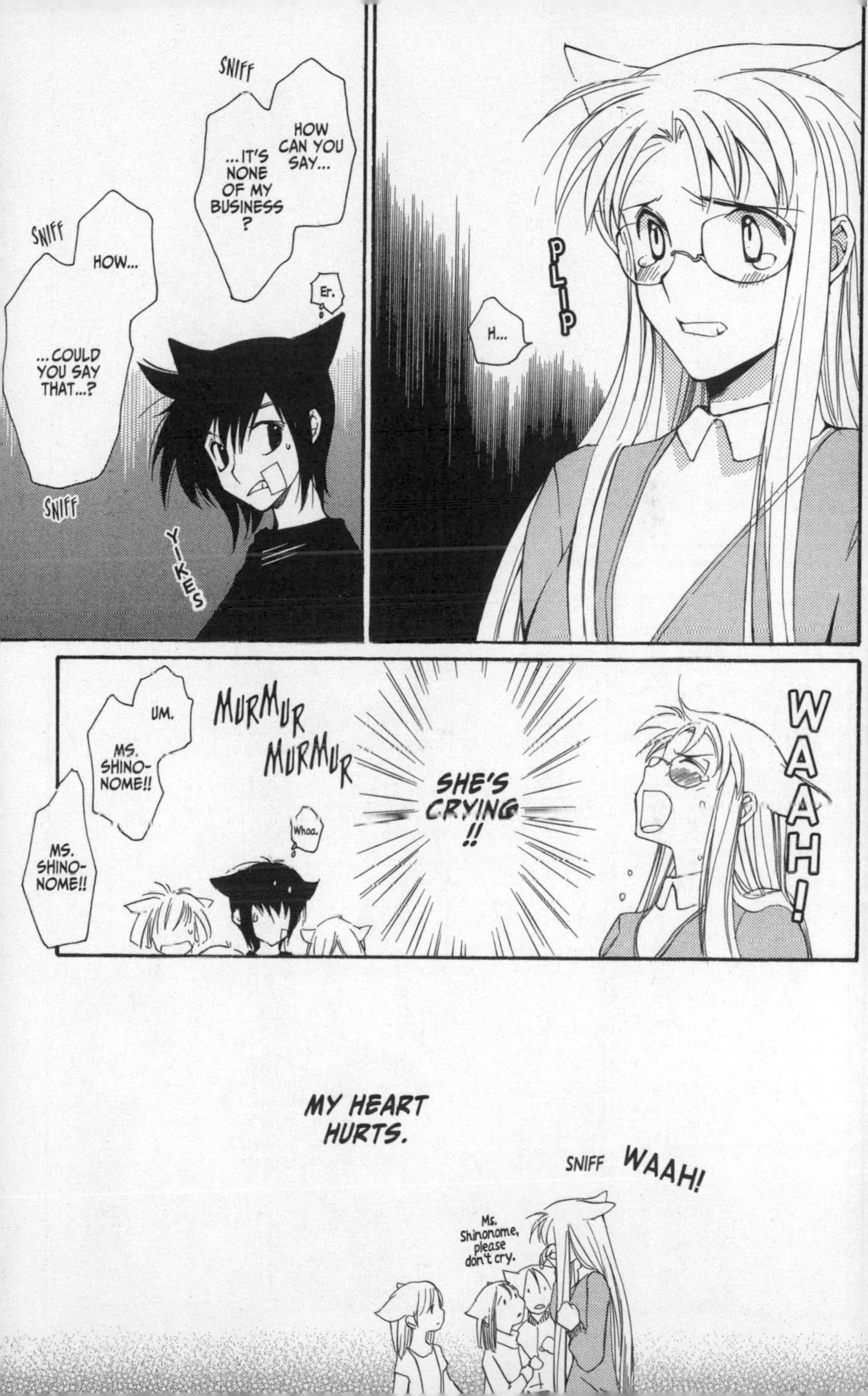
PLIP
H...
SNIFF
HOW CAN YOU SAY...
...IT'S NONE OF MY BUSINESS?
SNIFF
HOW...
...COULD YOU SAY THAT...?
SNIFF
Er.
YIKES
WAAH!
SHE'S CRYING!!
MURMUR MURMUR
Whoa.
UM. MS. SHINONOME!!
MS. SHINONOME!!
MY HEART HURTS.
WAAH!
SNIFF
Ms. Shinonome, please don't cry.

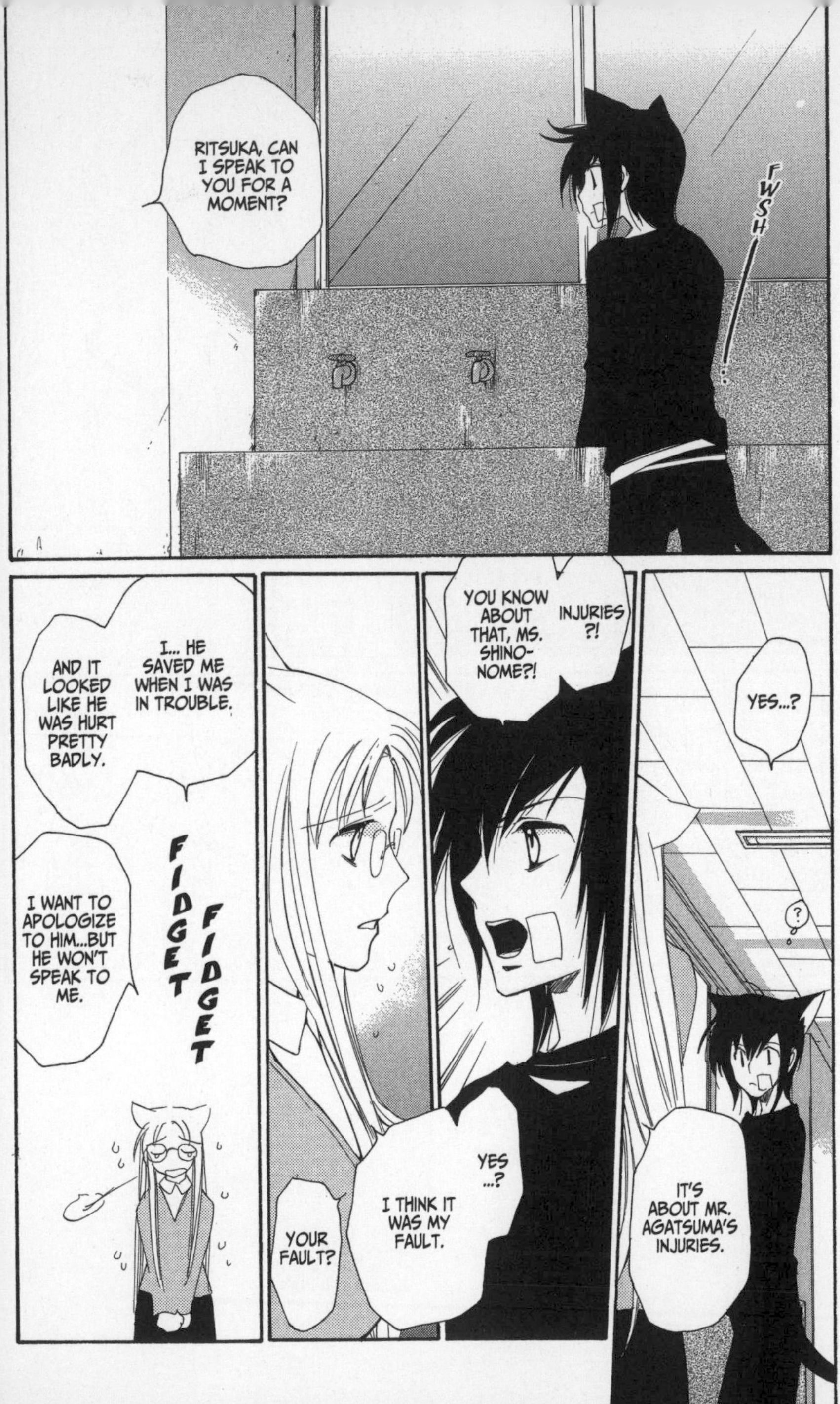
FWSH
RITSUKA, CAN I SPEAK TO YOU FOR A MOMENT?
YES...?
IT'S ABOUT MR. AGATSUMA'S INJURIES.
INJURIES?!
YOU KNOW ABOUT THAT, MS. SHINONOME?!
YES ...?
I THINK IT WAS MY FAULT.
YOUR FAULT?
I... HE SAVED ME WHEN I WAS IN TROUBLE.
AND IT LOOKED LIKE HE WAS HURT PRETTY BADLY.
FIDGET FIDGET
I WANT TO APOLOGIZE TO HIM...BUT HE WON'T SPEAK TO ME.

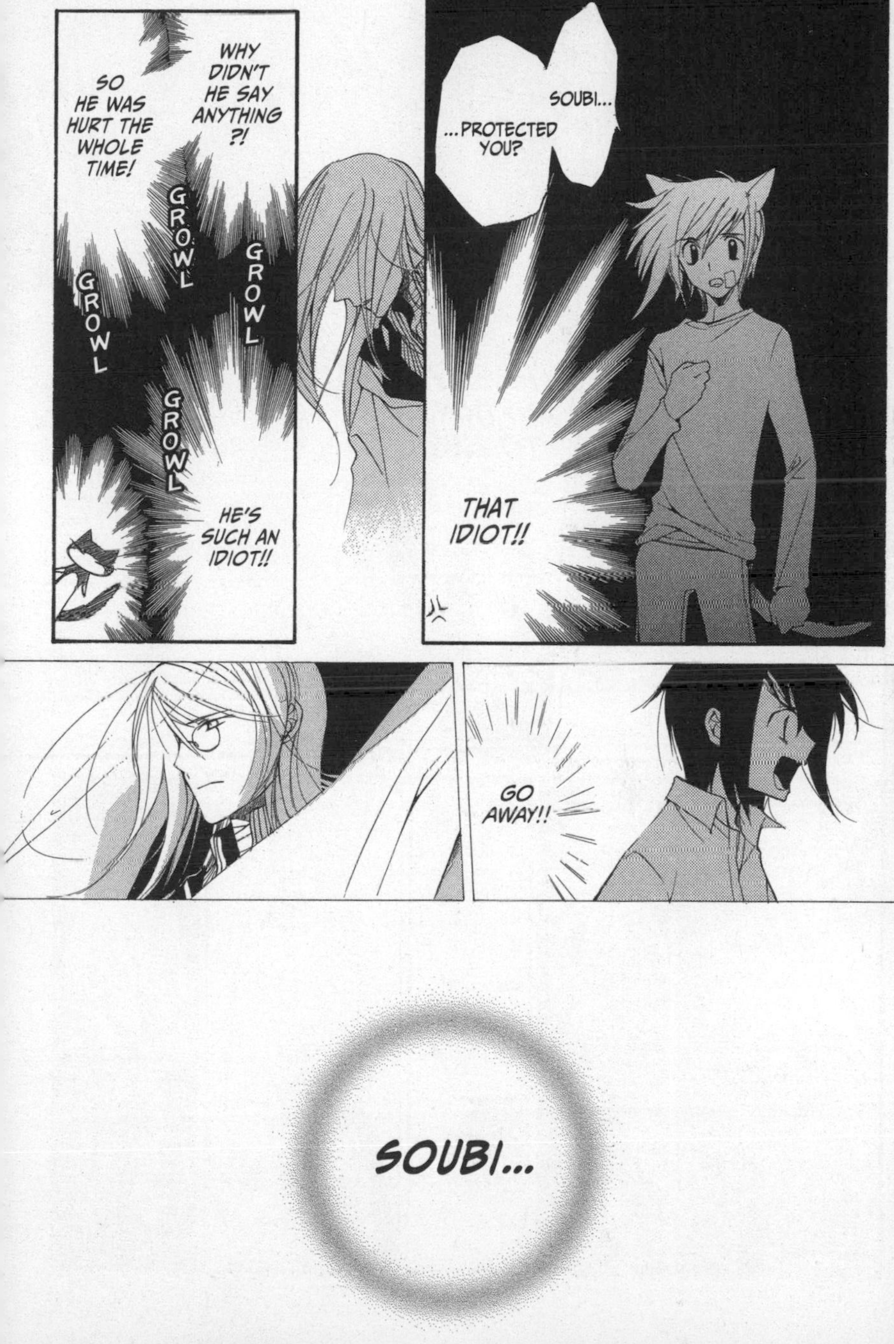
SOUBI...
...PROTECTED YOU?
THAT IDIOT!!
WHY DIDN'T HE SAY ANYTHING ?!
SO HE WAS HURT THE WHOLE TIME!
GROWL
GROWL
GROWL
GROWL
HE'S SUCH AN IDIOT!!
GO AWAY!!
SOUBI...

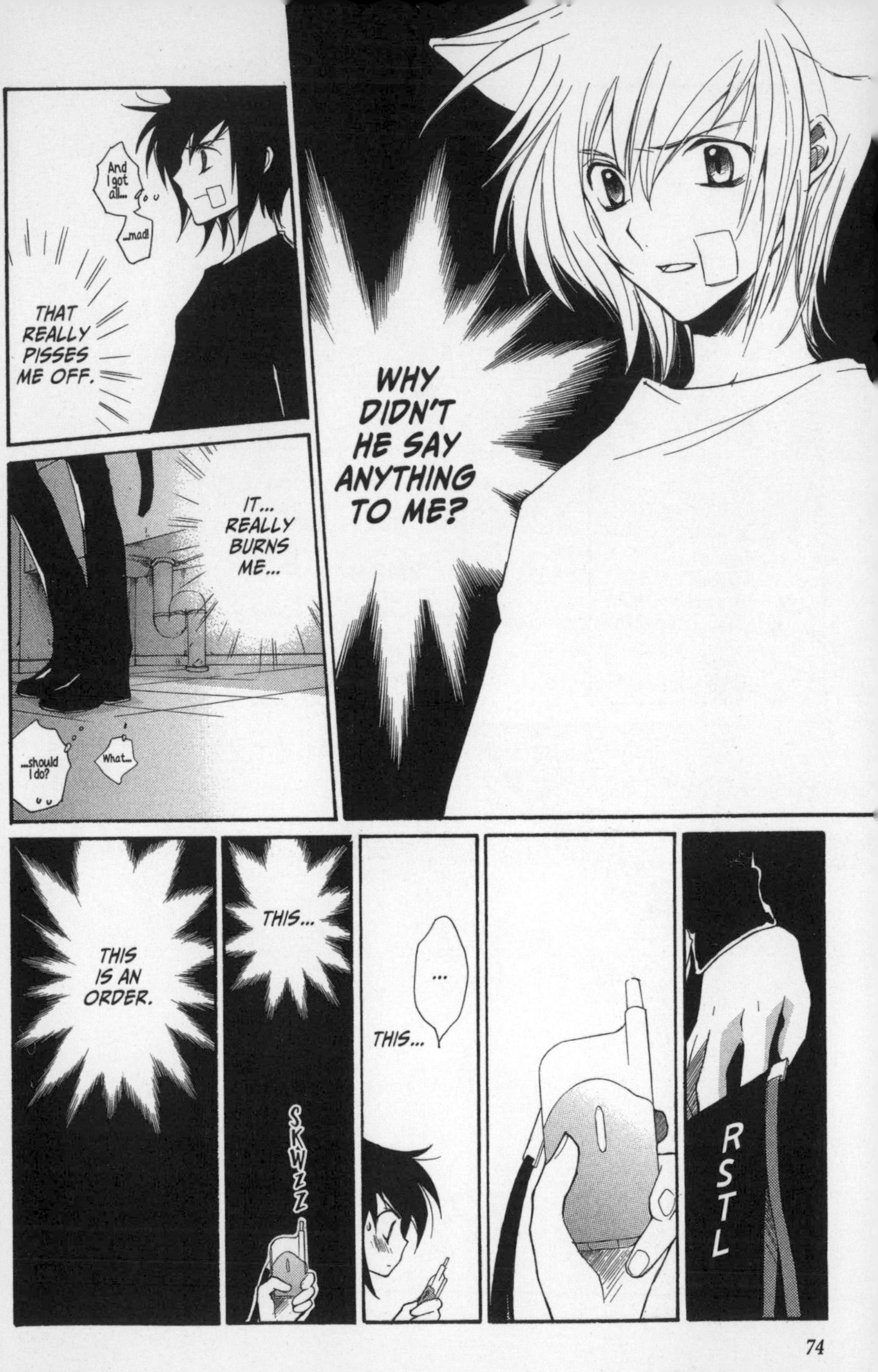
WHY DIDN'T HE SAY ANYTHING TO ME?
And I got all...
...mad!
THAT REALLY PISSES ME OFF.
IT... REALLY BURNS ME...
What...
...should I do?
RSTL
...
THIS...
THIS...
SKWZZ
THIS IS AN ORDER.

PWEEP
PWEEP

...

SO HE'S TRAINING ME BY EMAIL.

GOTTA HAND IT TO YOU, RITSUKA.

What should we do for lunch?

Udon'd be good.

KLAK

"THIS IS AN ORDER."

"YOU ARE NEVER TO LIE TO ME EVER AGAIN."

"NOT TELLING THE TRUTH COUNTS AS A LIE."

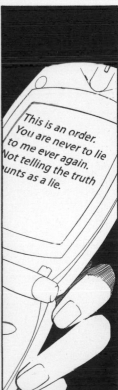

This is an order. You are never to lie to me ever again. Not telling the truth counts as a lie.

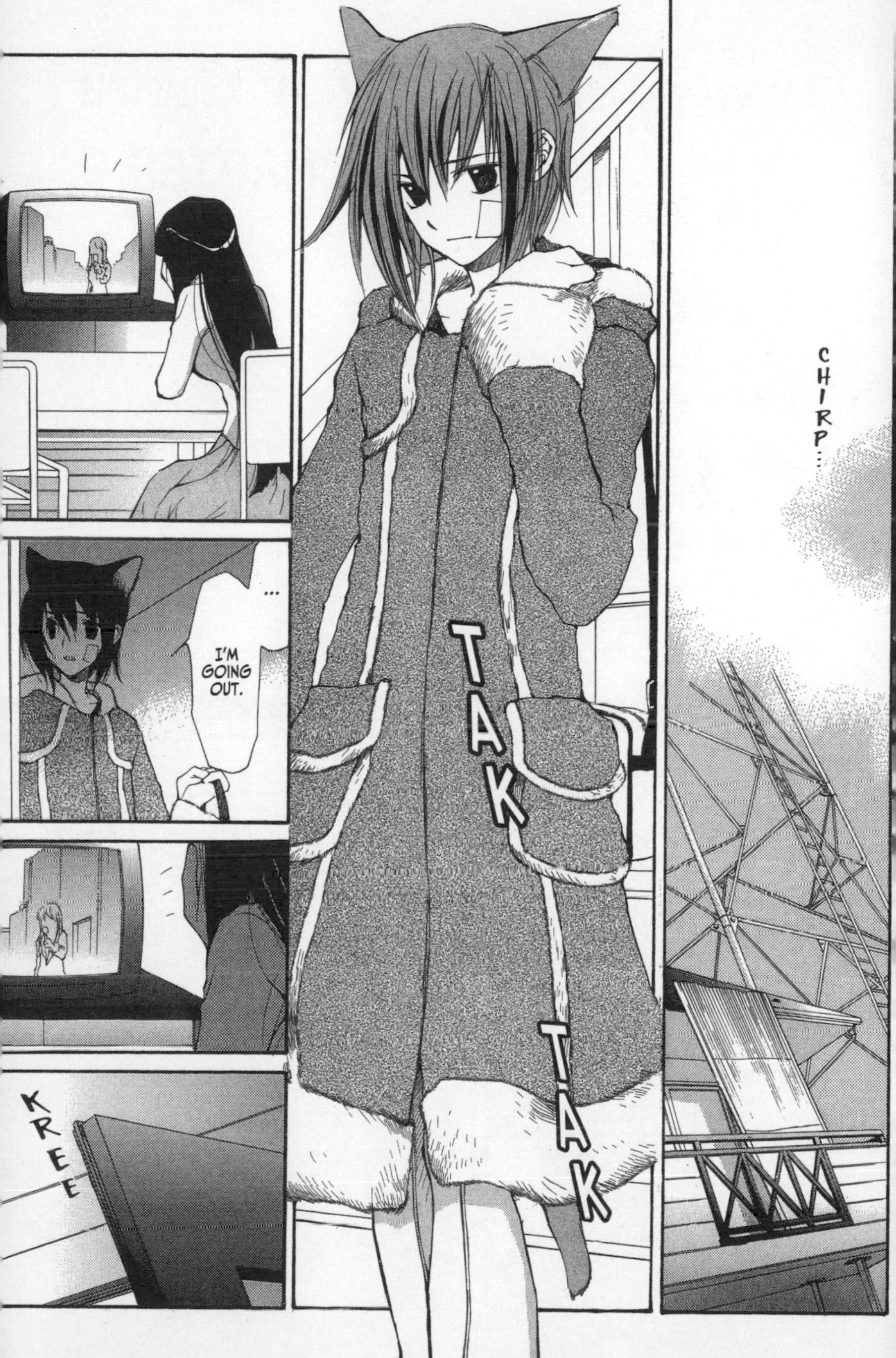
CHIRP...
TAK
TAK
...
I'M GOING OUT.
KREE

TOY'S MASTER / THE ABSOLUTE TOY MASTER CHAPTERS

CHAPTER 9

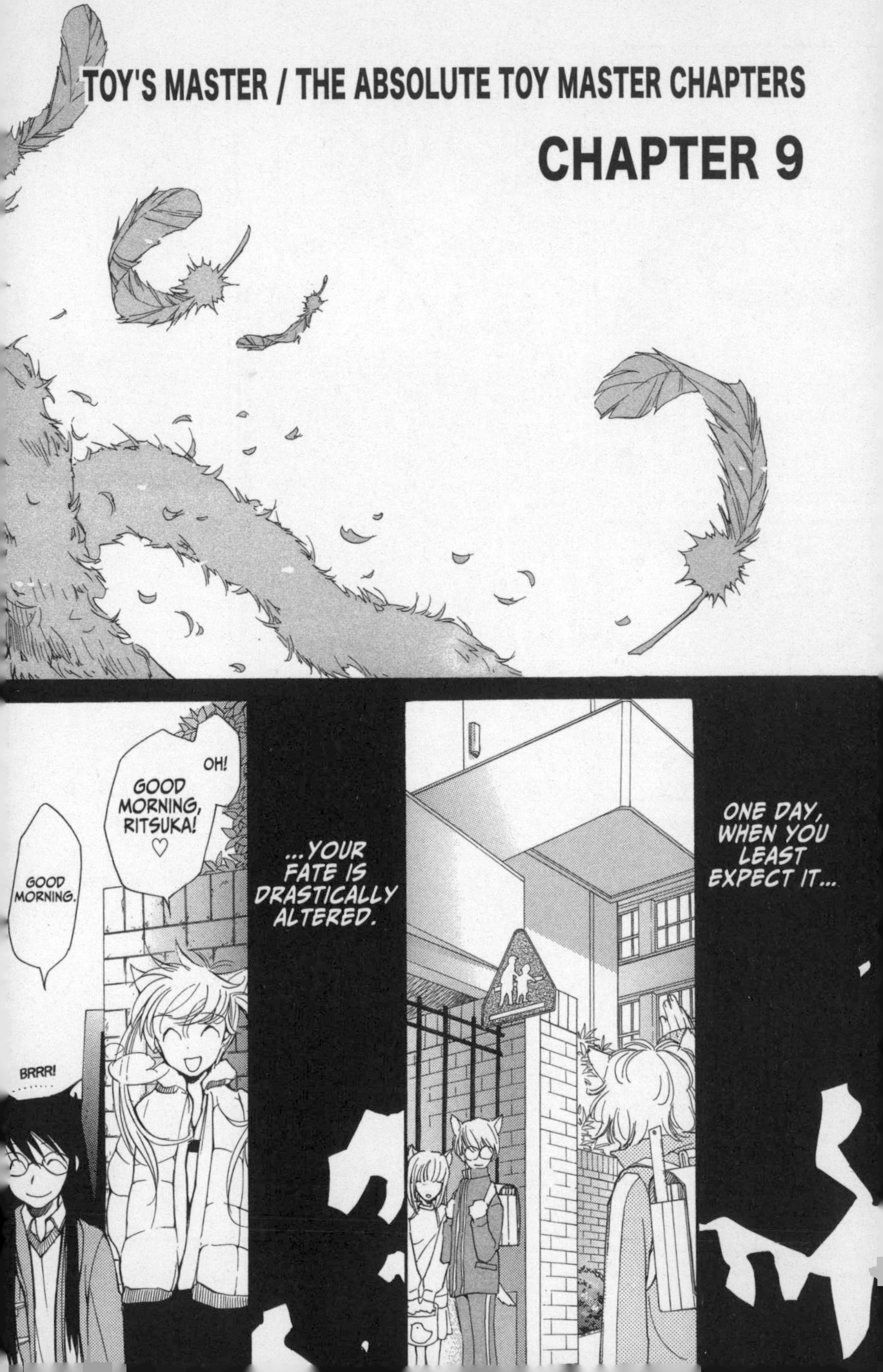
ONE DAY, WHEN YOU LEAST EXPECT IT...
...YOUR FATE IS DRASTICALLY ALTERED.
OH!
GOOD MORNING, RITSUKA! ♡
GOOD MORNING.
BRRR! ......

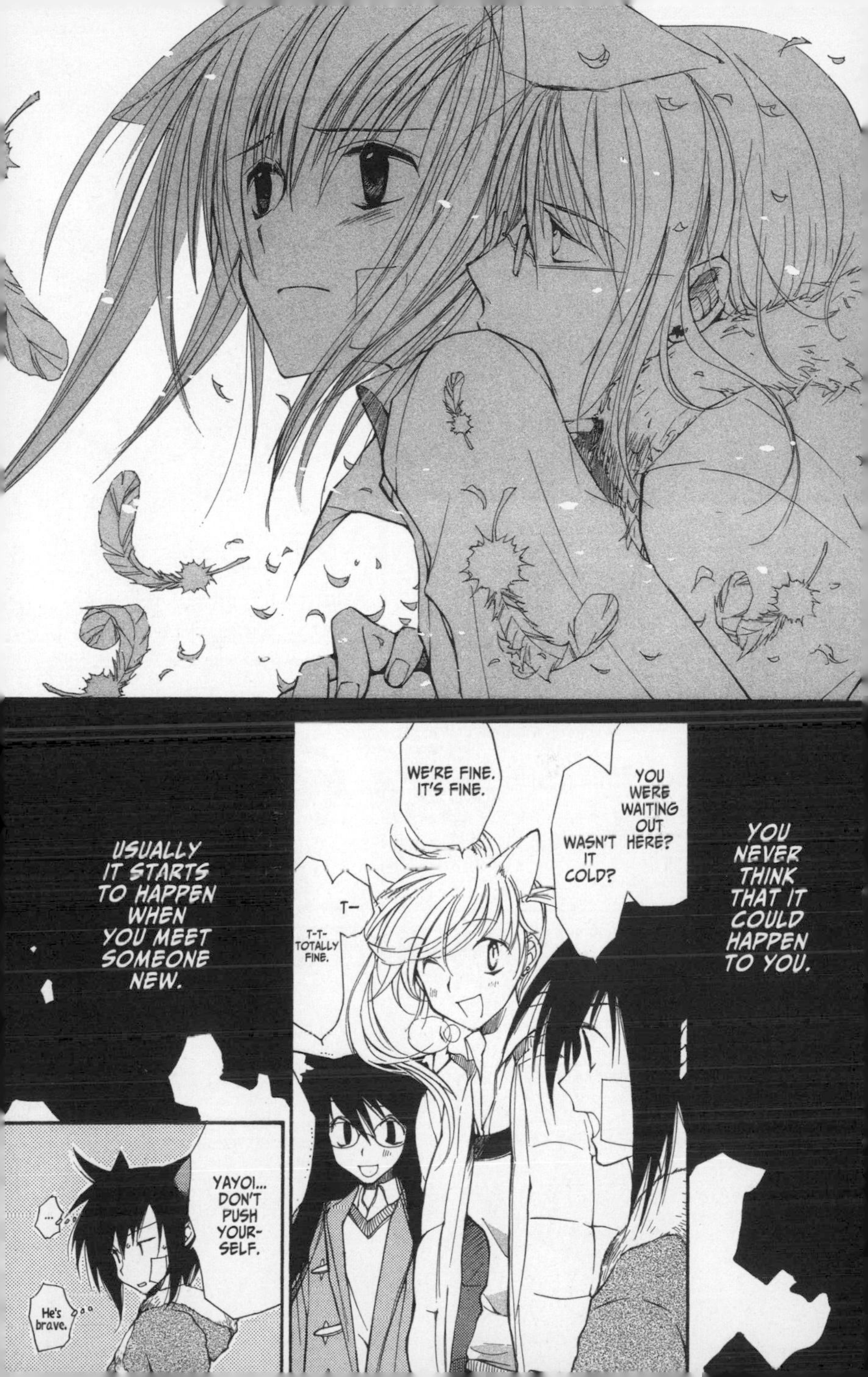
YOU NEVER THINK THAT IT COULD HAPPEN TO YOU.
YOU WERE WAITING OUT HERE?
WASN'T IT COLD?
WE'RE FINE. IT'S FINE.
T—
T-T-TOTALLY FINE.
...
USUALLY IT STARTS TO HAPPEN WHEN YOU MEET SOMEONE NEW.
YAYOI... DON'T PUSH YOUR-SELF.
...
He's brave.

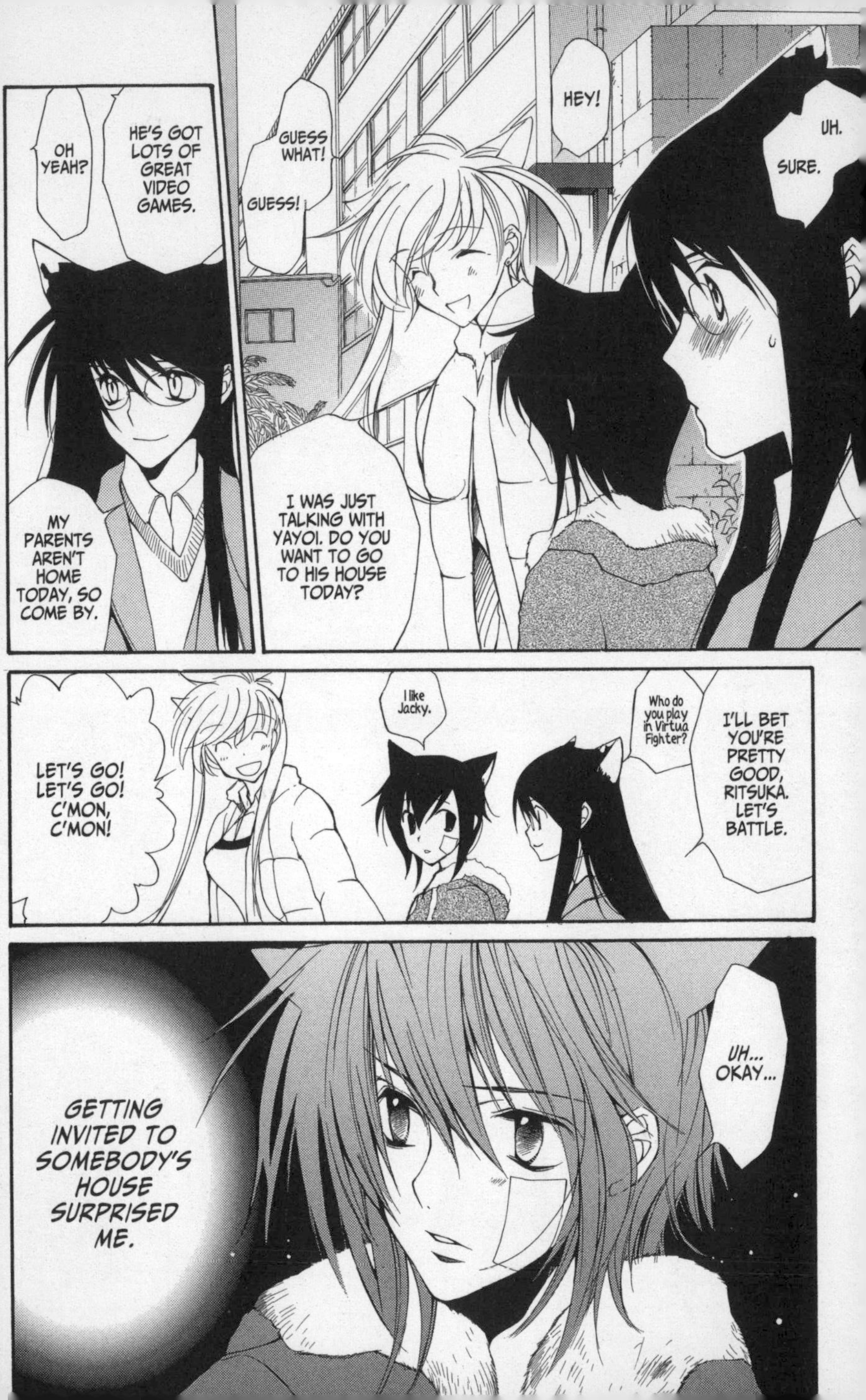
HEY!
GUESS WHAT!
GUESS!
I WAS JUST TALKING WITH YAYOI. DO YOU WANT TO GO TO HIS HOUSE TODAY?
UH.
SURE.
MY PARENTS AREN'T HOME TODAY, SO COME BY.
HE'S GOT LOTS OF GREAT VIDEO GAMES.
OH YEAH?
I'LL BET YOU'RE PRETTY GOOD, RITSUKA. LET'S BATTLE.
Who do you play in Virtua Fighter?
I like Jacky.
LET'S GO! LET'S GO! C'MON, C'MON!
UH... OKAY...
GETTING INVITED TO SOMEBODY'S HOUSE SURPRISED ME.

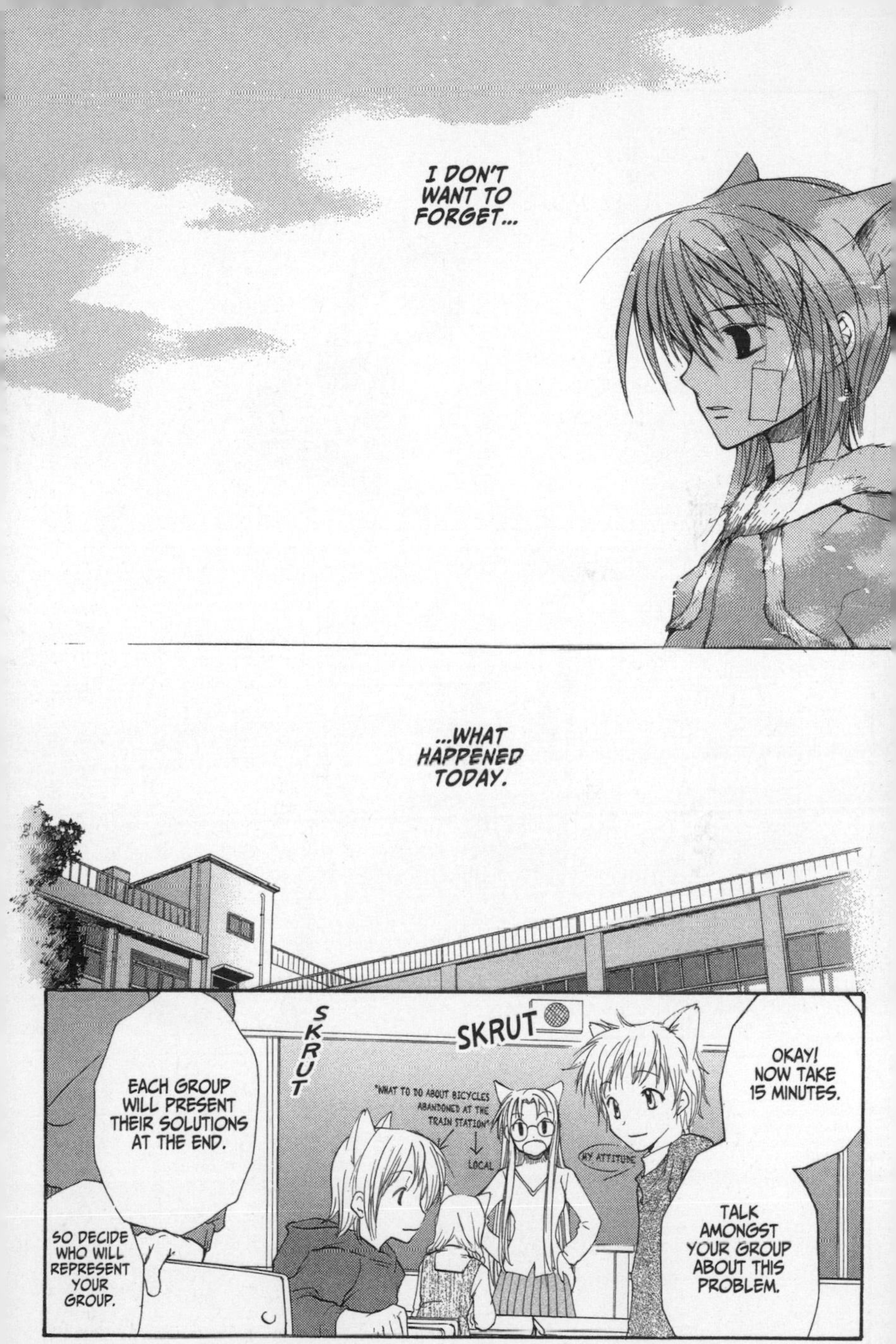
I DON'T WANT TO FORGET...
...WHAT HAPPENED TODAY.
OKAY! NOW TAKE 15 MINUTES.
TALK AMONGST YOUR GROUP ABOUT THIS PROBLEM.
SKRUT
"WHAT TO DO ABOUT BICYCLES ABANDONED AT THE TRAIN STATION"
LOCAL
MY ATTITUDE
SKRUT
EACH GROUP WILL PRESENT THEIR SOLUTIONS AT THE END.
SO DECIDE WHO WILL REPRESENT YOUR GROUP.

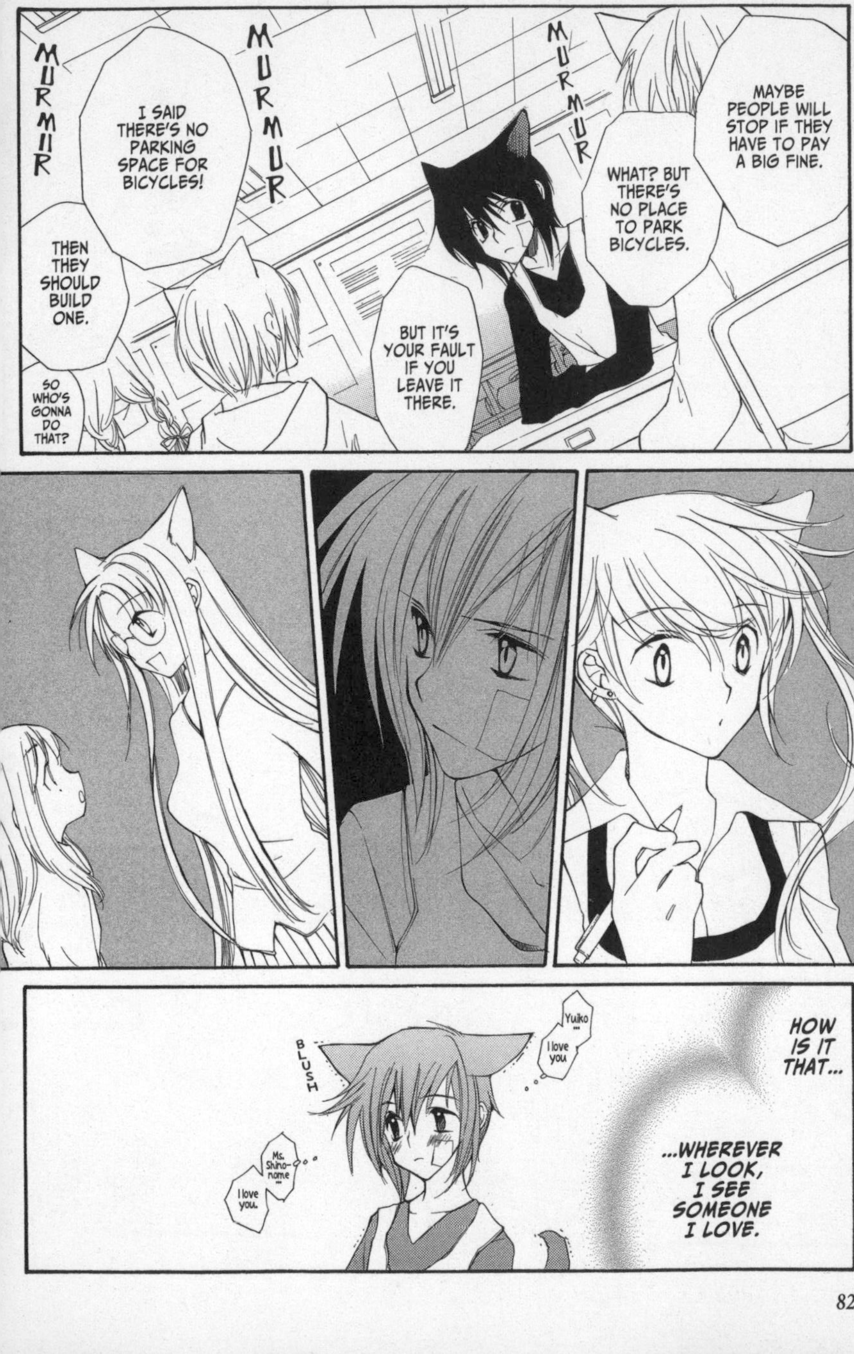
MAYBE PEOPLE WILL STOP IF THEY HAVE TO PAY A BIG FINE.
MURMUR
WHAT? BUT THERE'S NO PLACE TO PARK BICYCLES.
BUT IT'S YOUR FAULT IF YOU LEAVE IT THERE.
MURMUR
I SAID THERE'S NO PARKING SPACE FOR BICYCLES!
MURMUR
THEN THEY SHOULD BUILD ONE.
SO WHO'S GONNA DO THAT?
HOW IS IT THAT...
...WHEREVER I LOOK, I SEE SOMEONE I LOVE.
Yuiko... I love you
BLUSH
Ms. Shinonome... I love you.

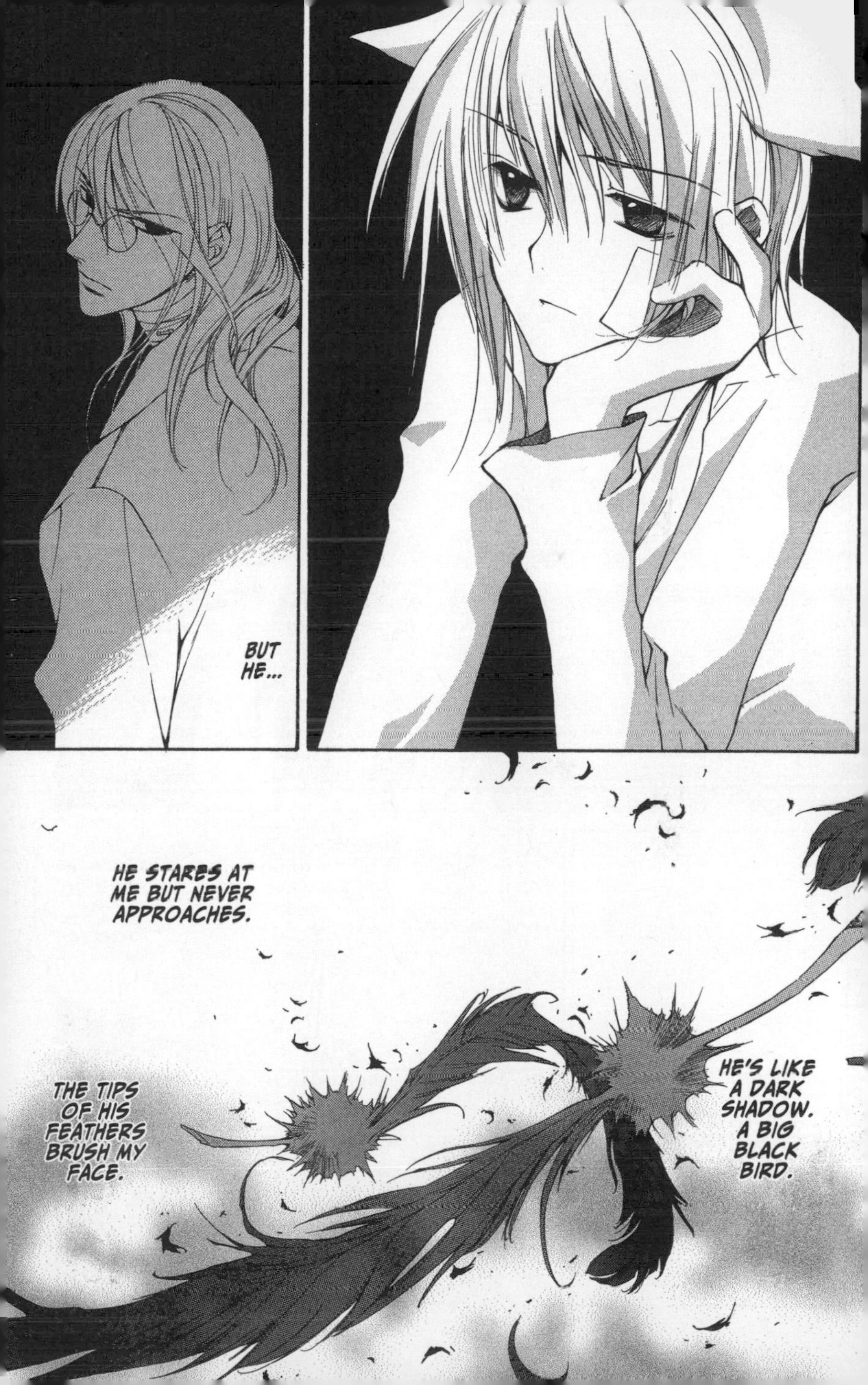
BUT HE...
HE STARES AT ME BUT NEVER APPROACHES.
HE'S LIKE A DARK SHADOW. A BIG BLACK BIRD.
THE TIPS OF HIS FEATHERS BRUSH MY FACE.

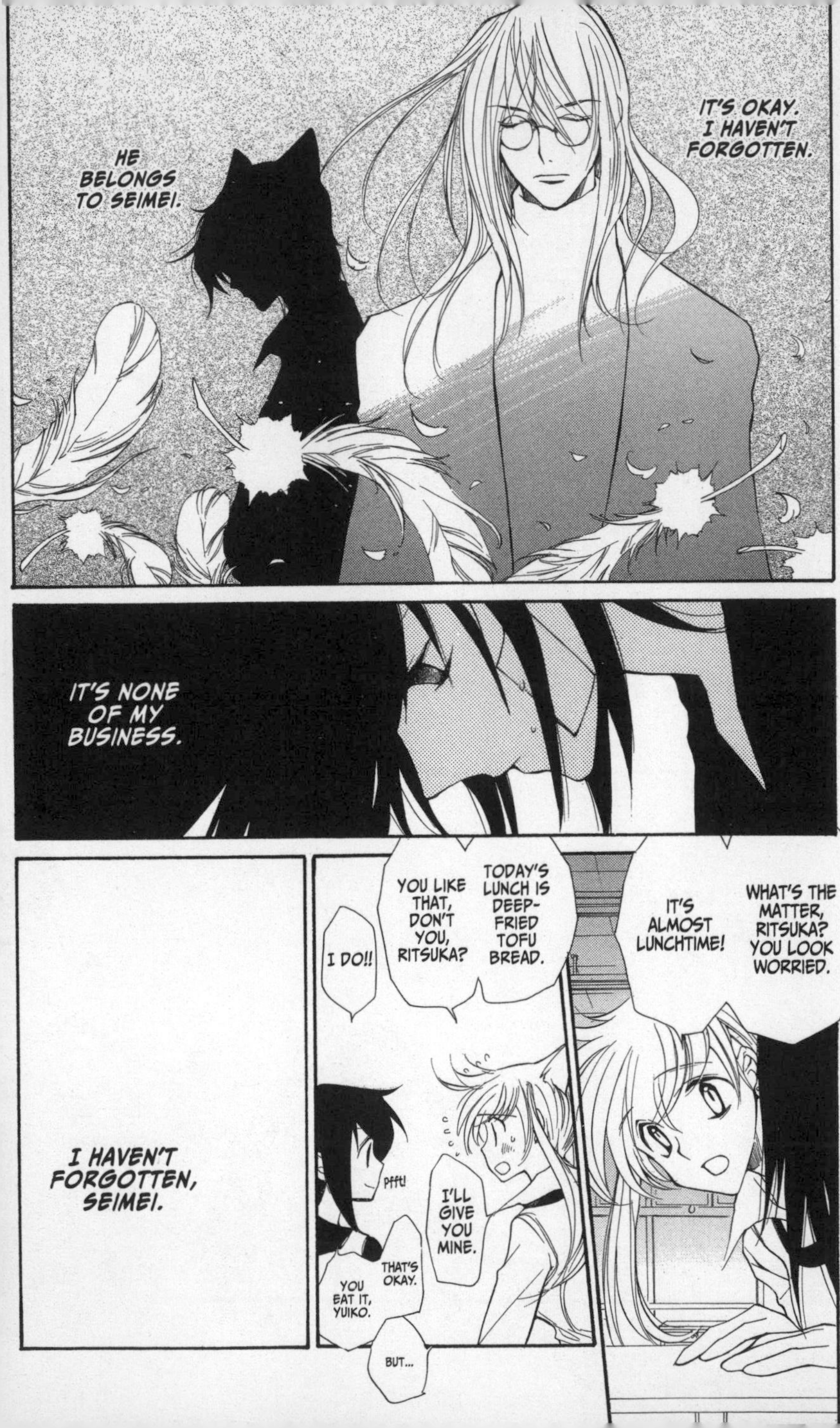
IT'S OKAY. I HAVEN'T FORGOTTEN.
HE BELONGS TO SEIMEI.
IT'S NONE OF MY BUSINESS.
WHAT'S THE MATTER, RITSUKA? YOU LOOK WORRIED.
IT'S ALMOST LUNCHTIME!
TODAY'S LUNCH IS DEEP-FRIED TOFU BREAD.
YOU LIKE THAT, DON'T YOU, RITSUKA?
I DO!!
I'LL GIVE YOU MINE.
pfft!
THAT'S OKAY.
YOU EAT IT, YUIKO.
BUT...
I HAVEN'T FORGOTTEN, SEIMEI.

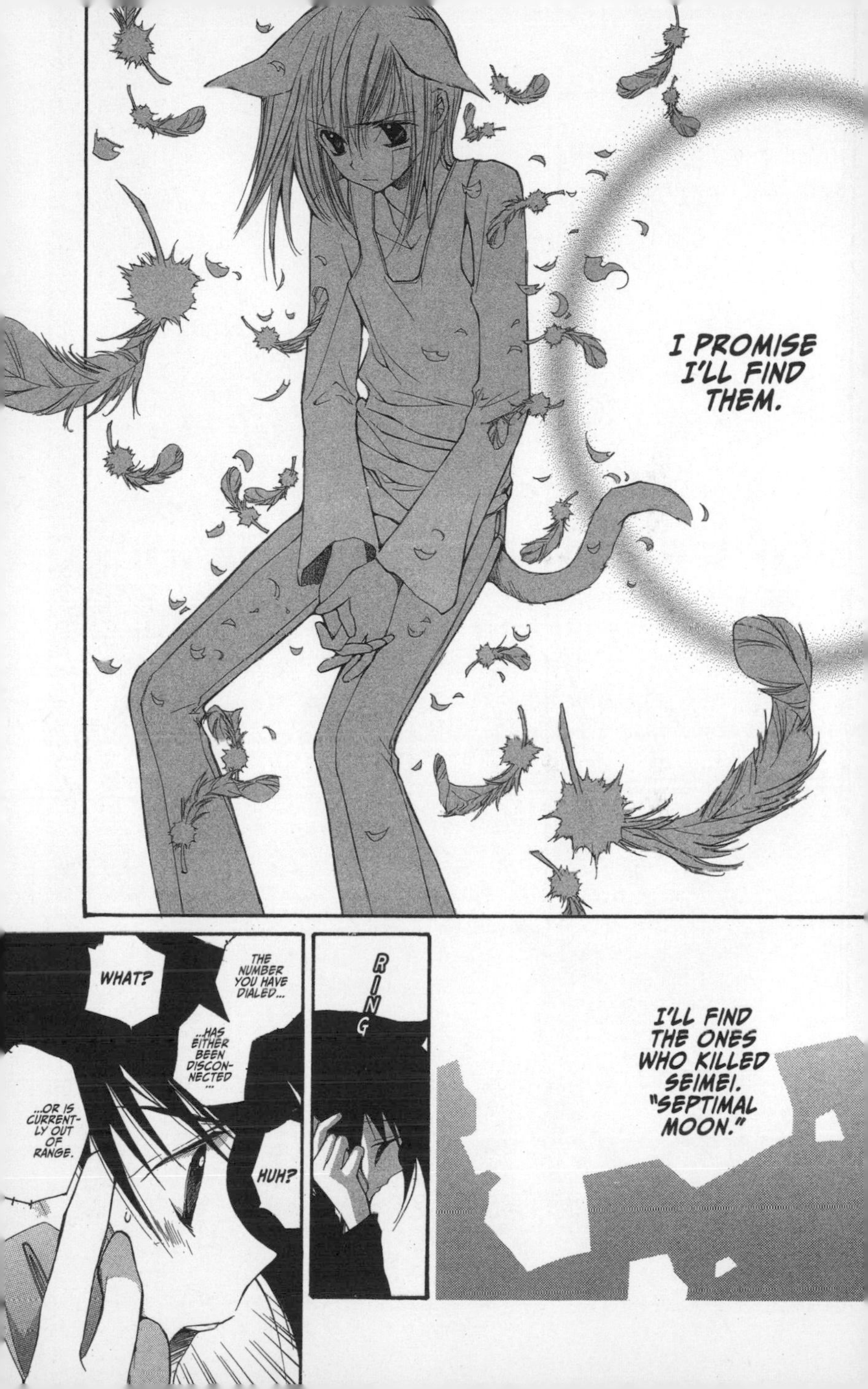
I PROMISE I'LL FIND THEM.
I'LL FIND THE ONES WHO KILLED SEIMEI. "SEPTIMAL MOON."
RING
THE NUMBER YOU HAVE DIALED...
WHAT?
...HAS EITHER BEEN DISCONNECTED...
...OR IS CURRENTLY OUT OF RANGE.
HUH?

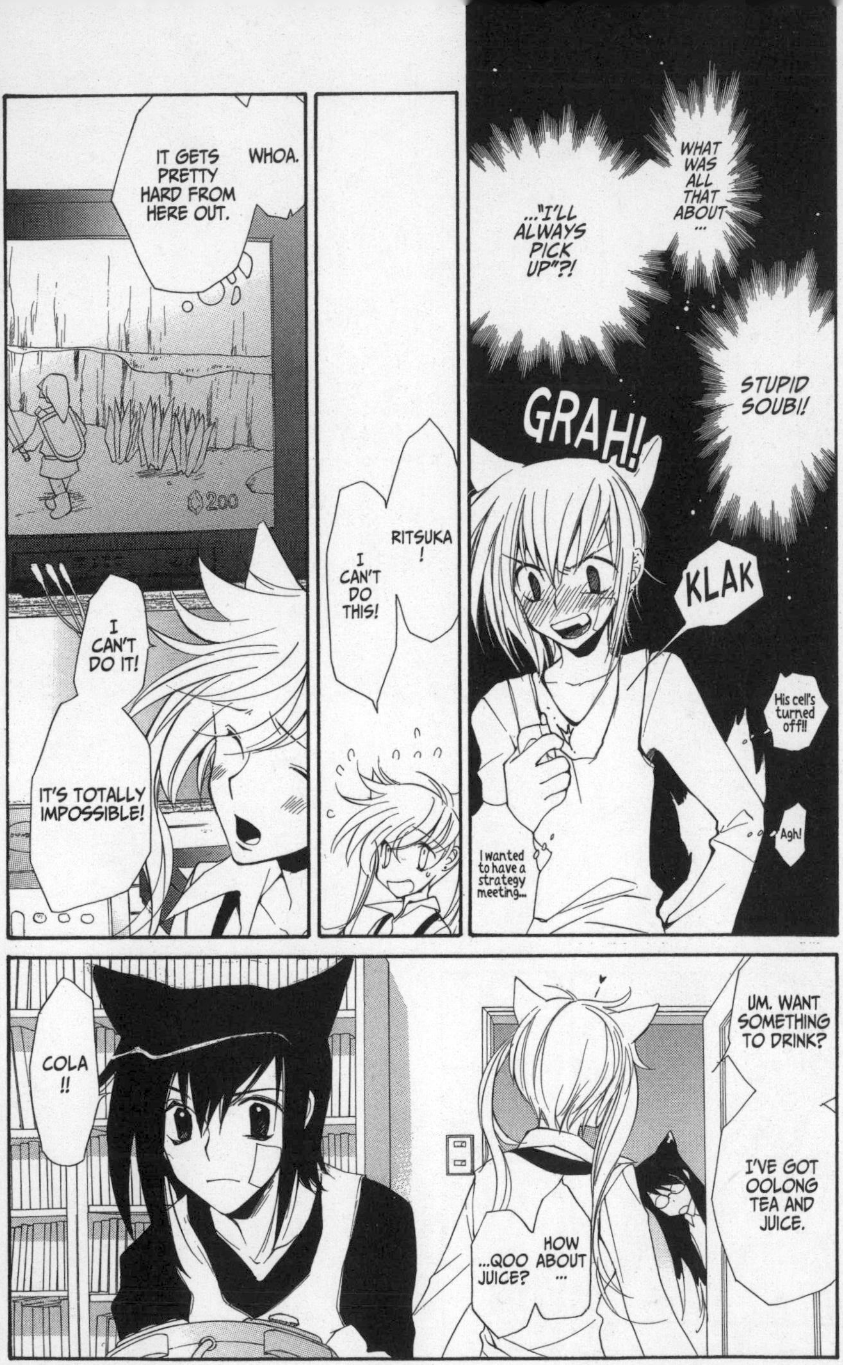
WHAT WAS ALL THAT ABOUT ...
..."I'LL ALWAYS PICK UP"?!
STUPID SOUBI!
GRAH!
KLAK
His cell's turned off!!
Agh!
I wanted to have a strategy meeting...
RITSUKA!
I CAN'T DO THIS!
WHOA.
IT GETS PRETTY HARD FROM HERE OUT.
200
I CAN'T DO IT!
IT'S TOTALLY IMPOSSIBLE!
UM. WANT SOMETHING TO DRINK?
I'VE GOT OOLONG TEA AND JUICE.
HOW ABOUT ...
...QOO JUICE?
COLA!!

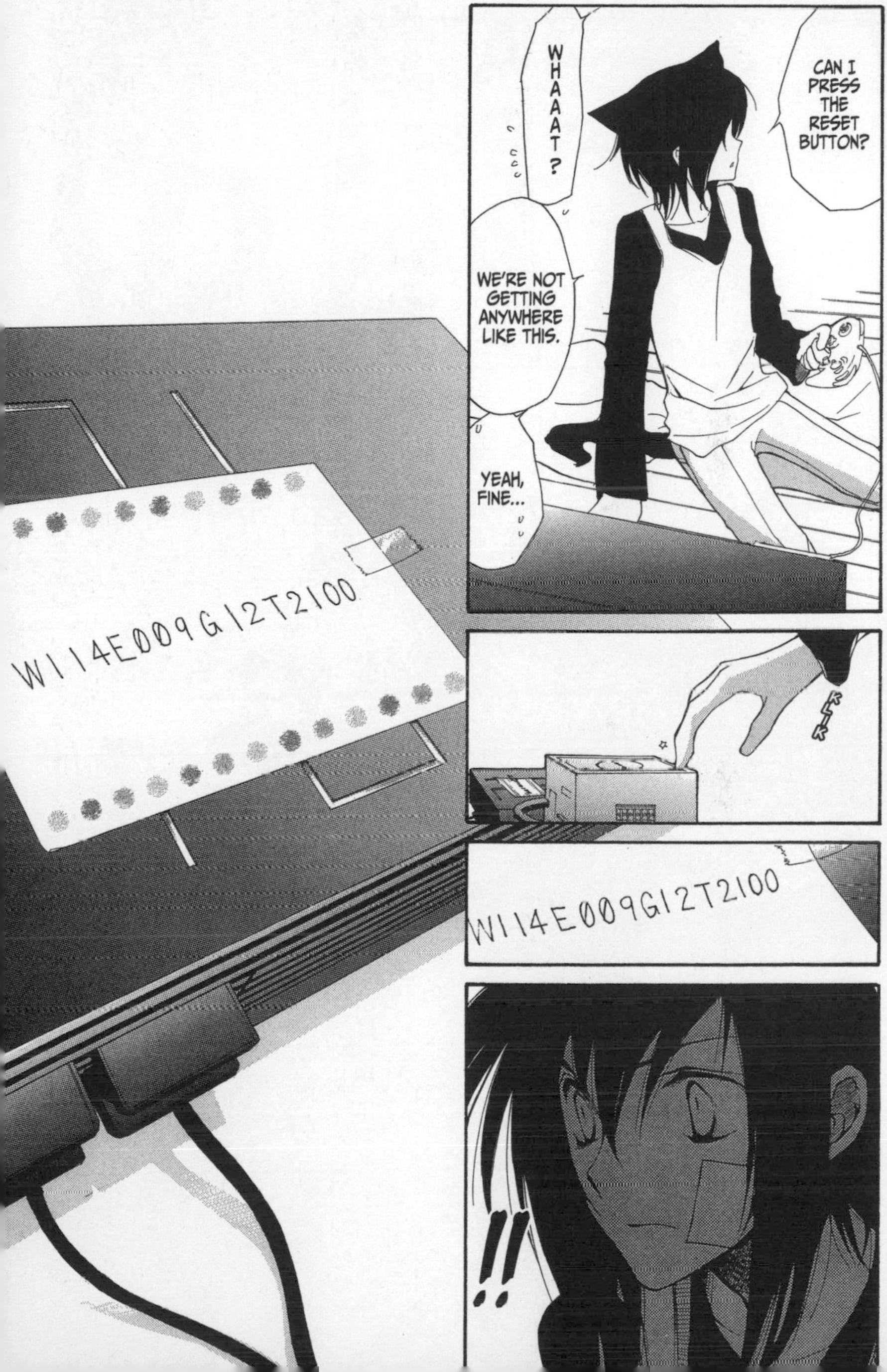
CAN I PRESS THE RESET BUTTON?
WHAAAT?
WE'RE NOT GETTING ANYWHERE LIKE THIS.
YEAH, FINE...
KLIK
W114E009G12T2100
!!
W114E009G12T2100

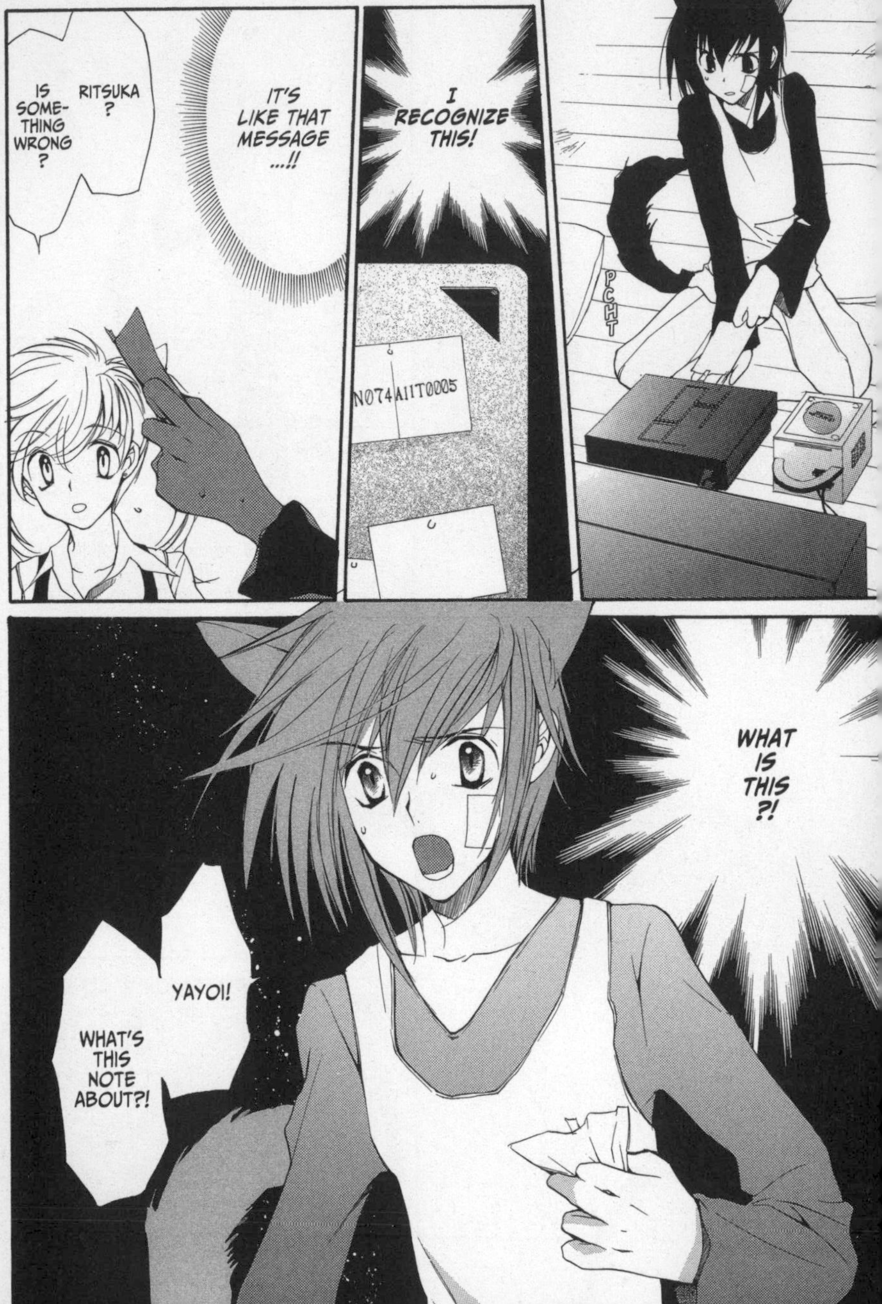
PCHT
I RECOGNIZE THIS!
N074 A1IT0005
IT'S LIKE THAT MESSAGE ...!!
RITSUKA?
IS SOMETHING WRONG?
WHAT IS THIS?!
YAYOI!
WHAT'S THIS NOTE ABOUT?!

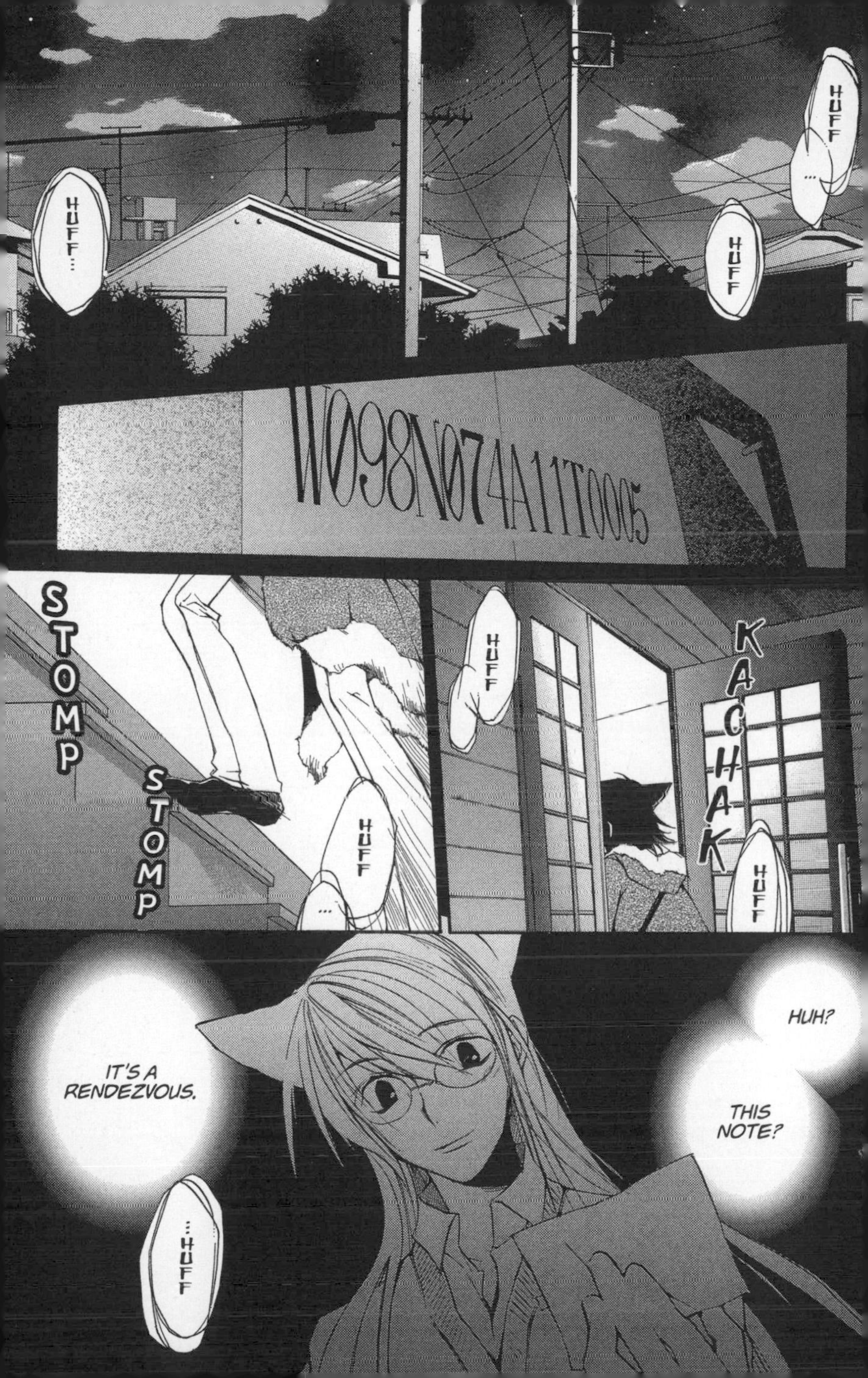
HUFF...
HUFF
HUFF...
W098N074A11T0005
KACHAK
HUFF
HUFF
STOMP
STOMP
HUFF...
HUH?
THIS NOTE?
IT'S A RENDEZVOUS.
...HUFF

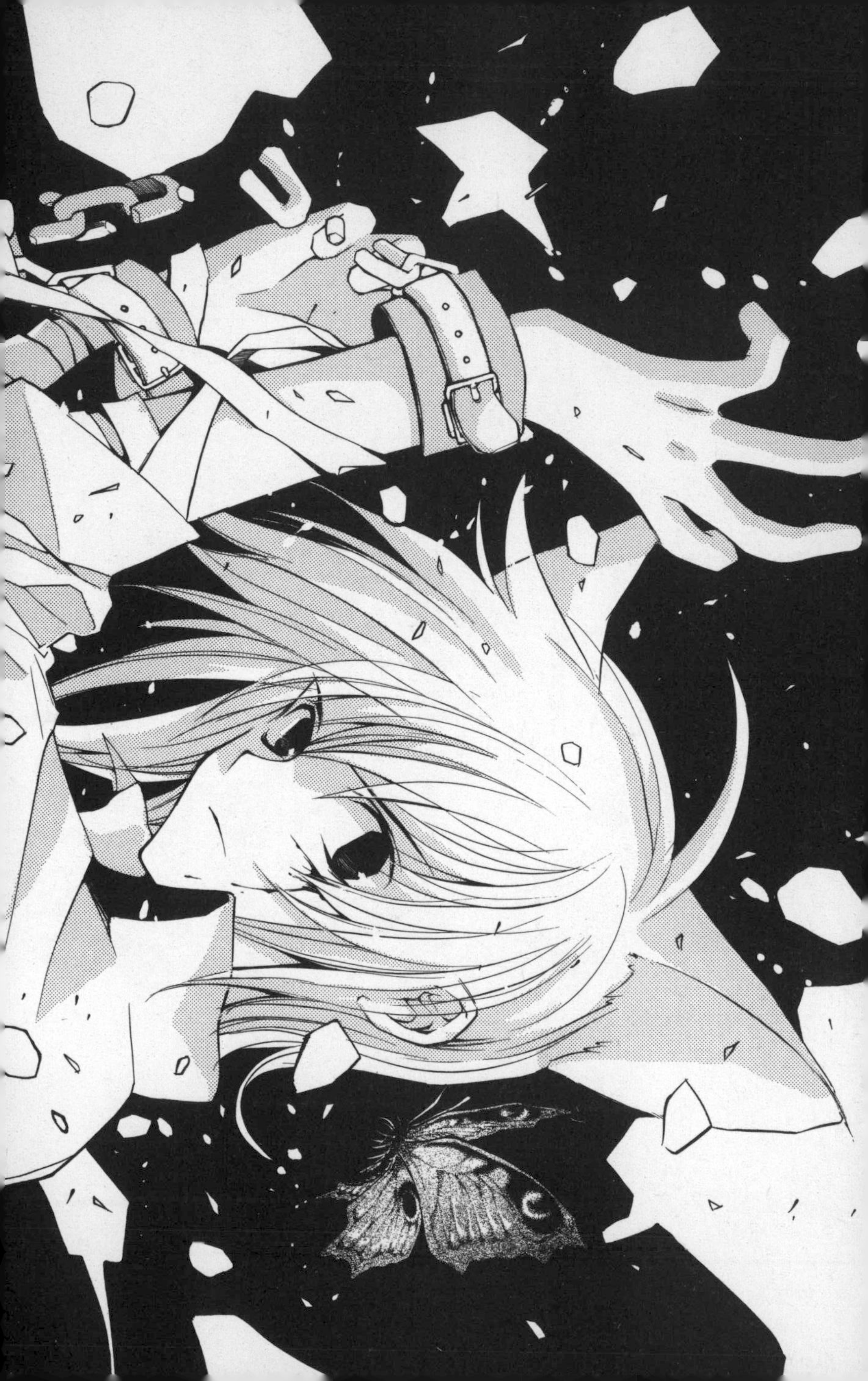

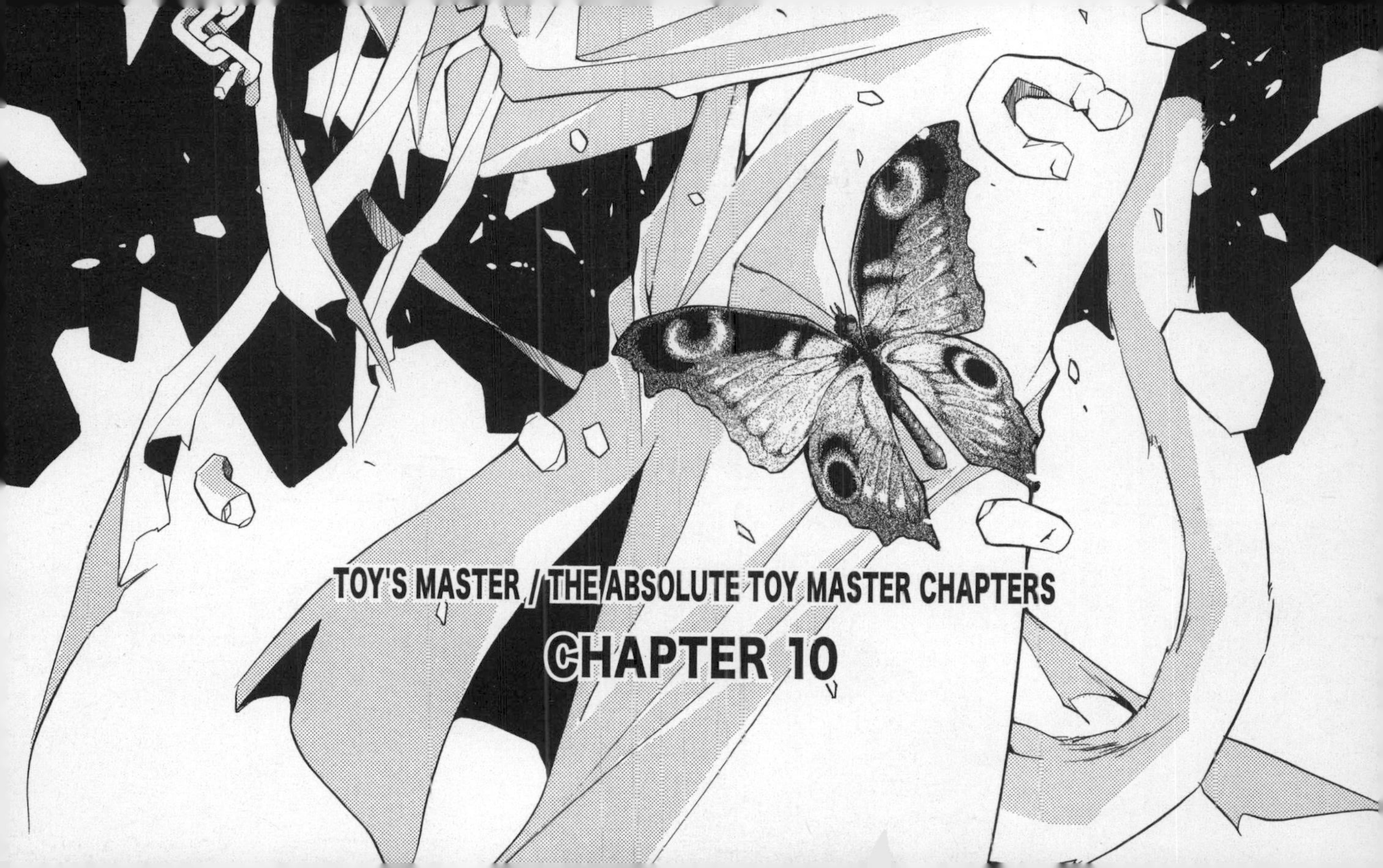
TOY'S MASTER // THE ABSOLUTE TOY MASTER CHAPTERS
CHAPTER 10

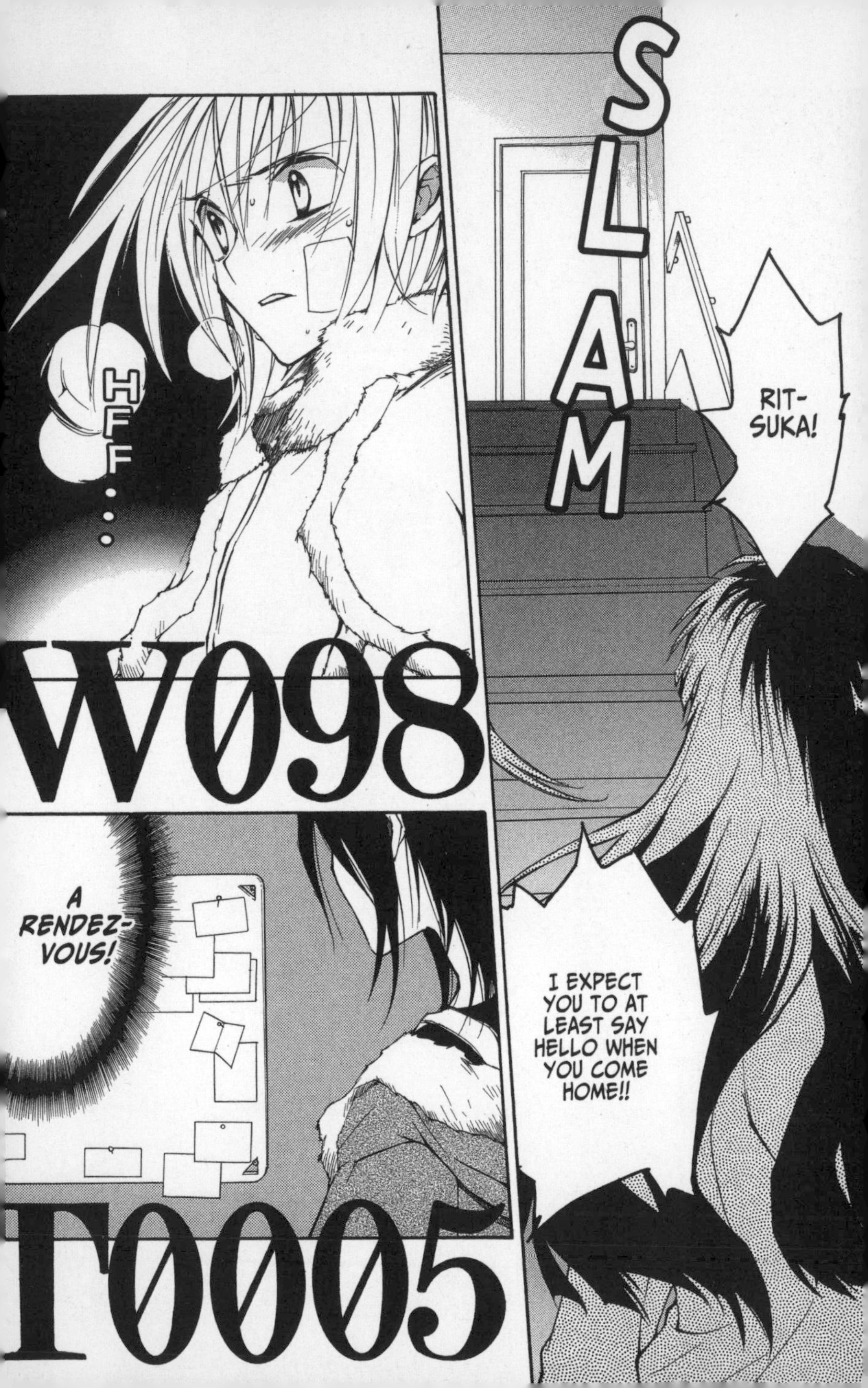
SLAM
RIT-SUKA!
I EXPECT YOU TO AT LEAST SAY HELLO WHEN YOU COME HOME!!
HFF...
W098
A RENDEZ-VOUS!
T0005

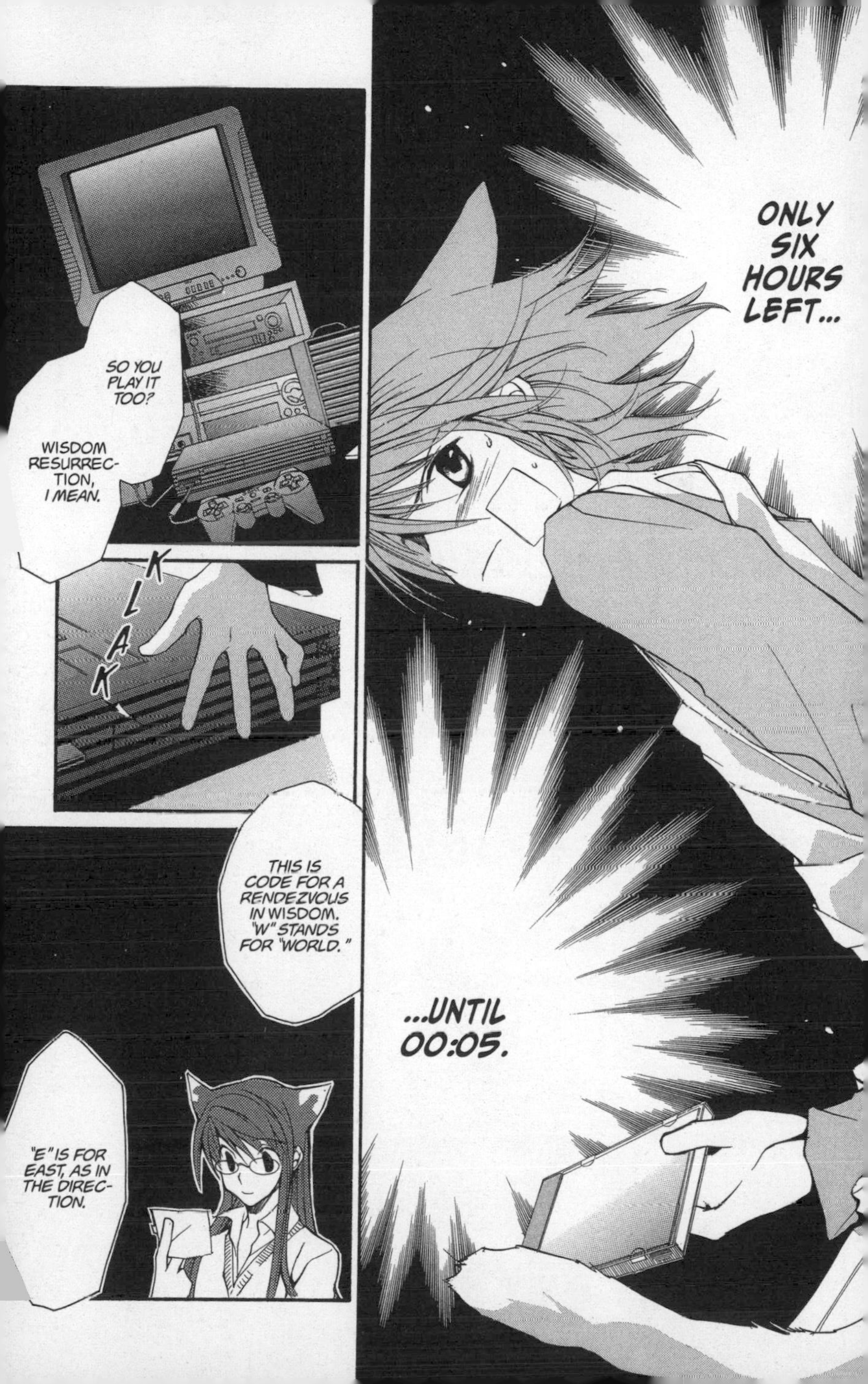
ONLY SIX HOURS LEFT...
...UNTIL 00:05.
SO YOU PLAY IT TOO?
WISDOM RESURREC-TION, I MEAN.
KLAK
THIS IS CODE FOR A RENDEZVOUS IN WISDOM. "W" STANDS FOR "WORLD."
"E" IS FOR EAST, AS IN THE DIREC-TION.

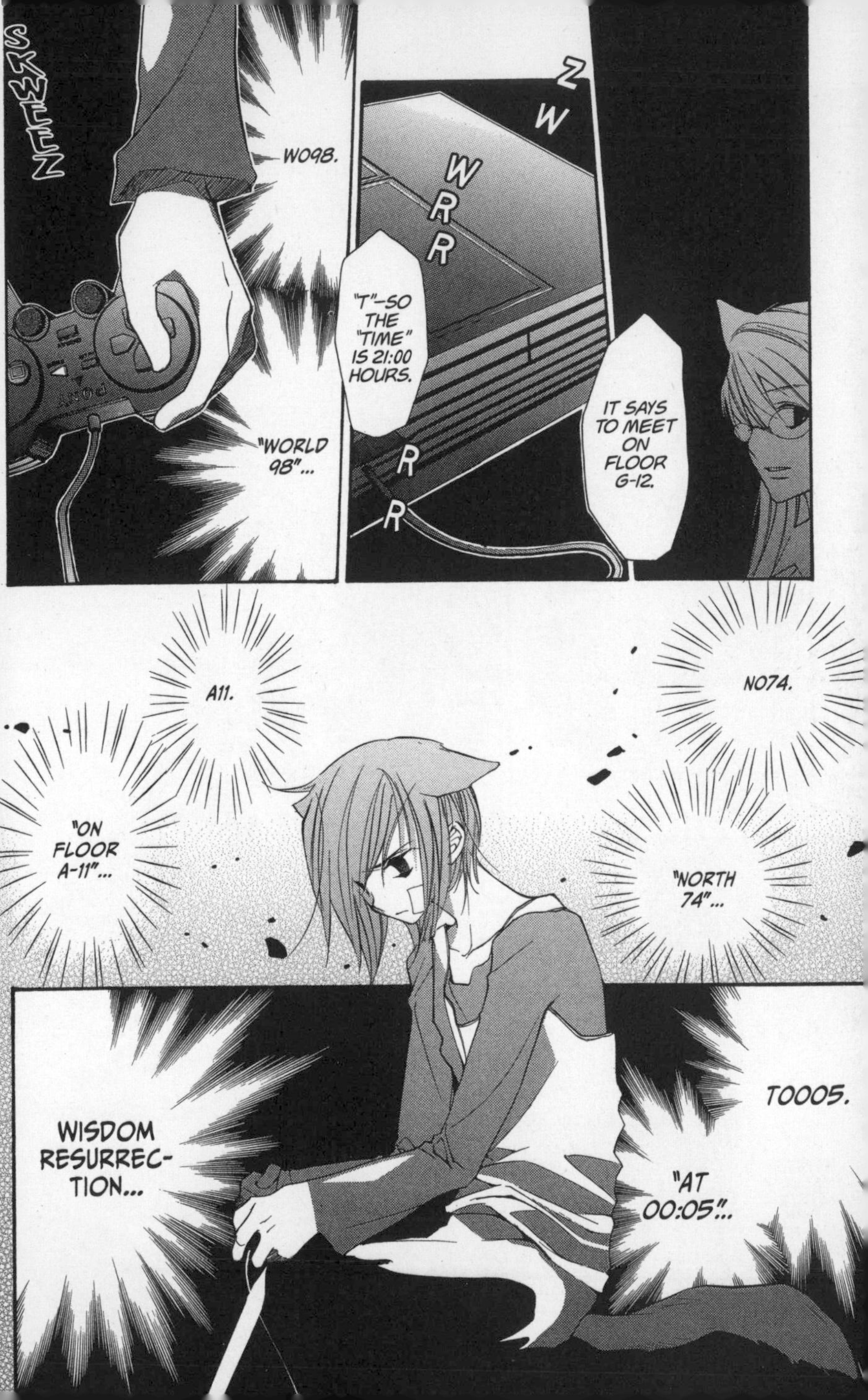
IT SAYS TO MEET ON FLOOR G-12.
ZW
WRRRR
"T"–SO THE "TIME" IS 21:00 HOURS.
SKWEEZ
W098.
"WORLD 98"...
N074.
A11.
"NORTH 74"...
"ON FLOOR A-11"...
T0005.
"AT 00:05"...
WISDOM RESURREC-TION...

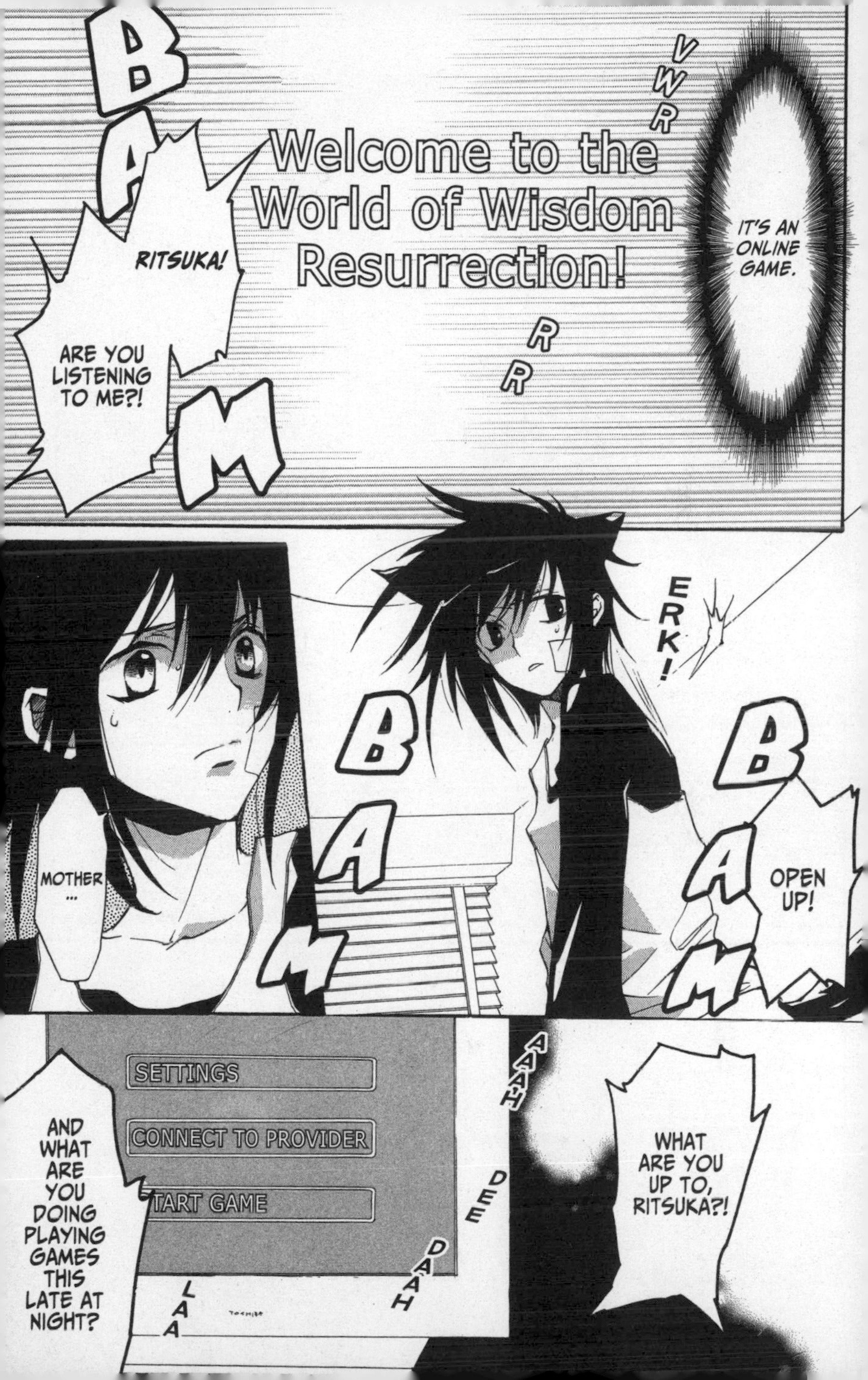
IT'S AN ONLINE GAME.
VWR
R
R
R
Welcome to the World of Wisdom Resurrection!
BAM
RITSUKA!
ARE YOU LISTENING TO ME?!
BAM
OPEN UP!
ERK!
BAM
MOTHER...
WHAT ARE YOU UP TO, RITSUKA?!
AAAAH
DEE
DAAAH
SETTINGS
CONNECT TO PROVIDER
TART GAME
LAA
AND WHAT ARE YOU DOING PLAYING GAMES THIS LATE AT NIGHT?

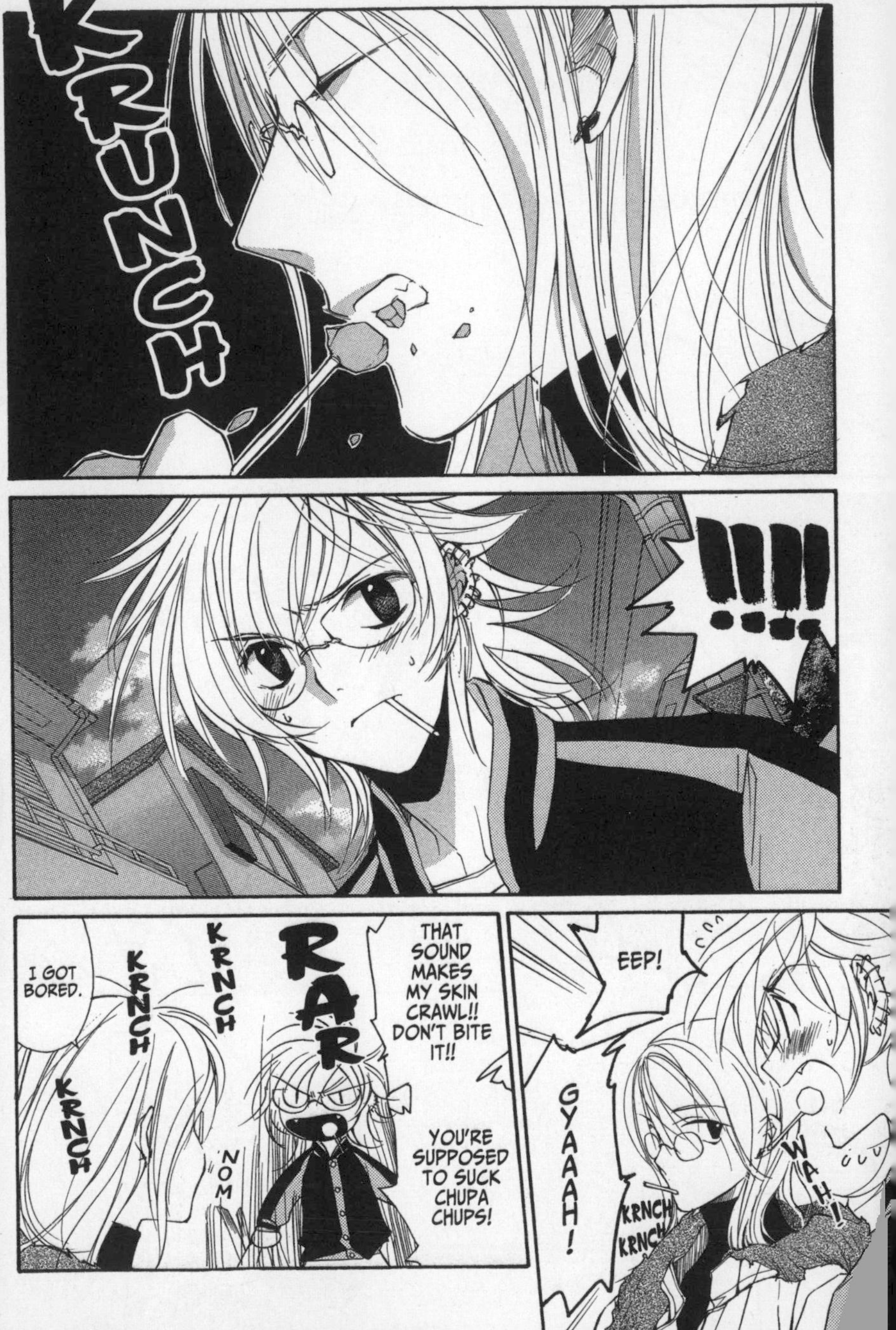
KRUNCH
!!!!
EEP!
WAH!
GYAAAH!
KRNCH KRNCH
THAT SOUND MAKES MY SKIN CRAWL!! DON'T BITE IT!!
RAR
KRNCH
KRNCH
I GOT BORED.
YOU'RE SUPPOSED TO SUCK CHUPA CHUPS!
NOM
KRNCH

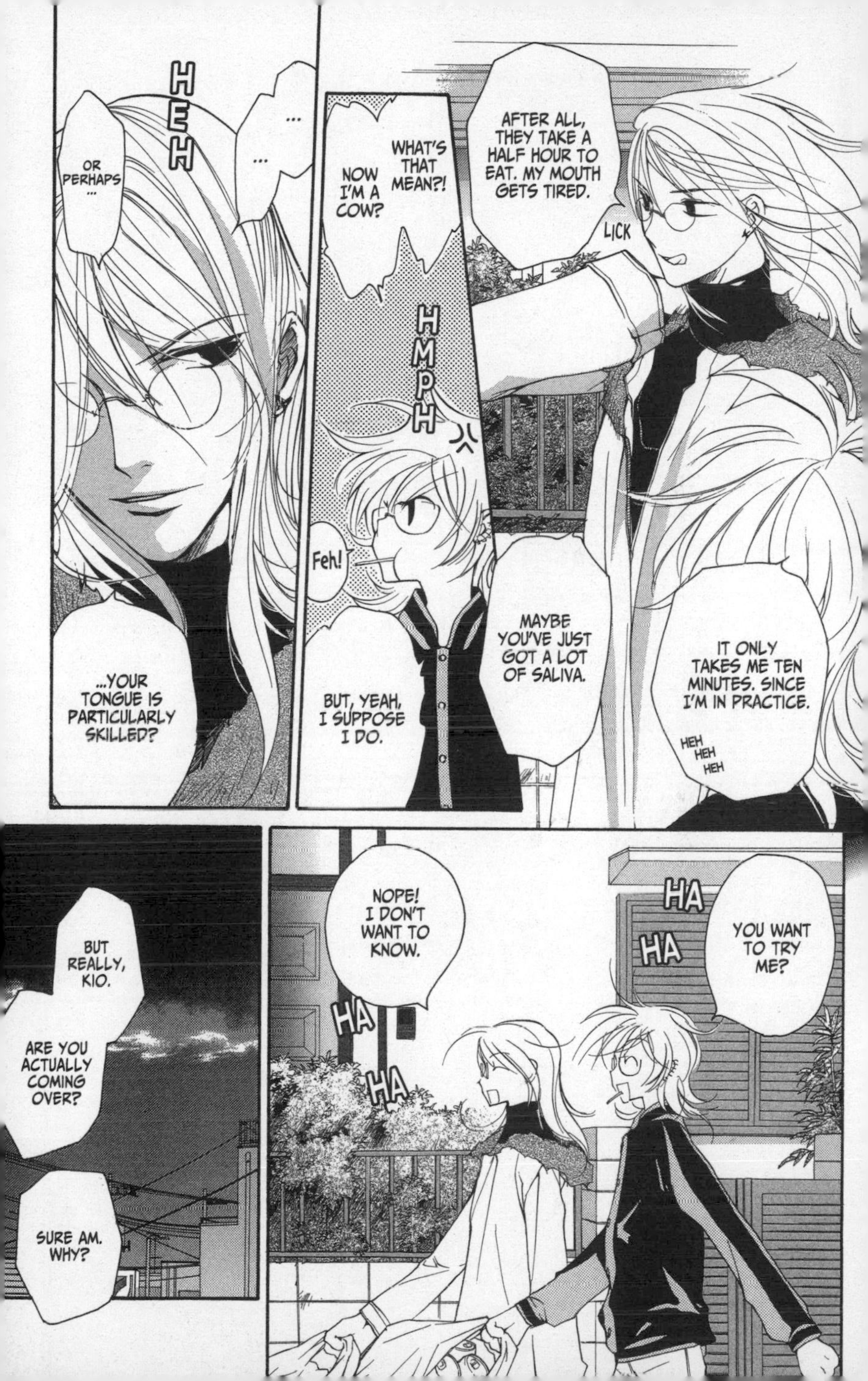
AFTER ALL, THEY TAKE A HALF HOUR TO EAT. MY MOUTH GETS TIRED.
LICK
IT ONLY TAKES ME TEN MINUTES. SINCE I'M IN PRACTICE.
HEH HEH HEH
MAYBE YOU'VE JUST GOT A LOT OF SALIVA.
WHAT'S THAT MEAN?!
NOW I'M A COW?
HMPH
Feh!
BUT, YEAH, I SUPPOSE I DO.
HEH
...
...
OR PERHAPS ...
...YOUR TONGUE IS PARTICULARLY SKILLED?
YOU WANT TO TRY ME?
HA
HA
NOPE! I DON'T WANT TO KNOW.
HA
HA
BUT REALLY, KIO.
ARE YOU ACTUALLY COMING OVER?
SURE AM. WHY?

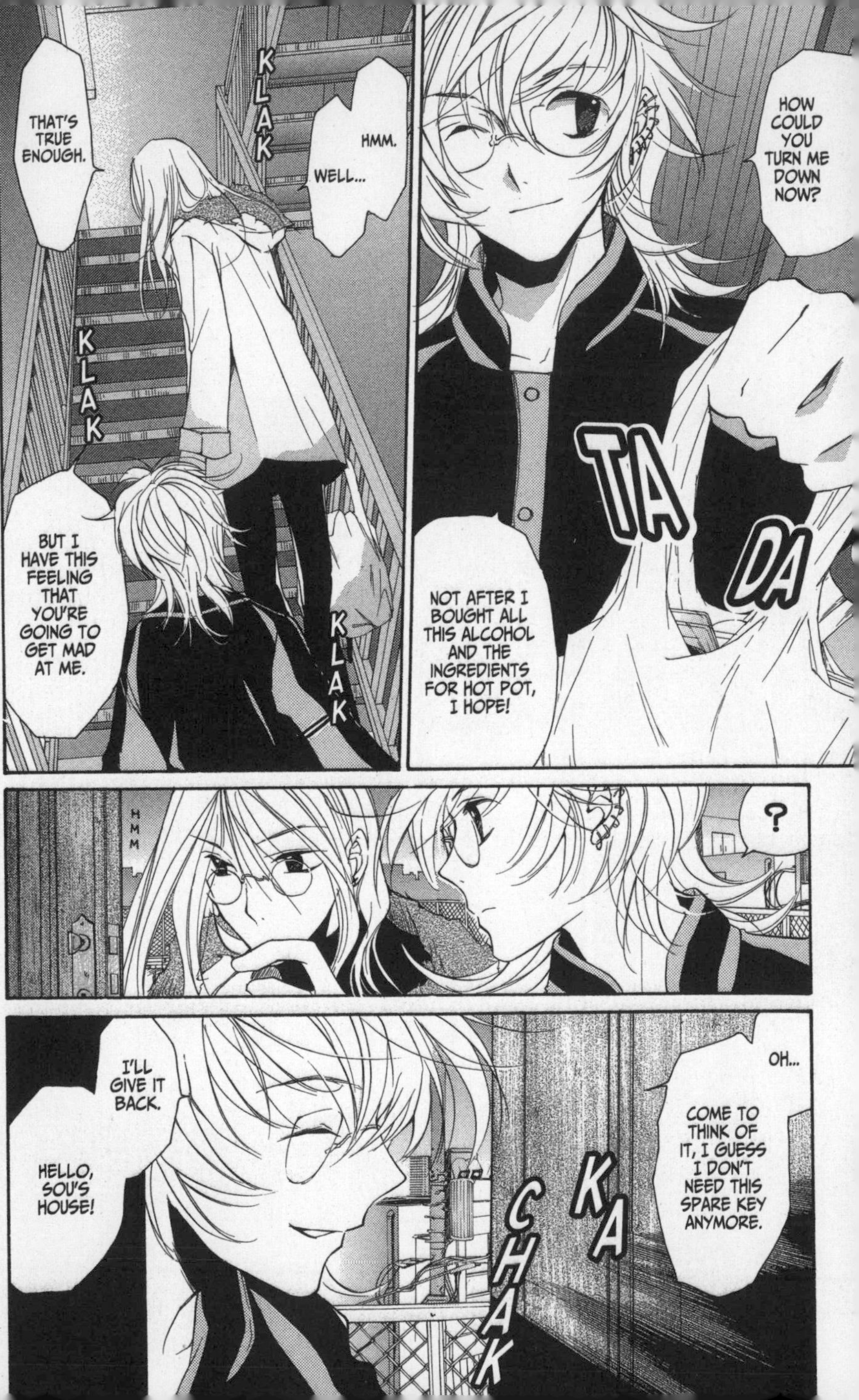
HOW COULD YOU TURN ME DOWN NOW?
TA DA
NOT AFTER I BOUGHT ALL THIS ALCOHOL AND THE INGREDIENTS FOR HOT POT, I HOPE!
HMM. WELL...
KLAK
THAT'S TRUE ENOUGH.
KLAK
BUT I HAVE THIS FEELING THAT YOU'RE GOING TO GET MAD AT ME.
KLAK
?
HMM
OH...
COME TO THINK OF IT, I GUESS I DON'T NEED THIS SPARE KEY ANYMORE.
KA CHAK
I'LL GIVE IT BACK.
HELLO, SOU'S HOUSE!

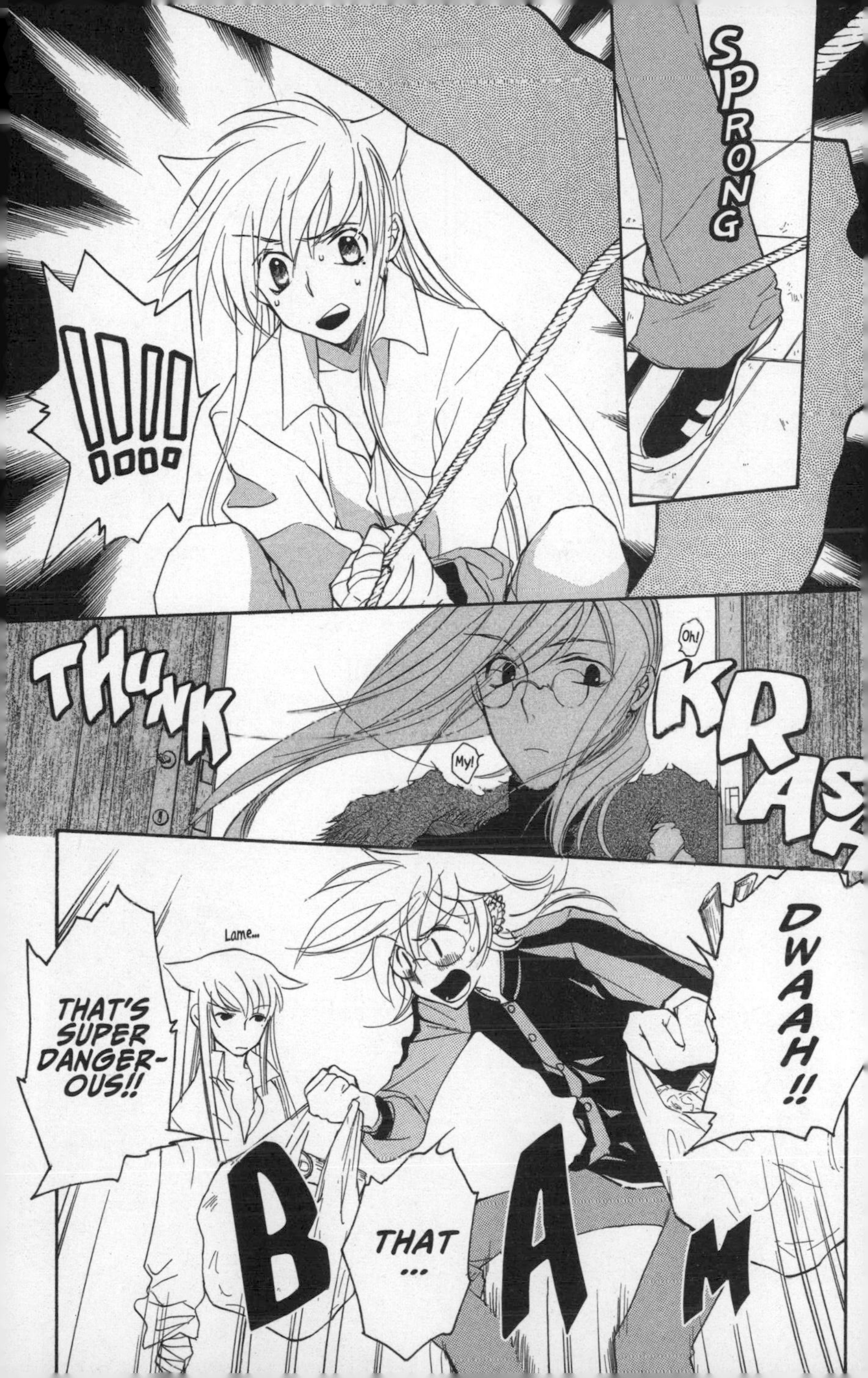
SPRONG
!!!!
THUNK
Oh!
KRAS
My!
DWAAH!!
Lame...
THAT'S SUPER DANGER-OUS!!
BAM
THAT ...

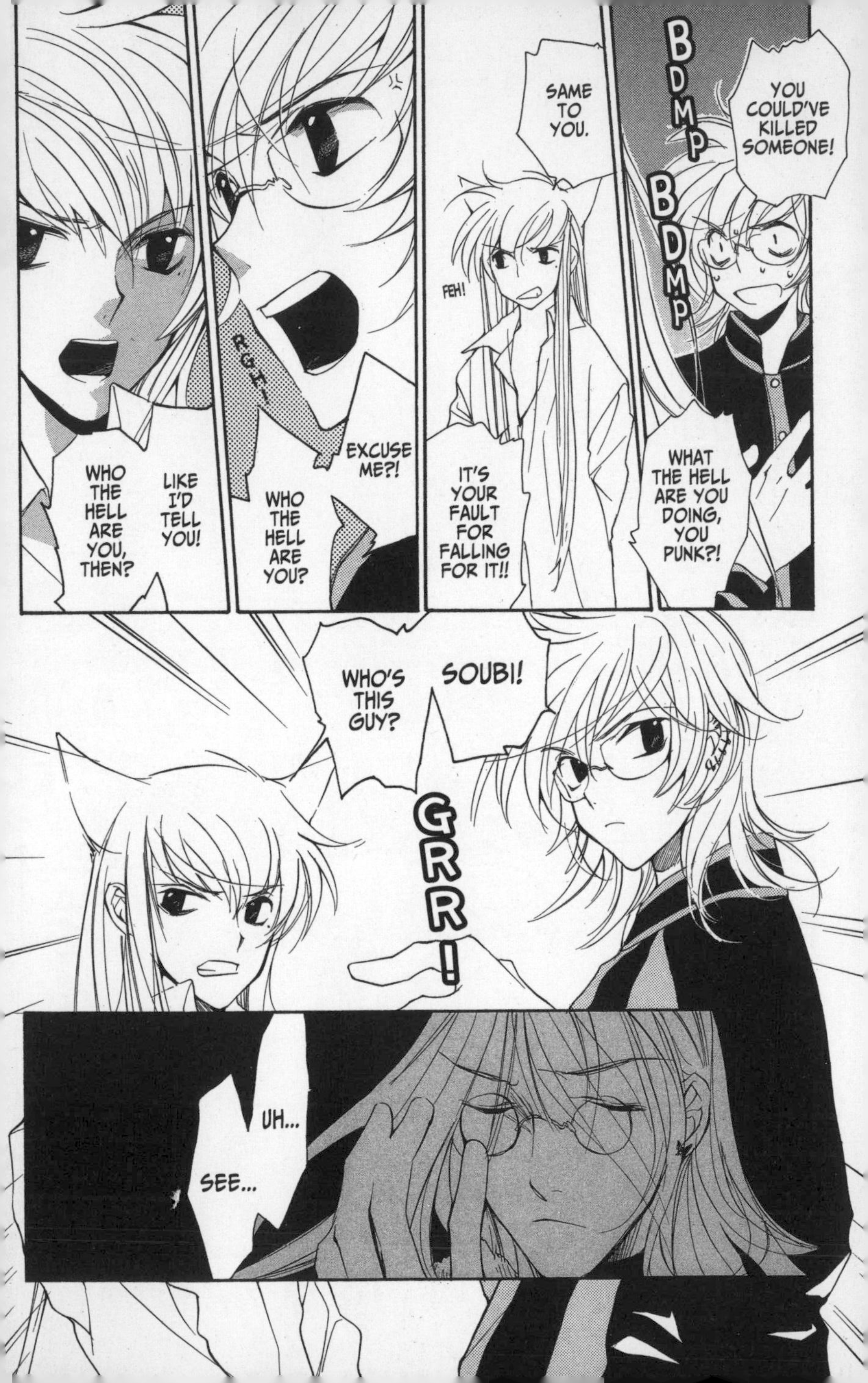
YOU COULD'VE KILLED SOMEONE!
BDMP
BDMP
WHAT THE HELL ARE YOU DOING, YOU PUNK?!
SAME TO YOU.
FEH!
IT'S YOUR FAULT FOR FALLING FOR IT!!
RGH!
EXCUSE ME?!
WHO THE HELL ARE YOU?
LIKE I'D TELL YOU!
WHO THE HELL ARE YOU, THEN?
SOUBI!
WHO'S THIS GUY?
GRR!
UH...
SEE...

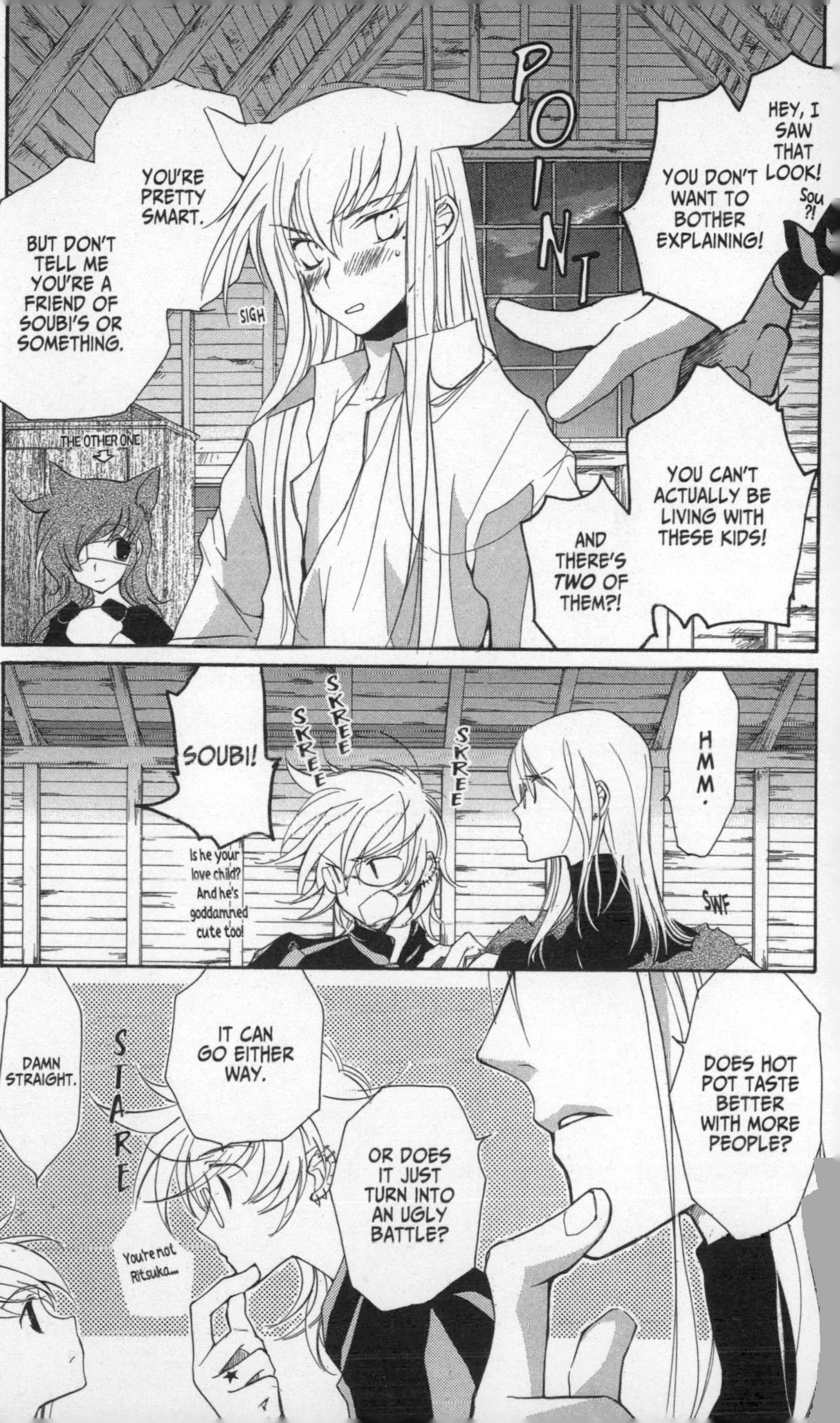
HEY, I SAW THAT LOOK!
Sou ?!
YOU DON'T WANT TO BOTHER EXPLAINING!
POINT
YOU'RE PRETTY SMART.
BUT DON'T TELL ME YOU'RE A FRIEND OF SOUBI'S OR SOMETHING.
SIGH
YOU CAN'T ACTUALLY BE LIVING WITH THESE KIDS!
AND THERE'S *TWO* OF THEM?!
THE OTHER ONE
HMM.
SWF
SKREE
SKREE
SKREE
SOUBI!
Is he your love child? And he's goddamned cute too!
DOES HOT POT TASTE BETTER WITH MORE PEOPLE?
OR DOES IT JUST TURN INTO AN UGLY BATTLE?
IT CAN GO EITHER WAY.
STARE
DAMN STRAIGHT.
You're not Ritsuka...

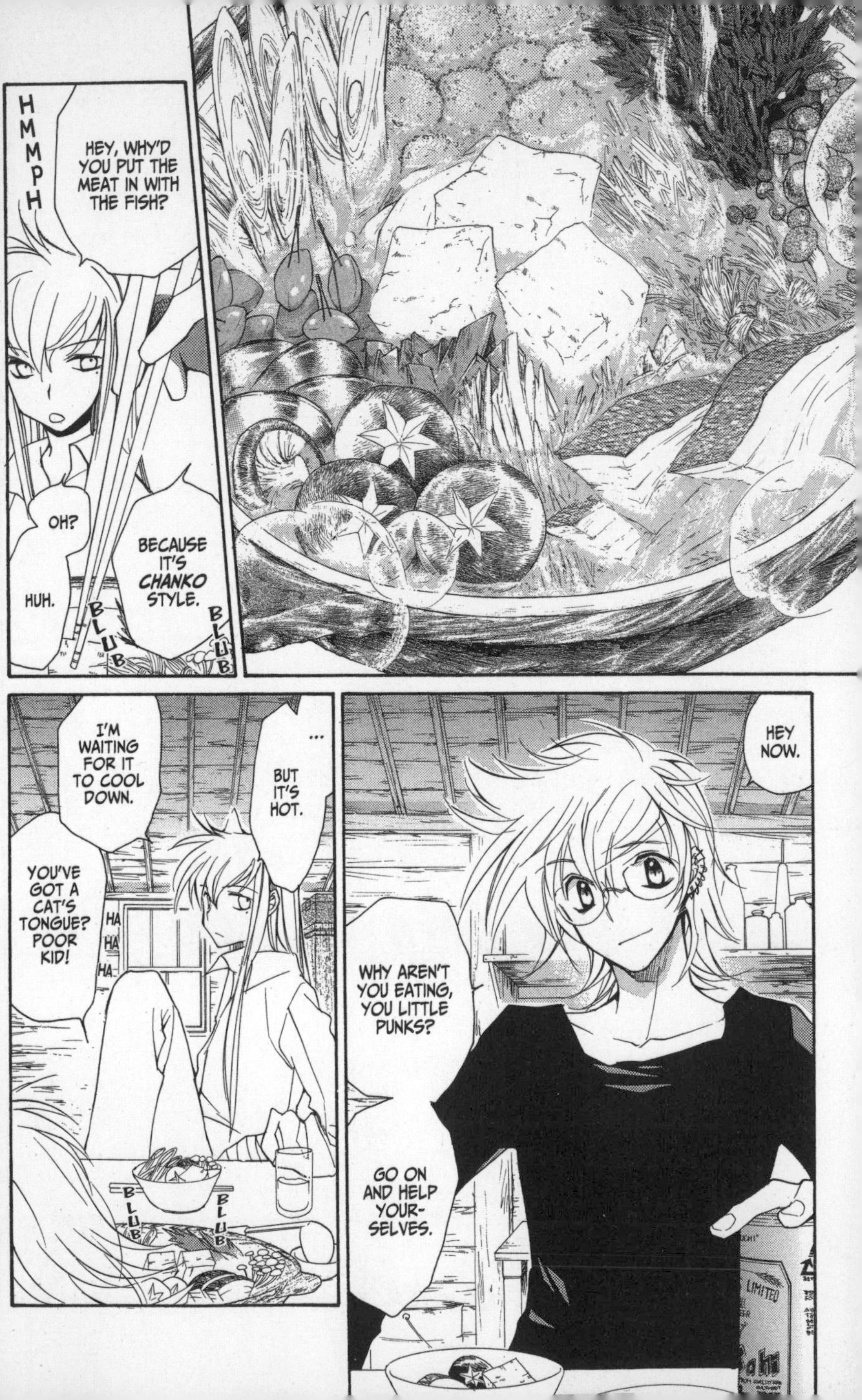
HMMPH
HEY, WHY'D YOU PUT THE MEAT IN WITH THE FISH?
BECAUSE IT'S *CHANKO* STYLE.
OH?
HUH.
BLUB
BLUB
HEY NOW.
WHY AREN'T YOU EATING, YOU LITTLE PUNKS?
GO ON AND HELP YOUR-SELVES.
...
BUT IT'S HOT.
I'M WAITING FOR IT TO COOL DOWN.
YOU'VE GOT A CAT'S TONGUE? POOR KID!
HA HA HA
BLUB
BLUB

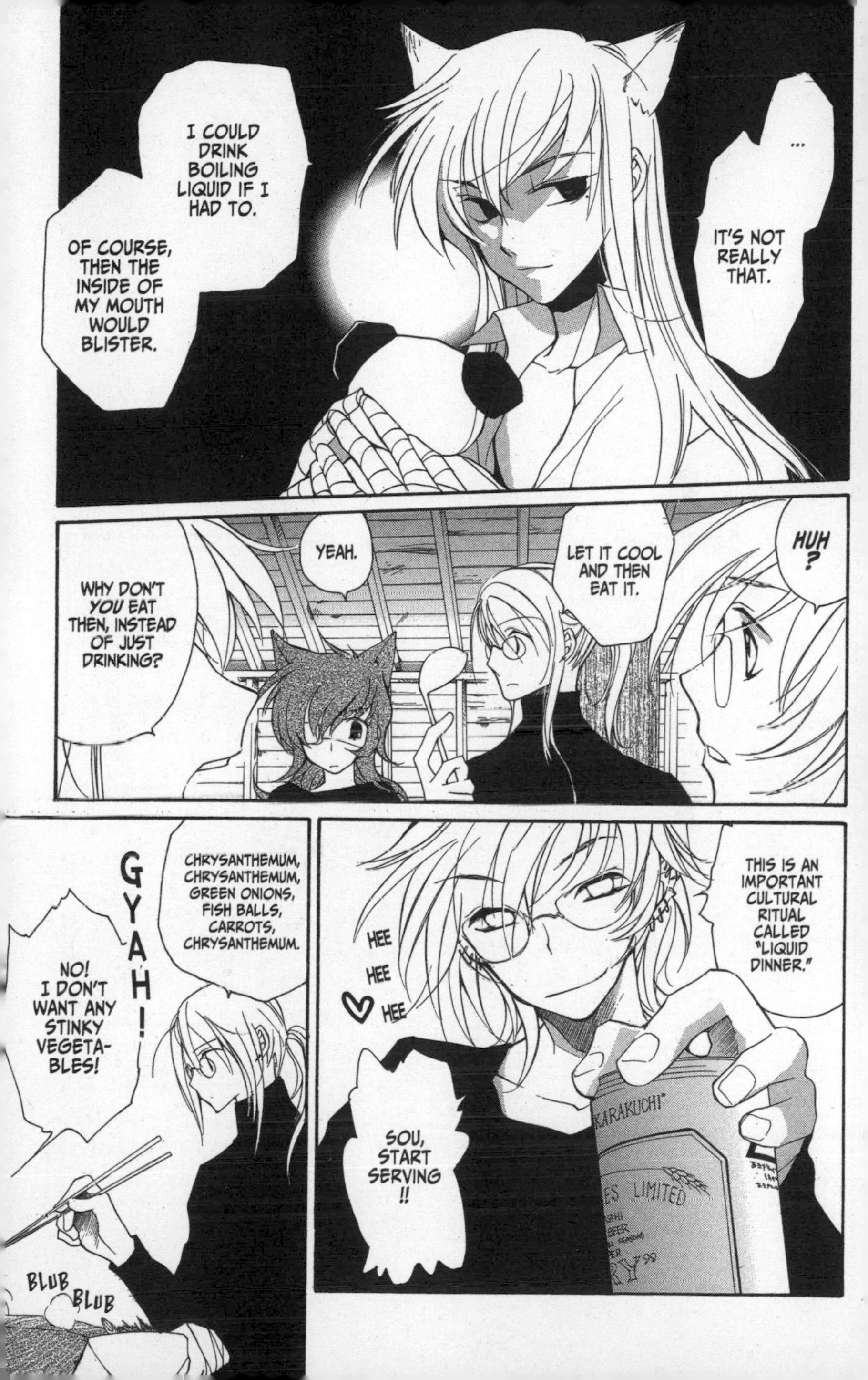
...
IT'S NOT REALLY THAT.
I COULD DRINK BOILING LIQUID IF I HAD TO.
OF COURSE, THEN THE INSIDE OF MY MOUTH WOULD BLISTER.
HUH?
LET IT COOL AND THEN EAT IT.
YEAH.
WHY DON'T *YOU* EAT THEN, INSTEAD OF JUST DRINKING?
THIS IS AN IMPORTANT CULTURAL RITUAL CALLED "LIQUID DINNER."
HEE HEE ♥ HEE
SOU, START SERVING!!
KARAKUCHI
CHRYSANTHEMUM, CHRYSANTHEMUM, GREEN ONIONS, FISH BALLS, CARROTS, CHRYSANTHEMUM.
GYAH!
NO! I DON'T WANT ANY STINKY VEGETA-BLES!
BLUB BLUB

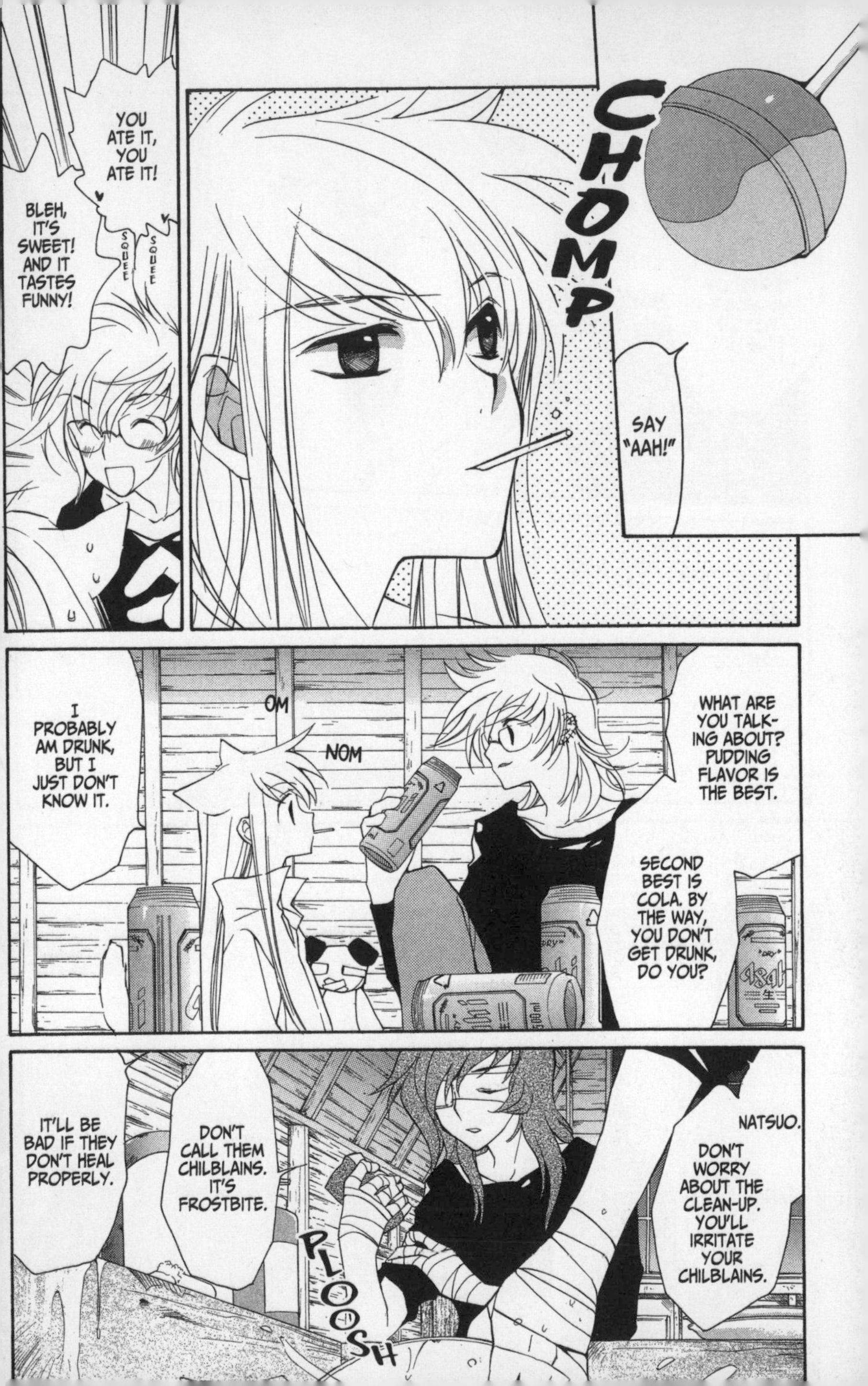
SAY "AAH!"
CHOMP
YOU ATE IT, YOU ATE IT!
BLEH, IT'S SWEET! AND IT TASTES FUNNY!
SQUEE
SQUEE
WHAT ARE YOU TALKING ABOUT? PUDDING FLAVOR IS THE BEST.
SECOND BEST IS COLA. BY THE WAY, YOU DON'T GET DRUNK, DO YOU?
NOM
OM
I PROBABLY AM DRUNK, BUT I JUST DON'T KNOW IT.
NATSUO.
DON'T WORRY ABOUT THE CLEAN-UP. YOU'LL IRRITATE YOUR CHILBLAINS.
PLOOSH
DON'T CALL THEM CHILBLAINS. IT'S FROSTBITE.
IT'LL BE BAD IF THEY DON'T HEAL PROPERLY.

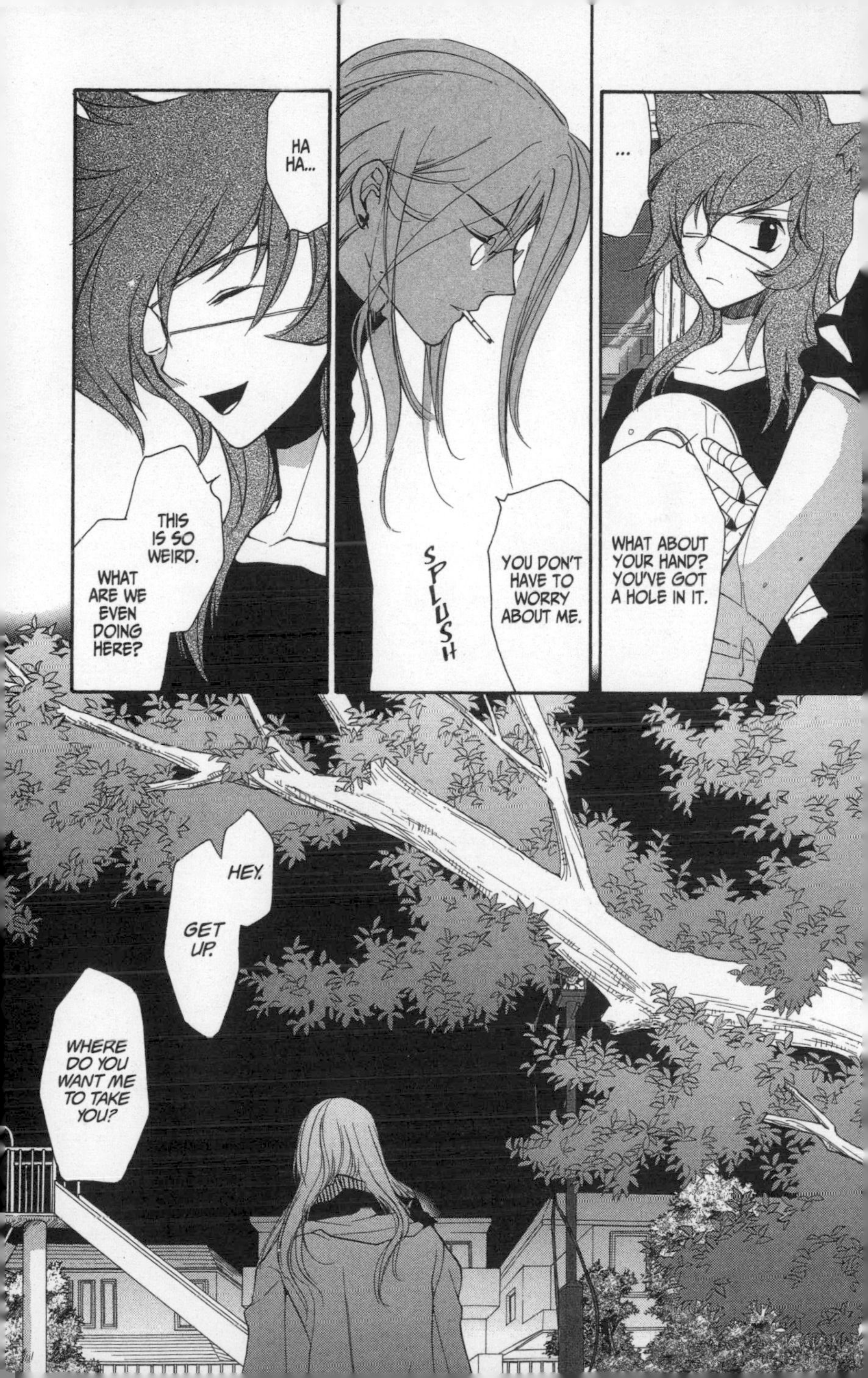
...
WHAT ABOUT YOUR HAND? YOU'VE GOT A HOLE IN IT.
YOU DON'T HAVE TO WORRY ABOUT ME.
SPLUSH
HA HA...
THIS IS SO WEIRD.
WHAT ARE WE EVEN DOING HERE?
HEY.
GET UP.
WHERE DO YOU WANT ME TO TAKE YOU?

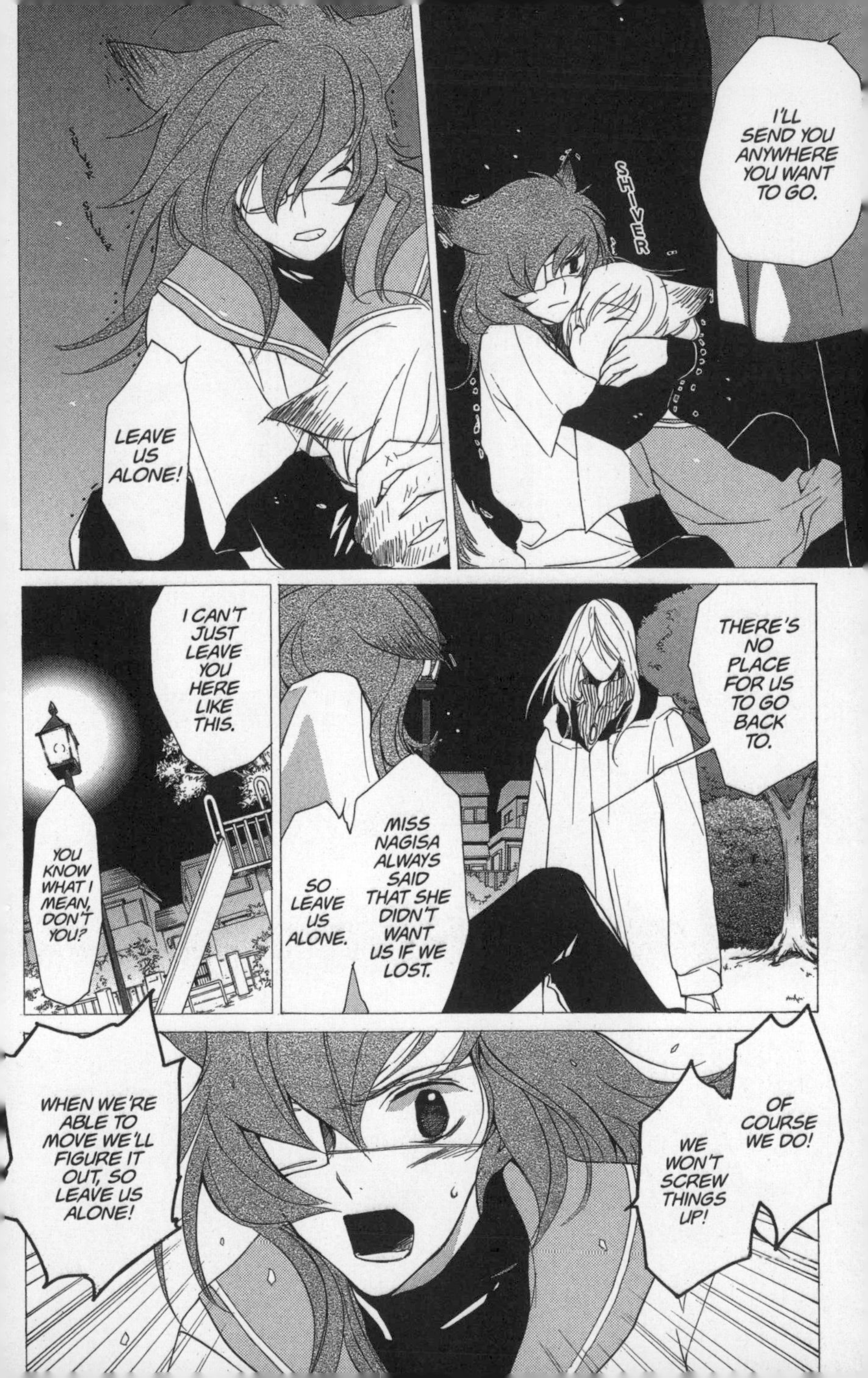
I'LL SEND YOU ANYWHERE YOU WANT TO GO.
SHIVER
SHIVER SHIVER
LEAVE US ALONE!
THERE'S NO PLACE FOR US TO GO BACK TO.
MISS NAGISA ALWAYS SAID THAT SHE DIDN'T WANT US IF WE LOST.
SO LEAVE US ALONE.
I CAN'T JUST LEAVE YOU HERE LIKE THIS.
YOU KNOW WHAT I MEAN, DON'T YOU?
OF COURSE WE DO!
WE WON'T SCREW THINGS UP!
WHEN WE'RE ABLE TO MOVE WE'LL FIGURE IT OUT, SO LEAVE US ALONE!

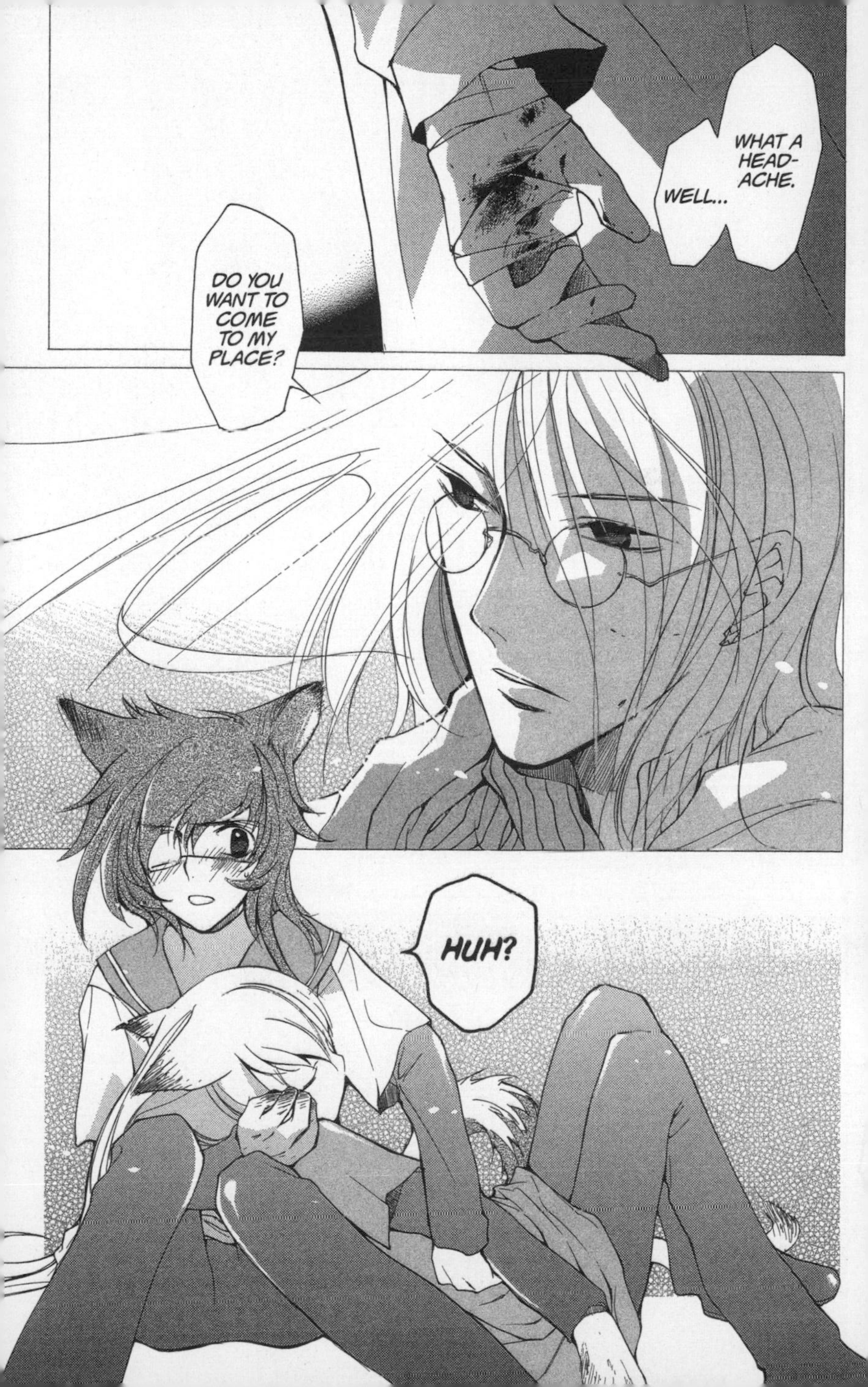
WHAT A HEAD-ACHE.
WELL...
DO YOU WANT TO COME TO MY PLACE?
HUH?

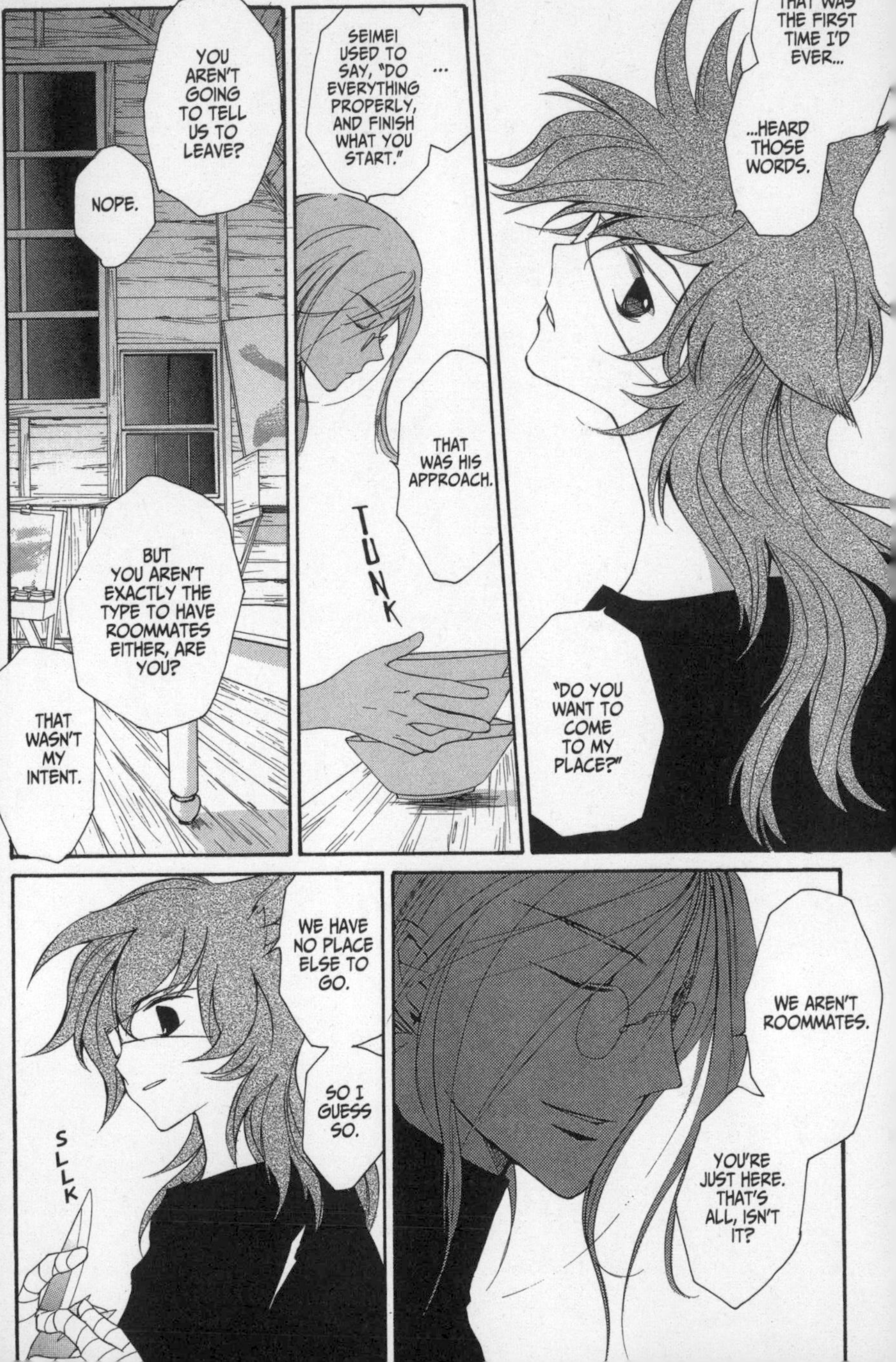
THAT WAS THE FIRST TIME I'D EVER...
...HEARD THOSE WORDS.
"DO YOU WANT TO COME TO MY PLACE?"
SEIMEI USED TO SAY, "DO EVERYTHING PROPERLY, AND FINISH WHAT YOU START."
...
THAT WAS HIS APPROACH.
TUNK
YOU AREN'T GOING TO TELL US TO LEAVE?
NOPE.
BUT YOU AREN'T EXACTLY THE TYPE TO HAVE ROOMMATES EITHER, ARE YOU?
THAT WASN'T MY INTENT.
WE AREN'T ROOMMATES.
YOU'RE JUST HERE. THAT'S ALL, ISN'T IT?
WE HAVE NO PLACE ELSE TO GO.
SO I GUESS SO.
SLLK

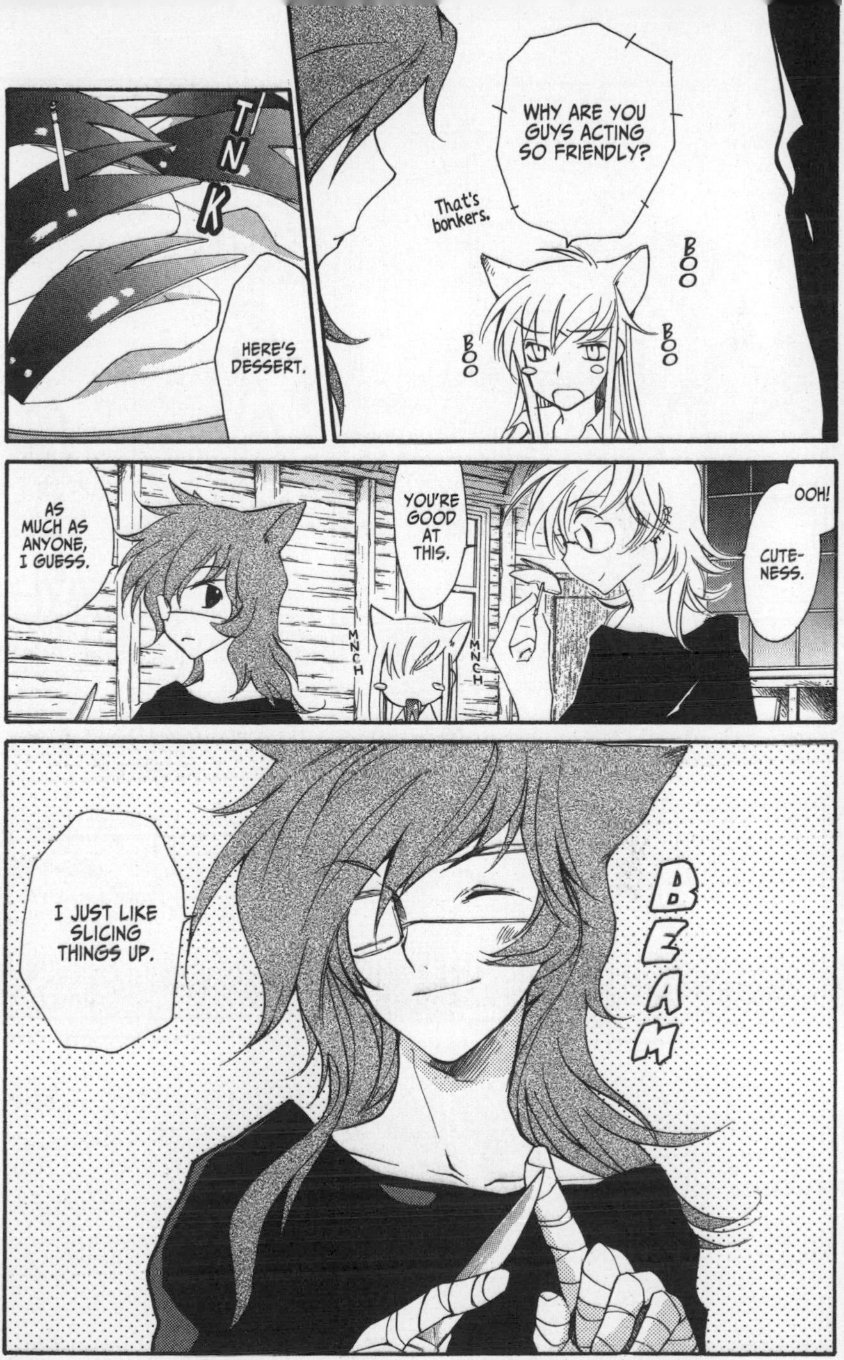
WHY ARE YOU GUYS ACTING SO FRIENDLY?
That's bonkers.
BOO
BOO
BOO
TNK
HERE'S DESSERT.
OOH!
CUTE-NESS.
YOU'RE GOOD AT THIS.
MNCH
MNCH
AS MUCH AS ANYONE, I GUESS.
BEAM
I JUST LIKE SLICING THINGS UP.

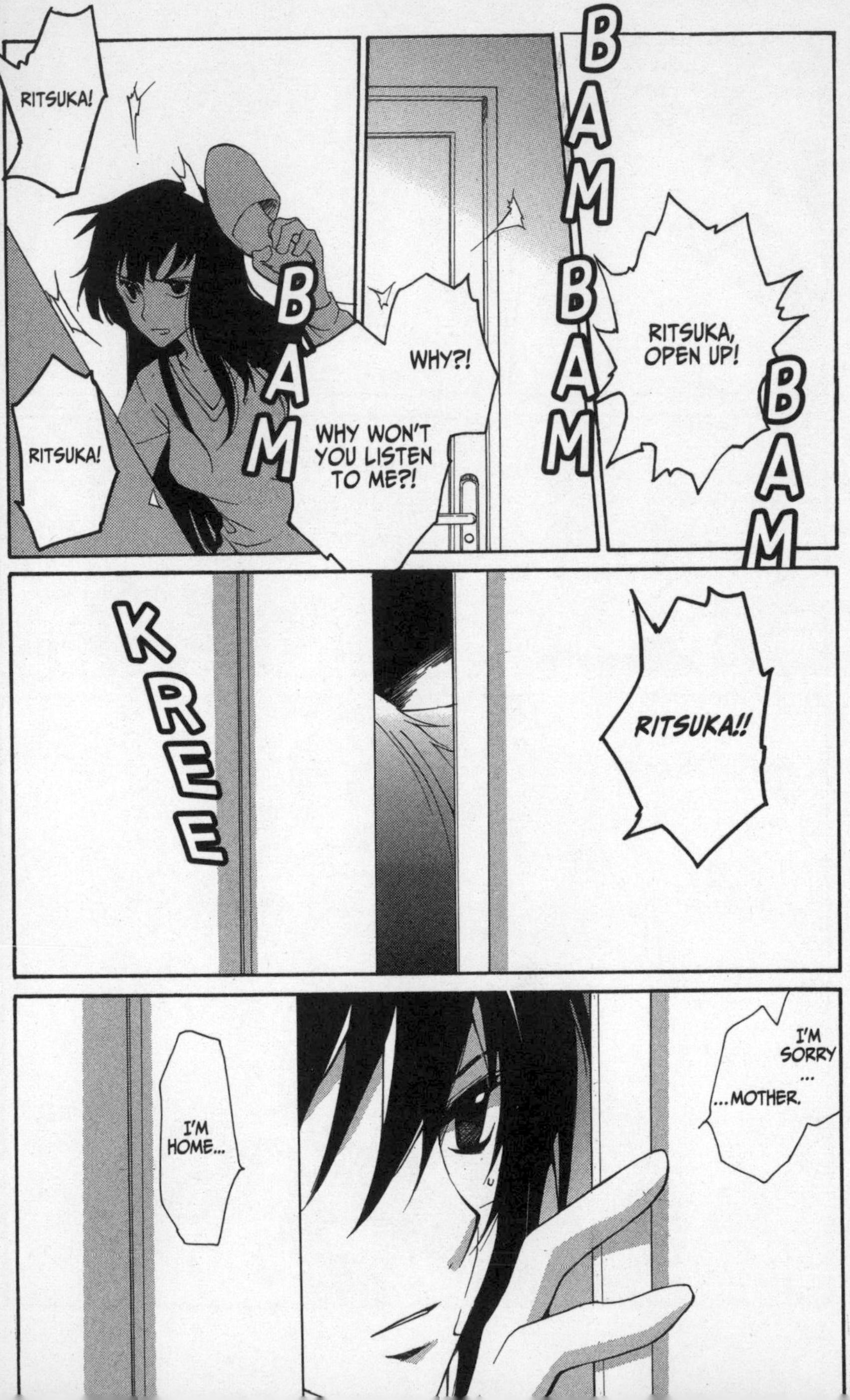
BAM
BAM
RITSUKA, OPEN UP!
BAM
WHY?!
WHY WON'T YOU LISTEN TO ME?!
BAM
RITSUKA!
RITSUKA!
RITSUKA!!
KREE
I'M SORRY ... ...MOTHER.
I'M HOME...

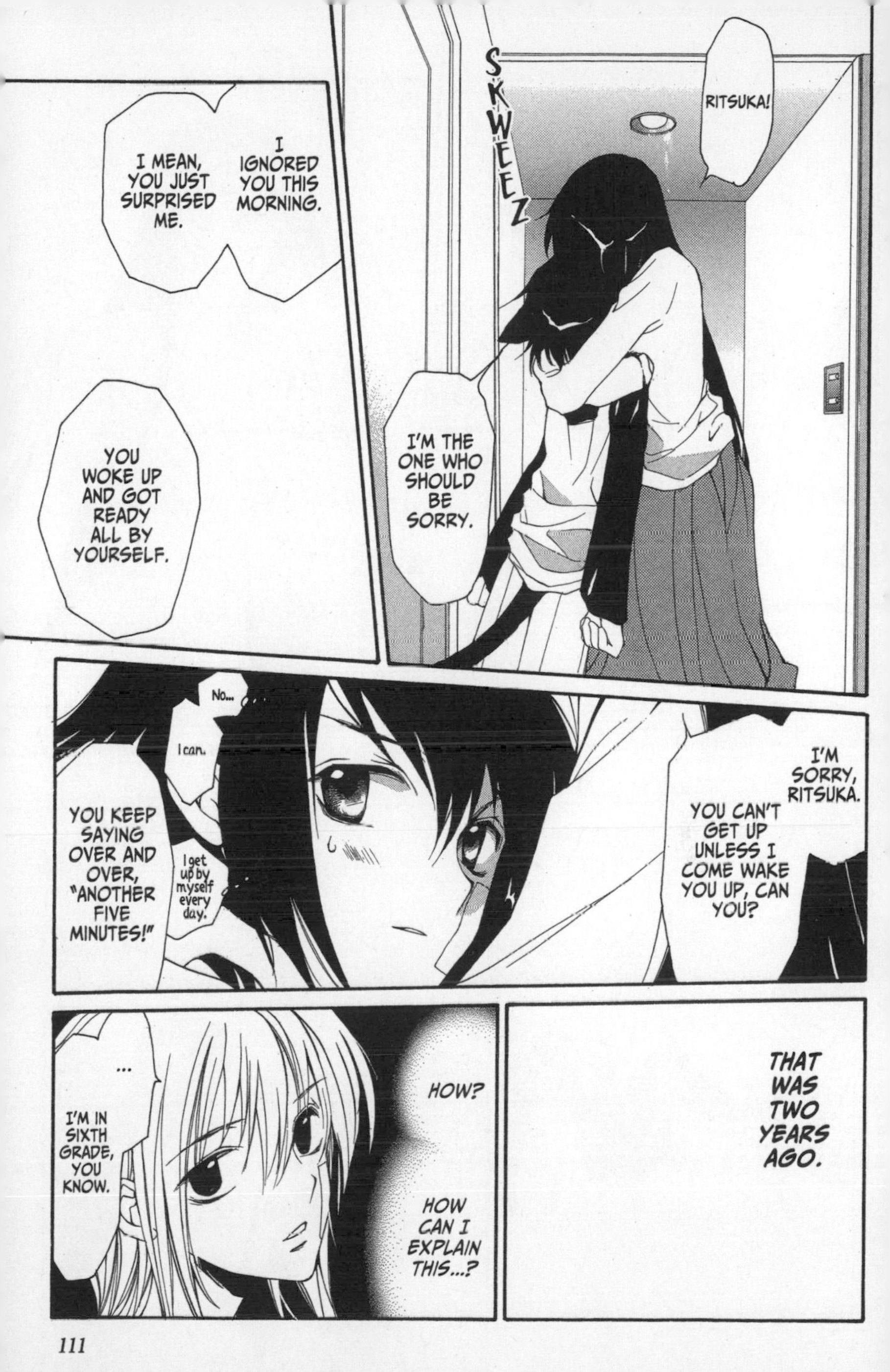
RITSUKA!
SKWEEZ
I'M THE ONE WHO SHOULD BE SORRY.
I IGNORED YOU THIS MORNING.
I MEAN, YOU JUST SURPRISED ME.
YOU WOKE UP AND GOT READY ALL BY YOURSELF.
I'M SORRY, RITSUKA.
YOU CAN'T GET UP UNLESS I COME WAKE YOU UP, CAN YOU?
No...
I can.
YOU KEEP SAYING OVER AND OVER, "ANOTHER FIVE MINUTES!"
I get up by myself every day.
THAT WAS TWO YEARS AGO.
...
I'M IN SIXTH GRADE, YOU KNOW.
HOW?
HOW CAN I EXPLAIN THIS...?

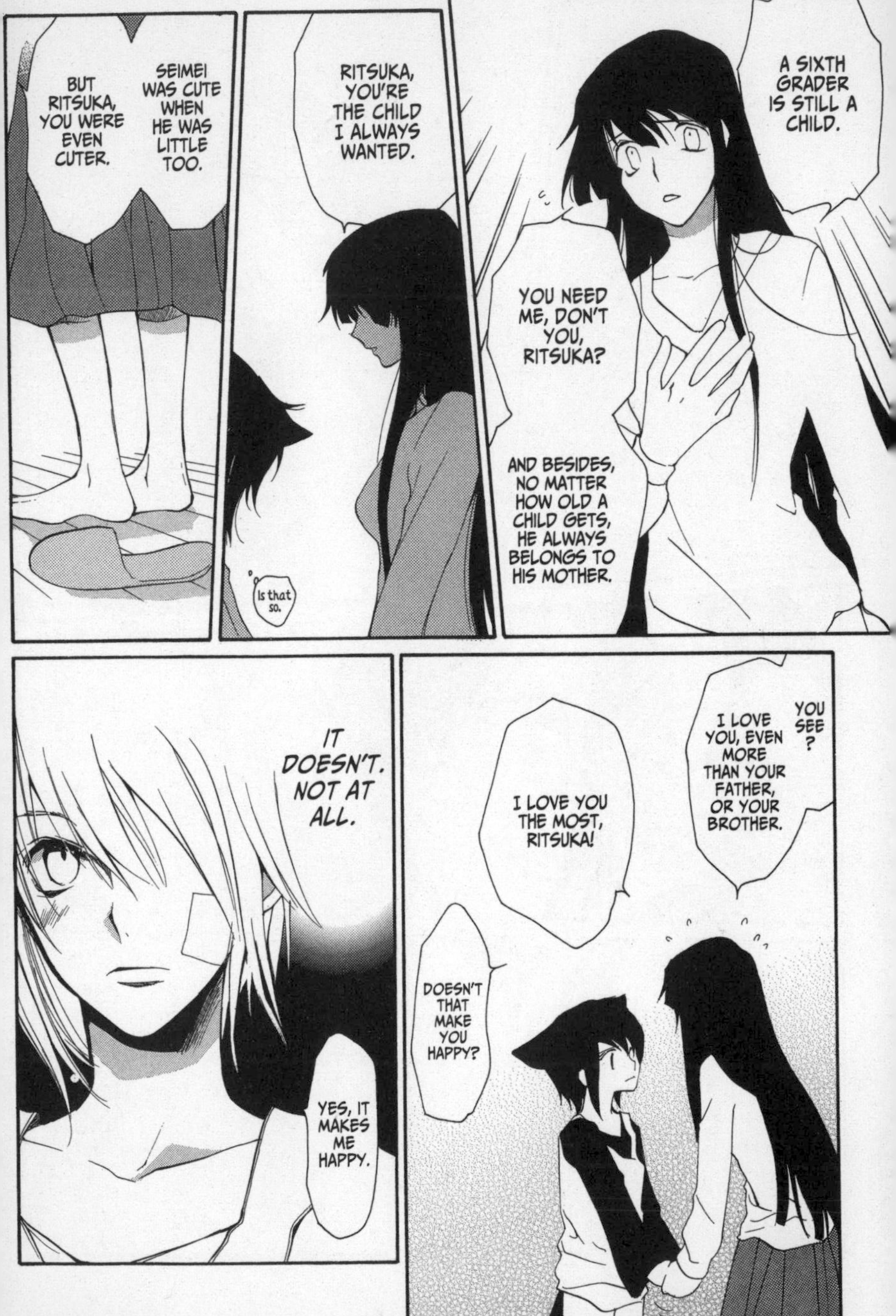
A SIXTH GRADER IS STILL A CHILD.
YOU NEED ME, DON'T YOU, RITSUKA?
AND BESIDES, NO MATTER HOW OLD A CHILD GETS, HE ALWAYS BELONGS TO HIS MOTHER.
RITSUKA, YOU'RE THE CHILD I ALWAYS WANTED.
Is that so.
SEIMEI WAS CUTE WHEN HE WAS LITTLE TOO.
BUT RITSUKA, YOU WERE EVEN CUTER.
YOU SEE?
I LOVE YOU, EVEN MORE THAN YOUR FATHER, OR YOUR BROTHER.
I LOVE YOU THE MOST, RITSUKA!
DOESN'T THAT MAKE YOU HAPPY?
IT DOESN'T. NOT AT ALL.
YES, IT MAKES ME HAPPY.

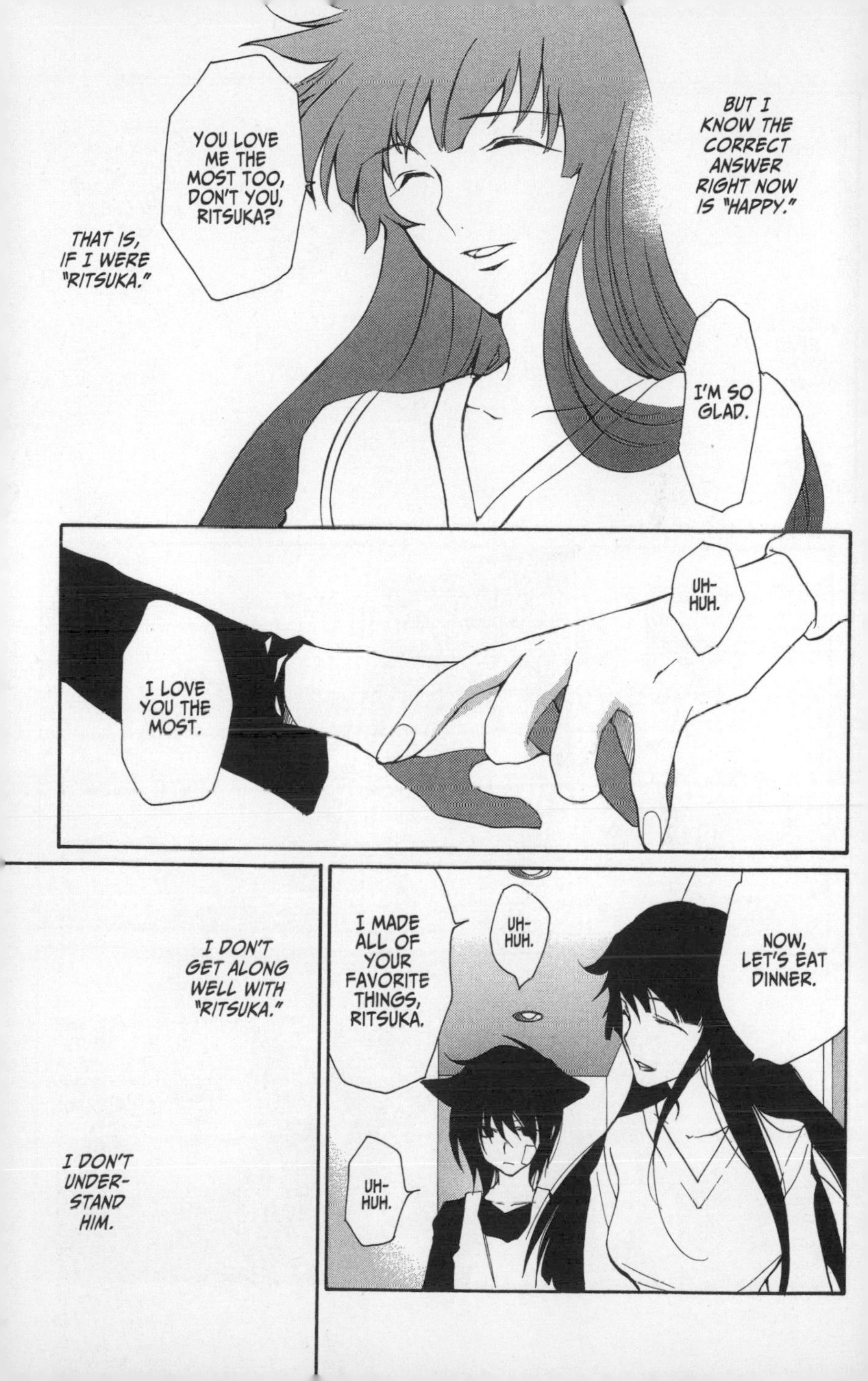
BUT I KNOW THE CORRECT ANSWER RIGHT NOW IS "HAPPY."
YOU LOVE ME THE MOST TOO, DON'T YOU, RITSUKA?
THAT IS, IF I WERE "RITSUKA."
I'M SO GLAD.
UH-HUH.
I LOVE YOU THE MOST.
NOW, LET'S EAT DINNER.
UH-HUH.
I MADE ALL OF YOUR FAVORITE THINGS, RITSUKA.
UH-HUH.
I DON'T GET ALONG WELL WITH "RITSUKA."
I DON'T UNDER-STAND HIM.

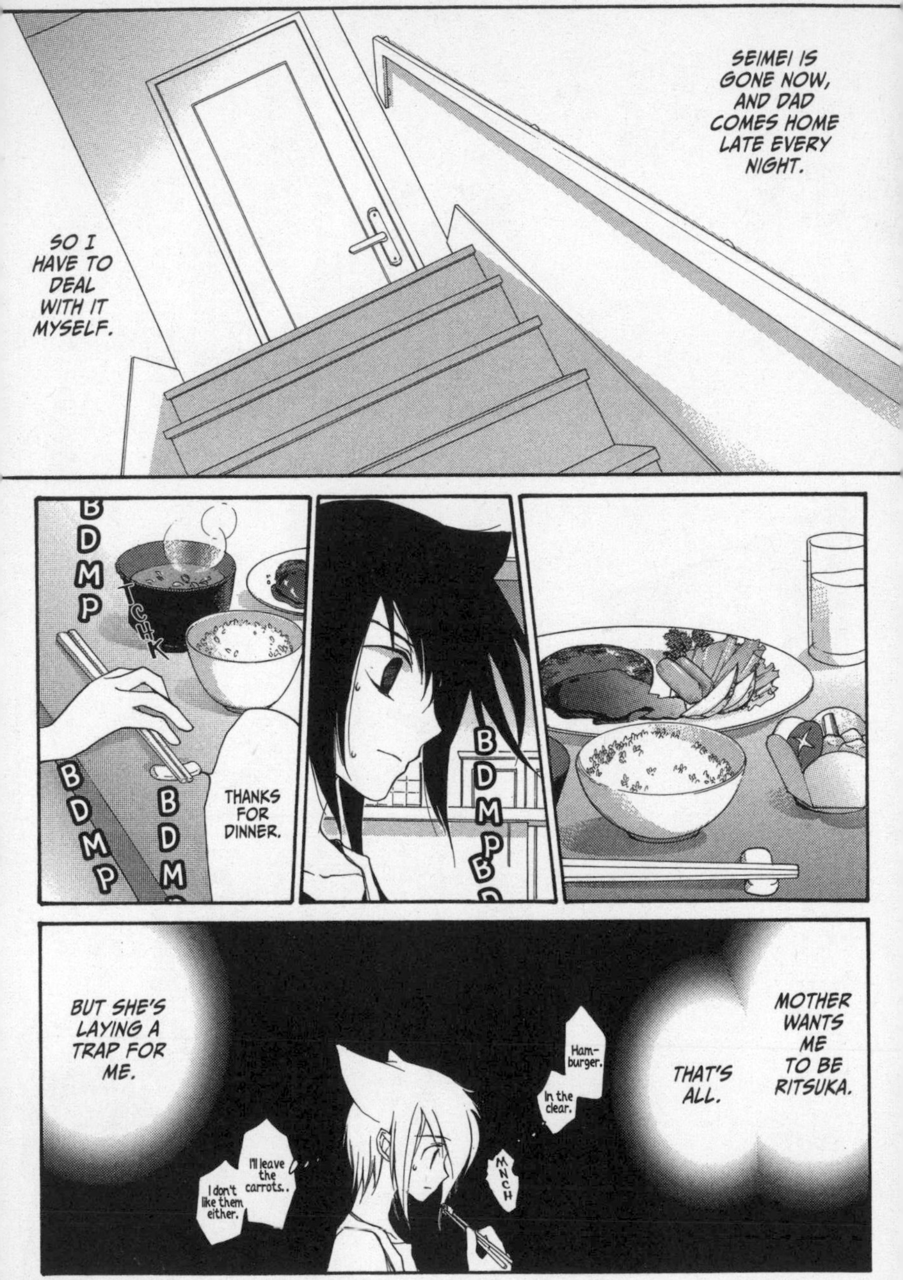
SEIMEI IS GONE NOW, AND DAD COMES HOME LATE EVERY NIGHT.
SO I HAVE TO DEAL WITH IT MYSELF.
BDMP
BD
BDMP
TCHK
BDMP
BDM
THANKS FOR DINNER.
MOTHER WANTS ME TO BE RITSUKA.
THAT'S ALL.
Ham-burger.
In the clear.
MNCH
I'll leave the carrots..
I don't like them either.
BUT SHE'S LAYING A TRAP FOR ME.

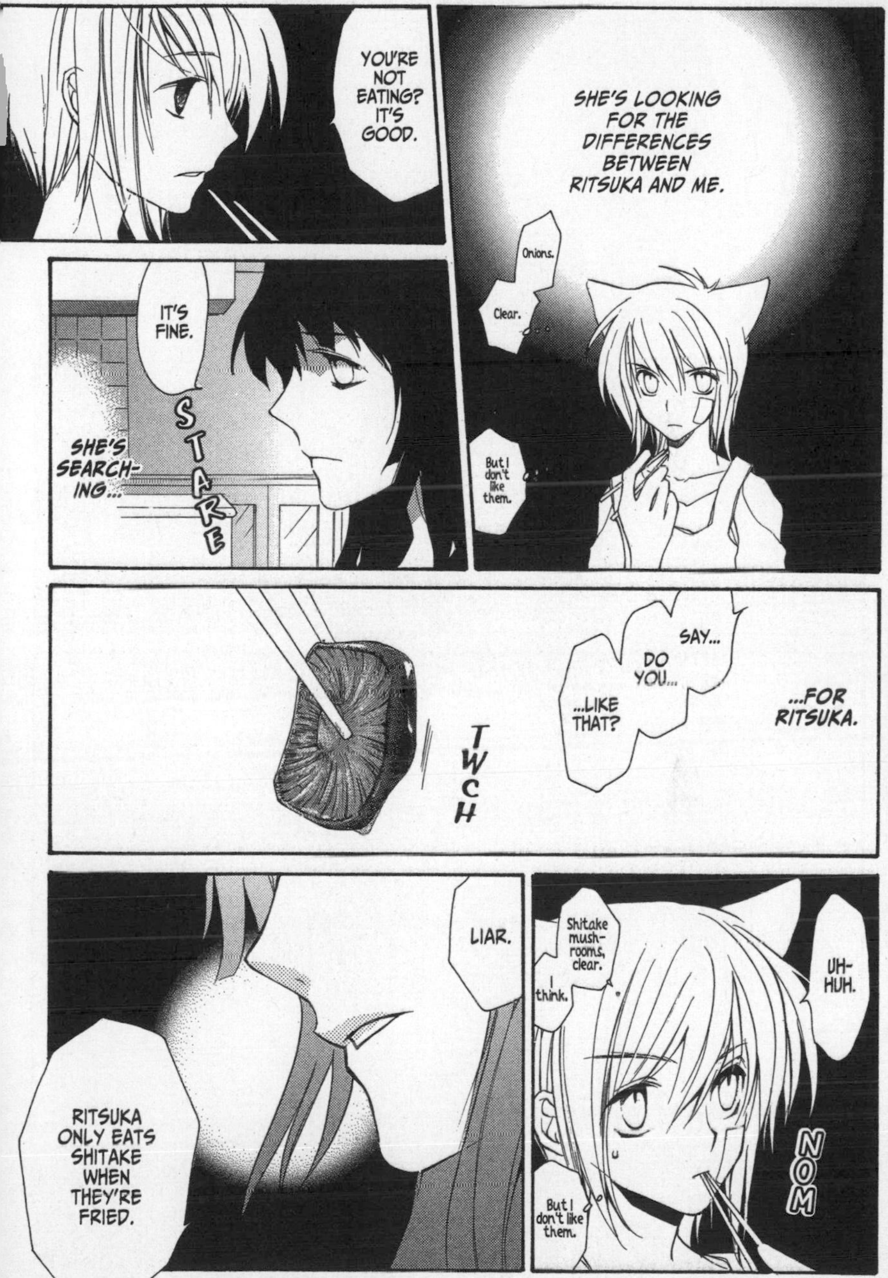
SHE'S LOOKING FOR THE DIFFERENCES BETWEEN RITSUKA AND ME.
Onions.
Clear.
But I don't like them.
YOU'RE NOT EATING? IT'S GOOD.
IT'S FINE.
STARE
SHE'S SEARCHING...
...FOR RITSUKA.
SAY... DO YOU... ...LIKE THAT?
TWCH
UH-HUH.
Shitake mush-rooms, clear.
I think.
NOM
But I don't like them.
LIAR.
RITSUKA ONLY EATS SHITAKE WHEN THEY'RE FRIED.

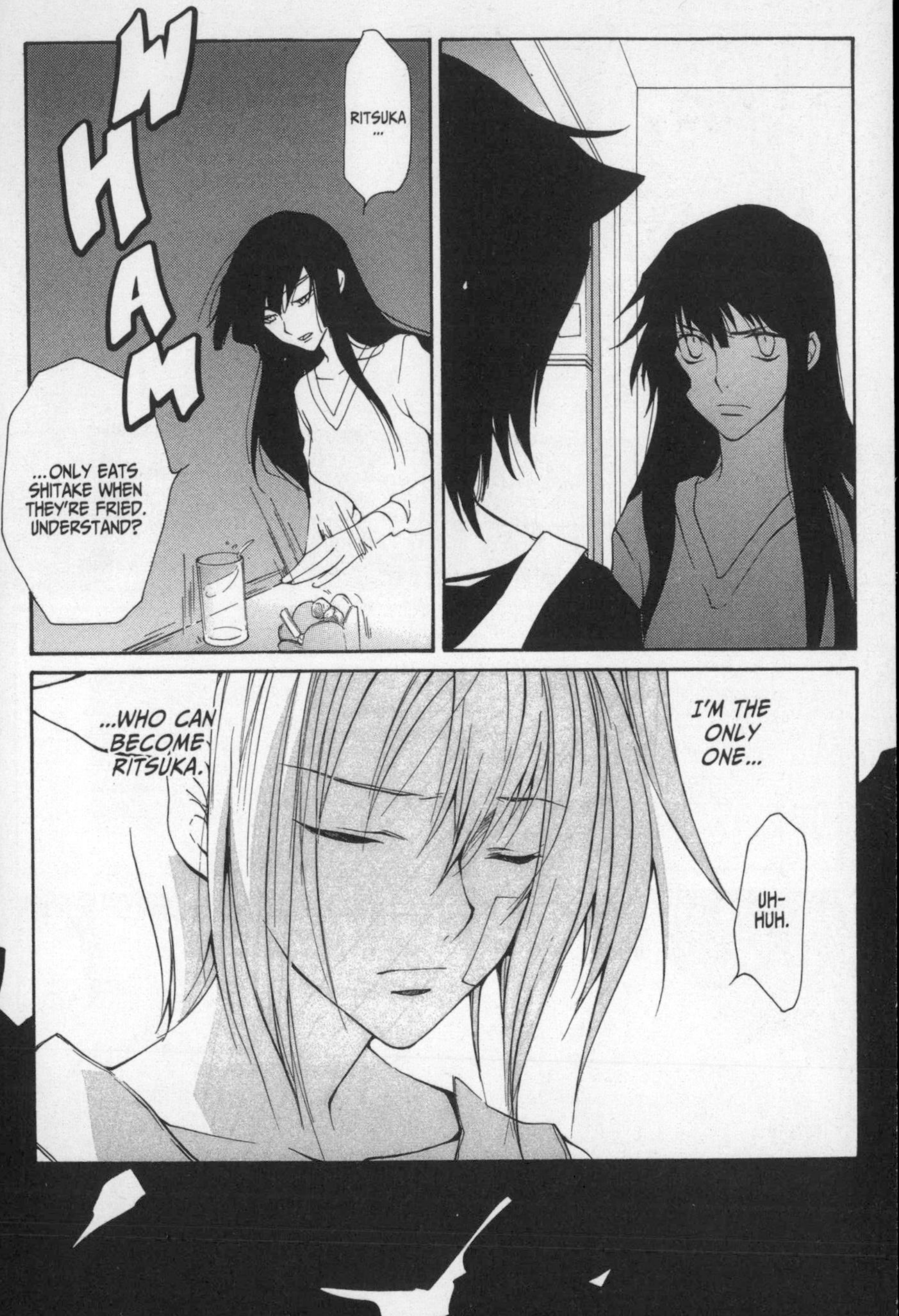
RITSUKA...
WHAM
...ONLY EATS SHITAKE WHEN THEY'RE FRIED. UNDERSTAND?
I'M THE ONLY ONE...
...WHO CAN BECOME RITSUKA.
UH-HUH.

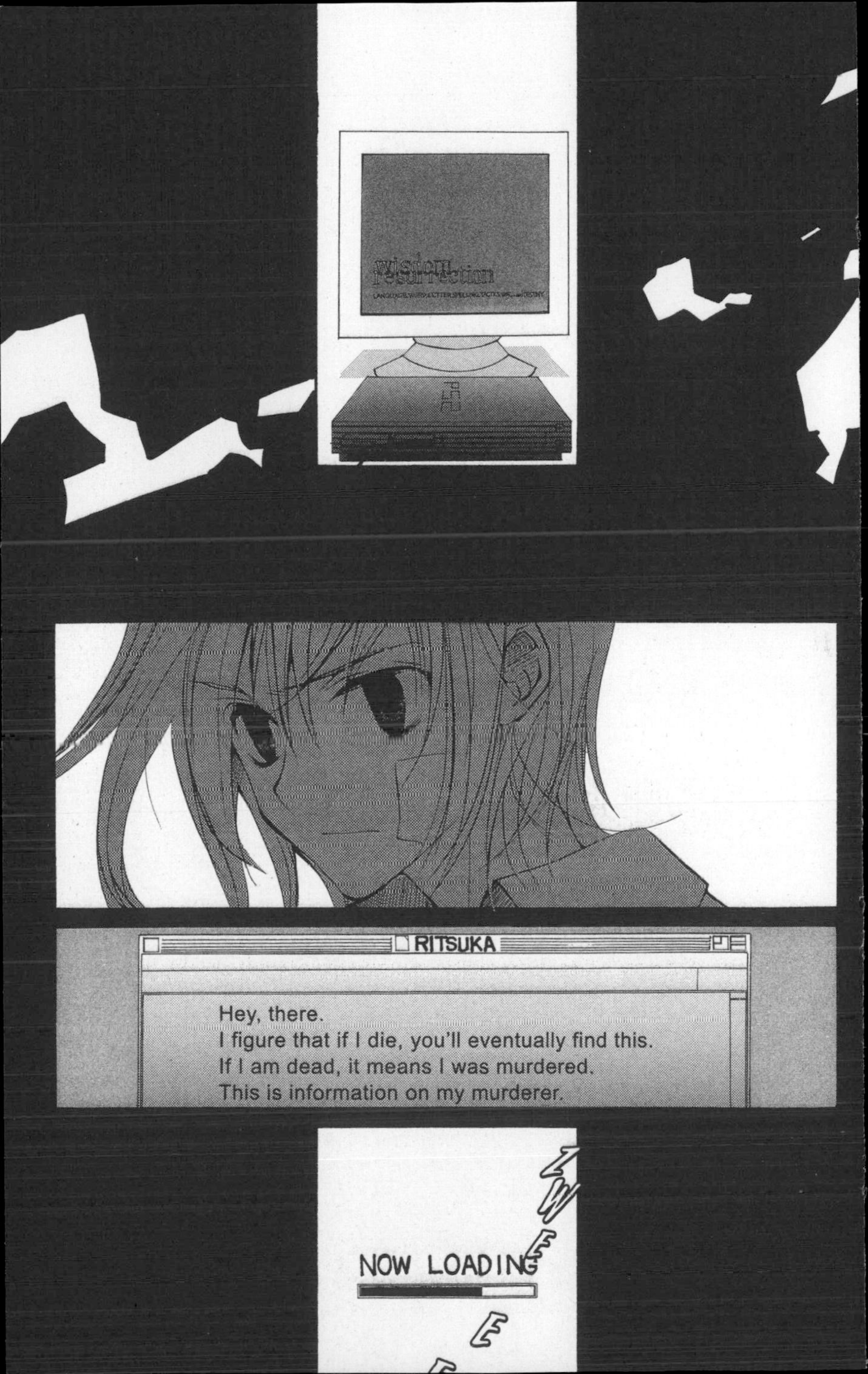
wisdom resurrection
RITSUKA
Hey, there.
I figure that if I die, you'll eventually find this.
If I am dead, it means I was murdered.
This is information on my murderer.
NOW LOADING

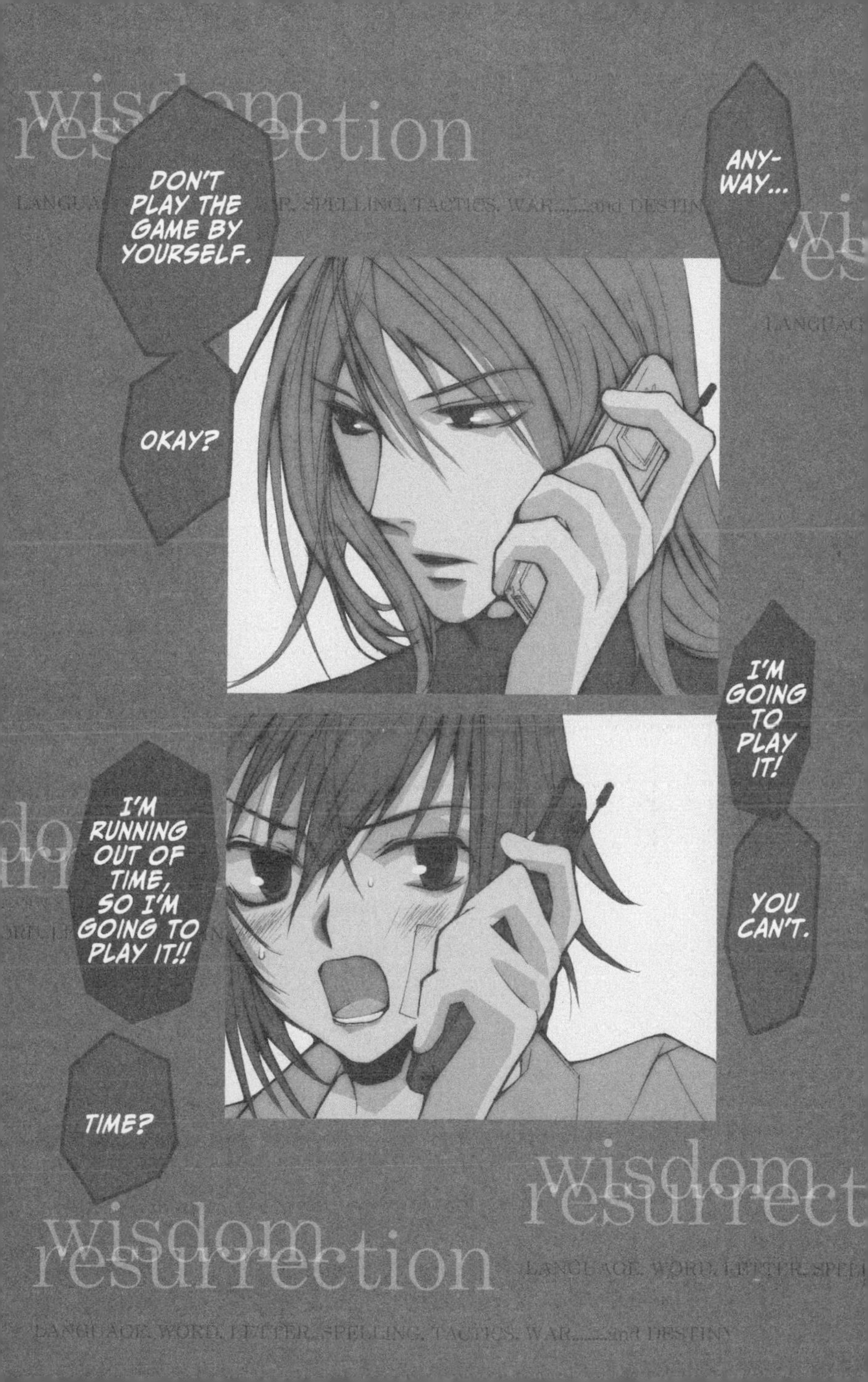
ANY-WAY...
DON'T PLAY THE GAME BY YOURSELF.
OKAY?
I'M GOING TO PLAY IT!
YOU CAN'T.
I'M RUNNING OUT OF TIME, SO I'M GOING TO PLAY IT!!
TIME?
wisdom
resurrection
LANGUAGE. WORD. LETTER. SPELLING. TACTICS. WAR.......and DESTINY

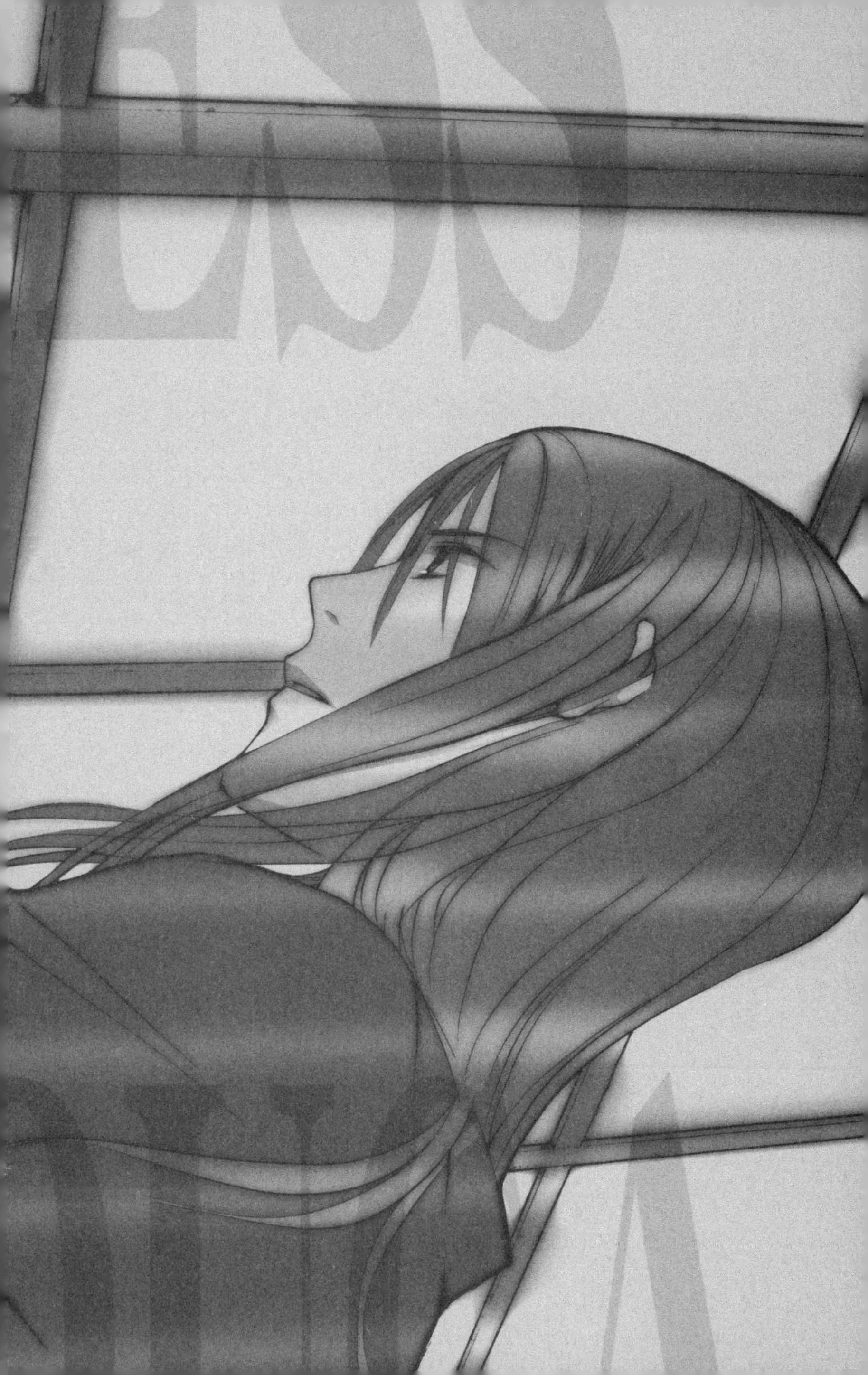

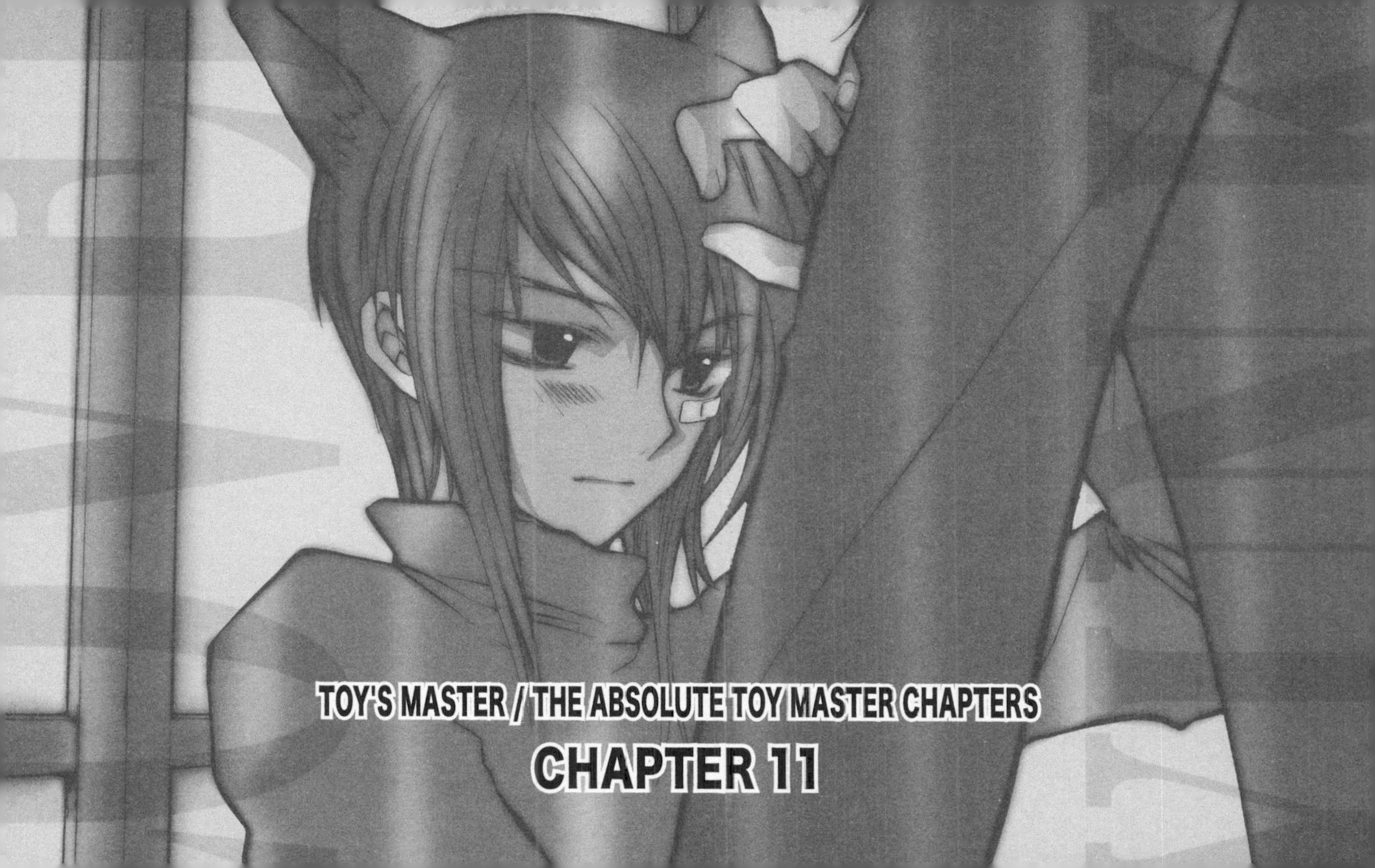
TOY'S MASTER / THE ABSOLUTE TOY MASTER CHAPTERS
CHAPTER 11

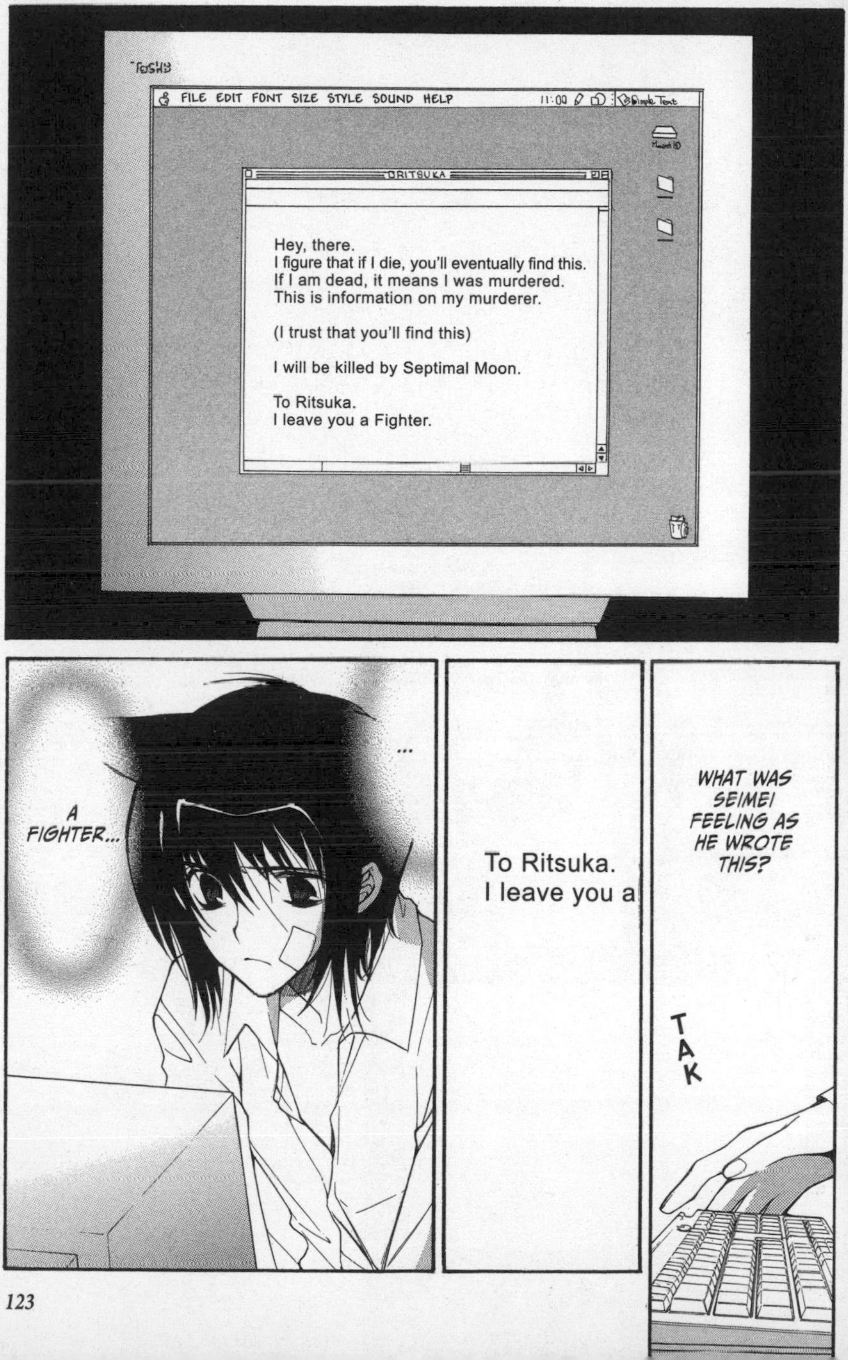
FILE EDIT FONT SIZE STYLE SOUND HELP
11:00
Simple Text
RITSUKA
Hey, there.
I figure that if I die, you'll eventually find this.
If I am dead, it means I was murdered.
This is information on my murderer.
(I trust that you'll find this)
I will be killed by Septimal Moon.
To Ritsuka.
I leave you a Fighter.
WHAT WAS SEIMEI FEELING AS HE WROTE THIS?
TAK
To Ritsuka.
I leave you a
...
A FIGHTER...

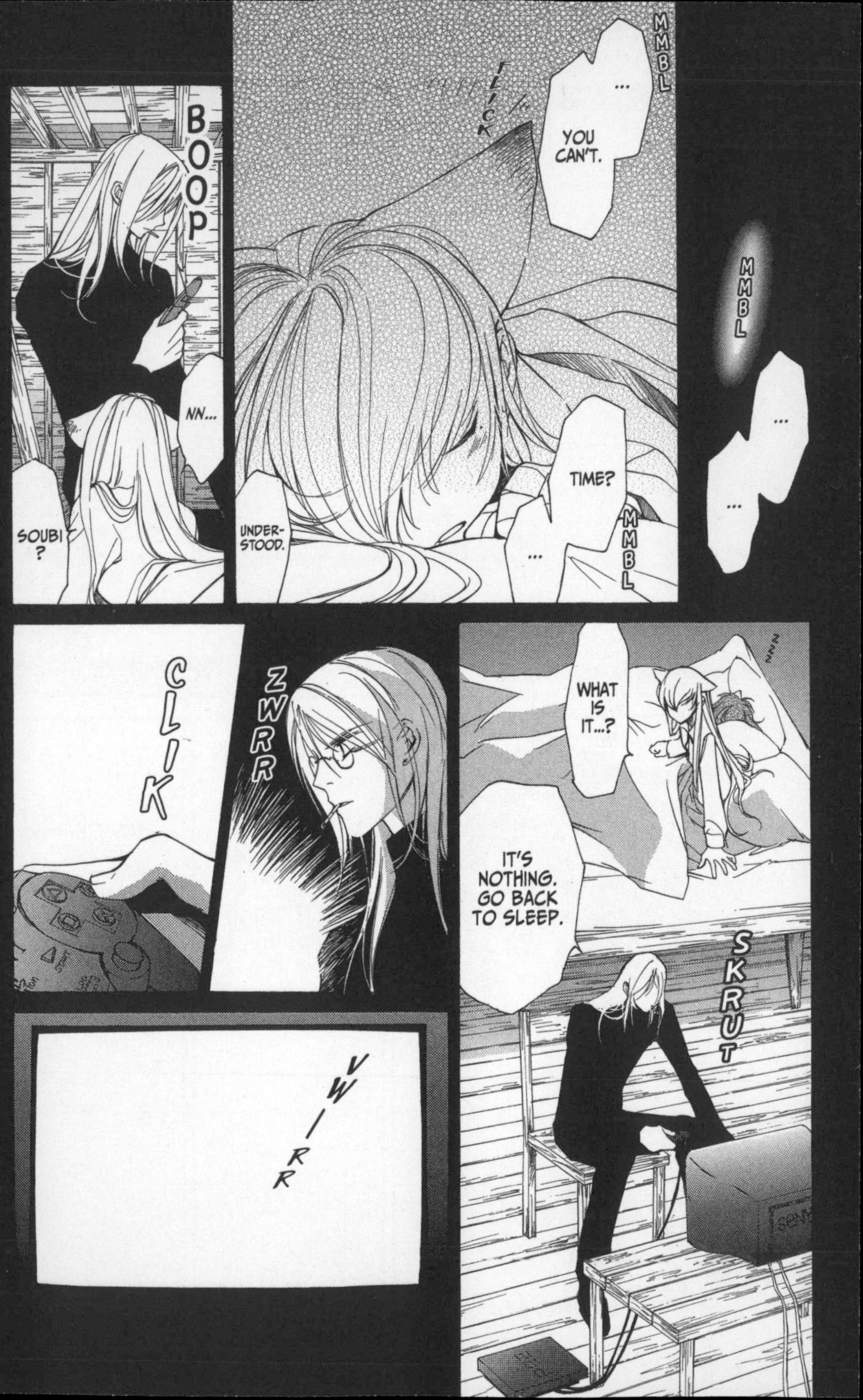
MMBL
...
...
MMBL
...
YOU CAN'T.
FLICK
TIME?
MMBL
...
UNDER-STOOD.
BOOP
NN...
SOUBI?
ZZZ
WHAT IS IT...?
IT'S NOTHING. GO BACK TO SLEEP.
SKRUT
ZWRR
CLIK
VWIRR

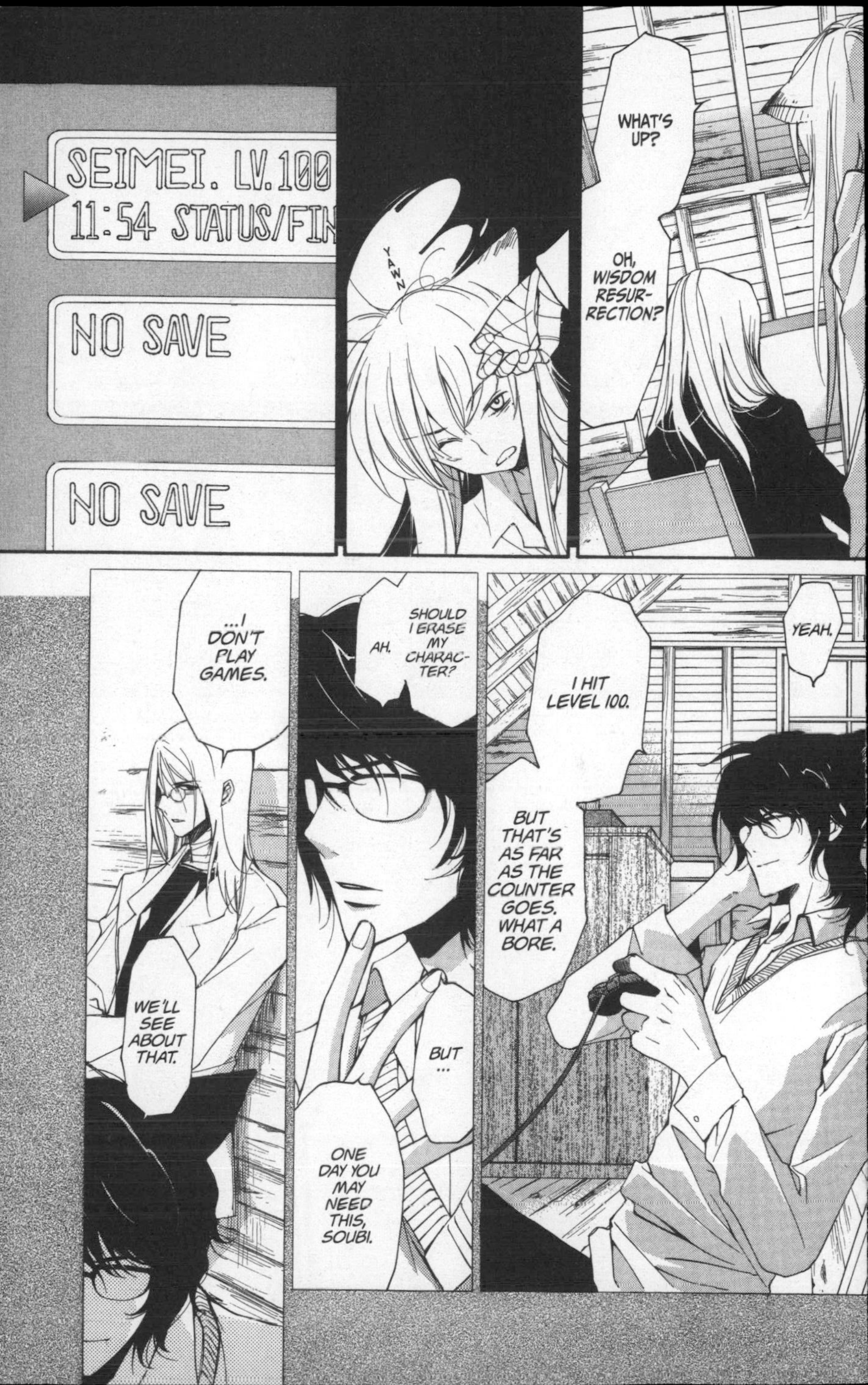
WHAT'S UP?
OH, WISDOM RESURRECTION?
YAWN
SEIMEI. LV.100
11:54 STATUS/FIN
NO SAVE
NO SAVE
YEAH.
I HIT LEVEL 100.
BUT THAT'S AS FAR AS THE COUNTER GOES. WHAT A BORE.
SHOULD I ERASE MY CHARACTER?
AH.
BUT...
ONE DAY YOU MAY NEED THIS, SOUBI.
...I DON'T PLAY GAMES.
WE'LL SEE ABOUT THAT.

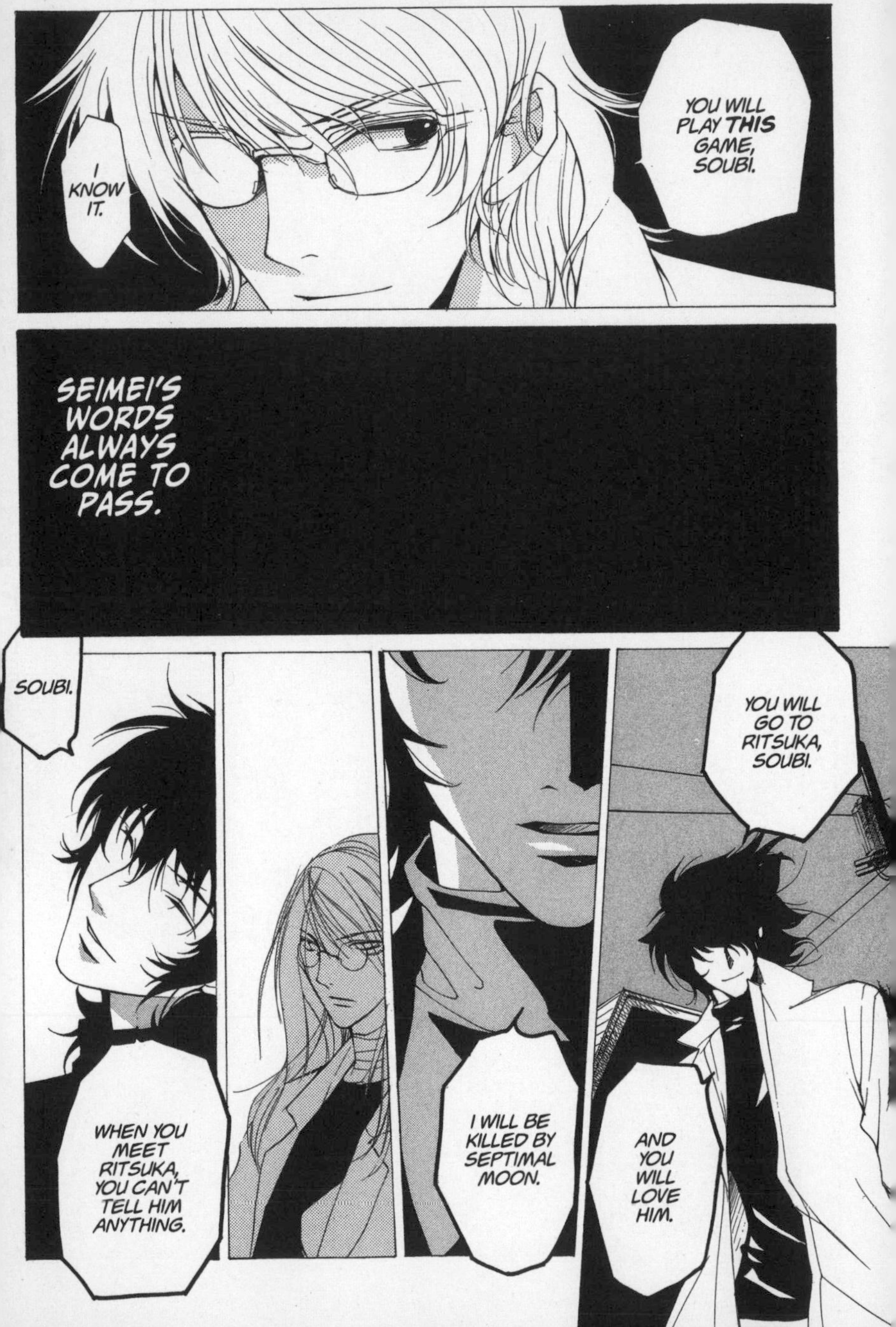
YOU WILL PLAY **THIS** GAME, SOUBI.
I KNOW IT.
SEIMEI'S WORDS ALWAYS COME TO PASS.
YOU WILL GO TO RITSUKA, SOUBI.
AND YOU WILL LOVE HIM.
I WILL BE KILLED BY SEPTIMAL MOON.
SOUBI.
WHEN YOU MEET RITSUKA, YOU CAN'T TELL HIM ANYTHING.

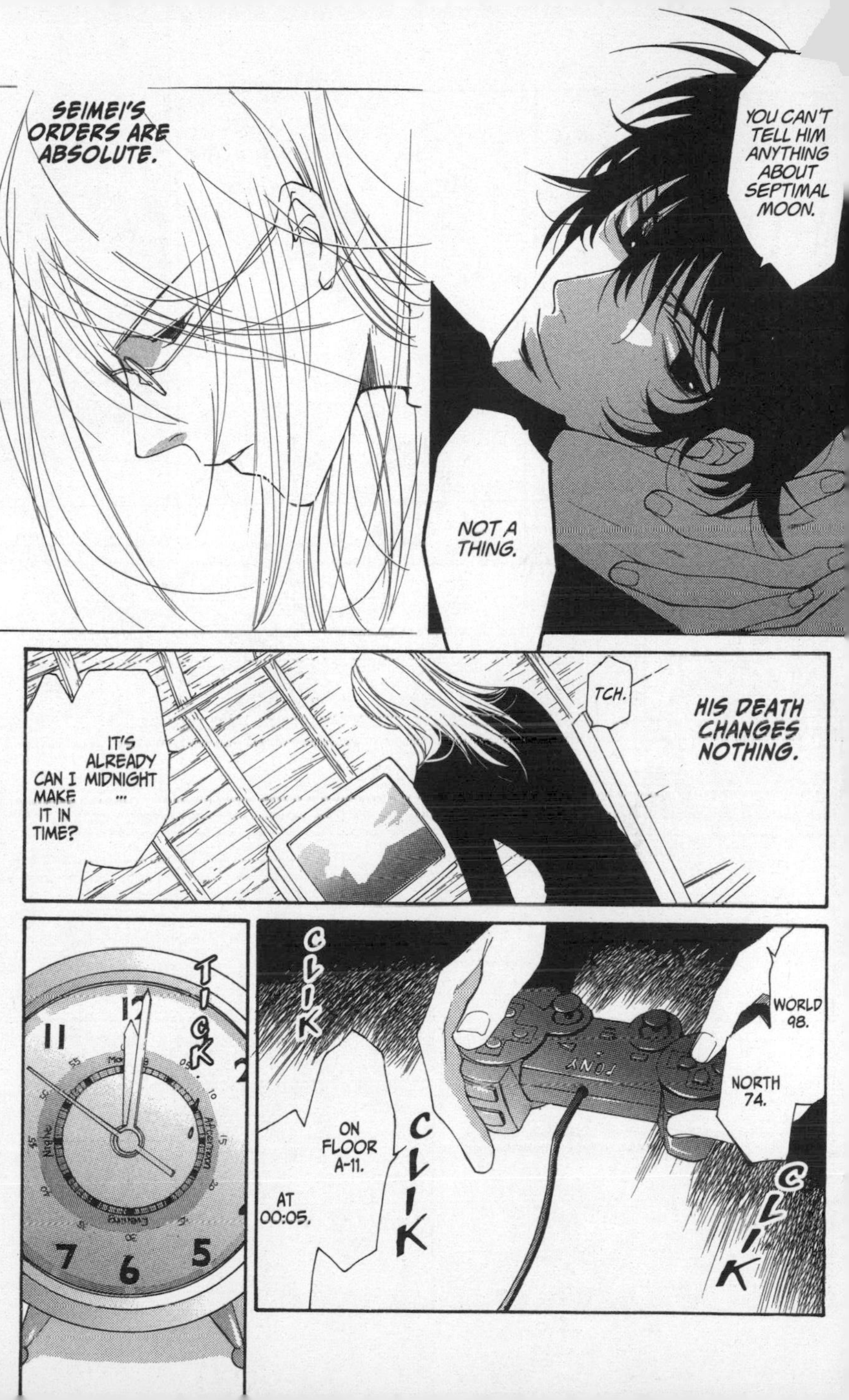
YOU CAN'T TELL HIM ANYTHING ABOUT SEPTIMAL MOON.
NOT A THING.
SEIMEI'S ORDERS ARE ABSOLUTE.
HIS DEATH CHANGES NOTHING.
TCH.
IT'S ALREADY MIDNIGHT...
CAN I MAKE IT IN TIME?
WORLD 98.
NORTH 74.
CLIK
ON FLOOR A-11.
AT 00:05.
CLIK
CLIK
TICK

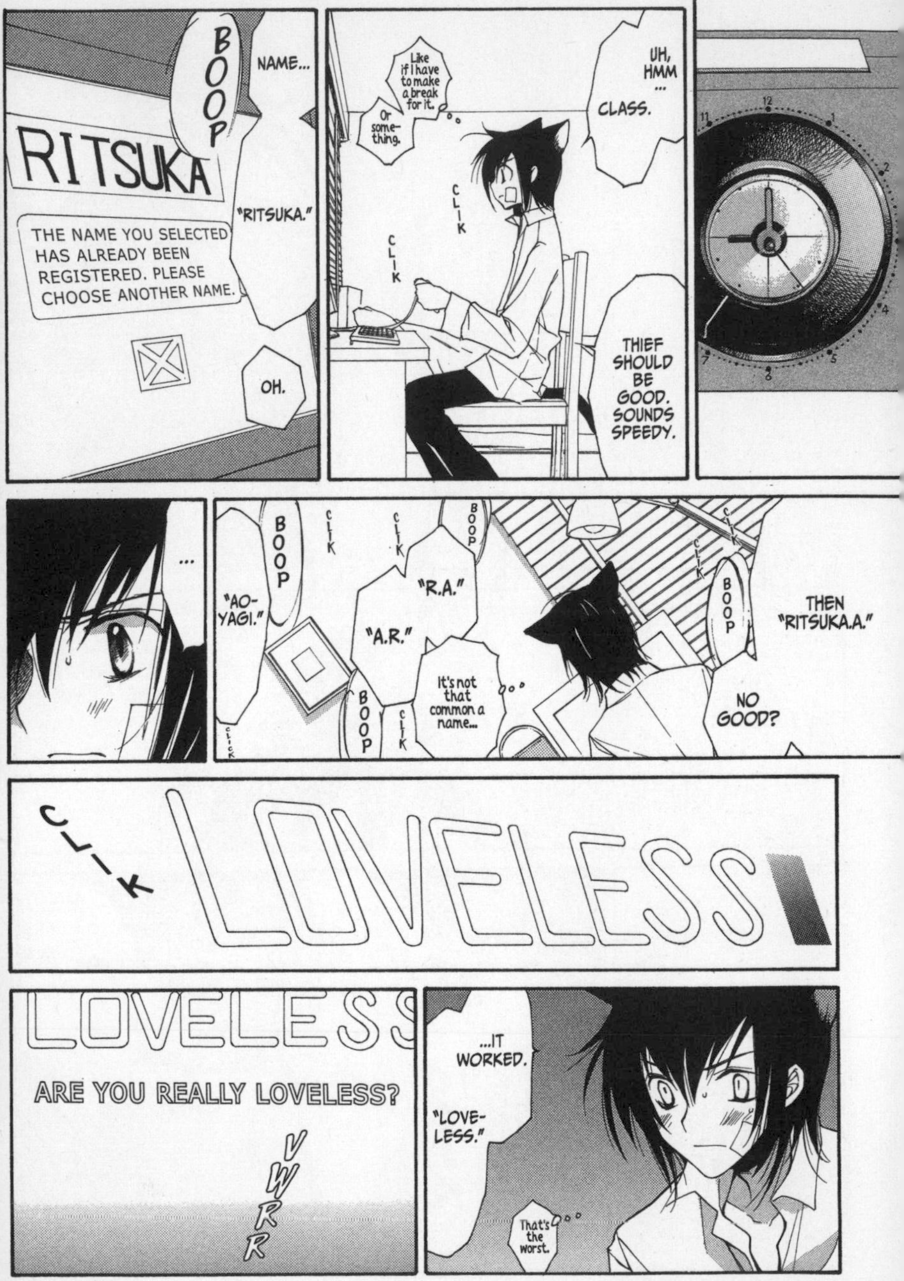
UH, HMM ... CLASS.
THIEF SHOULD BE GOOD. SOUNDS SPEEDY.
Like if I have to make a break for it.
Or something.
CLIK
CLIK
NAME...
BOOP
RITSUKA
"RITSUKA."
THE NAME YOU SELECTED HAS ALREADY BEEN REGISTERED. PLEASE CHOOSE ANOTHER NAME.
OH.
THEN "RITSUKA.A."
BOOP
CLIK
CLIK
NO GOOD?
It's not that common a name...
BOOP
"R.A."
CLIK
"A.R."
CLIK
BOOP
CLIK
BOOP
"AO-YAGI."
CLIK
CLICK
...
CLIK
LOVELESS
...IT WORKED.
"LOVE-LESS."
That's the worst.
LOVELESS
ARE YOU REALLY LOVELESS?
VWRR

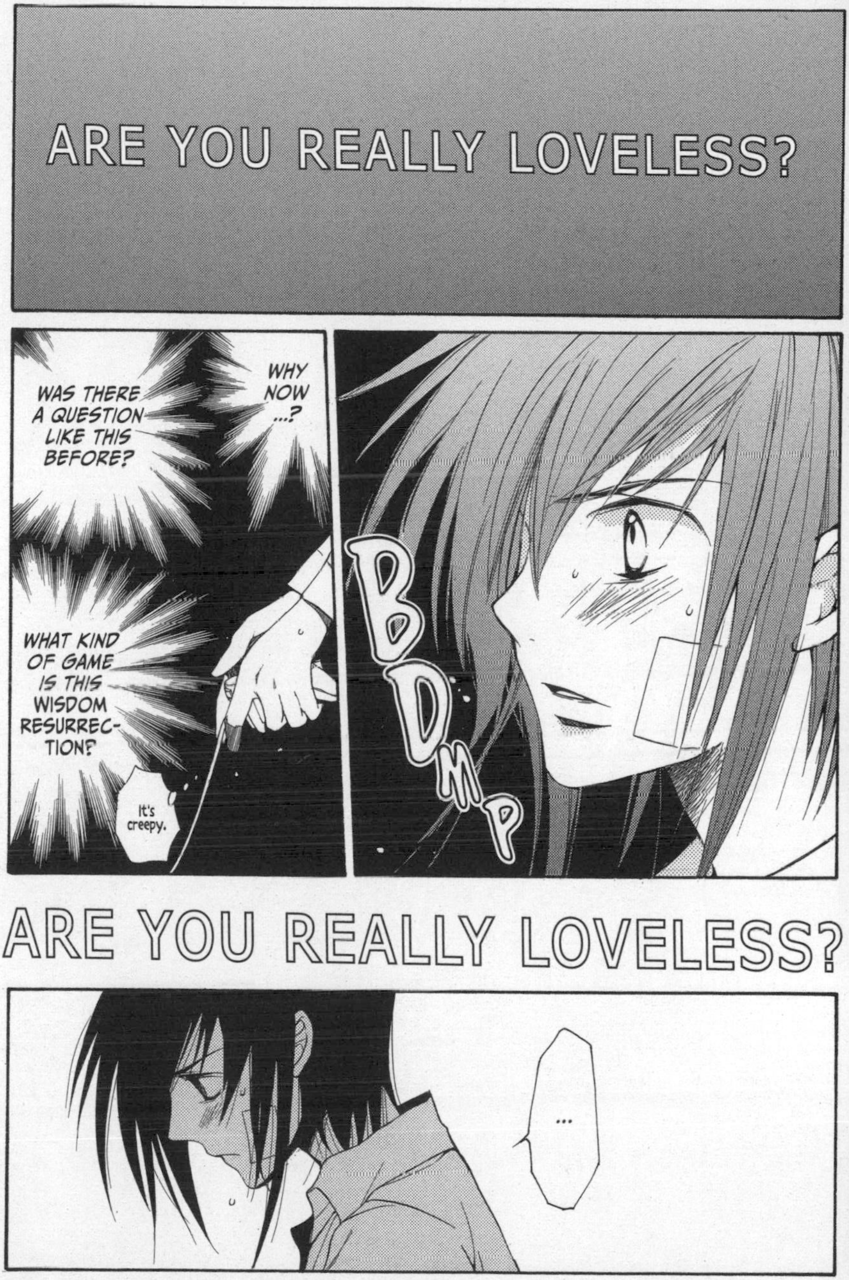
ARE YOU REALLY LOVELESS?
BDMP
WHY NOW ...?
WAS THERE A QUESTION LIKE THIS BEFORE?
WHAT KIND OF GAME IS THIS WISDOM RESURRECTION?
It's creepy.
ARE YOU REALLY LOVELESS?
...

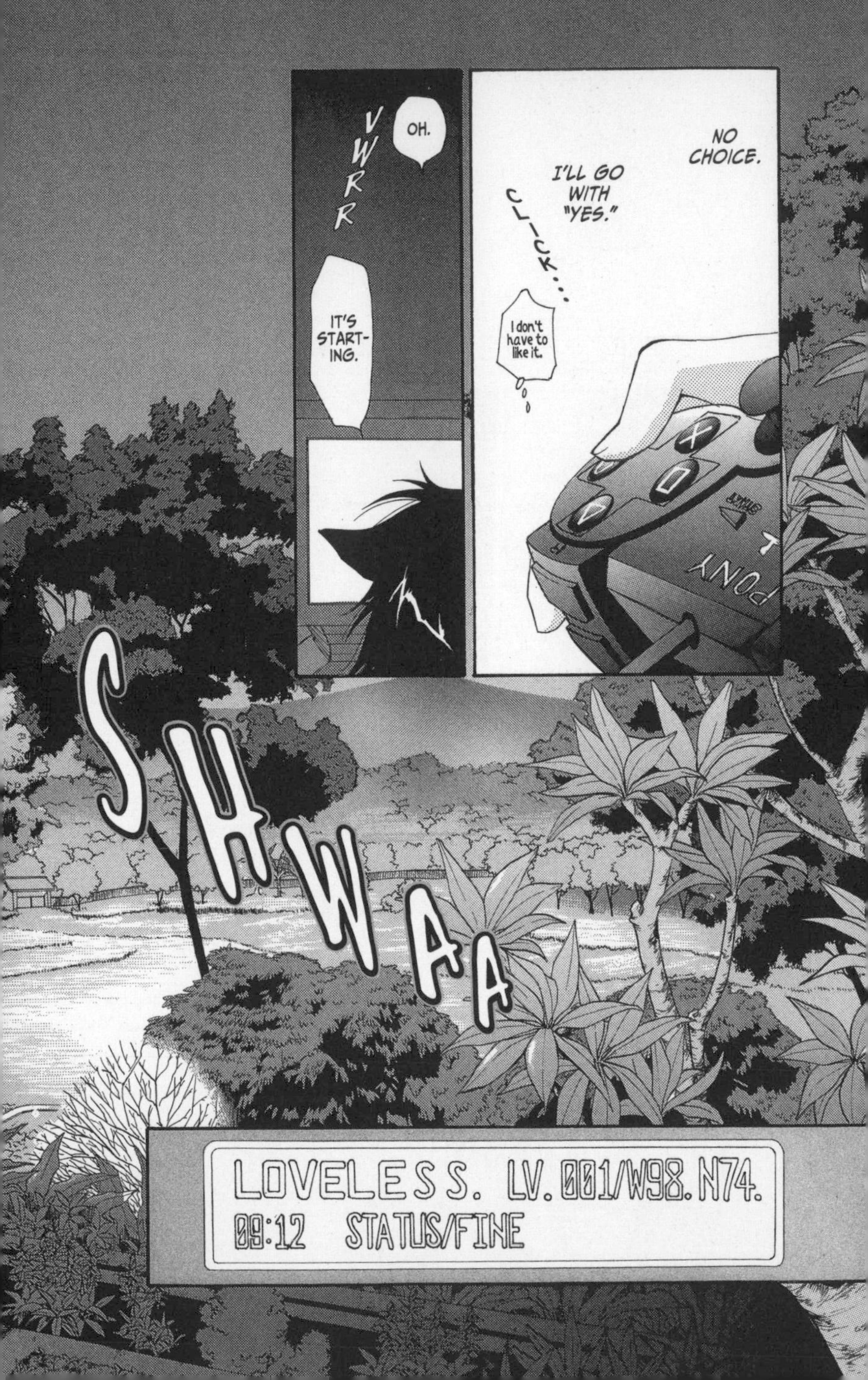
NO CHOICE.
I'LL GO WITH "YES."
CLICK...
I don't have to like it.
OH.
VWRR
IT'S START-ING.
SHWAA
LOVELESS. LV.001/W98.N74.
09:12 STATUS/FINE

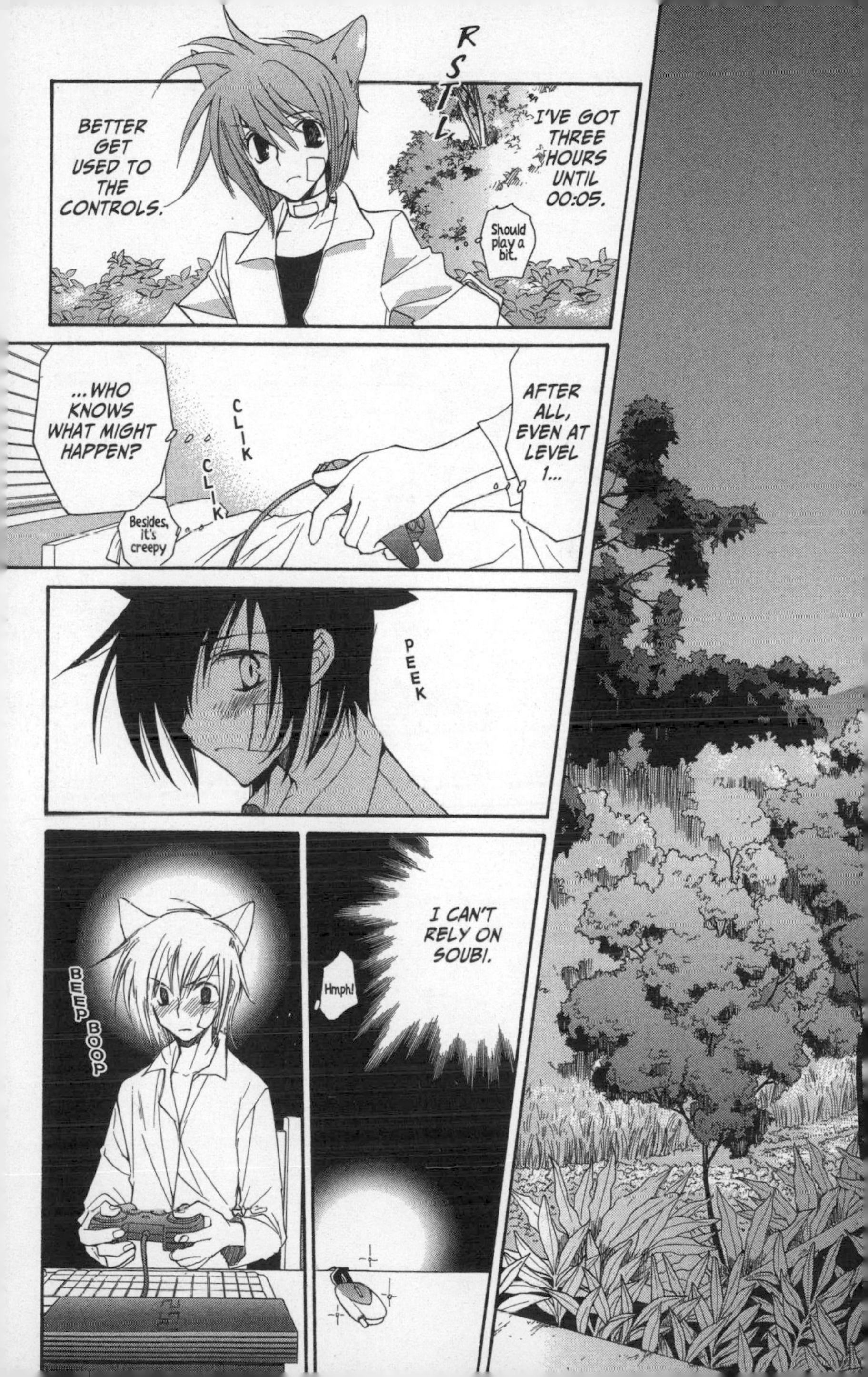
RSTL
I'VE GOT THREE HOURS UNTIL 00:05.
Should play a bit.
BETTER GET USED TO THE CONTROLS.
AFTER ALL, EVEN AT LEVEL 1...
CLIK
CLIK
...WHO KNOWS WHAT MIGHT HAPPEN?
Besides, it's creepy
PEEK
I CAN'T RELY ON SOUBI.
Hmph!
BEEP BOOP

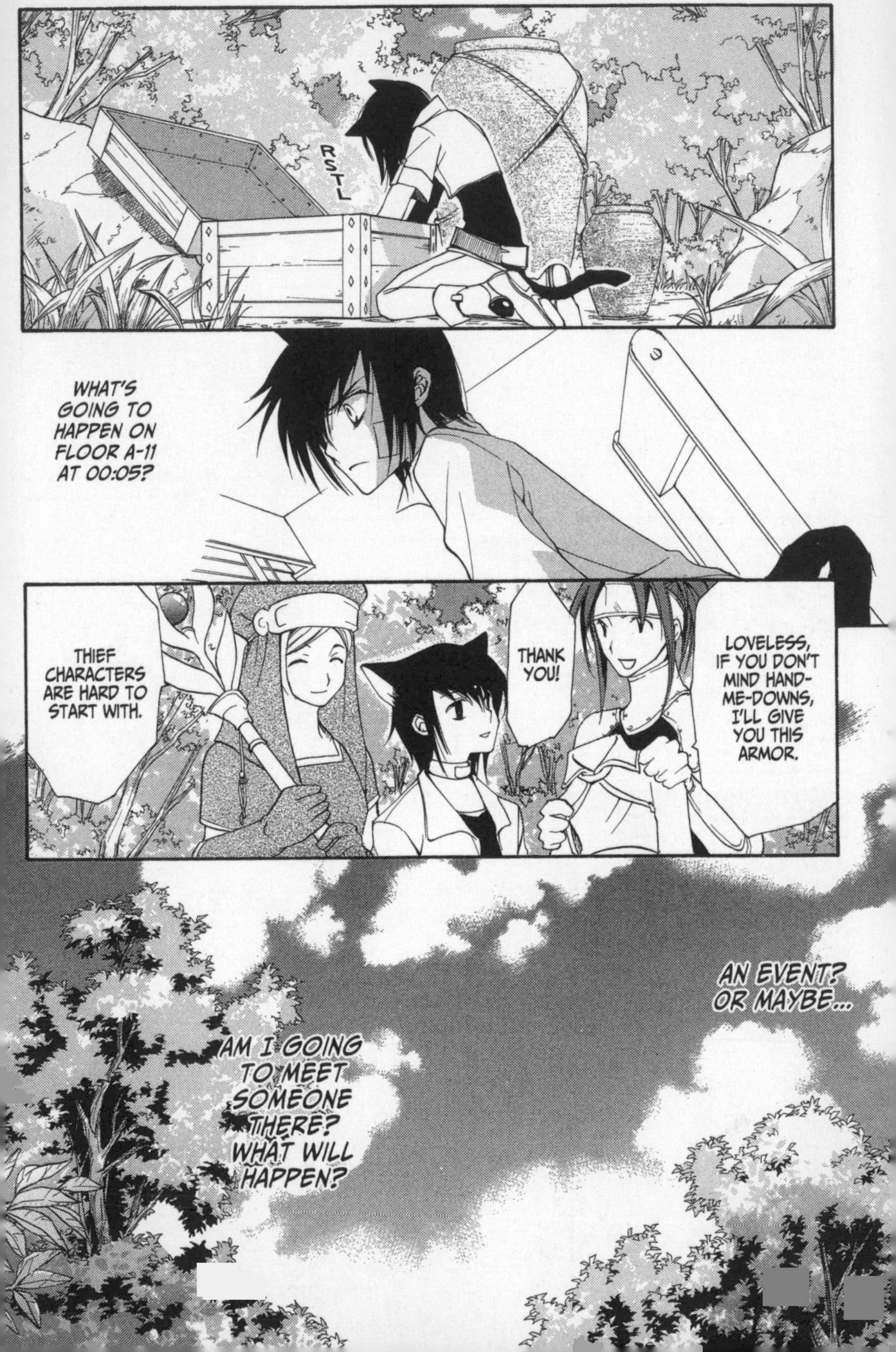
RSTL
WHAT'S GOING TO HAPPEN ON FLOOR A-11 AT 00:05?
LOVELESS, IF YOU DON'T MIND HAND-ME-DOWNS, I'LL GIVE YOU THIS ARMOR.
THANK YOU!
THIEF CHARACTERS ARE HARD TO START WITH.
AN EVENT? OR MAYBE...
AM I GOING TO MEET SOMEONE THERE? WHAT WILL HAPPEN?

Incoming Call
Souji Agatsuma

!!

PWEEP PWEEP PWEEP

PWEEP PWEEP PWEEP

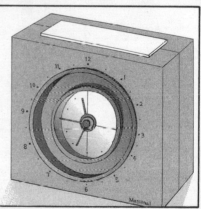

Marginal

THE MESSAGE? YOU FIGURED IT OUT?

FFT

HELLO...

RIT-SUKA?

WHAT?

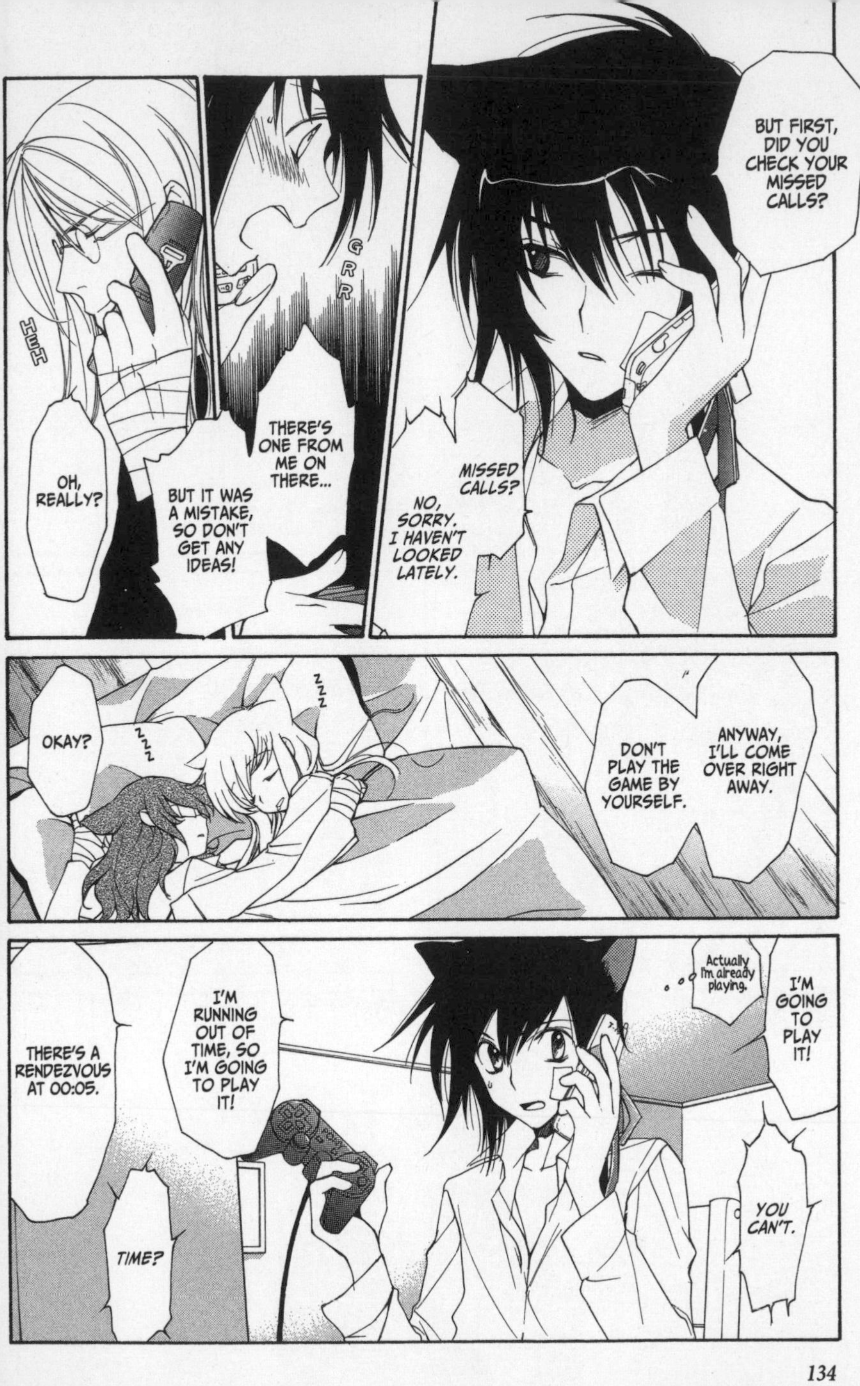
BUT FIRST, DID YOU CHECK YOUR MISSED CALLS?
MISSED CALLS?
NO, SORRY. I HAVEN'T LOOKED LATELY.
GRR
THERE'S ONE FROM ME ON THERE...
BUT IT WAS A MISTAKE, SO DON'T GET ANY IDEAS!
HEH
OH, REALLY?
ANYWAY, I'LL COME OVER RIGHT AWAY.
DON'T PLAY THE GAME BY YOURSELF.
ZZZ
ZZZ
OKAY?
I'M GOING TO PLAY IT!
Actually I'm already playing.
YOU CAN'T.
I'M RUNNING OUT OF TIME, SO I'M GOING TO PLAY IT!
THERE'S A RENDEZVOUS AT 00:05.
TIME?

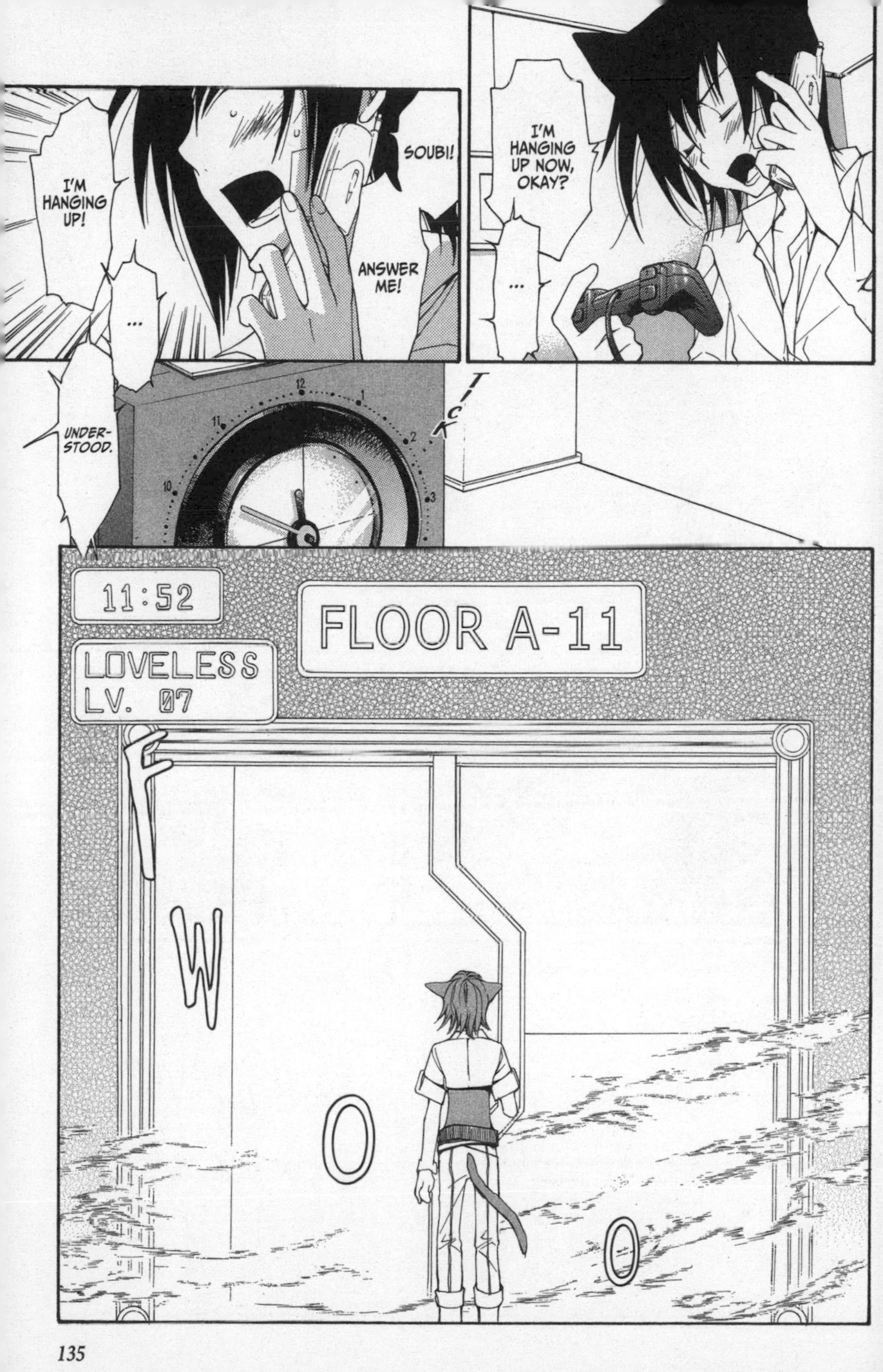
I'M HANGING UP NOW, OKAY?
...
SOUBI!
I'M HANGING UP!
ANSWER ME!
...
TICK
UNDER-STOOD.
FLOOR A-11
11:52
LOVELESS LV. 07
WOO

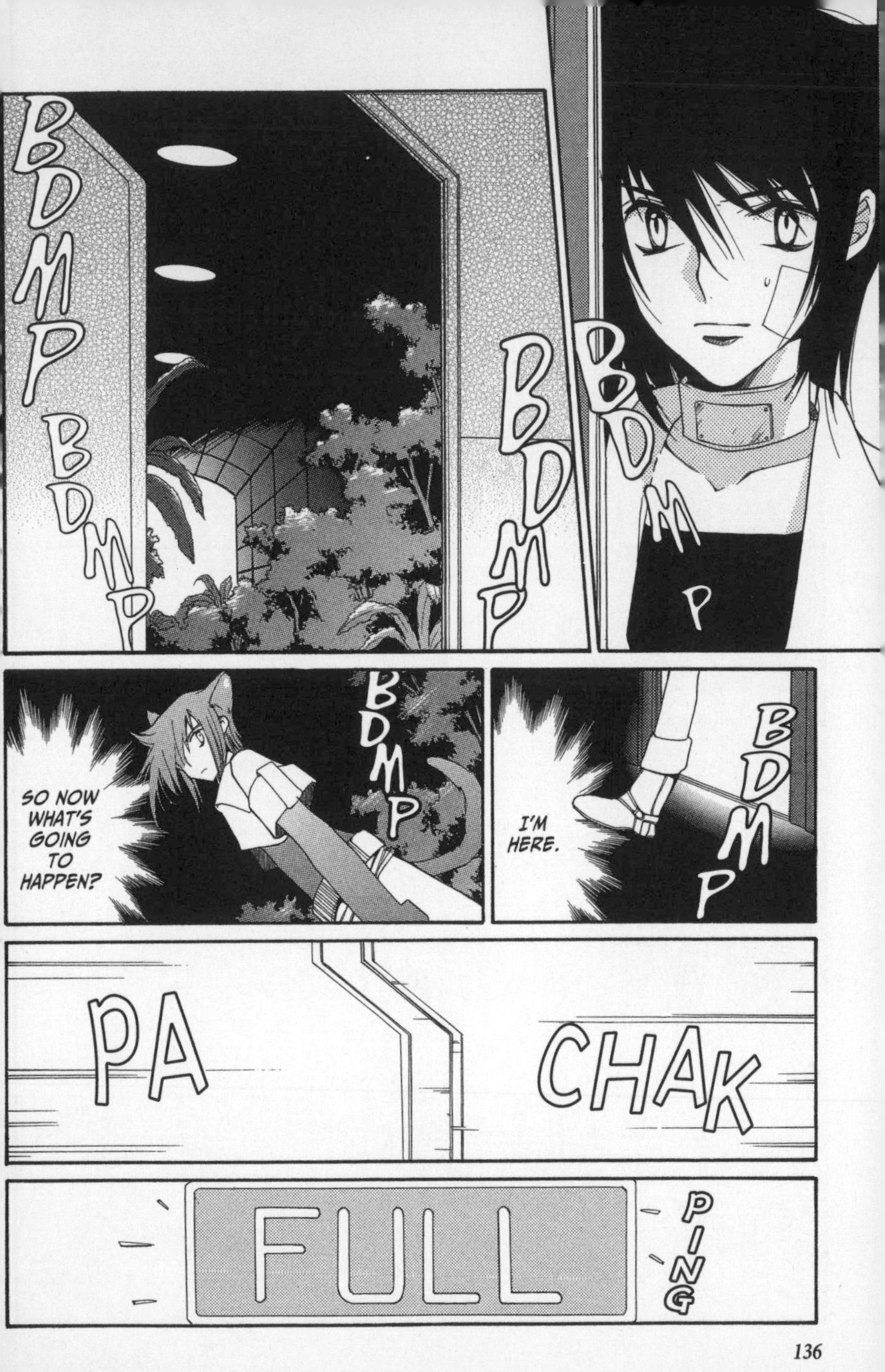

BDMP
BDMP
BDMP
BDMP
I'M HERE.
BDMP
SO NOW WHAT'S GOING TO HAPPEN?
BDMP
PA CHAK
PING
FULL

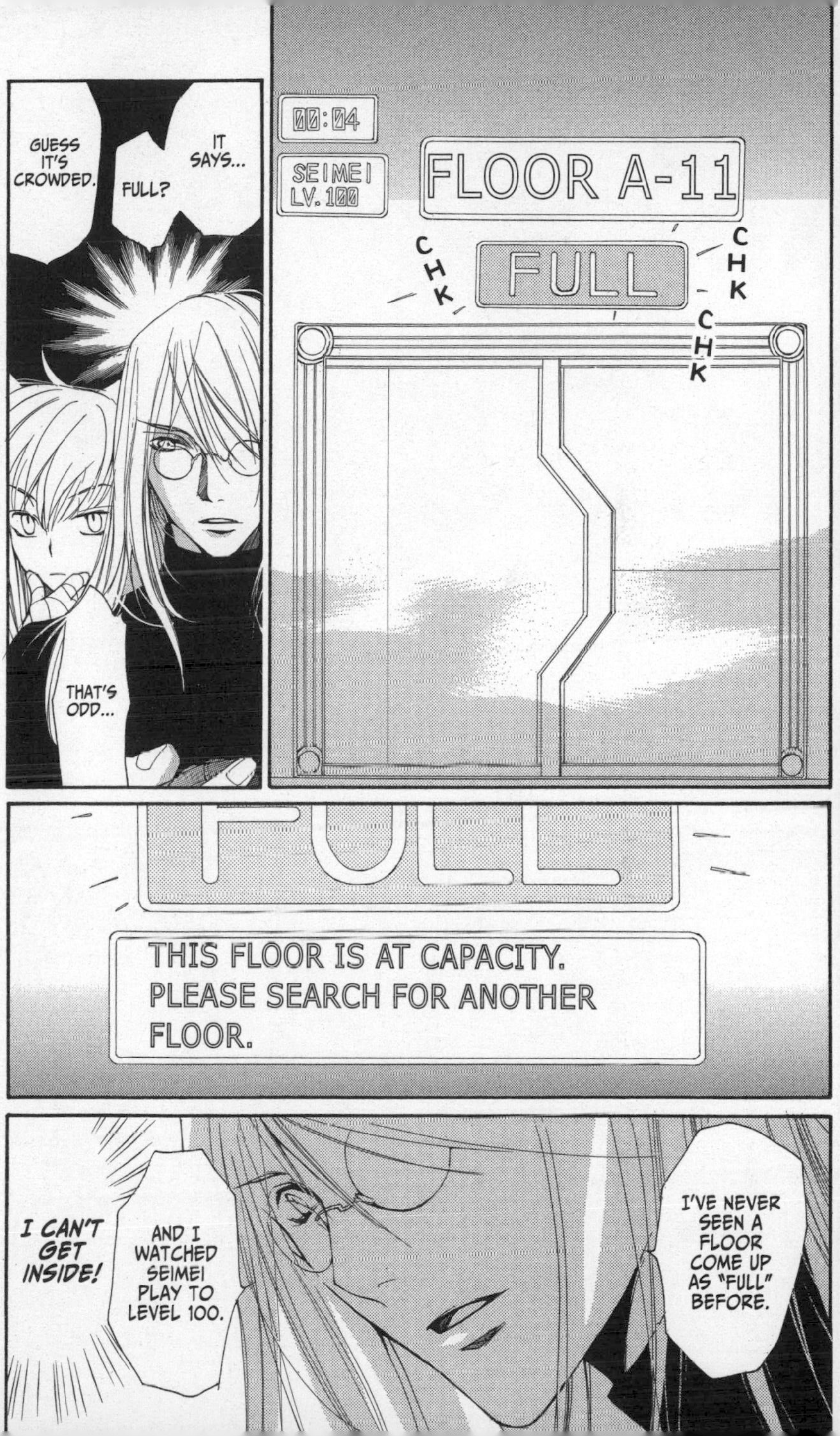

00:04
SEIMEI LV. 100
FLOOR A-11
CHK
CHK
CHK
FULL
IT SAYS... FULL?
GUESS IT'S CROWDED.
THAT'S ODD...
FULL
THIS FLOOR IS AT CAPACITY. PLEASE SEARCH FOR ANOTHER FLOOR.
I'VE NEVER SEEN A FLOOR COME UP AS "FULL" BEFORE.
AND I WATCHED SEIMEI PLAY TO LEVEL 100.
I CAN'T GET INSIDE!

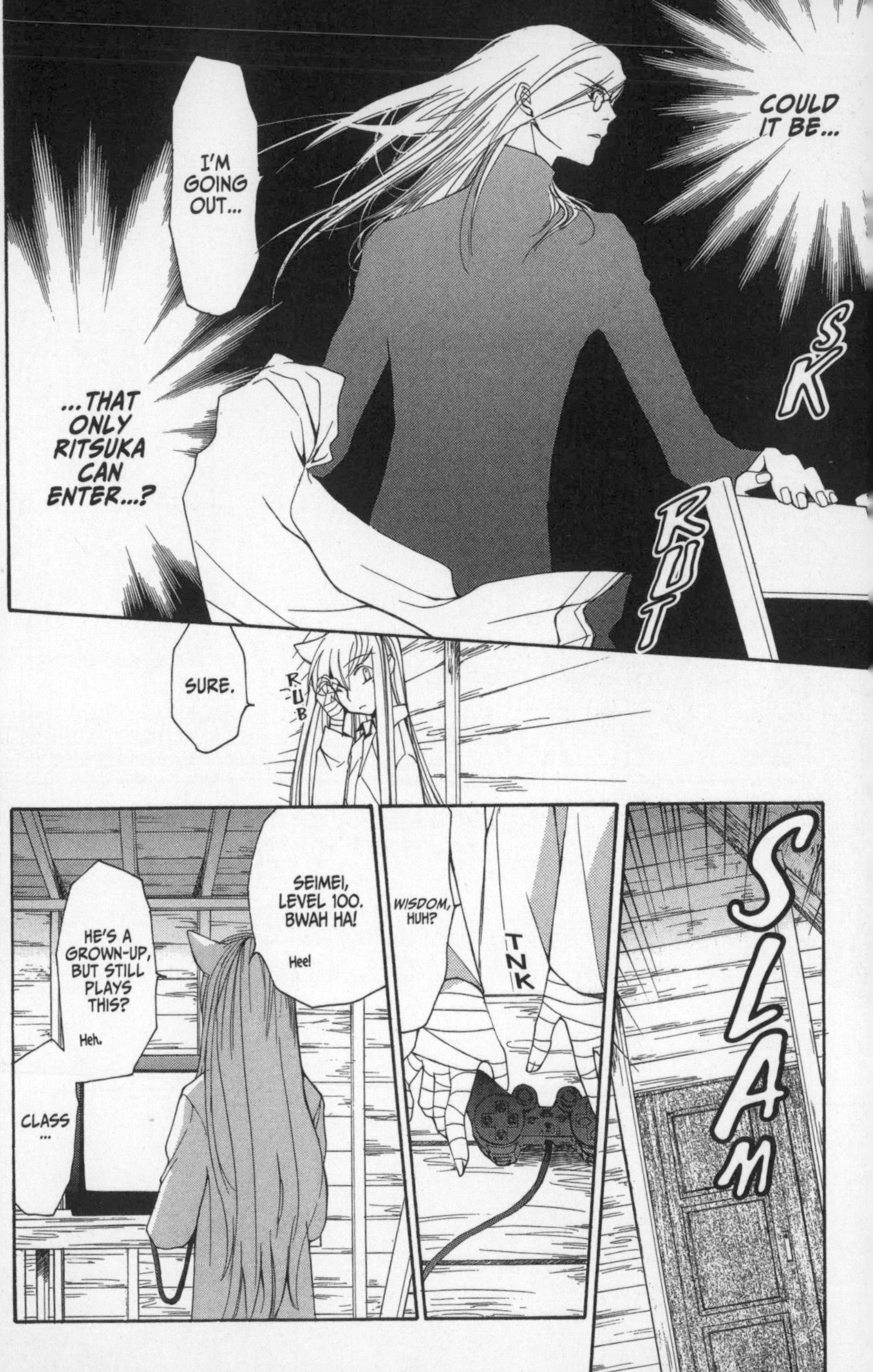
COULD IT BE...
I'M GOING OUT...
SSK
RUT
...THAT ONLY RITSUKA CAN ENTER...?
RUB
SURE.
SLAM
TNK
WISDOM, HUH?
SEIMEI, LEVEL 100. BWAH HA!
Hee!
HE'S A GROWN-UP, BUT STILL PLAYS THIS?
Heh.
CLASS...

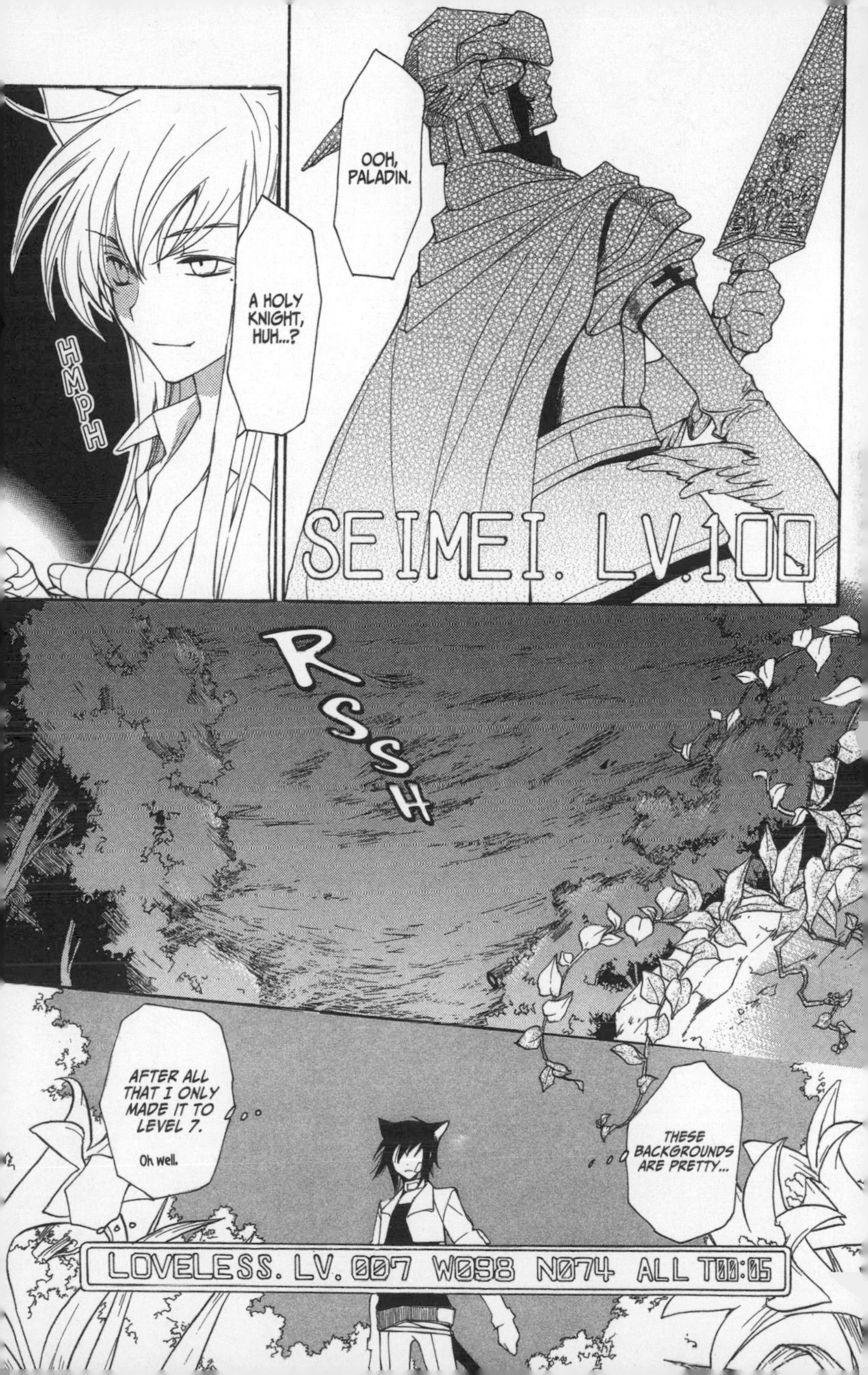
OOH, PALADIN.
A HOLY KNIGHT, HUH...?
HMPH
SEIMEI. LV.100
RSSH
THESE BACKGROUNDS ARE PRETTY...
AFTER ALL THAT I ONLY MADE IT TO LEVEL 7.
Oh well.
LOVELESS. LV. 007 W098 N074 ALL T00:05

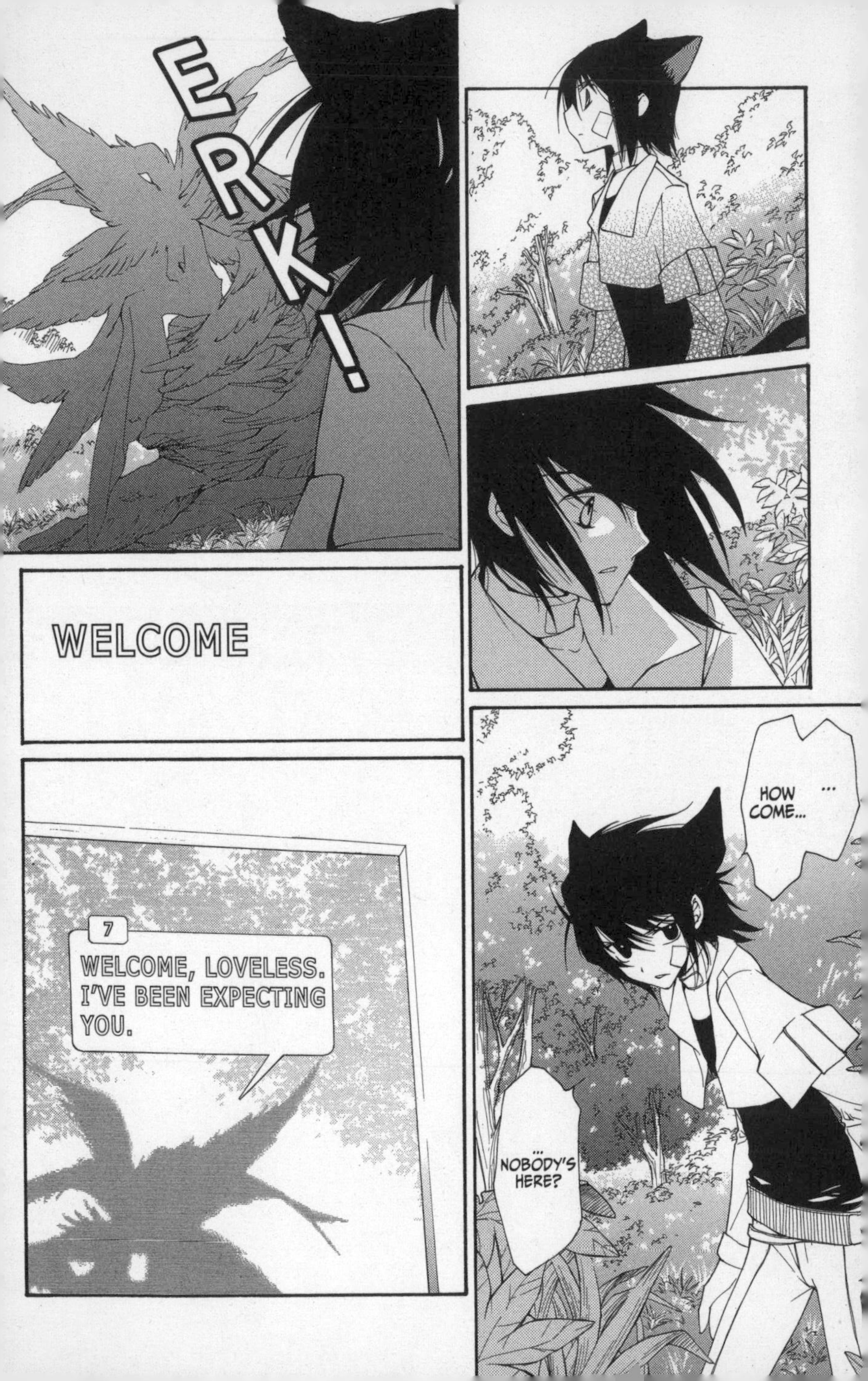
ERK!
... HOW COME...
... NOBODY'S HERE?
WELCOME
7
WELCOME, LOVELESS. I'VE BEEN EXPECTING YOU.

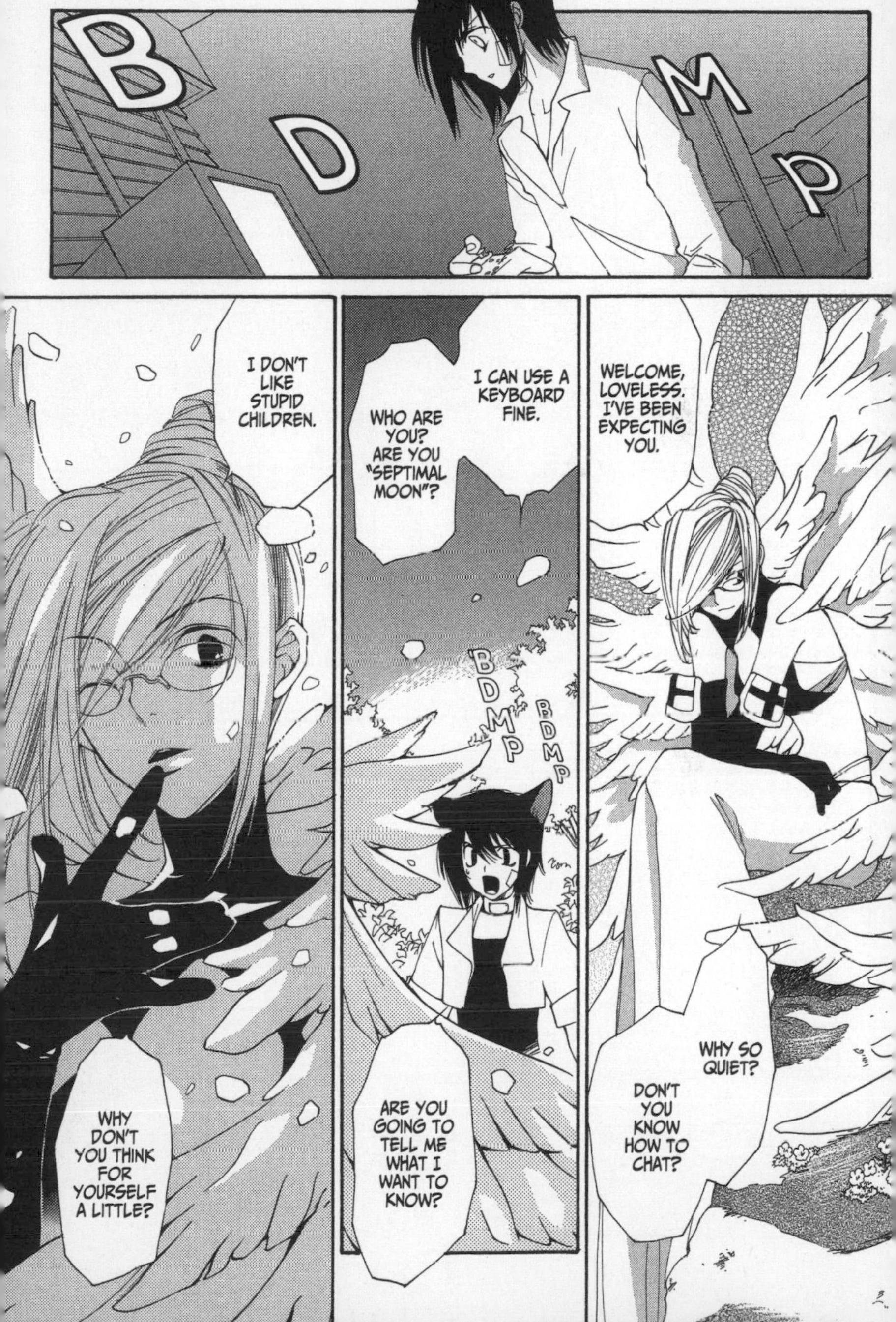
BDMP
WELCOME, LOVELESS. I'VE BEEN EXPECTING YOU.
WHY SO QUIET?
DON'T YOU KNOW HOW TO CHAT?
I CAN USE A KEYBOARD FINE.
WHO ARE YOU? ARE YOU "SEPTIMAL MOON"?
BDMP
BDMP
ARE YOU GOING TO TELL ME WHAT I WANT TO KNOW?
I DON'T LIKE STUPID CHILDREN.
WHY DON'T YOU THINK FOR YOURSELF A LITTLE?

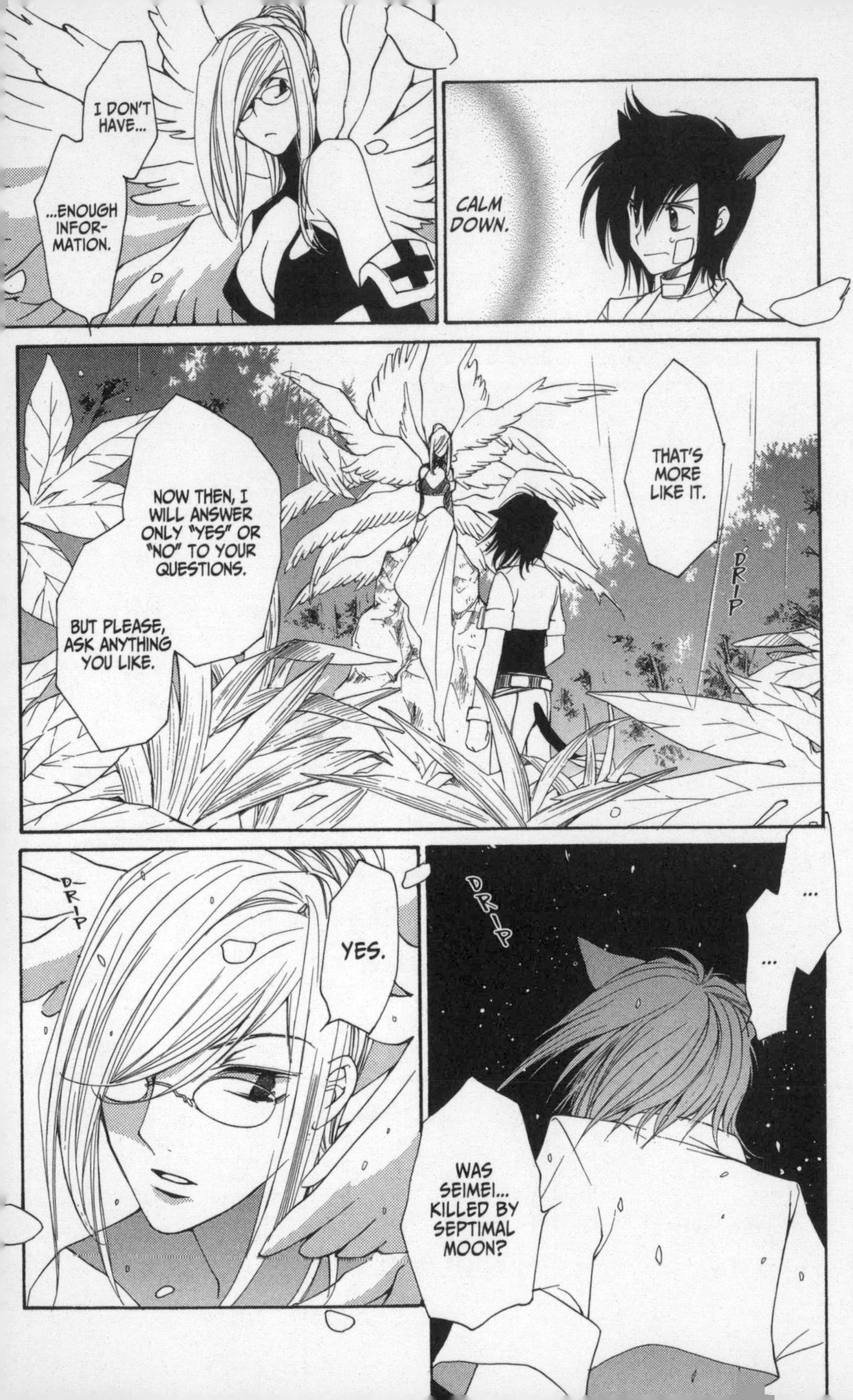
CALM DOWN.
I DON'T HAVE...
...ENOUGH INFORMATION.
THAT'S MORE LIKE IT.
DRIP
NOW THEN, I WILL ANSWER ONLY "YES" OR "NO" TO YOUR QUESTIONS.
BUT PLEASE, ASK ANYTHING YOU LIKE.
...
...
DRIP
WAS SEIMEI... KILLED BY SEPTIMAL MOON?
DRIP
YES.

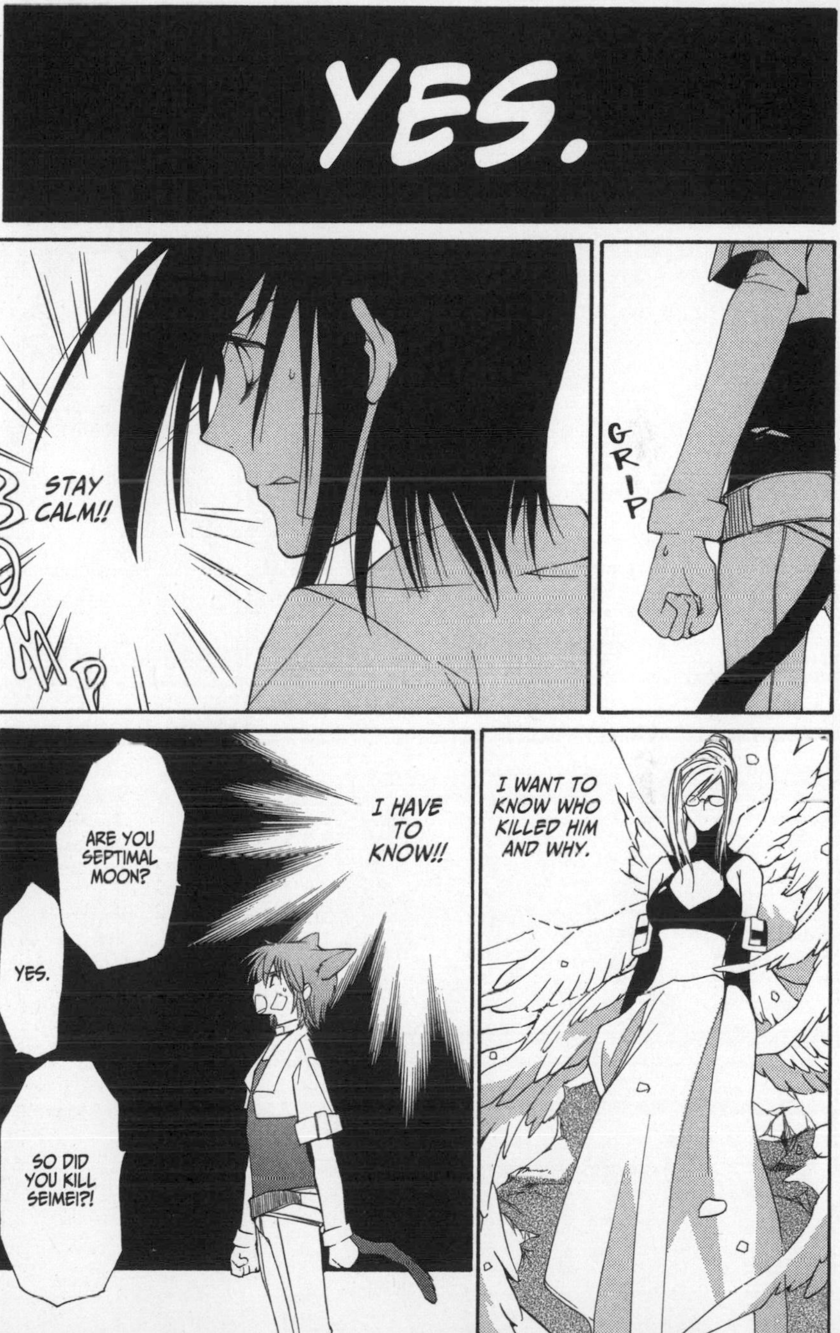
YES.
GRIP
BDMP
STAY CALM!!
I WANT TO KNOW WHO KILLED HIM AND WHY.
I HAVE TO KNOW!!
ARE YOU SEPTIMAL MOON?
YES.
SO DID YOU KILL SEIMEI?!

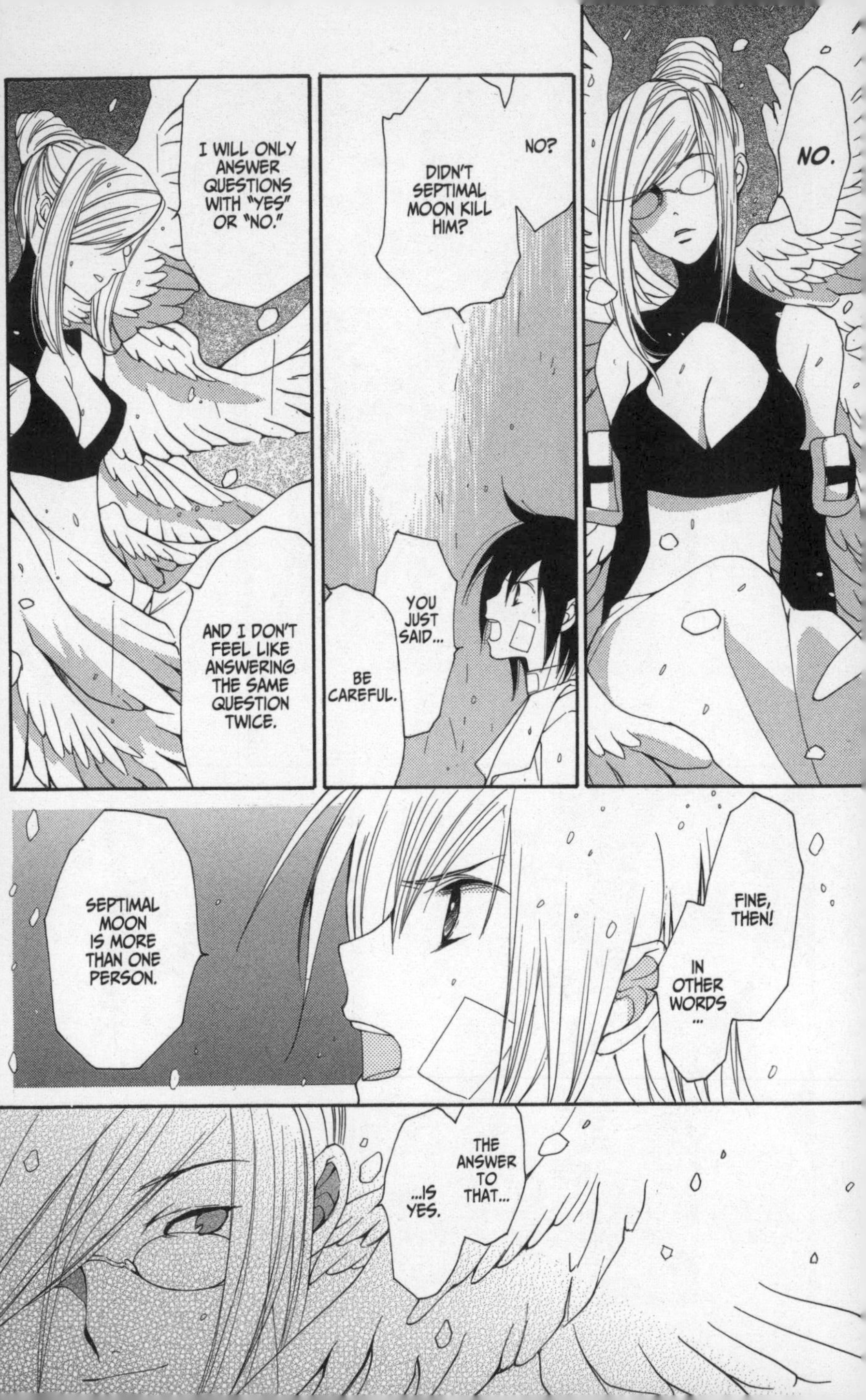
NO.
NO?
DIDN'T SEPTIMAL MOON KILL HIM?
YOU JUST SAID...
BE CAREFUL.
I WILL ONLY ANSWER QUESTIONS WITH "YES" OR "NO."
AND I DON'T FEEL LIKE ANSWERING THE SAME QUESTION TWICE.
FINE, THEN!
IN OTHER WORDS ...
SEPTIMAL MOON IS MORE THAN ONE PERSON.
THE ANSWER TO THAT...
...IS YES.

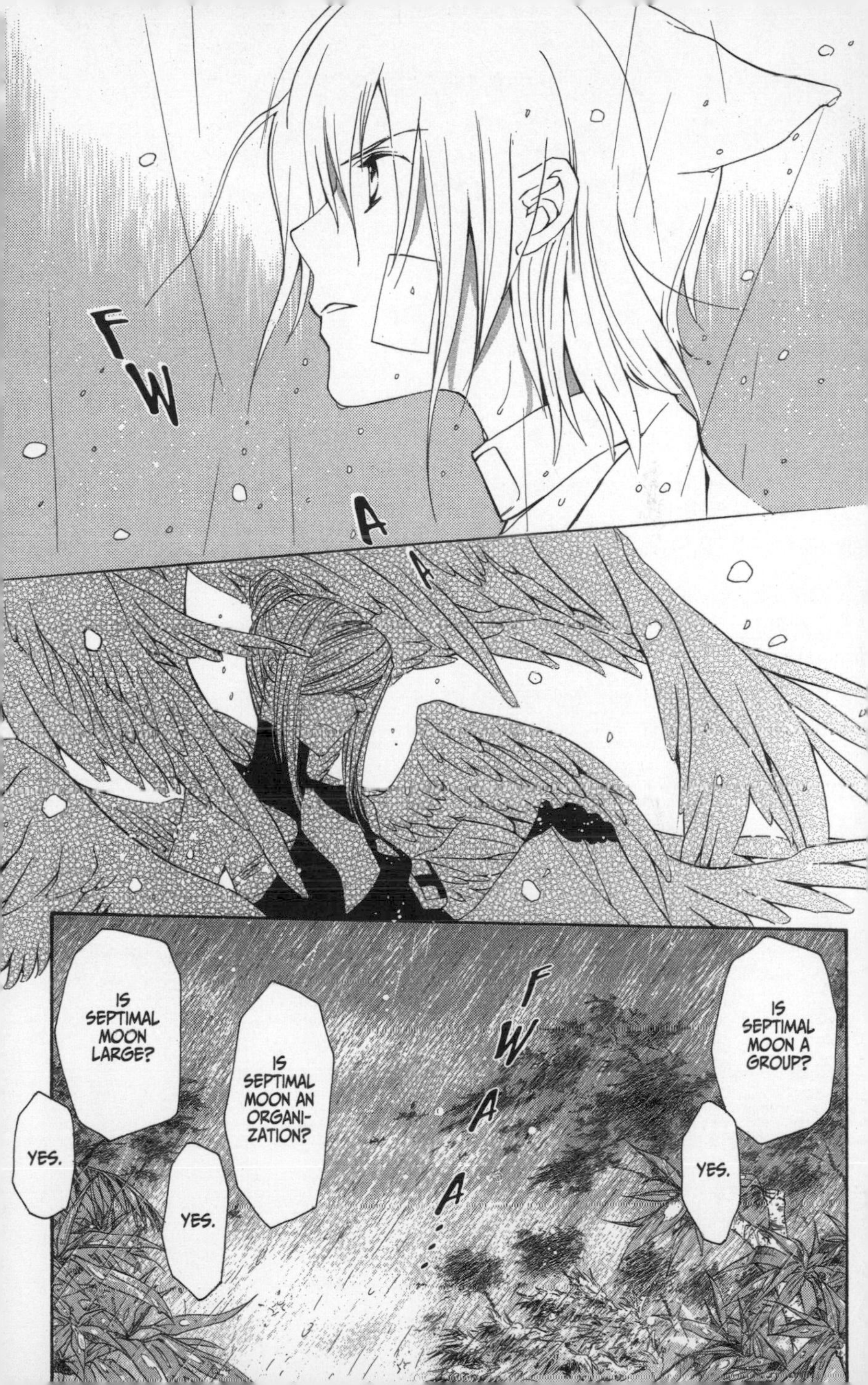
FWAA
IS SEPTIMAL MOON A GROUP?
YES.
FWAA...
IS SEPTIMAL MOON AN ORGANI-ZATION?
YES.
IS SEPTIMAL MOON LARGE?
YES.

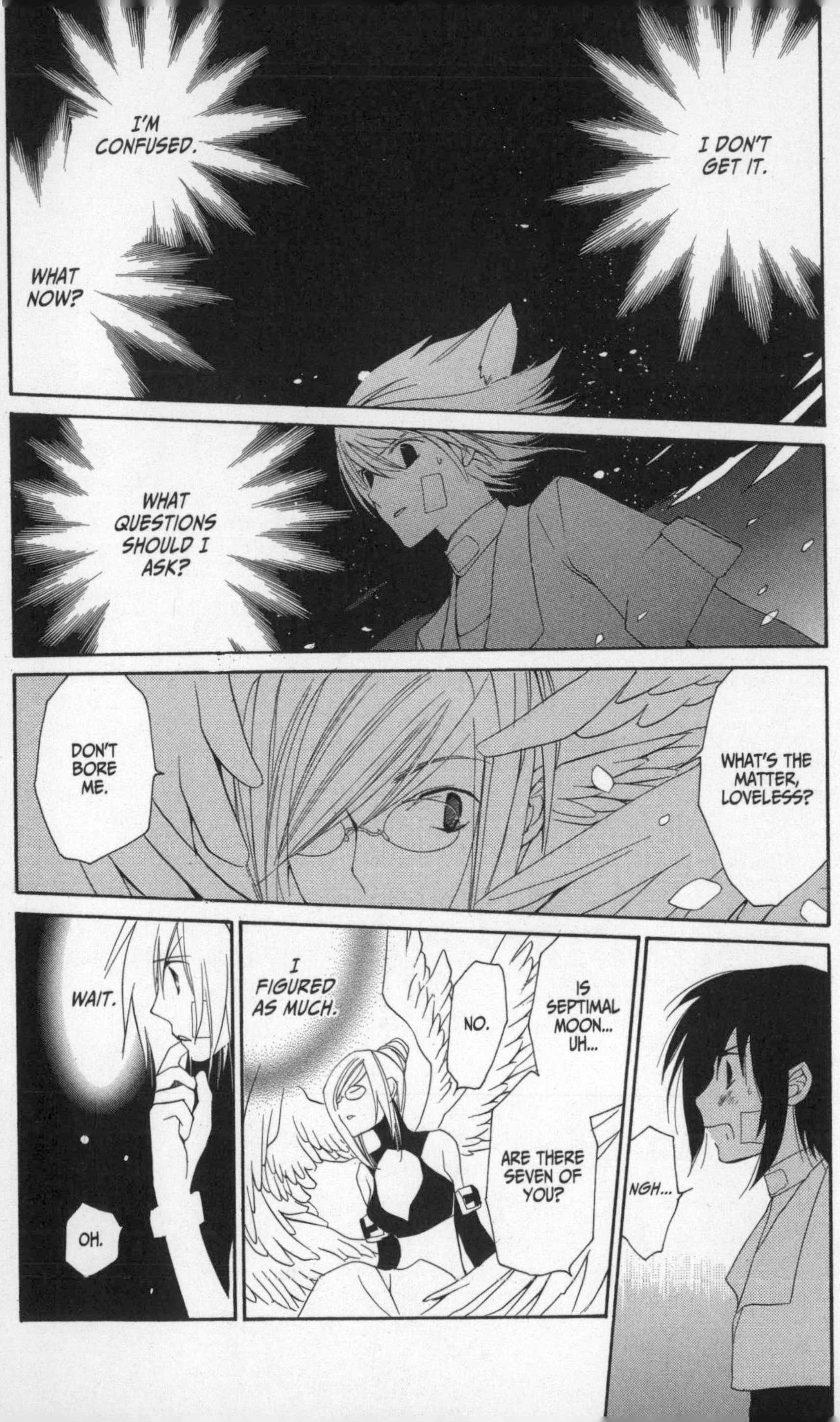
I DON'T GET IT.
I'M CONFUSED.
WHAT NOW?
WHAT QUESTIONS SHOULD I ASK?
WHAT'S THE MATTER, LOVELESS?
DON'T BORE ME.
IS SEPTIMAL MOON... UH...
ARE THERE SEVEN OF YOU?
NGH...
NO.
I FIGURED AS MUCH.
WAIT.
OH.

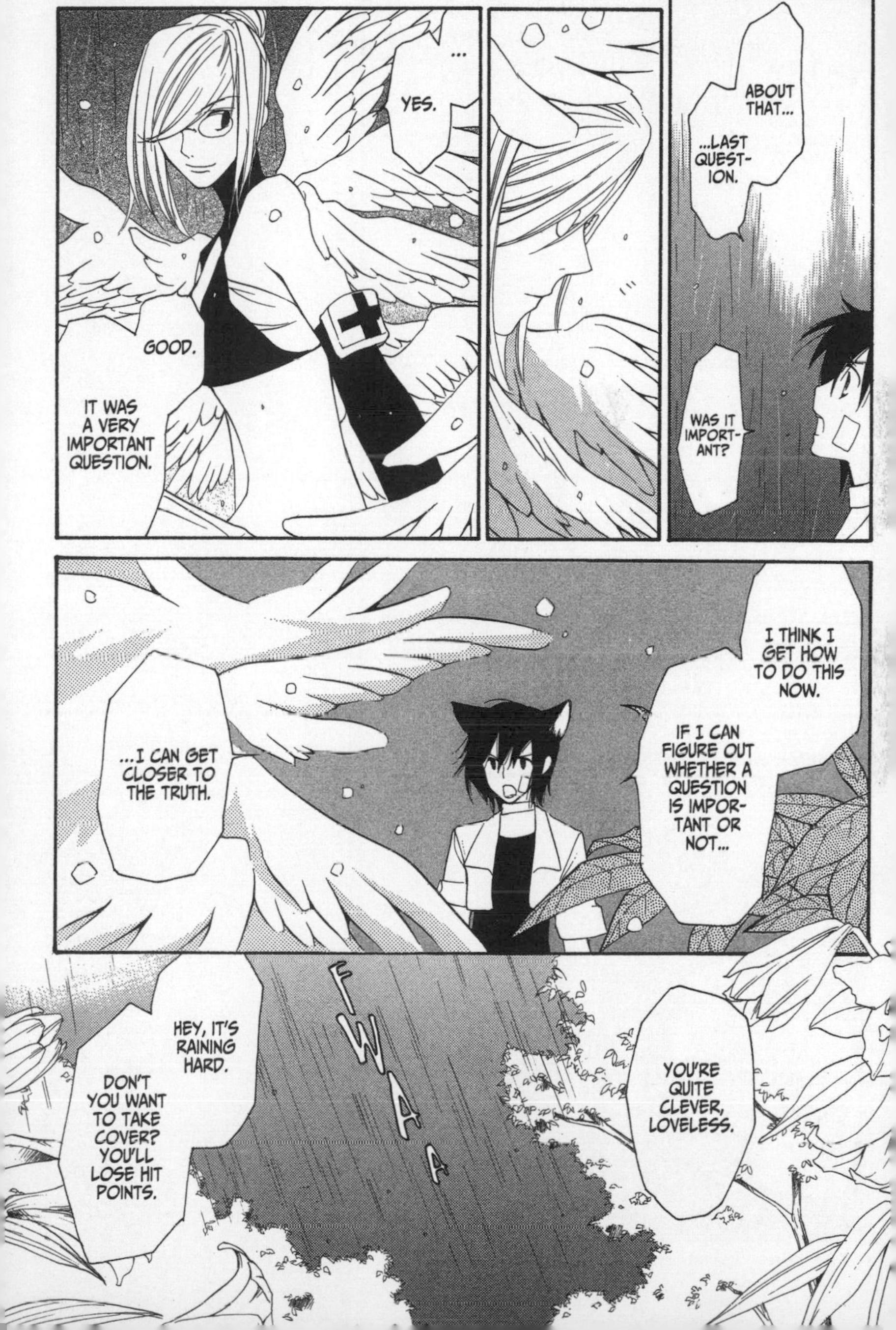
ABOUT THAT...
...LAST QUESTION.
WAS IT IMPORTANT?
...
YES.
GOOD.
IT WAS A VERY IMPORTANT QUESTION.
I THINK I GET HOW TO DO THIS NOW.
IF I CAN FIGURE OUT WHETHER A QUESTION IS IMPORTANT OR NOT...
...I CAN GET CLOSER TO THE TRUTH.
YOU'RE QUITE CLEVER, LOVELESS.
FWAA
HEY, IT'S RAINING HARD.
DON'T YOU WANT TO TAKE COVER? YOU'LL LOSE HIT POINTS.

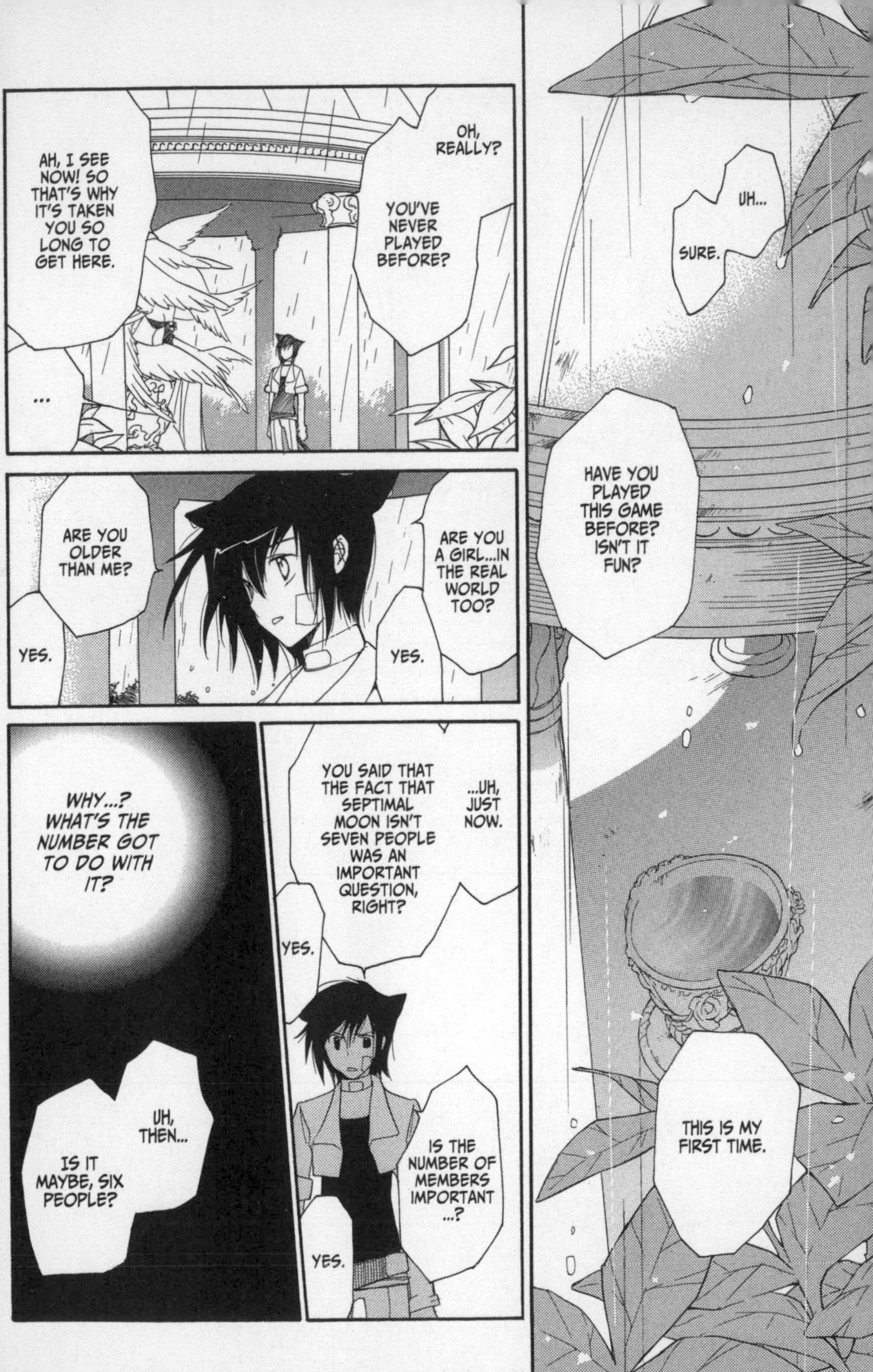
UH... SURE.
HAVE YOU PLAYED THIS GAME BEFORE? ISN'T IT FUN?
THIS IS MY FIRST TIME.
OH, REALLY?
YOU'VE NEVER PLAYED BEFORE?
AH, I SEE NOW! SO THAT'S WHY IT'S TAKEN YOU SO LONG TO GET HERE.
...
ARE YOU A GIRL...IN THE REAL WORLD TOO?
YES.
ARE YOU OLDER THAN ME?
YES.
...UH, JUST NOW.
YOU SAID THAT THE FACT THAT SEPTIMAL MOON ISN'T SEVEN PEOPLE WAS AN IMPORTANT QUESTION, RIGHT?
YES.
IS THE NUMBER OF MEMBERS IMPORTANT ...?
YES.
WHY...? WHAT'S THE NUMBER GOT TO DO WITH IT?
UH, THEN...
IS IT MAYBE, SIX PEOPLE?

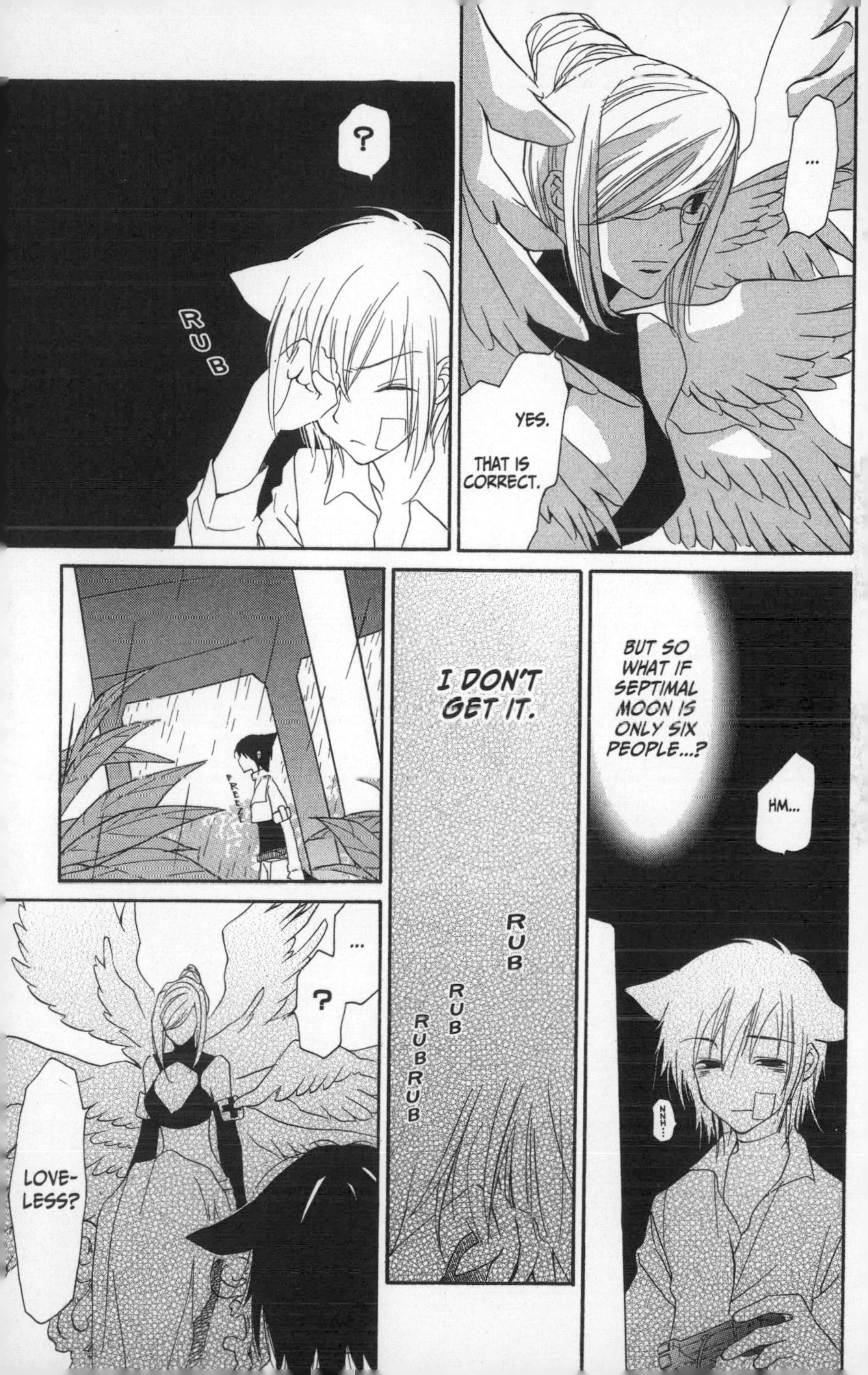
...
YES.
THAT IS CORRECT.
?
RUB
BUT SO WHAT IF SEPTIMAL MOON IS ONLY SIX PEOPLE...?
HM...
NNH...
I DON'T GET IT.
RUB
RUB
RUBRUB
FREEZE
...
?
LOVE-LESS?

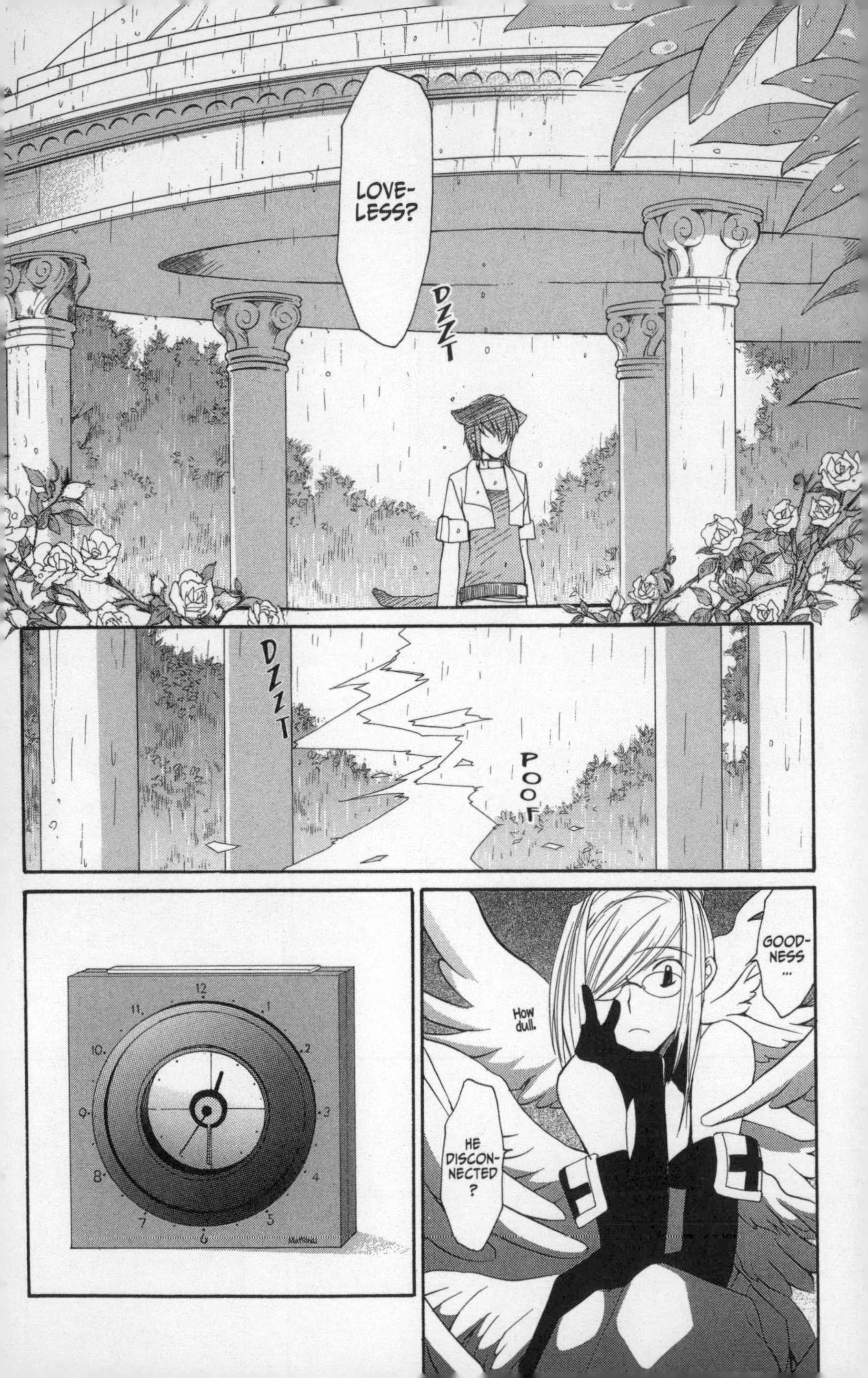
LOVE-LESS?
DZZT
DZZT
POOF
GOODNESS...
How dull.
HE DISCONNECTED?

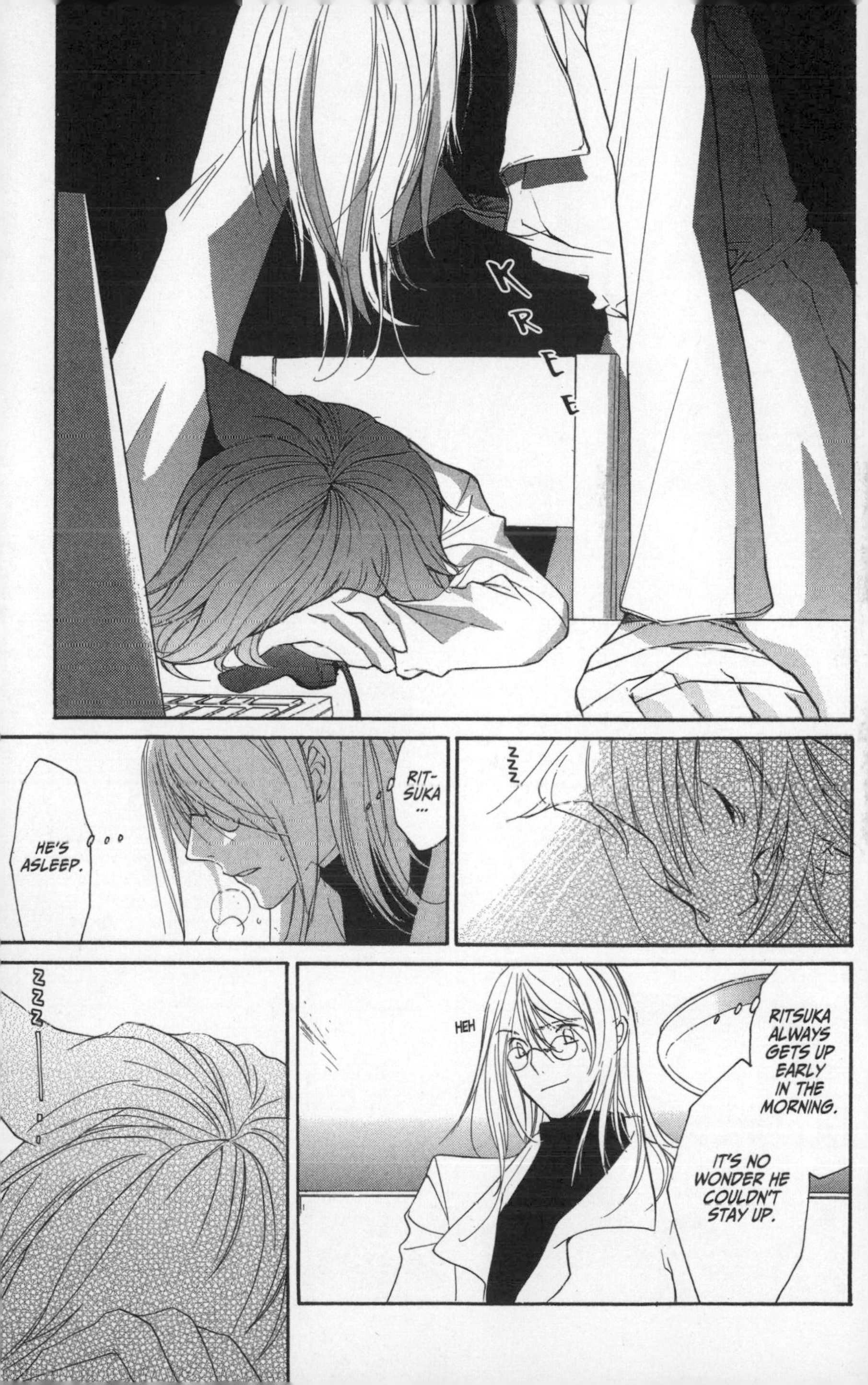
KREE
ZZZ
RIT-SUKA...
HE'S ASLEEP.
RITSUKA ALWAYS GETS UP EARLY IN THE MORNING.
IT'S NO WONDER HE COULDN'T STAY UP.
HEH
ZZZ...

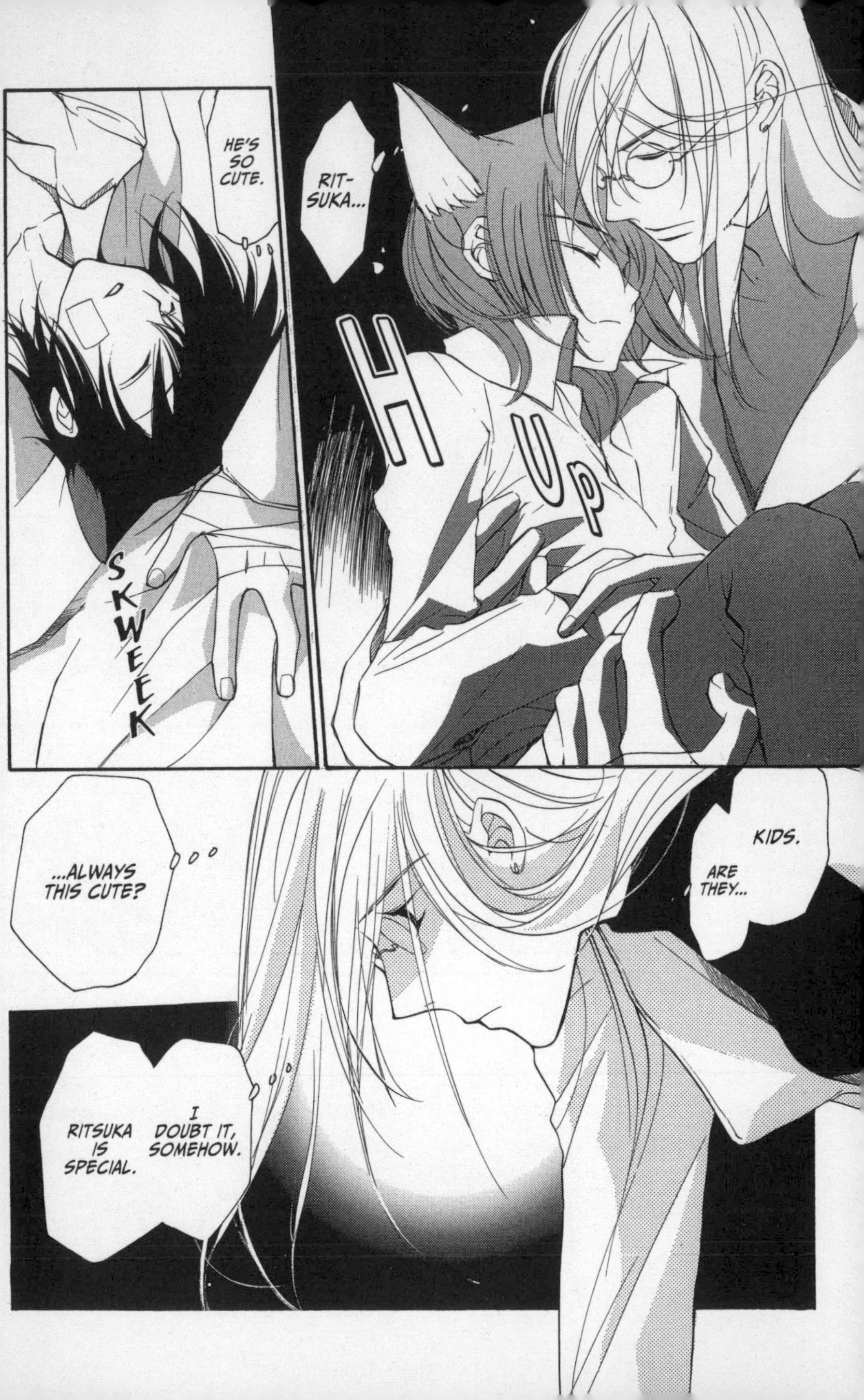
RIT-SUKA...
HUP
HE'S SO CUTE.
SKWEEK
KIDS.
ARE THEY...
...ALWAYS THIS CUTE?
I DOUBT IT, SOMEHOW.
RITSUKA IS SPECIAL.

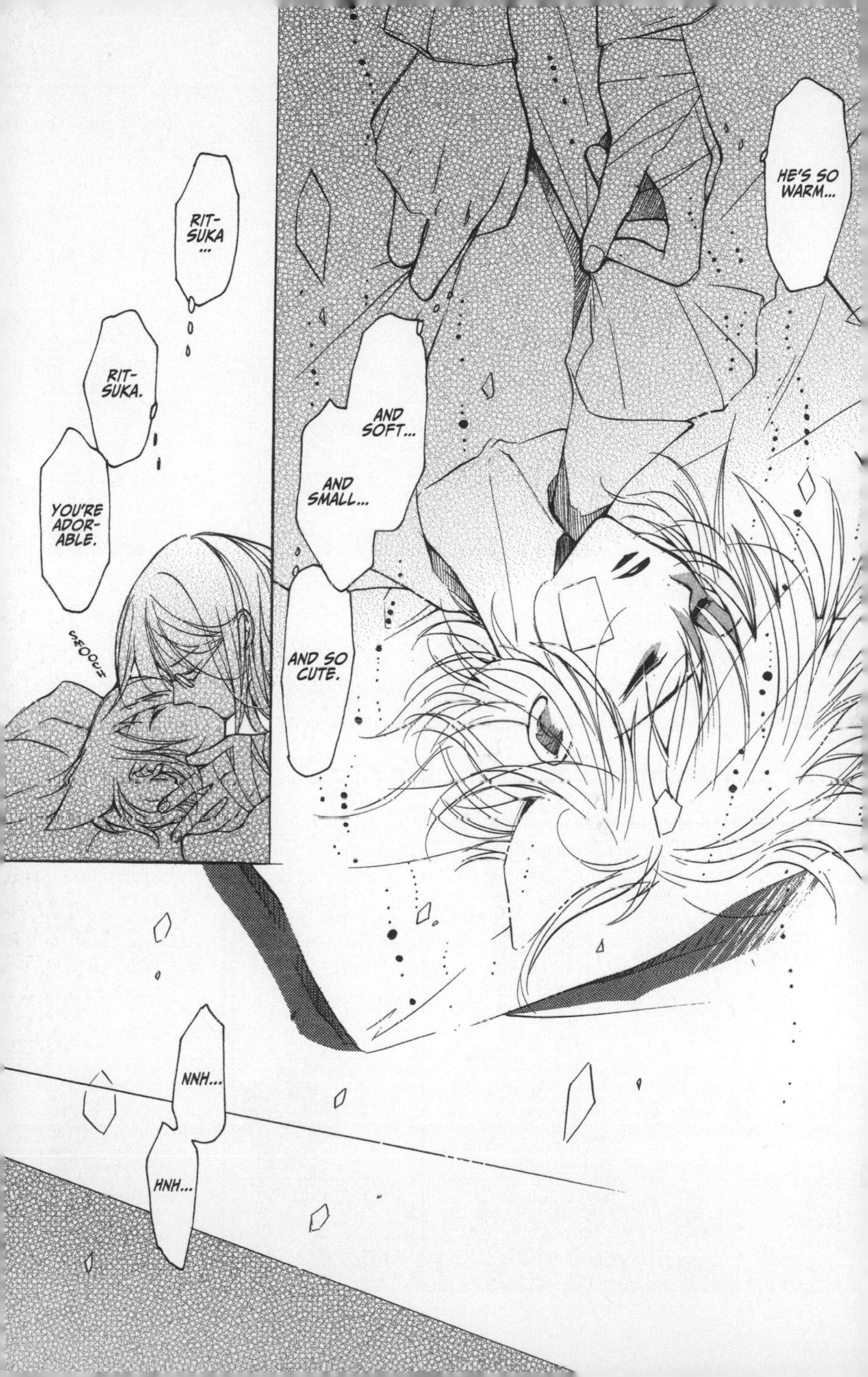
HE'S SO WARM...
AND SOFT...
AND SMALL...
AND SO CUTE.
RIT-SUKA...
RIT-SUKA.
YOU'RE ADORABLE.
SMOOCH
NNH...
HNH...

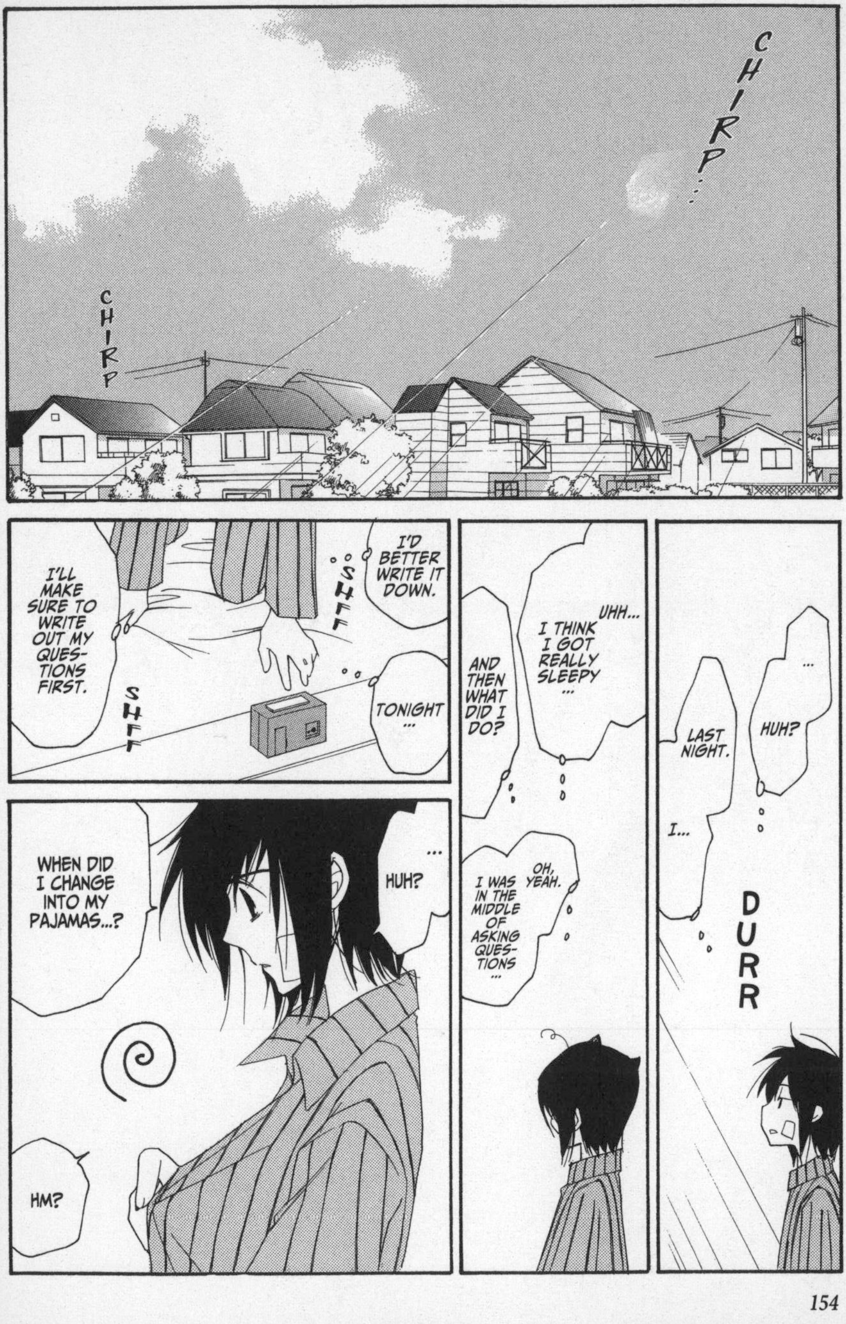
CHIRP...
CHIRP
...
HUH?
LAST NIGHT.
I...
DURR
UHH... I THINK I GOT REALLY SLEEPY...
AND THEN WHAT DID I DO?
OH, YEAH.
I WAS IN THE MIDDLE OF ASKING QUES-TIONS...
I'D BETTER WRITE IT DOWN.
SHFF
TONIGHT...
I'LL MAKE SURE TO WRITE OUT MY QUES-TIONS FIRST.
SHFF
...
HUH?
WHEN DID I CHANGE INTO MY PAJAMAS...?
HM?

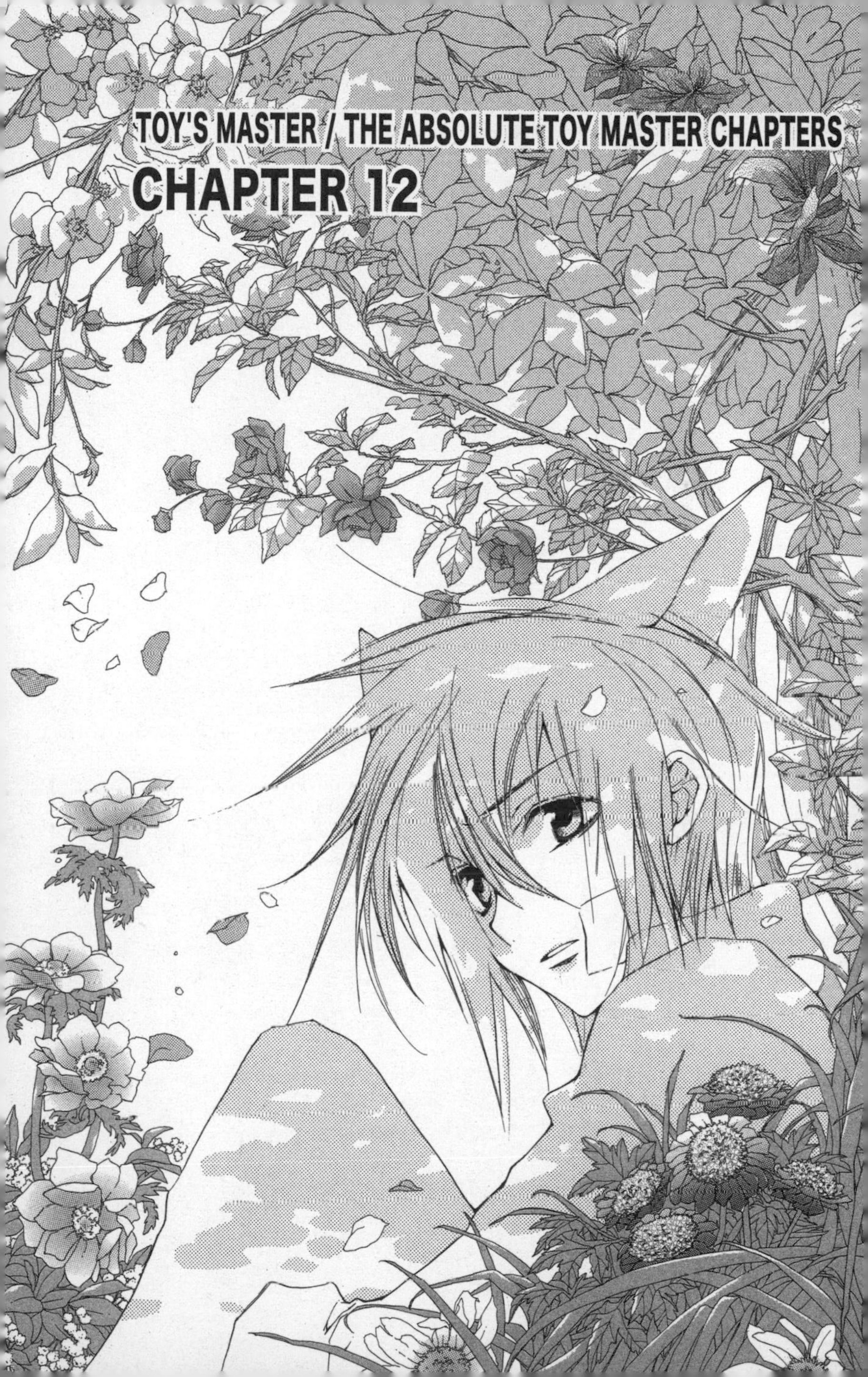
TOY'S MASTER / THE ABSOLUTE TOY MASTER CHAPTERS
CHAPTER 12

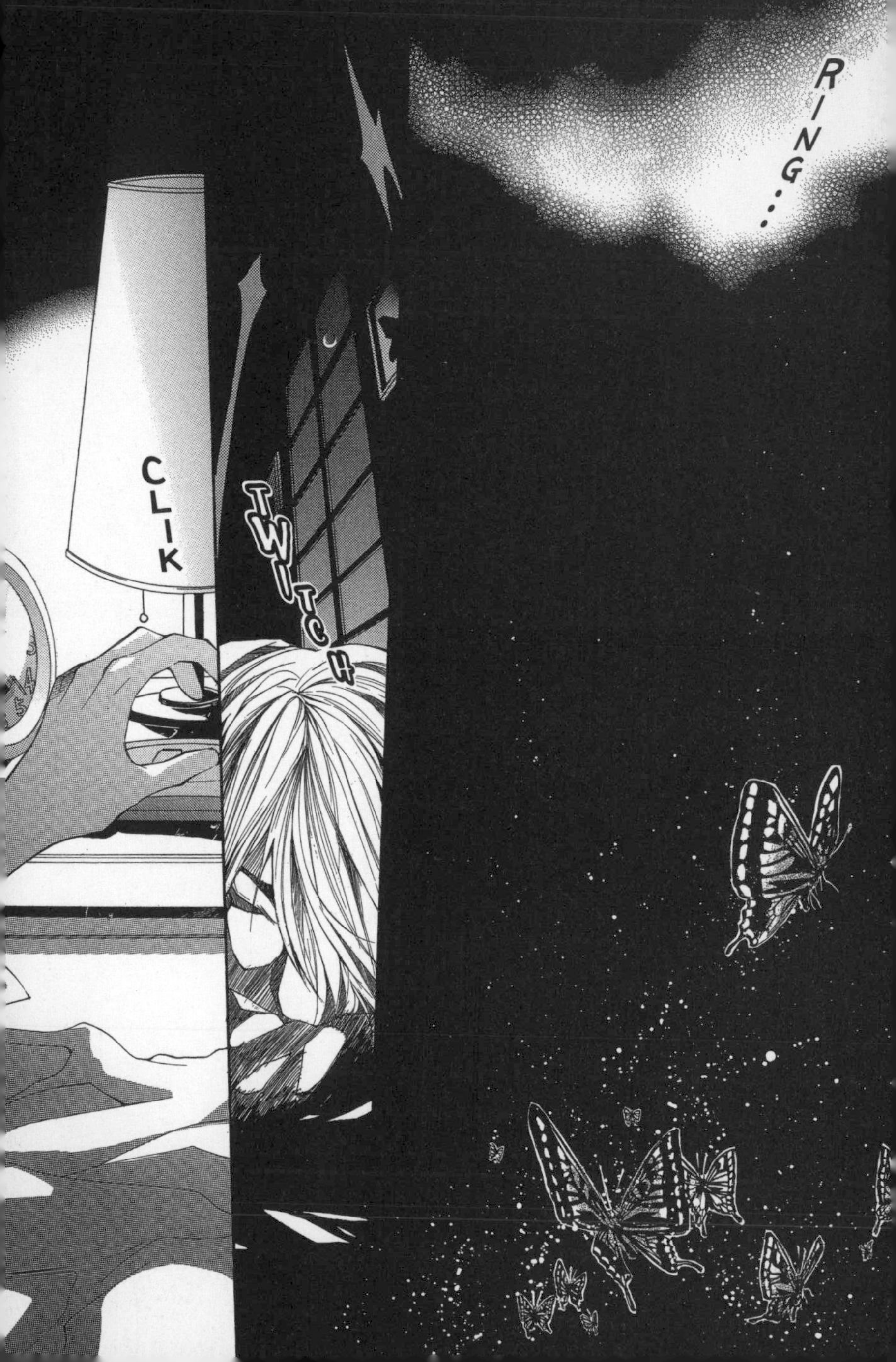
RING...
TWITCH
CLIK

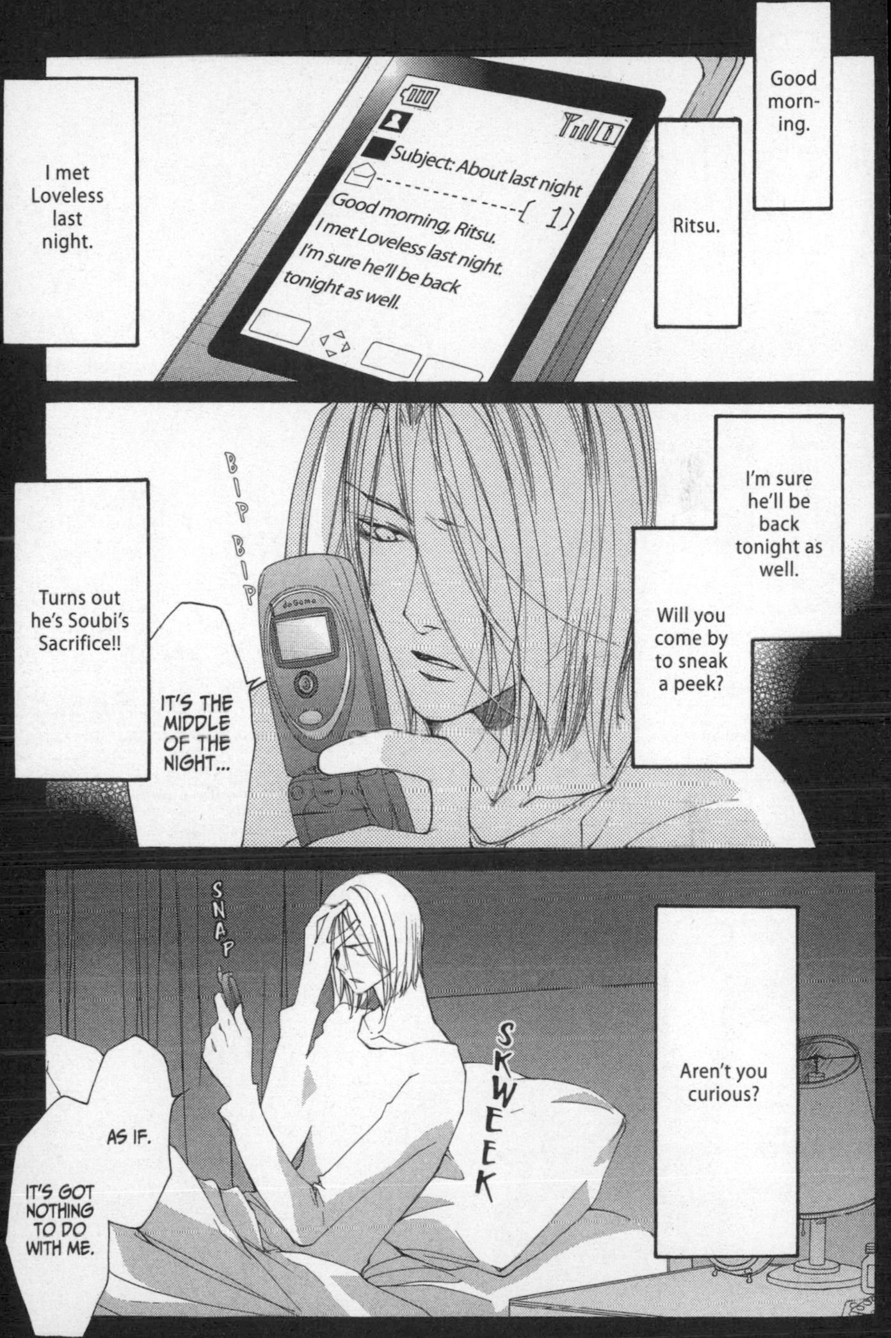
Good morn-ing.
Ritsu.
Subject: About last night
1
Good morning, Ritsu.
I met Loveless last night.
I'm sure he'll be back tonight as well.
I met Loveless last night.
I'm sure he'll be back tonight as well.
Will you come by to sneak a peek?
BIP BIP
Turns out he's Soubi's Sacrifice!!
IT'S THE MIDDLE OF THE NIGHT...
Aren't you curious?
SNAP
SKWEEK
AS IF.
IT'S GOT NOTHING TO DO WITH ME.

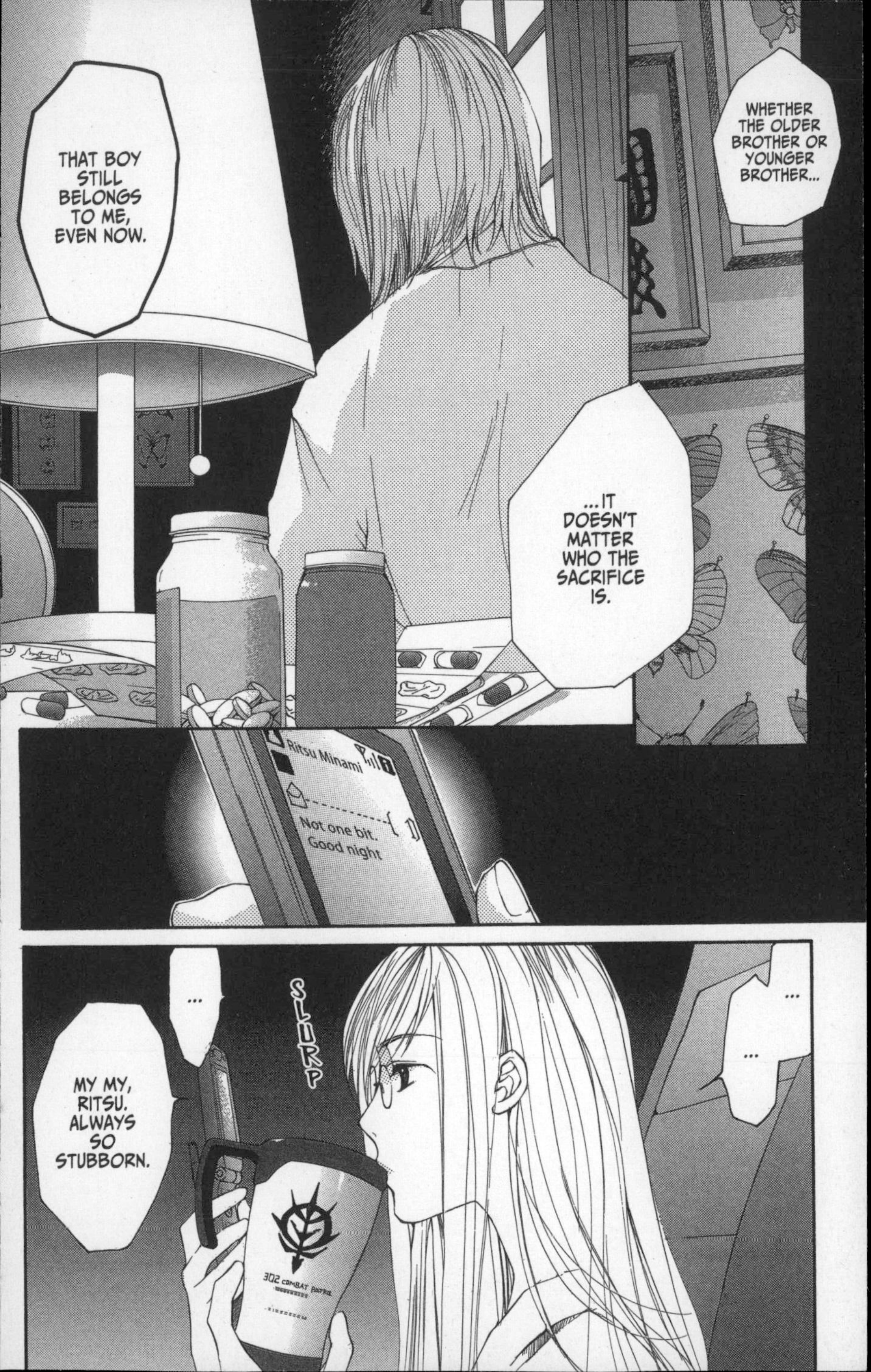
WHETHER THE OLDER BROTHER OR YOUNGER BROTHER...
...IT DOESN'T MATTER WHO THE SACRIFICE IS.
THAT BOY STILL BELONGS TO ME, EVEN NOW.
Ritsu Minami
Not one bit.
Good night
...
...
SLURP
...
MY MY, RITSU. ALWAYS SO STUBBORN.
302 COMBAT PATROL

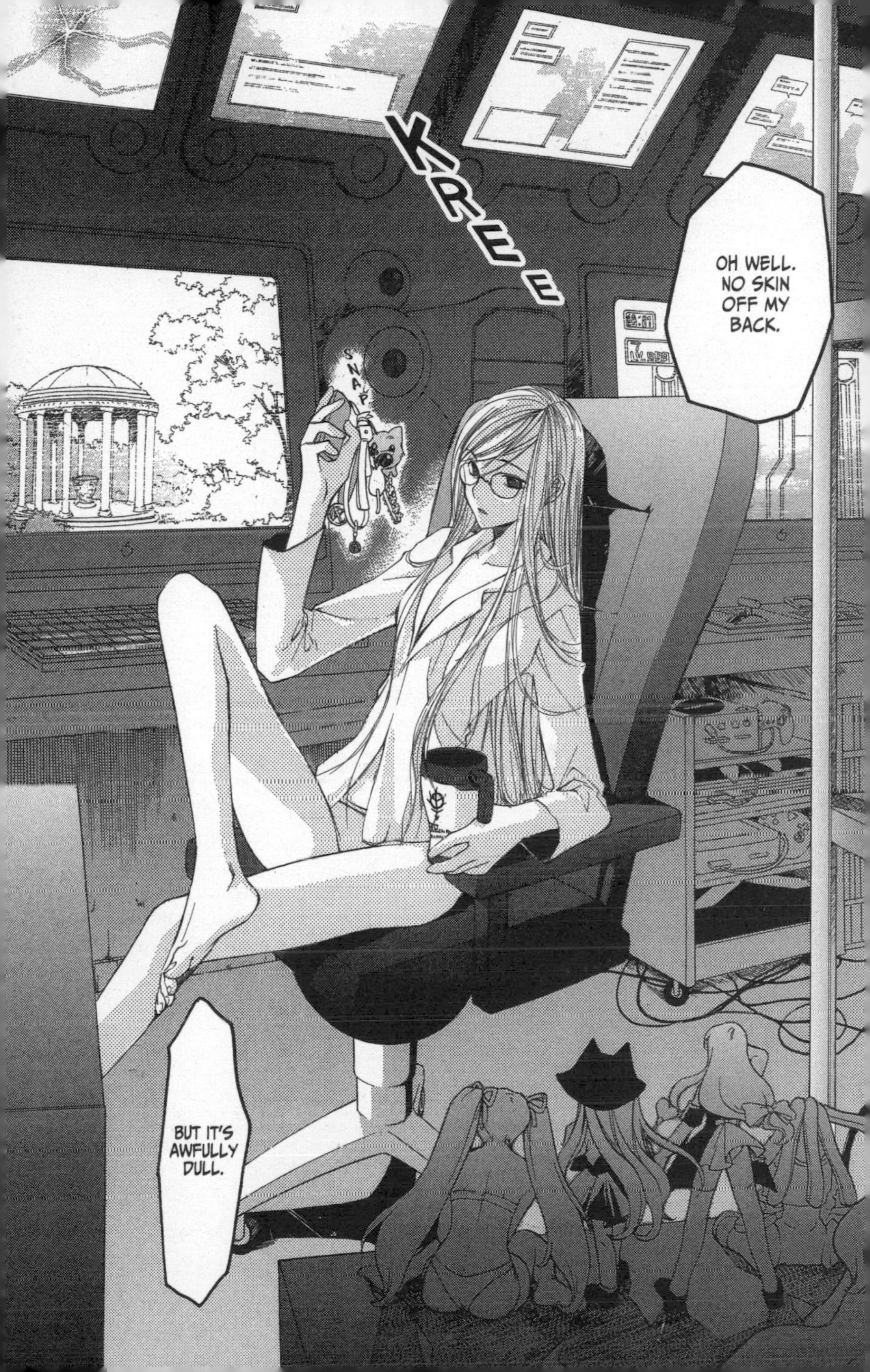
OH WELL. NO SKIN OFF MY BACK.
KREEE
SNAP
BUT IT'S AWFULLY DULL.

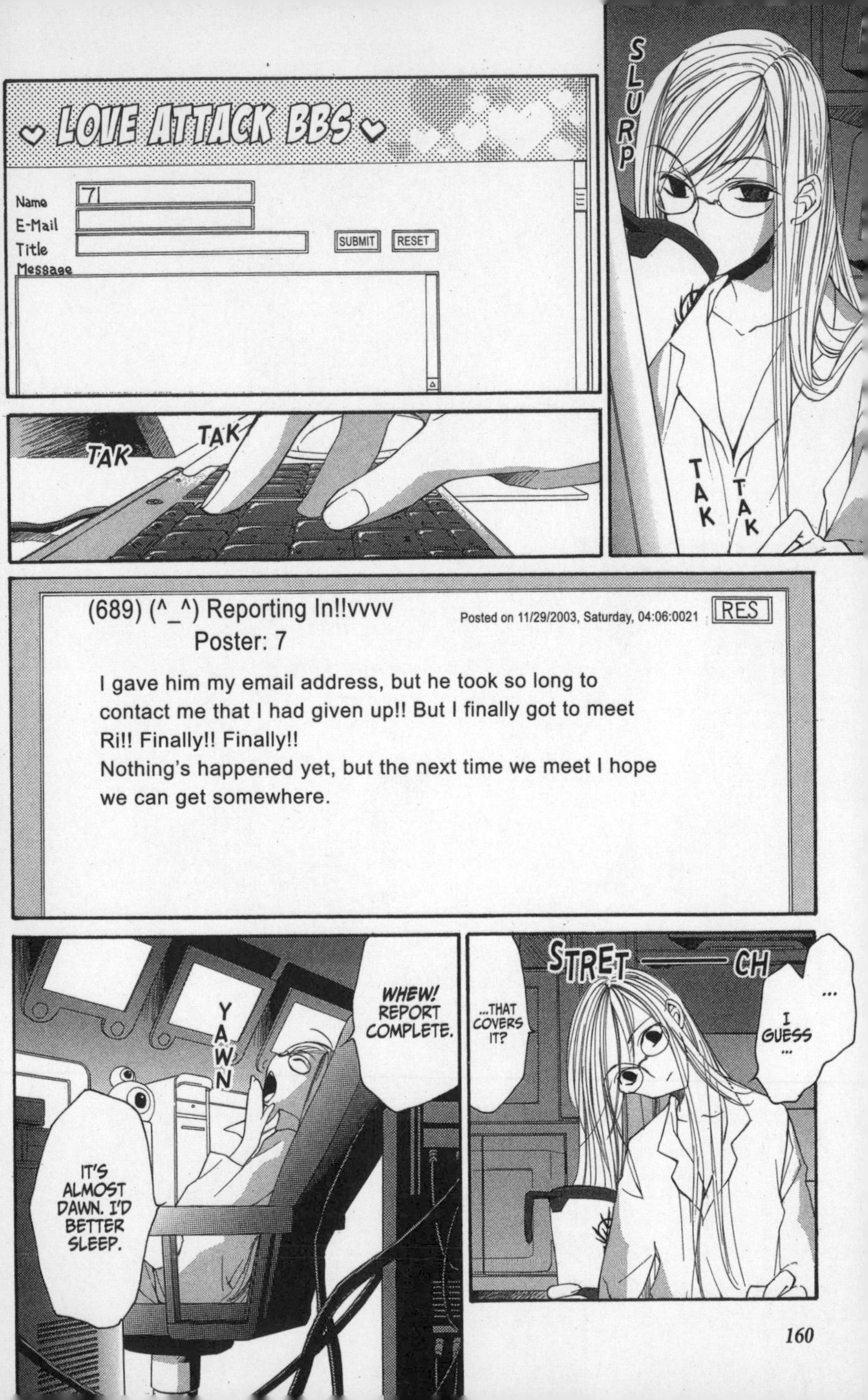
SLURP
TAK
TAK
♡ LOVE ATTACK BBS ♡
Name
7
E-Mail
Title
Message
SUBMIT
RESET
TAK
TAK
(689) (^_^) Reporting In!!vvvv
Posted on 11/29/2003, Saturday, 04:06:0021
RES
Poster: 7
I gave him my email address, but he took so long to contact me that I had given up!! But I finally got to meet Ri!! Finally!! Finally!!
Nothing's happened yet, but the next time we meet I hope we can get somewhere.
STRET——CH
... I GUESS ...
...THAT COVERS IT?
WHEW! REPORT COMPLETE.
YAWN
IT'S ALMOST DAWN. I'D BETTER SLEEP.

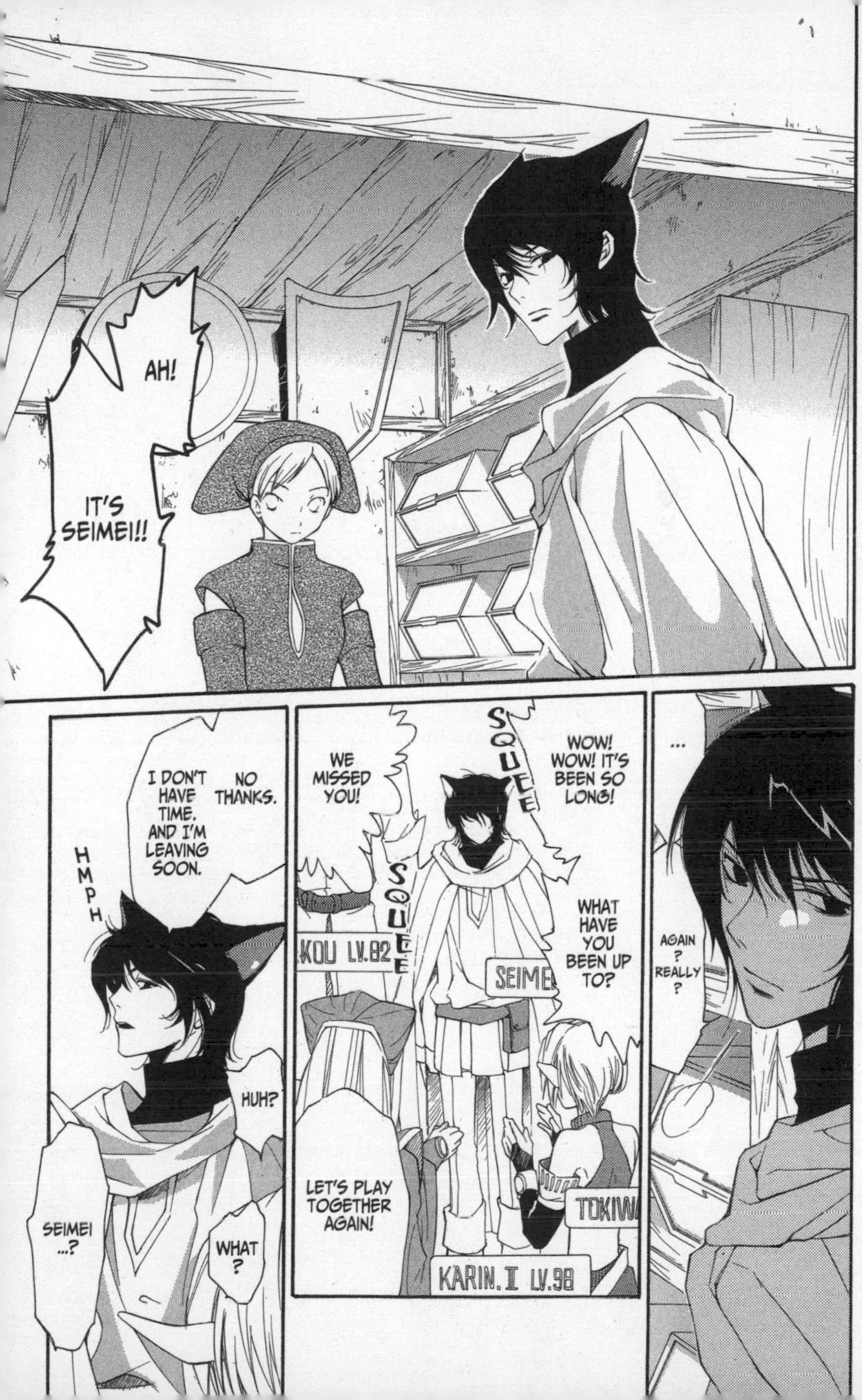
AH!
IT'S SEIMEI!!
...
AGAIN? REALLY?
WOW! WOW! IT'S BEEN SO LONG!
SQUEE
WE MISSED YOU!
SQUEE
WHAT HAVE YOU BEEN UP TO?
KOU LV.82
SEIME
TOKIW
LET'S PLAY TOGETHER AGAIN!
KARIN. II LV.98
NO THANKS.
I DON'T HAVE TIME. AND I'M LEAVING SOON.
HMPH
HUH?
WHAT?
SEIMEI ...?

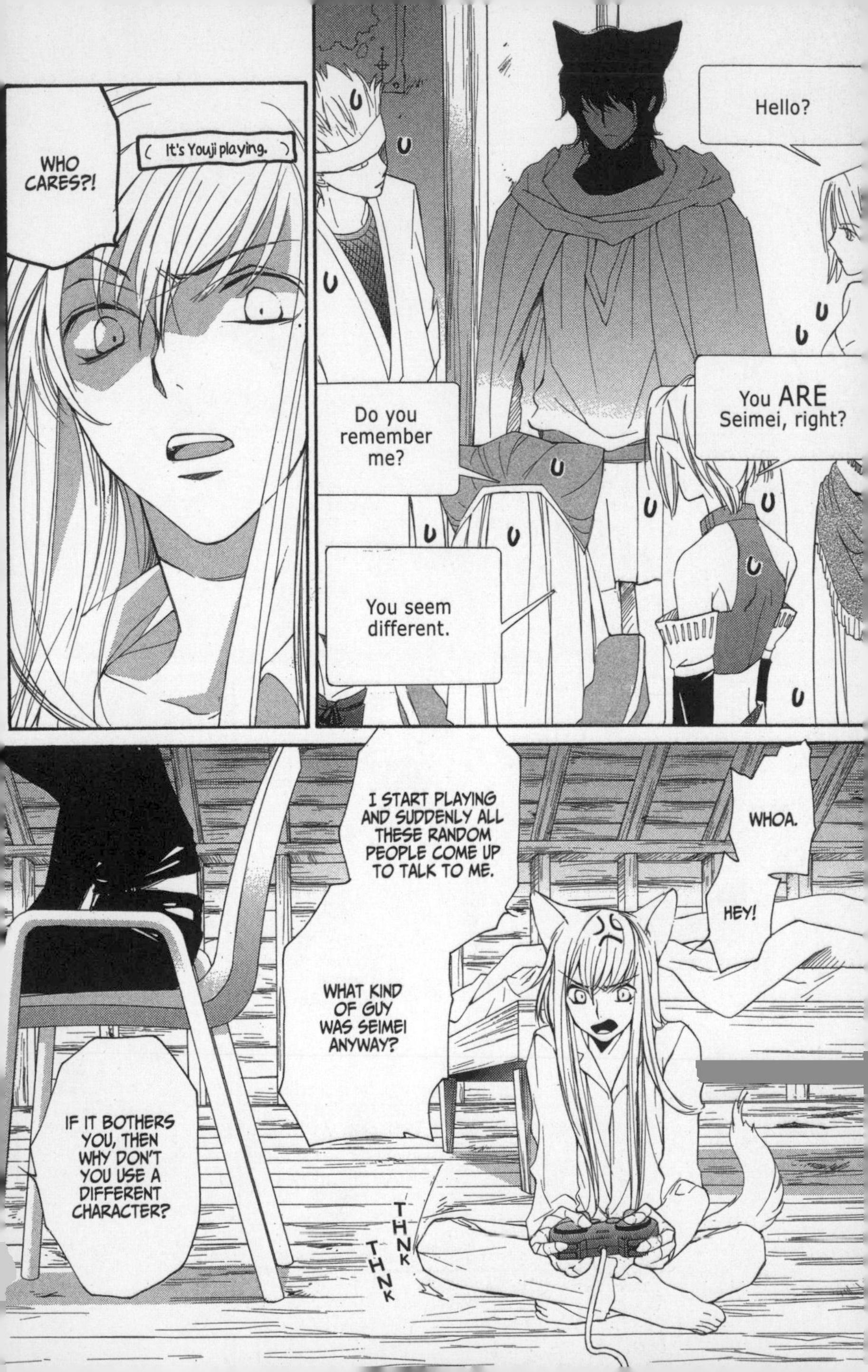
Hello?
You ARE Seimei, right?
Do you remember me?
You seem different.
(It's Youji playing.)
WHO CARES?!
WHOA.
HEY!
I START PLAYING AND SUDDENLY ALL THESE RANDOM PEOPLE COME UP TO TALK TO ME.
WHAT KIND OF GUY WAS SEIMEI ANYWAY?
THNK
THNK
IF IT BOTHERS YOU, THEN WHY DON'T YOU USE A DIFFERENT CHARACTER?

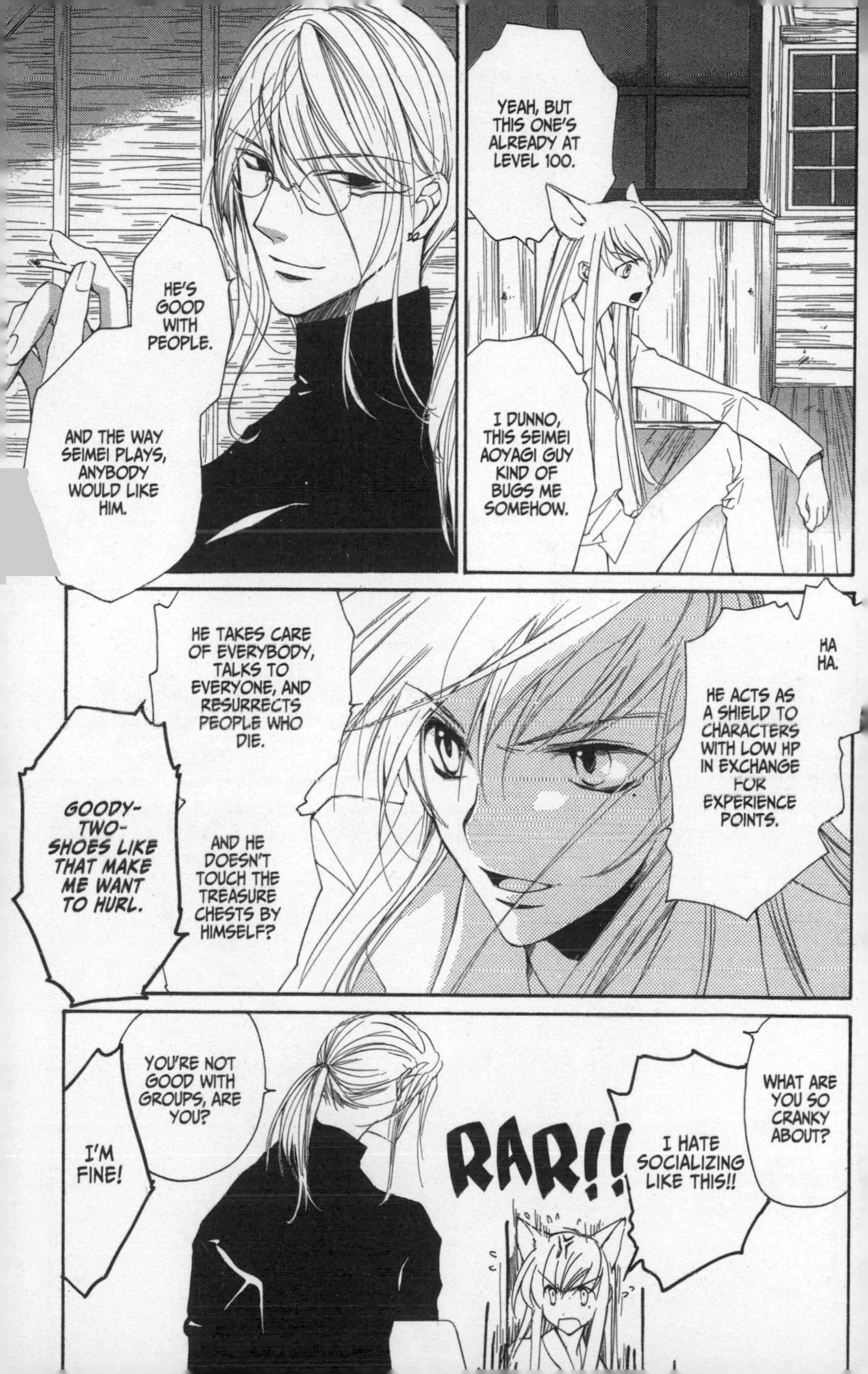
YEAH, BUT THIS ONE'S ALREADY AT LEVEL 100.
I DUNNO, THIS SEIMEI AOYAGI GUY KIND OF BUGS ME SOMEHOW.
HE'S GOOD WITH PEOPLE.
AND THE WAY SEIMEI PLAYS, ANYBODY WOULD LIKE HIM.
HA HA.
HE ACTS AS A SHIELD TO CHARACTERS WITH LOW HP IN EXCHANGE FOR EXPERIENCE POINTS.
HE TAKES CARE OF EVERYBODY, TALKS TO EVERYONE, AND RESURRECTS PEOPLE WHO DIE.
AND HE DOESN'T TOUCH THE TREASURE CHESTS BY HIMSELF?
GOODY-TWO-SHOES LIKE THAT MAKE ME WANT TO HURL.
WHAT ARE YOU SO CRANKY ABOUT?
I HATE SOCIALIZING LIKE THIS!!
RAR!!
YOU'RE NOT GOOD WITH GROUPS, ARE YOU?
I'M FINE!

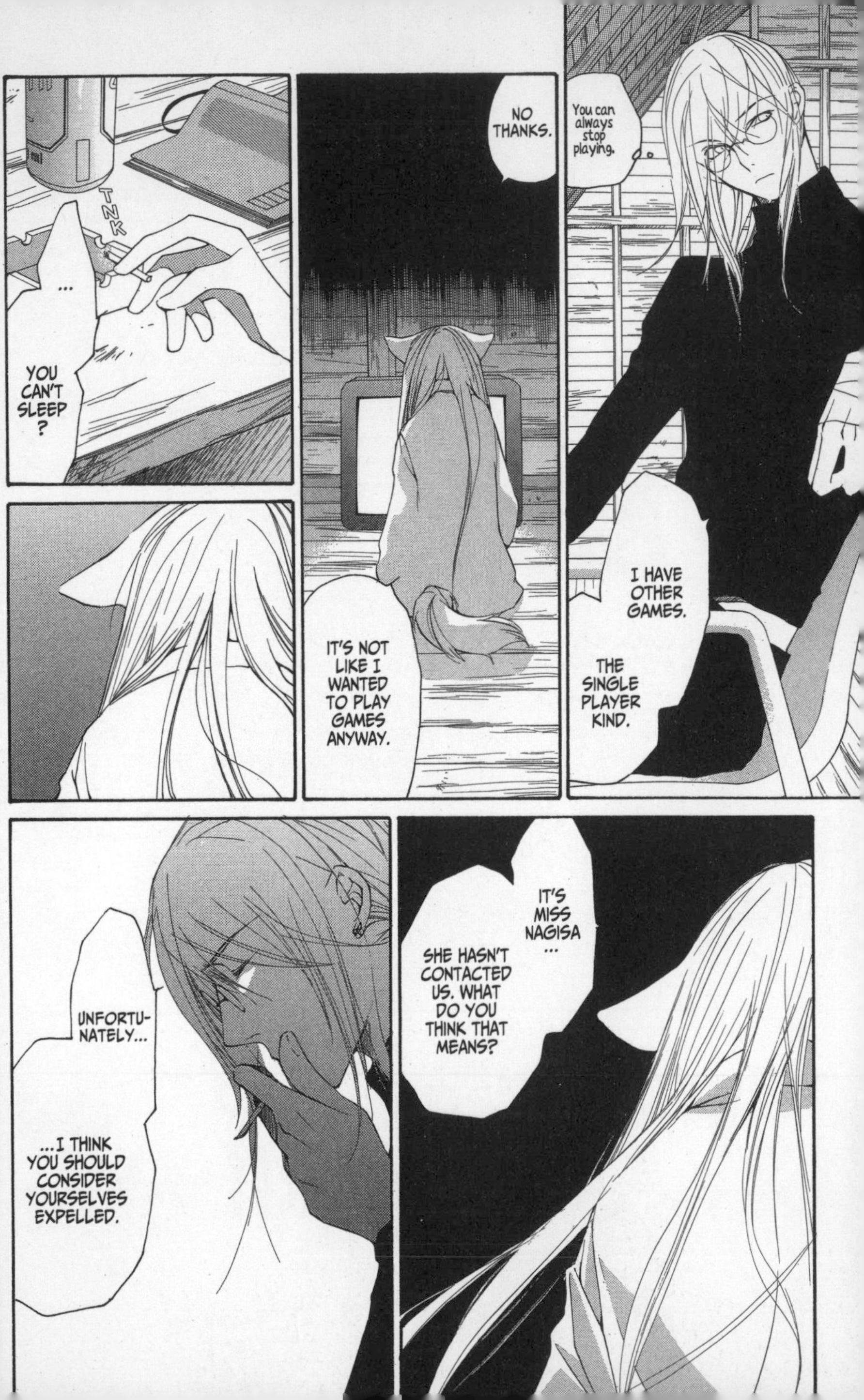
You can always stop playing.
I HAVE OTHER GAMES.
THE SINGLE PLAYER KIND.
NO THANKS.
IT'S NOT LIKE I WANTED TO PLAY GAMES ANYWAY.
TNK
...
YOU CAN'T SLEEP?
IT'S MISS NAGISA...
SHE HASN'T CONTACTED US. WHAT DO YOU THINK THAT MEANS?
UNFORTUNATELY...
...I THINK YOU SHOULD CONSIDER YOURSELVES EXPELLED.

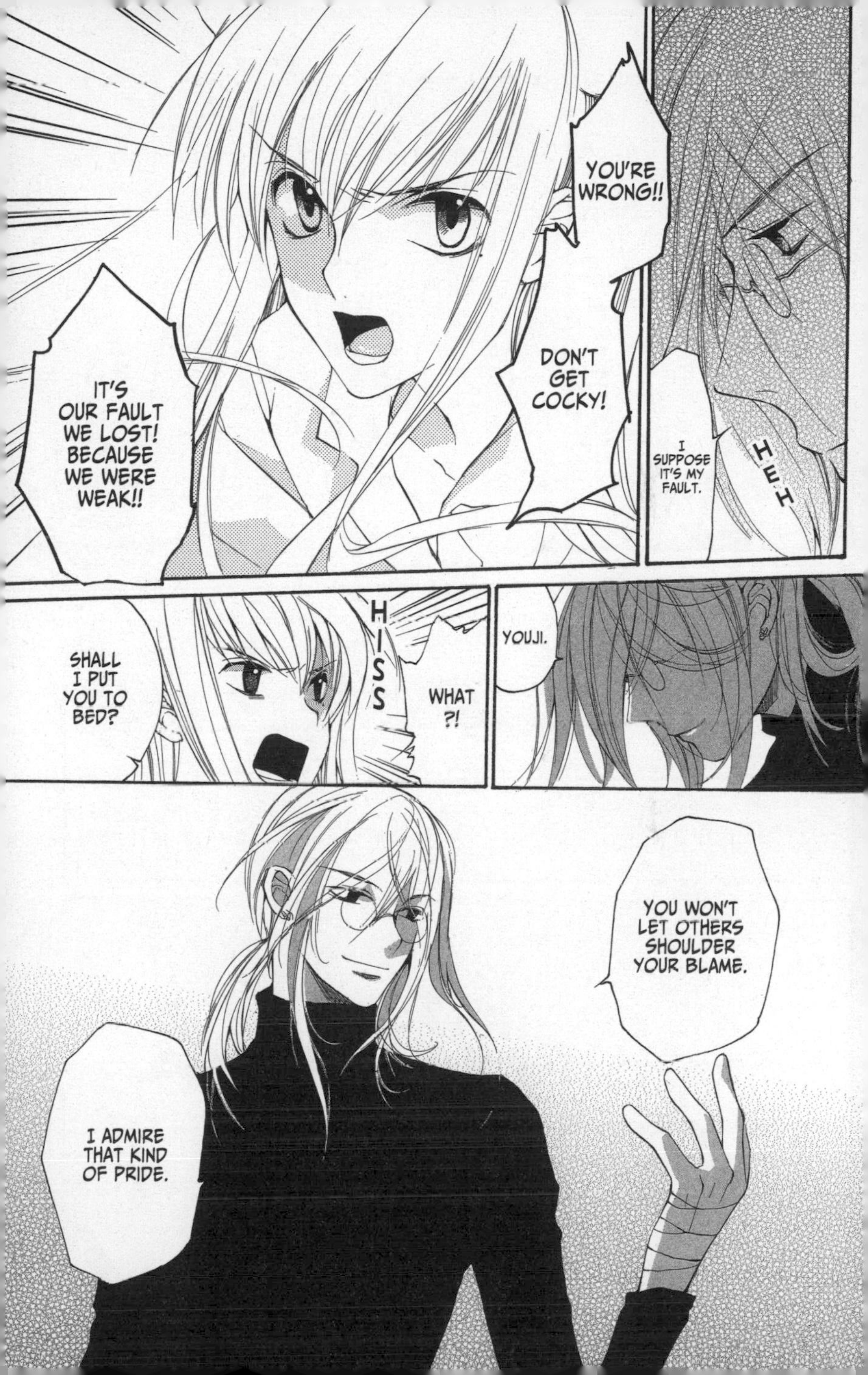
HEH
I SUPPOSE IT'S MY FAULT.
YOU'RE WRONG!!
DON'T GET COCKY!
IT'S OUR FAULT WE LOST! BECAUSE WE WERE WEAK!!
YOUJI.
WHAT?!
HISS
SHALL I PUT YOU TO BED?
YOU WON'T LET OTHERS SHOULDER YOUR BLAME.
I ADMIRE THAT KIND OF PRIDE.

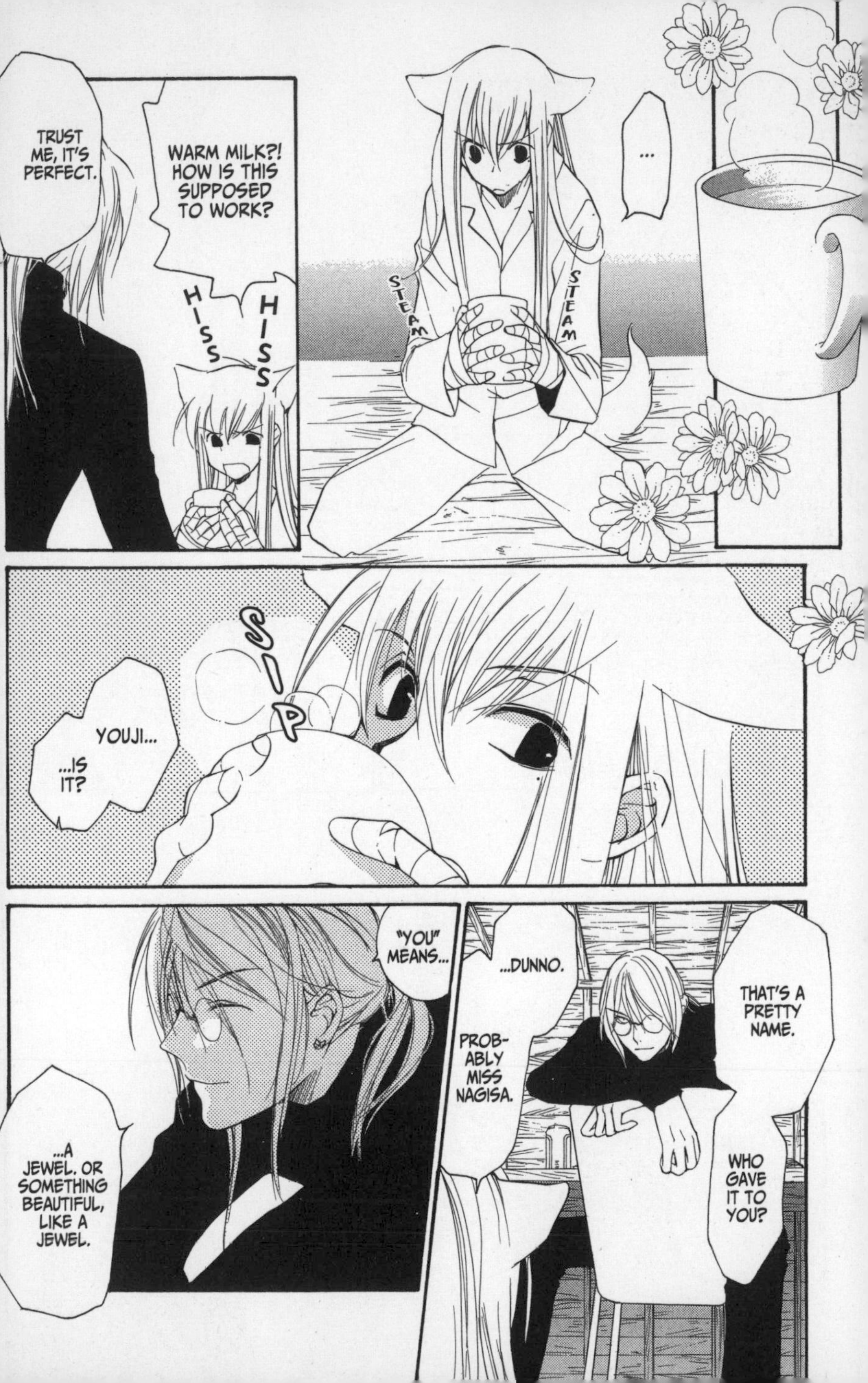
...
STEAM
STEAM
WARM MILK?! HOW IS THIS SUPPOSED TO WORK?
TRUST ME, IT'S PERFECT.
HISS
HISS
SIP
YOUJI...
...IS IT?
THAT'S A PRETTY NAME.
WHO GAVE IT TO YOU?
...DUNNO.
PROB-ABLY MISS NAGISA.
"YOU" MEANS...
...A JEWEL. OR SOMETHING BEAUTIFUL, LIKE A JEWEL.

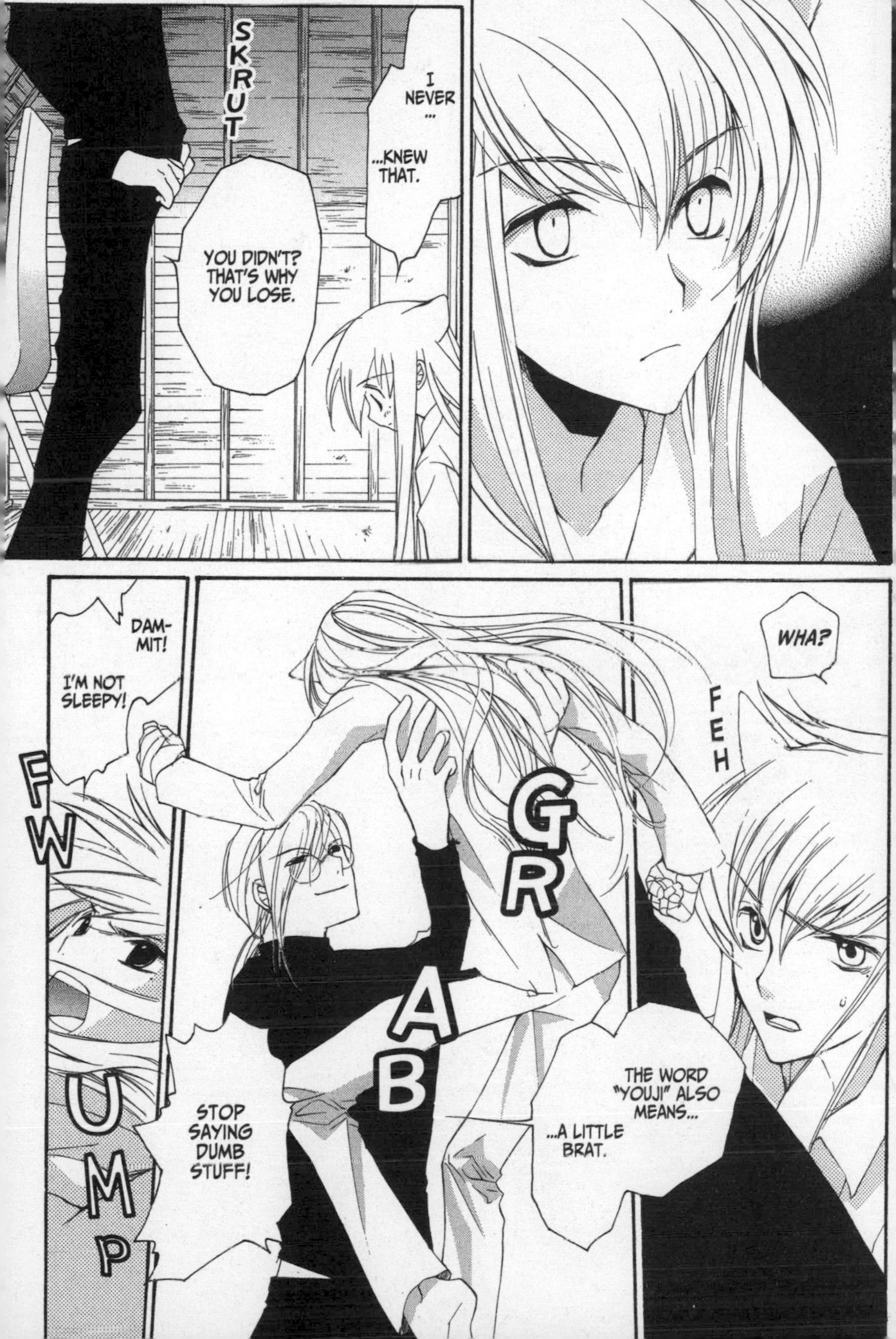
I NEVER ...
...KNEW THAT.
SKRUT
YOU DIDN'T? THAT'S WHY YOU LOSE.
WHA?
FEH
THE WORD "YOUJI" ALSO MEANS...
...A LITTLE BRAT.
GRAB
STOP SAYING DUMB STUFF!
DAM-MIT!
I'M NOT SLEEPY!
FWUMP

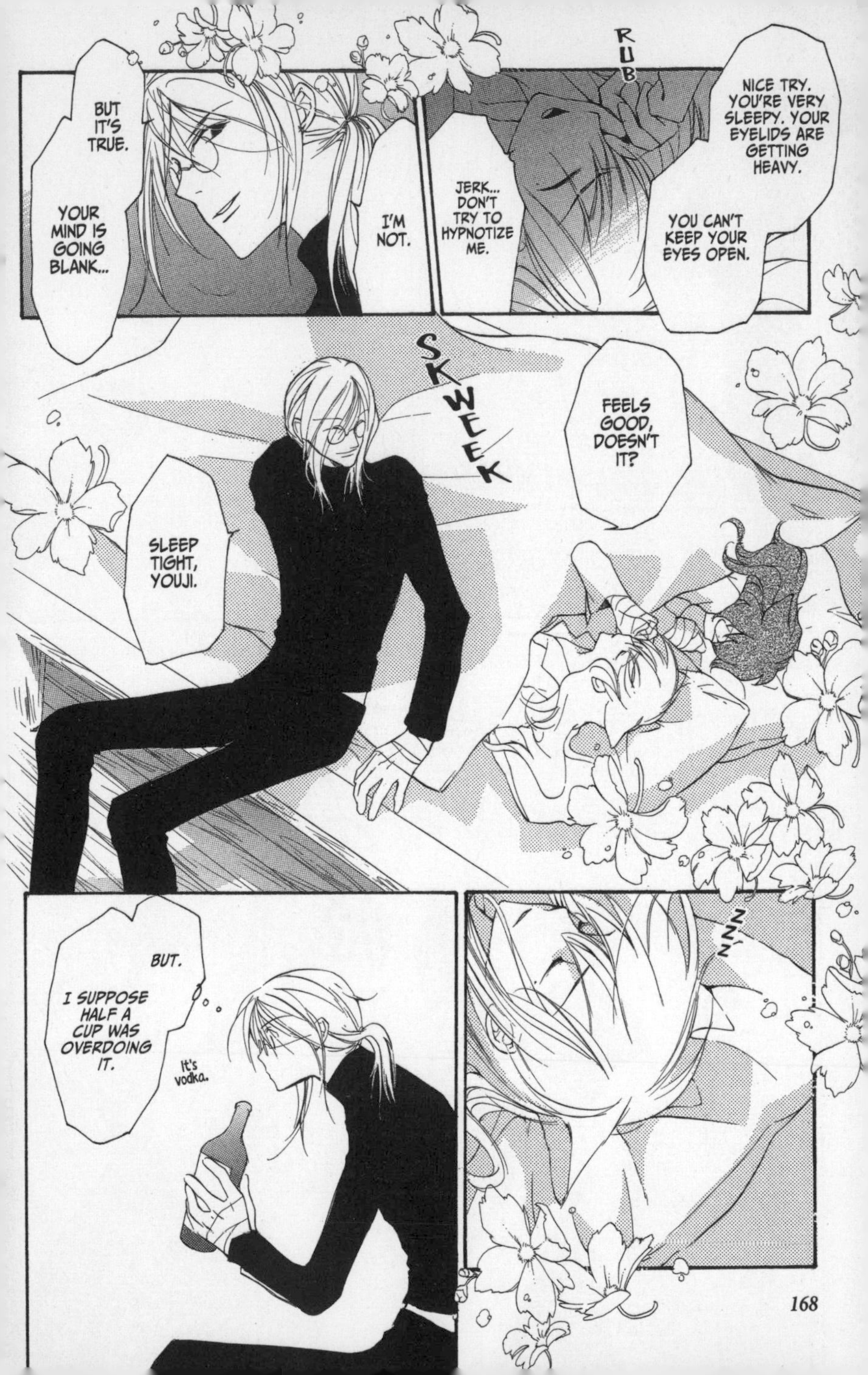
RUB
NICE TRY. YOU'RE VERY SLEEPY. YOUR EYELIDS ARE GETTING HEAVY.
YOU CAN'T KEEP YOUR EYES OPEN.
JERK... DON'T TRY TO HYPNOTIZE ME.
I'M NOT.
BUT IT'S TRUE.
YOUR MIND IS GOING BLANK...
SKWEEK
FEELS GOOD, DOESN'T IT?
SLEEP TIGHT, YOUJI.
ZZZ
BUT.
I SUPPOSE HALF A CUP WAS OVERDOING IT.
It's vodka.

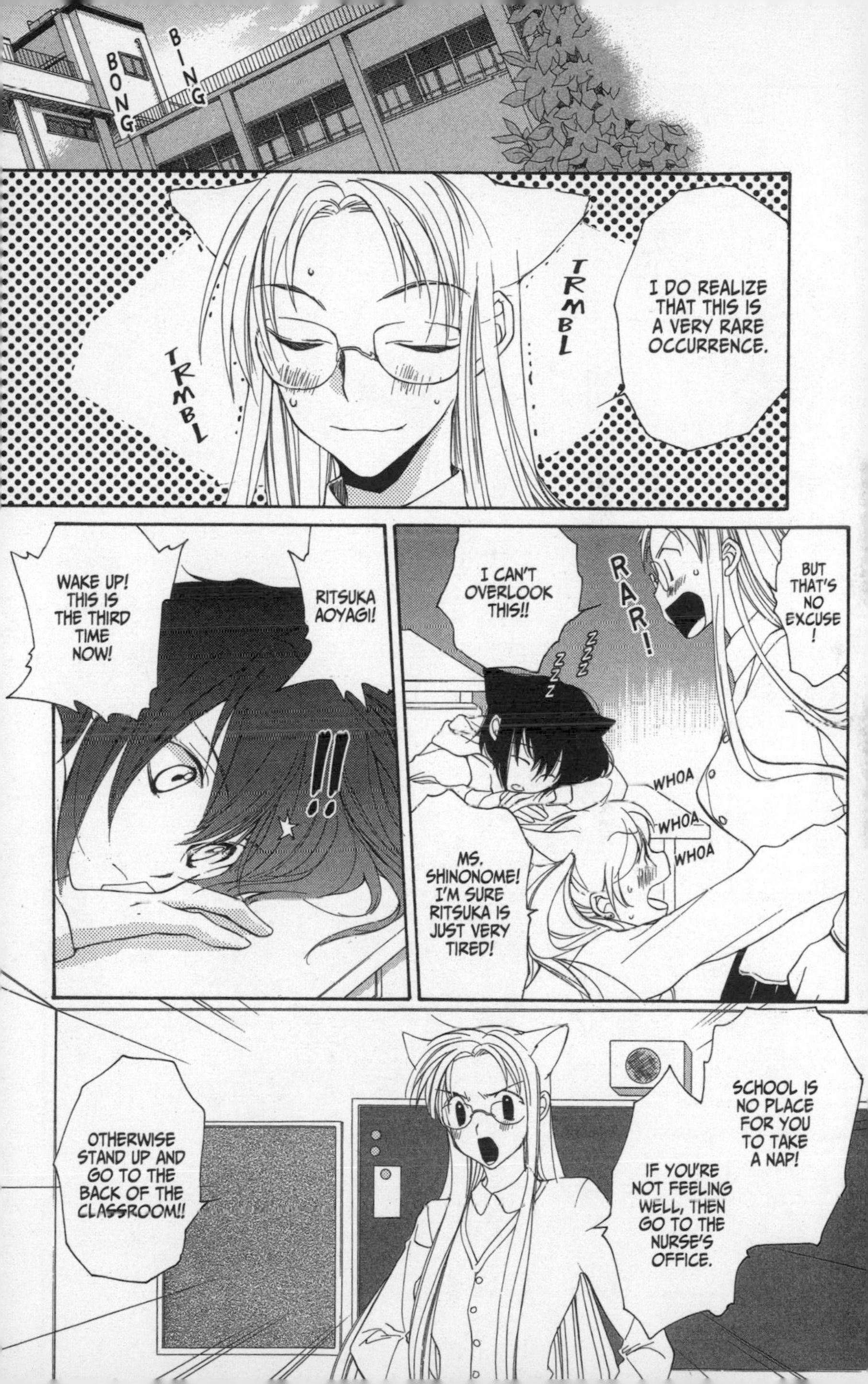
BING
BONG
TRMBL
I DO REALIZE THAT THIS IS A VERY RARE OCCURRENCE.
TRMBL
BUT THAT'S NO EXCUSE!
RARI!
I CAN'T OVERLOOK THIS!!
ZZZ
WHOA
WHOA
WHOA
MS. SHINONOME! I'M SURE RITSUKA IS JUST VERY TIRED!
RITSUKA AOYAGI!
WAKE UP! THIS IS THE THIRD TIME NOW!
!!
SCHOOL IS NO PLACE FOR YOU TO TAKE A NAP!
IF YOU'RE NOT FEELING WELL, THEN GO TO THE NURSE'S OFFICE.
OTHERWISE STAND UP AND GO TO THE BACK OF THE CLASSROOM!!

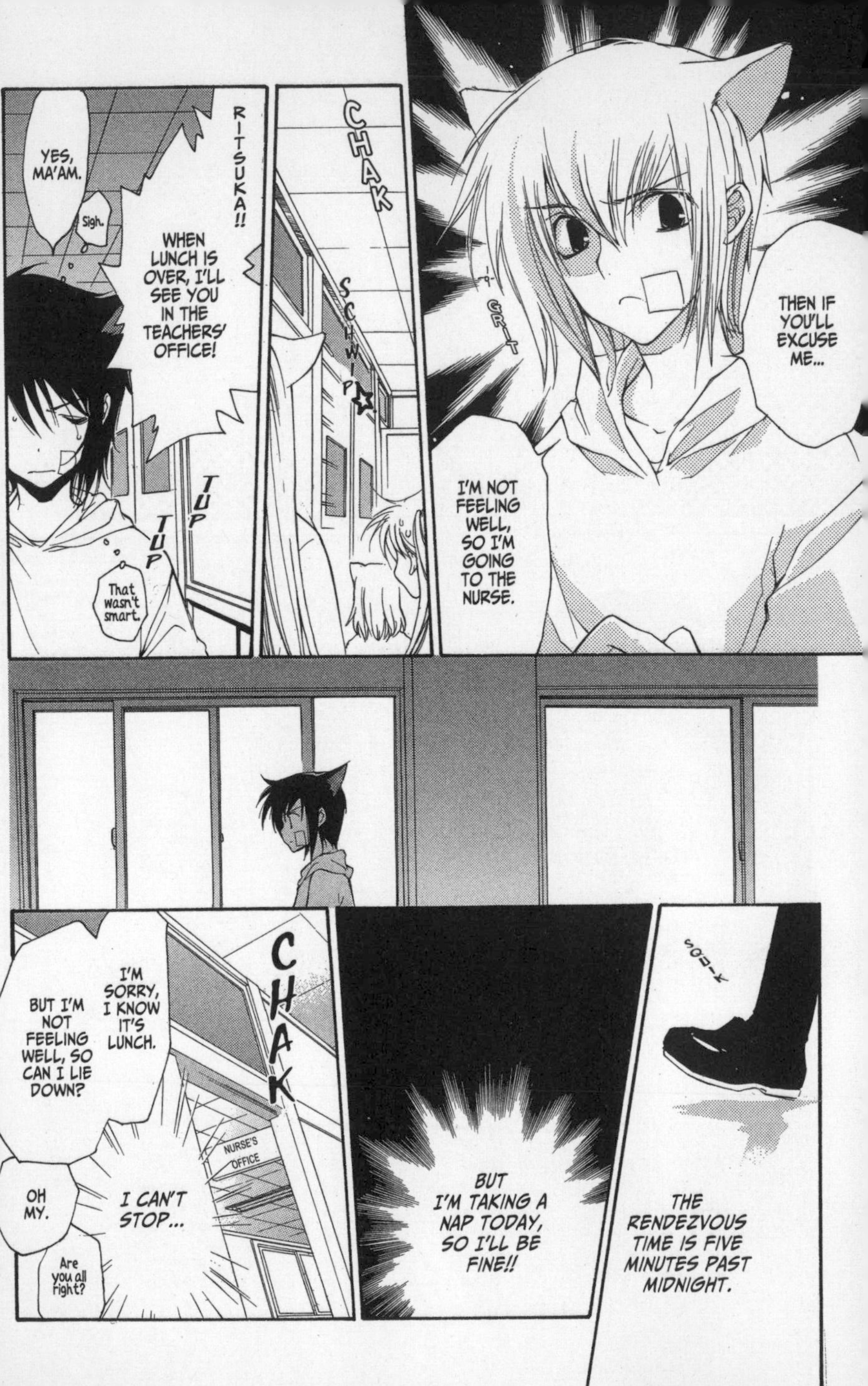
THEN IF YOU'LL EXCUSE ME...
GRIT
I'M NOT FEELING WELL, SO I'M GOING TO THE NURSE.
CHAK
SCHWIP☆
RITSUKA!!
WHEN LUNCH IS OVER, I'LL SEE YOU IN THE TEACHERS' OFFICE!
YES, MA'AM.
Sigh.
TUP TUP
That wasn't smart.
THE RENDEZVOUS TIME IS FIVE MINUTES PAST MIDNIGHT.
BUT I'M TAKING A NAP TODAY, SO I'LL BE FINE!!
CHAK
I'M SORRY, I KNOW IT'S LUNCH.
BUT I'M NOT FEELING WELL, SO CAN I LIE DOWN?
NURSE'S OFFICE
I CAN'T STOP...
OH MY.
Are you all right?

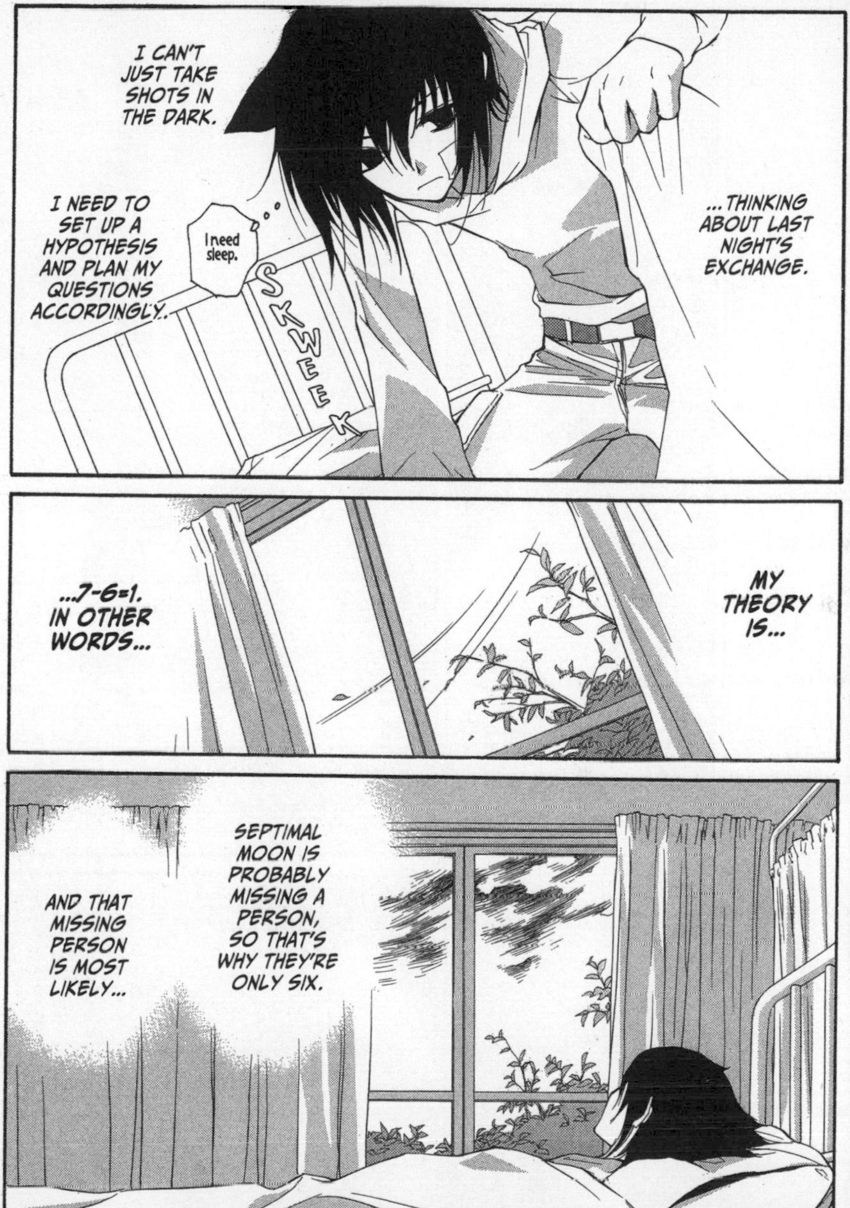
...THINKING ABOUT LAST NIGHT'S EXCHANGE.
I CAN'T JUST TAKE SHOTS IN THE DARK.
I NEED TO SET UP A HYPOTHESIS AND PLAN MY QUESTIONS ACCORDINGLY.
I need sleep.
SKWEEK
MY THEORY IS...
...7-6=1. IN OTHER WORDS...
SEPTIMAL MOON IS PROBABLY MISSING A PERSON, SO THAT'S WHY THEY'RE ONLY SIX.
AND THAT MISSING PERSON IS MOST LIKELY...

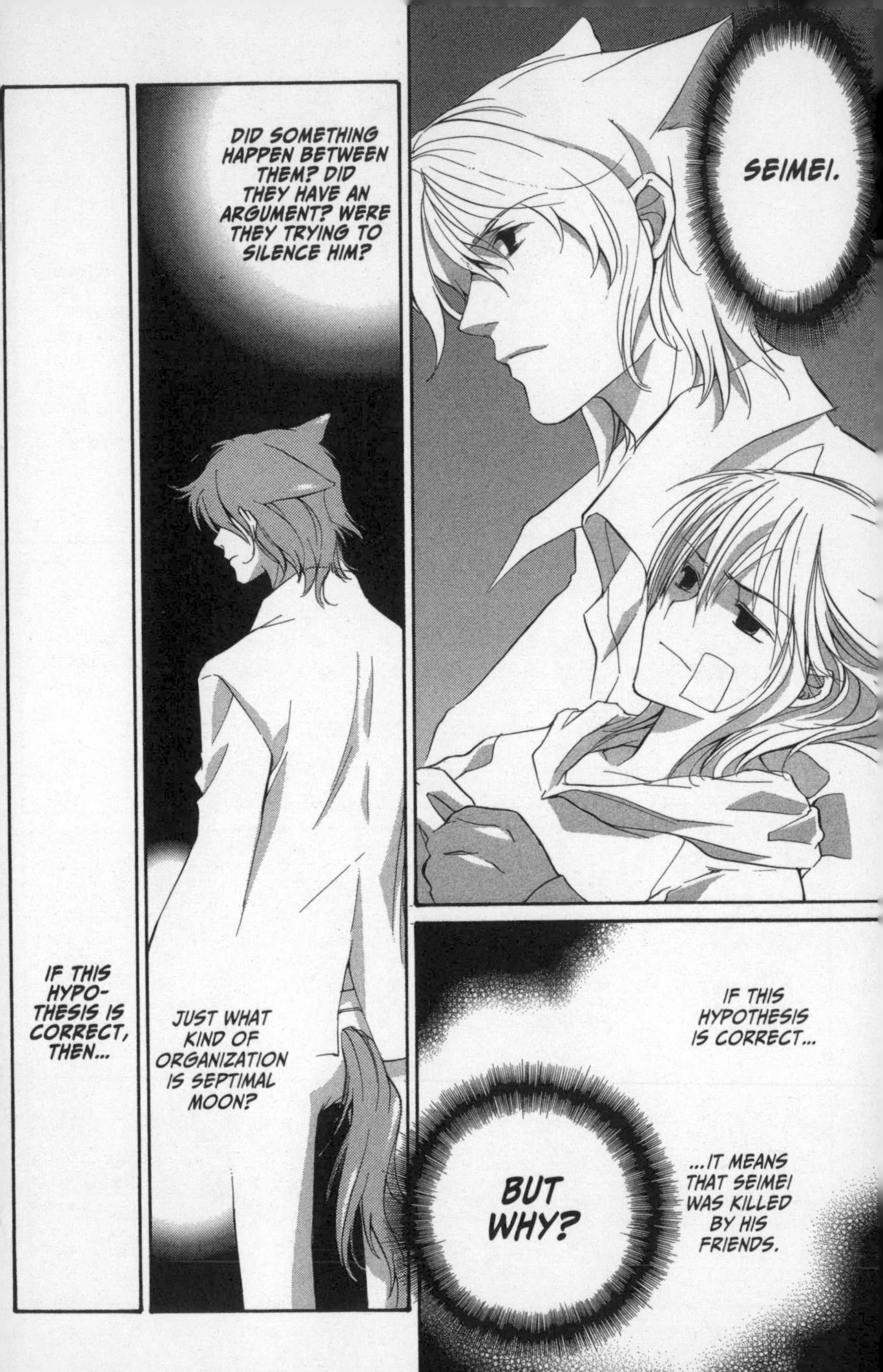
SEIMEI.
IF THIS HYPOTHESIS IS CORRECT...
...IT MEANS THAT SEIMEI WAS KILLED BY HIS FRIENDS.
BUT WHY?
DID SOMETHING HAPPEN BETWEEN THEM? DID THEY HAVE AN ARGUMENT? WERE THEY TRYING TO SILENCE HIM?
JUST WHAT KIND OF ORGANIZATION IS SEPTIMAL MOON?
IF THIS HYPOTHESIS IS CORRECT, THEN...

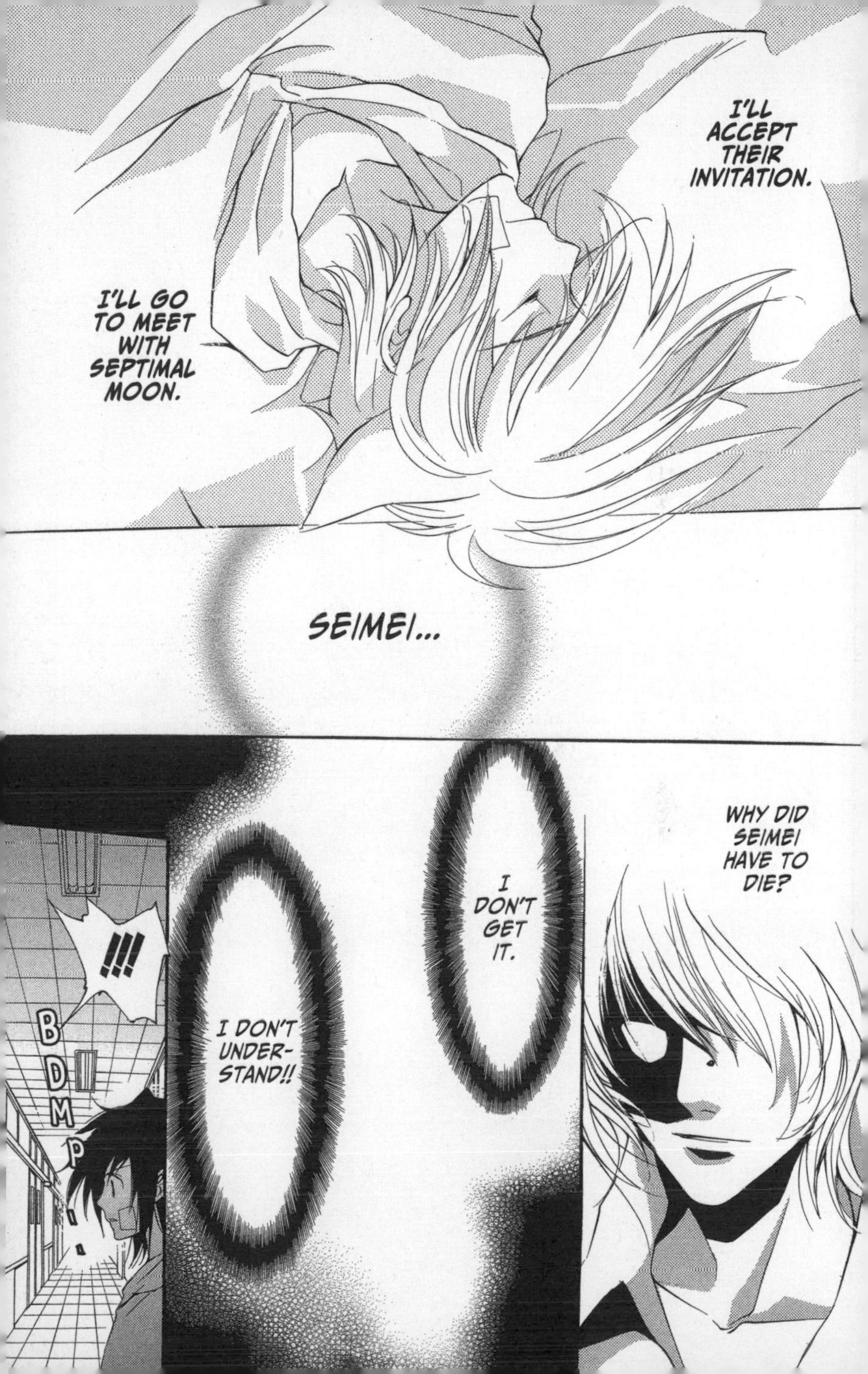
I'LL ACCEPT THEIR INVITATION.
I'LL GO TO MEET WITH SEPTIMAL MOON.
SEIMEI...
WHY DID SEIMEI HAVE TO DIE?
I DON'T GET IT.
I DON'T UNDER-STAND!!
!!!
BDMP

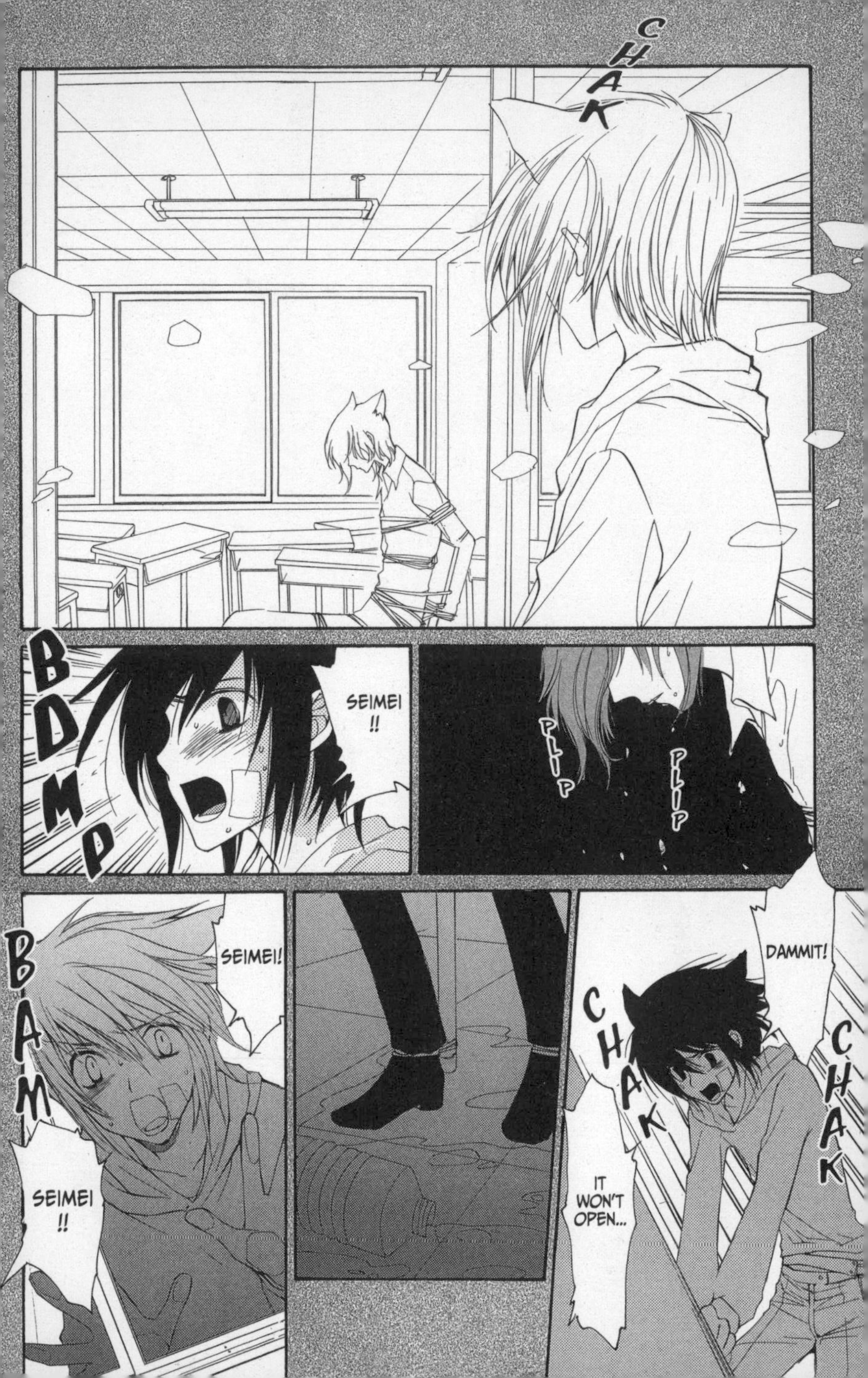
CHAK
PLIP
PLIP
SEIMEI !!
BDMP
DAMMIT!
CHAK
CHAK
IT WON'T OPEN...
SEIMEI!
BAM
SEIMEI !!

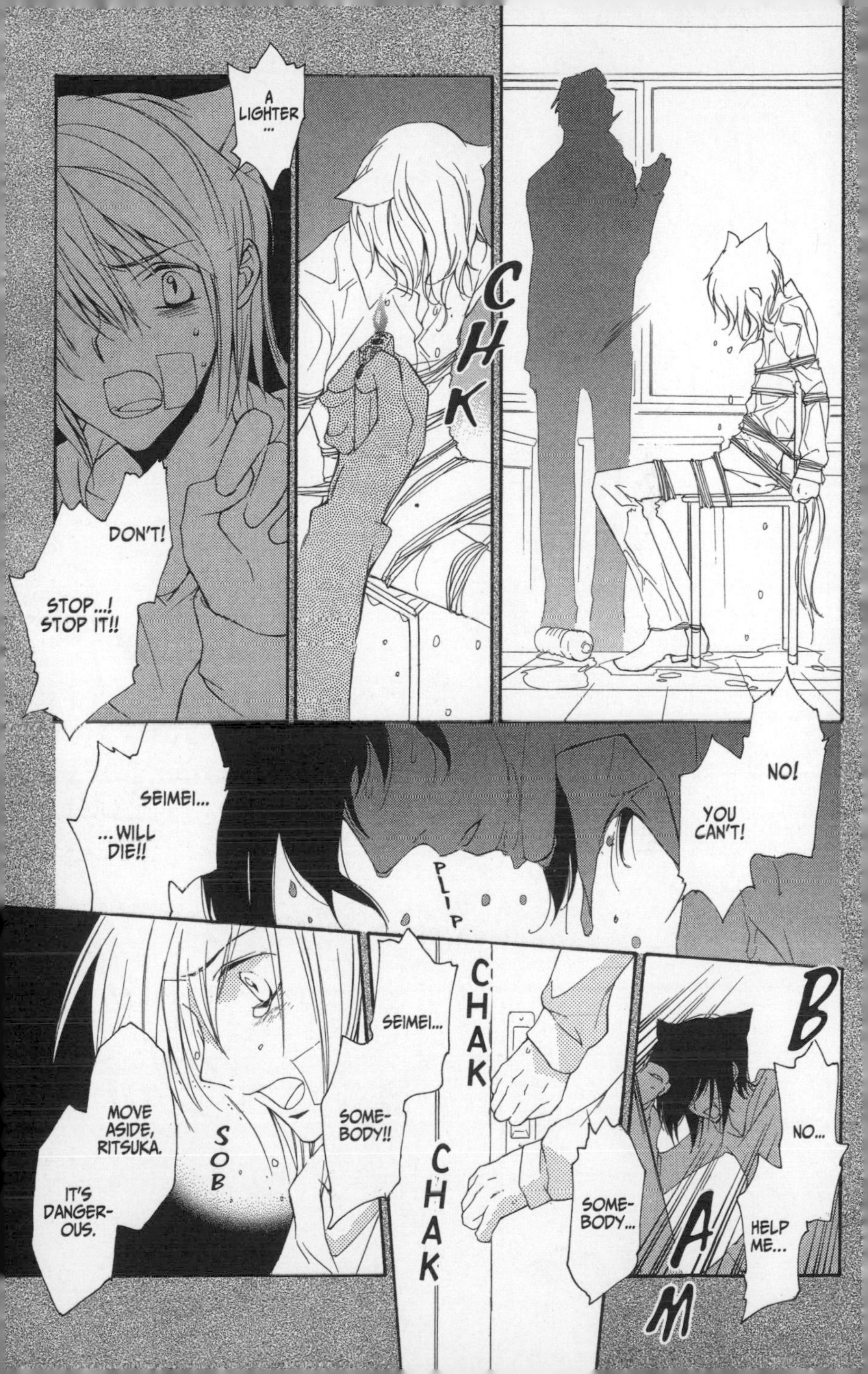
A LIGHTER...
CHK
DON'T!
STOP...! STOP IT!!
NO!
YOU CAN'T!
PLIP
SEIMEI...
...WILL DIE!!
BAM
NO...
HELP ME...
SOME-BODY...
SEIMEI...
CHAK
CHAK
SOME-BODY!!
MOVE ASIDE, RITSUKA.
IT'S DANGER-OUS.
SOB

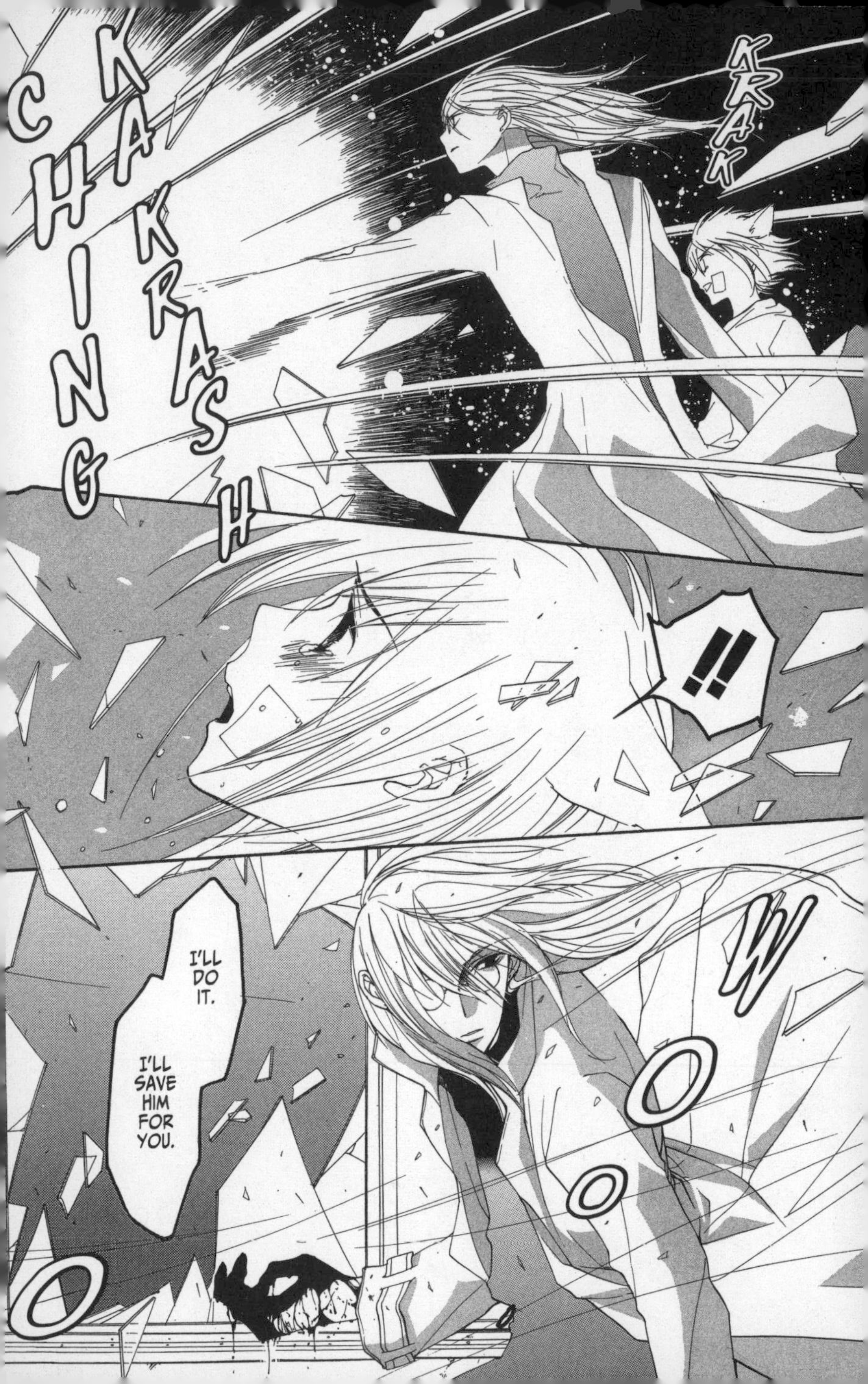
KRAK
KRAKRASH
CHAKKING
!!
WOOOO
I'LL DO IT.
I'LL SAVE HIM FOR YOU.

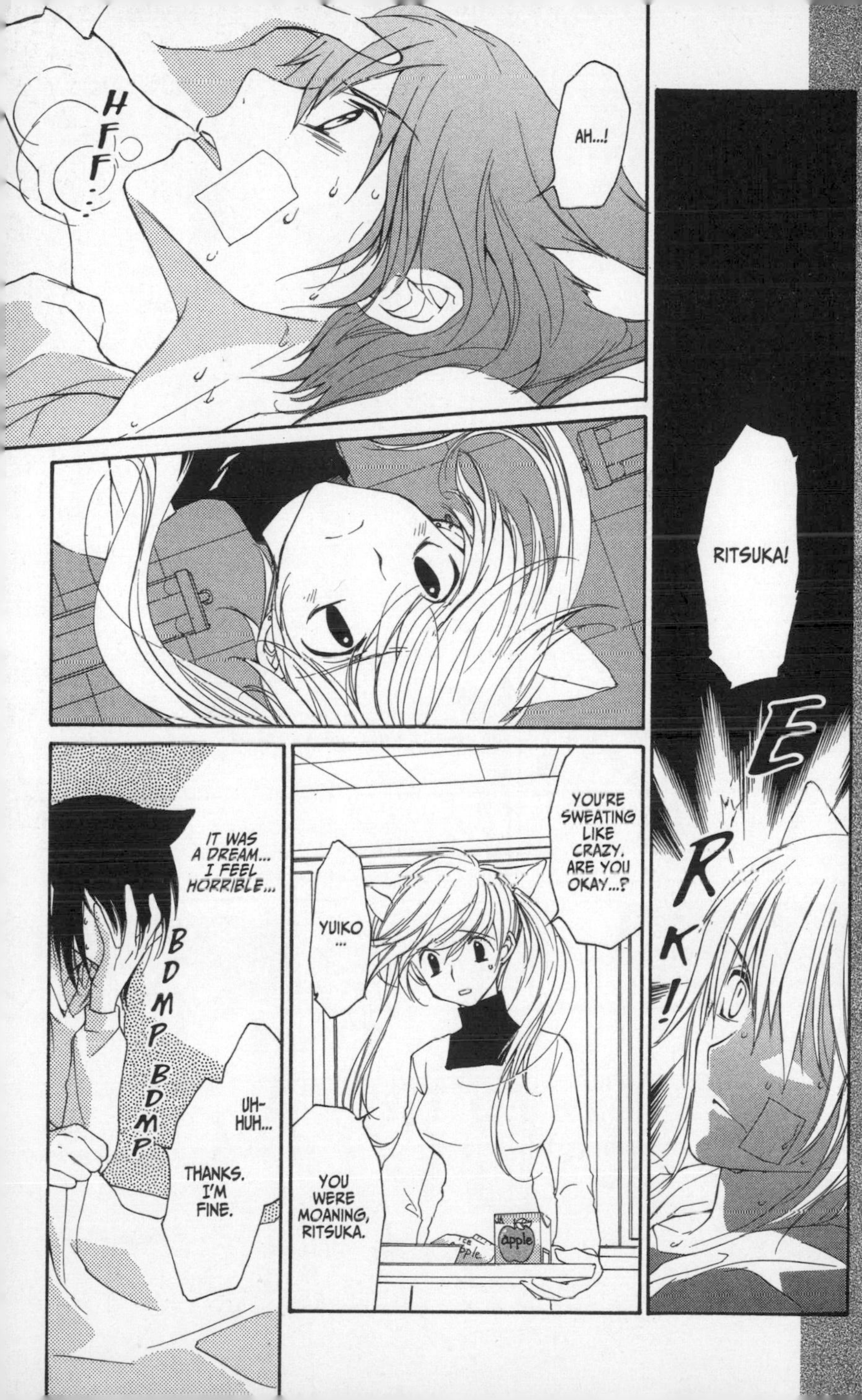
AH...!
HFF...
RITSUKA!
ERK!
YOU'RE SWEATING LIKE CRAZY. ARE YOU OKAY...?
YUIKO...
YOU WERE MOANING, RITSUKA.
apple
IT WAS A DREAM... I FEEL HORRIBLE...
BDMP BDMP
UH-HUH...
THANKS. I'M FINE.

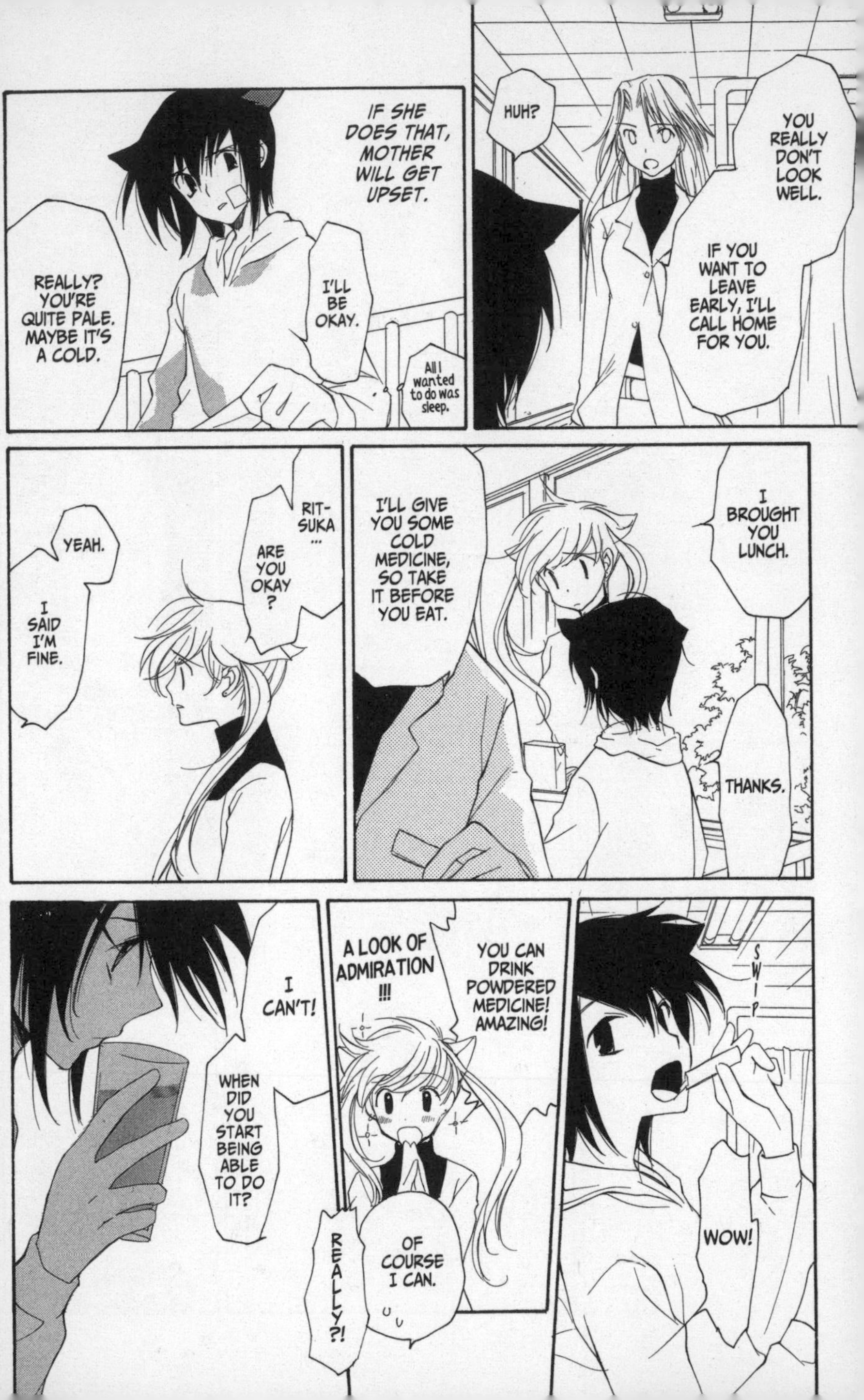
YOU REALLY DON'T LOOK WELL.
HUH?
IF YOU WANT TO LEAVE EARLY, I'LL CALL HOME FOR YOU.
IF SHE DOES THAT, MOTHER WILL GET UPSET.
I'LL BE OKAY.
REALLY? YOU'RE QUITE PALE. MAYBE IT'S A COLD.
All I wanted to do was sleep.
I BROUGHT YOU LUNCH.
I'LL GIVE YOU SOME COLD MEDICINE, SO TAKE IT BEFORE YOU EAT.
THANKS.
RIT-SUKA...
ARE YOU OKAY?
YEAH.
I SAID I'M FINE.
SWIP
WOW!
YOU CAN DRINK POWDERED MEDICINE! AMAZING!
A LOOK OF ADMIRATION!!!
OF COURSE I CAN.
REALLY?!
I CAN'T!
WHEN DID YOU START BEING ABLE TO DO IT?

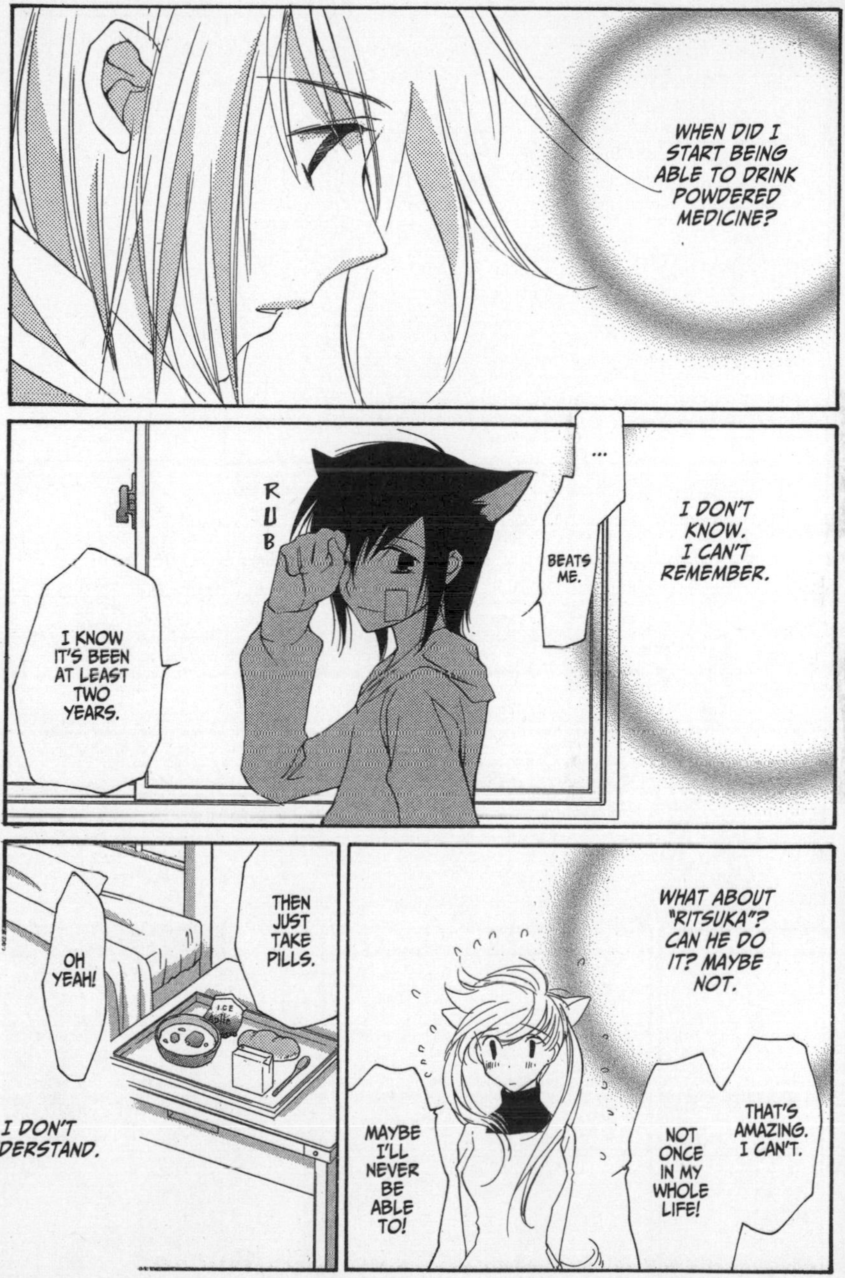
WHEN DID I START BEING ABLE TO DRINK POWDERED MEDICINE?
...
I DON'T KNOW. I CAN'T REMEMBER.
BEATS ME.
RUB
I KNOW IT'S BEEN AT LEAST TWO YEARS.
WHAT ABOUT "RITSUKA"? CAN HE DO IT? MAYBE NOT.
THAT'S AMAZING. I CAN'T.
NOT ONCE IN MY WHOLE LIFE!
MAYBE I'LL NEVER BE ABLE TO!
THEN JUST TAKE PILLS.
OH YEAH!
I DON'T UNDERSTAND.

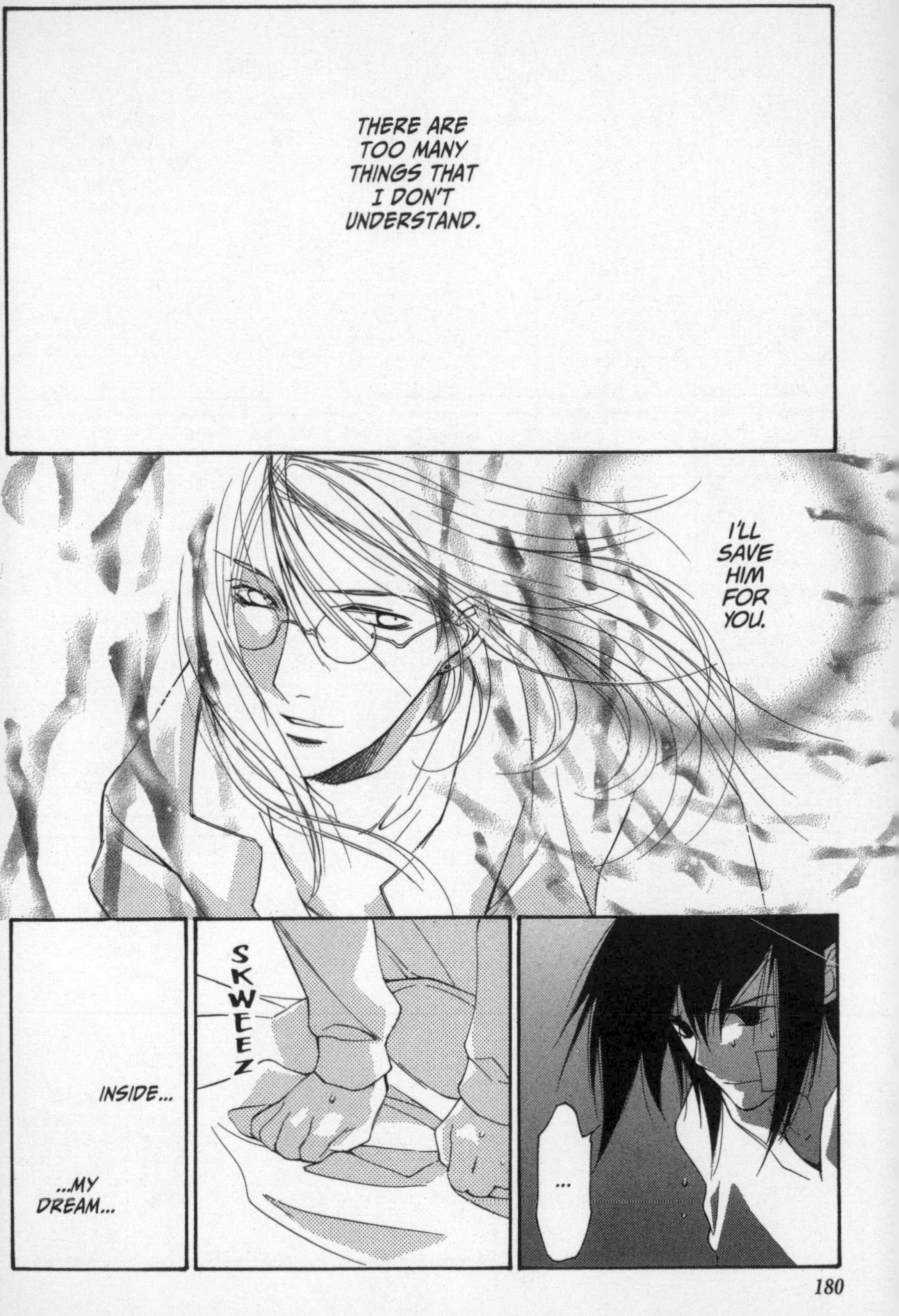
THERE ARE TOO MANY THINGS THAT I DON'T UNDERSTAND.
I'LL SAVE HIM FOR YOU.
...
SKWEEZ
INSIDE...
...MY DREAM...

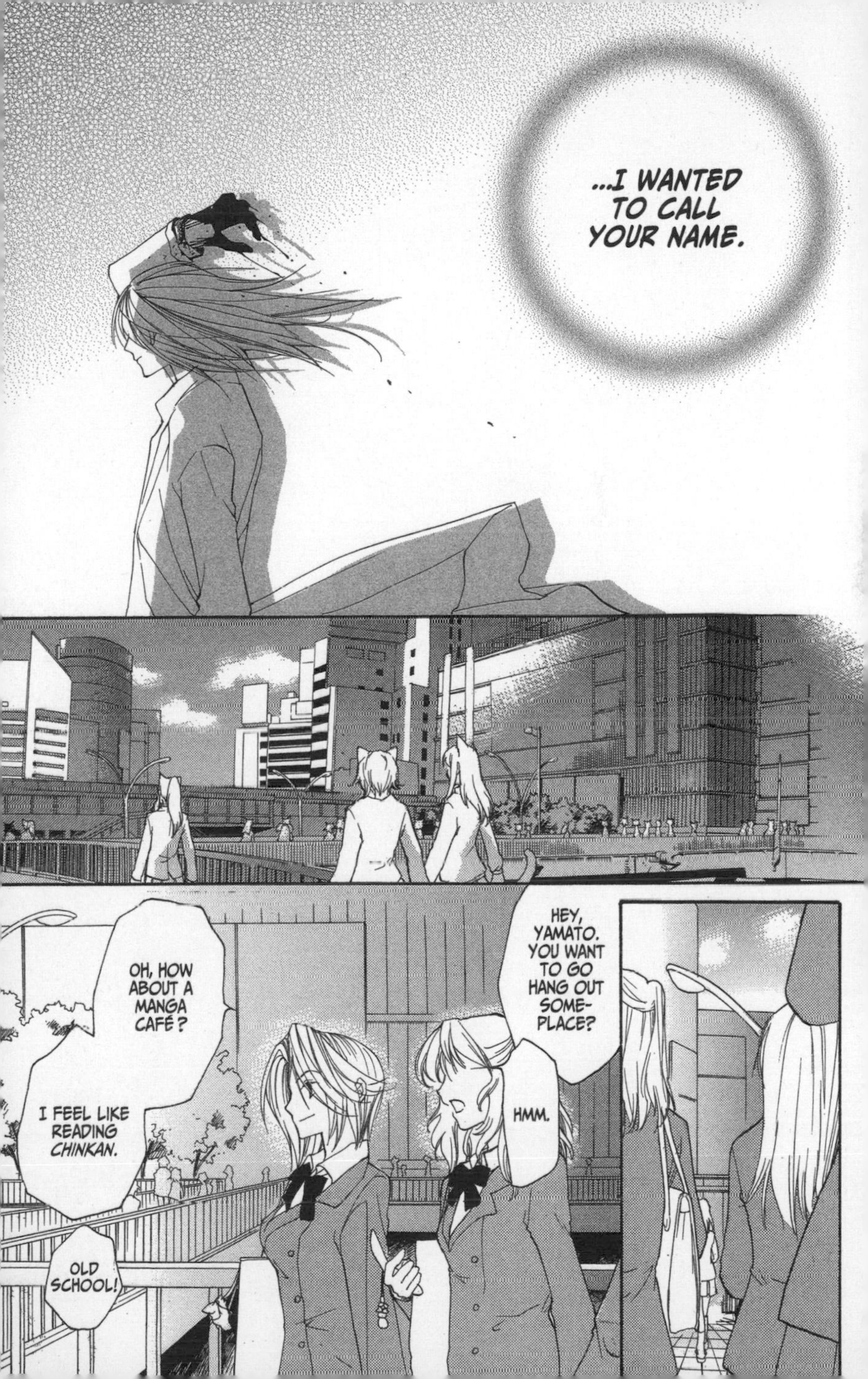
...I WANTED TO CALL YOUR NAME.
HEY, YAMATO. YOU WANT TO GO HANG OUT SOME-PLACE?
HMM.
OH, HOW ABOUT A MANGA CAFÉ?
I FEEL LIKE READING CHINKAN.
OLD SCHOOL!

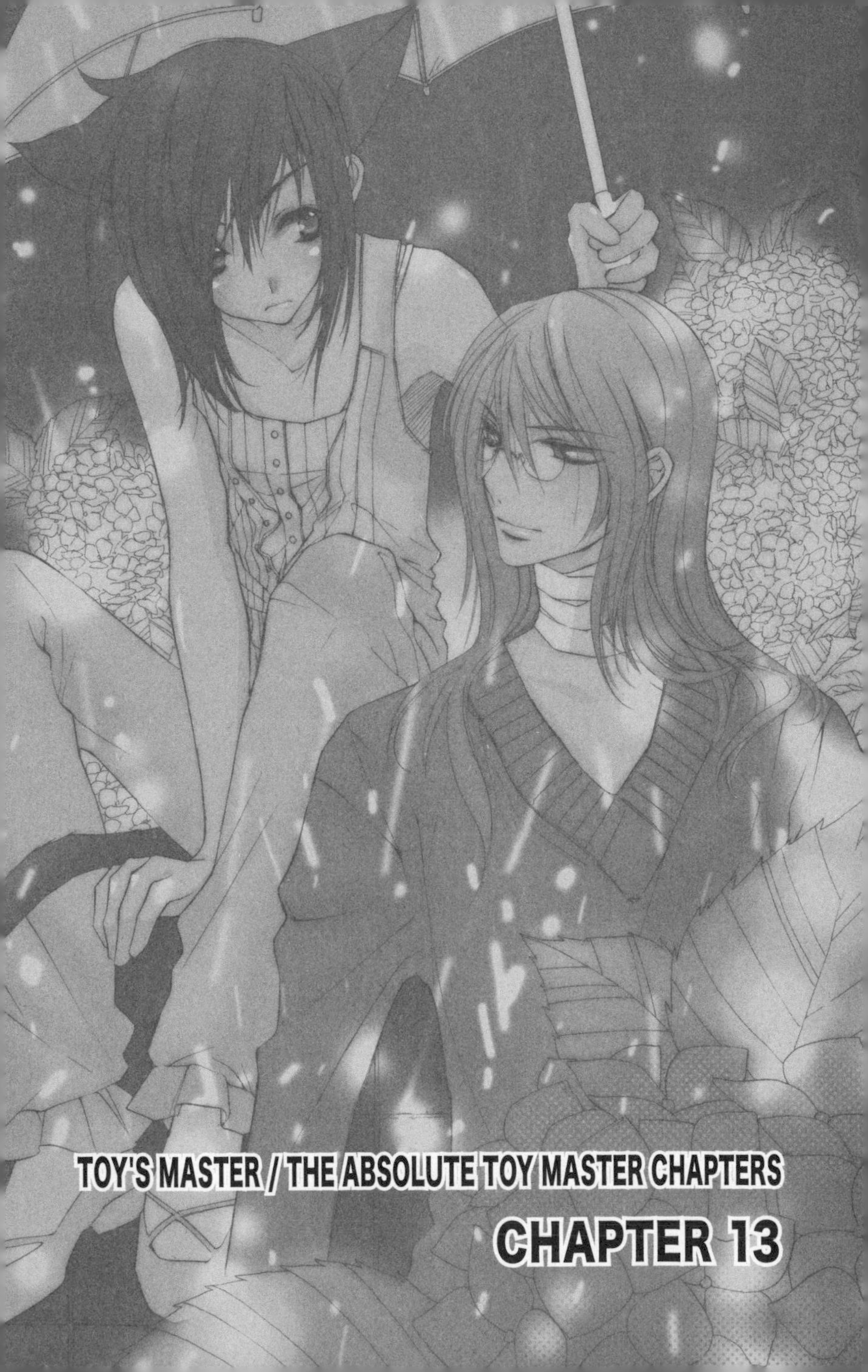
TOY'S MASTER // THE ABSOLUTE TOY MASTER CHAPTERS
CHAPTER 13

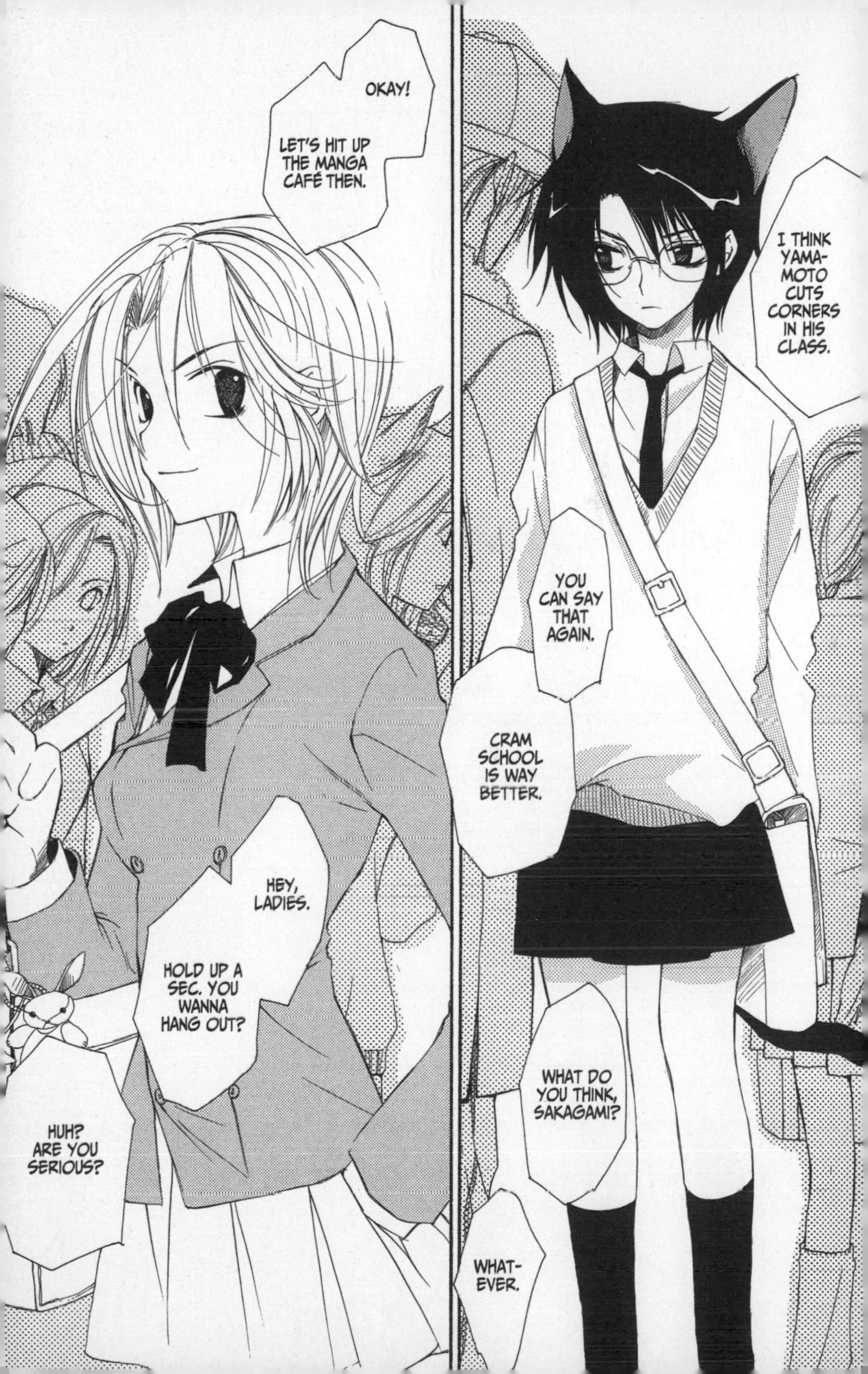
I THINK YAMA-MOTO CUTS CORNERS IN HIS CLASS.
YOU CAN SAY THAT AGAIN.
CRAM SCHOOL IS WAY BETTER.
WHAT DO YOU THINK, SAKAGAMI?
WHAT-EVER.
OKAY!
LET'S HIT UP THE MANGA CAFÉ THEN.
HEY, LADIES.
HOLD UP A SEC. YOU WANNA HANG OUT?
HUH? ARE YOU SERIOUS?

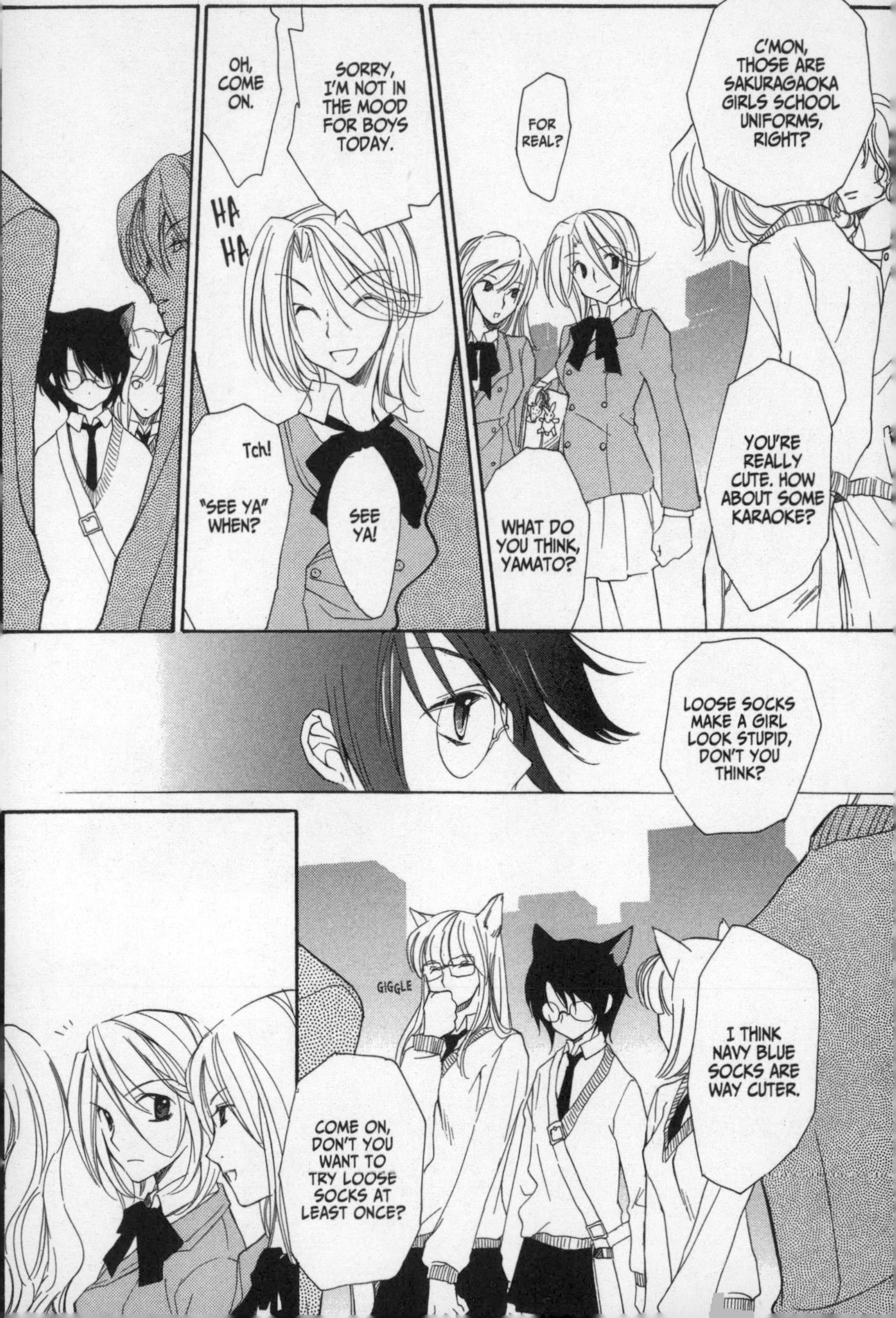
C'MON, THOSE ARE SAKURAGAOKA GIRLS SCHOOL UNIFORMS, RIGHT?
YOU'RE REALLY CUTE. HOW ABOUT SOME KARAOKE?
FOR REAL?
WHAT DO YOU THINK, YAMATO?
SORRY, I'M NOT IN THE MOOD FOR BOYS TODAY.
OH, COME ON.
HA HA
SEE YA!
Tch!
"SEE YA" WHEN?
LOOSE SOCKS MAKE A GIRL LOOK STUPID, DON'T YOU THINK?
I THINK NAVY BLUE SOCKS ARE WAY CUTER.
GIGGLE
COME ON, DON'T YOU WANT TO TRY LOOSE SOCKS AT LEAST ONCE?

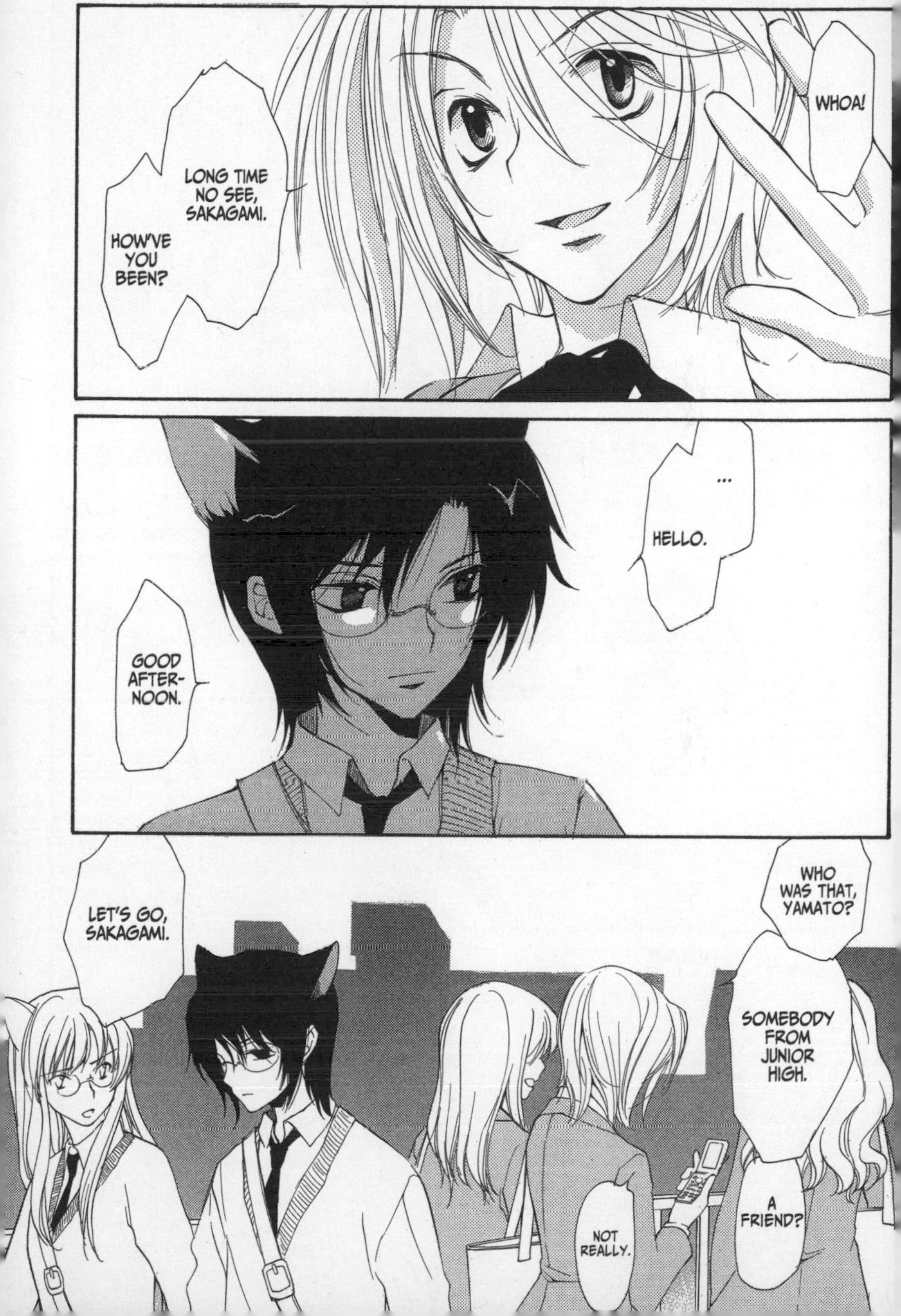
WHOA!
LONG TIME NO SEE, SAKAGAMI.
HOW'VE YOU BEEN?
...
HELLO.
GOOD AFTER-NOON.
WHO WAS THAT, YAMATO?
SOMEBODY FROM JUNIOR HIGH.
A FRIEND?
NOT REALLY.
LET'S GO, SAKAGAMI.

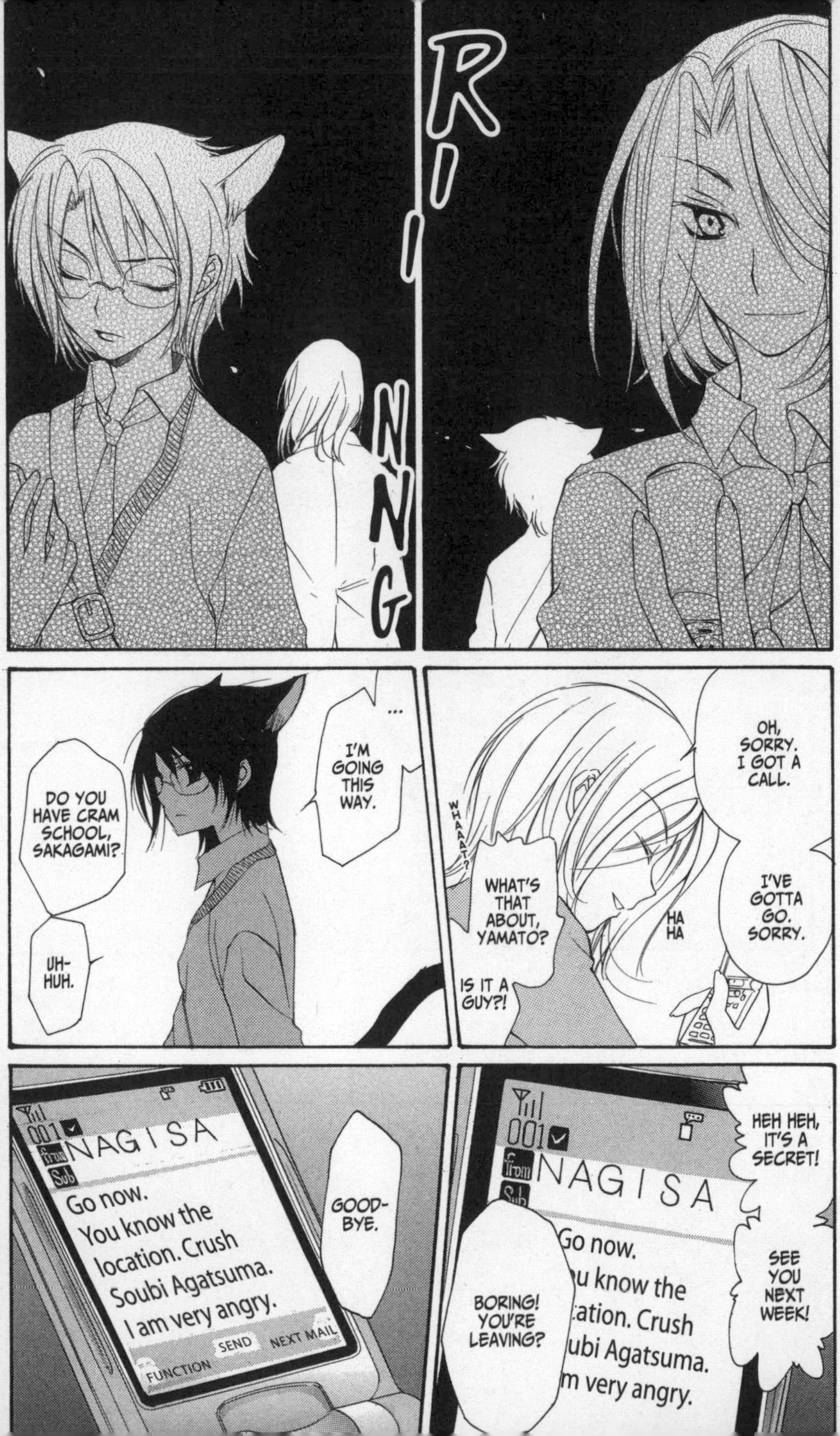
RIIINNNG
OH, SORRY. I GOT A CALL.
I'VE GOTTA GO. SORRY.
HA HA
WHAAAAT?
WHAT'S THAT ABOUT, YAMATO?
IS IT A GUY?!
...
I'M GOING THIS WAY.
DO YOU HAVE CRAM SCHOOL, SAKAGAMI?
UH-HUH.
HEH HEH, IT'S A SECRET!
SEE YOU NEXT WEEK!
001
From NAGISA
Sub
Go now.
u know the
cation. Crush
ubi Agatsuma.
m very angry.
BORING! YOU'RE LEAVING?
GOOD-BYE.
001
From NAGISA
Sub
Go now.
You know the location. Crush Soubi Agatsuma.
I am very angry.
SEND
NEXT MAIL
FUNCTION

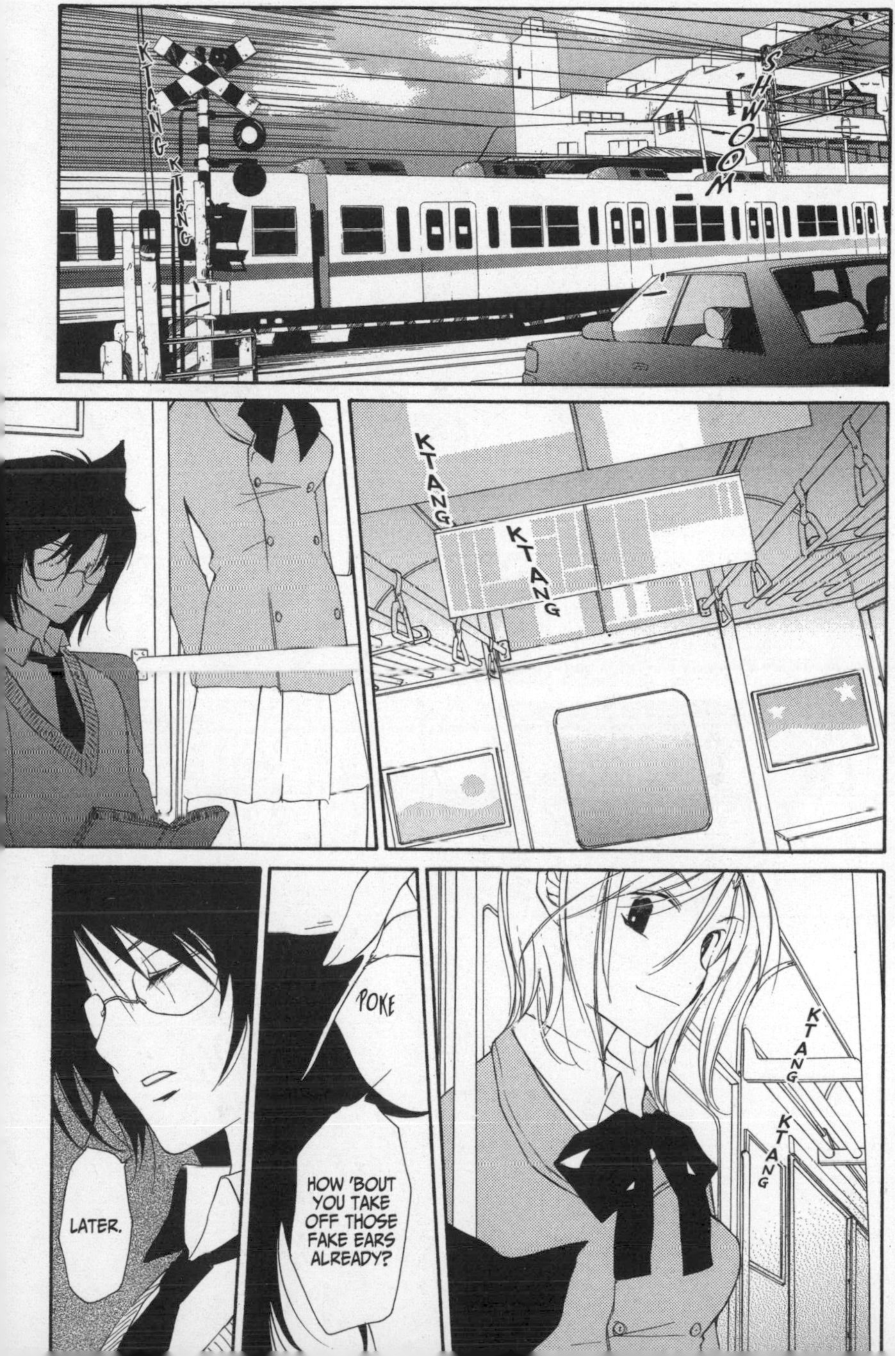
SHWOOM
KTANG
KTANG
KTANG
KTANG
KTANG
KTANG
POKE
HOW 'BOUT YOU TAKE OFF THOSE FAKE EARS ALREADY?
LATER.

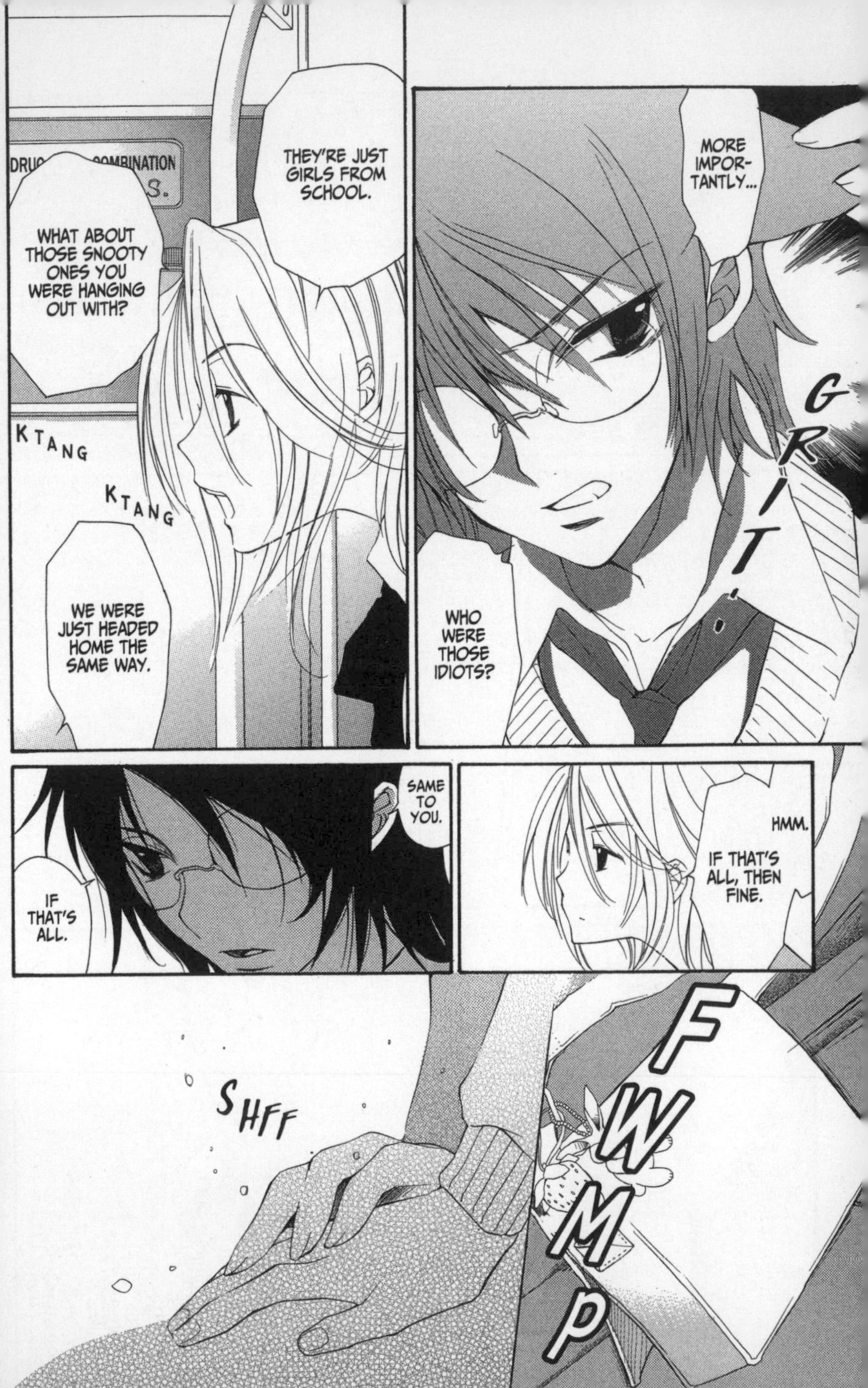
MORE IMPORTANTLY...
GRIT!
WHO WERE THOSE IDIOTS?
THEY'RE JUST GIRLS FROM SCHOOL.
WHAT ABOUT THOSE SNOOTY ONES YOU WERE HANGING OUT WITH?
KTANG
KTANG
WE WERE JUST HEADED HOME THE SAME WAY.
HMM.
IF THAT'S ALL, THEN FINE.
SAME TO YOU.
IF THAT'S ALL.
FWMP
SHFF

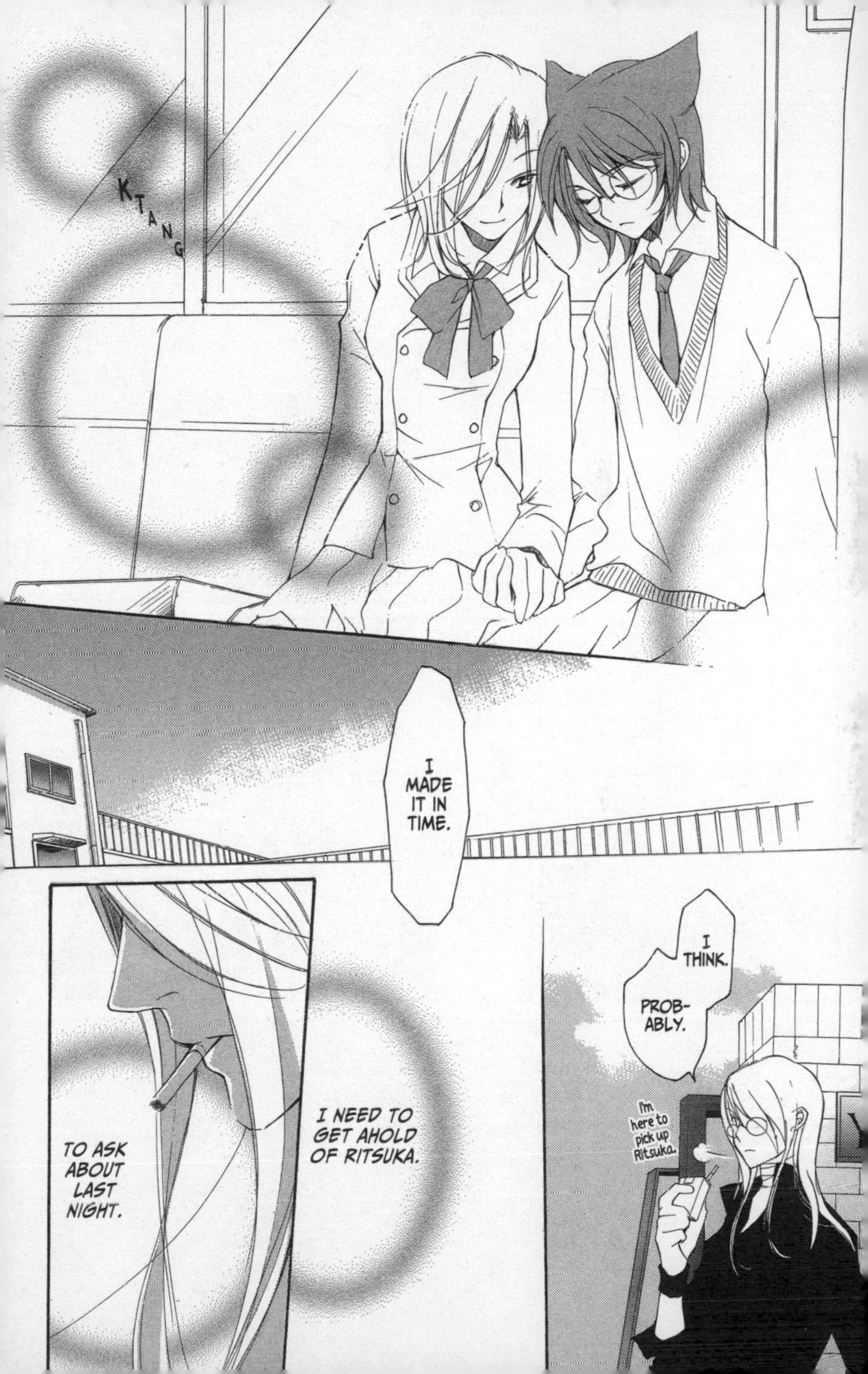
KTANG
I MADE IT IN TIME.
I THINK.
PROBABLY.
I'm here to pick up Ritsuka.
I NEED TO GET AHOLD OF RITSUKA.
TO ASK ABOUT LAST NIGHT.

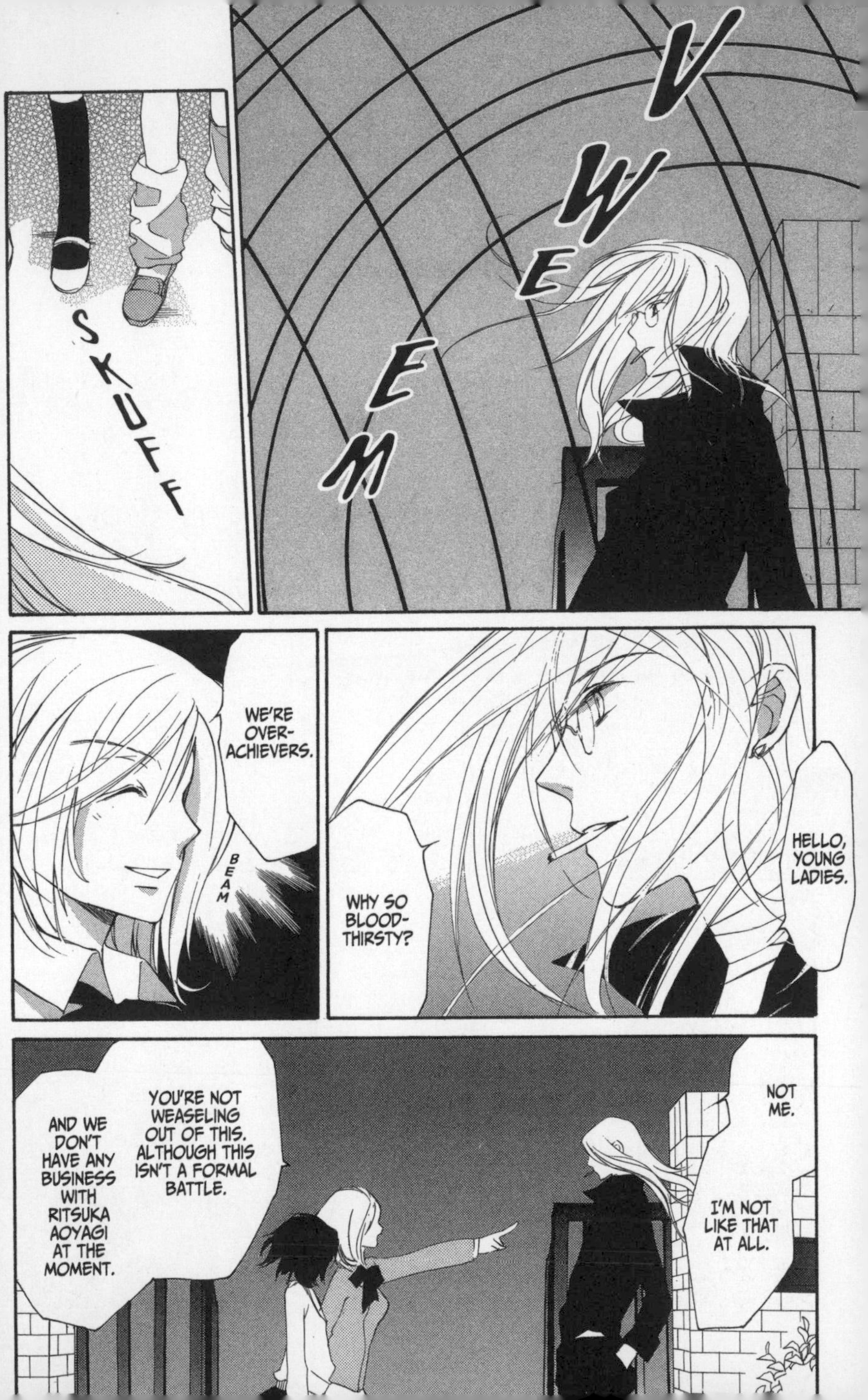
VWEEM
SKUFF
HELLO, YOUNG LADIES.
WHY SO BLOOD-THIRSTY?
WE'RE OVER-ACHIEVERS.
BEAM
NOT ME.
I'M NOT LIKE THAT AT ALL.
YOU'RE NOT WEASELING OUT OF THIS. ALTHOUGH THIS ISN'T A FORMAL BATTLE.
AND WE DON'T HAVE ANY BUSINESS WITH RITSUKA AOYAGI AT THE MOMENT.

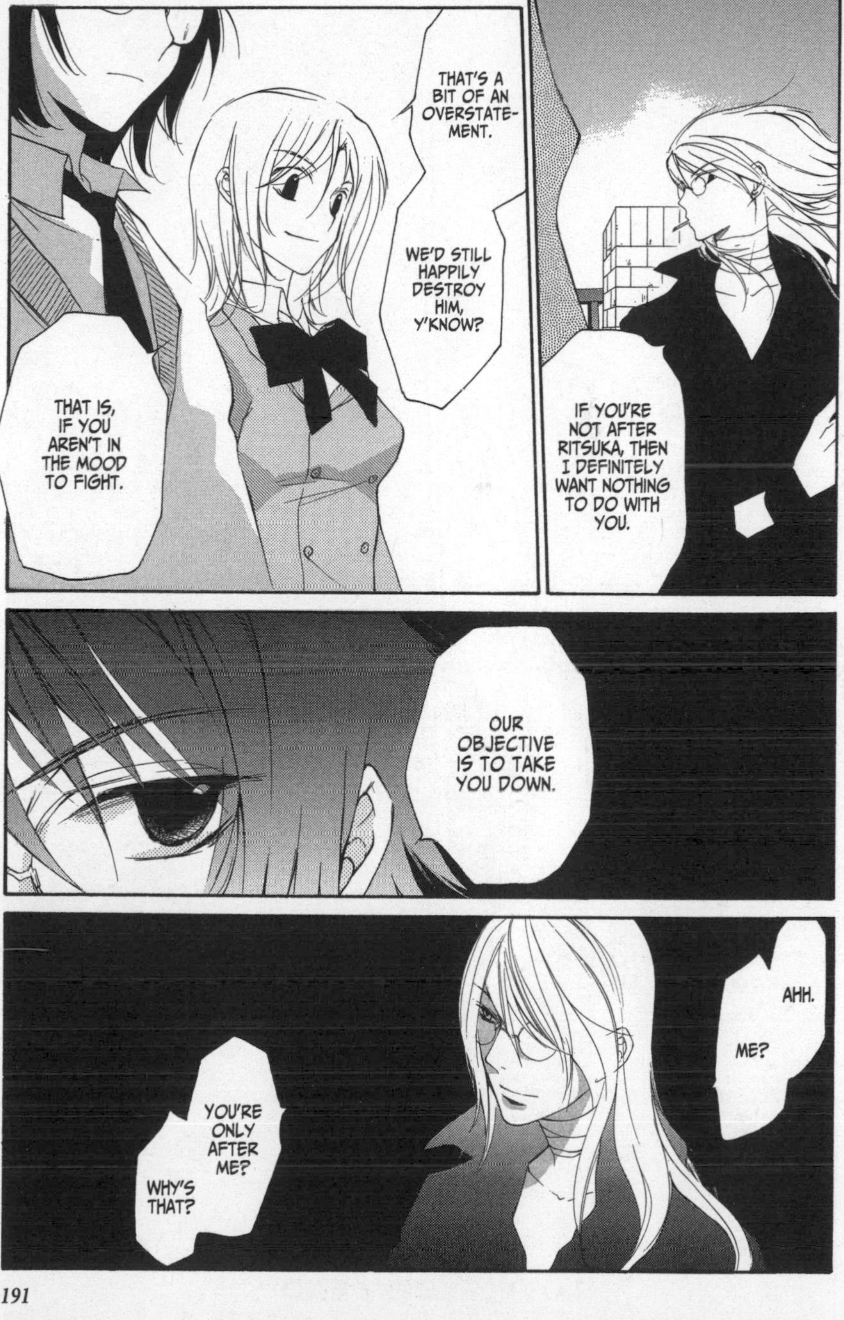
IF YOU'RE NOT AFTER RITSUKA, THEN I DEFINITELY WANT NOTHING TO DO WITH YOU.
THAT'S A BIT OF AN OVERSTATE-MENT.
WE'D STILL HAPPILY DESTROY HIM, Y'KNOW?
THAT IS, IF YOU AREN'T IN THE MOOD TO FIGHT.
OUR OBJECTIVE IS TO TAKE YOU DOWN.
AHH.
ME?
YOU'RE ONLY AFTER ME?
WHY'S THAT?

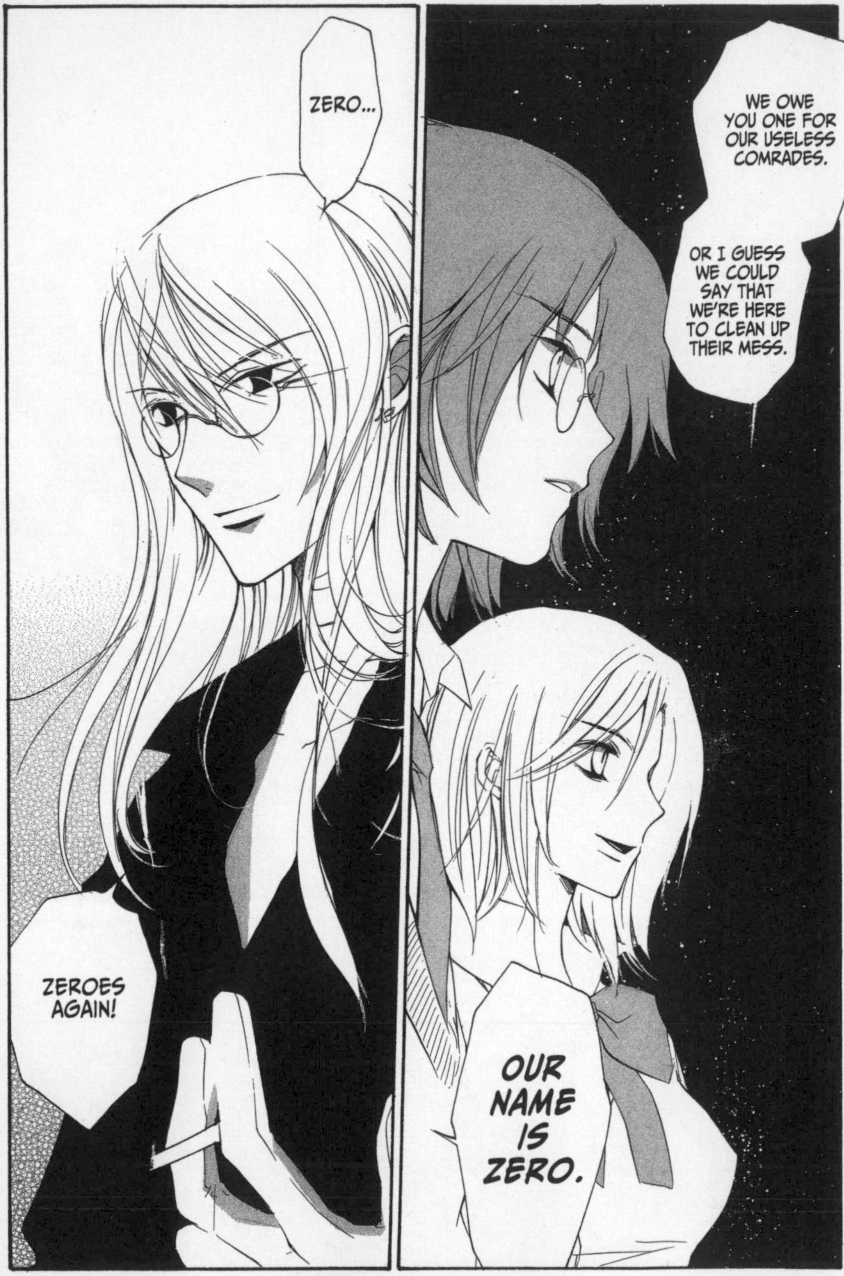
WE OWE YOU ONE FOR OUR USELESS COMRADES.
OR I GUESS WE COULD SAY THAT WE'RE HERE TO CLEAN UP THEIR MESS.
OUR NAME IS ZERO.
ZERO...
ZEROES AGAIN!

LOVELESS 3 / END

I love Hanazono *manju*, said to be the most expensive manju in Japan. (Dare I doubt this and ruin their reputation?) Since *Zero-Sum*'s editorial office is in Shinjuku, my editor often brings me manju from Hanazono as a present! I scarf them down without giving much thought to the fact that 30 pieces cost 10,000 yen! What's with me, eating all of them in only two days?! And by the way, Hanazono manju only show their true value after three days! You rarely find manju that still taste good after three days! Yup.

—*Yun Kouga, 2003*

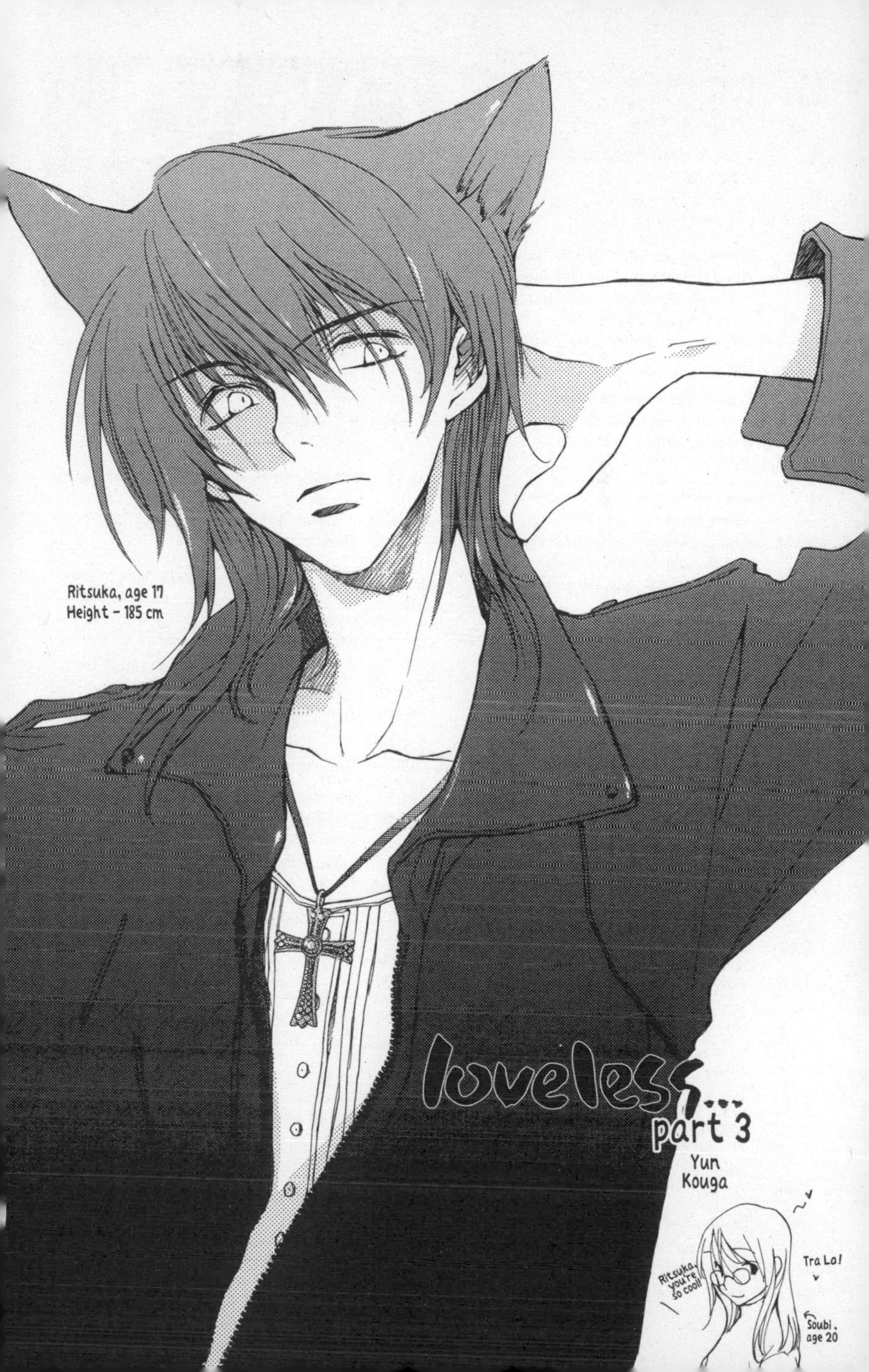
loveless...
part 3
Yun
Kouga
Ritsuka, age 17
Height - 185 cm
Tra La!
Ritsuka, you're so cool!
Soubi. age 20

Q&A with Soubi and Ritsuka!

1: Describe your family.
Soubi: I'm alone.
Ritsuka: It's just my parents and myself. I had an older brother but he died.

2: How would you describe your personality, in a word?
Soubi: Irresponsible.
Ritsuka: Serious.

3: What's the most expensive thing in your room?
Soubi: If it's something I bought, it would be the refrigerator. If it's something I received, then it would be a watch.
Ritsuka: My computer.

4: Do you go for tans? Or prefer pale skin?
Soubi: Neither. I go natural.
Ritsuka: I don't care. I like the sun.

5: Ever done any part-time jobs?
Soubi: I've been an art teacher and a layout artist at a design studio; I've done traffic surveys, delivery services, etc.
Ritsuka: Nope.

6: What kind of computer do you use?
Soubi: A Sony VAIO.
Ritsuka: A Macintosh G4.

7: How many piercings do you have?
Soubi: Two...oh, three.
Ritsuka: Zero.

8: How long do you spend in the bath? What part of your body do you wash first?
Soubi: About 30 minutes. I start with my left arm.
Ritsuka: About 25 minutes, and I start by washing my hair.

9: Do you smoke?
Soubi: About a pack a day of Seven Stars.
Ritsuka: I don't smoke. And I don't think I'll smoke when I grow up either.

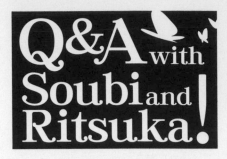

10: Are you fast at typing on your phone?
Soubi: I think I'm average.
Ritsuka: I'm probably fast.

11: What do you want to be when you grow up?
Soubi: I'm already grown up.
Ritsuka: I haven't thought about it.

12: Where do you usually spend time?
Soubi: Aside from things involving Ritsuka, I'm at the art supply store, and around Ikebukuro and Akihabara.
Ritsuka: School, sometimes Yuiko's house or the river.

13: What is your favorite flower?
Soubi: I like all flowers, but if I had to pick one it would be the Casablanca lily.
Ritsuka: Tulips.

14: Are you the humanities type or the science type?
Soubi: A science type among the humanities.
Ritsuka: I'm probably a humanities type, but I'm thinking of going to a science-focused middle school...

15: Are you the indoor type or outdoor type?
Soubi: I'm the indoor type.
Ritsuka: I'm an indoor type but I like being outside too.

16: Please tell us your gaming history.
Soubi: About 15 years?
Ritsuka: These past two years I've mainly played the PS2, X-Box and online PC games. I don't really play too many portable games.

17: If you were reborn, would you want to remain yourself?
Soubi: Not at all.
Ritsuka: I pass.

18: Where do you buy your food?
Soubi: The supermarket next to the train station (open until 11 PM).
Ritsuka: I don't. I buy my snacks at the convenience store.

19: Are you a *Shonen Jump* fan? A *Shonen Magazine* fan? Or *Shonen Sunday*?
Soubi: All of them. I borrow whatever Kio is reading.
Ritsuka: *Jump*!!

20: How much do you have in your wallet right now?
Soubi: I think about 20,000 yen.
Ritsuka: About 1,200 yen.

Ritsuka: Seimei Aoyagi. If not, then the person who killed Seimei.

34: Could you secretly tell me how much money you have saved up?
Soubi: A bit. Maybe about 10,000,000 yen?
Ritsuka: Sorry, I can't tell you.

35: Do you have any dreams?
Soubi: Hmmm...
Ritsuka: I don't really know.

36: Do you want power?
Soubi: I want it.
Ritsuka: Yes.

37: If you have any special skills or qualifications please tell us about them.
Soubi: I don't in particular. I have a driver's license that I got when I was 18, though.
Ritsuka: None. I have a Class 4 English rating, though.

38: Is there any food you're good at cooking?
Soubi: Japanese food. I like home-cooked meals.
Ritsuka: Nothing! Nope! None at all!!

39: When was the last time you cried and why?
Soubi: I don't cry.
Ritsuka: When I had a scary dream, because I was frightened.

40: At what point do you think you could kill a person?
Soubi: If I am ordered to kill.
Ritsuka: If someone important to me was killed. But I probably wouldn't be able to do it.

Likes&Dislikes

1: What is your favorite fast food?
Soubi: I don't really like fast food. But if I had to choose, I would say Mos Burger.
Ritsuka: McDonald's.

2: What is your favorite kind of music?
Soubi: Like, Enigma?
Ritsuka: Asuka Hayashi.

3: What's your favorite part of a cat?
Soubi: The fur?
Ritsuka: The ears and tail.

4: What kind of alcohol do you like?
Soubi: Beer (especially Asahi Super Dry)
Ritsuka: I don't.

5: What are your favorite movies?

21: Can you fake a smile?
Soubi: I cannot.
Ritsuka: I can.

22: What is your body temperature?
Soubi: About 36.5 °C. On the high side.
Ritsuka: 36 °C.

23: What do you do every night before you sleep?
Soubi: I open the curtains. And open the window about 2 cm.
Ritsuka: I brush my teeth.

24: What is the first thing you do in the morning?
Soubi: I check my cell phone, and then go on the internet.
Ritsuka: I change my clothes.

25: Oda Nobunaga, Toyotomi Hideyoshi, or Tokugawa Ieyasu—which one are you most like?
Soubi: I might be like Tokugawa Ieyasu.
Ritsuka: If the bush warbler does not sing, then it should be left alone. Because it doesn't want to sing.

26: Is there any place you would like to visit?
Soubi: Ayers Rock.
Ritsuka: A tropical island!! The North Sea!!

27: What curse word do you use the most?
Soubi: I do not use dirty words.
Ritsuka: "Jerk."

28: What kind of toothbrush do you use?
Soubi: An electric one.
Ritsuka: A regular one.

29: Are you good at arm-wrestling?
Soubi: Yes, I am.
Ritsuka: ...I don't think I am...

30: What do you always carry with you in your bag?
Soubi: I don't carry a bag.
Ritsuka: My digital camera, my cell phone, my wallet.

31: Do you have a best friend?
Soubi: I do. In a sense.
Ritsuka: I think I do.

32: What do you do on your days off?
Soubi: Maybe...stalking? :D
Ritsuka: If my mother is in a good mood I stay home. If not, I go out.

33: Is there a person you wish you could see right now?
Soubi: Ritsuka.

Ritsuka: Social Studies.

6: **What is your favorite color (paint colors)?**
Soubi: Off-white, or bluish-gray shades. I also like rust green and mustard colors.

7: **What is your favorite school lunch?**
Ritsuka: Deep-fried tofu bread.

8: **Is there something you absolutely cannot do without when painting?**
Soubi: Everyone listens to music, but I can't work unless it's silent. I need cigarettes while waiting for the paints to dry.

9: **Who is your favorite teacher?**
Ritsuka: My homeroom teacher, Hitomi Shinonome.

10: **You can't finish your assignment in time! What will you do?**
Soubi: I'll either sneak in during breaks or take it home to work on (but I'll get in trouble if I'm found out).

11: **Do you enjoy painting/drawing?**
Ritsuka: I don't draw. I can't draw.

12: **Where's your favorite place at school?**
Soubi: The studio.
Ritsuka: The hallway.

13: **Will you be able to graduate?**
Soubi: ...probably...
Ritsuka: Of course I will. (What kind of question is that?)

What if

1: **Tell us one thing that you want to have.**
Soubi: A car, I think.
Ritsuka: Nothing in particular.

2: **If the world were to end in one week, what would you do?**
Soubi: What indeed? First I'd go to Ritsuka's place and think about it.
Ritsuka: I'd search for the least painful way to die.

3: **If you could erase the past, is there an event you would like to erase?**
Soubi: There is, but I don't have to tell you, right?
Ritsuka: Nothing for myself.

4: **If you could call forth a demon, what kind would you choose? And what would you ask for?**

Soubi: Reservoir Dogs, The Negotiator, Storm, The Crucible, Speed, Scream, Enemy of the State, Starship Troopers, Mission: Impossible, Quiz Show, L.A. Confidential, The Shawshank Redemption, The Sixth Sense. I like popular Hollywood films.
Ritsuka: The Matrix: Reloaded! It's cool.

6: **Who is your favorite celebrity?**
Soubi: Miwako Ichikawa.
Ritsuka: That's not really my thing.

7: **What is your favorite sport?**
Soubi: I don't play sports. :D If it's just to watch, F1. And pro-wrestling. Cycling.
Ritsuka: I don't have any in particular, but maybe swimming?

8: **What is your favorite animal?**
Soubi: Cats, I guess?
Ritsuka: I like just about all animals. I like monkeys and elephants too.

9: **Is there a type of person you don't like?**
Soubi: Not really... If I had to say, a person with no sense of aesthetics.
Ritsuka: Selfish people. People who lie.

10: **Is there a type of person you like?**
Soubi: Not really...but maybe I like tender people.
Ritsuka: Strong people.

School

1: **Is school fun?**
Soubi: It's fun.
Ritsuka: Sort of.

2: **A word for the principal and teachers!!**
Soubi: Please put more entrees on the cafeteria menu.
Ritsuka: I think your hairstyles are weird.

3: **Do you arrive late for school?**
Soubi: I never arrive on time. Period.
Ritsuka: I do not.

4: **If you were to date, would it be with someone at your school, or outside your school? And why?**
Soubi: Someone from outside school. Dating someone from the same school would be problematic in lots of ways.
Ritsuka: ...I wouldn't date, but if I did it would be someone from the same school. We could spend more time together.

5: **What is your favorite class?**
Soubi: Study of Painting/Materials.

Soubi: Nothing.
Ritsuka: I wouldn't cheat.

6: **You've found out your girlfriend has been cheating on you! What do you do?**

Soubi: I'd save myself the bother and break up with her.

Ritsuka: ...I'd talk it over. I'd want to find out the reason.

7: **Is friendship between a man and a woman possible?**

Soubi: I kind of think...it's impossible.

Ritsuka: I think it's doable.

8: **When was your first love?**

Soubi: I don't remember having one.

Ritsuka: I pass on answering that.

9: **Would you ever be the first to declare your love?**

Soubi: No.

Ritsuka: If I fall in love I'll probably be the first to say it.

10: **What is love?**

Soubi: Obsession.

Ritsuka: I pass.

11: **What is sex?**

Soubi: A union of flesh, and a management of sexual desires.

Ritsuka: I pass!!

12: **Do you have any intention of marrying?**

Soubi: I do not.

Ritsuka: No.

13: **What do you think of same-sex love?**

Soubi: If people love each other, it's fine. As long as it doesn't involve me.

Ritsuka: I feel a little scared about it.

14: **Can love make people happy?**

Soubi: For that one instant, yes.

Ritsuka: Yes... I think so, but that alone isn't enough. I don't know.

15: **What do you think when you see someone without ears?**

Soubi: If I had to say, its, "Ah, they did it."

Ritsuka: I think, "There goes an adult."

Soubi: Lucifer, so we could chat. :D

Ritsuka: Satan, and I'd ask him to revive dead people.

5: **Rate your level of honesty on a scale of 1 to 100.**

Soubi: 50.

Ritsuka: About 95. A perfect score is impossible.

6: **What item would you take with you to a deserted island?**

Soubi: Ritsuka.

Ritsuka: A digital camera?

7: **Suppose that one day you found an enormous amount of money in your bank account! What would you do?**

Soubi: I'd pretend I never saw it.

Ritsuka: I'd contact the bank, because it must be some kind of mistake.

8: **If you were to meet someone who was the spitting image of yourself, what would you do?**

Soubi: I'd kill him.

Ritsuka: I'd be surprised! The first thing I'd do is take a picture with him.

9: **What will you be like a year from now?**

Soubi: Probably not the same?

Ritsuka: ...I really don't know.

10: **If you could have one wish granted, what would it be?**

Soubi: I would hand that right over to Ritsuka.

Ritsuka: I don't want to say.

Love

1: **Have you ever received a ring?**

Soubi: Yes. (Although I think I lost it.)

Ritsuka: I have not.

2: **Do you have a lover?**

Soubi: No, I don't.

Ritsuka: I don't.

3: **What attribute do you look for in a potential date, looks or personality?**

Soubi: Nice face and body?

Ritsuka: Personality.

4: **Are marriage and love separate things?**

Soubi: Of course they're separate.

Ritsuka: I thought you got married because you're in love? I don't know.

5: **Your girlfriend finds out you've been cheating on her! What do you do?**

A TALE OF EARS AND TAIL

In this mini-comic, which has absolutely nothing to do with the *Loveless* story, Soubi is 12 years old (sixth grade, homeroom 1).

homeroom 2 → Yayoi
homeroom 3 → Ritsuka & Yuiko

In honor of little Soubi's first appearance in volume 3!!

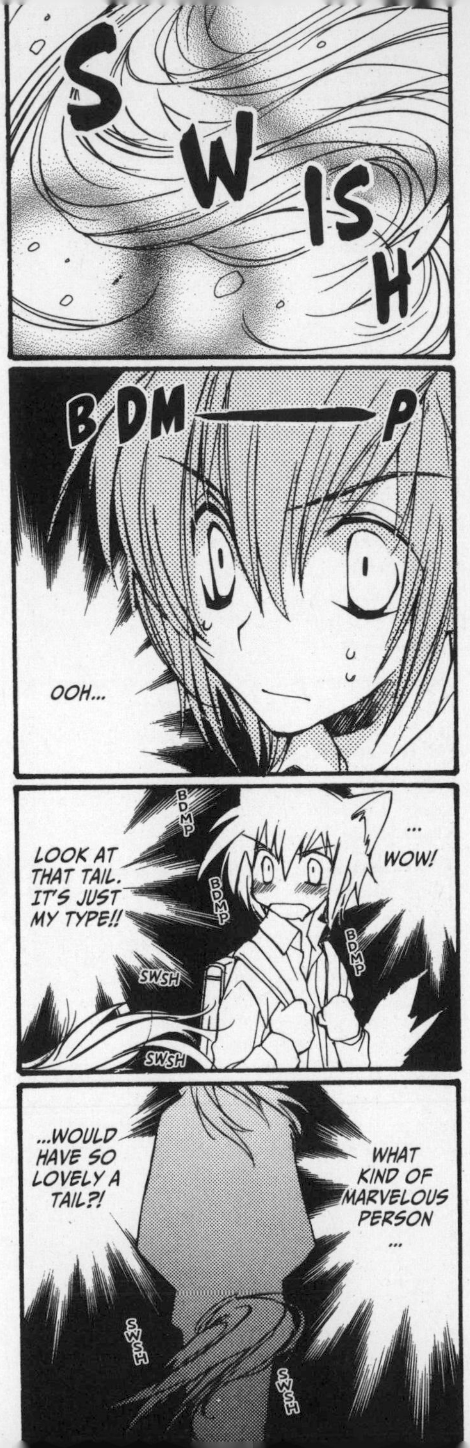
SWISH
BDM——P
OOH...
... WOW!
BDMP
LOOK AT THAT TAIL. IT'S JUST MY TYPE!!
BDMP
BDMP
SWSH
SWSH
WHAT KIND OF MARVELOUS PERSON ...
...WOULD HAVE SO LOVELY A TAIL?!
SWSH
SWSH

■ THE MEETING, FIRST LOVE AND THE END ■

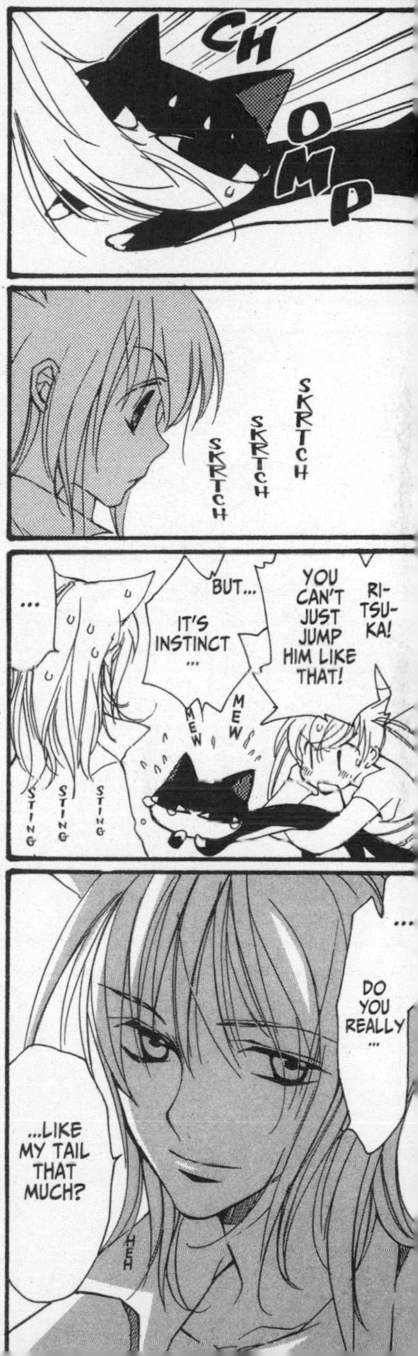
CHOMP
SKRTCH
SKRTCH
SKRTCH
RI-TSUKA!
YOU CAN'T JUST JUMP HIM LIKE THAT!
BUT...
IT'S INSTINCT...
...
MEW
MEW
STING
STING
STING
...
DO YOU REALLY...
...LIKE MY TAIL THAT MUCH?
HEH

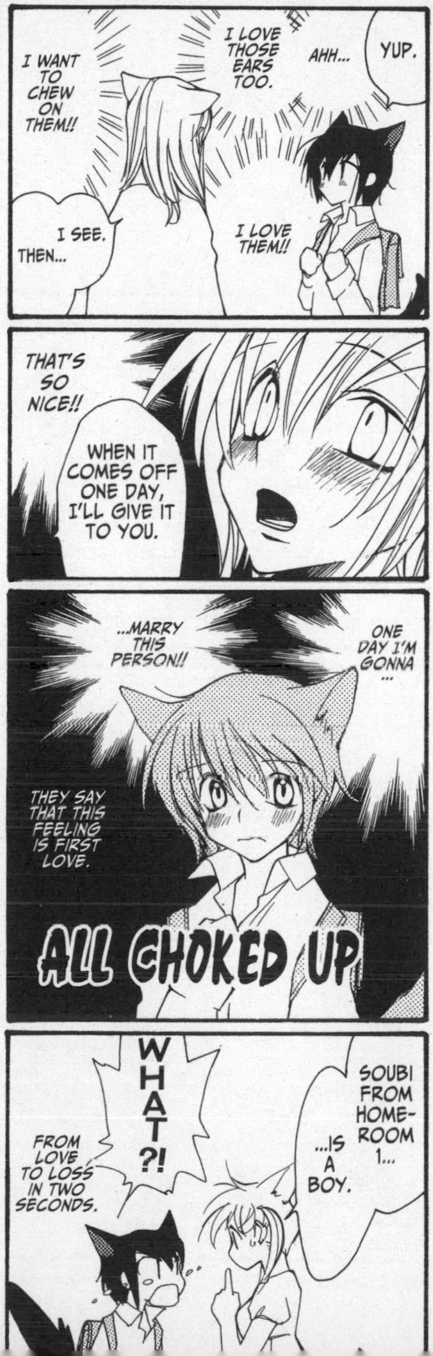
YUP.
AHH...
I LOVE THOSE EARS TOO.
I WANT TO CHEW ON THEM!!
I LOVE THEM!!
I SEE. THEN...
WHEN IT COMES OFF ONE DAY, I'LL GIVE IT TO YOU.
THAT'S SO NICE!!
ONE DAY I'M GONNA...
...MARRY THIS PERSON!!
THEY SAY THAT THIS FEELING IS FIRST LOVE.
ALL CHOKED UP
SOUBI FROM HOME-ROOM 1...
...IS A BOY.
WHAT?!
FROM LOVE TO LOSS IN TWO SECONDS.

■ THE RUMORED BOYFRIEND (IN HOMEROOM 1) ■

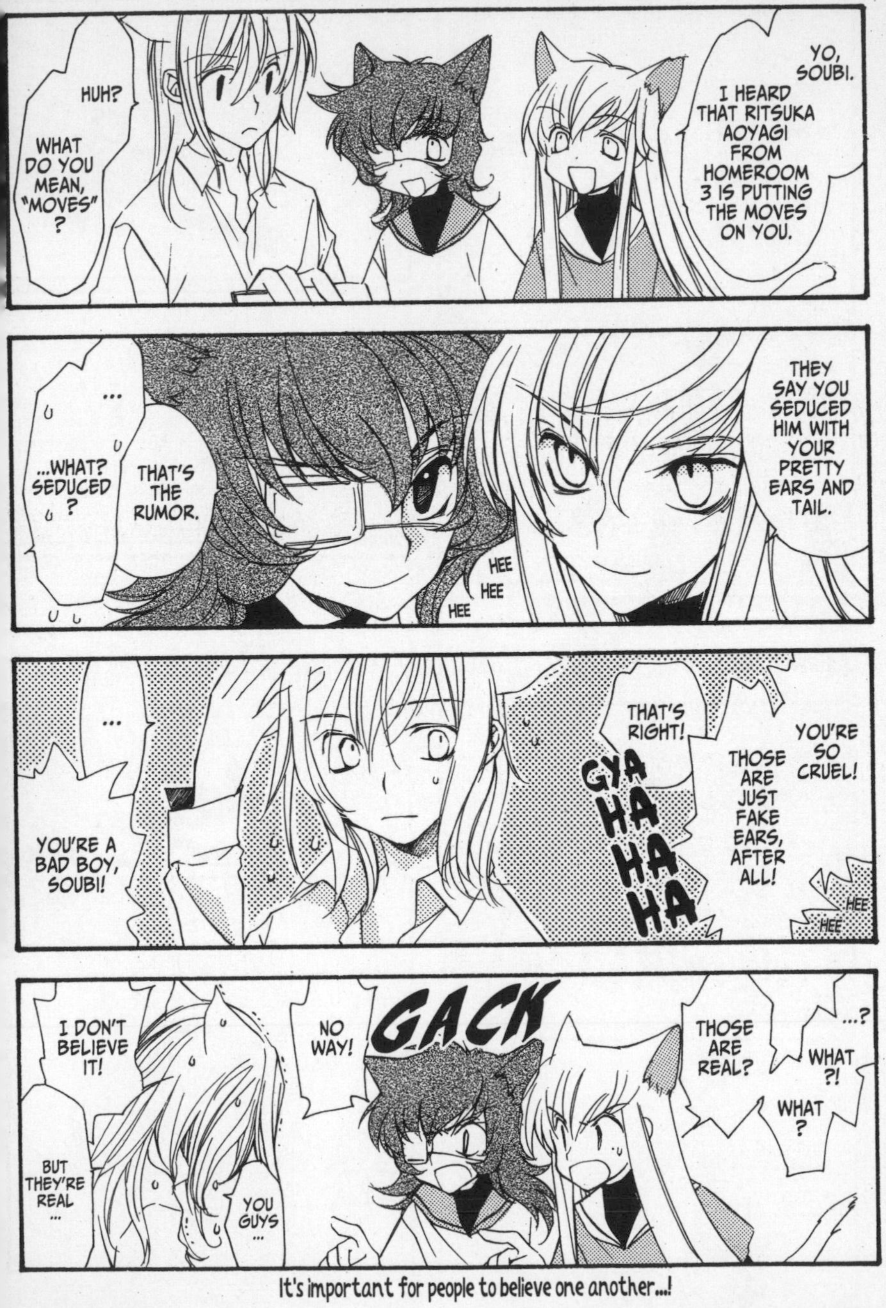
YO, SOUBI. I HEARD THAT RITSUKA AOYAGI FROM HOMEROOM 3 IS PUTTING THE MOVES ON YOU.
HUH?
WHAT DO YOU MEAN, "MOVES"?
THEY SAY YOU SEDUCED HIM WITH YOUR PRETTY EARS AND TAIL.
HEE HEE HEE
THAT'S THE RUMOR.
...
...WHAT? SEDUCED?
YOU'RE SO CRUEL!
THAT'S RIGHT!
THOSE ARE JUST FAKE EARS, AFTER ALL!
GYA HA HA HA HA
HEE HEE
...
YOU'RE A BAD BOY, SOUBI!
...?
WHAT?!
WHAT?
THOSE ARE REAL?
GACK
NO WAY!
I DON'T BELIEVE IT!
YOU GUYS...
BUT THEY'RE REAL...

It's important for people to believe one another...!

■ CONFUSION, A GROUNDLESS RUMOR, AND A PROPOSAL (IN HOMEROOM 3) ■

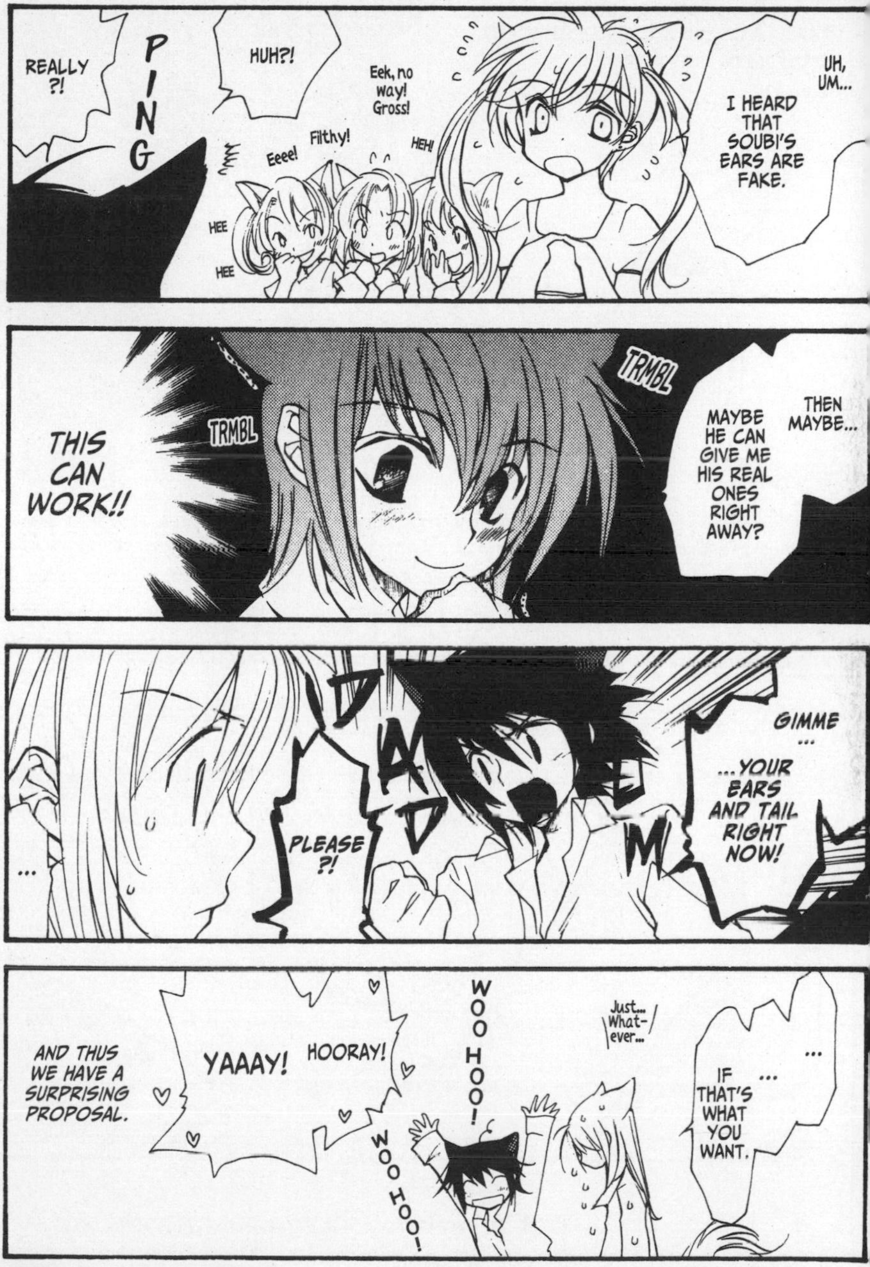
UH, UM...
I HEARD THAT SOUBI'S EARS ARE FAKE.
HEH!
Eek, no way! Gross!
Filthy!
Eeee!
HUH?!
PING
REALLY?!
HEE HEE
THEN MAYBE...
MAYBE HE CAN GIVE ME HIS REAL ONES RIGHT AWAY?
TRMBL
TRMBL
THIS CAN WORK!!
GIMME...
...YOUR EARS AND TAIL RIGHT NOW!
DADM
PLEASE?!
...
...
...
IF THAT'S WHAT YOU WANT.
Just... Whatever...
WOO HOO!
WOO HOO!
HOORAY!
YAAAY!
AND THUS WE HAVE A SURPRISING PROPOSAL.

END! There's no continuation!! This is it!!

Eisen Mädchen

17-year old Ritsuka x 12-year old Soubi
Drawing little Soubi sparked the idea of this sort of pairing in my head.

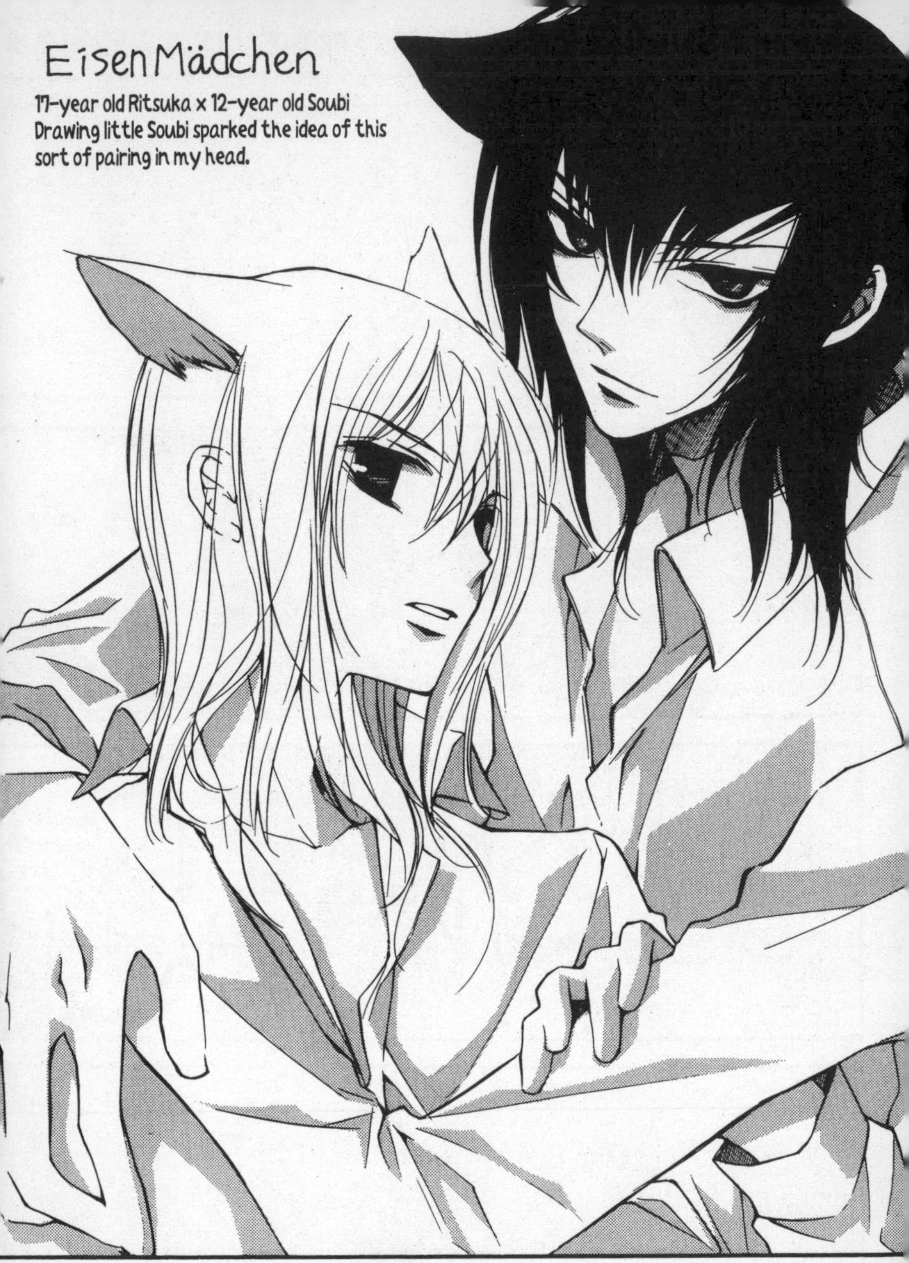

• Soubi: "I'm here because Seimei ordered it. I will protect you."
• Ritsuka: "...Whuh..."

What a different story that would be! :D

A Let's-Read-It-On-The-Homepage
AFTERWORD CHAT!

http://ichijinsha.co.jp/
Over here!!

Kouga: No one's better at eating snacks with chopsticks than a manga artist. *MUNCH MUNCH*

Sugino: No greeting?! Hello, everyone! Does that taste good?

Ⓚ: Oops. H-hello! Yun Kouga here. I'm eating again. This is a Cinnabon. *MUNCH MUNCH*

Ⓢ: Can you really eat that with chopsticks? By the way, now that volume 3 has wrapped up, how'd it go?

Ⓚ: It was tough. The end. Why am I writing in such tiny letters? I was sleepy.

Ⓢ: ...That's it? Your penmanship is...fine. And I guess you were tired. Thanks for the hard work.

Ⓚ: It seems like you're trying to make meaningful conversation, but it won't work!

Ⓢ: Don't you realize this is an important part of the book too? Don't you have
any juicy scoops or stories you've been saving or any secrets?

Ⓚ: Every time, y'know, I'm writing these at the very end of everything, and my heart is just frazzled.

Ⓢ: ...Your heart? ...Your HEART? Are you trying some new sexy talk?

Ⓚ: ...I don't like books that have no heart behind them... Oh!! Oops. I meant
to write "brain" and wrote "heart" instead! You joker! ⚡

Ⓢ: That's a silly mistake. :D But really. You end up in a panic every time. You're taking
years off your life...but anyway, a book on sale is always a joyous occasion!

Ⓚ: It is joyous, but I have to say maybe this time was the worst? In terms of workflow...

Ⓢ: My apologies and thanks to all involved. We keep re-writing the record for being
"worst" each time. But despite that, we did a good job...I believe.

Ⓚ: Which means that next time, we'll aim for the worst workflow and the absolute best work, right? Go team...

Ⓢ: Bad workflow is a bad goal!! But we'll work hard on the manga! And on that note, I'm sorry about "the incident"...

Ⓚ: Oh, you're going to fess up?! I mean, it wasn't really your fault that there was no afterword in the book itself.

Ⓢ: I'm so sorry! :(But anyway! I'll do something about the Phantom Afterword.

Ⓚ: Due to an issue with our final page count, the afterword we were planning to
have at the end of volume 3 will be up on Ichijinsha's website instead.

Ⓢ: ... P-please check it out. Y'know, when you throw in the special limited edition
booklet (this one), Soubi gets a lot of screen time in volume 3!

Ⓚ: Uh...

Ⓢ: Do you like him that much?

Ⓚ: That's strange. I didn't plan it this way... ᵕᵤᵕ Mmm... Mmm... No, I like Ritsuka.

Ⓢ: The 17-year-old Ritsuka looks intense. Give Yuiko and Shinonome more to do. Don't play favorites with Soubi.

Ⓚ: Come to think of it, you said that Ritsuka at 17 looks like a different
person...and that's exactly what's going to happen!!

Ⓢ: Really? I wonder... It's like, I'm looking forward to it, so I'm not sure how to say it... Man, I'm sleepy.

Ⓚ: I'm sleepy too... 😴 There're going to be various awful things that happen
to Ritsuka, and that's why he'll probably end up like that.

Ⓢ: Well, as far as the story goes, we can discuss it in our meetings. Oh yes, let's go at it full force. Full force!

Ⓚ: But more importantly, I thought that I managed to draw little Soubi
very cute... I think. Well, whatever. ᵕᵤᵕ Is Hee doing well?

Ⓢ: That's true. It was surprising, but cute. Hee? You mean my cat. :(Yup. Doing great.

Ⓚ: She's a big one... If you're a cat lover does that make you an ear and tail fan? (I guess that's more me!)

Ⓢ: You have a lot of cats at your place, don't you, Kouga? Ears and tails, huh? What
other fetish could there be? :D Like for a round face or nice hind legs?

Ⓚ: Oh! ᵕᵤᵕ I remember you were a "heel" fetishist. For you it's the ears, tail, and footpads!! ᵕᵤᵕ

Ⓢ: I'm totally into those hind legs! But in any case, we should aim for a
more meaningful conversation!! What's next for you?

Ⓚ: I would like to get volume 4 out within the year. And I want to work harder on the special
limited edition booklet for volume 4. In terms of both quality and length.

Ⓢ: In order for that to happen you'll have to really work hard... Let's crack that whip!!

Ⓚ: R-really...yeah...ᵕᵤᵕ It's fun to draw little loveless side stories.

Ⓢ: little loveless is nice... but let's work hard on the main story too. Will volume 4 be the girls' high school part?

Ⓚ: It means more weirdos showing up. I'll do my best. Look forward to it!

Ⓢ: There's a scarcity of normal people, isn't there? I wonder why...

Ⓚ: It's normal enough...I think. *MUMBLE MUMBLE*... after all, I like weirdos...

Ⓢ: It's not so much that you like weirdos, as you're a weir—Uh, never mind. So, let's keep working hard!!

Ⓚ: Thanks for everything you've done for me! See you again tomorrow! Or, it's actually today! See you later.

Ⓢ: No, no! You have to say it to the readers! Please continue to give us
your kind readerly support and love! It'll be fun...

Ⓚ: Really? Yay! Regards! Thank you very much!

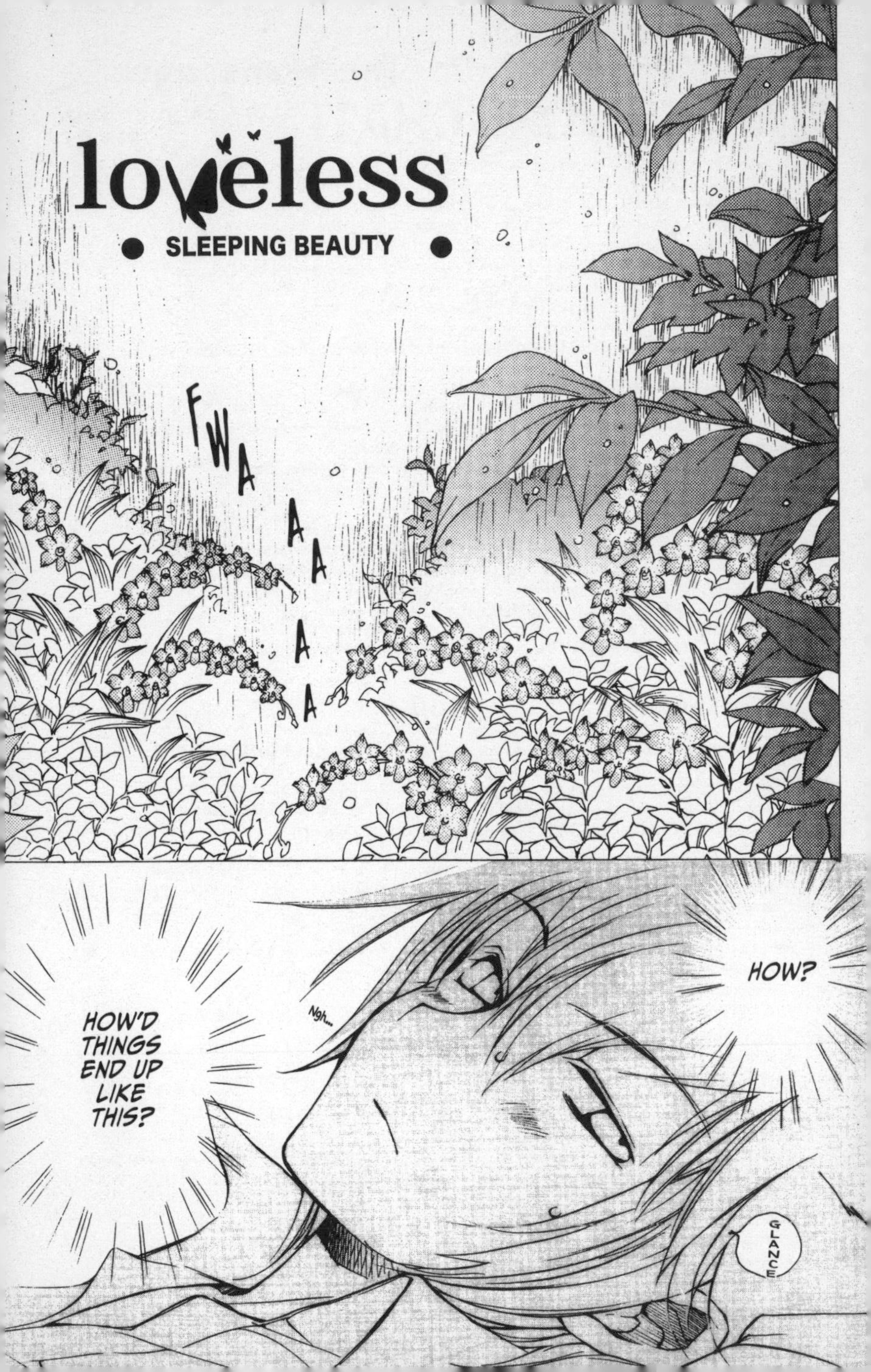
loveless
SLEEPING BEAUTY
FWAAAAA
HOW?
Ngh...
HOW'D THINGS END UP LIKE THIS?
GLANCE

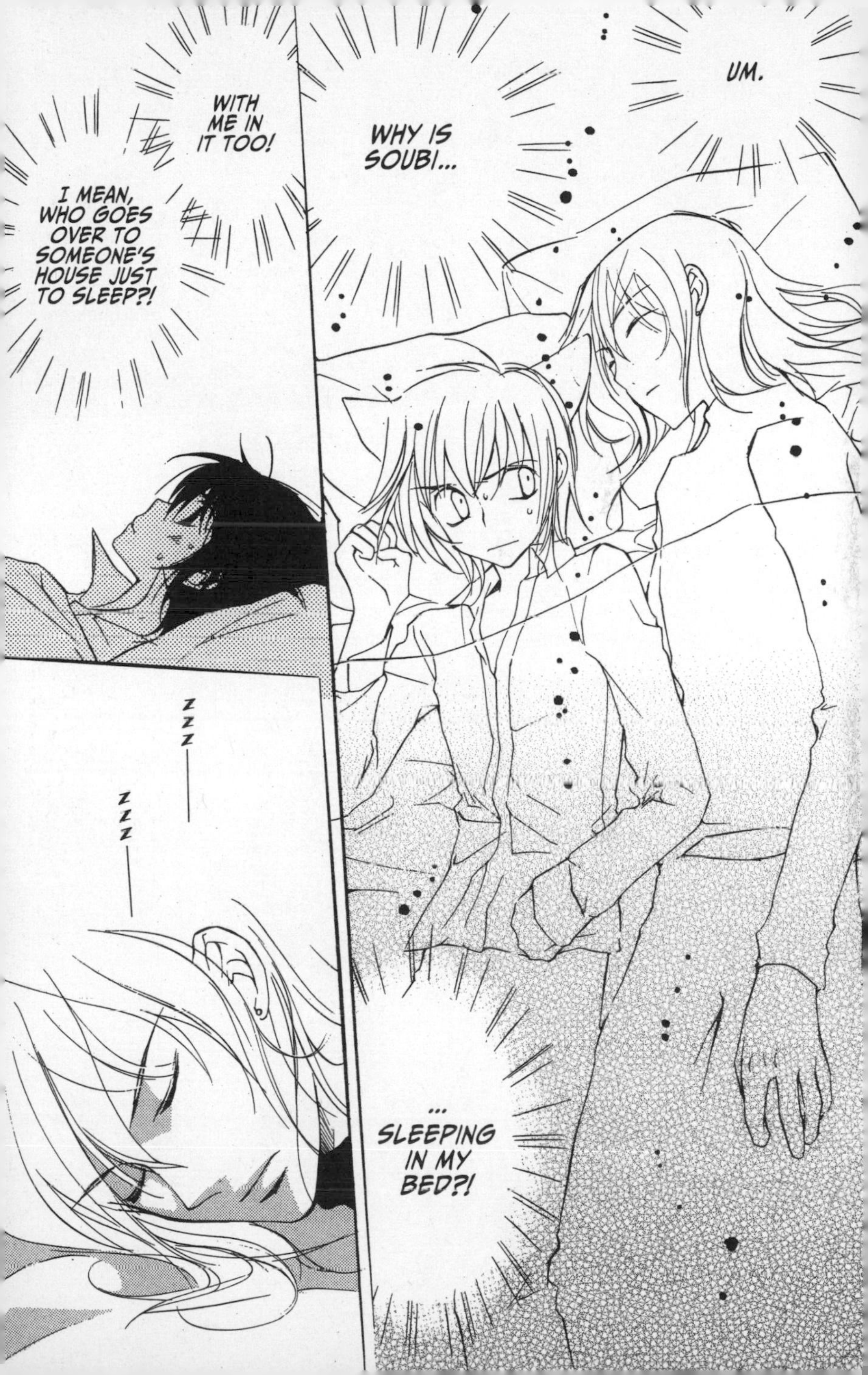
UM.
WHY IS SOUBI...
... SLEEPING IN MY BED?!
WITH ME IN IT TOO!
I MEAN, WHO GOES OVER TO SOMEONE'S HOUSE JUST TO SLEEP?!
ZZZ——
ZZZ——

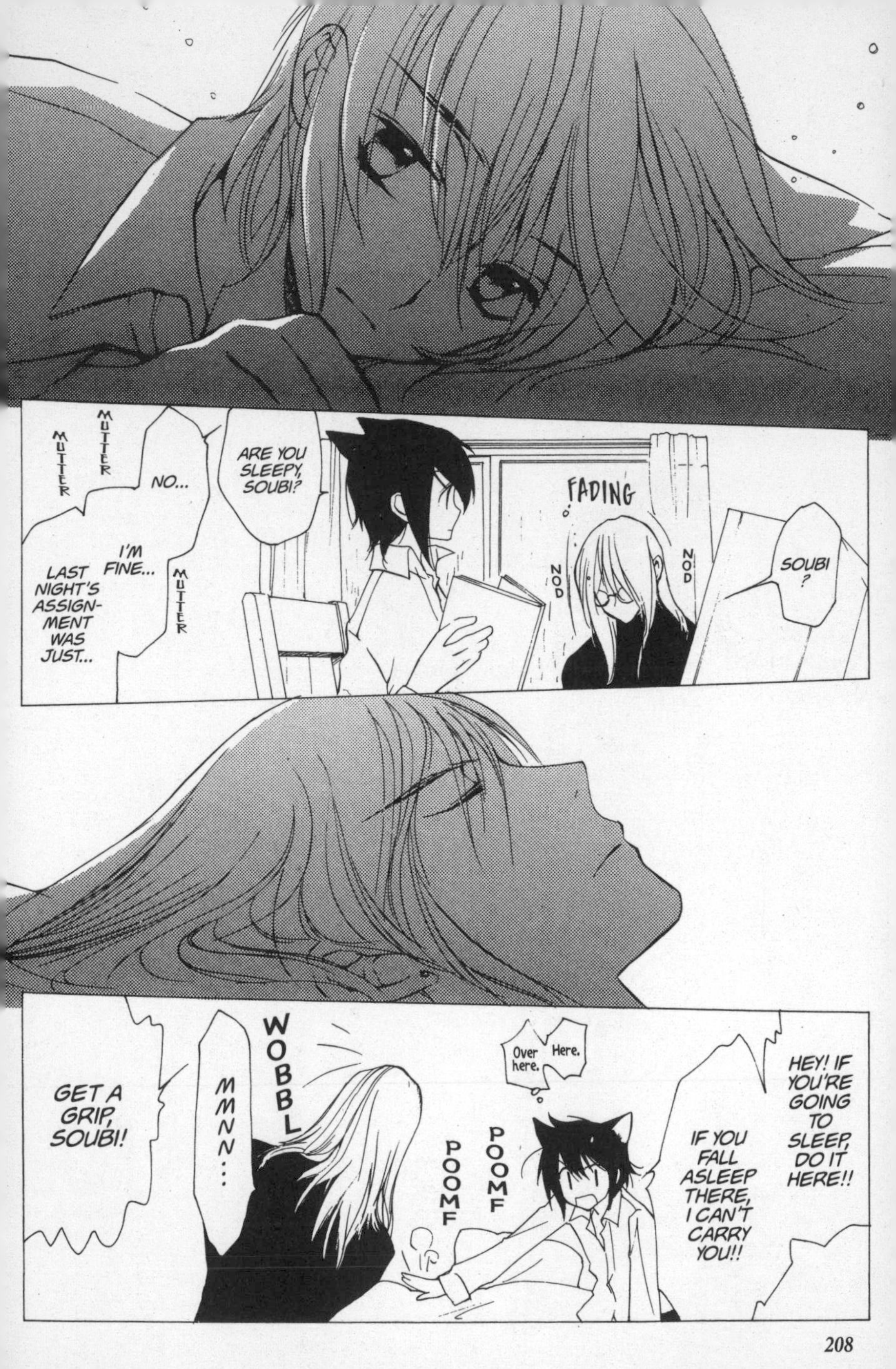
SOUBI?
NOD NOD
FADING
ARE YOU SLEEPY, SOUBI?
NO...
MUTTER MUTTER
I'M FINE...
LAST NIGHT'S ASSIGNMENT WAS JUST...
MUTTER
HEY! IF YOU'RE GOING TO SLEEP, DO IT HERE!!
IF YOU FALL ASLEEP THERE, I CAN'T CARRY YOU!!
Here.
Over here.
POOMF
POOMF
WOBBL
MMNN...
GET A GRIP, SOUBI!

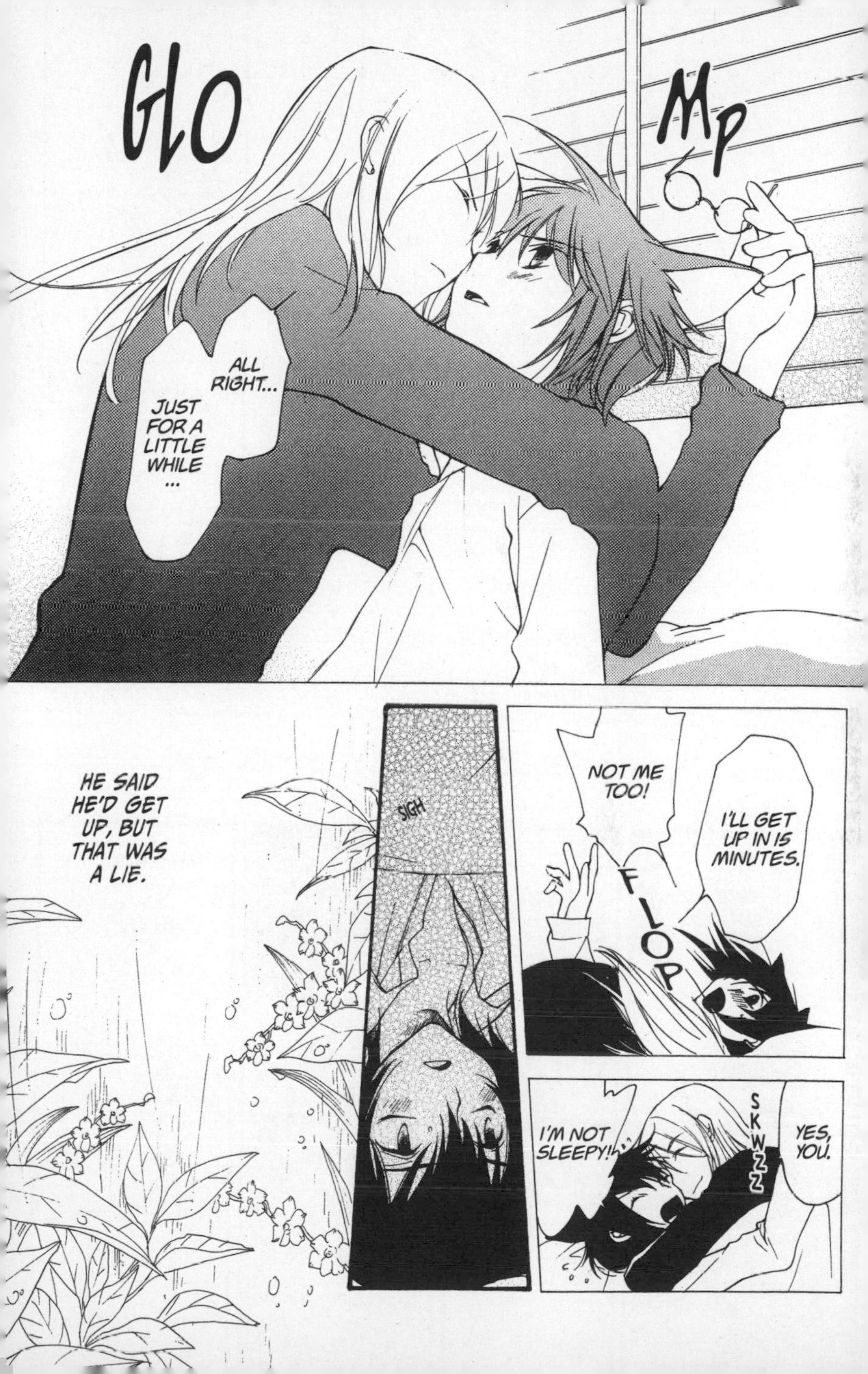
GLOMP
ALL RIGHT... JUST FOR A LITTLE WHILE ...
I'LL GET UP IN 15 MINUTES.
NOT ME TOO!
FLOP
YES, YOU.
SKWZZ
I'M NOT SLEEPY!!
SIGH
HE SAID HE'D GET UP, BUT THAT WAS A LIE.

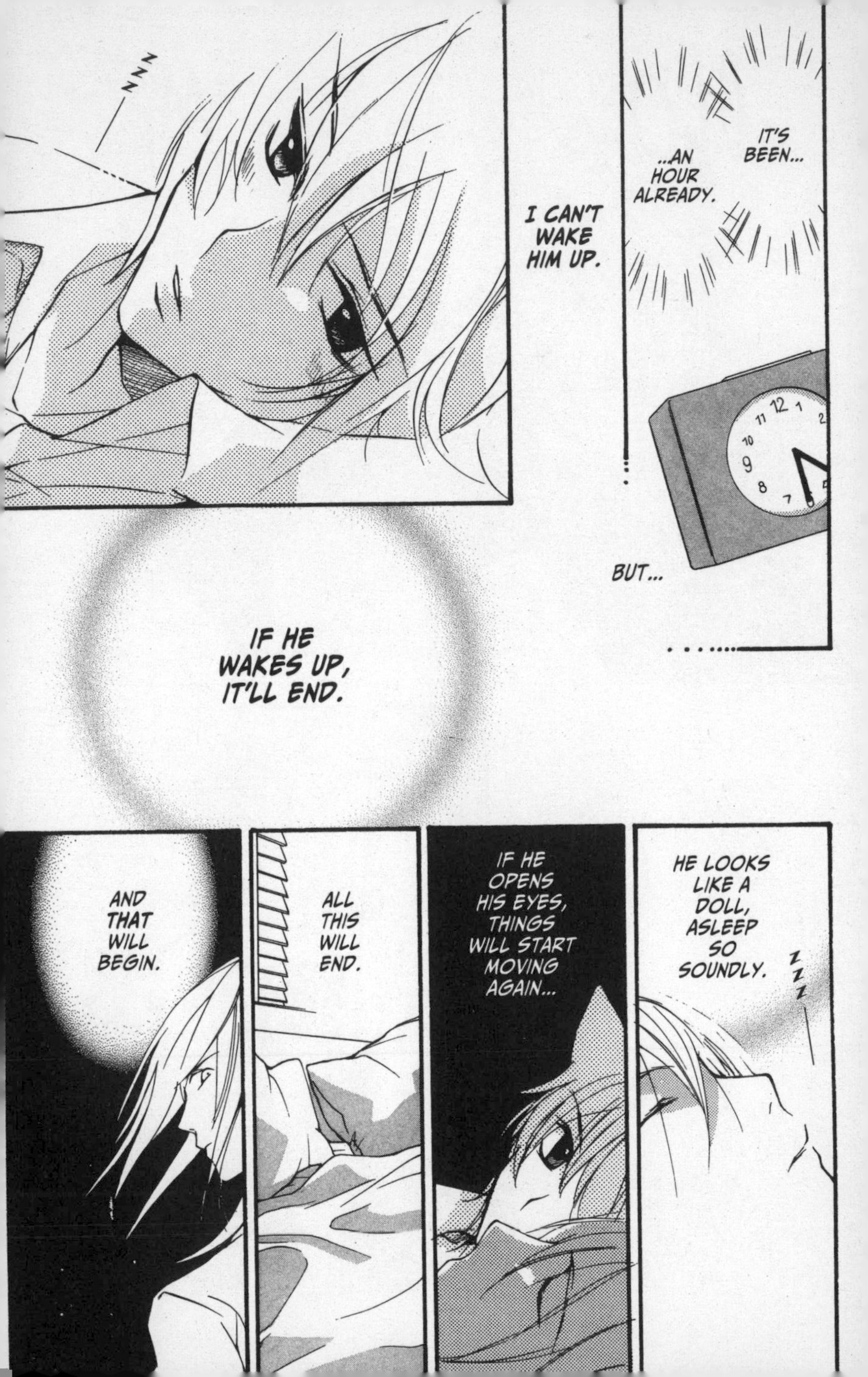
IT'S BEEN...
...AN HOUR ALREADY.
I CAN'T WAKE HIM UP.
BUT...
IF HE WAKES UP, IT'LL END.
HE LOOKS LIKE A DOLL, ASLEEP SO SOUNDLY.
ZZZ
IF HE OPENS HIS EYES, THINGS WILL START MOVING AGAIN...
ALL THIS WILL END.
AND THAT WILL BEGIN.

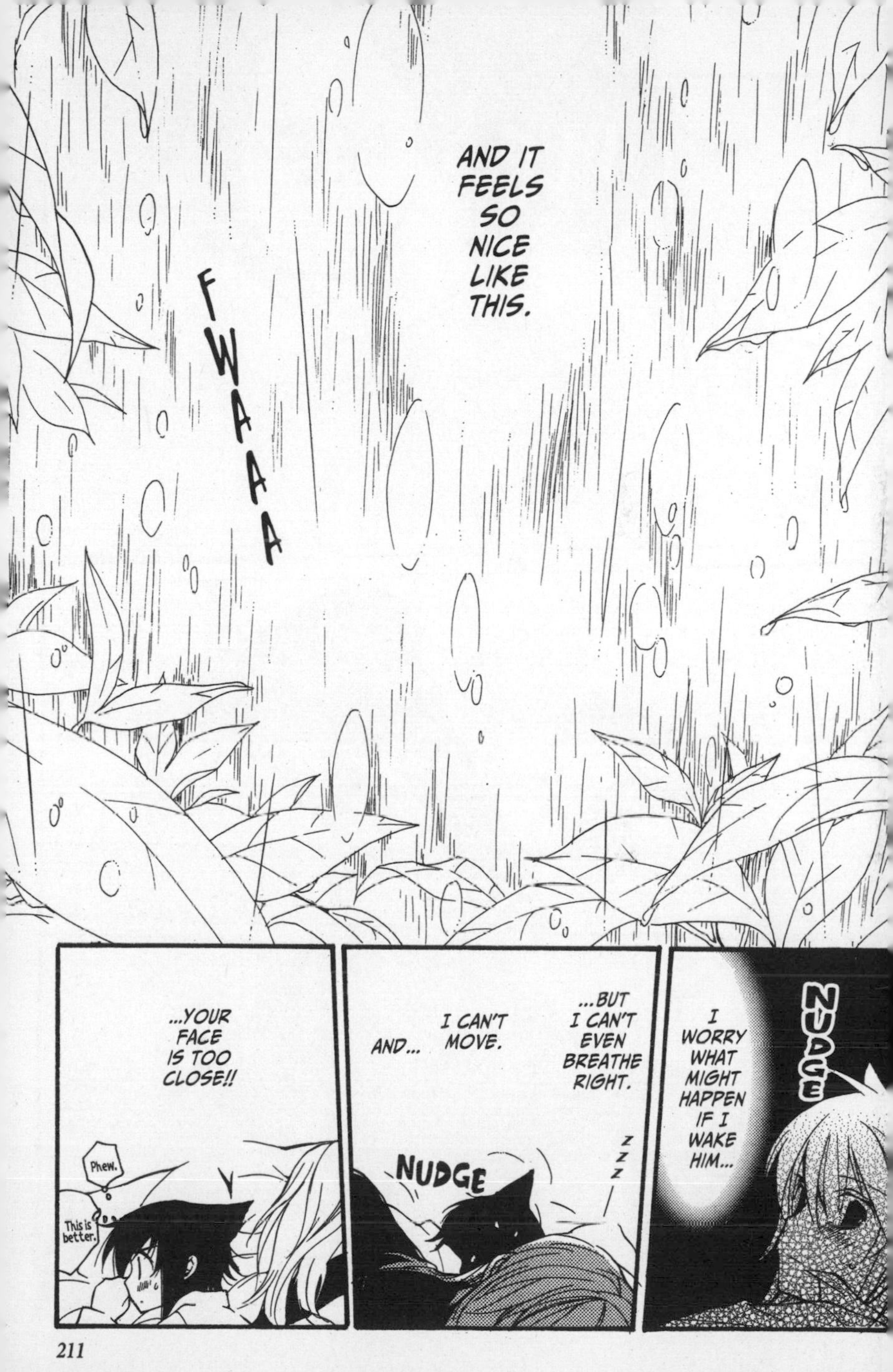
AND IT FEELS SO NICE LIKE THIS.
FWAAA
NUDGE
I WORRY WHAT MIGHT HAPPEN IF I WAKE HIM...
...BUT I CAN'T EVEN BREATHE RIGHT.
I CAN'T MOVE.
AND...
Z Z Z
NUDGE
...YOUR FACE IS TOO CLOSE!!
Phew.
This is better.

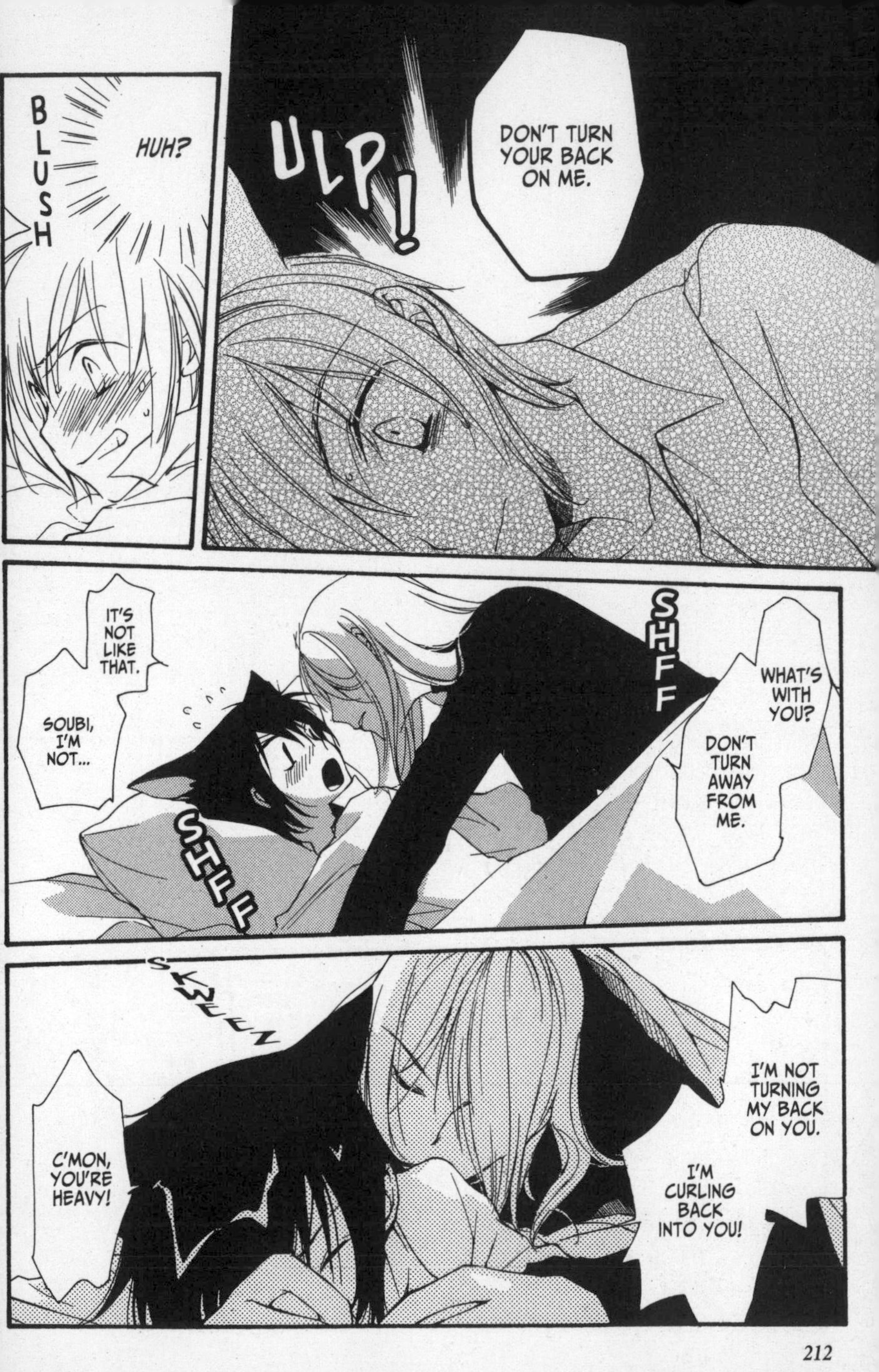
DON'T TURN YOUR BACK ON ME.
ULP!
HUH?
BLUSH
WHAT'S WITH YOU?
DON'T TURN AWAY FROM ME.
SHFF
SHFF
IT'S NOT LIKE THAT.
SOUBI, I'M NOT...
I'M NOT TURNING MY BACK ON YOU.
I'M CURLING BACK INTO YOU!
SKWEEN
C'MON, YOU'RE HEAVY!

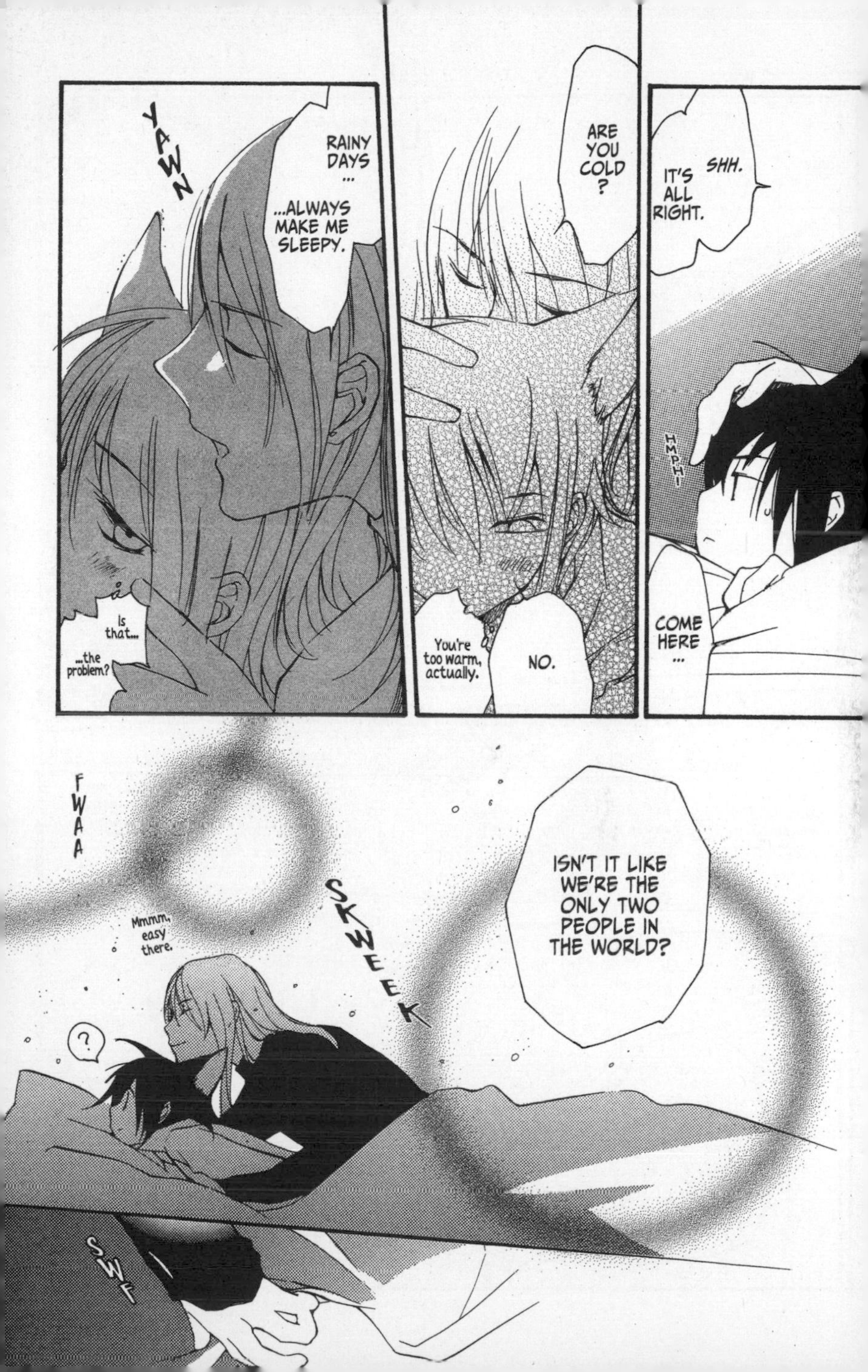
SHH.
IT'S ALL RIGHT.
HMPH!
COME HERE ...
ARE YOU COLD ?
NO.
You're too warm, actually.
YAWN
RAINY DAYS ...
...ALWAYS MAKE ME SLEEPY.
Is that...
...the problem?
ISN'T IT LIKE WE'RE THE ONLY TWO PEOPLE IN THE WORLD?
SKWEEK
Mmmm, easy there.
FWAA
?
SWF

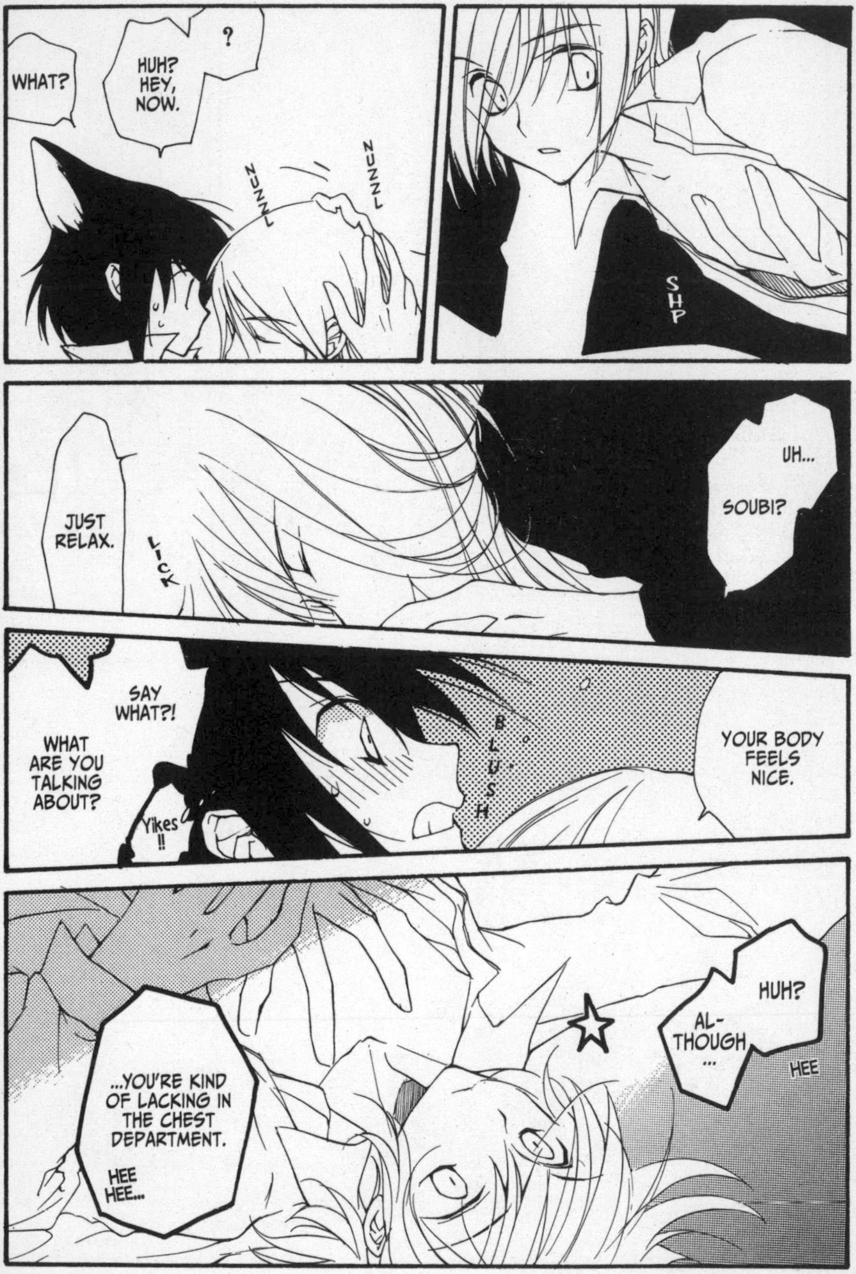
SHP
?
HUH? HEY, NOW.
NUZZL
WHAT?
NUZZL
UH... SOUBI?
JUST RELAX.
LICK
YOUR BODY FEELS NICE.
BLUSH
SAY WHAT?!
WHAT ARE YOU TALKING ABOUT?
Yikes!!
HUH?
AL-THOUGH...
HEE
...YOU'RE KIND OF LACKING IN THE CHEST DEPARTMENT.
HEE HEE...

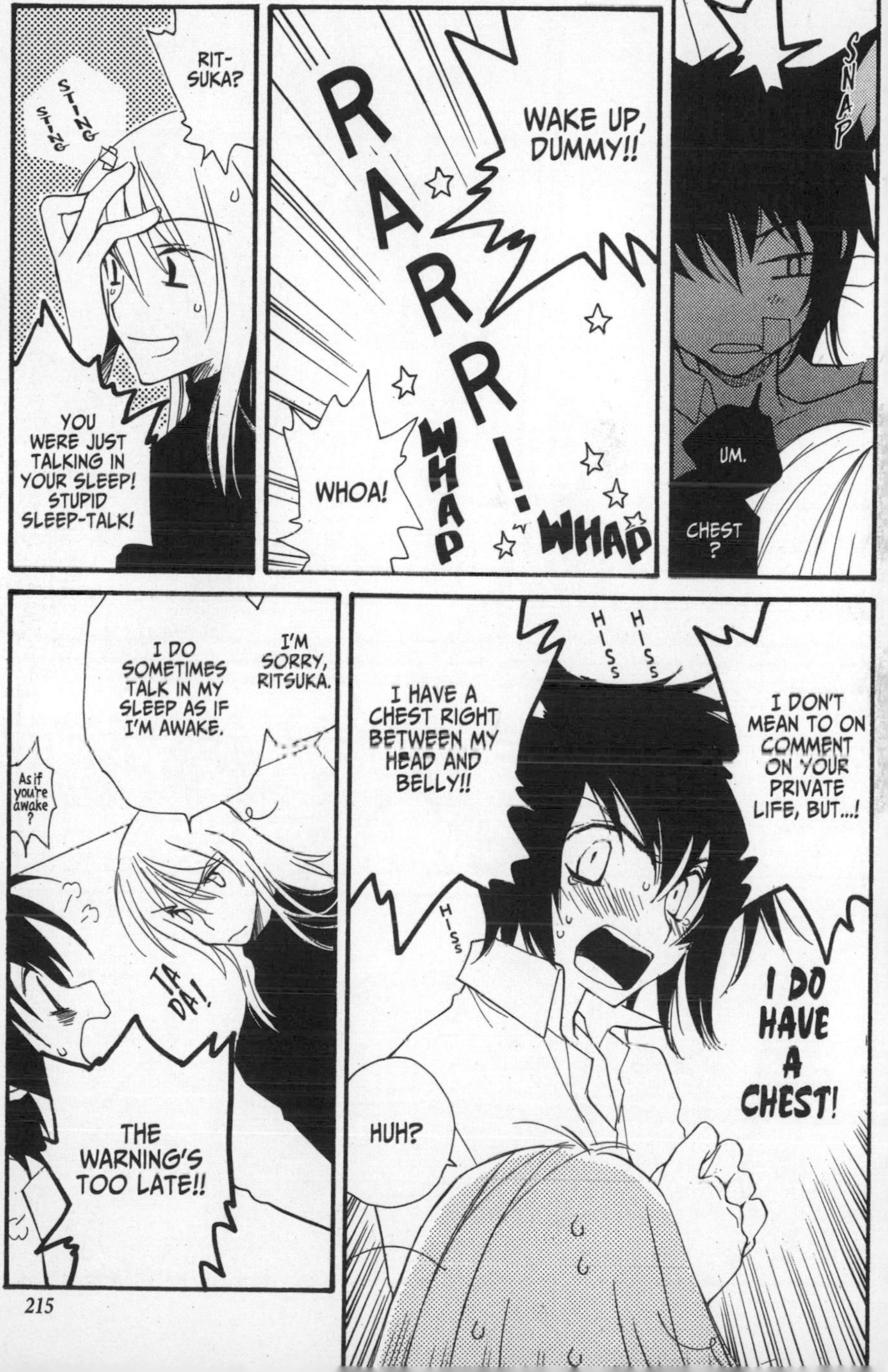
SNAP
UM.
CHEST?
WAKE UP, DUMMY!!
RARRRI!
WHAP
WHAP
WHOA!
RIT-SUKA?
STING STING
YOU WERE JUST TALKING IN YOUR SLEEP! STUPID SLEEP-TALK!
HISS HISS
I DON'T MEAN TO ON COMMENT ON YOUR PRIVATE LIFE, BUT...!
I HAVE A CHEST RIGHT BETWEEN MY HEAD AND BELLY!!
HISS
I DO HAVE A CHEST!
HUH?
I'M SORRY, RITSUKA.
I DO SOMETIMES TALK IN MY SLEEP AS IF I'M AWAKE.
As if you're awake?
TA DA!
THE WARNING'S TOO LATE!!

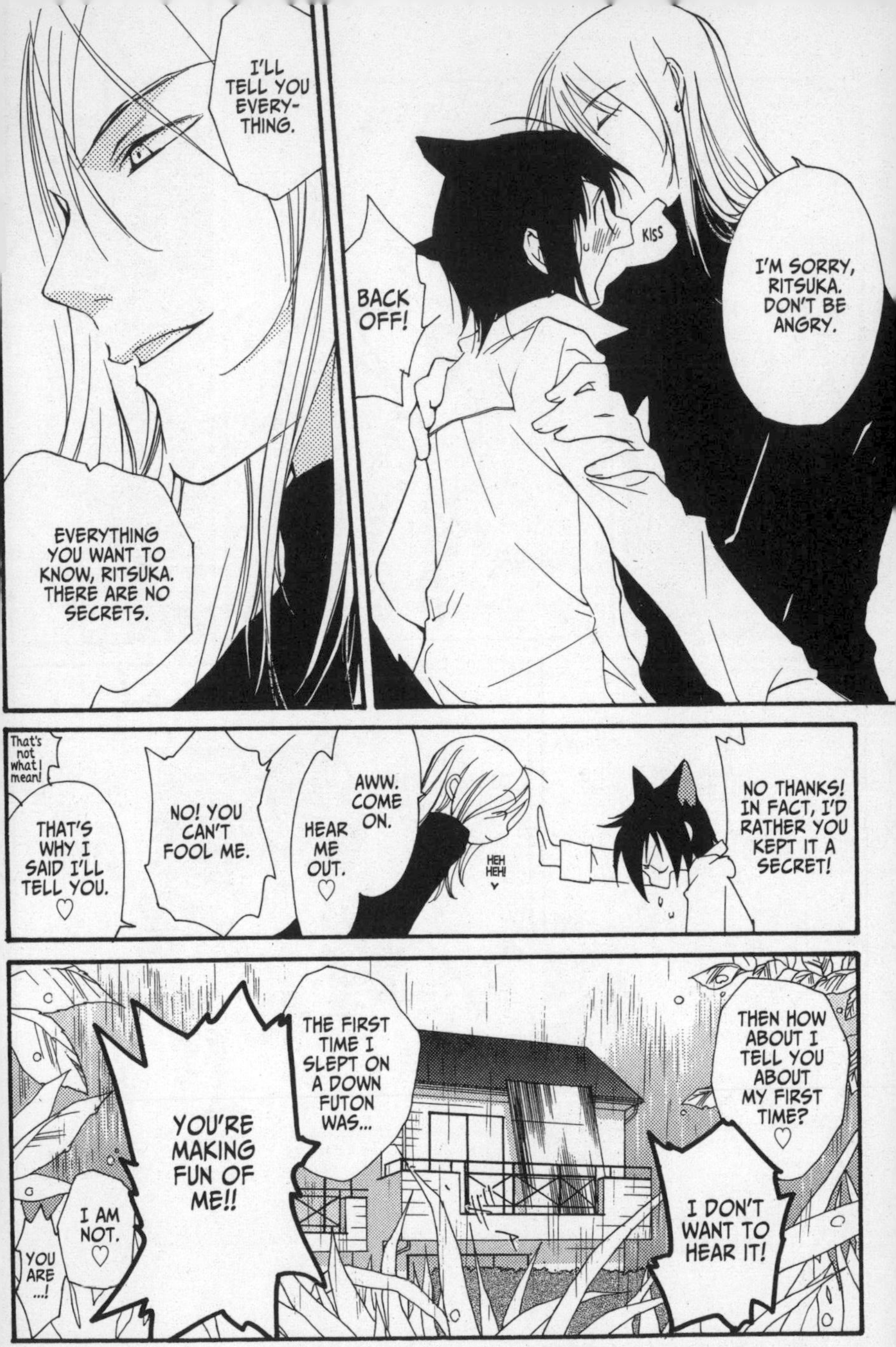
I'M SORRY, RITSUKA. DON'T BE ANGRY.
KISS
BACK OFF!
I'LL TELL YOU EVERY-THING.
EVERYTHING YOU WANT TO KNOW, RITSUKA. THERE ARE NO SECRETS.
NO THANKS! IN FACT, I'D RATHER YOU KEPT IT A SECRET!
HEH HEH! ♥
AWW. COME ON. HEAR ME OUT. ♡
NO! YOU CAN'T FOOL ME.
THAT'S WHY I SAID I'LL TELL YOU. ♡
That's not what I mean!
THEN HOW ABOUT I TELL YOU ABOUT MY FIRST TIME? ♡
I DON'T WANT TO HEAR IT!
THE FIRST TIME I SLEPT ON A DOWN FUTON WAS...
YOU'RE MAKING FUN OF ME!!
I AM NOT. ♡
YOU ARE ...!

little loveless 3 / END

If possible, please read the book first and then read the bonus section as a "+α" bit of chatter.

There are several parts of volume 3 that I particularly like (ones that I always wanted to do). The piercing of flesh is well, one of those things too, but that's a story for another time. The scene where Soubi comes to Ritsuka's window is patterned after the motif of "the man who comes courting," and "the woman who waits for him" as found in *Romeo and Juliet*, the story of *Ono no Komachi*, and *Fukakusa no Shosho*. (At least that is what I intended!)

Of course, Ritsuka is not a girl, he's only occupying the traditionally female position. This is a metaphor for the courtier's passion and the unbridgeable distance between the two (a simile!), but it started to bug me as I drew, thinking, in what part of the world does a guy go home after being told that his love was "waiting for him"?

After all, it must have taken a lot of courage for Ritsuka to say that he was "waiting." (I mean, wasn't that horrible for Soubi to just up and leave when he knew that?) And also a visit via windowsill bears a premonition of tragedy. A love by the windowsill goes unrequited. (What will happen to Ritsuka x Soubi! Is it love?!)

If it is unrequited, Soubi should just shut up and go home. If he goes too far, he's just going to have regrets! Soubi is putting a lot of stress on Ritsuka, y'know. (*grumble grumble*)

Love is stress. When you put stress on a person, sometimes it turns into love. If you can settle things smoothly, the love affair can continue after you get past your issues. But Ritsuka is completely unable to control his stress, mostly because he is inexperienced. In the end, Soubi is putting Ritsuka through the wringer, but that's okay. Romance is about getting smashed to bits (I think).

When I decided on Ritsuka's name, I liked the kanji character for "to stand." I thought that it was a word that wasn't commonly used for names, and as you can plainly see, I've invested the meaning of "to stand" into Ritsuka. I also like the shape of it, drawn with a minimum of brushstrokes. It also has connection to *rikka*, the beginning of summer in the traditional Japanese calendar. In other words, no matter what happens, Ritsuka will stand strong.

If you must know why, it's because I wanted to draw a character like that. A person who never get messed up, or a person who only fails—both are uninteresting. I like someone who continues to stand up, even if he is confused and loses himself. I like someone who falls but gets back up.

I don't think there's anything as dumb as someone who tries to interpret their own manga, so keep this between us!

"I CAN ARMOR MYSELF WITH WORDS."

THANK YOU FOR THE HARD WORK!

See you soon! See you soon!!
Volume 4 is coming right up!!

This has been Yun Kouga.
2003, beginning of summer
The rainy season...

Special Thanks to Yakumo Izumi
Thanks always!!

Soubi, age 12

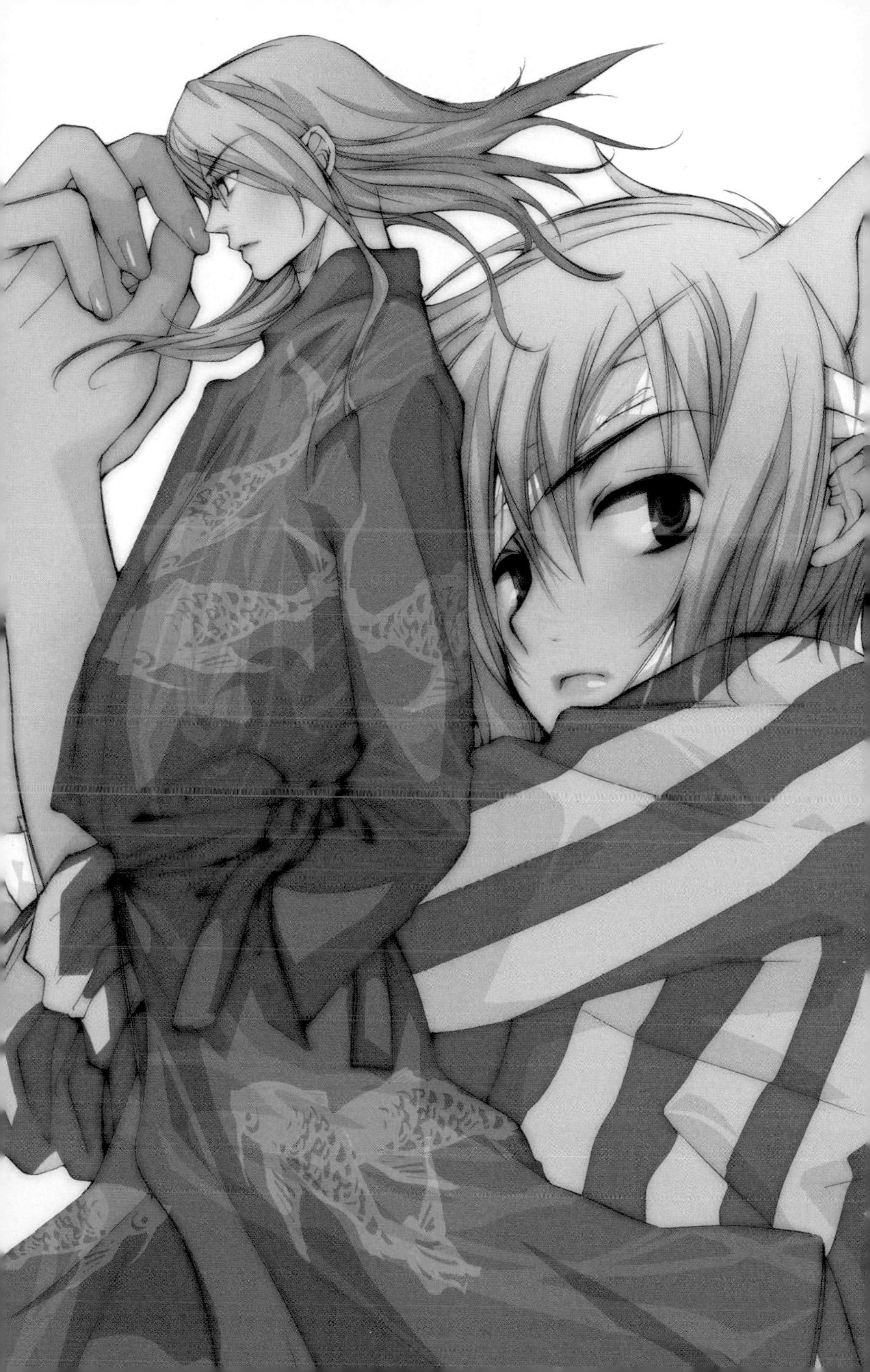

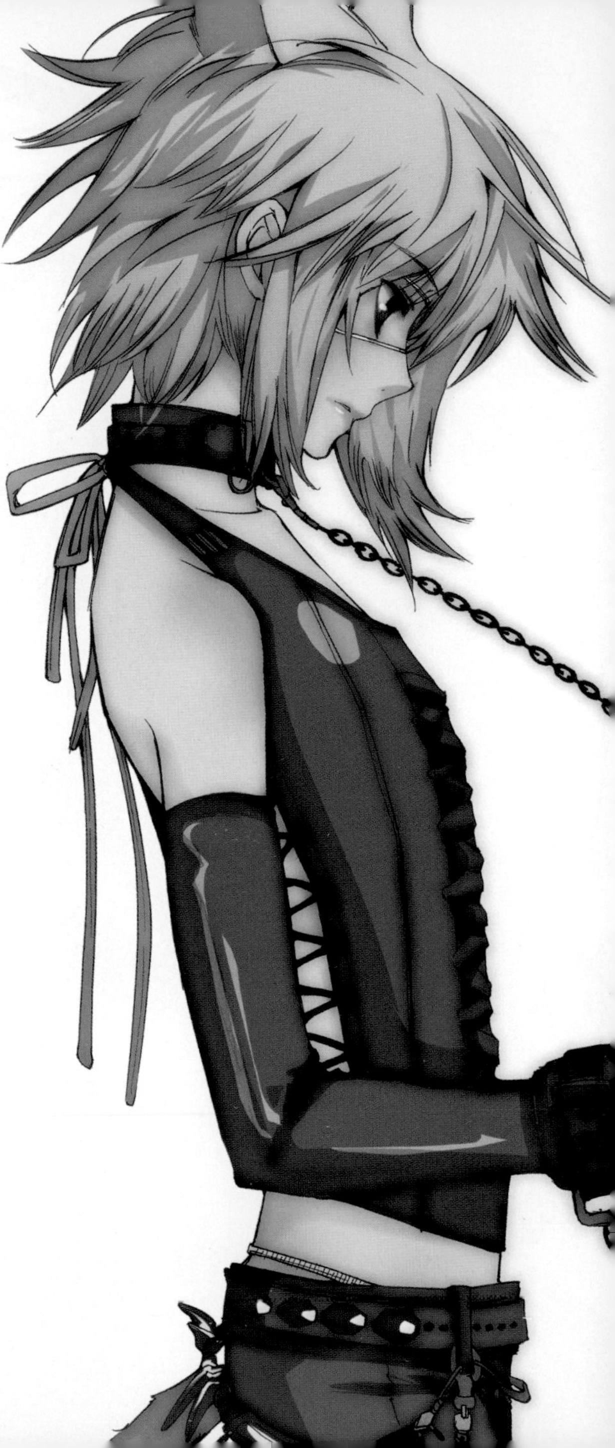

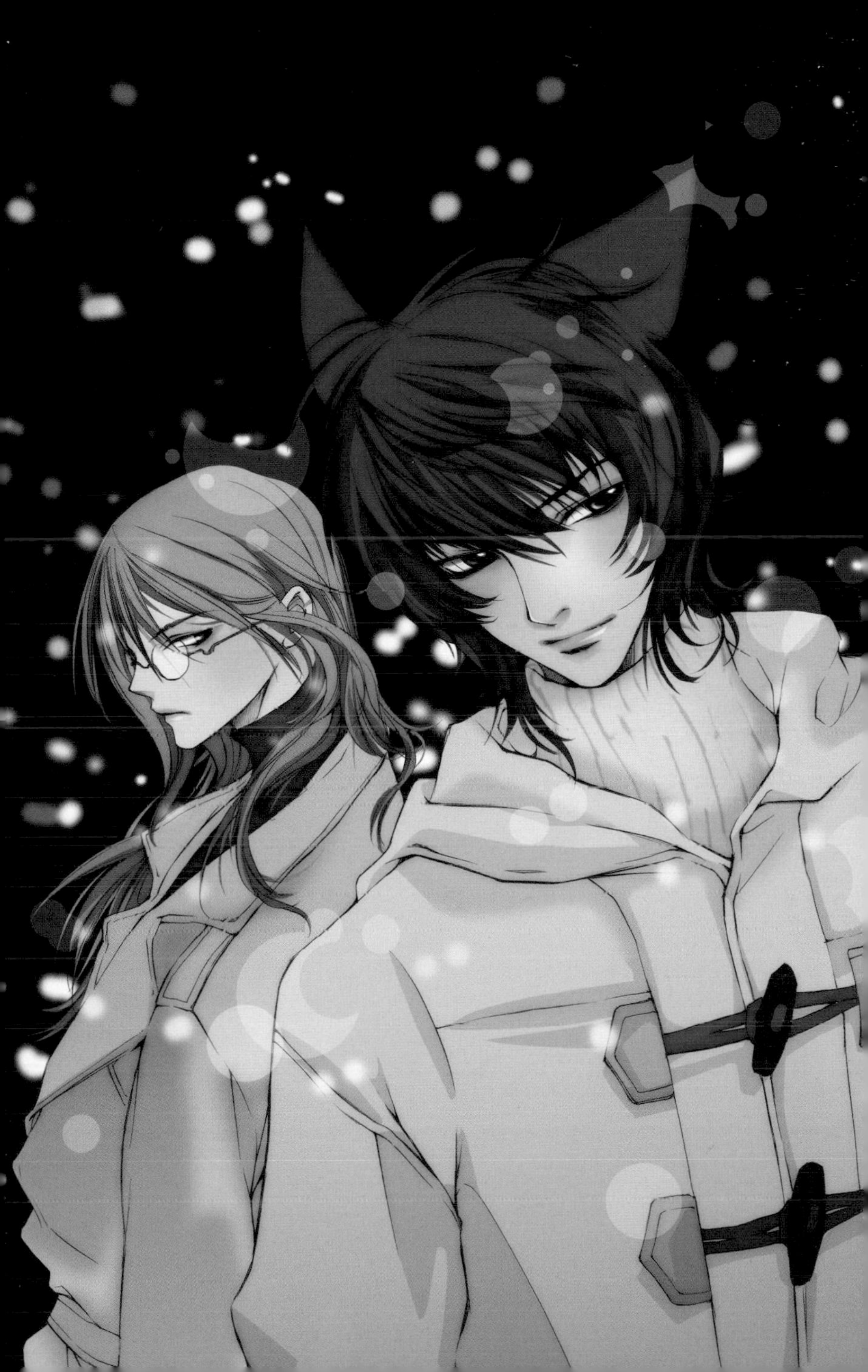

The Absolute Toy Master Chapters

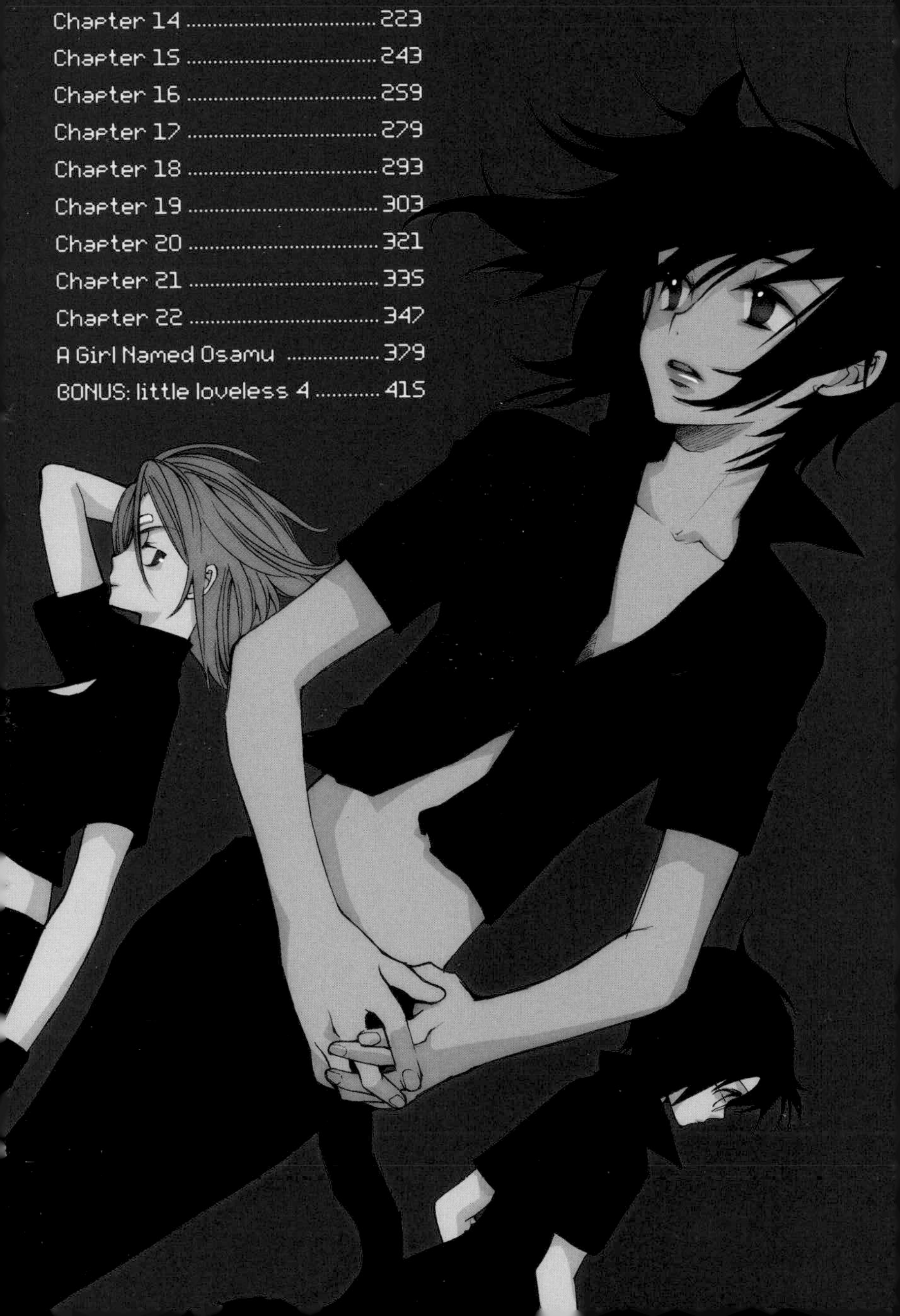

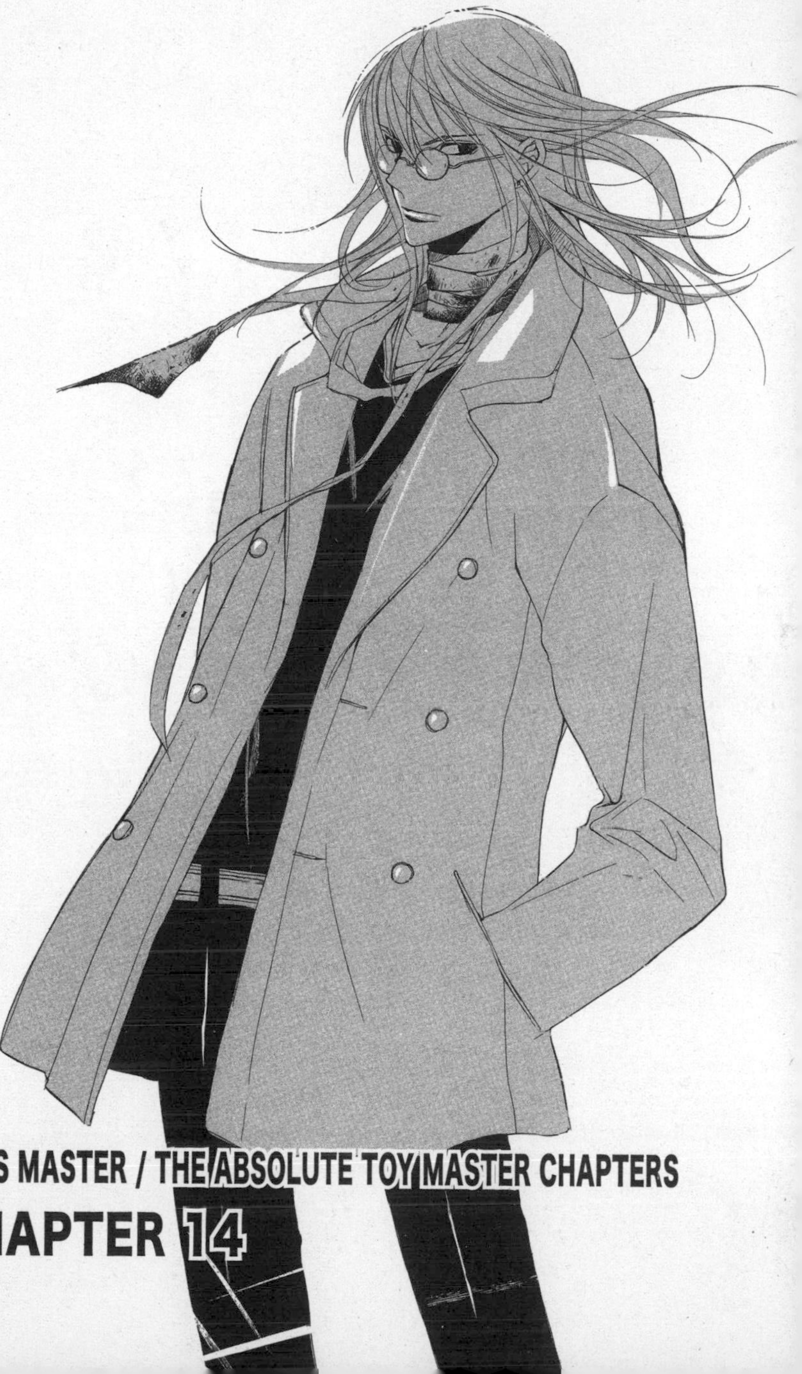

TOY'S MASTER / THE ABSOLUTE TOY MASTER CHAPTERS

CHAPTER 14

THIS IS NO GAME.
IN ORDER TO SPARK THE FIRE...
COME...

CAST YOUR WEAPONS TO
THE GROUND.

THERE IS NOTHING TO FEAR.

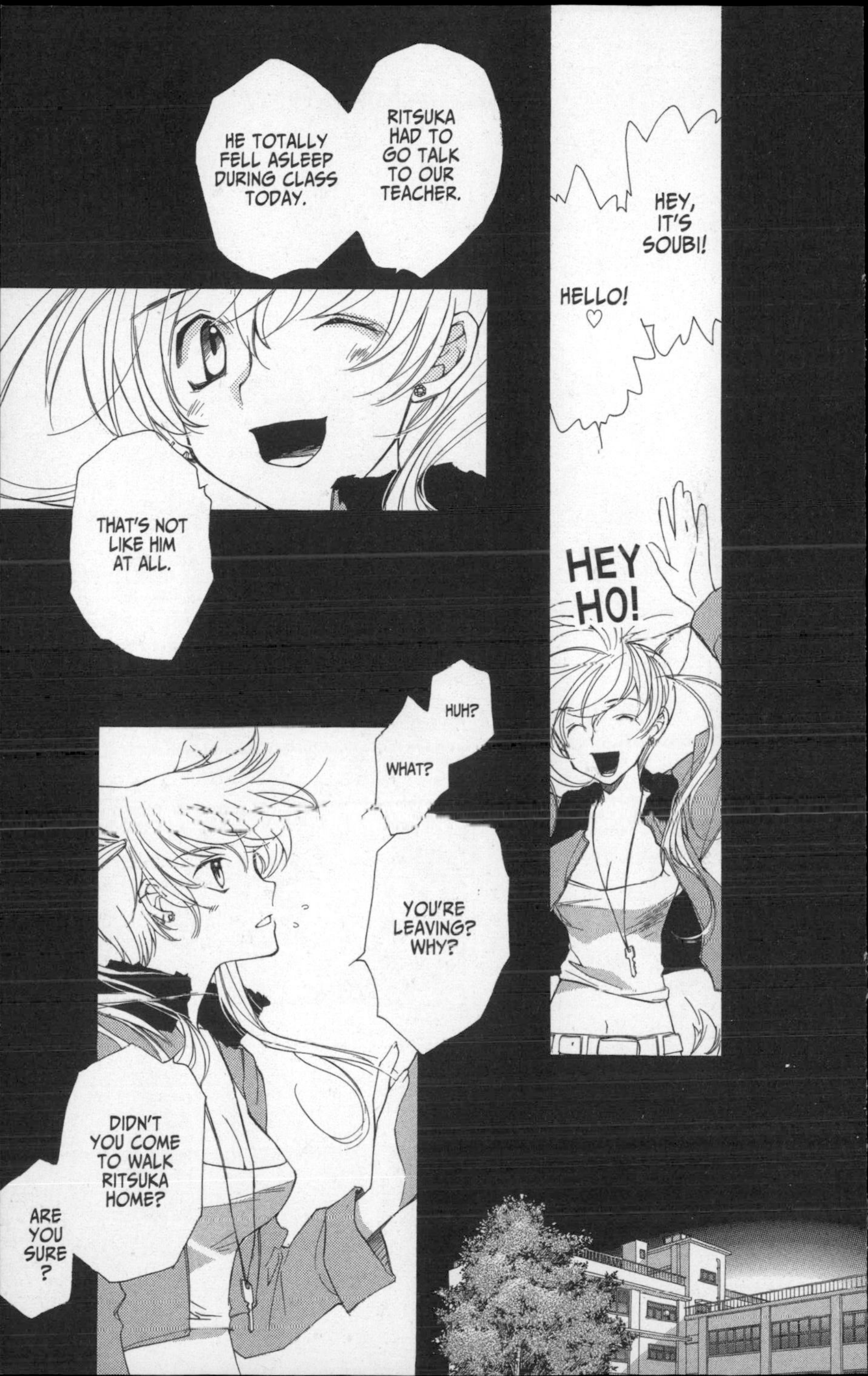
HEY, IT'S SOUBI!
HELLO! ♡
HEY HO!
RITSUKA HAD TO GO TALK TO OUR TEACHER.
HE TOTALLY FELL ASLEEP DURING CLASS TODAY.
THAT'S NOT LIKE HIM AT ALL.
HUH?
WHAT?
YOU'RE LEAVING? WHY?
DIDN'T YOU COME TO WALK RITSUKA HOME?
ARE YOU SURE?

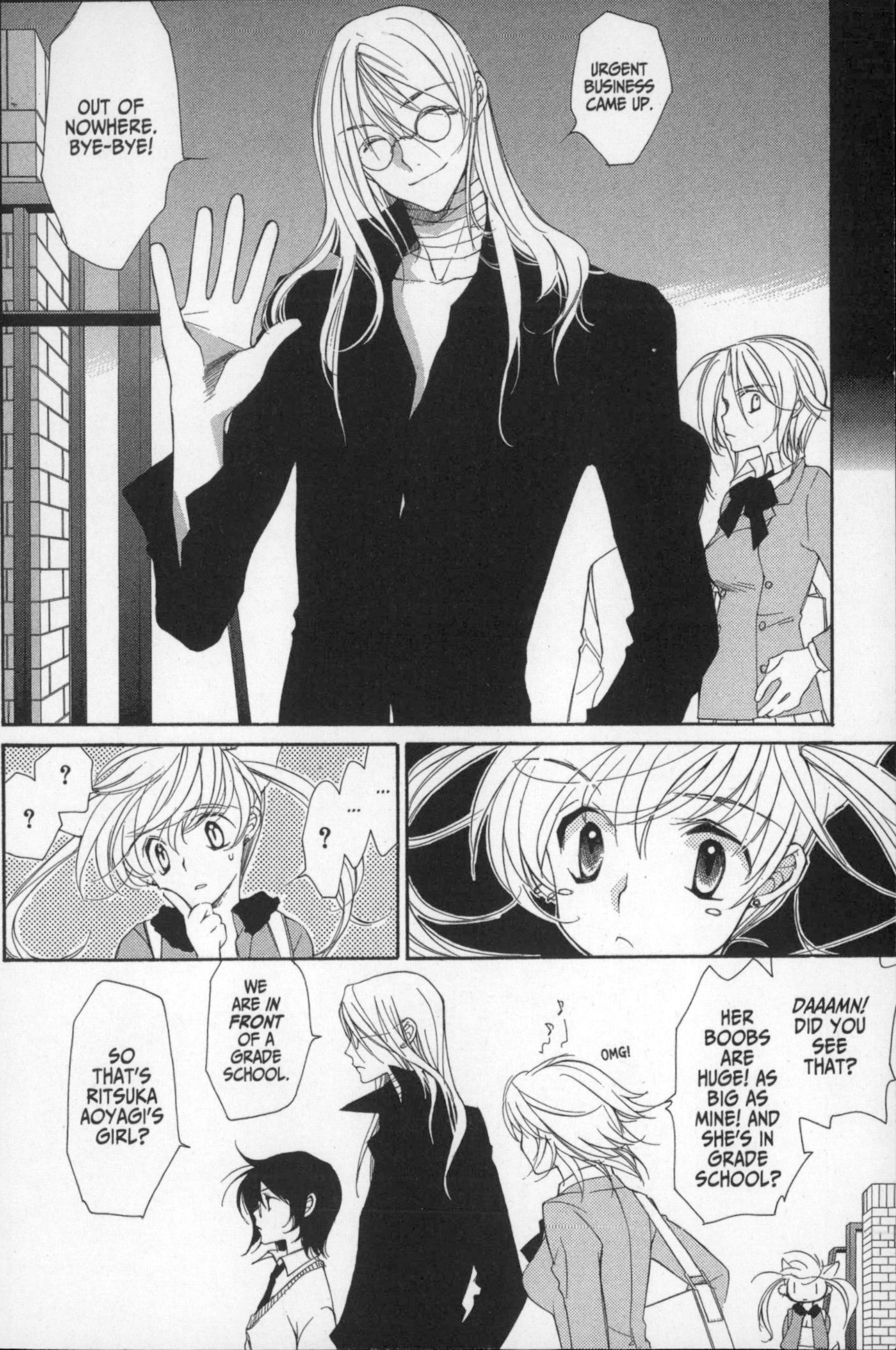
URGENT BUSINESS CAME UP.
OUT OF NOWHERE. BYE-BYE!
...
...
?
?
?
DAAAMN! DID YOU SEE THAT?
HER BOOBS ARE HUGE! AS BIG AS MINE! AND SHE'S IN GRADE SCHOOL?
OMG!
WE ARE IN FRONT OF A GRADE SCHOOL.
SO THAT'S RITSUKA AOYAGI'S GIRL?

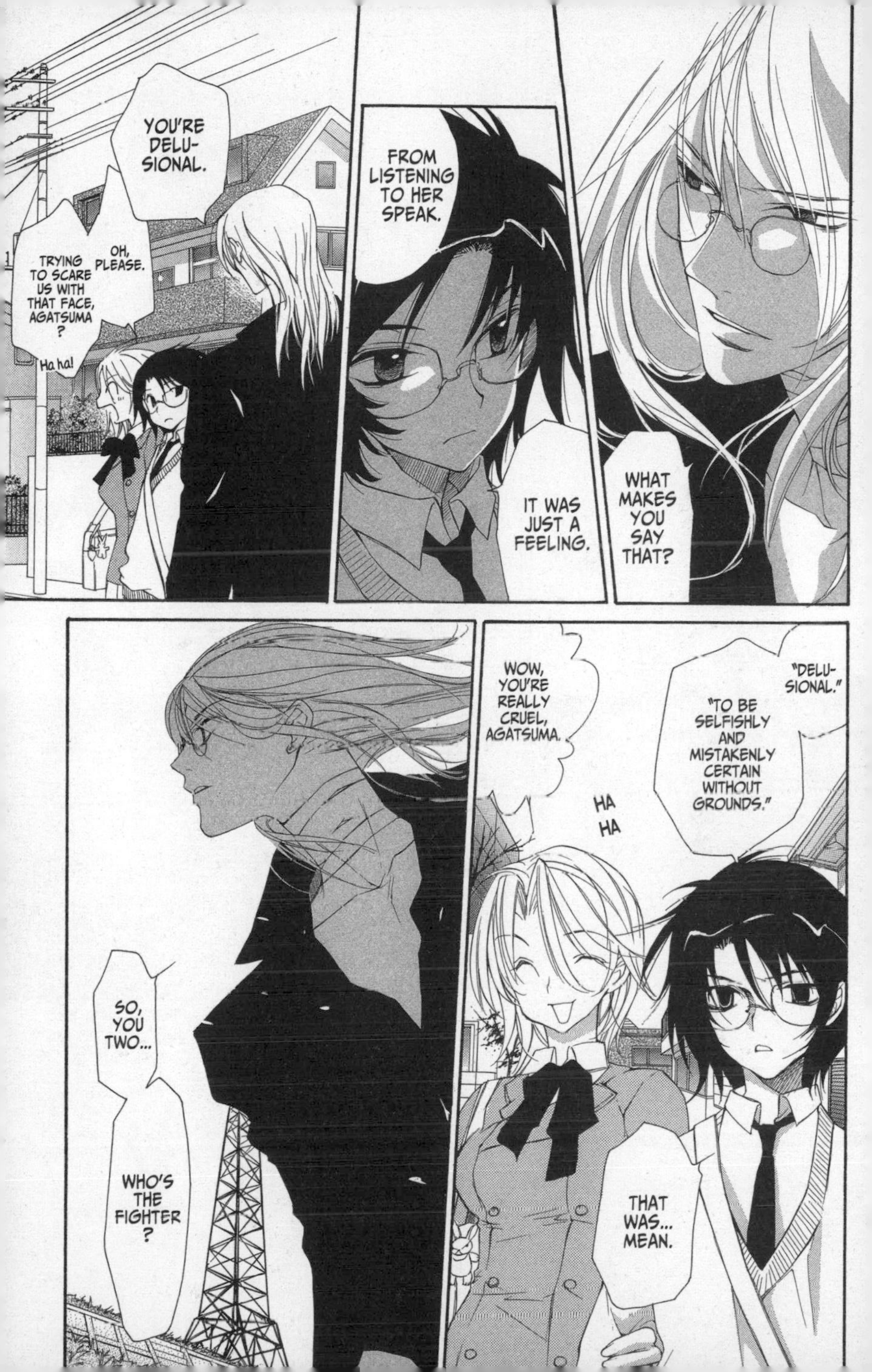
WHAT MAKES YOU SAY THAT?
IT WAS JUST A FEELING.
FROM LISTENING TO HER SPEAK.
YOU'RE DELU-SIONAL.
OH, PLEASE.
TRYING TO SCARE US WITH THAT FACE, AGATSUMA?
Ha ha!
"DELU-SIONAL."
"TO BE SELFISHLY AND MISTAKENLY CERTAIN WITHOUT GROUNDS."
WOW, YOU'RE REALLY CRUEL, AGATSUMA.
HA HA
THAT WAS... MEAN.
SO, YOU TWO...
WHO'S THE FIGHTER?

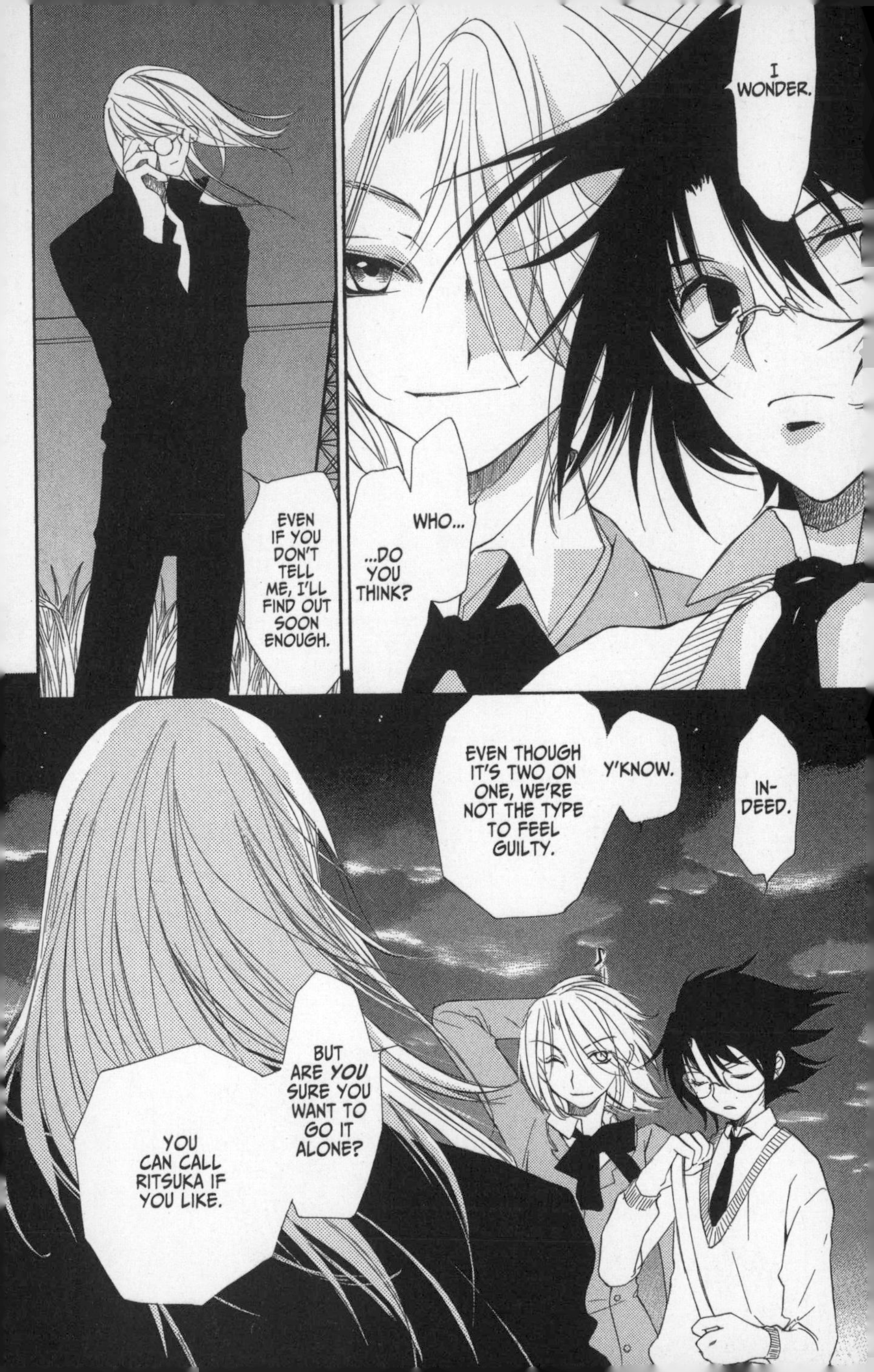
I WONDER.
WHO...
...DO YOU THINK?
EVEN IF YOU DON'T TELL ME, I'LL FIND OUT SOON ENOUGH.
IN-DEED.
Y'KNOW.
EVEN THOUGH IT'S TWO ON ONE, WE'RE NOT THE TYPE TO FEEL GUILTY.
BUT ARE *YOU* SURE YOU WANT TO GO IT ALONE?
YOU CAN CALL RITSUKA IF YOU LIKE.

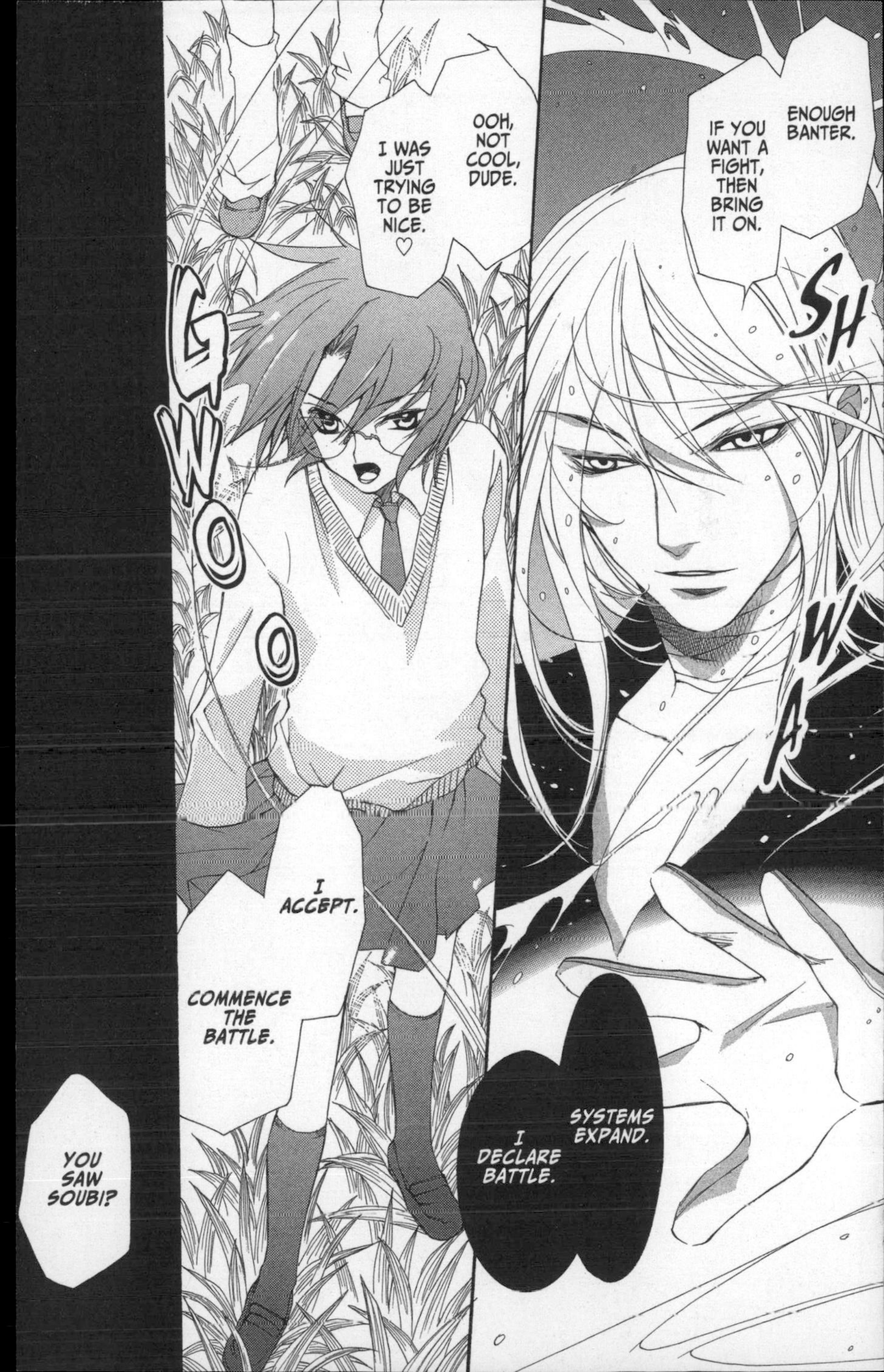
ENOUGH BANTER.
IF YOU WANT A FIGHT, THEN BRING IT ON.
SHWA
SYSTEMS EXPAND.
I DECLARE BATTLE.
OOH, NOT COOL, DUDE.
I WAS JUST TRYING TO BE NICE. ♡
GWOOO
I ACCEPT.
COMMENCE THE BATTLE.
YOU SAW SOUBI?

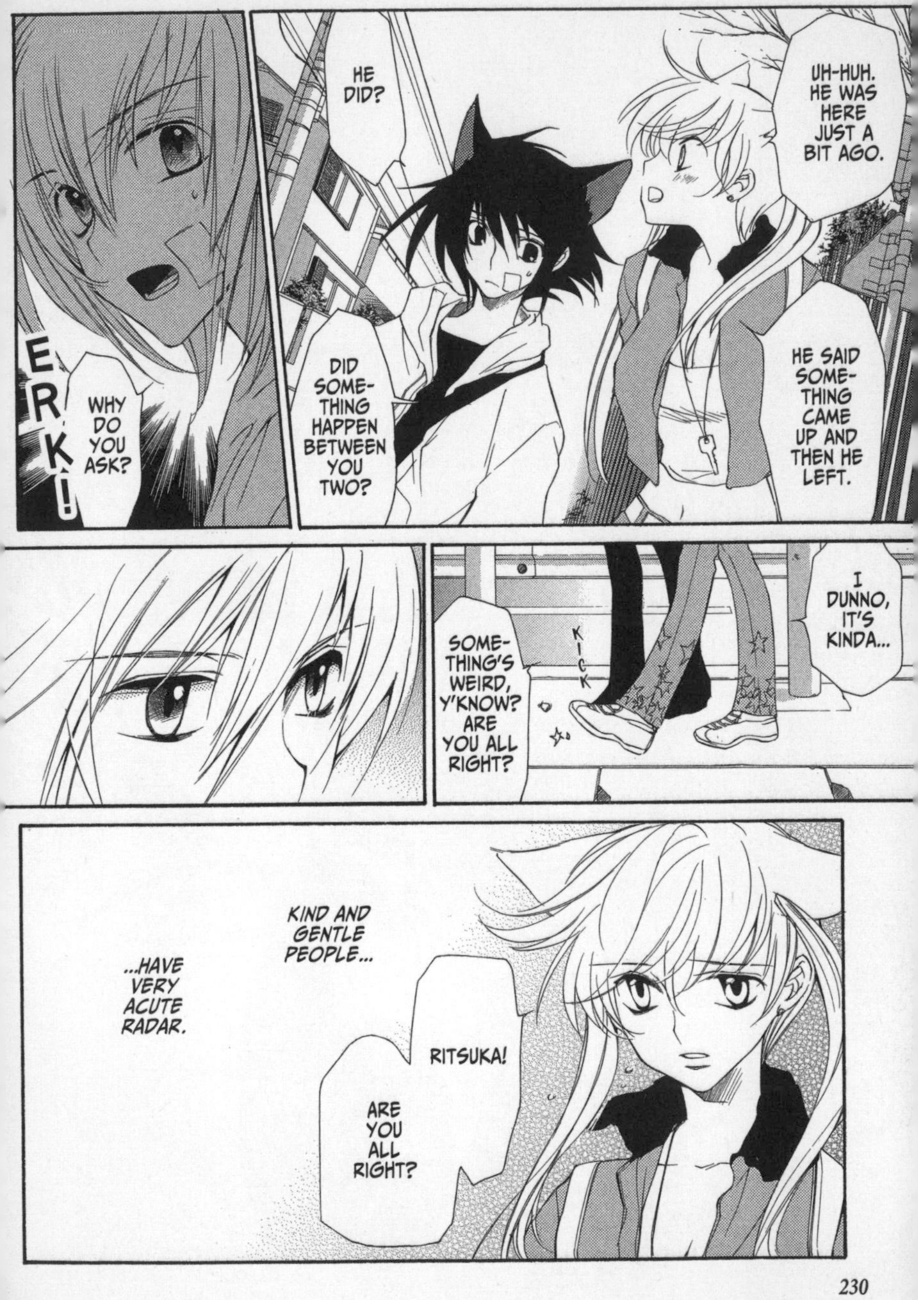
UH-HUH. HE WAS HERE JUST A BIT AGO.
HE DID?
HE SAID SOMETHING CAME UP AND THEN HE LEFT.
DID SOMETHING HAPPEN BETWEEN YOU TWO?
ERK!
WHY DO YOU ASK?
I DUNNO, IT'S KINDA...
KICK
SOMETHING'S WEIRD, Y'KNOW? ARE YOU ALL RIGHT?
KIND AND GENTLE PEOPLE...
...HAVE VERY ACUTE RADAR.
RITSUKA!
ARE YOU ALL RIGHT?

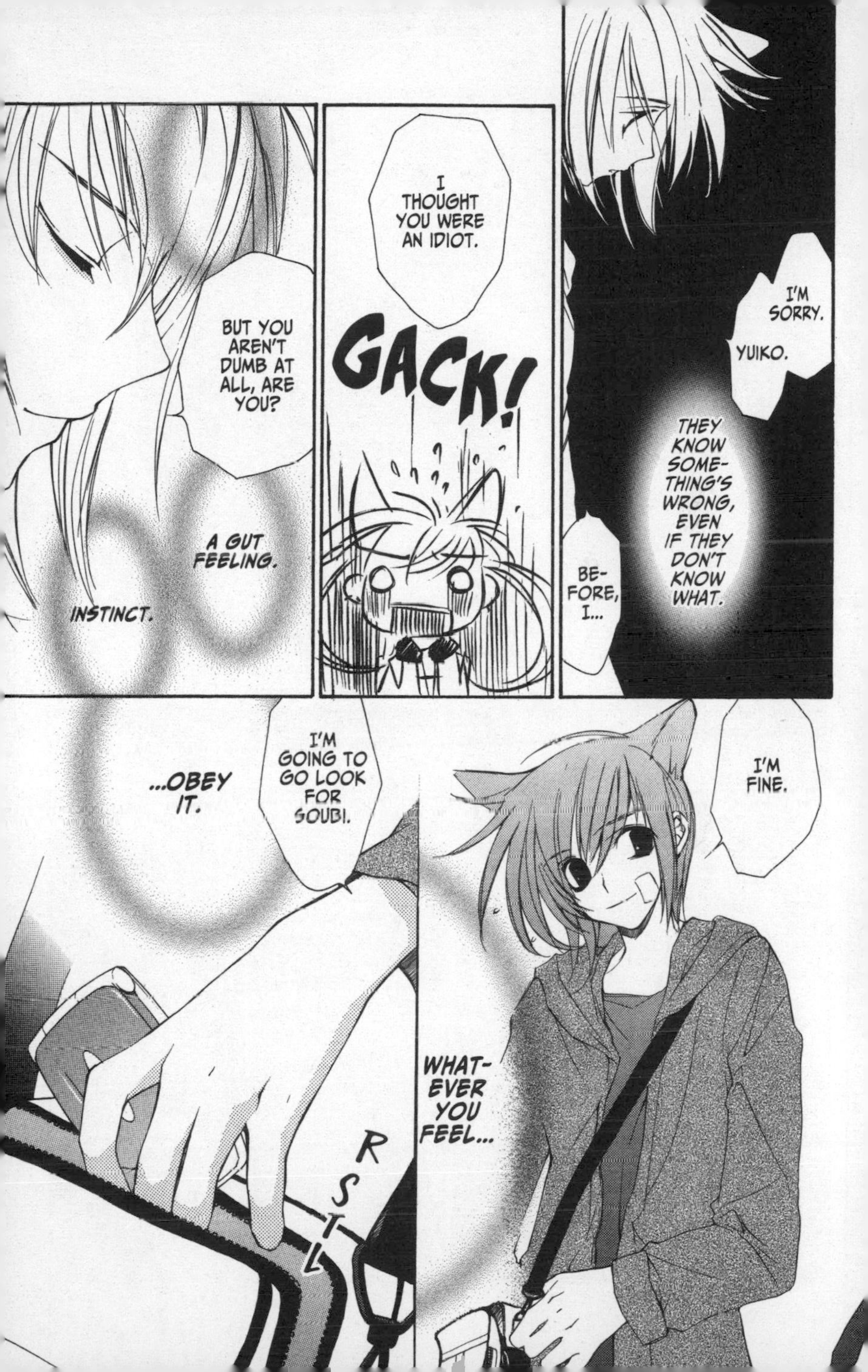
I'M SORRY.
YUIKO.
THEY KNOW SOME-THING'S WRONG, EVEN IF THEY DON'T KNOW WHAT.
BE-FORE, I...
I THOUGHT YOU WERE AN IDIOT.
GACK!
BUT YOU AREN'T DUMB AT ALL, ARE YOU?
A GUT FEELING.
INSTINCT.
I'M FINE.
WHAT-EVER YOU FEEL...
I'M GOING TO GO LOOK FOR SOUBI.
...OBEY IT.
RSTL

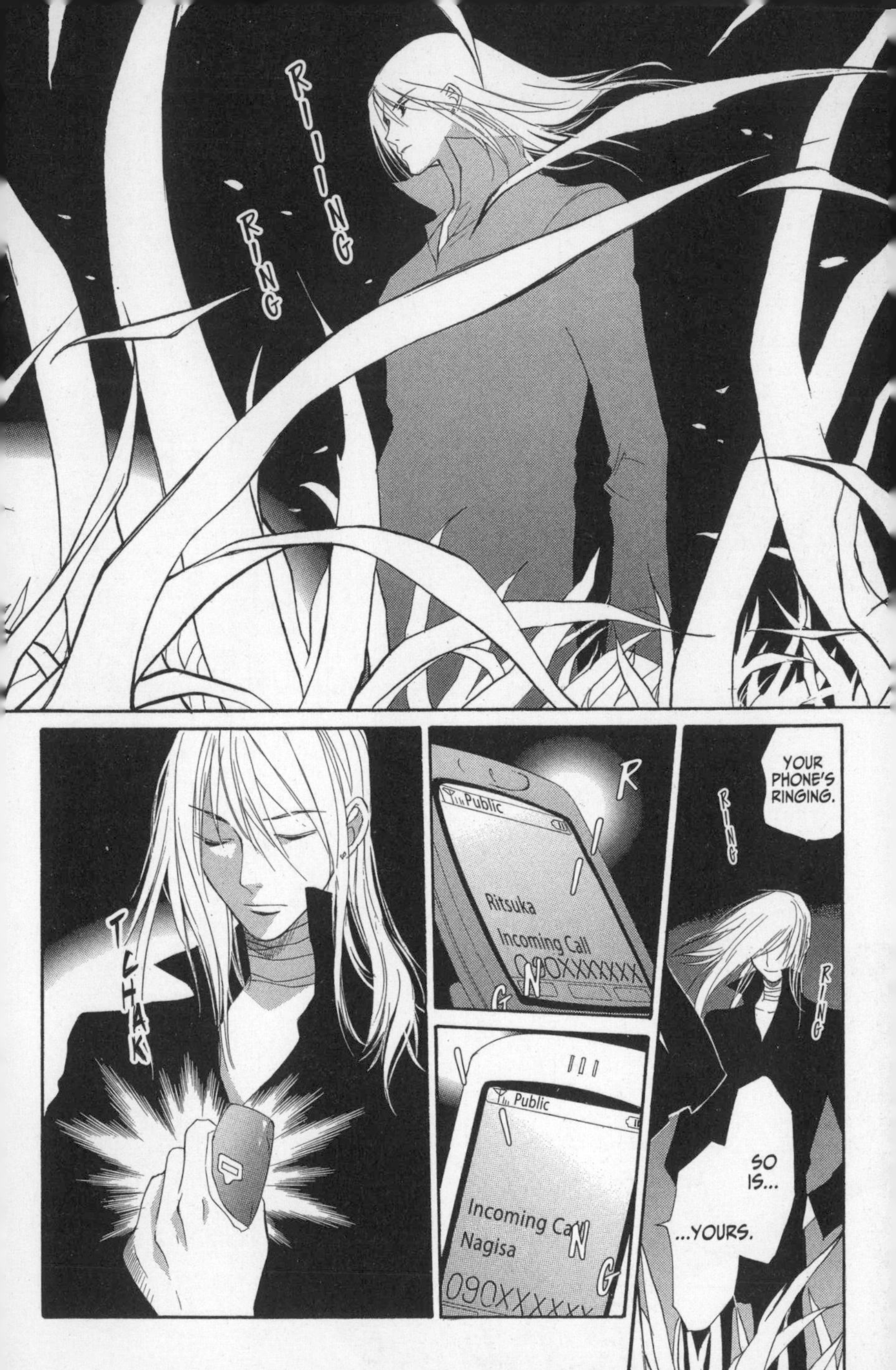
RIIIING
RING
YOUR PHONE'S RINGING.
RING
RING
SO IS...
...YOURS.
RIIING
Public
Ritsuka
Incoming Call
Public
Incoming Ca
Nagisa
NG
TCHAK

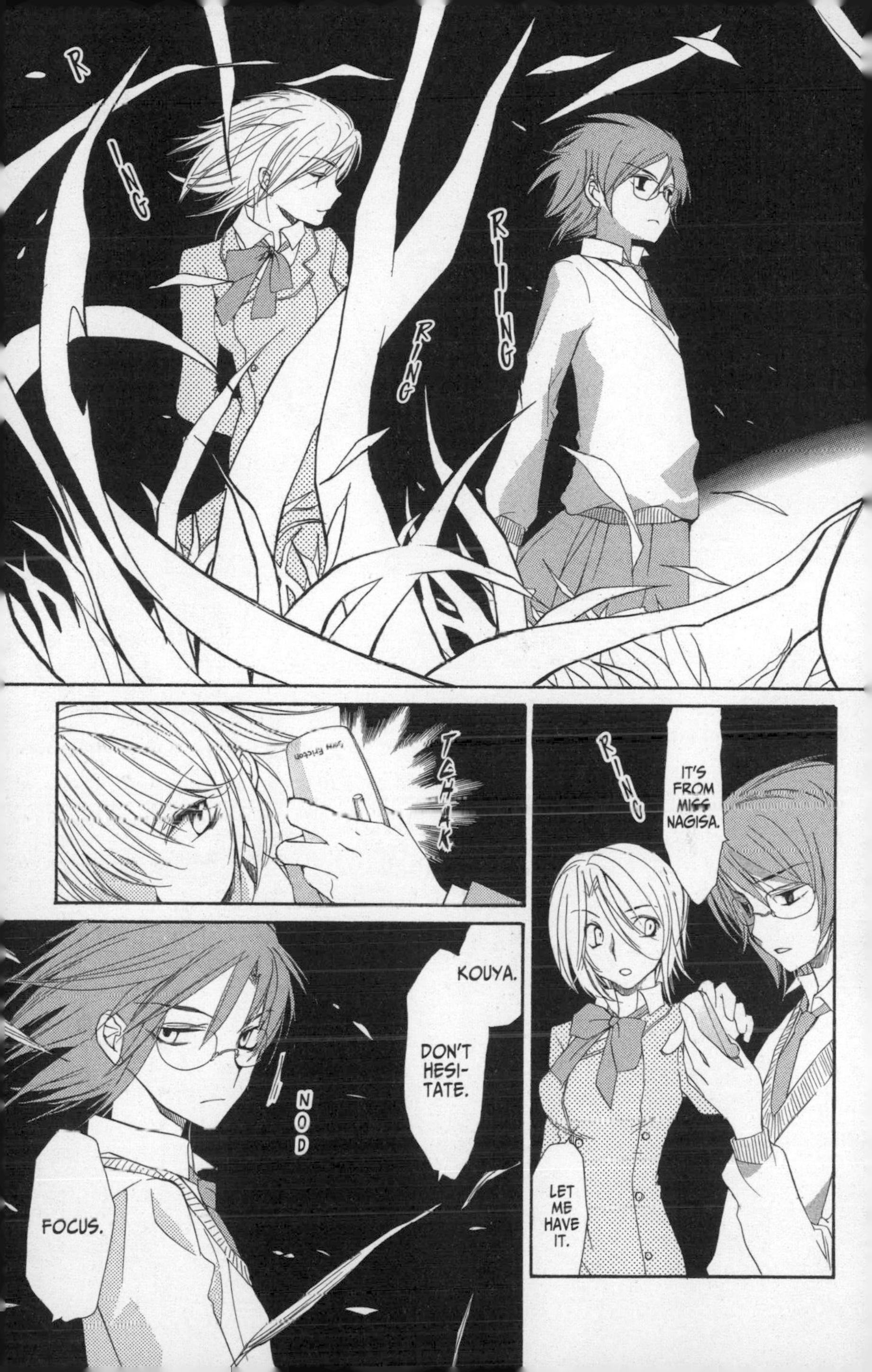
RIIIING
RING
RING
RING
IT'S FROM MISS NAGISA.
LET ME HAVE IT.
TSHAK
KOUYA.
DON'T HESI-TATE.
NOD
FOCUS.

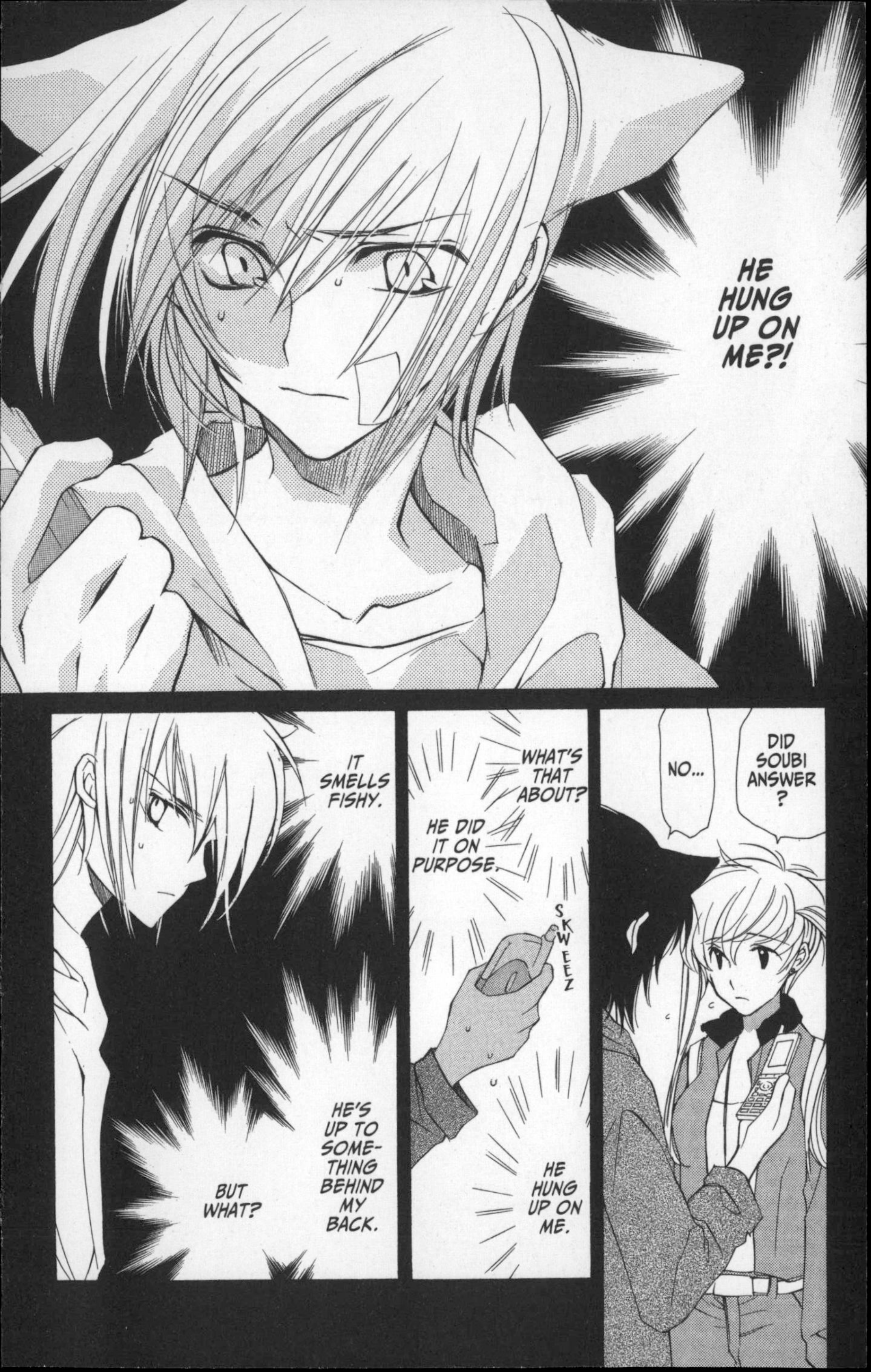
HE HUNG UP ON ME?!
DID SOUBI ANSWER?
NO...
WHAT'S THAT ABOUT?
HE DID IT ON PURPOSE.
SKWEEZ
HE HUNG UP ON ME.
IT SMELLS FISHY.
HE'S UP TO SOME-THING BEHIND MY BACK.
BUT WHAT?

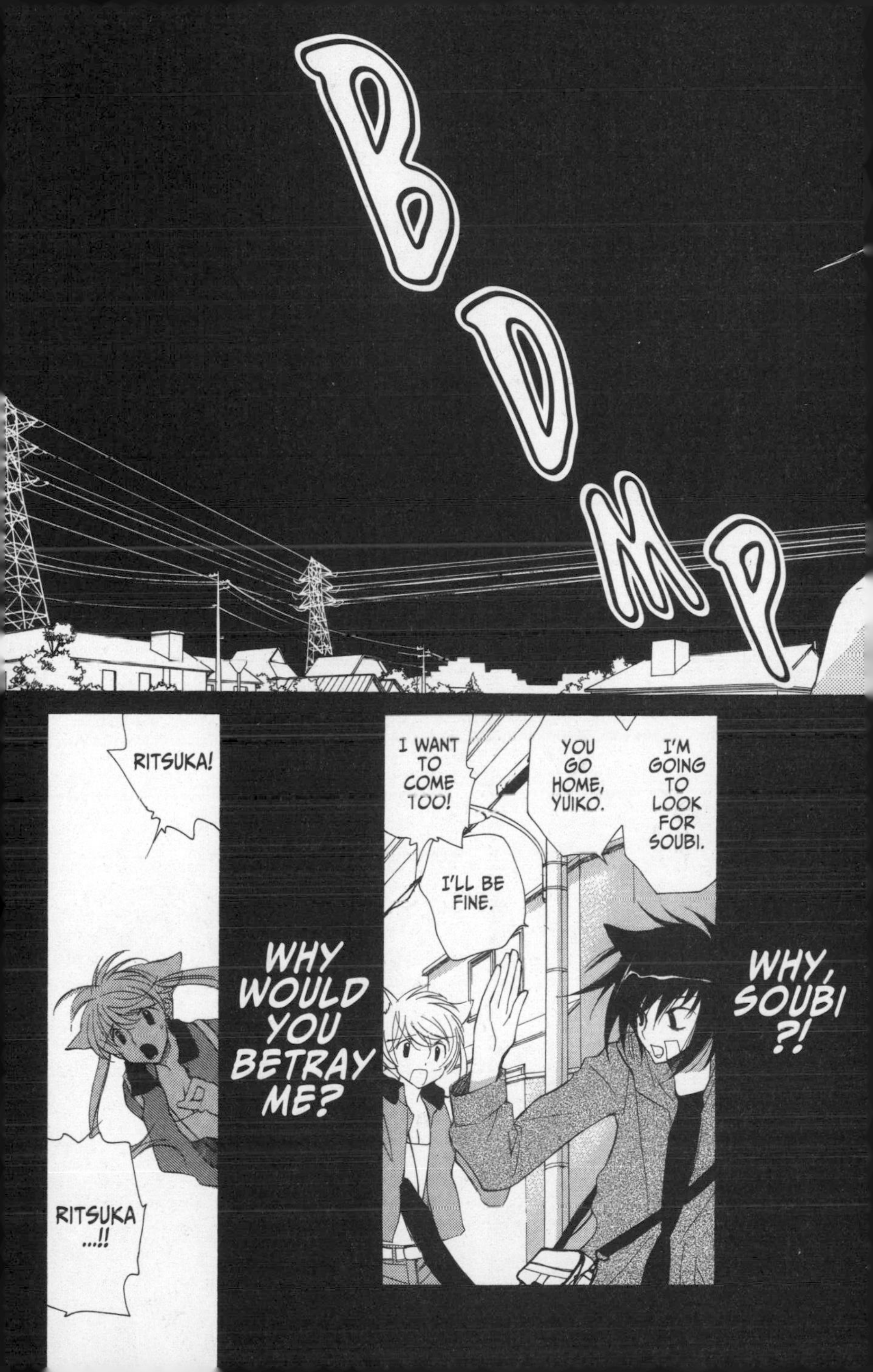
BDMP
WHY, SOUBI?!
I'M GOING TO LOOK FOR SOUBI.
YOU GO HOME, YUIKO.
I WANT TO COME TOO!
I'LL BE FINE.
WHY WOULD YOU BETRAY ME?
RITSUKA!
RITSUKA ...!!

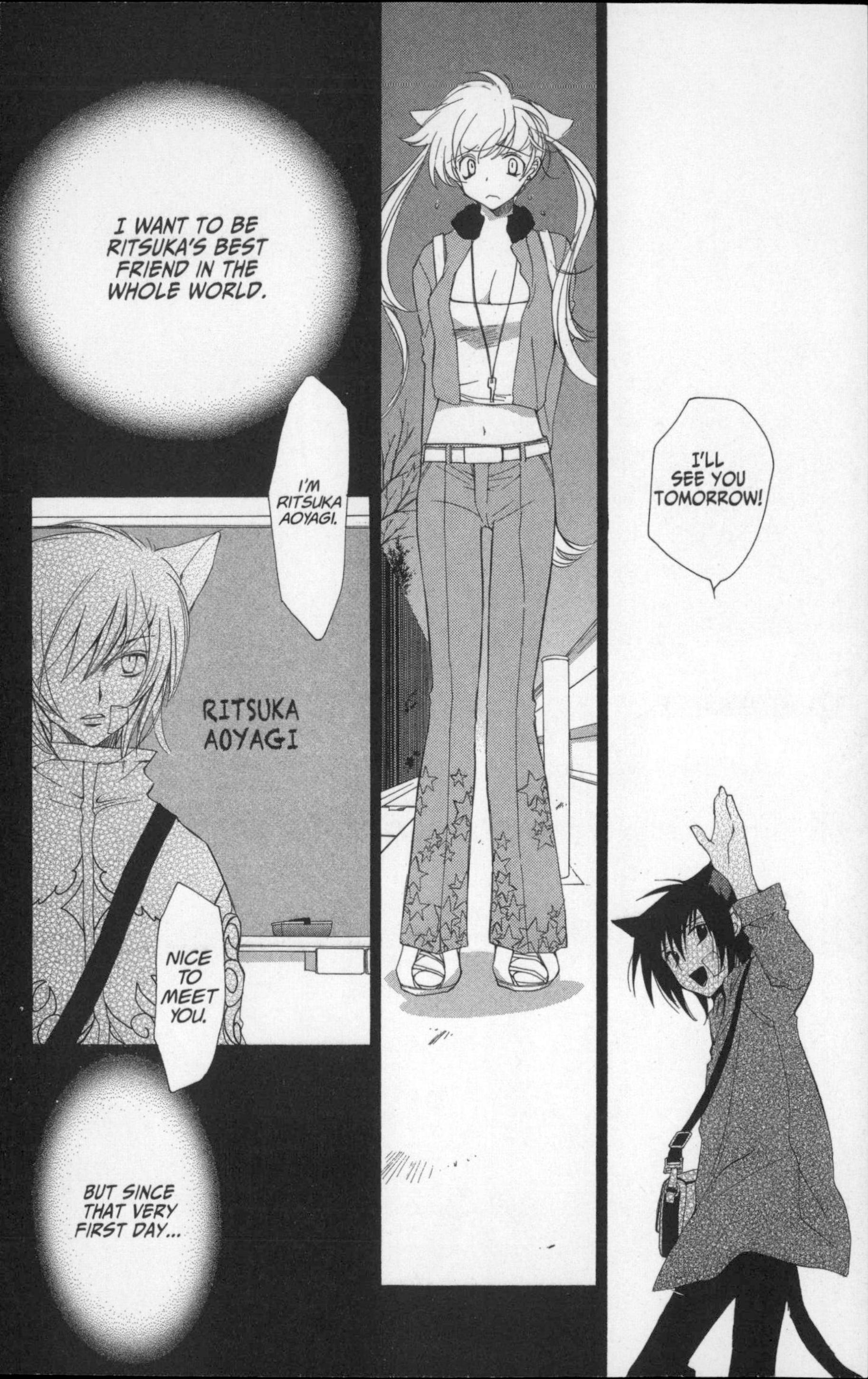
I'LL SEE YOU TOMORROW!
I WANT TO BE RITSUKA'S BEST FRIEND IN THE WHOLE WORLD.
I'M RITSUKA AOYAGI.
RITSUKA AOYAGI
NICE TO MEET YOU.
BUT SINCE THAT VERY FIRST DAY...

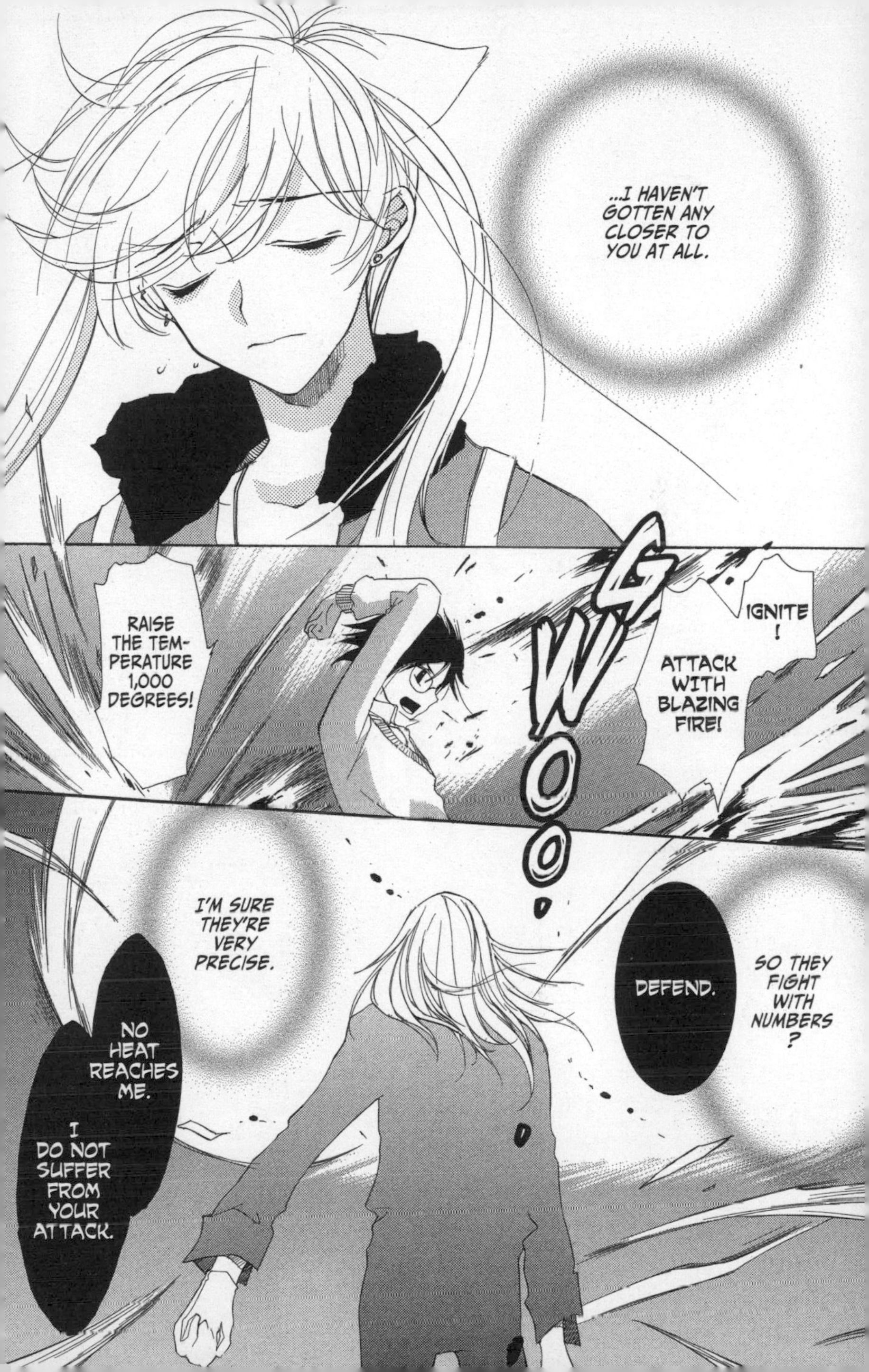
...I HAVEN'T GOTTEN ANY CLOSER TO YOU AT ALL.
IGNITE!
ATTACK WITH BLAZING FIRE!
GWOOOO
RAISE THE TEM-PERATURE 1,000 DEGREES!
SO THEY FIGHT WITH NUMBERS?
DEFEND.
I'M SURE THEY'RE VERY PRECISE.
NO HEAT REACHES ME.
I DO NOT SUFFER FROM YOUR ATTACK.

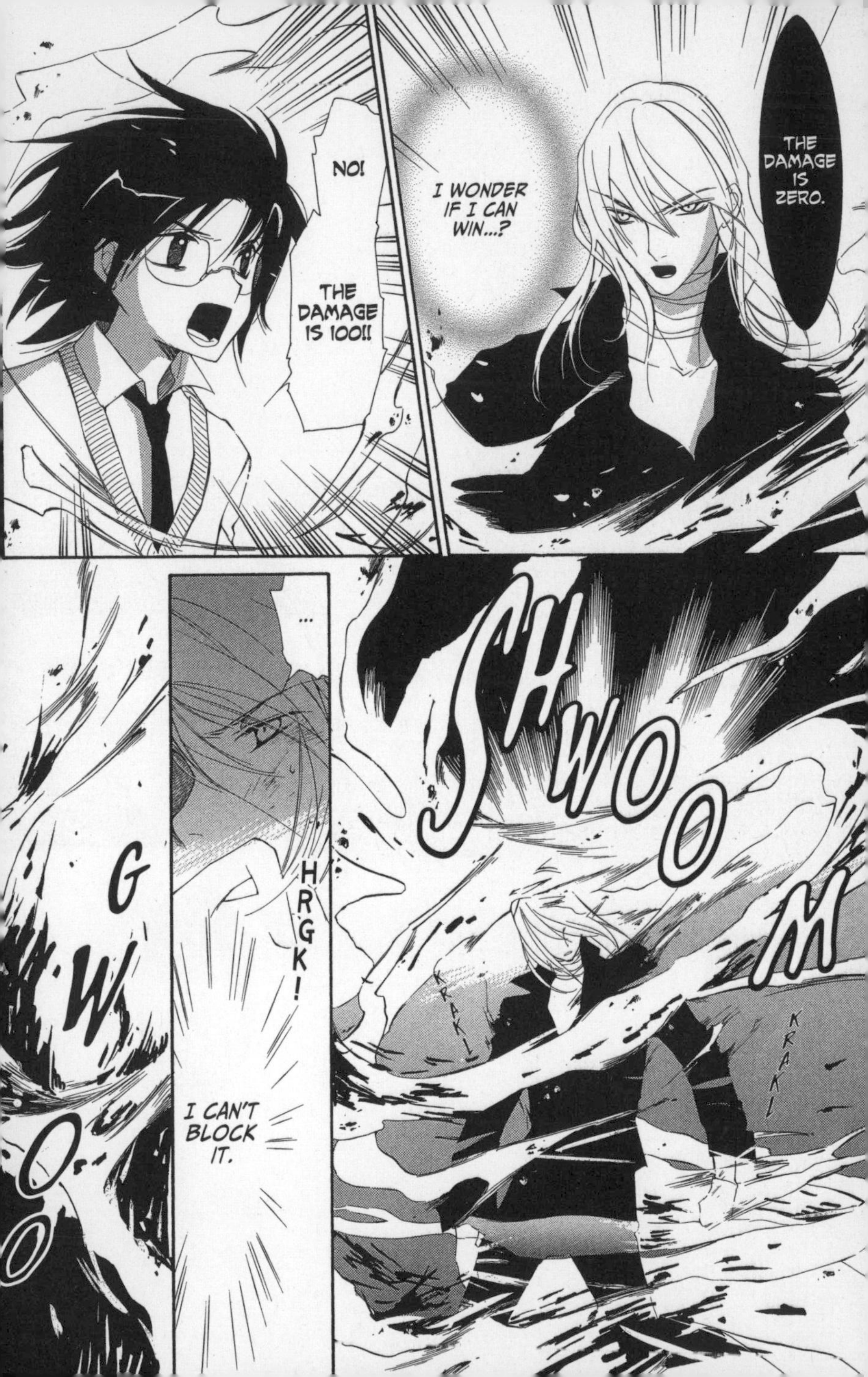
THE DAMAGE IS ZERO.
I WONDER IF I CAN WIN...?
NO!
THE DAMAGE IS 100!!
SHWOOOM
KRAKL
KRAKL
...
HRGK!
I CAN'T BLOCK IT.
GWOOO

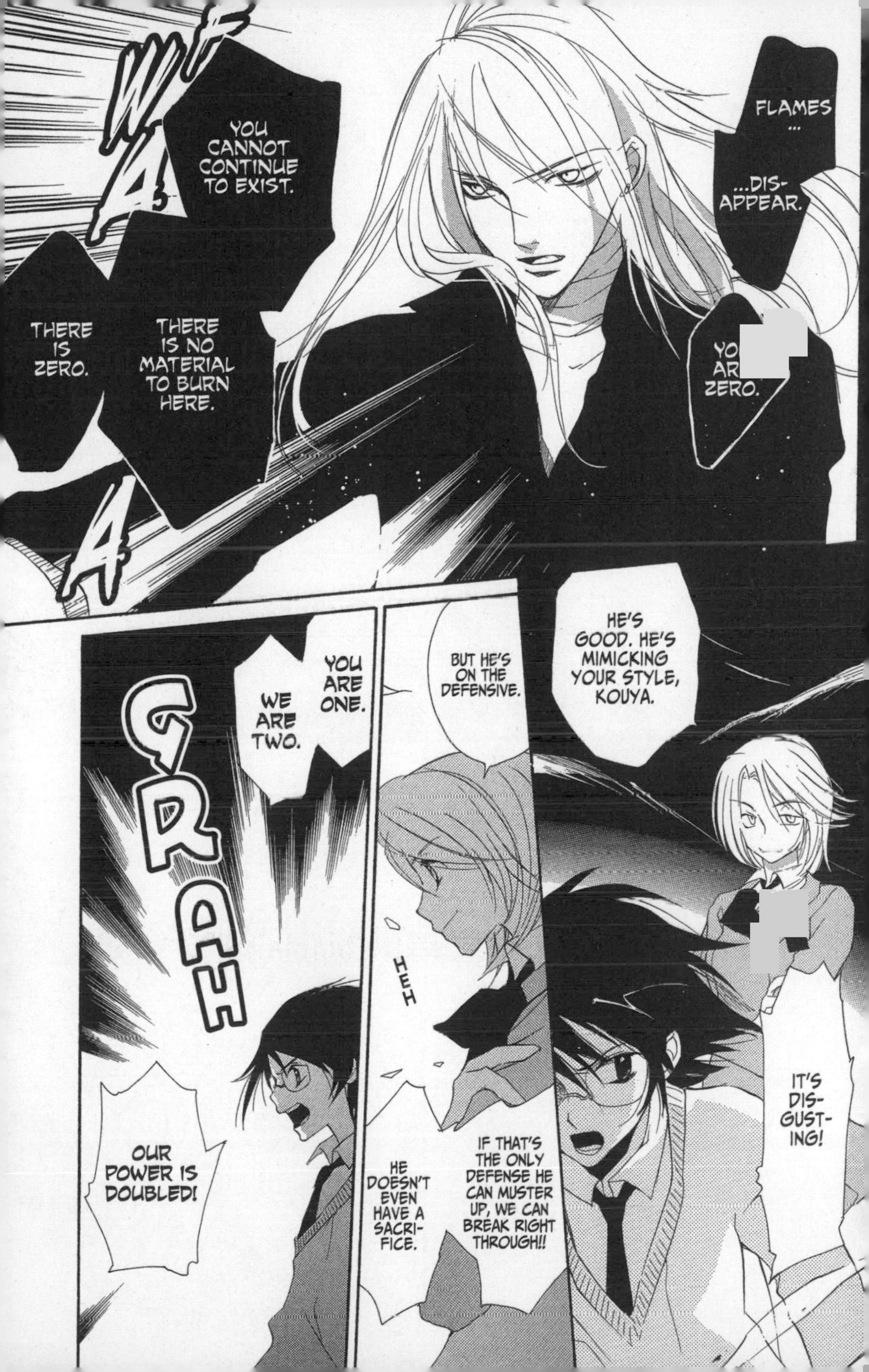
FLAMES ...
...DIS-APPEAR.
YO AR ZERO.
YOU CANNOT CONTINUE TO EXIST.
THERE IS NO MATERIAL TO BURN HERE.
THERE IS ZERO.
HE'S GOOD. HE'S MIMICKING YOUR STYLE, KOUYA.
IT'S DIS-GUST-ING!
IF THAT'S THE ONLY DEFENSE HE CAN MUSTER UP, WE CAN BREAK RIGHT THROUGH!!
BUT HE'S ON THE DEFENSIVE.
HEH
HE DOESN'T EVEN HAVE A SACRI-FICE.
YOU ARE ONE.
WE ARE TWO.
OUR POWER IS DOUBLED!

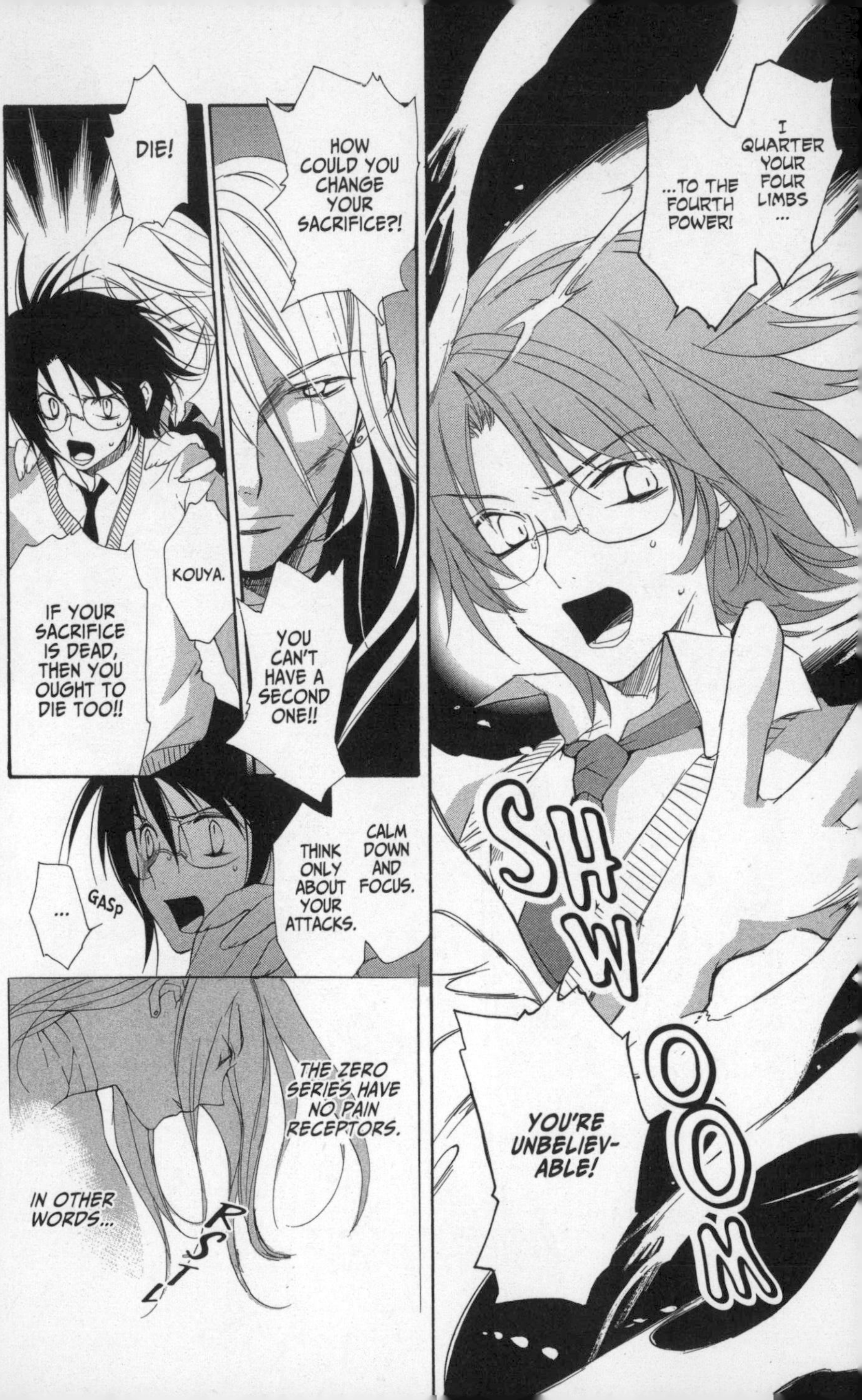
I QUARTER YOUR FOUR LIMBS...
...TO THE FOURTH POWER!
SHWOOOM
YOU'RE UNBELIEV-ABLE!
HOW COULD YOU CHANGE YOUR SACRIFICE?!
YOU CAN'T HAVE A SECOND ONE!!
DIE!
KOUYA.
IF YOUR SACRIFICE IS DEAD, THEN YOU OUGHT TO DIE TOO!!
CALM DOWN AND FOCUS.
THINK ONLY ABOUT YOUR ATTACKS.
GASp
...
THE ZERO SERIES HAVE NO PAIN RECEPTORS.
IN OTHER WORDS...
RUSTL

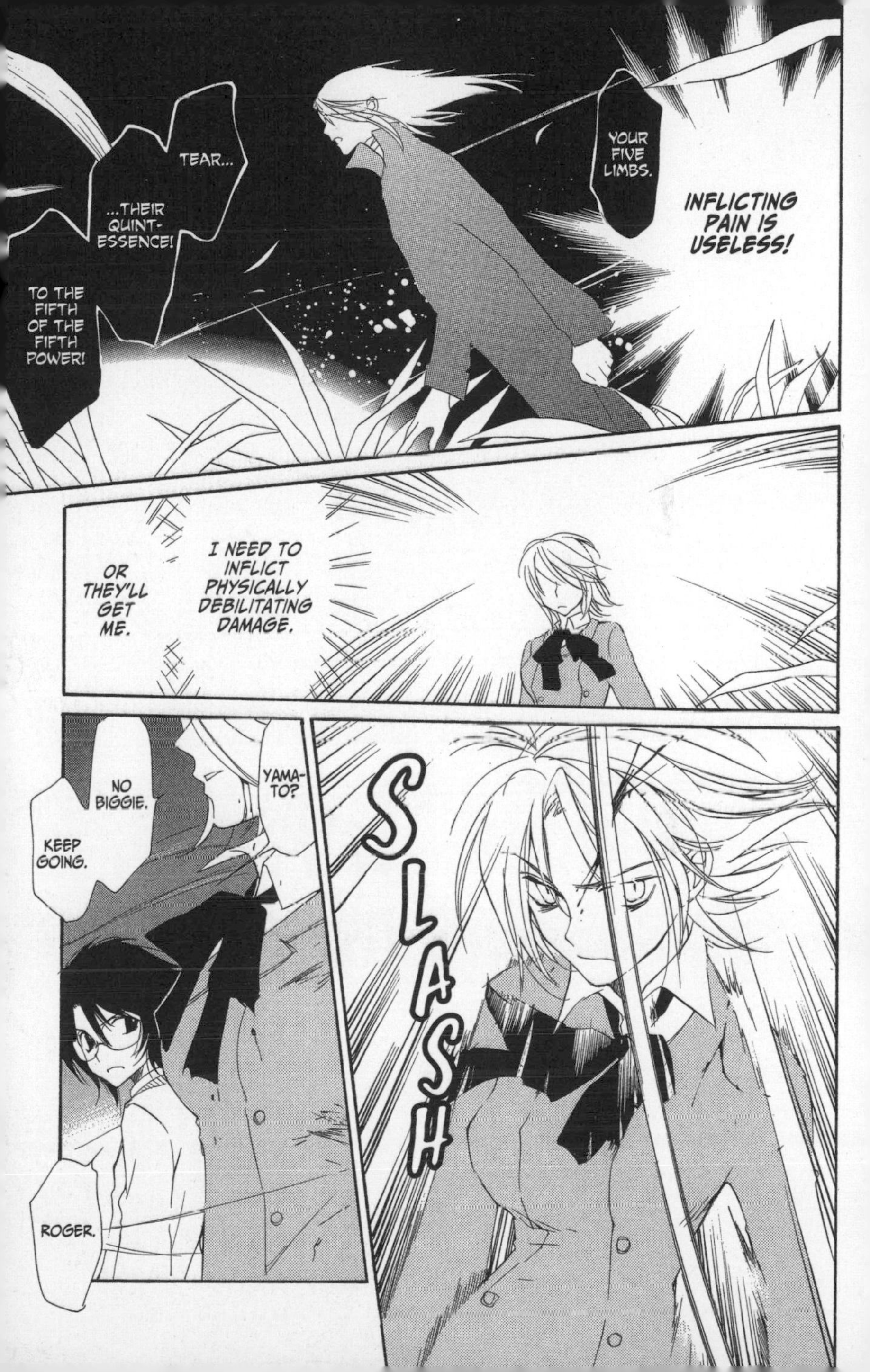
YOUR FIVE LIMBS.
INFLICTING PAIN IS USELESS!
TEAR...
...THEIR QUINT-ESSENCE!
TO THE FIFTH OF THE FIFTH POWER!
I NEED TO INFLICT PHYSICALLY DEBILITATING DAMAGE.
OR THEY'LL GET ME.
SLASH
YAMA-TO?
NO BIGGIE.
KEEP GOING.
ROGER.

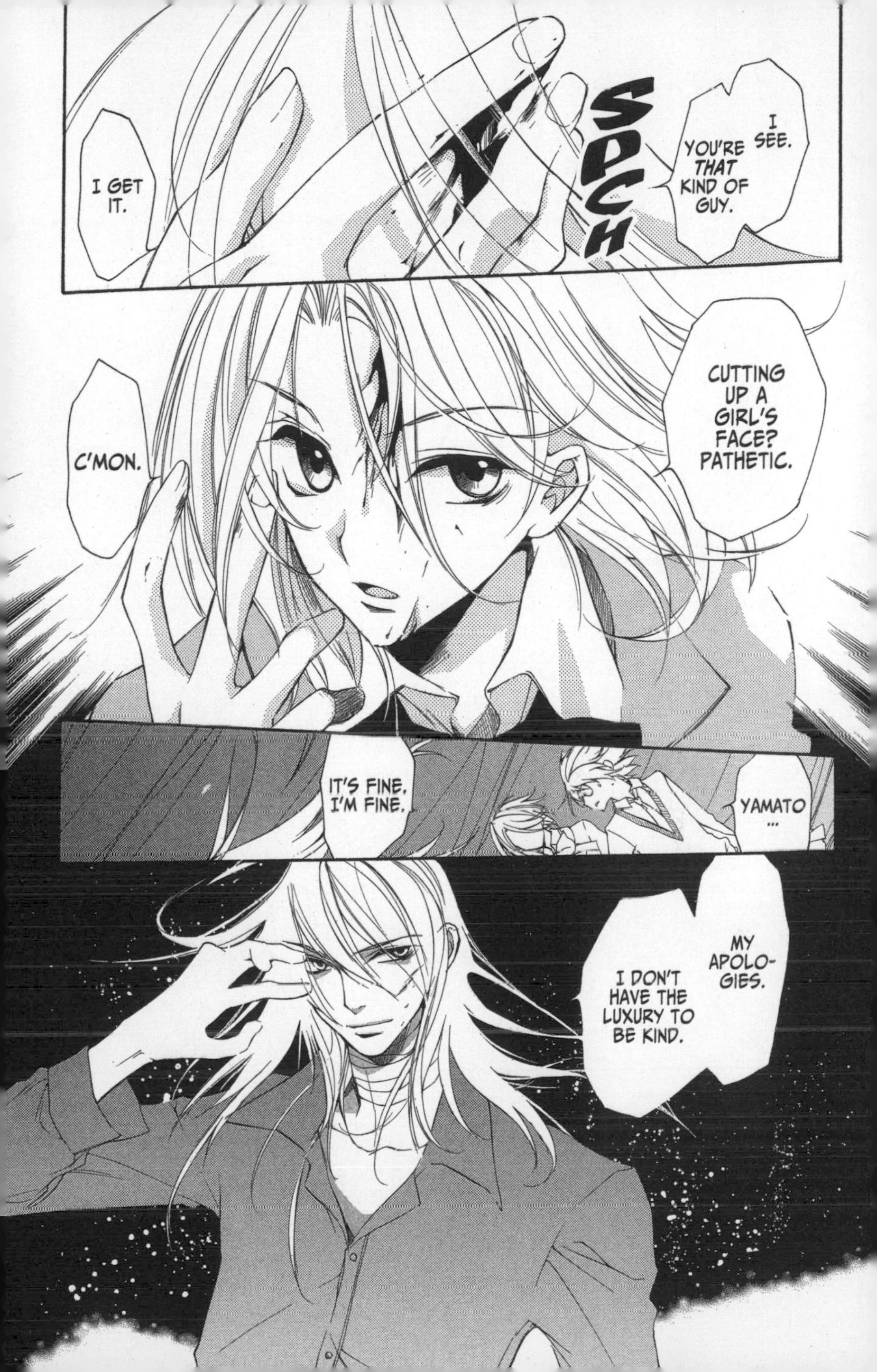
I SEE. YOU'RE THAT KIND OF GUY.
SPCH
I GET IT.
CUTTING UP A GIRL'S FACE? PATHETIC.
C'MON.
YAMATO ...
IT'S FINE. I'M FINE.
MY APOLOGIES.
I DON'T HAVE THE LUXURY TO BE KIND.

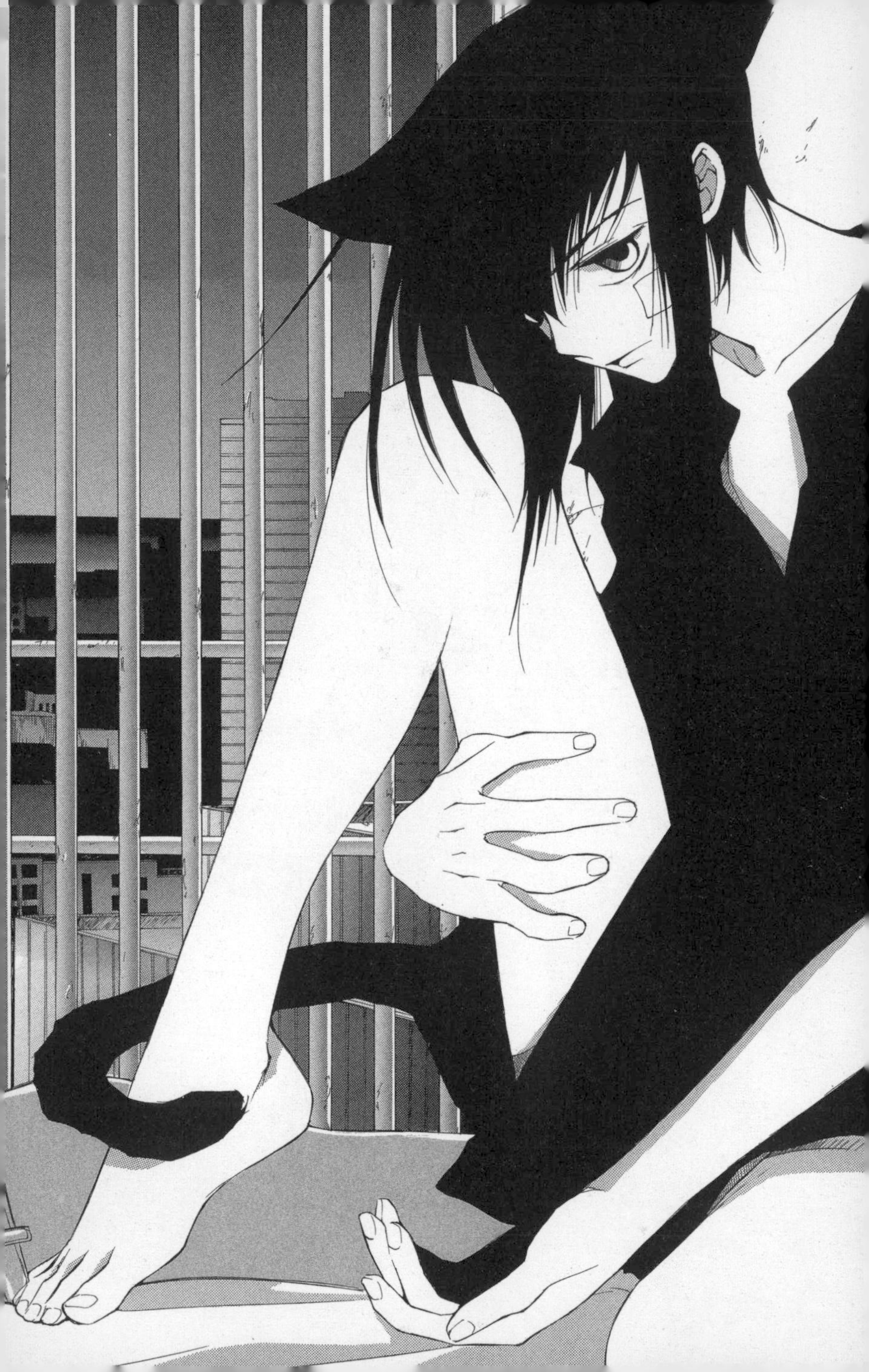

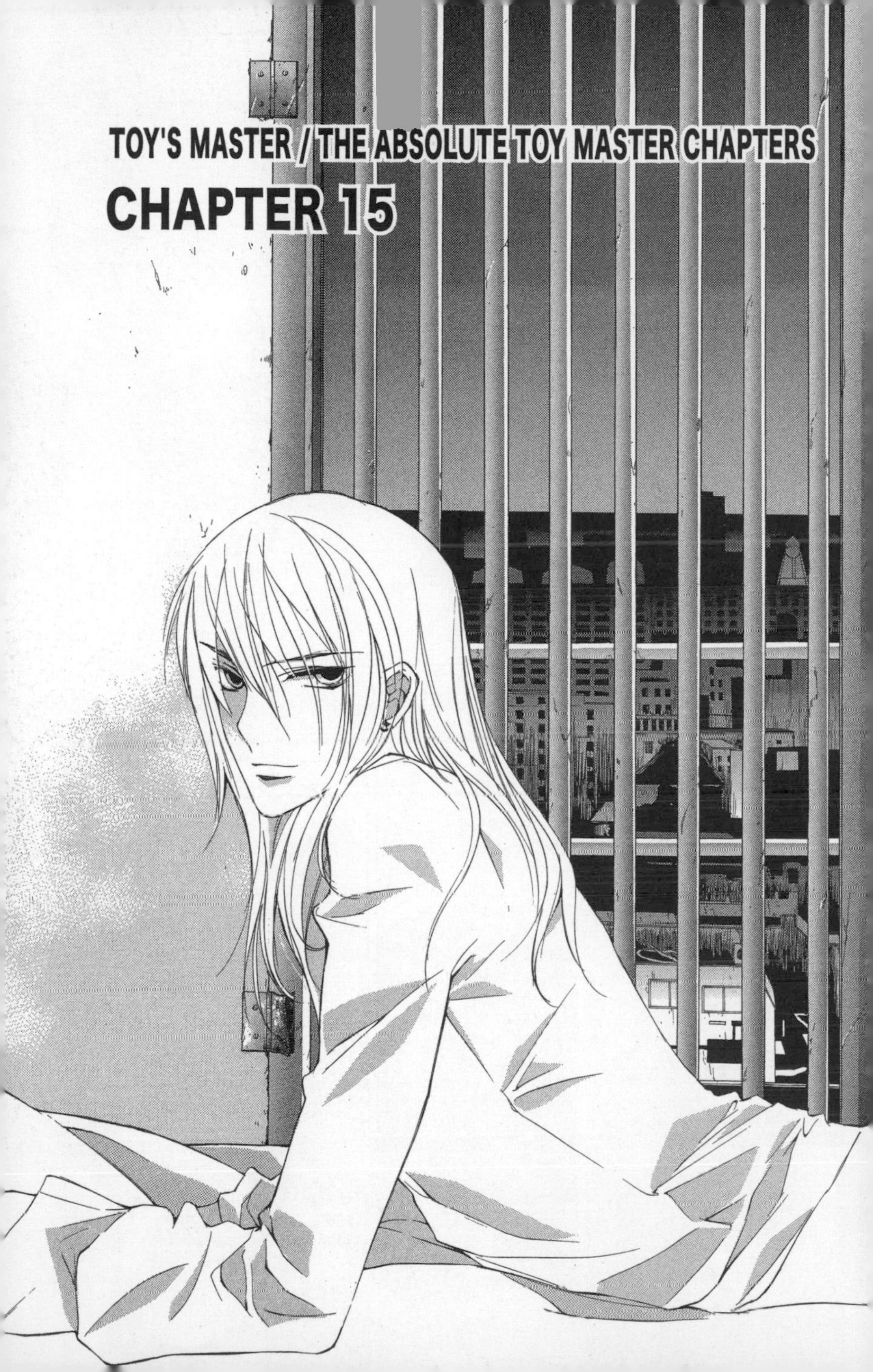
TOY'S MASTER / THE ABSOLUTE TOY MASTER CHAPTERS
CHAPTER 15

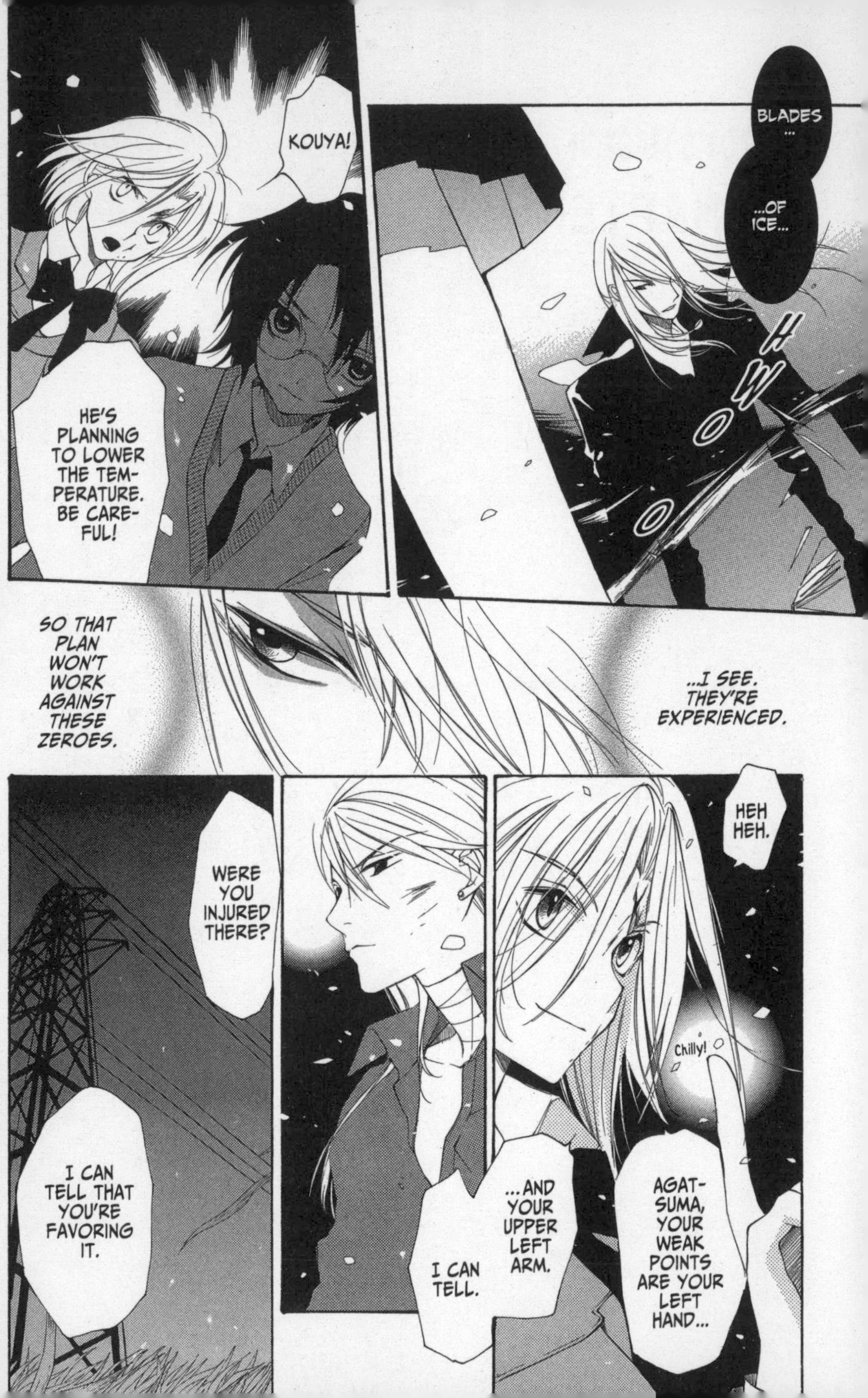
BLADES...
...OF ICE...
HWOOO
KOUYA!
HE'S PLANNING TO LOWER THE TEMPERATURE. BE CAREFUL!
...I SEE. THEY'RE EXPERIENCED.
SO THAT PLAN WON'T WORK AGAINST THESE ZEROES.
HEH HEH.
Chilly!
AGATSUMA, YOUR WEAK POINTS ARE YOUR LEFT HAND...
...AND YOUR UPPER LEFT ARM.
I CAN TELL.
WERE YOU INJURED THERE?
I CAN TELL THAT YOU'RE FAVORING IT.

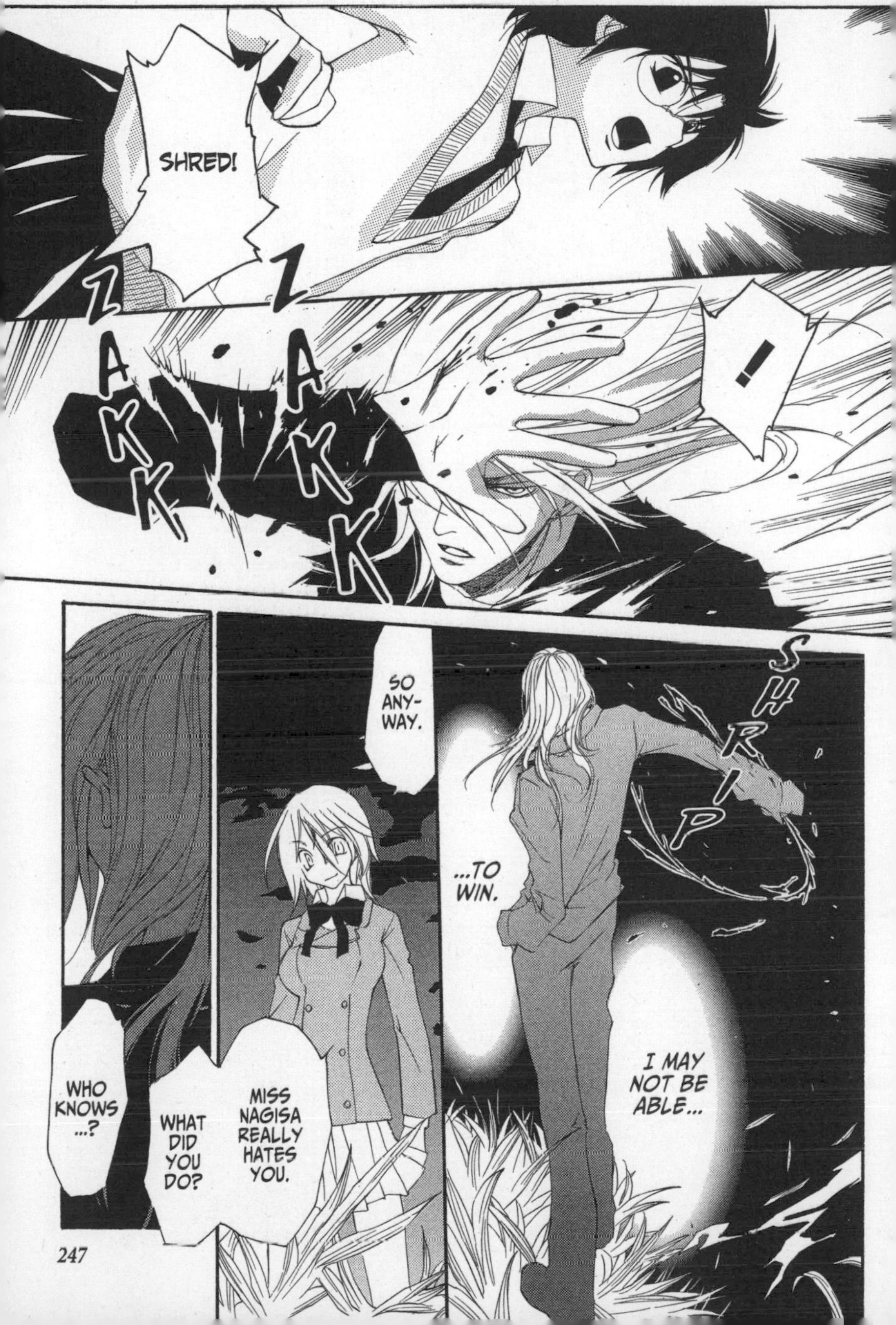
SHRED!
ZAKK
ZAKK
!
SHRIP
SO ANYWAY.
I MAY NOT BE ABLE...
...TO WIN.
MISS NAGISA REALLY HATES YOU.
WHAT DID YOU DO?
WHO KNOWS ...?

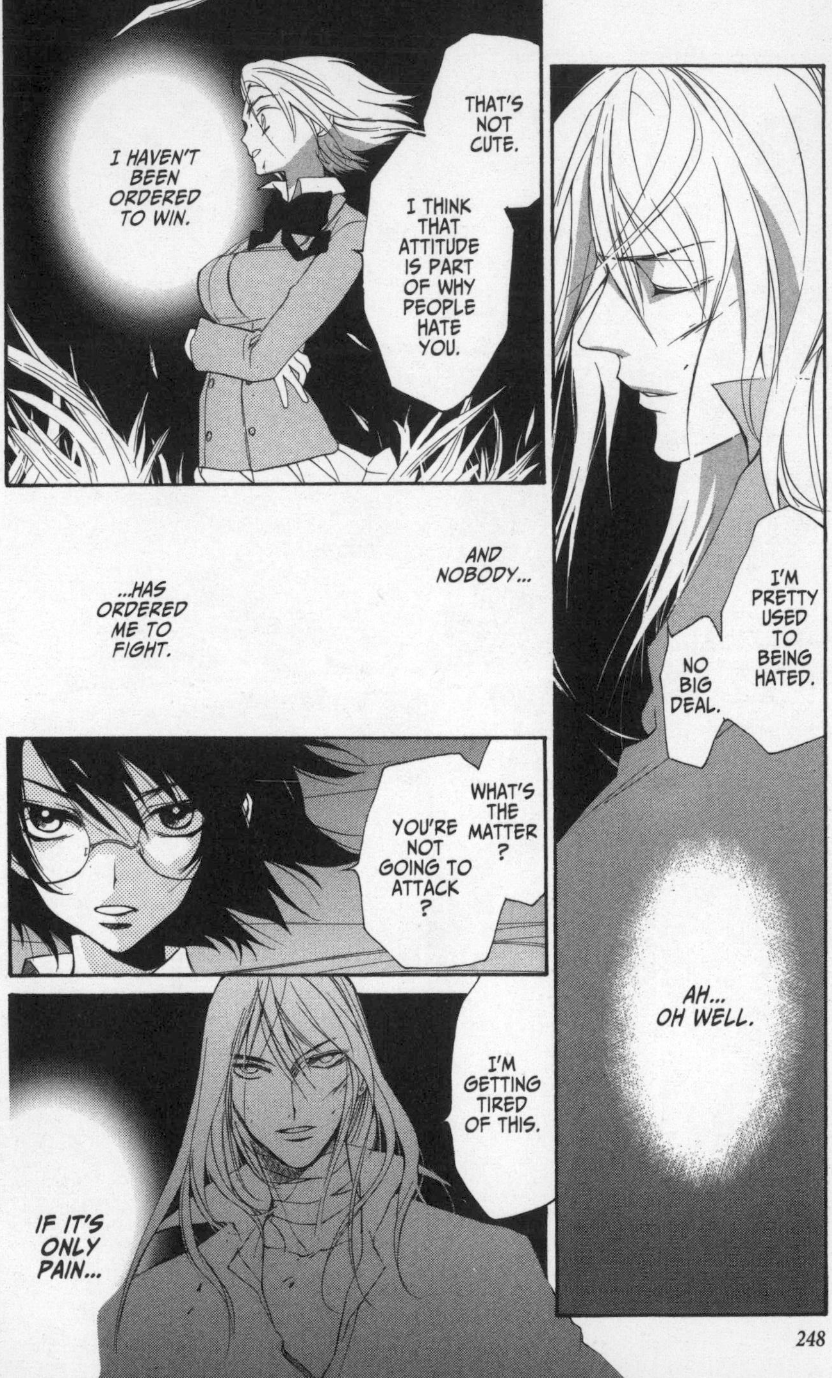
I'M PRETTY USED TO BEING HATED.
NO BIG DEAL.
AH... OH WELL.
THAT'S NOT CUTE.
I THINK THAT ATTITUDE IS PART OF WHY PEOPLE HATE YOU.
I HAVEN'T BEEN ORDERED TO WIN.
AND NOBODY...
...HAS ORDERED ME TO FIGHT.
WHAT'S THE MATTER?
YOU'RE NOT GOING TO ATTACK?
I'M GETTING TIRED OF THIS.
IF IT'S ONLY PAIN...

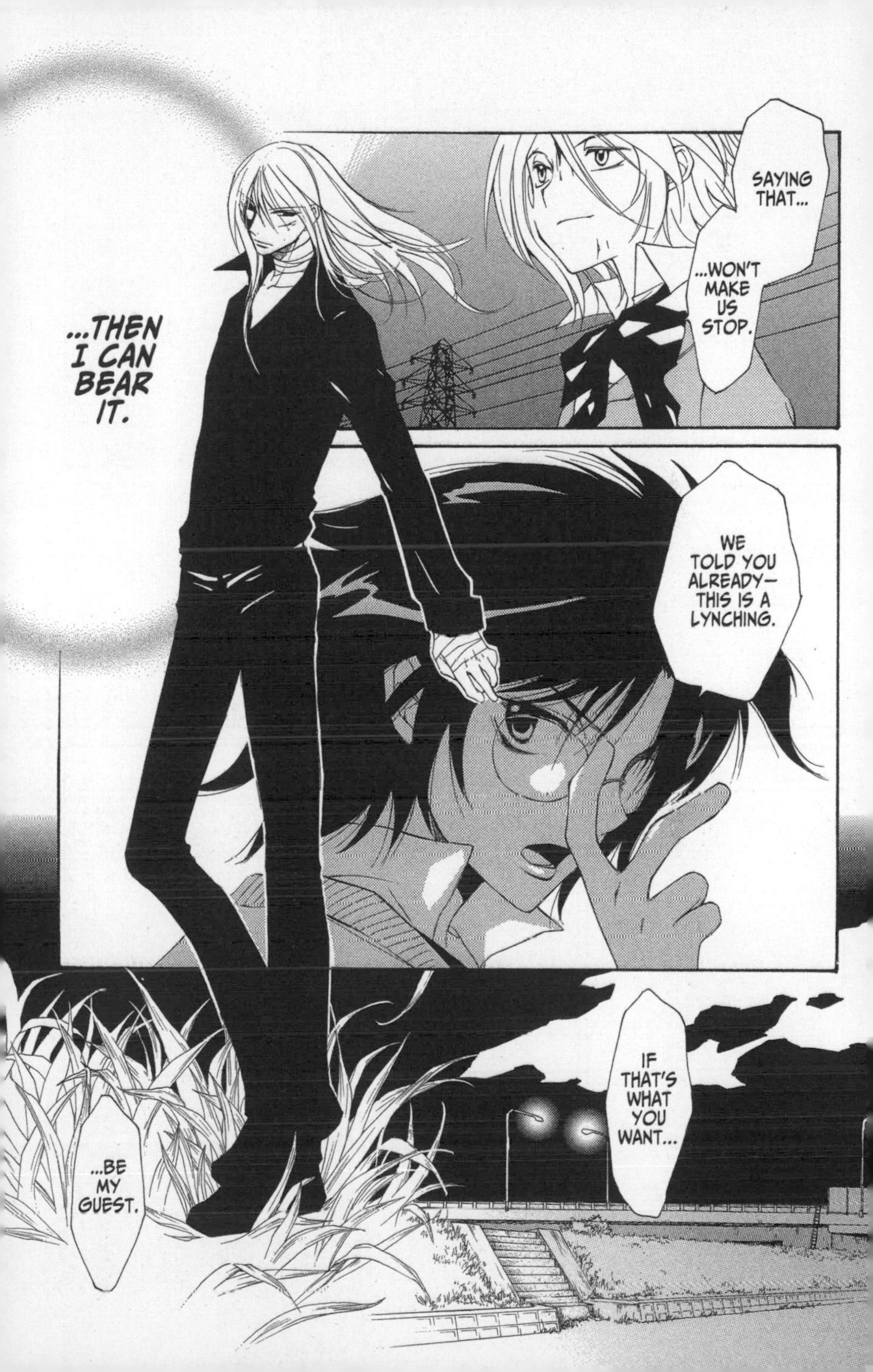
SAYING THAT...
...WON'T MAKE US STOP.
...THEN I CAN BEAR IT.
WE TOLD YOU ALREADY—THIS IS A LYNCHING.
IF THAT'S WHAT YOU WANT...
...BE MY GUEST.

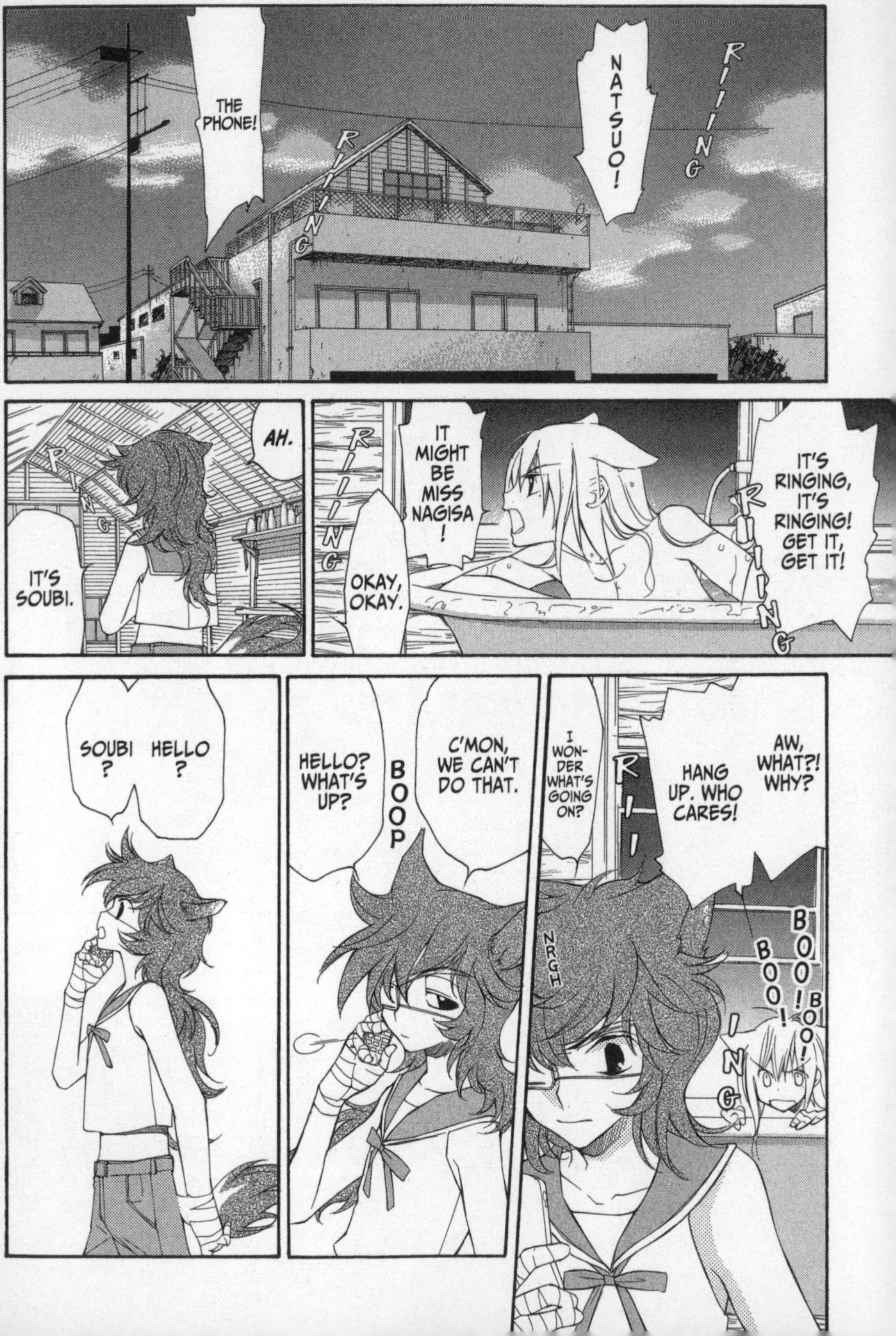
RIIIING
NATSUO!
RIIIING
THE PHONE!
IT'S RINGING, IT'S RINGING! GET IT, GET IT!
RIIING
IT MIGHT BE MISS NAGISA!
RIIIING
OKAY, OKAY.
AH.
RING
IT'S SOUBI.
AW, WHAT?! WHY?
HANG UP. WHO CARES!
I WONDER WHAT'S GOING ON?
RIIING
NRGH
BOO! BOO! BOO!
C'MON, WE CAN'T DO THAT.
BOOP
HELLO? WHAT'S UP?
HELLO?
SOUBI?

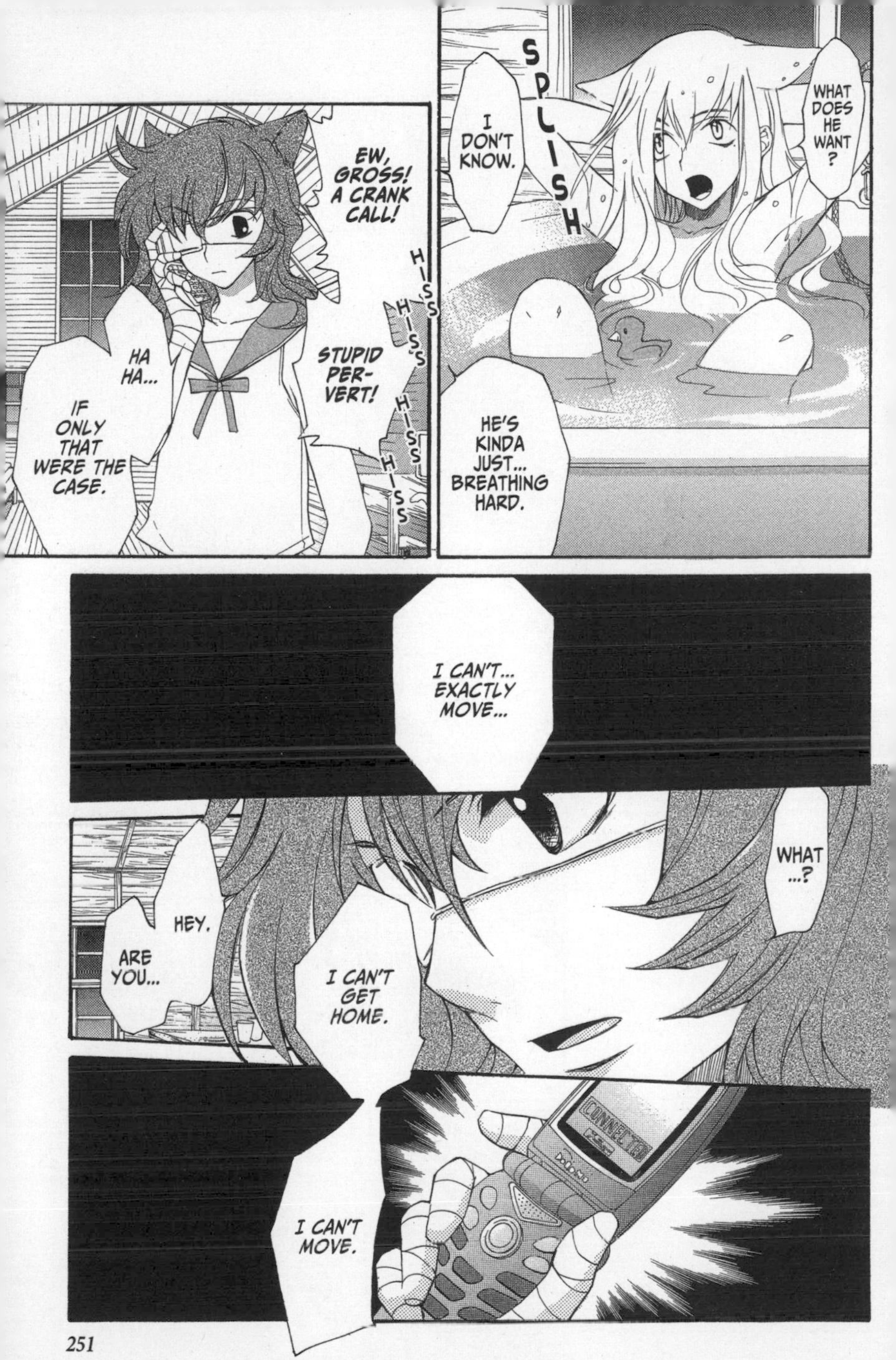
WHAT DOES HE WANT?
I DON'T KNOW.
SPLISH
HE'S KINDA JUST... BREATHING HARD.
EW, GROSS! A CRANK CALL!
STUPID PER-VERT!
HISS HISS HISS HISS
HA HA...
IF ONLY THAT WERE THE CASE.
I CAN'T... EXACTLY MOVE...
WHAT ...?
HEY.
ARE YOU...
I CAN'T GET HOME.
CONNECTED
I CAN'T MOVE.

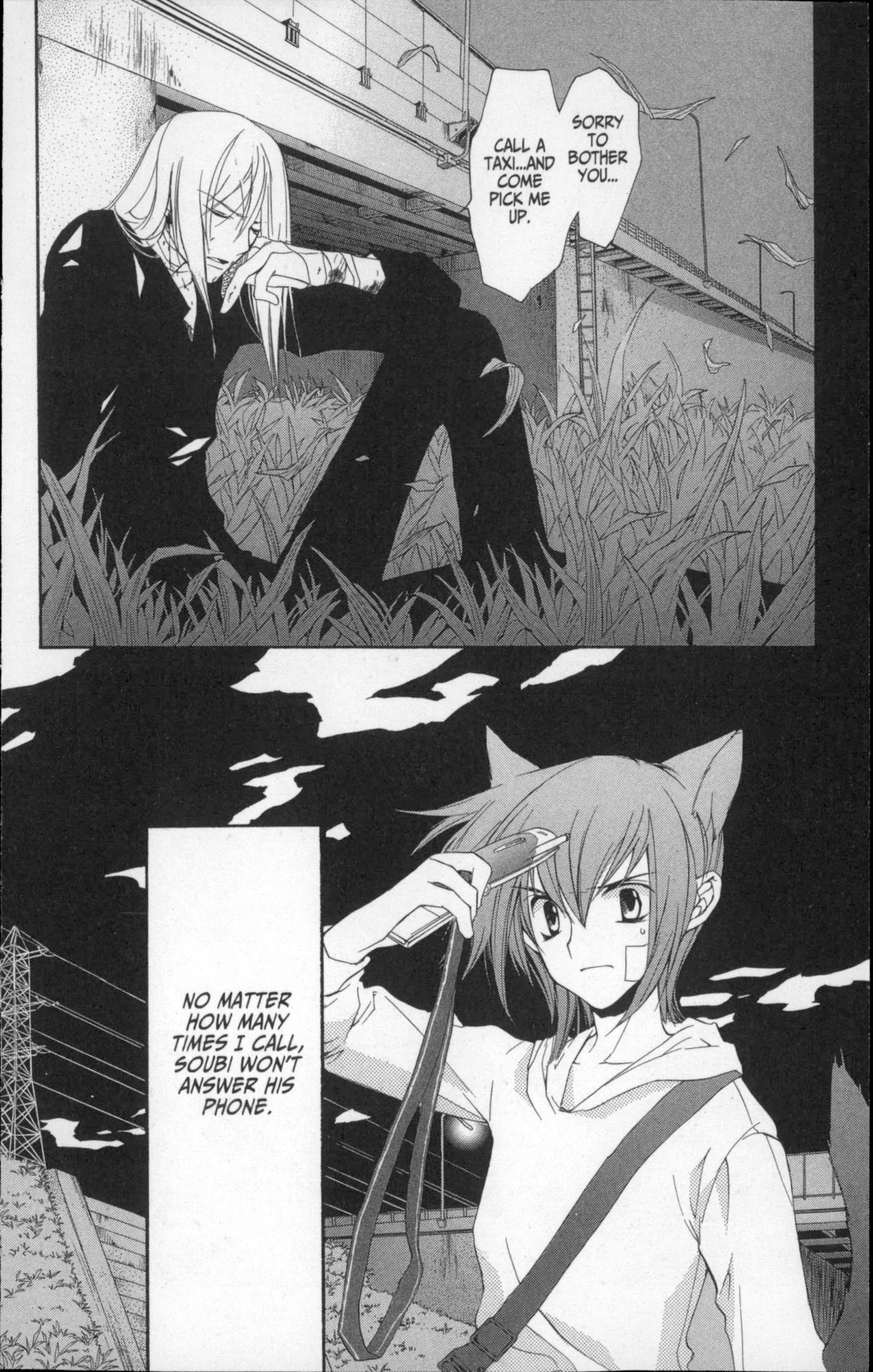
SORRY TO BOTHER YOU...
CALL A TAXI...AND COME PICK ME UP.
NO MATTER HOW MANY TIMES I CALL, SOUBI WON'T ANSWER HIS PHONE.

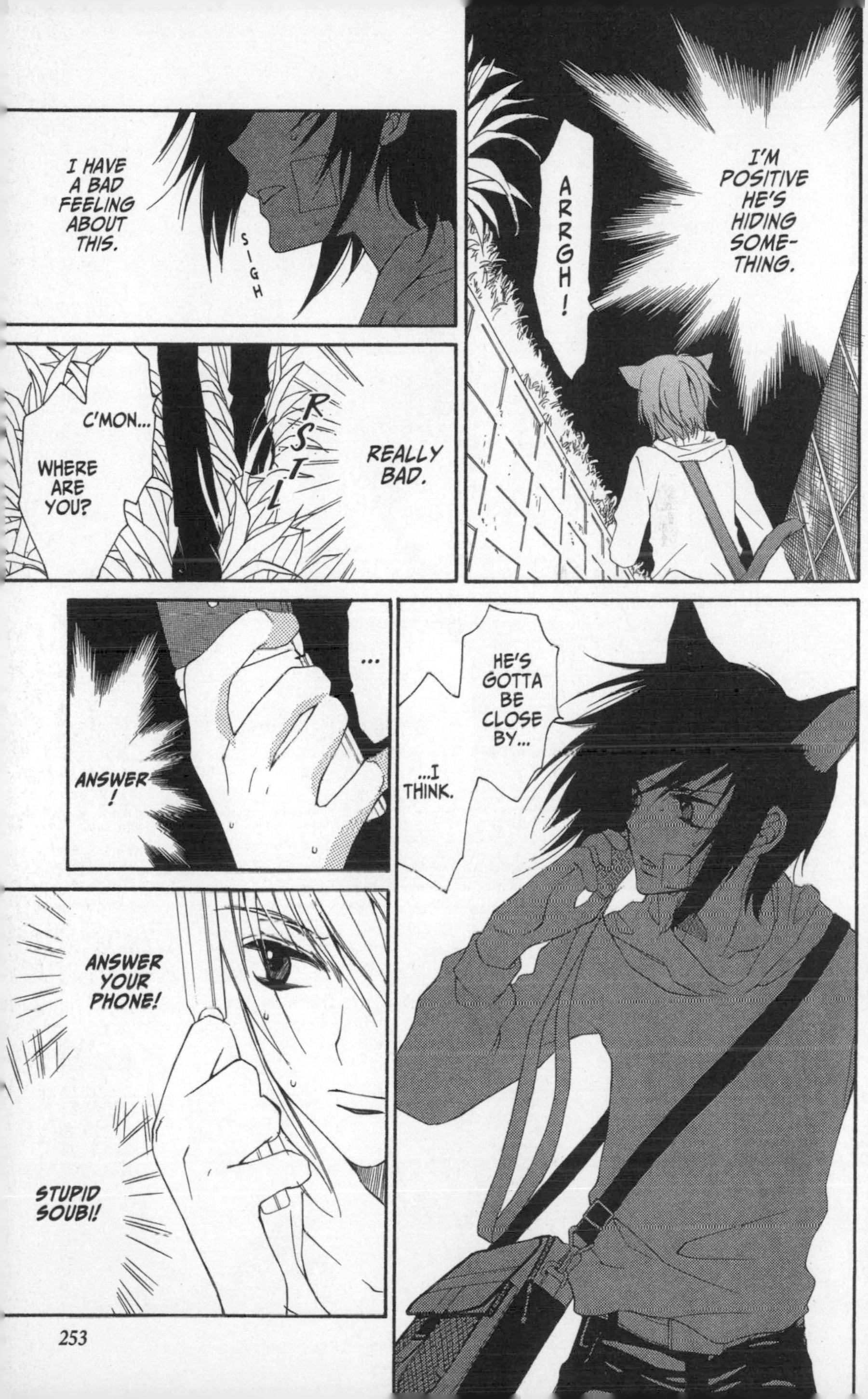
I'M POSITIVE HE'S HIDING SOME-THING.
ARRGH!
I HAVE A BAD FEELING ABOUT THIS.
SIGH
REALLY BAD.
RSTL
C'MON...
WHERE ARE YOU?
HE'S GOTTA BE CLOSE BY...
...I THINK.
...
ANSWER!
ANSWER YOUR PHONE!
STUPID SOUBI!

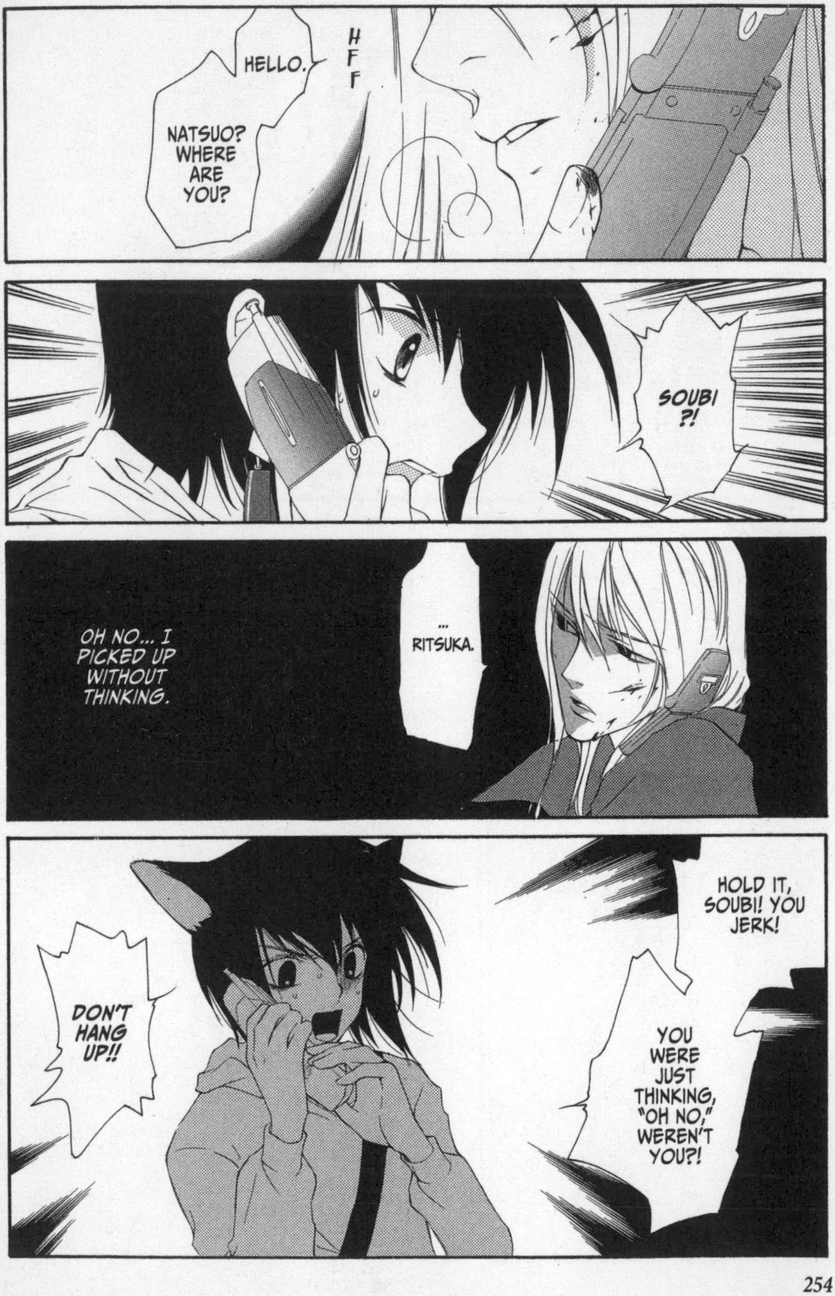
HFF
HELLO.
NATSUO? WHERE ARE YOU?
SOUBI ?!
... RITSUKA.
OH NO... I PICKED UP WITHOUT THINKING.
HOLD IT, SOUBI! YOU JERK!
YOU WERE JUST THINKING, "OH NO," WEREN'T YOU?!
DON'T HANG UP!!

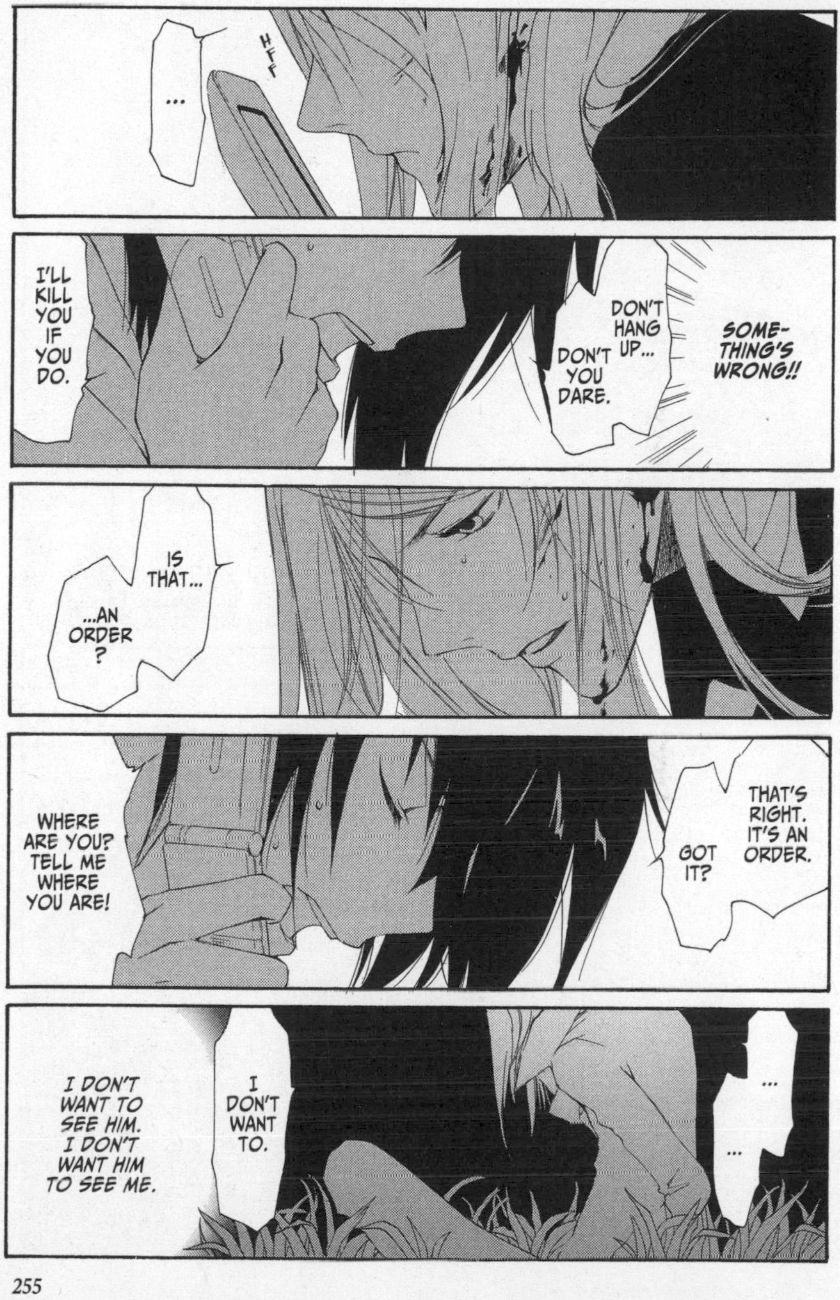
HFF
...
SOME-THING'S WRONG!!
DON'T HANG UP...
DON'T YOU DARE.
I'LL KILL YOU IF YOU DO.
IS THAT...
...AN ORDER?
THAT'S RIGHT. IT'S AN ORDER.
GOT IT?
WHERE ARE YOU? TELL ME WHERE YOU ARE!
...
...
I DON'T WANT TO.
I DON'T WANT TO SEE HIM. I DON'T WANT HIM TO SEE ME.

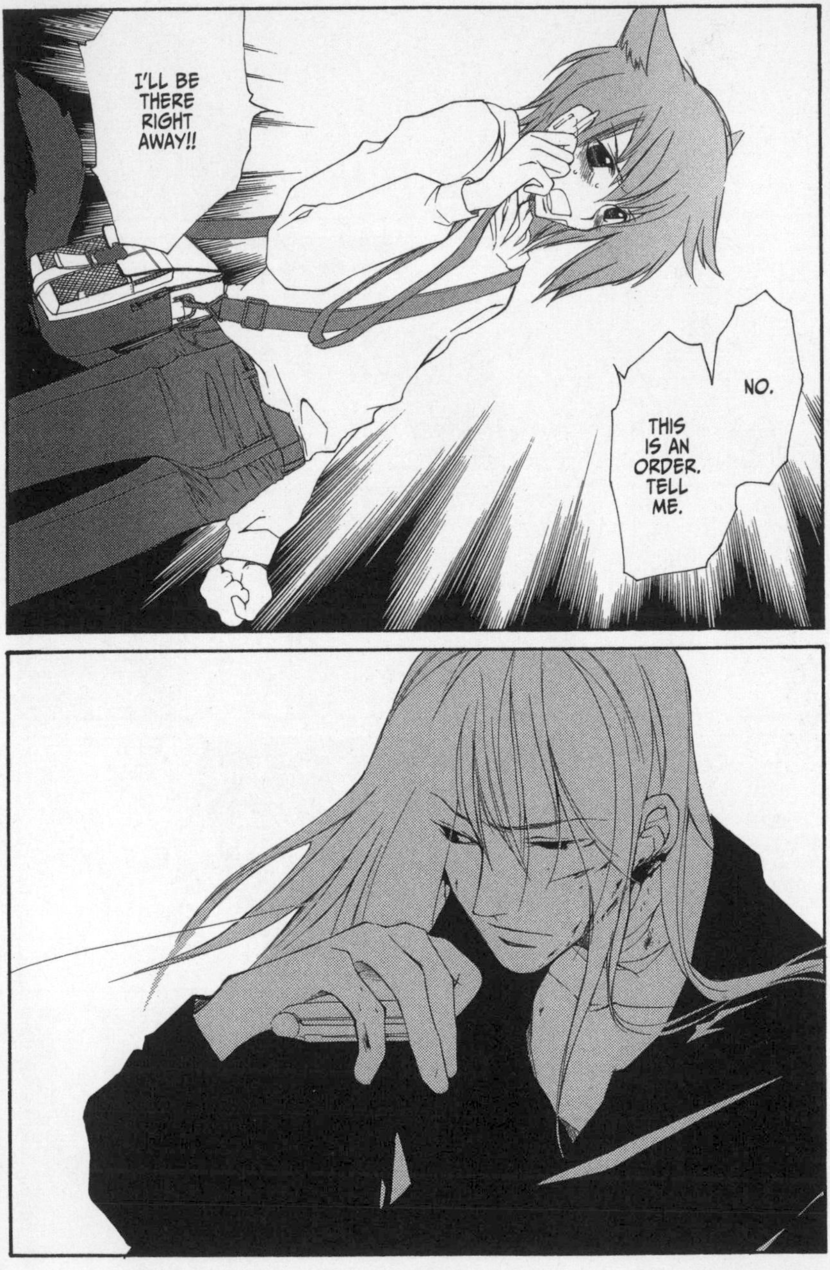
NO.
THIS IS AN ORDER. TELL ME.
I'LL BE THERE RIGHT AWAY!!

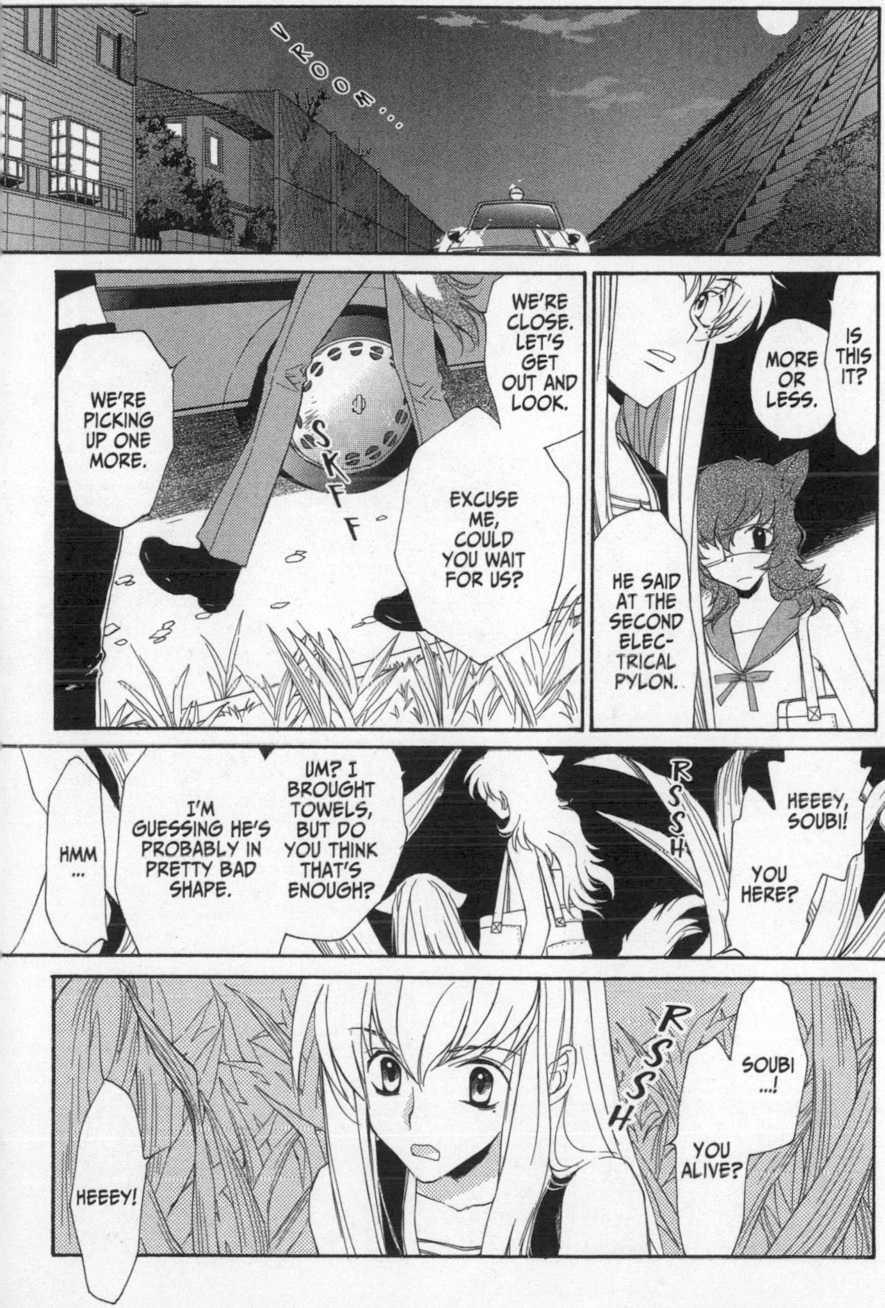
VROOM...
IS THIS IT?
MORE OR LESS.
HE SAID AT THE SECOND ELEC-TRICAL PYLON.
WE'RE CLOSE. LET'S GET OUT AND LOOK.
SKFF
EXCUSE ME, COULD YOU WAIT FOR US?
WE'RE PICKING UP ONE MORE.
HEEEY, SOUBI!
YOU HERE?
RSSH
UM? I BROUGHT TOWELS, BUT DO YOU THINK THAT'S ENOUGH?
I'M GUESSING HE'S PROBABLY IN PRETTY BAD SHAPE.
HMM ...
SOUBI ...!
YOU ALIVE?
RSSH
HEEEY!

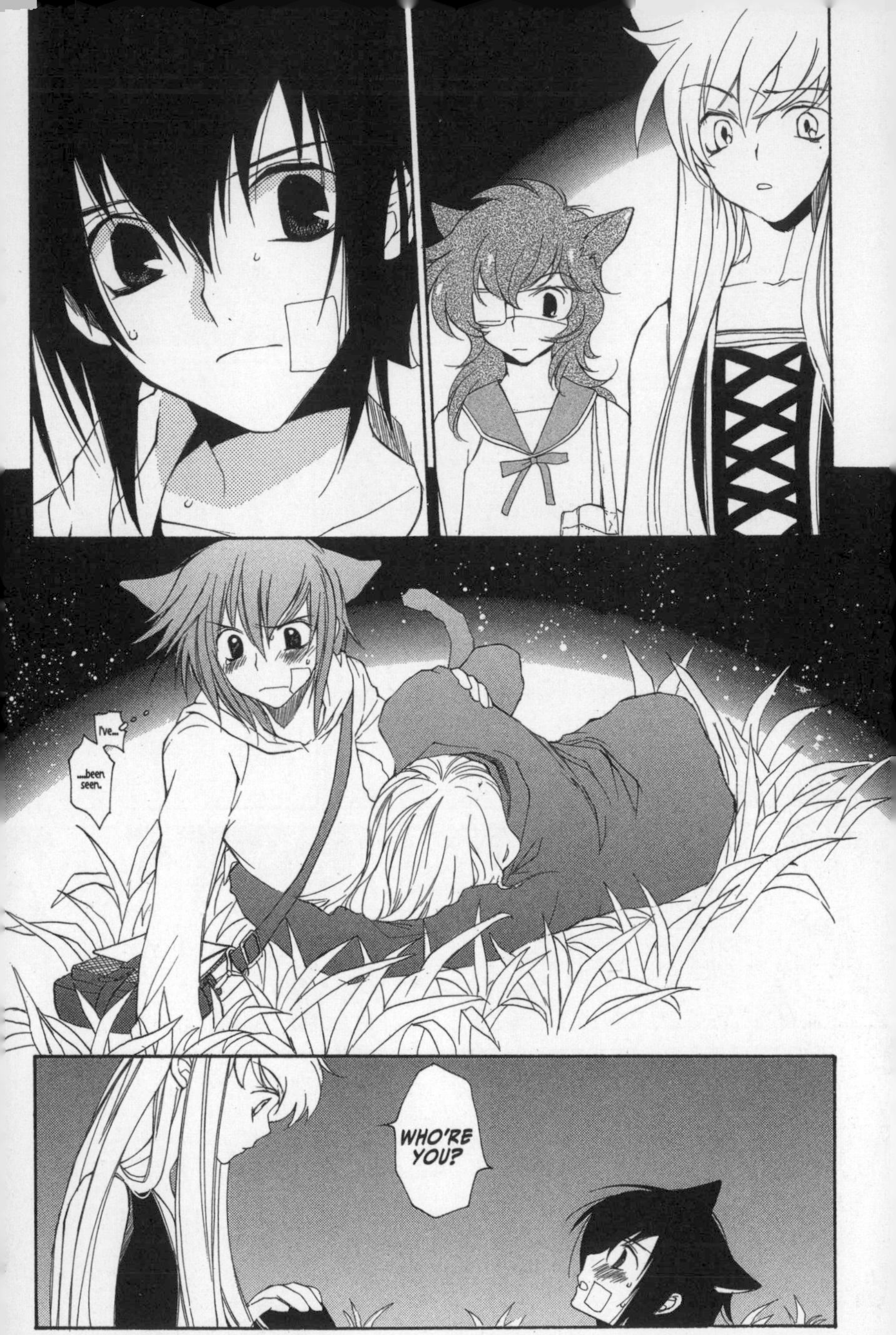
I've...
...been seen.
WHO'RE YOU?

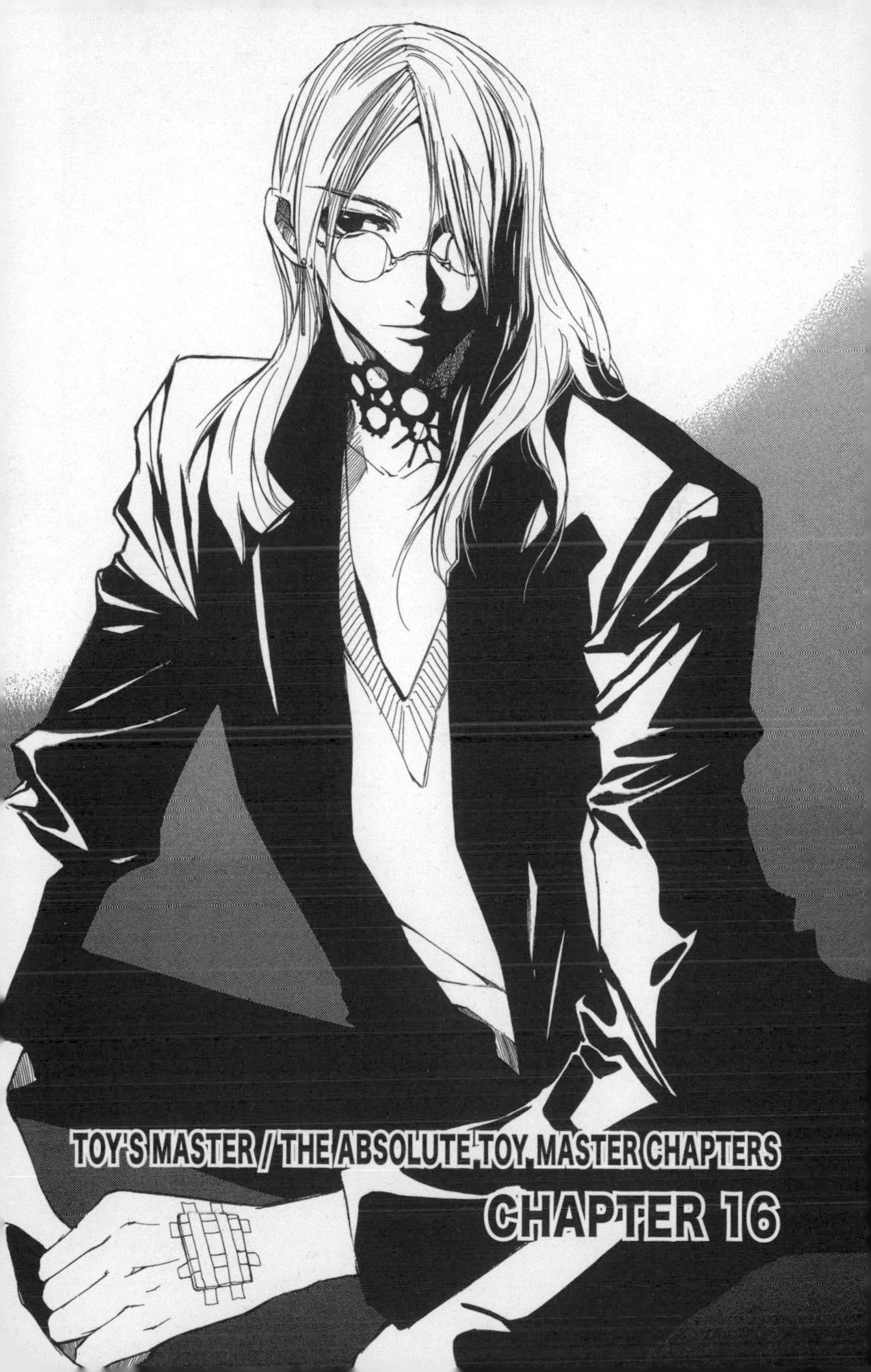
TOY'S MASTER // THE ABSOLUTE TOY MASTER CHAPTERS
CHAPTER 16

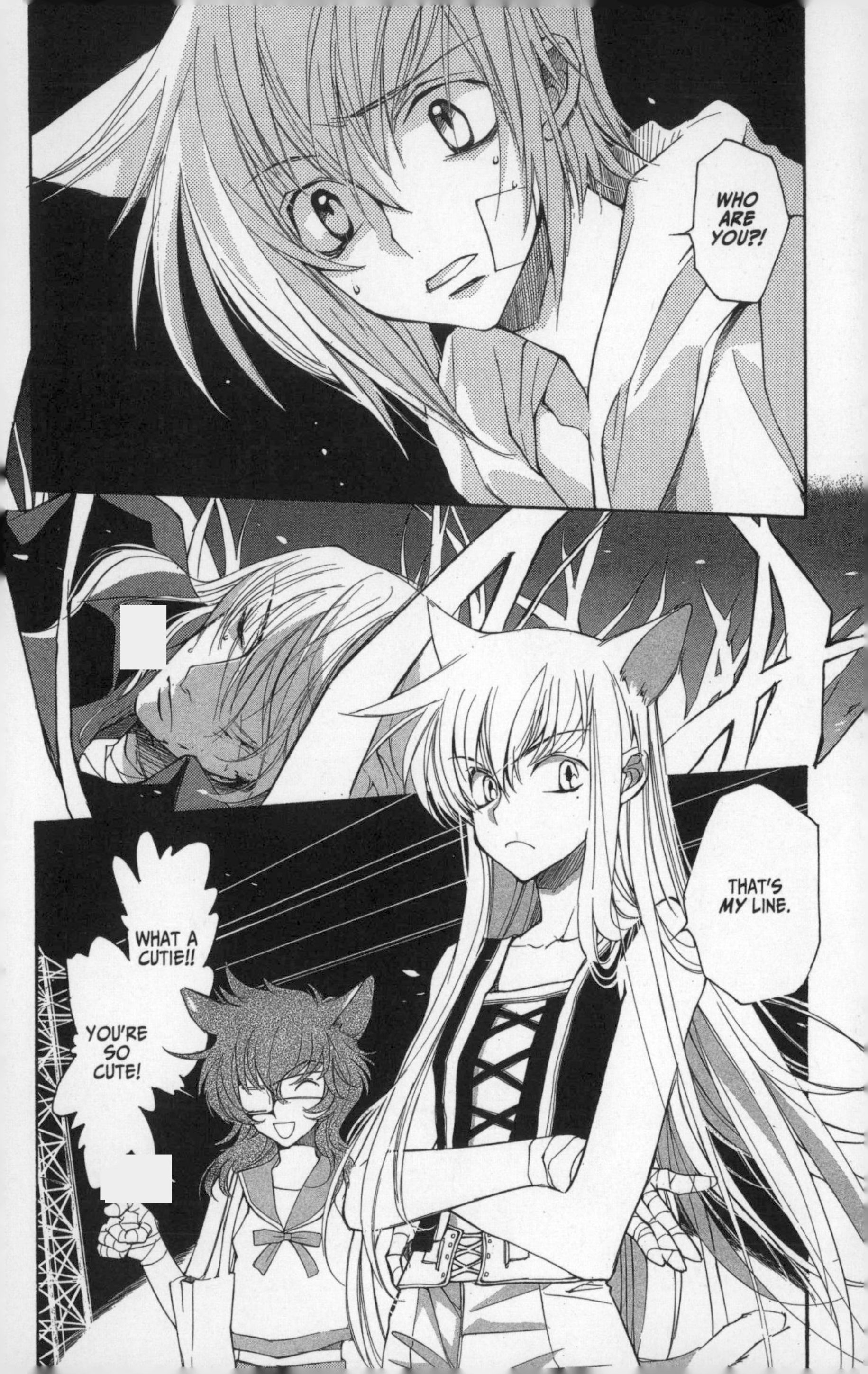
WHO ARE YOU?!
THAT'S MY LINE.
WHAT A CUTIE!!
YOU'RE SO CUTE!

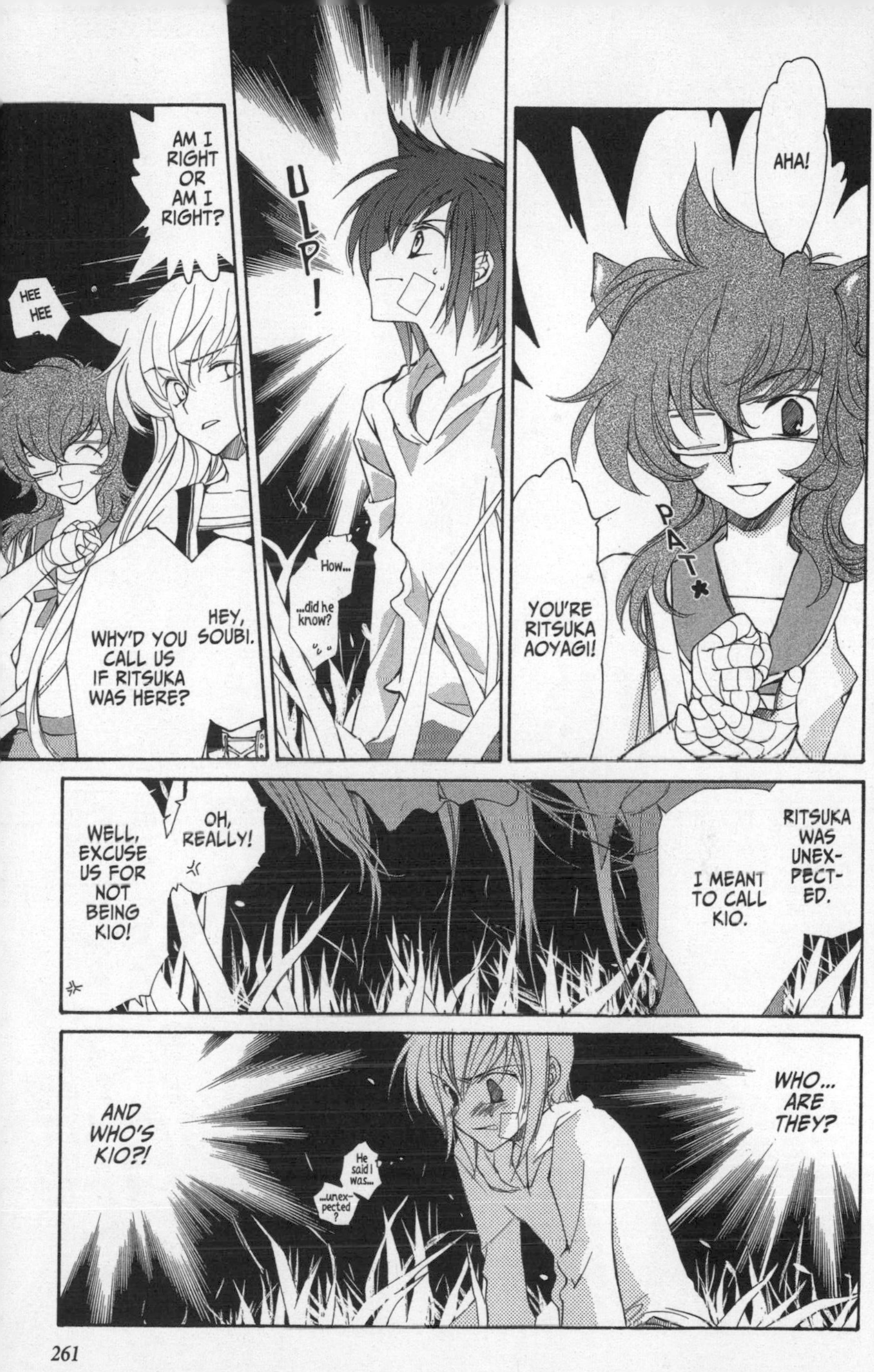
AHA!
YOU'RE RITSUKA AOYAGI!
PAT*
ULP!
How...
...did he know?
AM I RIGHT OR AM I RIGHT?
HEE HEE
HEY, SOUBI.
WHY'D YOU CALL US IF RITSUKA WAS HERE?
RITSUKA WAS UNEXPECTED.
I MEANT TO CALL KIO.
OH, REALLY!
WELL, EXCUSE US FOR NOT BEING KIO!
WHO... ARE THEY?
He said I was...
...unexpected?
AND WHO'S KIO?!

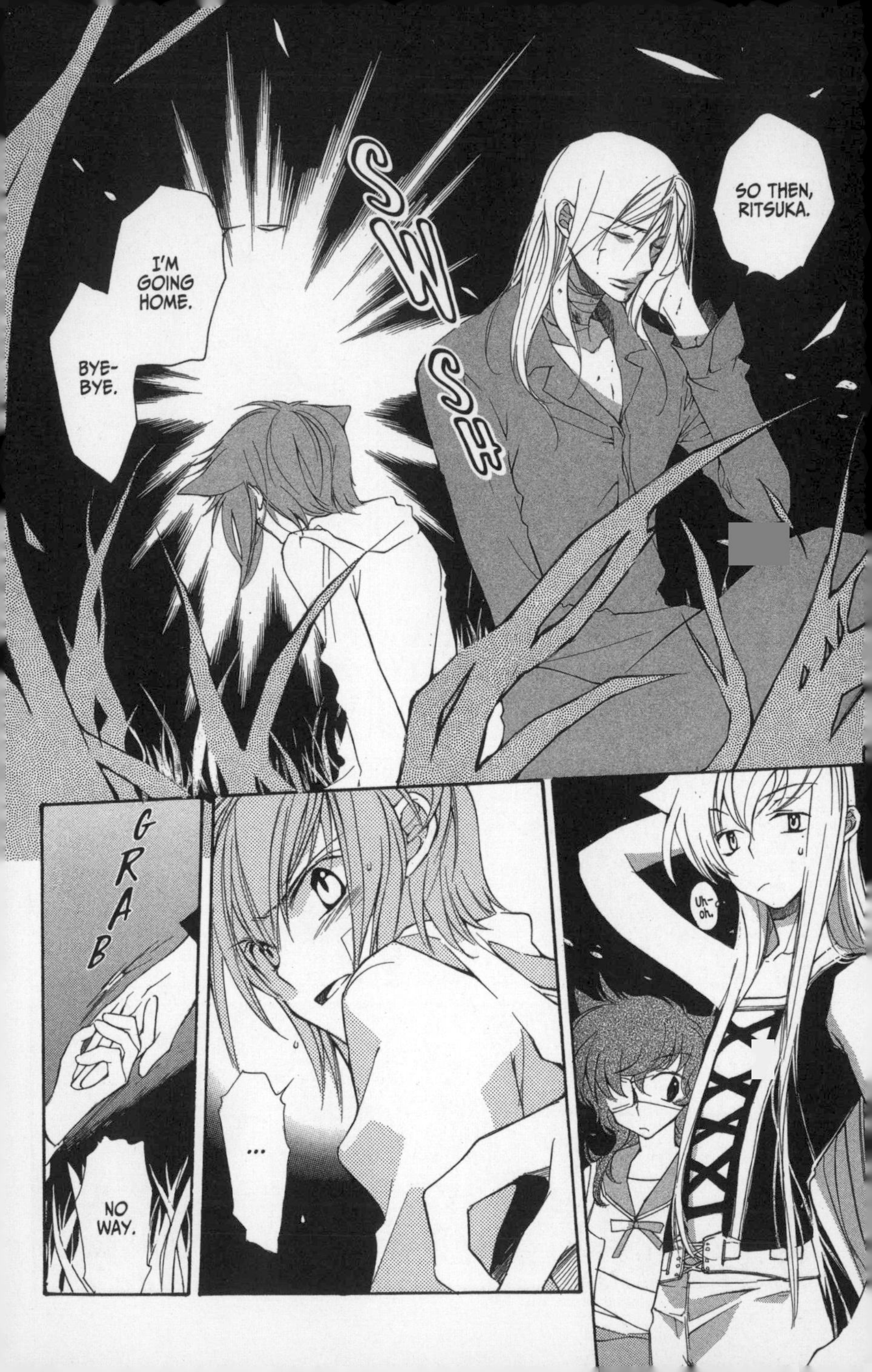
SO THEN, RITSUKA.
SWSH
I'M GOING HOME.
BYE-BYE.
Uh-oh.
...
GRAB
NO WAY.

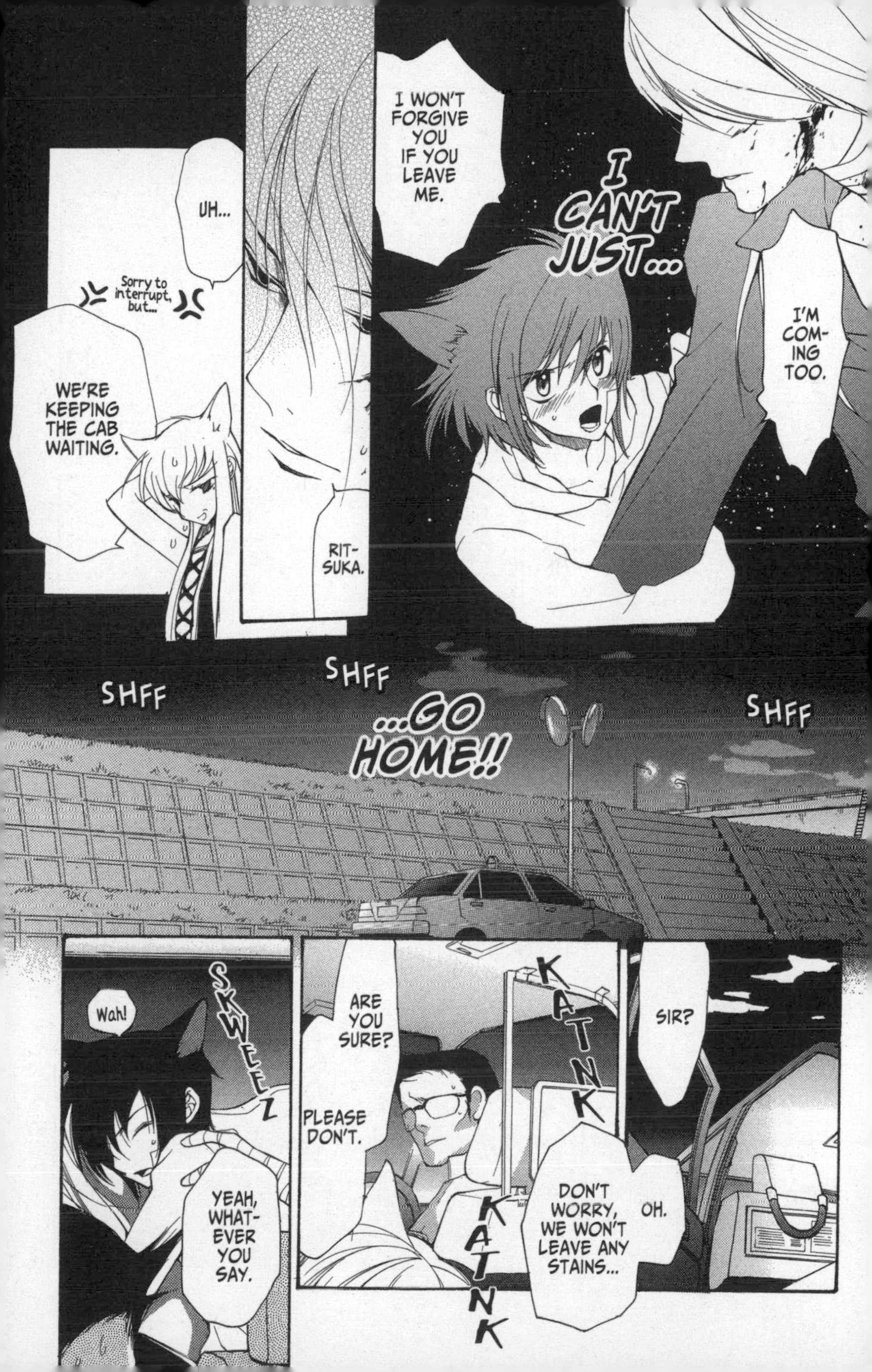
I WON'T FORGIVE YOU IF YOU LEAVE ME.
I'M COMING TOO.
I CAN'T JUST...
RIT-SUKA.
UH...
Sorry to interrupt, but...
WE'RE KEEPING THE CAB WAITING.
SHFF
SHFF
SHFF
...GO HOME!!
SIR?
OH.
DON'T WORRY, WE WON'T LEAVE ANY STAINS...
KATNK
KATNK
ARE YOU SURE?
PLEASE DON'T.
SKWEEZ
Wah!
YEAH, WHATEVER YOU SAY.

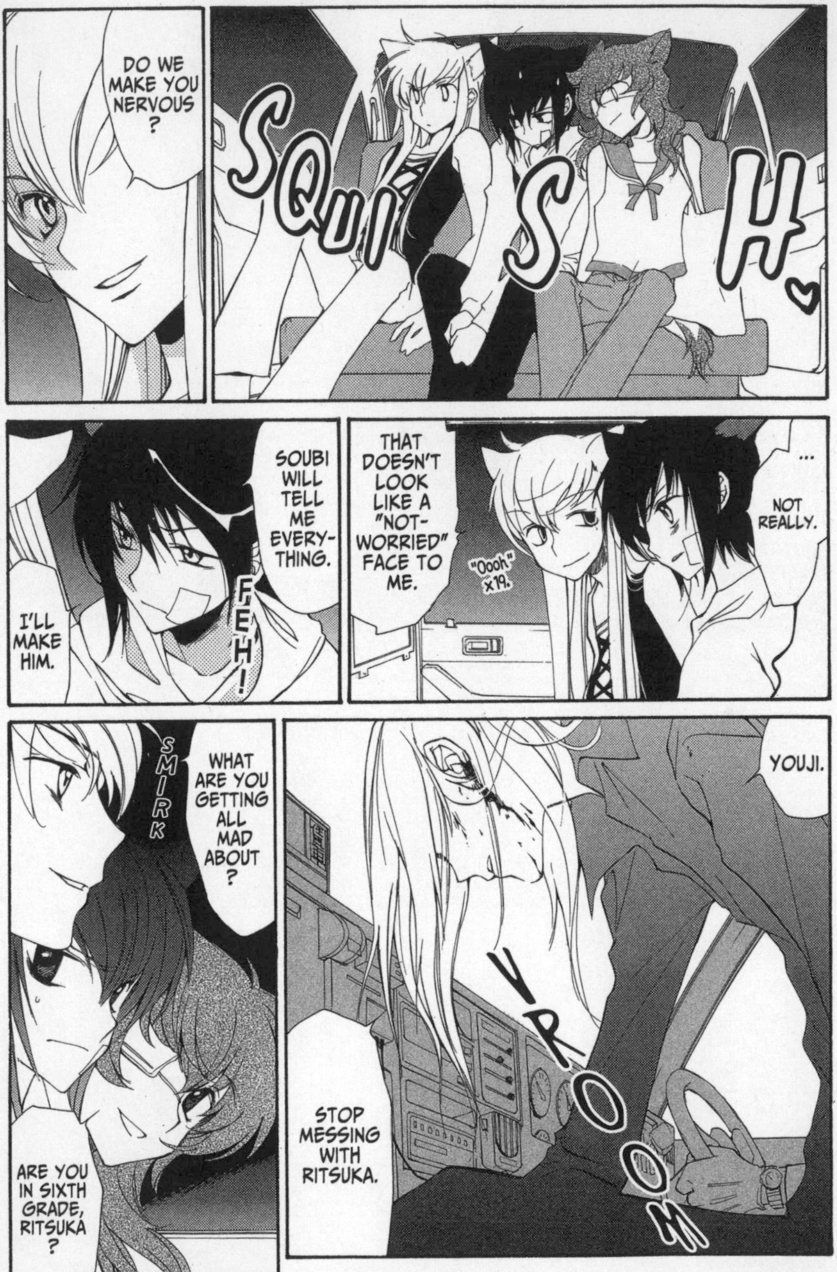
SQUISH ♥
DO WE MAKE YOU NERVOUS?
...
NOT REALLY.
THAT DOESN'T LOOK LIKE A "NOT-WORRIED" FACE TO ME.
"Oooh" x19.
SOUBI WILL TELL ME EVERYTHING.
FEH!
I'LL MAKE HIM.
YOUJI.
VROOOM
STOP MESSING WITH RITSUKA.
SMIRK
WHAT ARE YOU GETTING ALL MAD ABOUT?
ARE YOU IN SIXTH GRADE, RITSUKA?

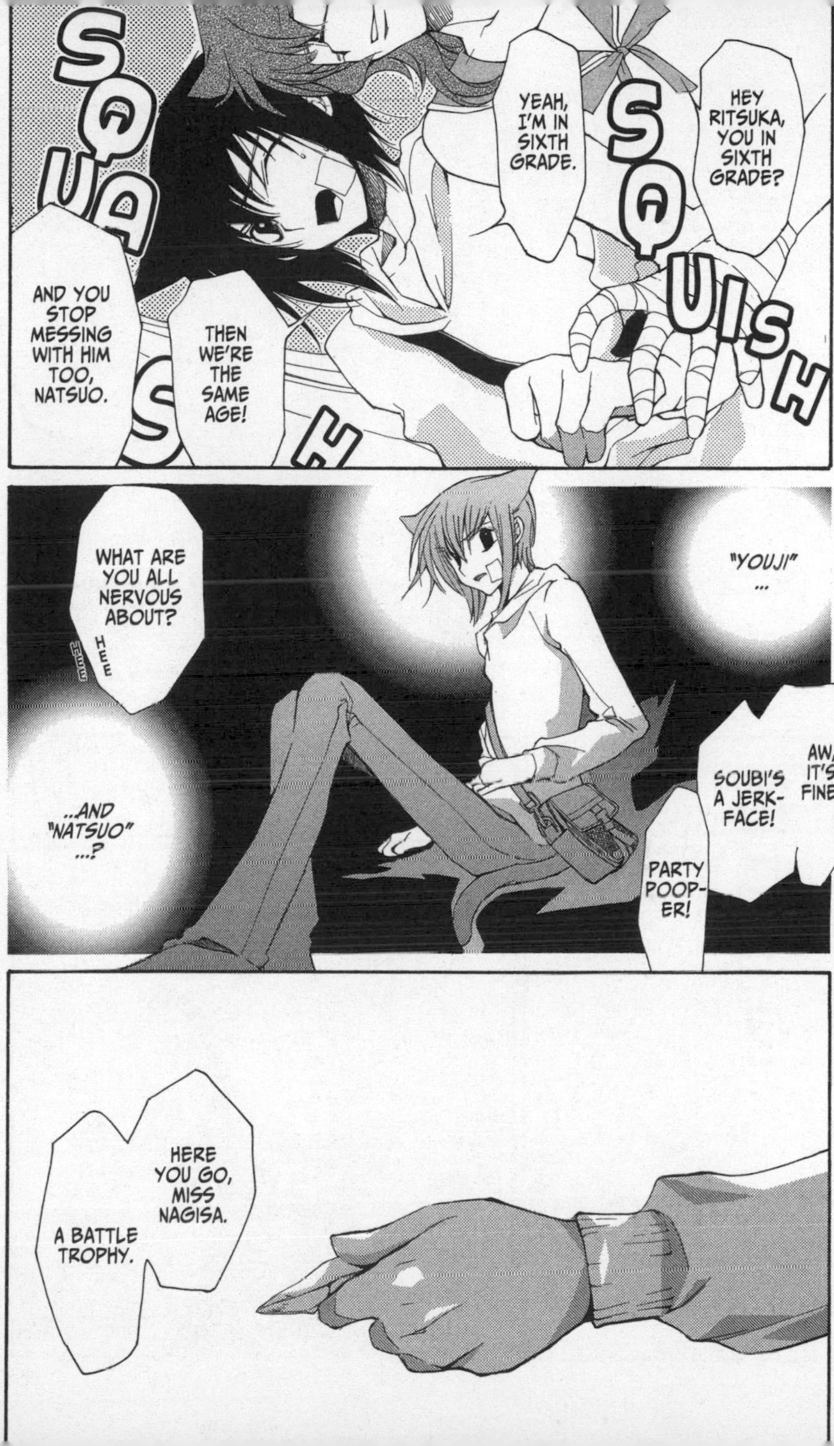
HEY RITSUKA, YOU IN SIXTH GRADE?
SQUISH
YEAH, I'M IN SIXTH GRADE.
SQUASH
THEN WE'RE THE SAME AGE!
AND YOU STOP MESSING WITH HIM TOO, NATSUO.
"YOUJI" ...
AW, IT'S FINE!
SOUBI'S A JERK-FACE!
PARTY POOPER!
WHAT ARE YOU ALL NERVOUS ABOUT?
HEE HEE
...AND "NATSUO" ...?
HERE YOU GO, MISS NAGISA.
A BATTLE TROPHY.

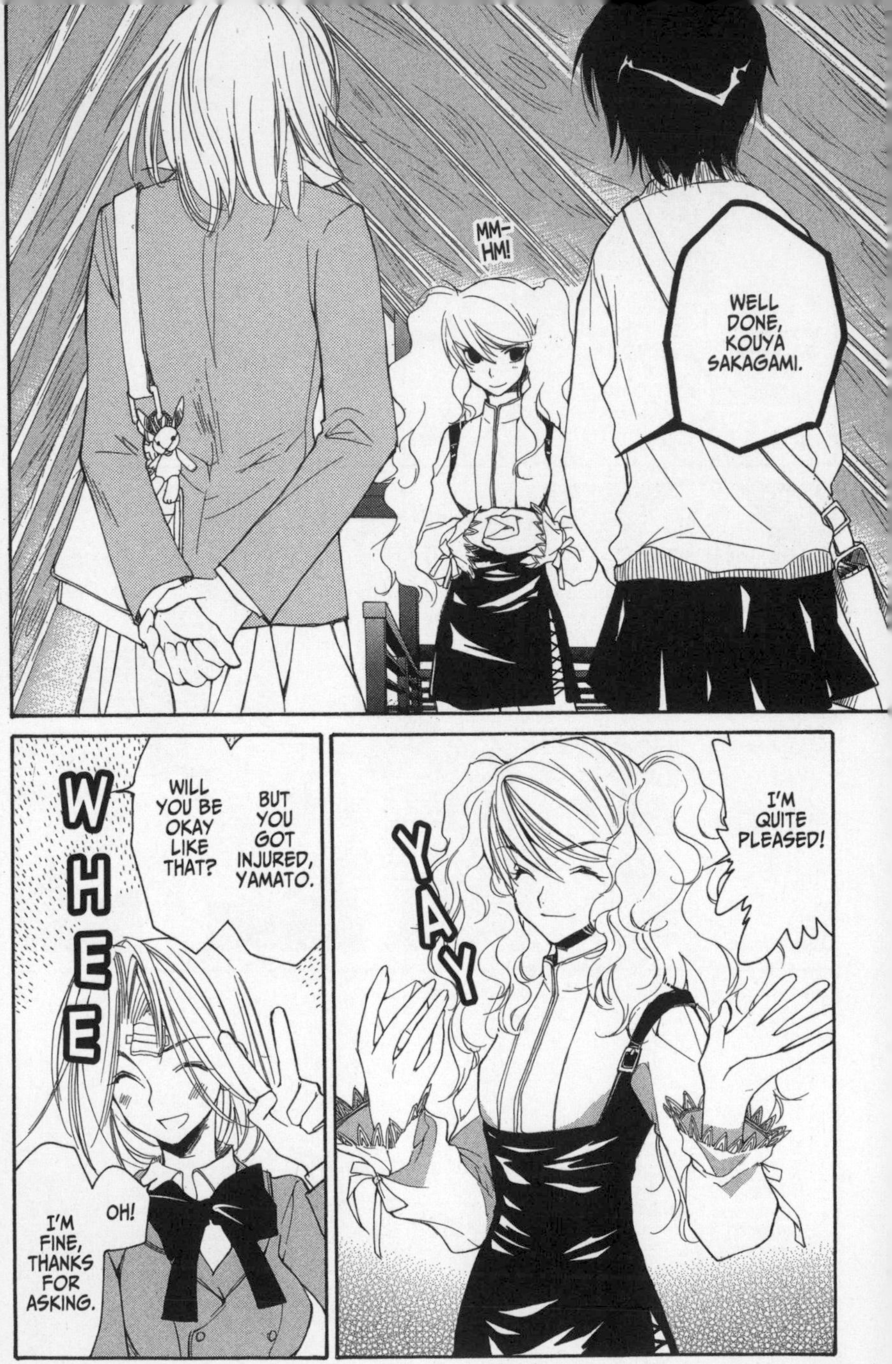
WELL DONE, KOUYA SAKAGAMI.
MM-HM!
I'M QUITE PLEASED!
YAY
BUT YOU GOT INJURED, YAMATO.
WILL YOU BE OKAY LIKE THAT?
WHEE
OH!
I'M FINE, THANKS FOR ASKING.

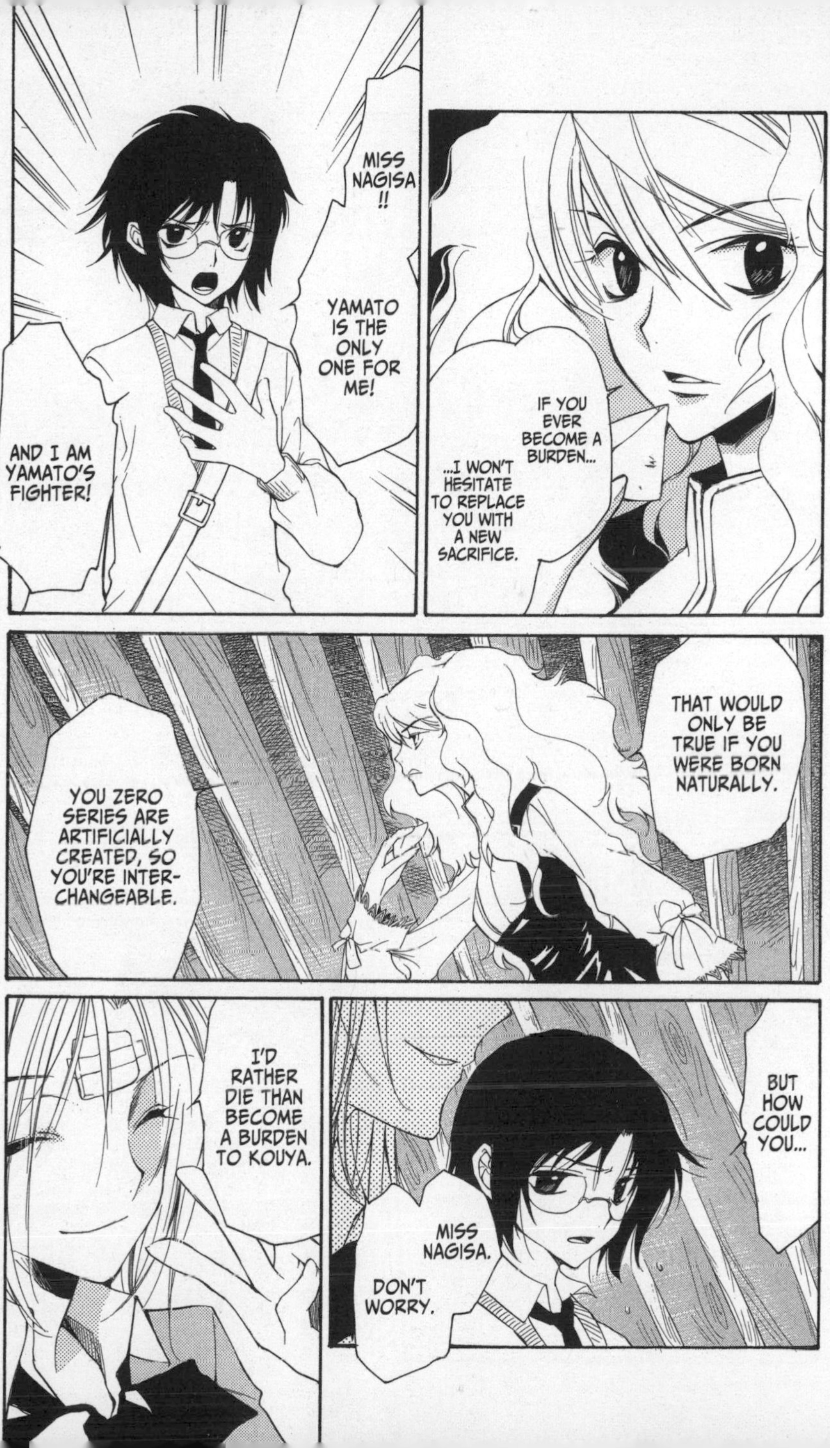
IF YOU EVER BECOME A BURDEN...
...I WON'T HESITATE TO REPLACE YOU WITH A NEW SACRIFICE.
MISS NAGISA !!
YAMATO IS THE ONLY ONE FOR ME!
AND I AM YAMATO'S FIGHTER!
THAT WOULD ONLY BE TRUE IF YOU WERE BORN NATURALLY.
YOU ZERO SERIES ARE ARTIFICIALLY CREATED, SO YOU'RE INTER-CHANGEABLE.
BUT HOW COULD YOU...
MISS NAGISA.
DON'T WORRY.
I'D RATHER DIE THAN BECOME A BURDEN TO KOUYA.

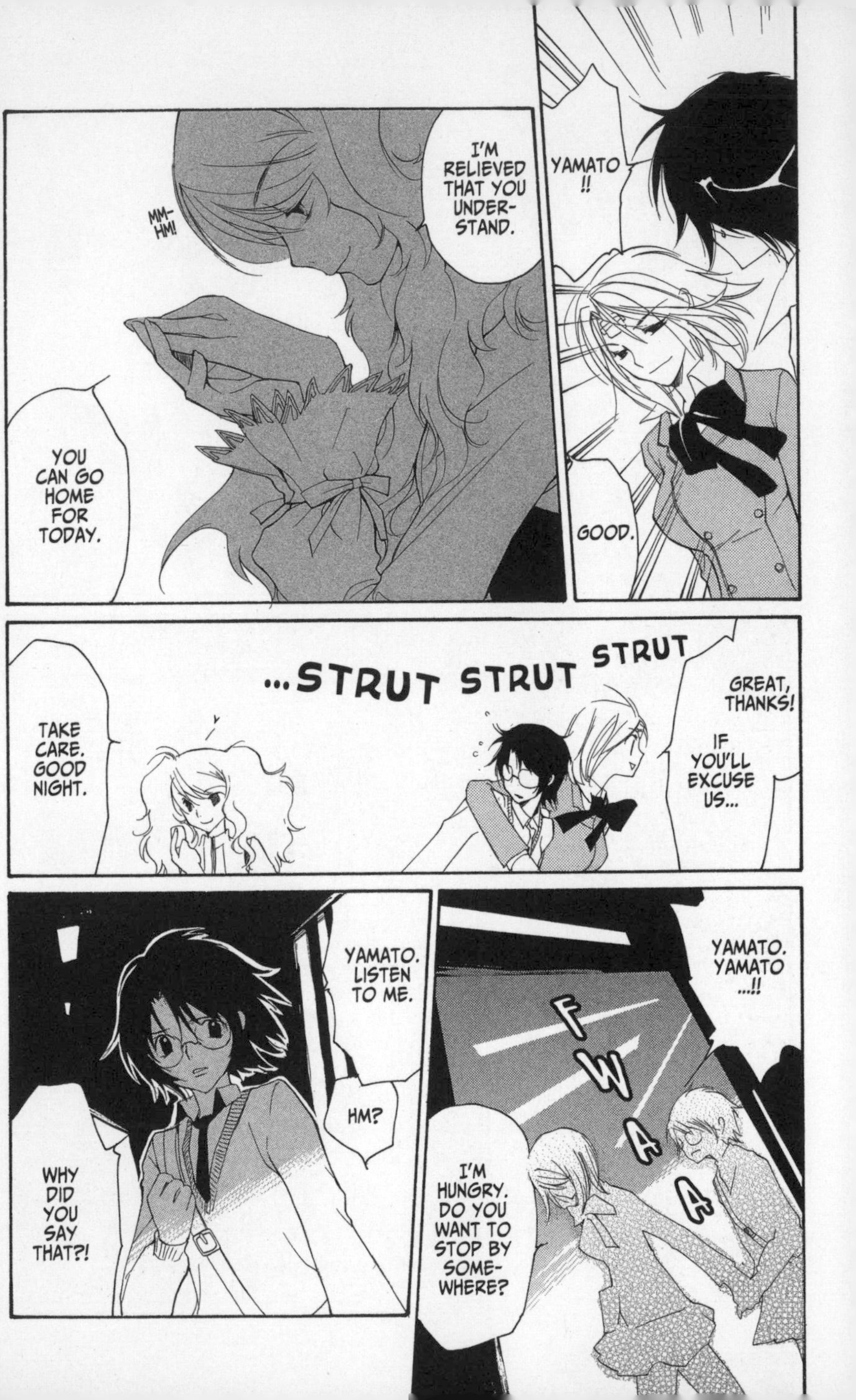
YAMATO !!
GOOD.
I'M RELIEVED THAT YOU UNDER-STAND.
MM-HM!
YOU CAN GO HOME FOR TODAY.
GREAT, THANKS!
IF YOU'LL EXCUSE US...
...STRUT STRUT STRUT
TAKE CARE. GOOD NIGHT.
YAMATO. YAMATO ...!!
FWAA
I'M HUNGRY. DO YOU WANT TO STOP BY SOME-WHERE?
YAMATO. LISTEN TO ME.
HM?
WHY DID YOU SAY THAT?!

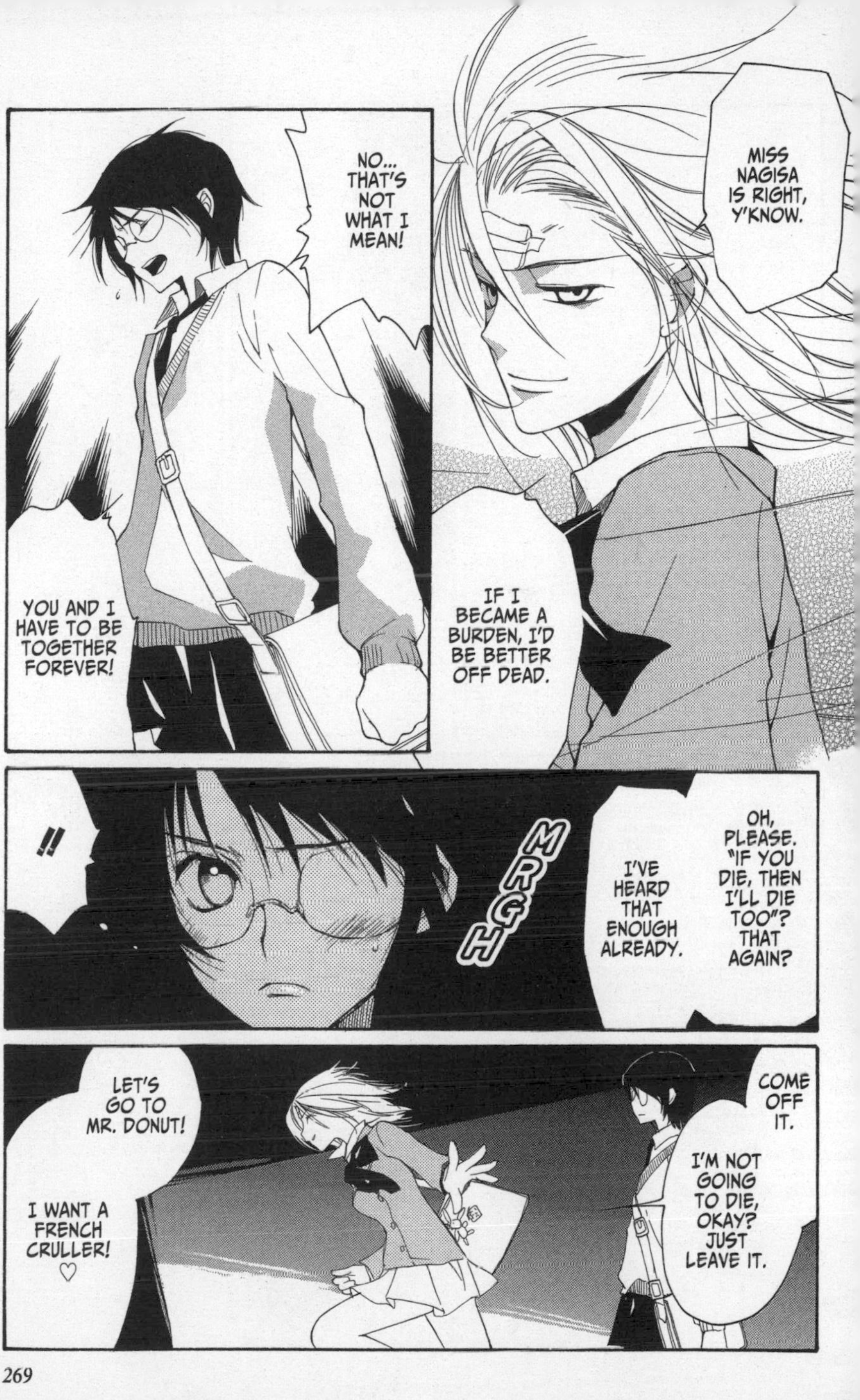
MISS NAGISA IS RIGHT, Y'KNOW.
IF I BECAME A BURDEN, I'D BE BETTER OFF DEAD.
NO... THAT'S NOT WHAT I MEAN!
YOU AND I HAVE TO BE TOGETHER FOREVER!
OH, PLEASE. "IF YOU DIE, THEN I'LL DIE TOO"? THAT AGAIN?
I'VE HEARD THAT ENOUGH ALREADY.
MRGH
!!
COME OFF IT.
I'M NOT GOING TO DIE, OKAY? JUST LEAVE IT.
LET'S GO TO MR. DONUT!
I WANT A FRENCH CRULLER! ♡

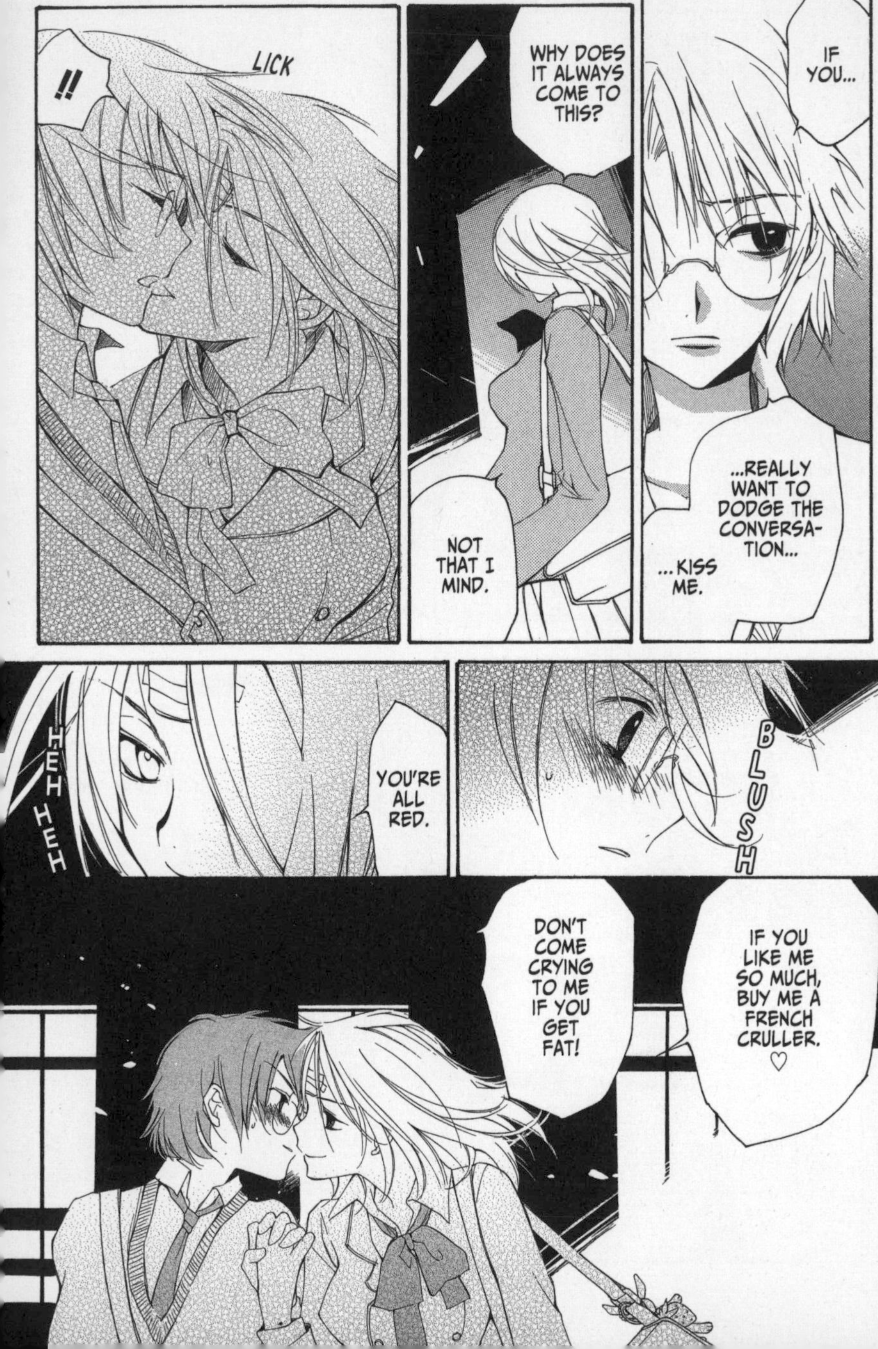
IF YOU...
...REALLY WANT TO DODGE THE CONVERSATION...
...KISS ME.
WHY DOES IT ALWAYS COME TO THIS?
NOT THAT I MIND.
LICK
!!
BLUSH
YOU'RE ALL RED.
HEH HEH
IF YOU LIKE ME SO MUCH, BUY ME A FRENCH CRULLER. ♡
DON'T COME CRYING TO ME IF YOU GET FAT!

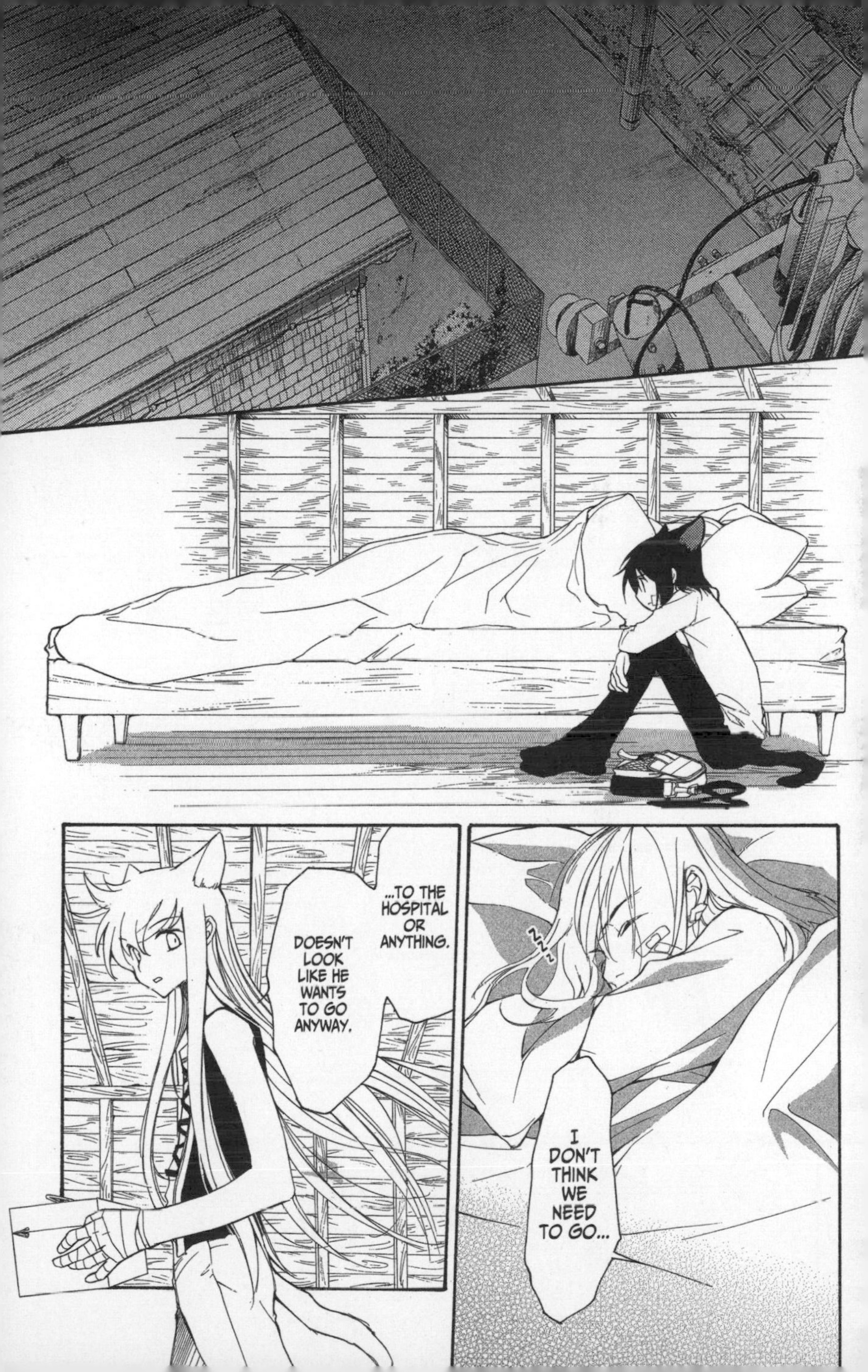
Z Z Z
I DON'T THINK WE NEED TO GO...
...TO THE HOSPITAL OR ANYTHING.
DOESN'T LOOK LIKE HE WANTS TO GO ANYWAY.

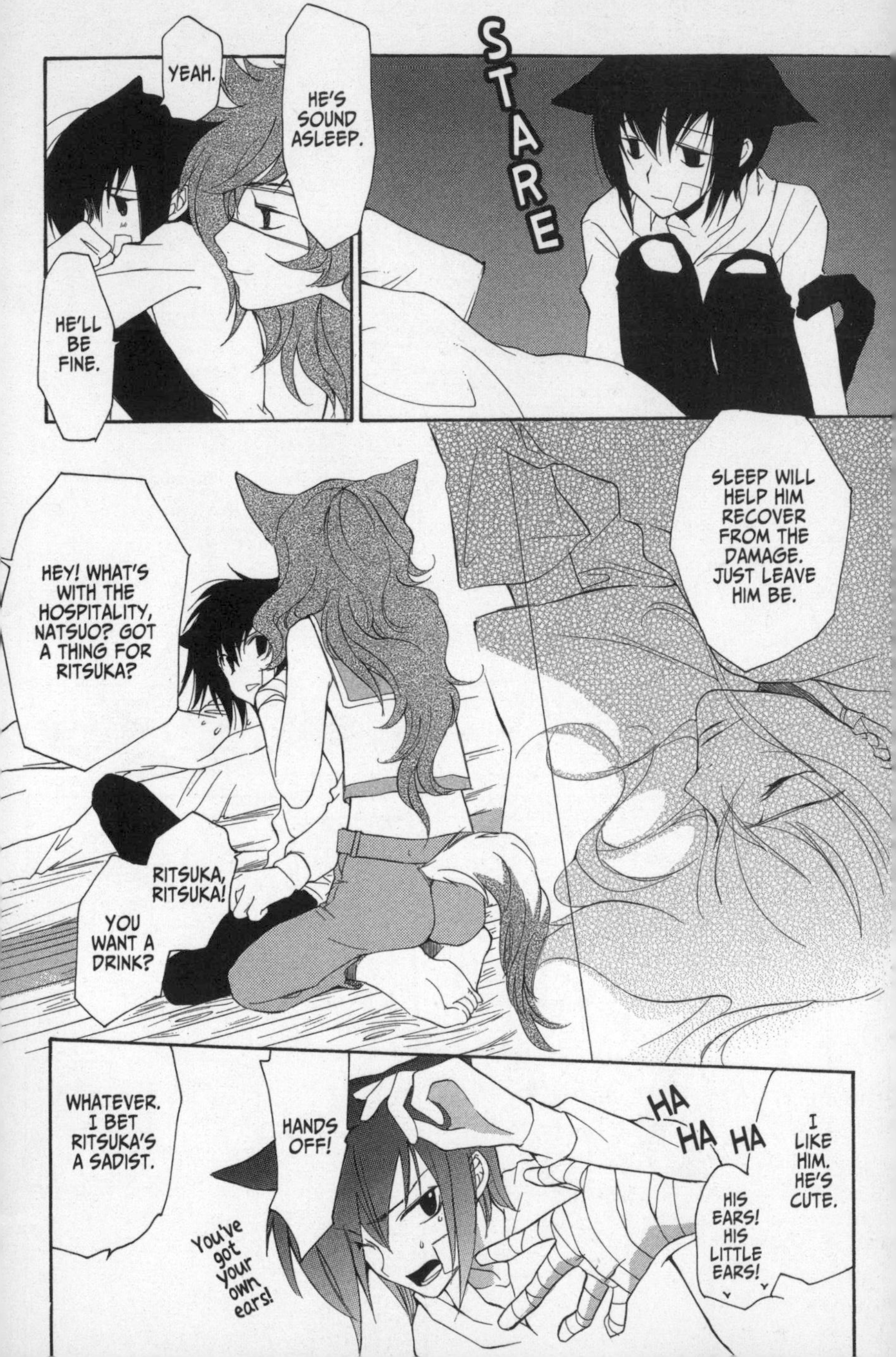
STARE
HE'S SOUND ASLEEP.
YEAH.
HE'LL BE FINE.
SLEEP WILL HELP HIM RECOVER FROM THE DAMAGE. JUST LEAVE HIM BE.
HEY! WHAT'S WITH THE HOSPITALITY, NATSUO? GOT A THING FOR RITSUKA?
RITSUKA, RITSUKA!
YOU WANT A DRINK?
I LIKE HIM. HE'S CUTE.
HA HA HA
HIS EARS! HIS LITTLE EARS!
HANDS OFF!
WHATEVER. I BET RITSUKA'S A SADIST.
You've got your own ears!

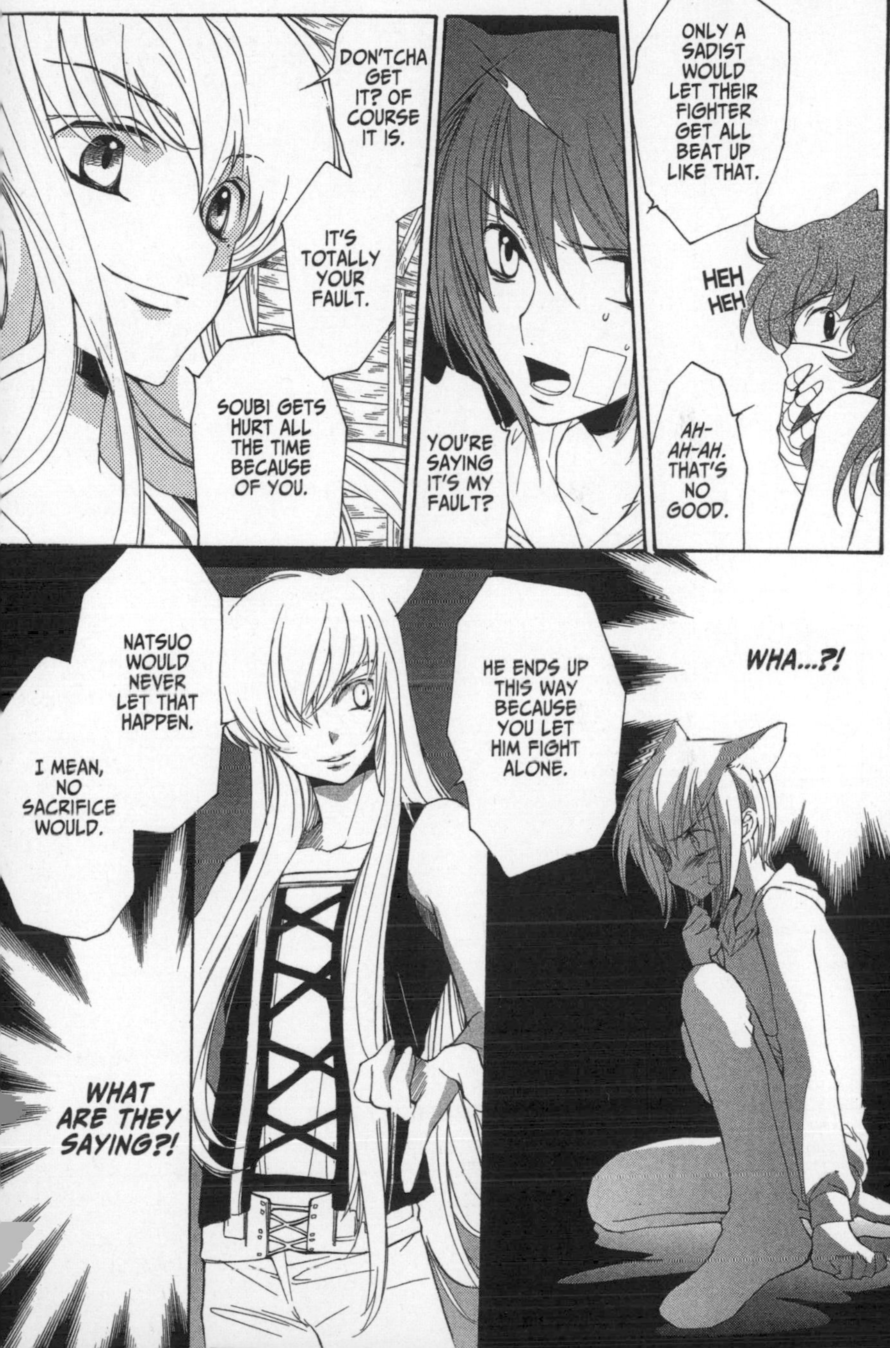
ONLY A SADIST WOULD LET THEIR FIGHTER GET ALL BEAT UP LIKE THAT.
HEH HEH
AH-AH-AH. THAT'S NO GOOD.
YOU'RE SAYING IT'S MY FAULT?
DON'TCHA GET IT? OF COURSE IT IS.
IT'S TOTALLY YOUR FAULT.
SOUBI GETS HURT ALL THE TIME BECAUSE OF YOU.
WHA...?!
HE ENDS UP THIS WAY BECAUSE YOU LET HIM FIGHT ALONE.
NATSUO WOULD NEVER LET THAT HAPPEN.
I MEAN, NO SACRIFICE WOULD.
WHAT ARE THEY SAYING?!

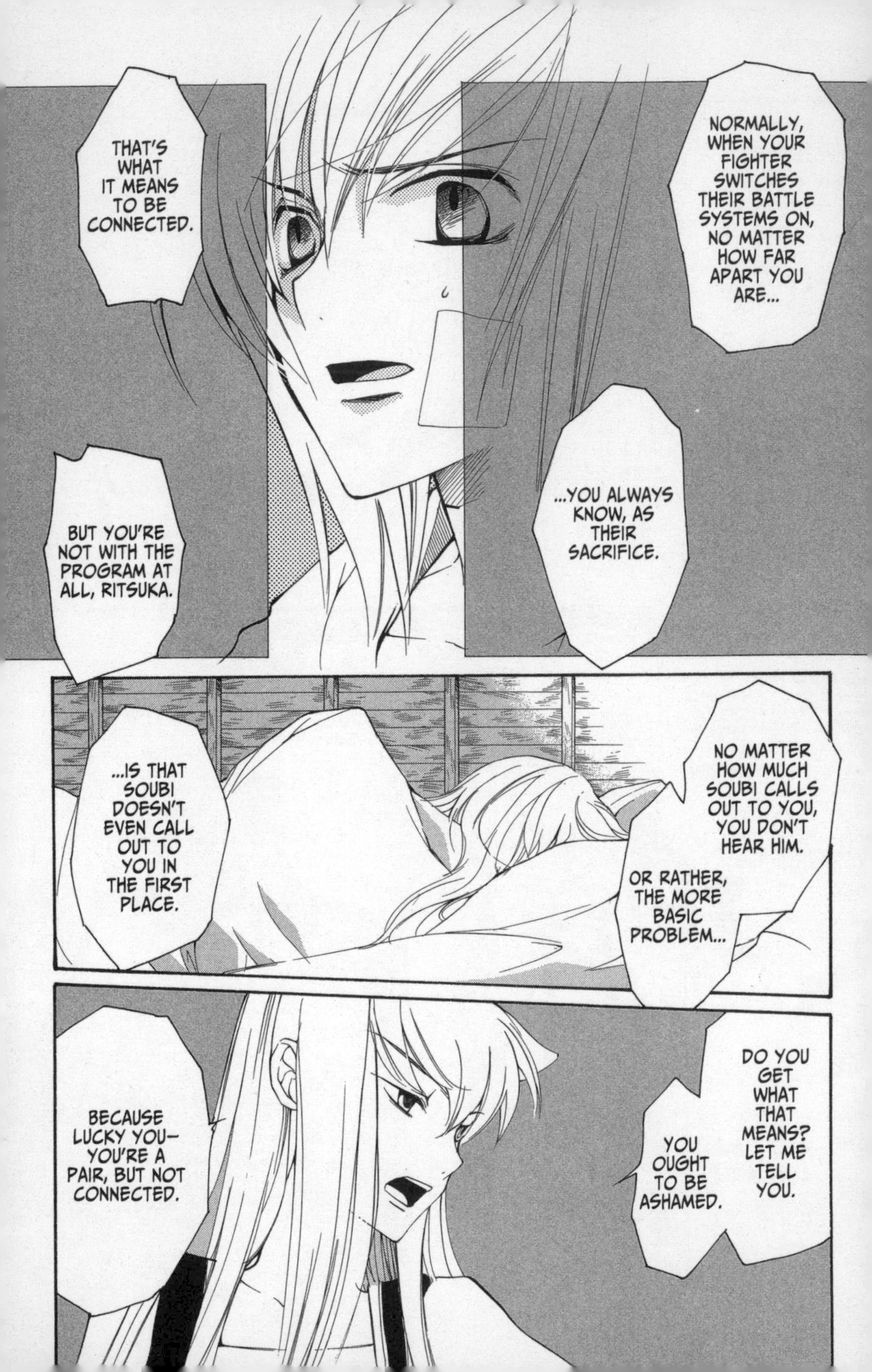
NORMALLY, WHEN YOUR FIGHTER SWITCHES THEIR BATTLE SYSTEMS ON, NO MATTER HOW FAR APART YOU ARE...
...YOU ALWAYS KNOW, AS THEIR SACRIFICE.
THAT'S WHAT IT MEANS TO BE CONNECTED.
BUT YOU'RE NOT WITH THE PROGRAM AT ALL, RITSUKA.
NO MATTER HOW MUCH SOUBI CALLS OUT TO YOU, YOU DON'T HEAR HIM.
OR RATHER, THE MORE BASIC PROBLEM...
...IS THAT SOUBI DOESN'T EVEN CALL OUT TO YOU IN THE FIRST PLACE.
DO YOU GET WHAT THAT MEANS? LET ME TELL YOU.
YOU OUGHT TO BE ASHAMED.
BECAUSE LUCKY YOU—YOU'RE A PAIR, BUT NOT CONNECTED.

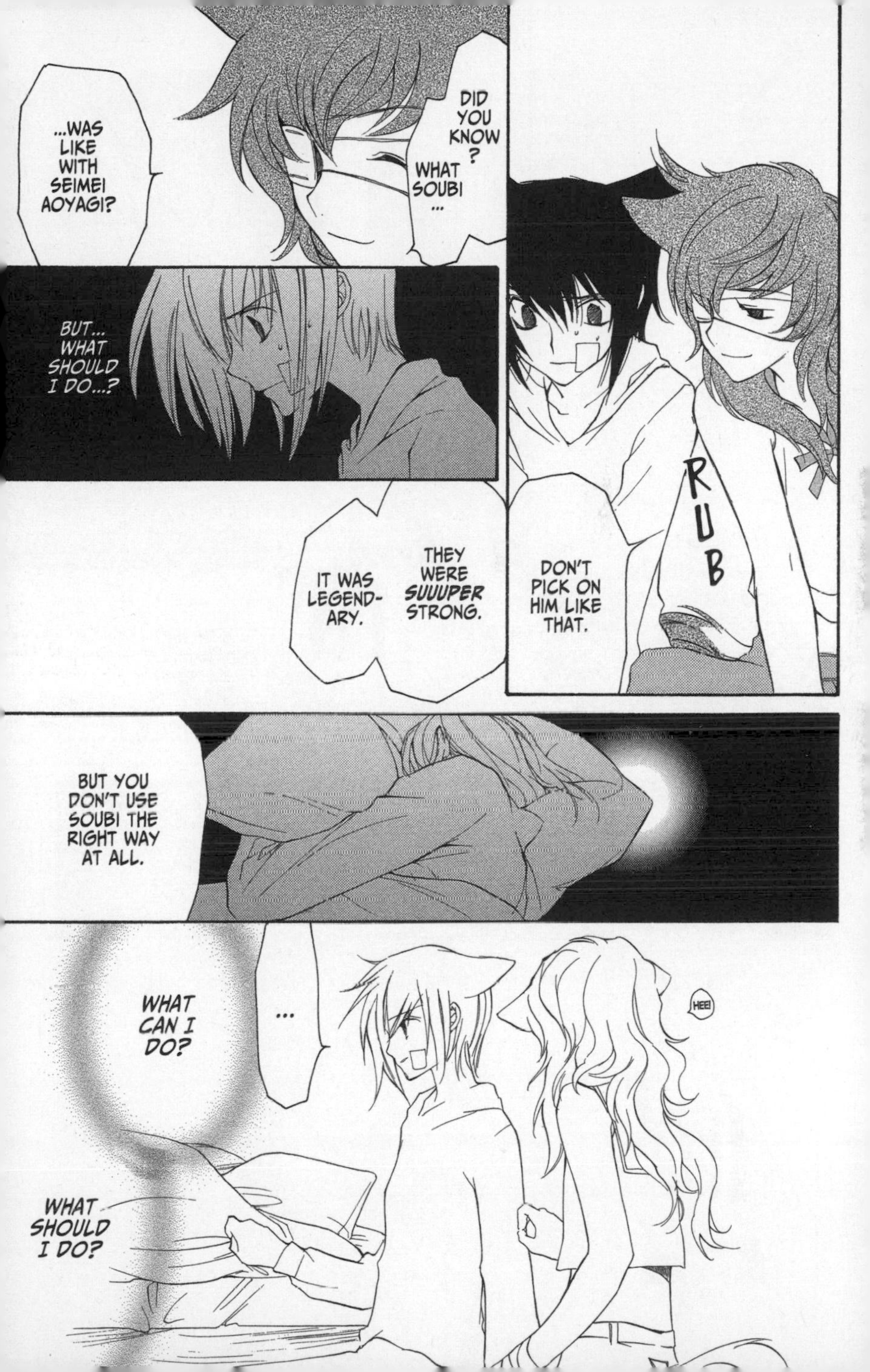
DON'T PICK ON HIM LIKE THAT.
RUB
DID YOU KNOW? WHAT SOUBI...
...WAS LIKE WITH SEIMEI AOYAGI?
BUT... WHAT SHOULD I DO...?
THEY WERE *SUUUPER* STRONG.
IT WAS LEGENDARY.
BUT YOU DON'T USE SOUBI THE RIGHT WAY AT ALL.
HEE!
...
WHAT CAN I DO?
WHAT SHOULD I DO?

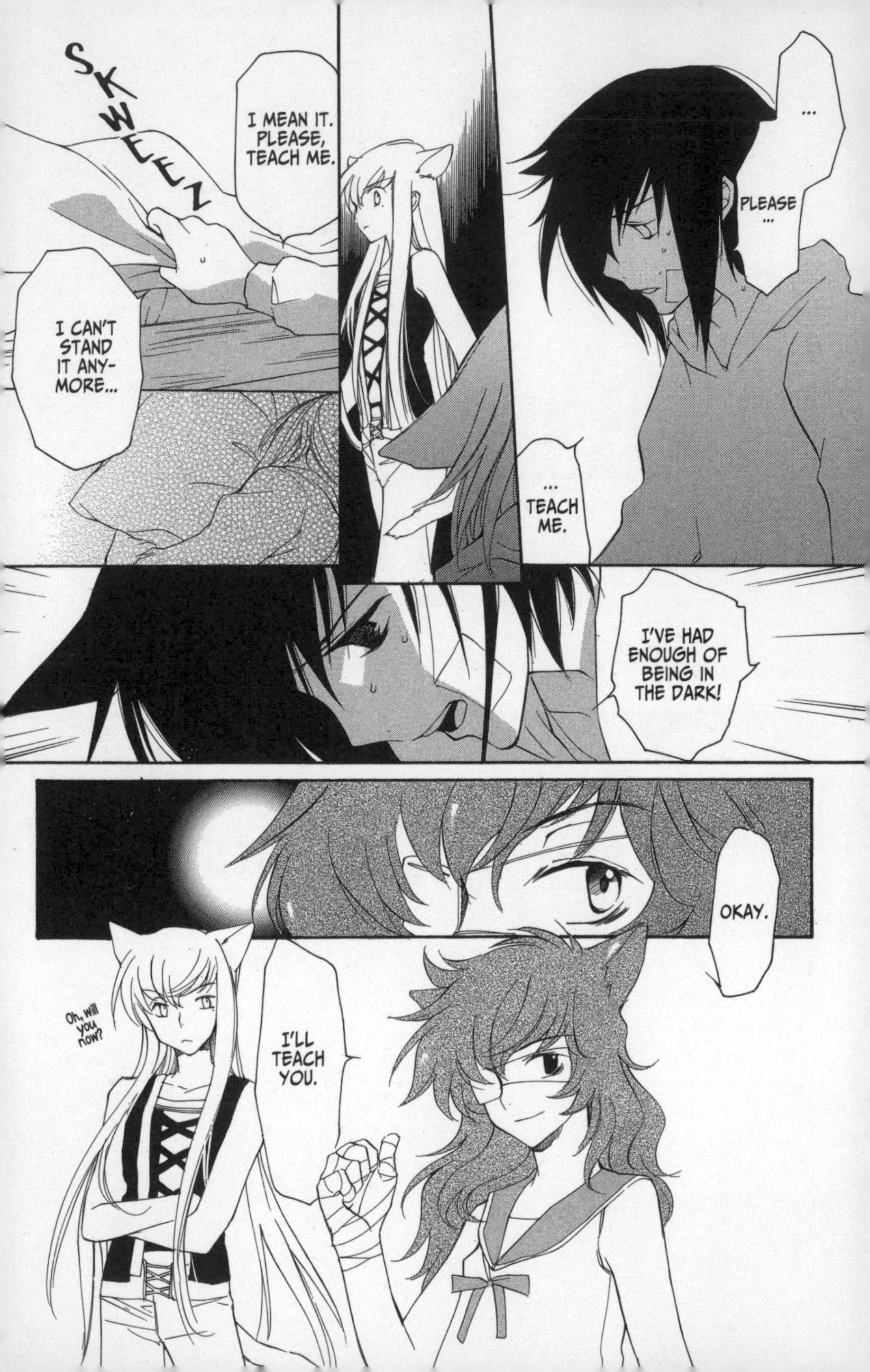
...
PLEASE ...
... TEACH ME.
I MEAN IT. PLEASE, TEACH ME.
SKWEEZ
I CAN'T STAND IT ANYMORE...
I'VE HAD ENOUGH OF BEING IN THE DARK!
OKAY.
I'LL TEACH YOU.
Oh, will you now?

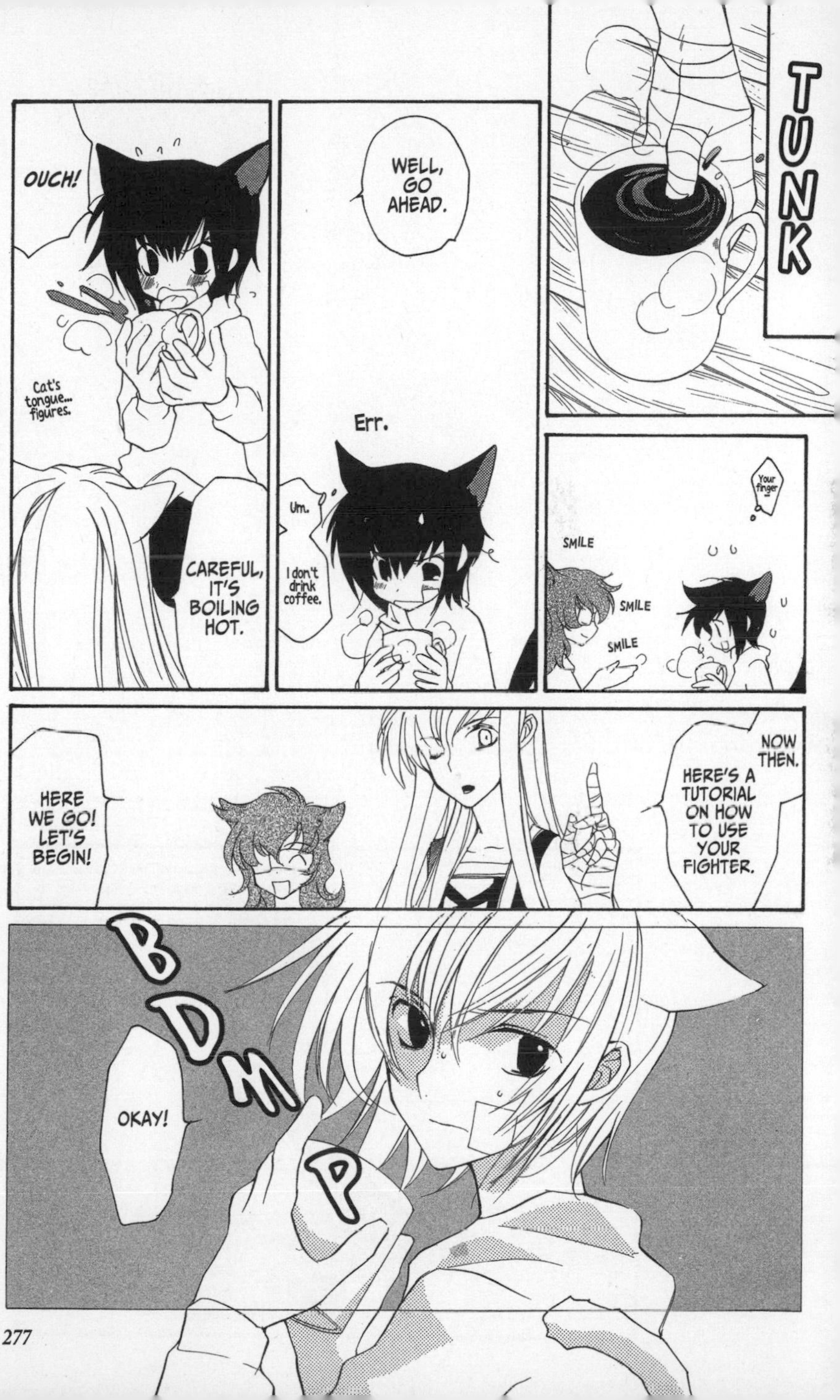
TUNK
Your finger...
SMILE
SMILE
SMILE
WELL, GO AHEAD.
Err.
Um.
I don't drink coffee.
OUCH!
Cat's tongue... figures.
CAREFUL, IT'S BOILING HOT.
NOW THEN.
HERE'S A TUTORIAL ON HOW TO USE YOUR FIGHTER.
HERE WE GO! LET'S BEGIN!
BDMP
OKAY!

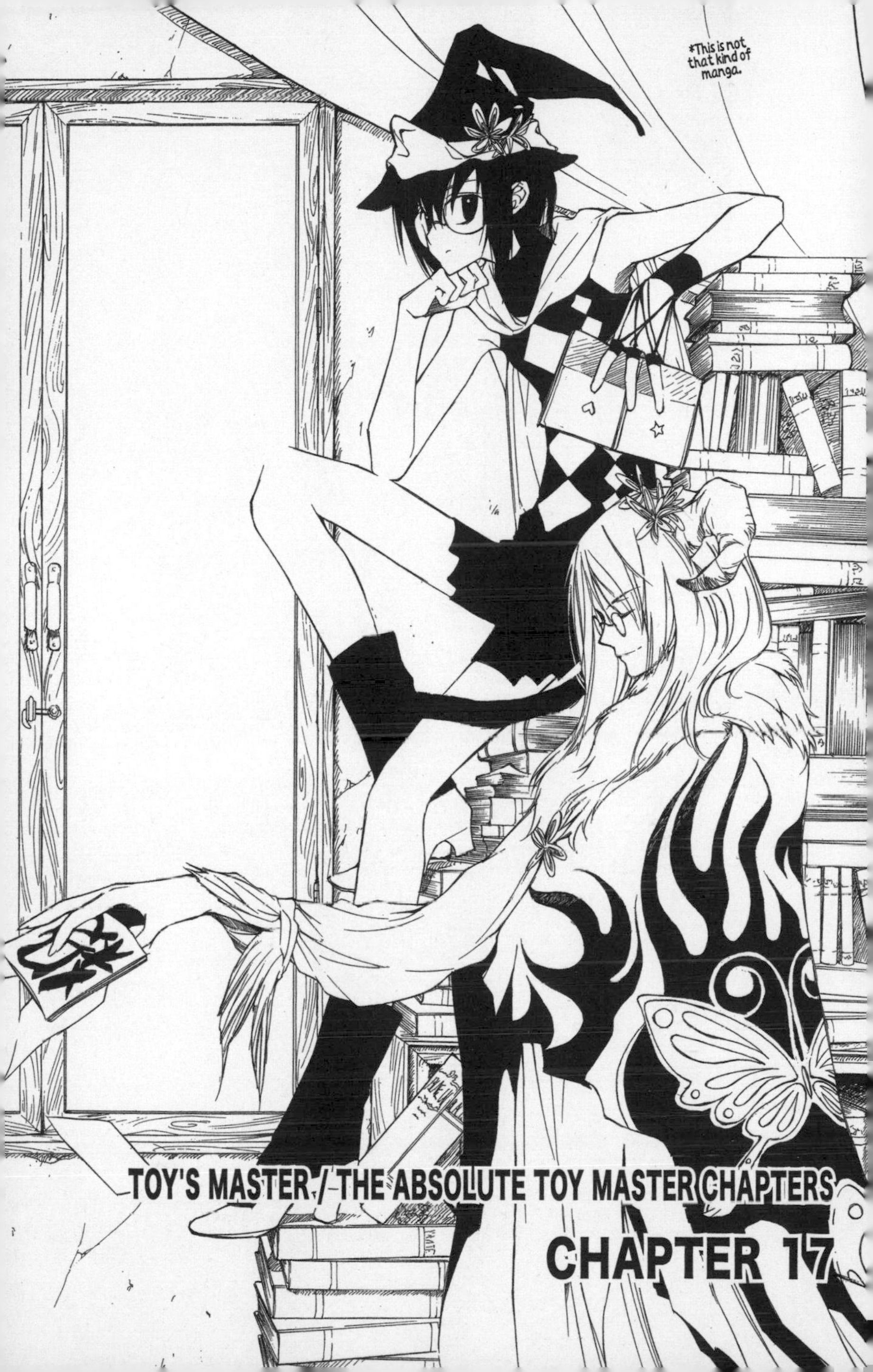
*This is not that kind of manga.
TOY'S MASTER / THE ABSOLUTE TOY MASTER CHAPTERS
CHAPTER 17

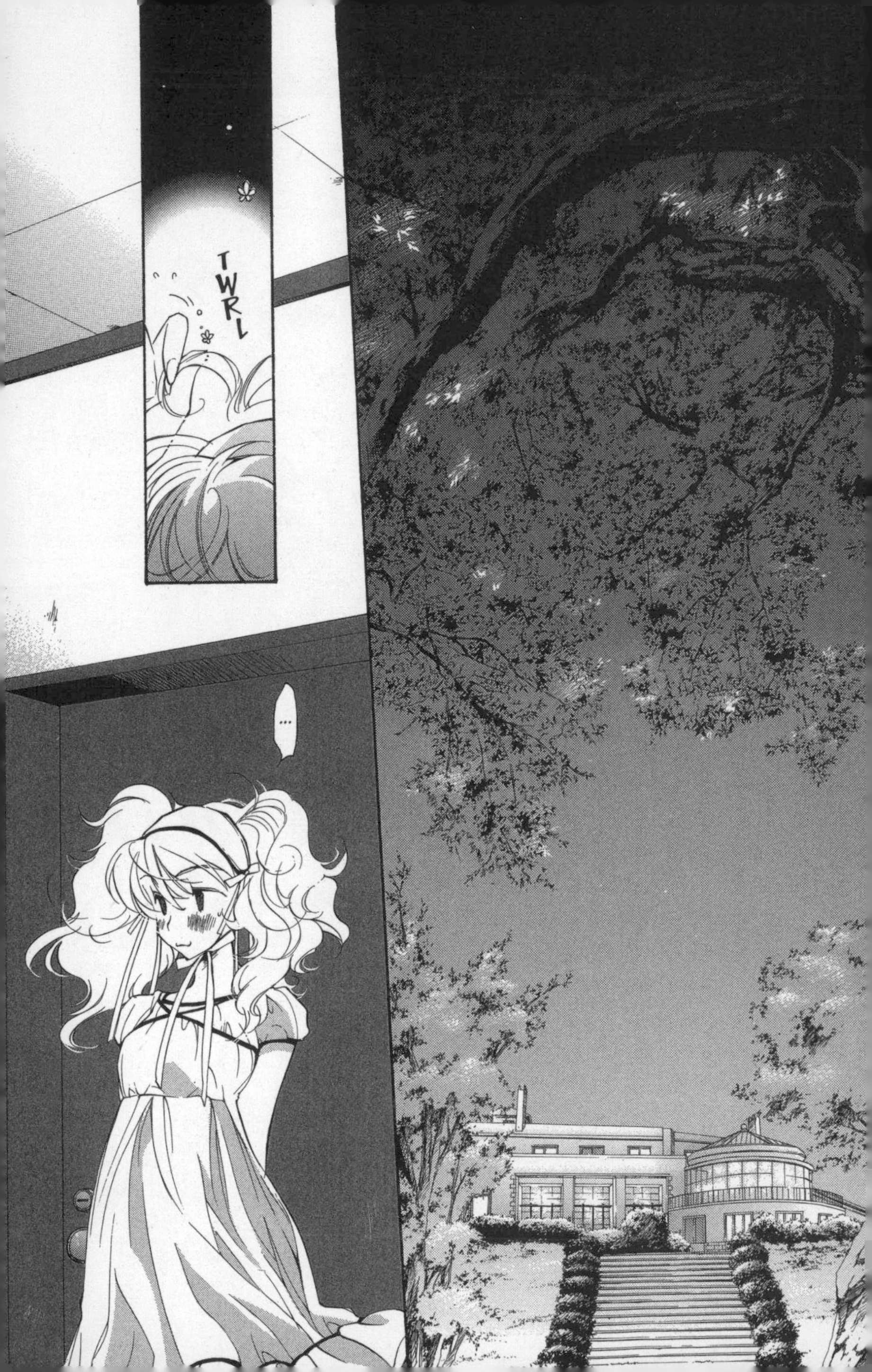
TWRL
...

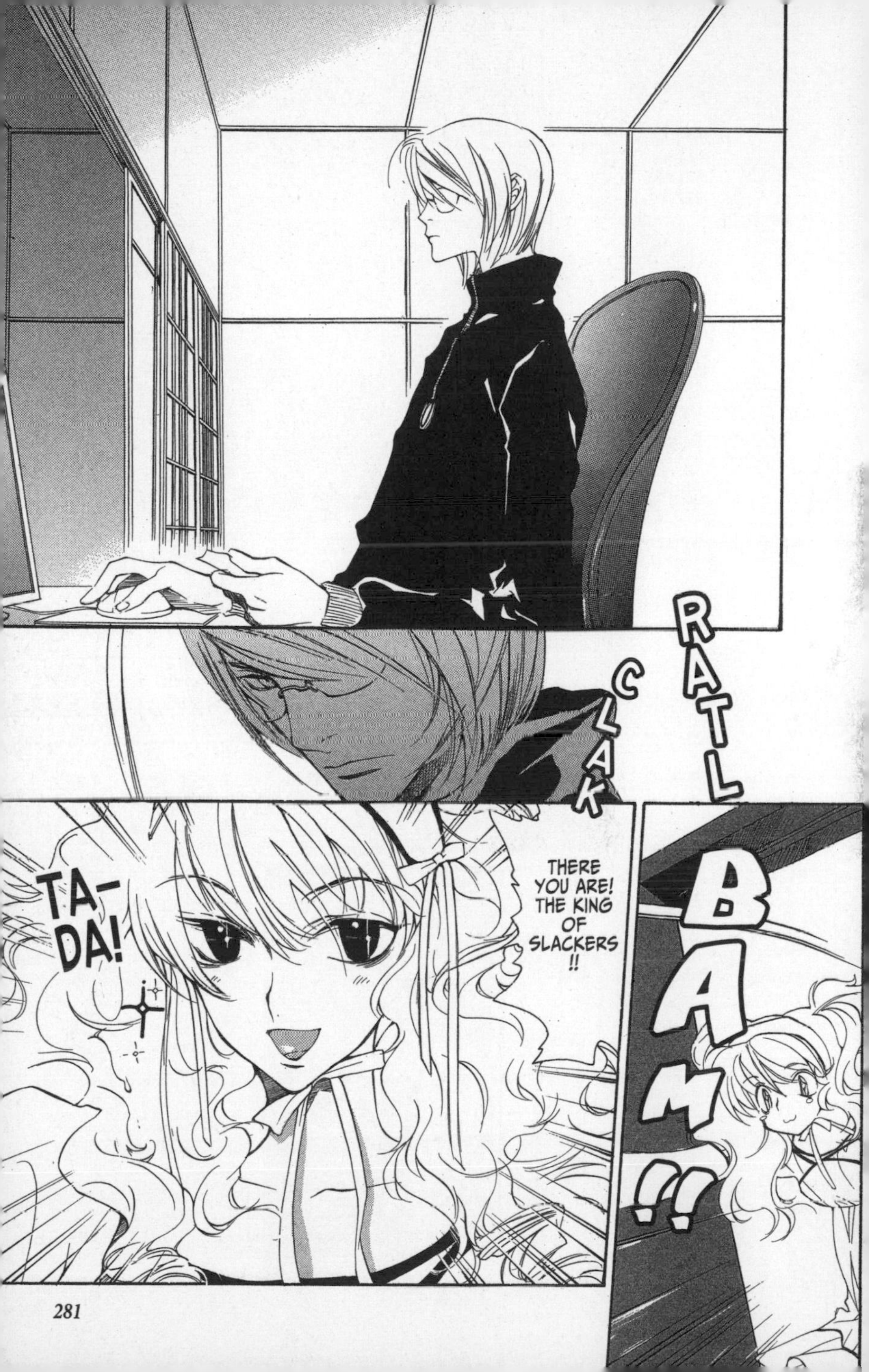
RATTL
CLAK
BAM!!
THERE YOU ARE! THE KING OF SLACKERS!!
TA-DA!

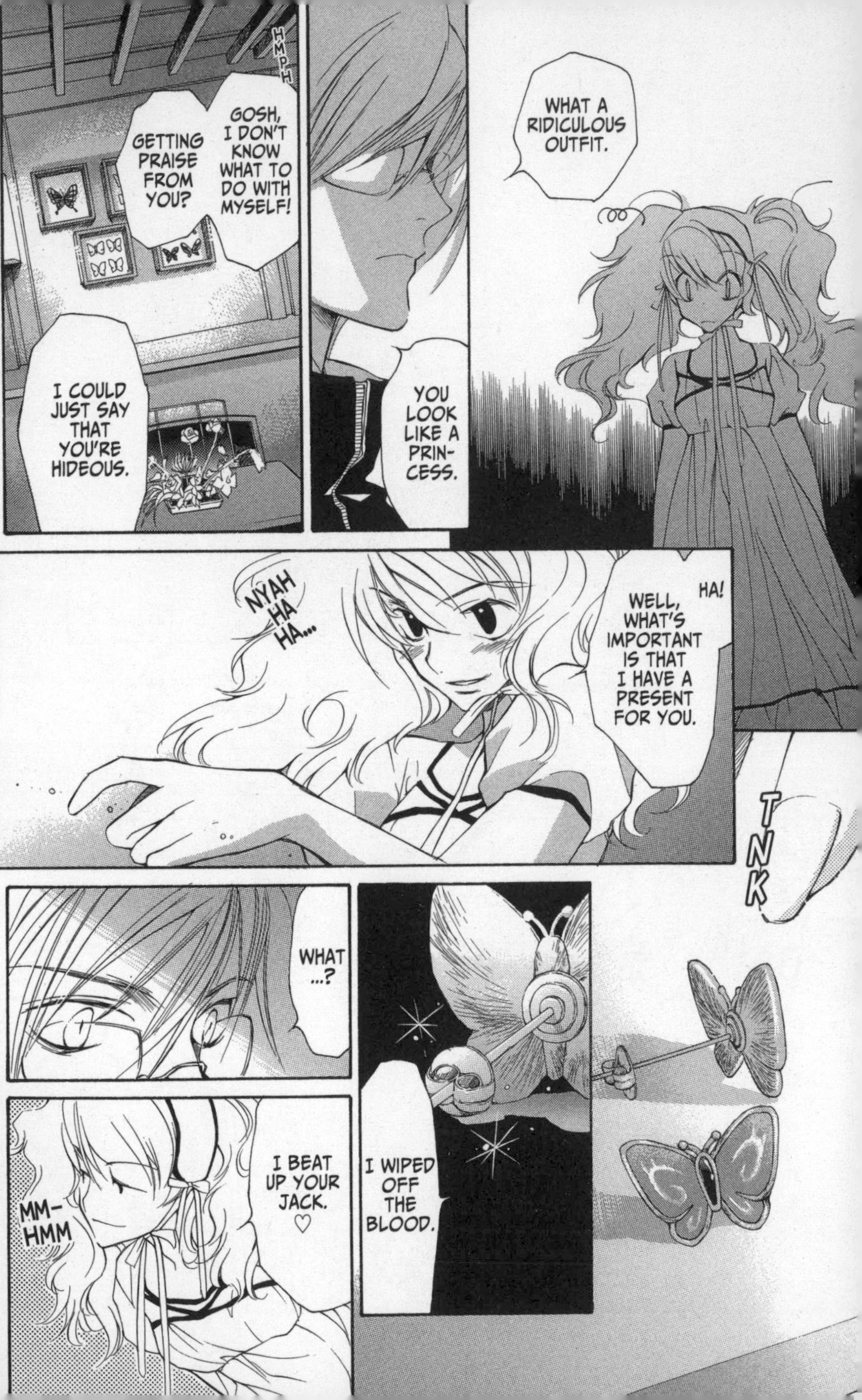
WHAT A RIDICULOUS OUTFIT.
YOU LOOK LIKE A PRIN-CESS.
HMPH
GOSH, I DON'T KNOW WHAT TO DO WITH MYSELF!
GETTING PRAISE FROM YOU?
I COULD JUST SAY THAT YOU'RE HIDEOUS.
HA!
WELL, WHAT'S IMPORTANT IS THAT I HAVE A PRESENT FOR YOU.
NYAH HA HA...
TNK
I WIPED OFF THE BLOOD.
WHAT ...?
I BEAT UP YOUR JACK. ♡
MM-HMM

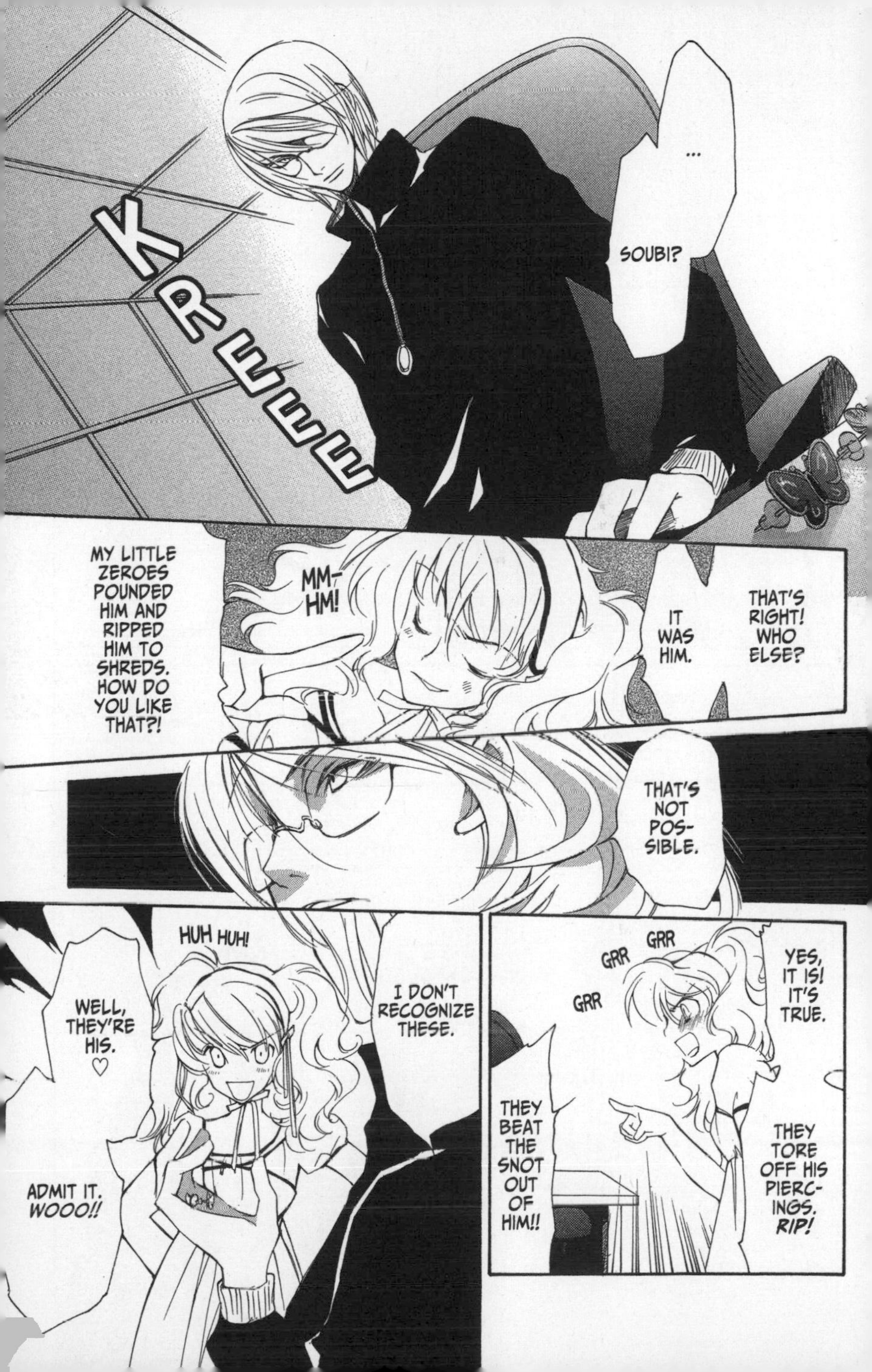
...
SOUBI?
KREEEE
THAT'S RIGHT! WHO ELSE?
IT WAS HIM.
MM-HM!
MY LITTLE ZEROES POUNDED HIM AND RIPPED HIM TO SHREDS. HOW DO YOU LIKE THAT?!
THAT'S NOT POS-SIBLE.
YES, IT IS! IT'S TRUE.
GRR GRR
GRR
THEY TORE OFF HIS PIERC-INGS. RIP!
THEY BEAT THE SNOT OUT OF HIM!!
I DON'T RECOGNIZE THESE.
HUH HUH!
WELL, THEY'RE HIS. ♡
ADMIT IT. WOOO!!

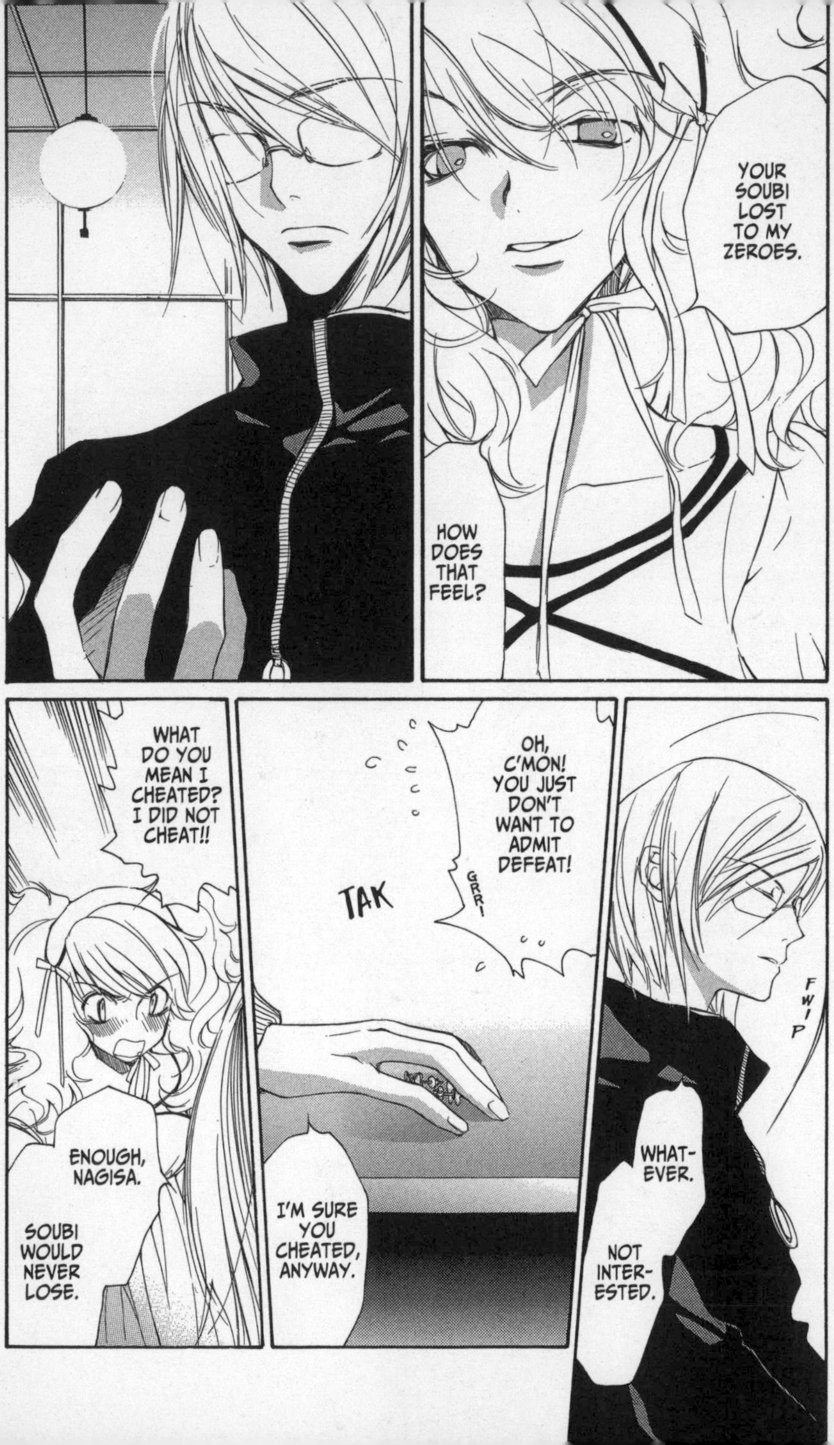
YOUR SOUBI LOST TO MY ZEROES.
HOW DOES THAT FEEL?
FWIP
WHAT-EVER.
NOT INTER-ESTED.
OH, C'MON! YOU JUST DON'T WANT TO ADMIT DEFEAT!
GRR!
TAK
I'M SURE YOU CHEATED, ANYWAY.
WHAT DO YOU MEAN I CHEATED? I DID NOT CHEAT!!
ENOUGH, NAGISA.
SOUBI WOULD NEVER LOSE.

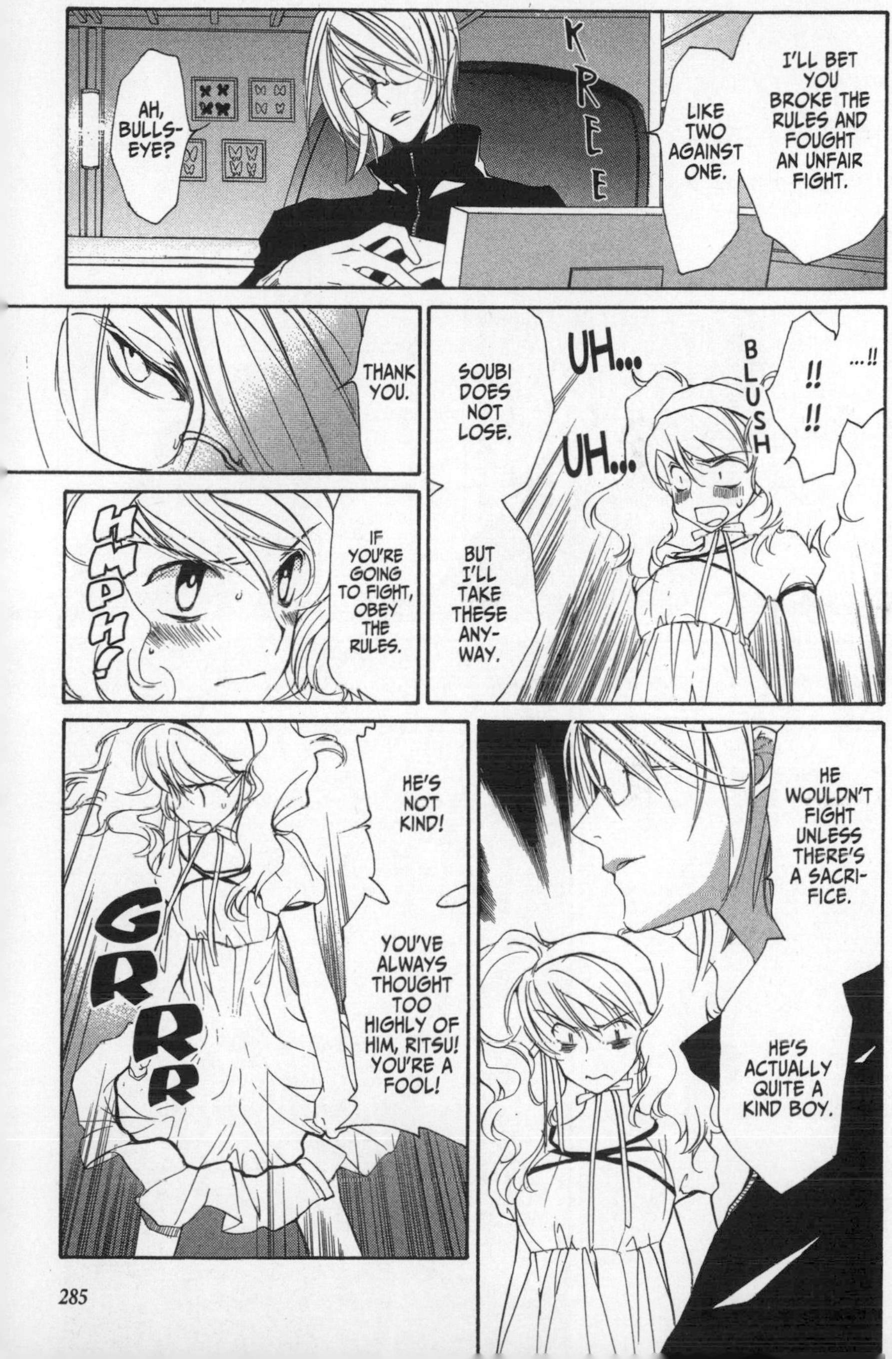
I'LL BET YOU BROKE THE RULES AND FOUGHT AN UNFAIR FIGHT.
LIKE TWO AGAINST ONE.
KREE
AH, BULLS-EYE?
...!!
!!
!!
BLUSH
UH...
UH...
SOUBI DOES NOT LOSE.
BUT I'LL TAKE THESE ANY-WAY.
THANK YOU.
IF YOU'RE GOING TO FIGHT, OBEY THE RULES.
HMPH!
HE WOULDN'T FIGHT UNLESS THERE'S A SACRI-FICE.
HE'S ACTUALLY QUITE A KIND BOY.
HE'S NOT KIND!
YOU'VE ALWAYS THOUGHT TOO HIGHLY OF HIM, RITSU! YOU'RE A FOOL!
GRRR

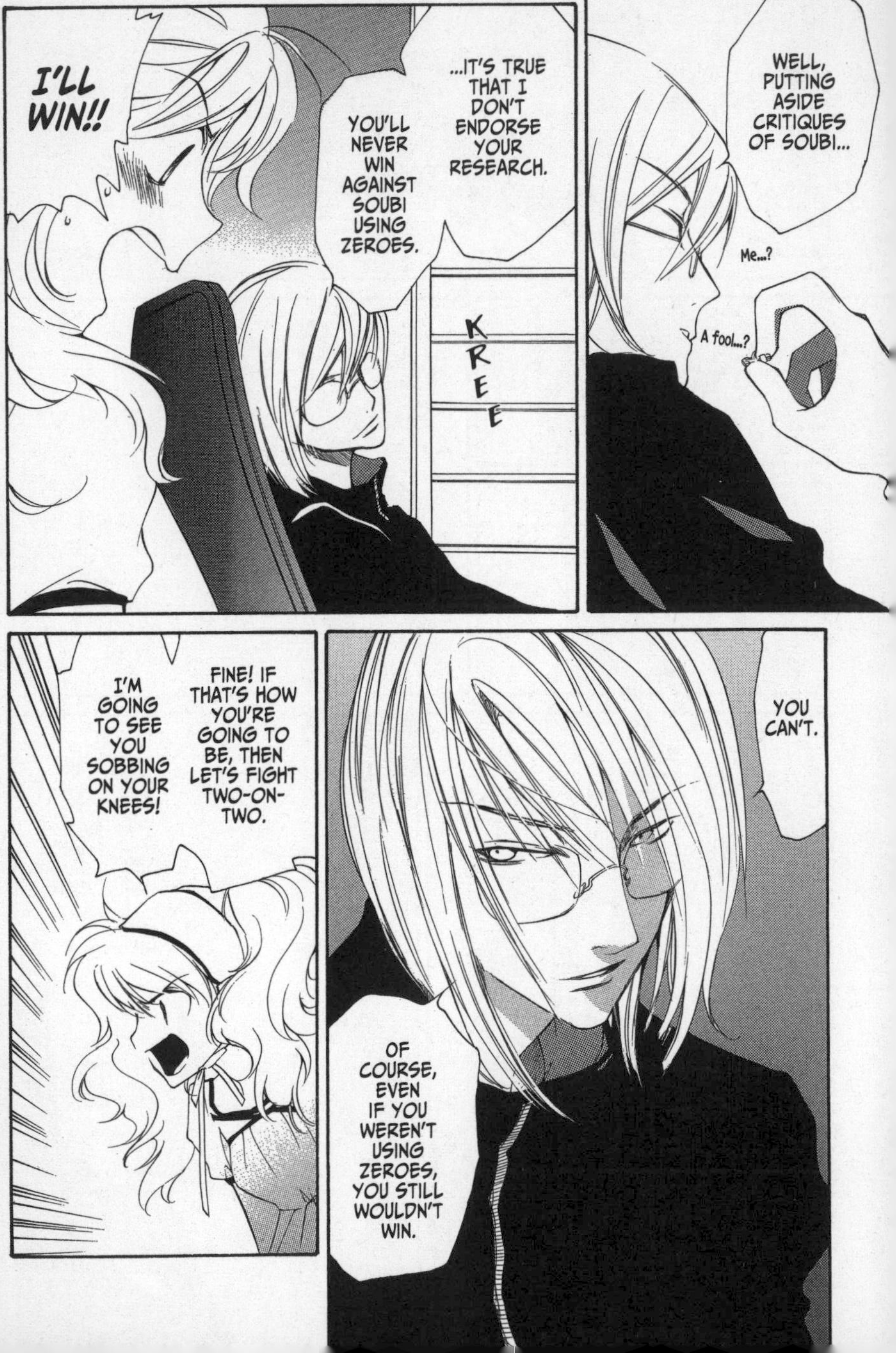
WELL, PUTTING ASIDE CRITIQUES OF SOUBI...
Me...?
A fool...?
...IT'S TRUE THAT I DON'T ENDORSE YOUR RESEARCH.
YOU'LL NEVER WIN AGAINST SOUBI USING ZEROES.
KREE
I'LL WIN!!
YOU CAN'T.
OF COURSE, EVEN IF YOU WEREN'T USING ZEROES, YOU STILL WOULDN'T WIN.
FINE! IF THAT'S HOW YOU'RE GOING TO BE, THEN LET'S FIGHT TWO-ON-TWO.
I'M GOING TO SEE YOU SOBBING ON YOUR KNEES!

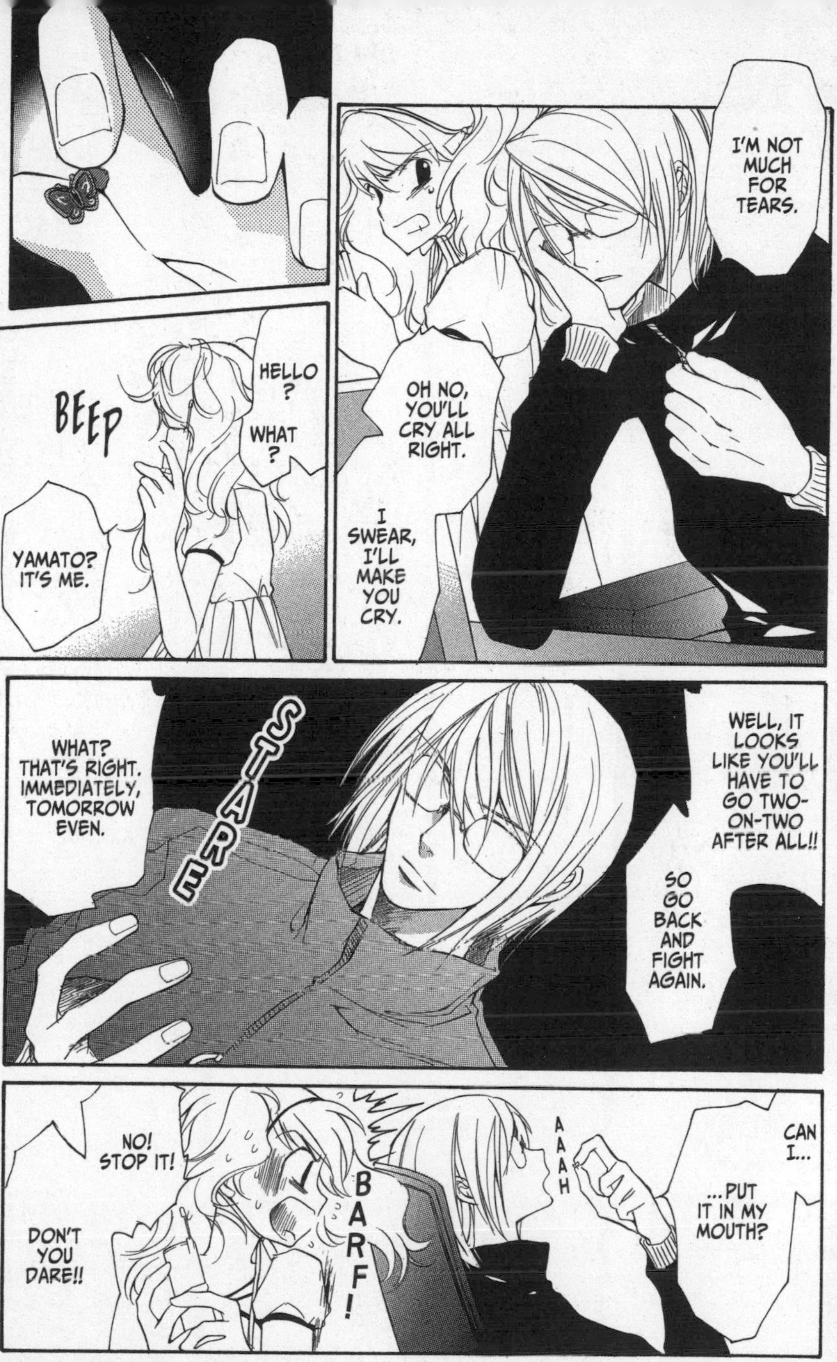
I'M NOT MUCH FOR TEARS.
OH NO, YOU'LL CRY ALL RIGHT.
I SWEAR, I'LL MAKE YOU CRY.
HELLO?
WHAT?
BEEP
YAMATO? IT'S ME.
WELL, IT LOOKS LIKE YOU'LL HAVE TO GO TWO-ON-TWO AFTER ALL!!
SO GO BACK AND FIGHT AGAIN.
STARE
WHAT? THAT'S RIGHT. IMMEDIATELY, TOMORROW EVEN.
CAN I...
...PUT IT IN MY MOUTH?
AAAH
BARF!
NO! STOP IT!
DON'T YOU DARE!!

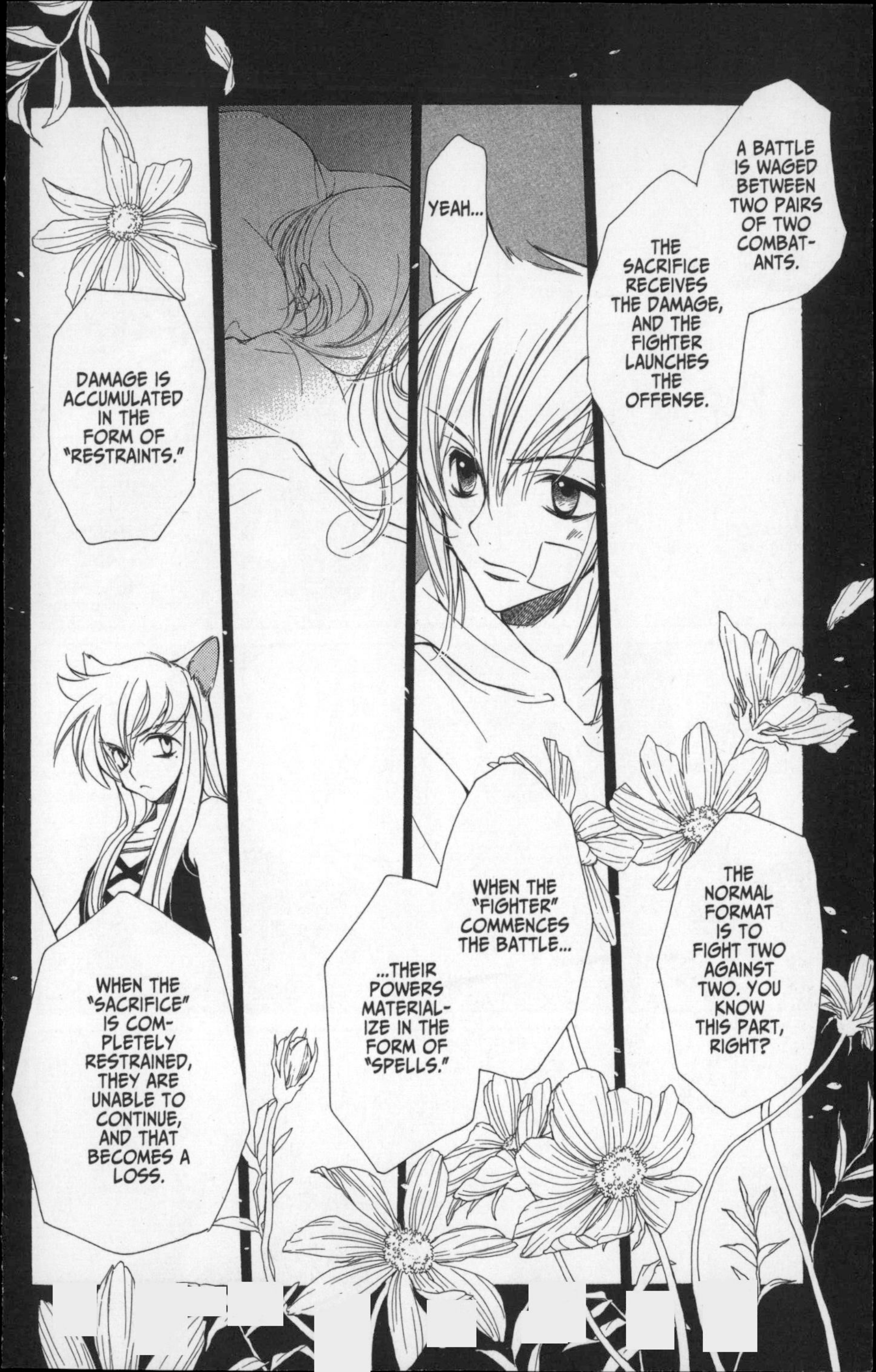
A BATTLE IS WAGED BETWEEN TWO PAIRS OF TWO COMBAT-ANTS.
THE SACRIFICE RECEIVES THE DAMAGE, AND THE FIGHTER LAUNCHES THE OFFENSE.
THE NORMAL FORMAT IS TO FIGHT TWO AGAINST TWO. YOU KNOW THIS PART, RIGHT?
YEAH...
WHEN THE "FIGHTER" COMMENCES THE BATTLE...
...THEIR POWERS MATERIAL-IZE IN THE FORM OF "SPELLS."
DAMAGE IS ACCUMULATED IN THE FORM OF "RESTRAINTS."
WHEN THE "SACRIFICE" IS COM-PLETELY RESTRAINED, THEY ARE UNABLE TO CONTINUE, AND THAT BECOMES A LOSS.

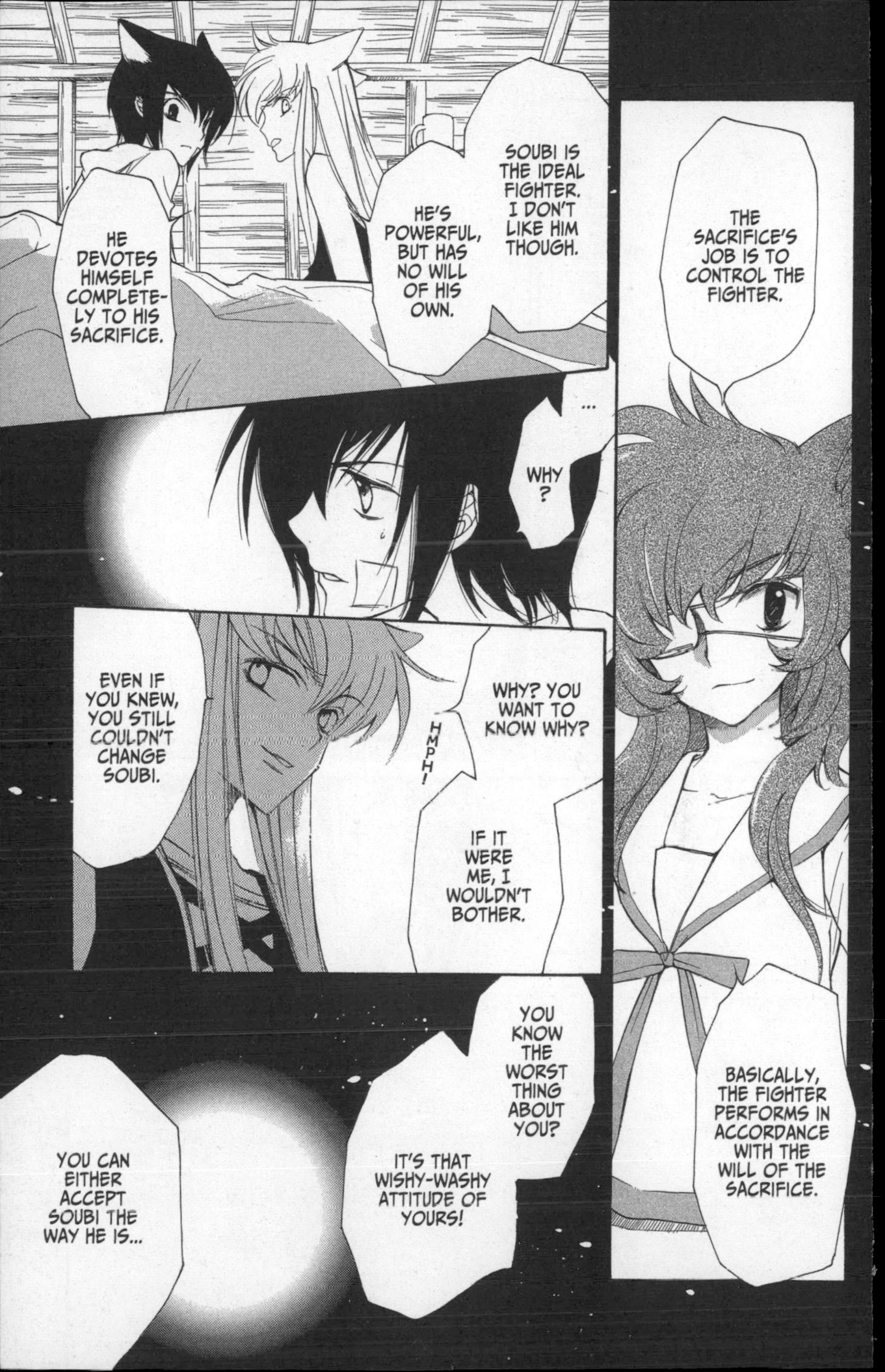
THE SACRIFICE'S JOB IS TO CONTROL THE FIGHTER.
BASICALLY, THE FIGHTER PERFORMS IN ACCORDANCE WITH THE WILL OF THE SACRIFICE.
SOUBI IS THE IDEAL FIGHTER. I DON'T LIKE HIM THOUGH.
HE'S POWERFUL, BUT HAS NO WILL OF HIS OWN.
HE DEVOTES HIMSELF COMPLETE-LY TO HIS SACRIFICE.
...
WHY?
WHY? YOU WANT TO KNOW WHY?
HMPH!
IF IT WERE ME, I WOULDN'T BOTHER.
EVEN IF YOU KNEW, YOU STILL COULDN'T CHANGE SOUBI.
YOU KNOW THE WORST THING ABOUT YOU?
IT'S THAT WISHY-WASHY ATTITUDE OF YOURS!
YOU CAN EITHER ACCEPT SOUBI THE WAY HE IS...

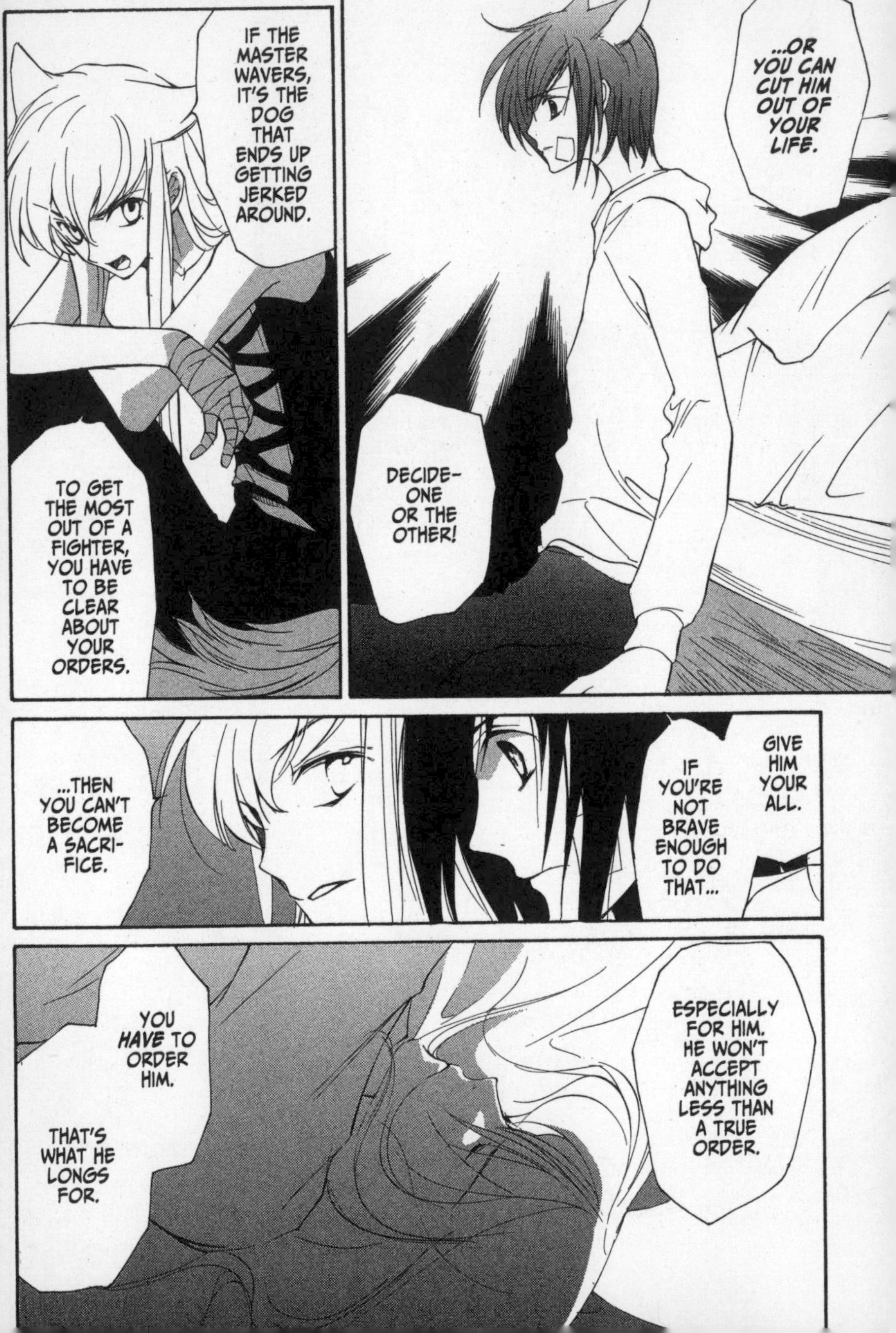

...OR YOU CAN CUT HIM OUT OF YOUR LIFE.
DECIDE-ONE OR THE OTHER!
IF THE MASTER WAVERS, IT'S THE DOG THAT ENDS UP GETTING JERKED AROUND.
TO GET THE MOST OUT OF A FIGHTER, YOU HAVE TO BE CLEAR ABOUT YOUR ORDERS.
GIVE HIM YOUR ALL.
IF YOU'RE NOT BRAVE ENOUGH TO DO THAT...
...THEN YOU CAN'T BECOME A SACRIFICE.
ESPECIALLY FOR HIM. HE WON'T ACCEPT ANYTHING LESS THAN A TRUE ORDER.
YOU *HAVE* TO ORDER HIM.
THAT'S WHAT HE LONGS FOR.

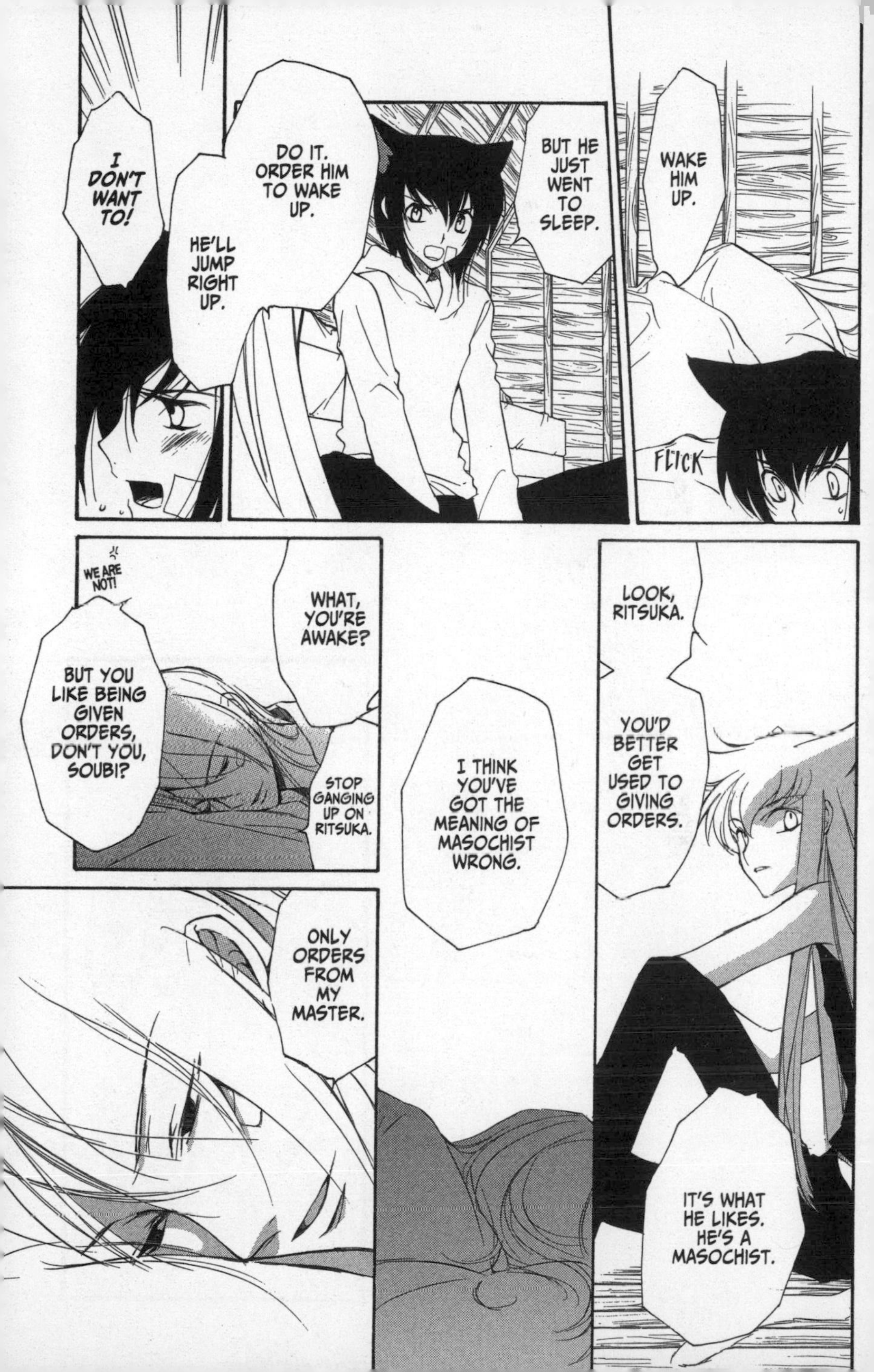
WAKE HIM UP.
FLICK
BUT HE JUST WENT TO SLEEP.
DO IT. ORDER HIM TO WAKE UP.
HE'LL JUMP RIGHT UP.
I DON'T WANT TO!
LOOK, RITSUKA.
YOU'D BETTER GET USED TO GIVING ORDERS.
IT'S WHAT HE LIKES. HE'S A MASOCHIST.
I THINK YOU'VE GOT THE MEANING OF MASOCHIST WRONG.
WHAT, YOU'RE AWAKE?
STOP GANGING UP ON RITSUKA.
BUT YOU LIKE BEING GIVEN ORDERS, DON'T YOU, SOUBI?
WE ARE NOT!
ONLY ORDERS FROM MY MASTER.

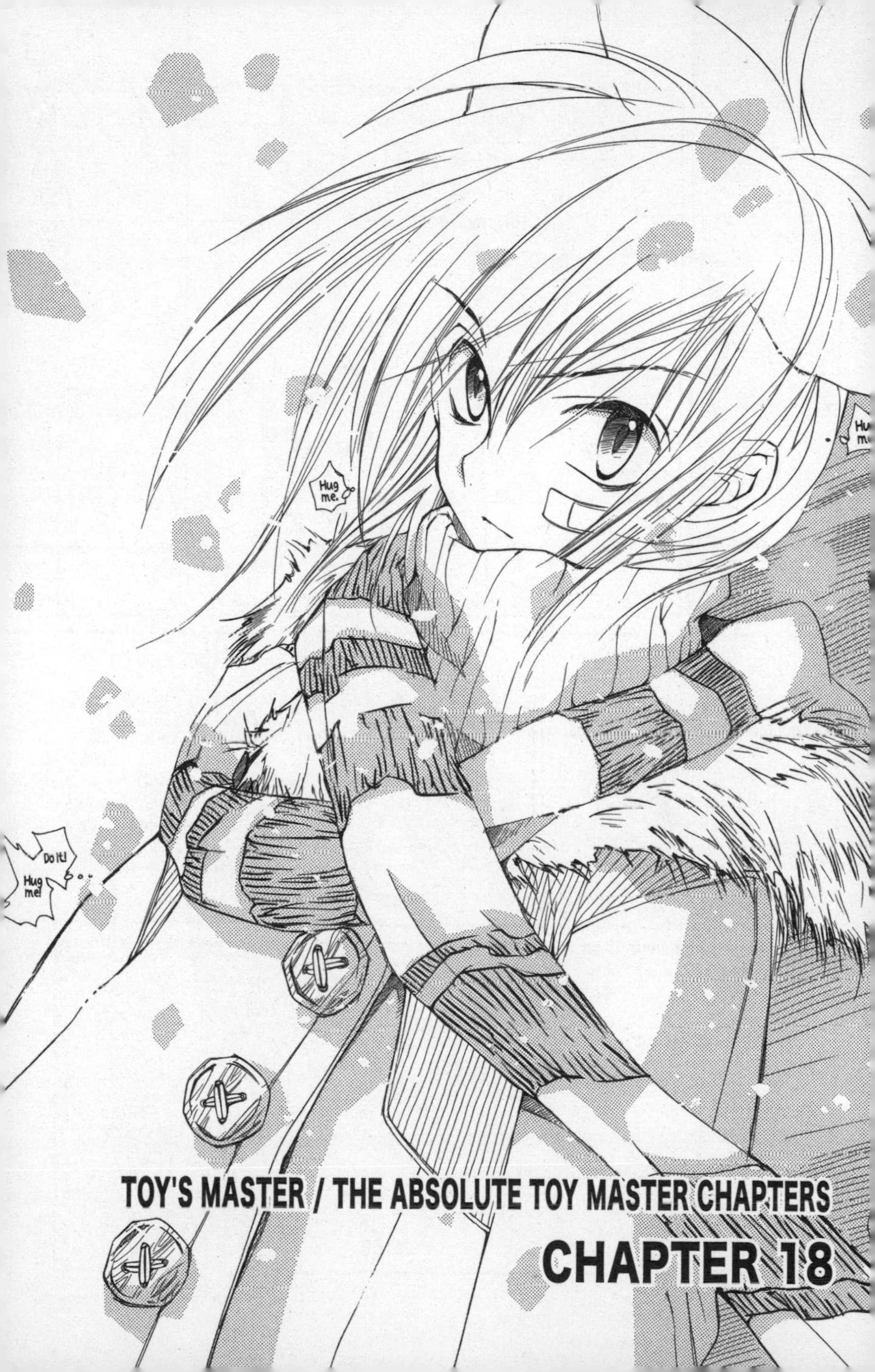
Hug me.
Do it! Hug me!

TOY'S MASTER / THE ABSOLUTE TOY MASTER CHAPTERS

CHAPTER 18

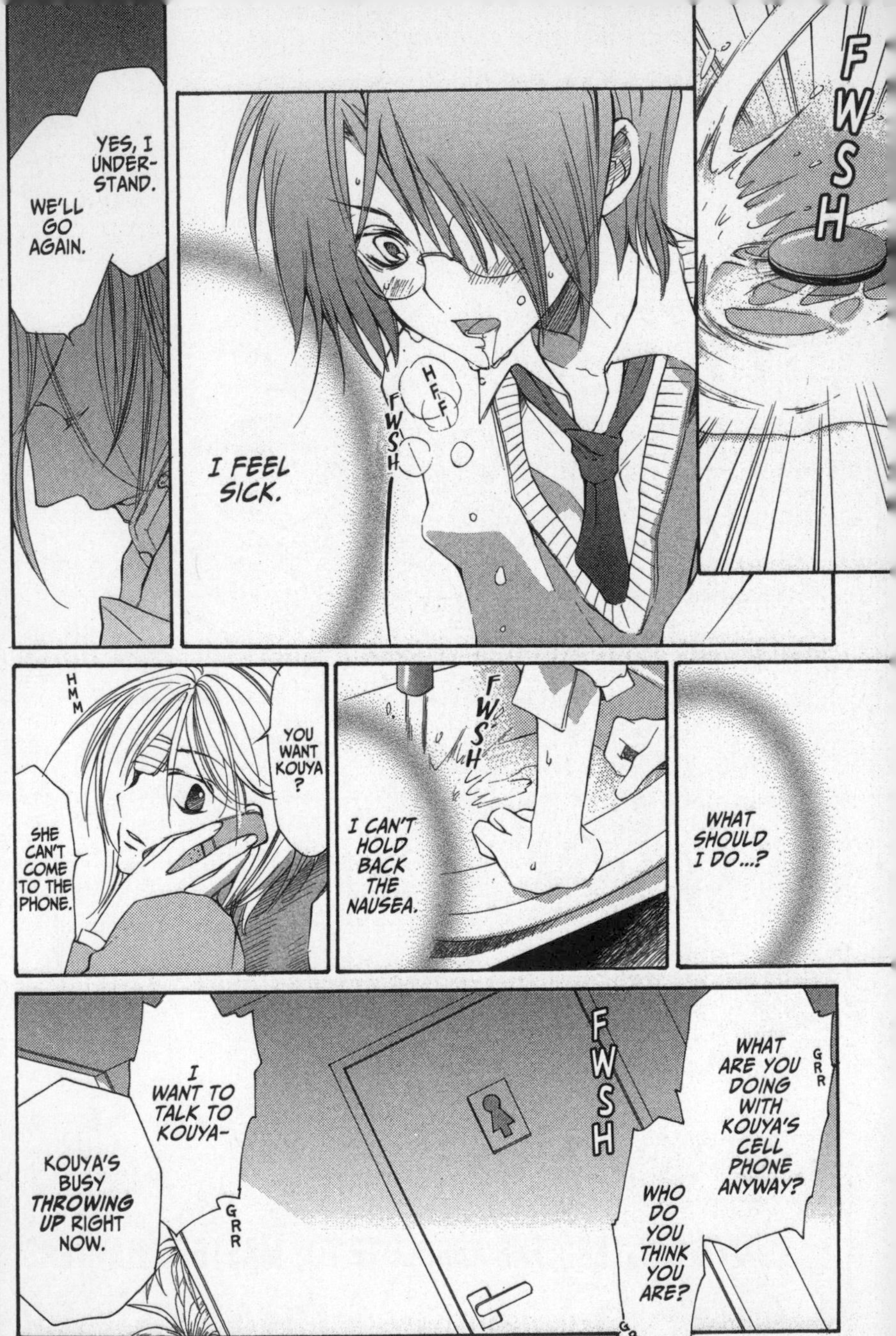
FWSH
I FEEL SICK.
HFF
FWSH
YES, I UNDERSTAND.
WE'LL GO AGAIN.
WHAT SHOULD I DO...?
FWSH
I CAN'T HOLD BACK THE NAUSEA.
YOU WANT KOUYA?
HMM
SHE CAN'T COME TO THE PHONE.
WHAT ARE YOU DOING WITH KOUYA'S CELL PHONE ANYWAY?
GRR
FWSH
I WANT TO TALK TO KOUYA-
WHO DO YOU THINK YOU ARE?
GRR
KOUYA'S BUSY THROWING UP RIGHT NOW.
GRR

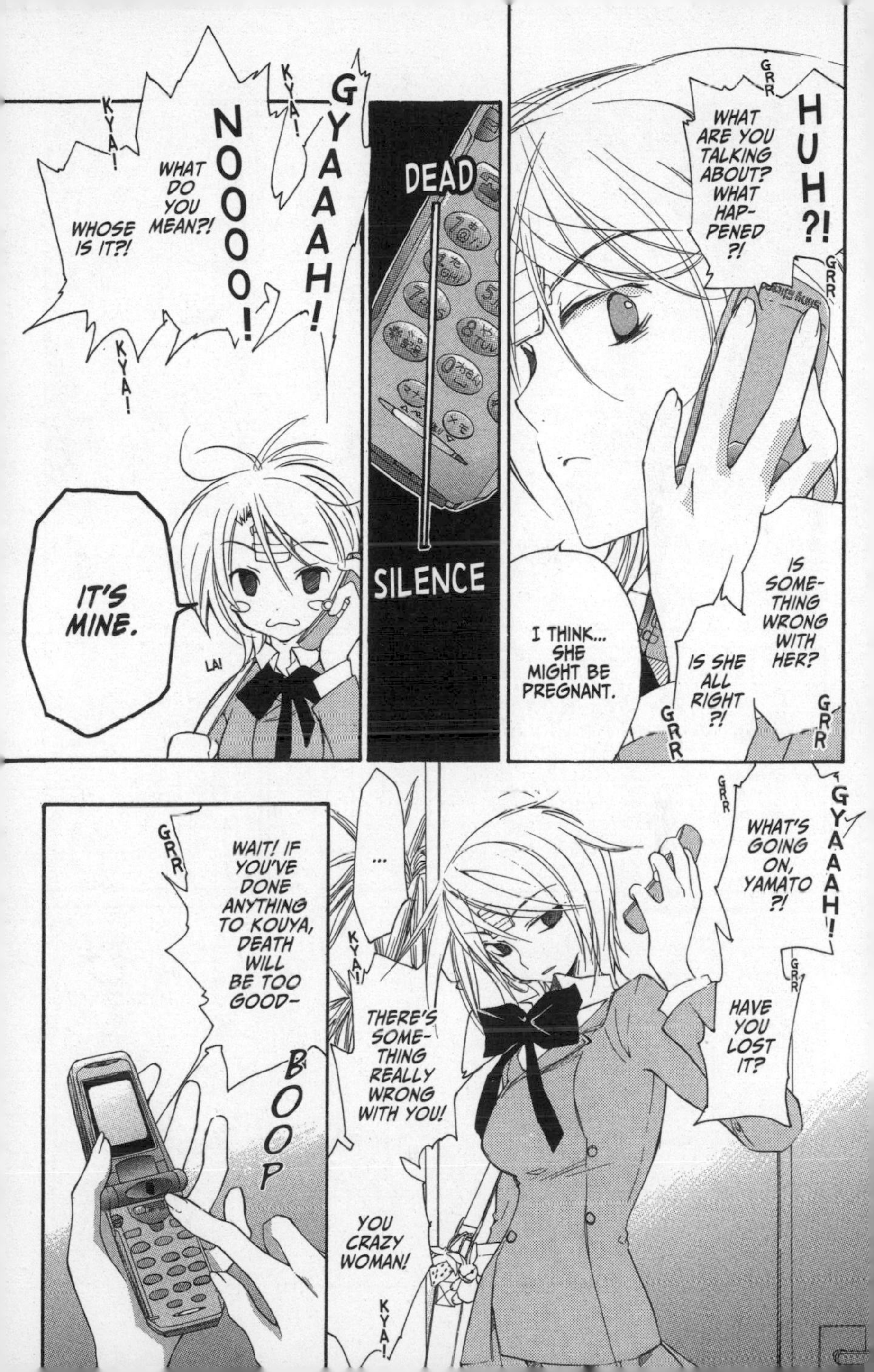
GRR
HUH?!
WHAT ARE YOU TALKING ABOUT? WHAT HAP-PENED?!
GRR
IS SOMETHING WRONG WITH HER?
IS SHE ALL RIGHT?!
I THINK... SHE MIGHT BE PREGNANT.
GRR
GRR
DEAD
SILENCE
GYAAAH!
KYA!
NOOOOO!
WHAT DO YOU MEAN?!
KYA!
WHOSE IS IT?!
KYA!
IT'S MINE.
LA!
GYAAAH!
GRR
WHAT'S GOING ON, YAMATO?!
GRR
HAVE YOU LOST IT?
...
KYA!
THERE'S SOME-THING REALLY WRONG WITH YOU!
YOU CRAZY WOMAN!
KYA!
GRR
WAIT! IF YOU'VE DONE ANYTHING TO KOUYA, DEATH WILL BE TOO GOOD-
BOOP

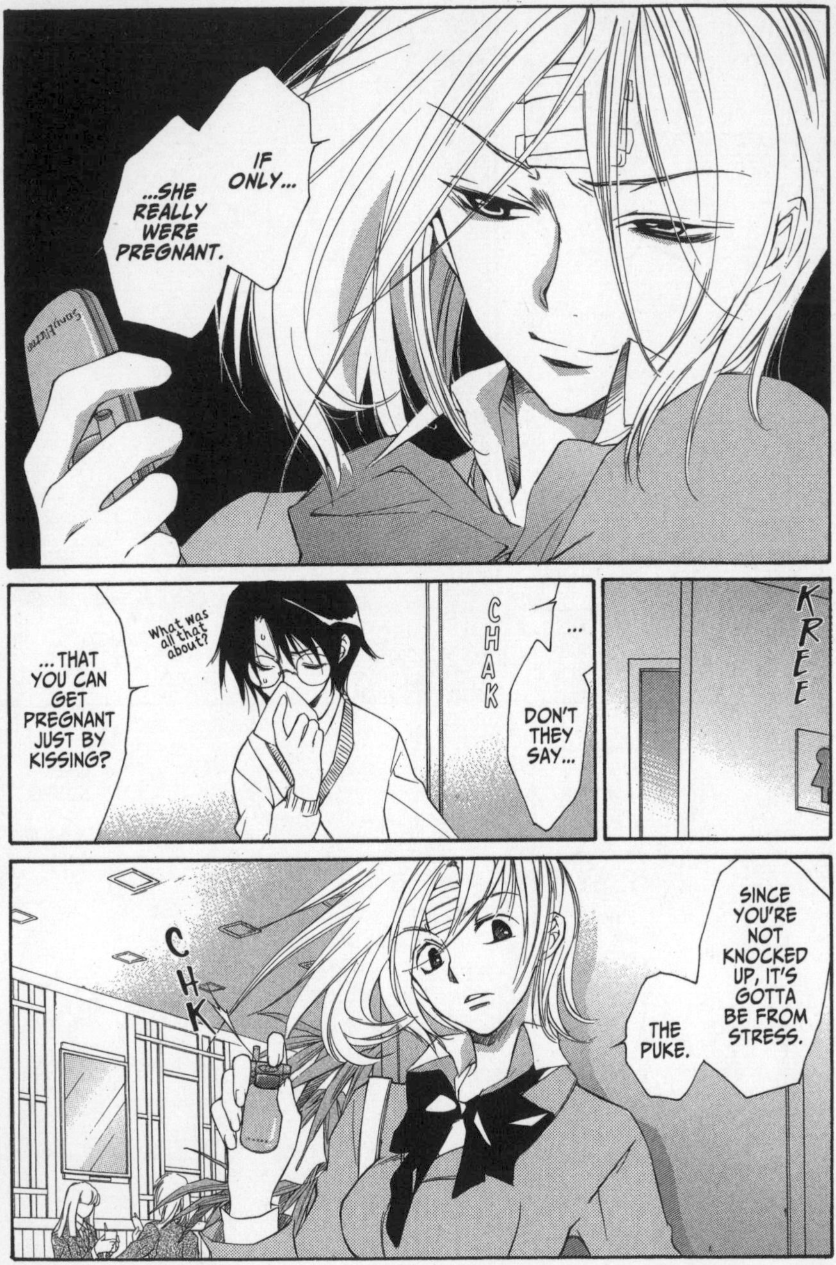
IF ONLY...
...SHE REALLY WERE PREGNANT.
KREE
CHAK
...
DON'T THEY SAY...
What was all that about?
...THAT YOU CAN GET PREGNANT JUST BY KISSING?
SINCE YOU'RE NOT KNOCKED UP, IT'S GOTTA BE FROM STRESS.
THE PUKE.
CHK

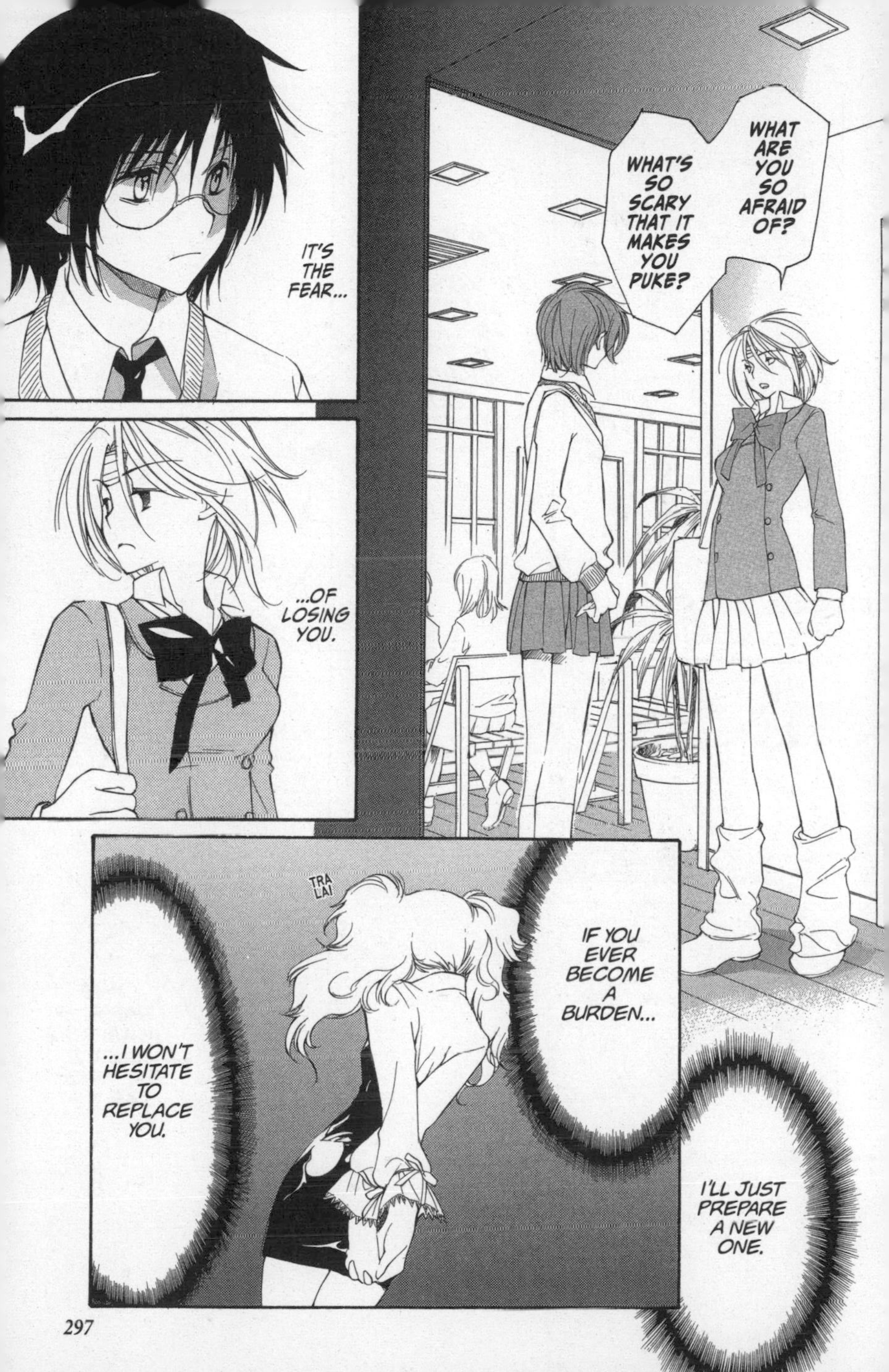
WHAT ARE YOU SO AFRAID OF?
WHAT'S SO SCARY THAT IT MAKES YOU PUKE?
IT'S THE FEAR...
...OF LOSING YOU.
IF YOU EVER BECOME A BURDEN...
TRA LAI
...I WON'T HESITATE TO REPLACE YOU.
I'LL JUST PREPARE A NEW ONE.

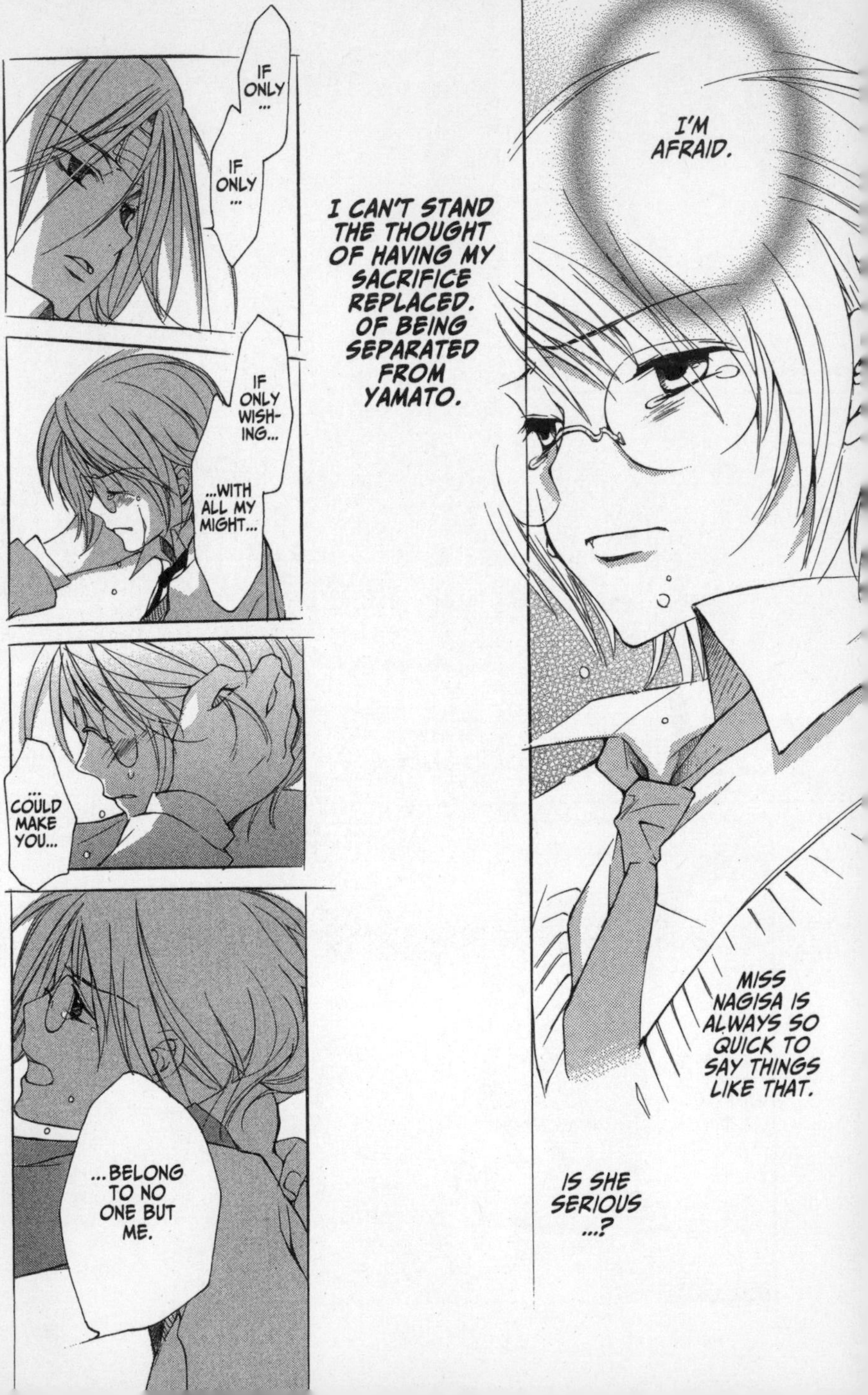
I'M AFRAID.
MISS NAGISA IS ALWAYS SO QUICK TO SAY THINGS LIKE THAT.
IS SHE SERIOUS ...?
I CAN'T STAND THE THOUGHT OF HAVING MY SACRIFICE REPLACED. OF BEING SEPARATED FROM YAMATO.
IF ONLY ...
IF ONLY ...
IF ONLY WISHING...
...WITH ALL MY MIGHT...
... COULD MAKE YOU...
...BELONG TO NO ONE BUT ME.

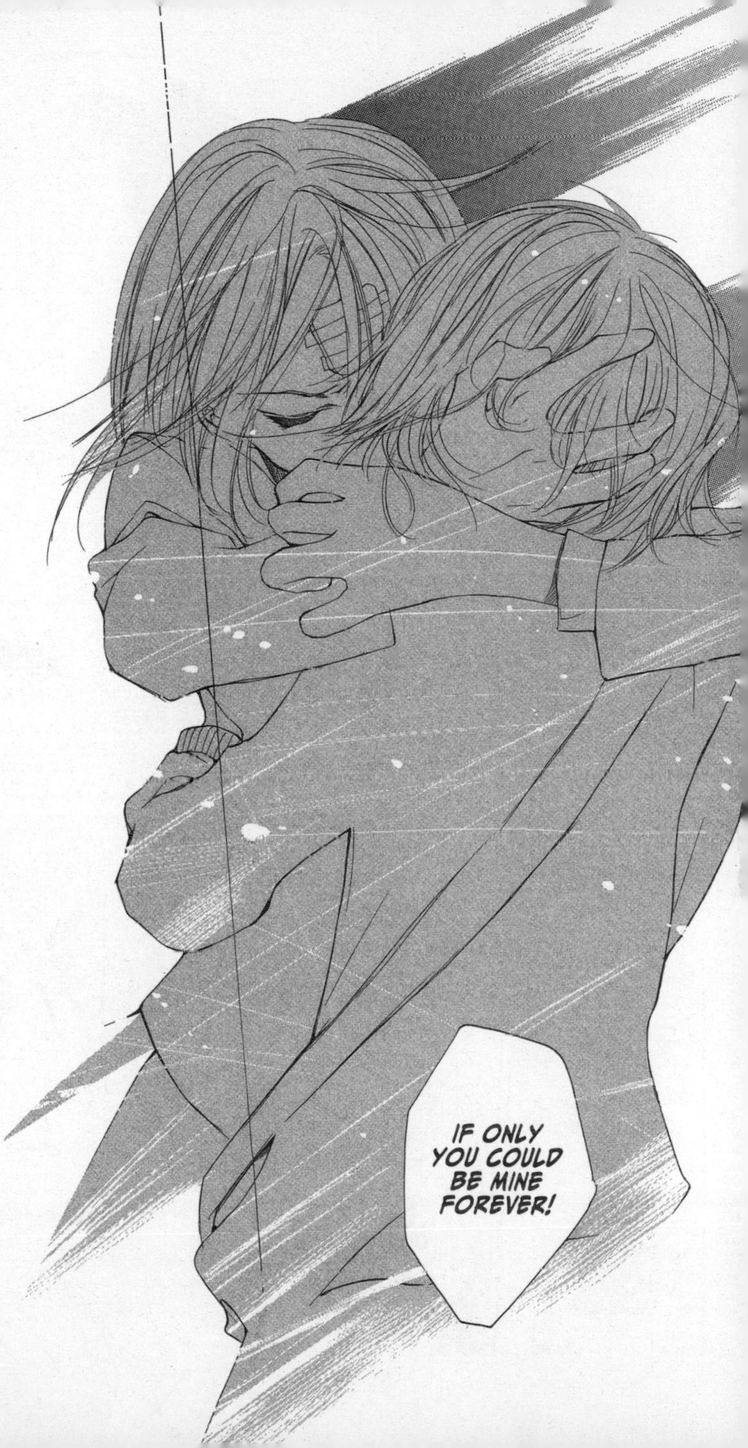
IF ONLY YOU COULD BE MINE FOREVER!

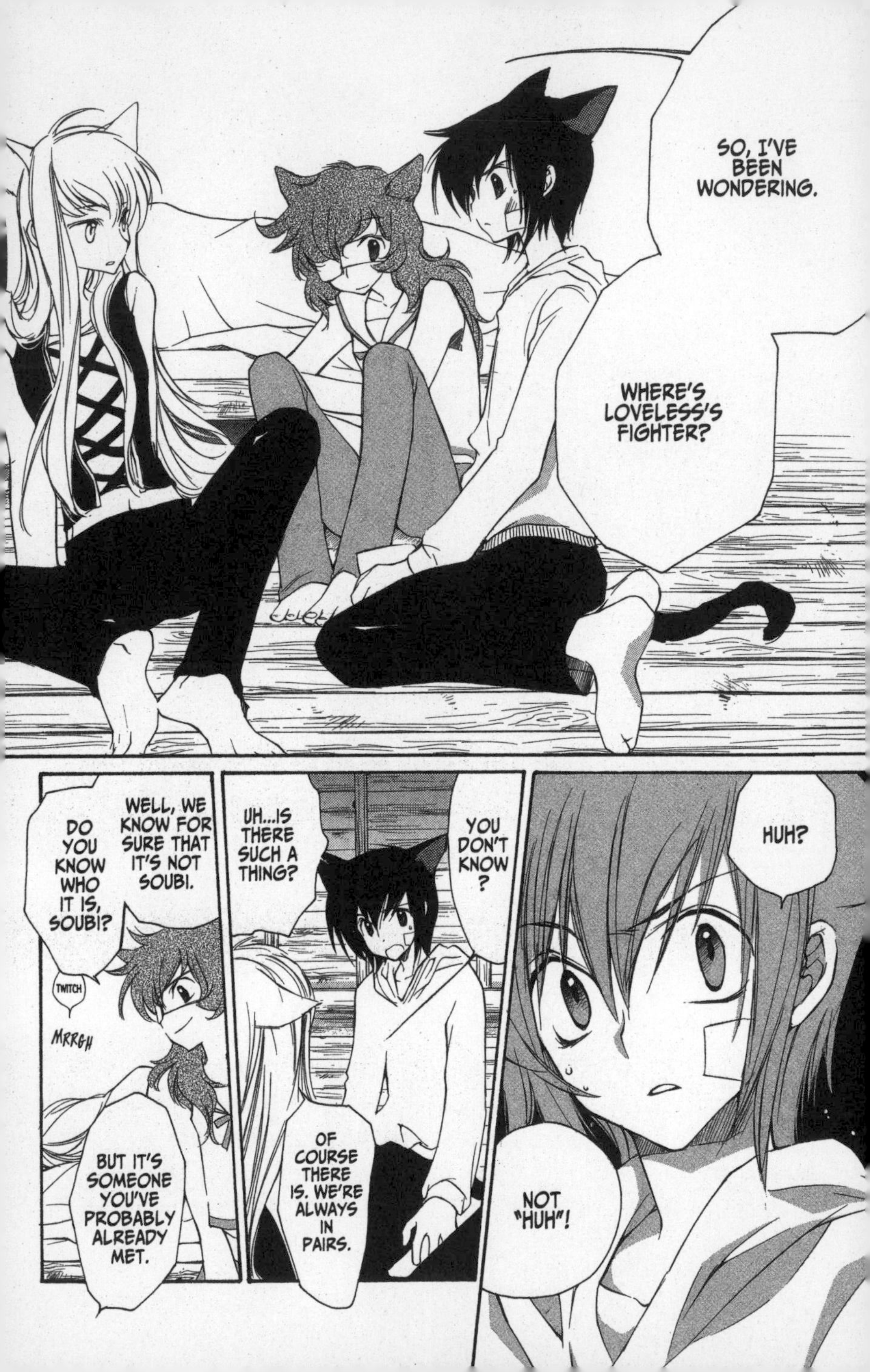
SO, I'VE BEEN WONDERING.
WHERE'S LOVELESS'S FIGHTER?
HUH?
NOT "HUH"!
YOU DON'T KNOW?
UH...IS THERE SUCH A THING?
OF COURSE THERE IS. WE'RE ALWAYS IN PAIRS.
WELL, WE KNOW FOR SURE THAT IT'S NOT SOUBI.
DO YOU KNOW WHO IT IS, SOUBI?
TWITCH
MRRGH
BUT IT'S SOMEONE YOU'VE PROBABLY ALREADY MET.

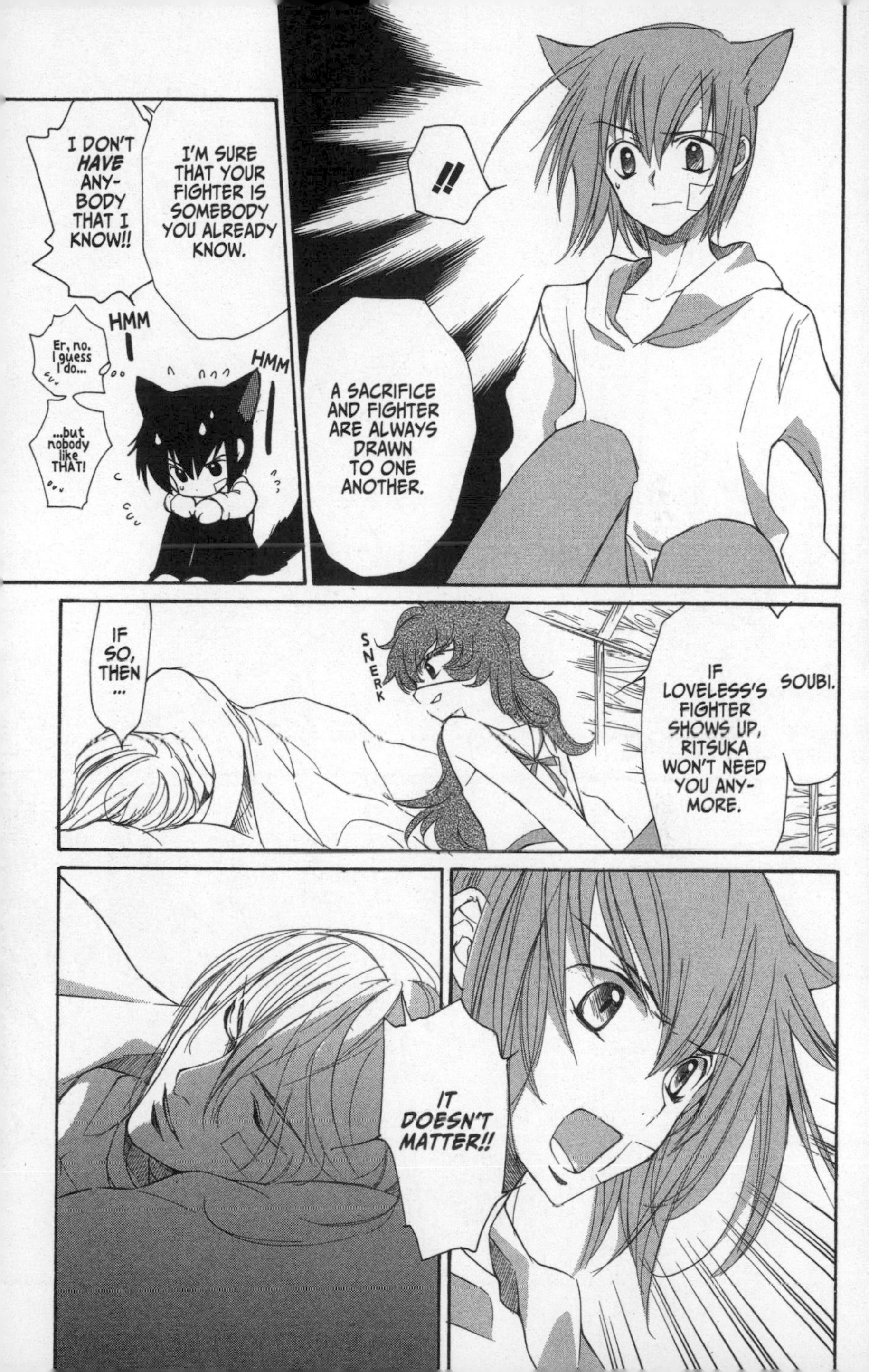
!!
A SACRIFICE AND FIGHTER ARE ALWAYS DRAWN TO ONE ANOTHER.
I'M SURE THAT YOUR FIGHTER IS SOMEBODY YOU ALREADY KNOW.
I DON'T *HAVE* ANYBODY THAT I KNOW!!
HMM
HMM
Er, no. I guess I do...
...but nobody like THAT!
SOUBI.
IF LOVELESS'S FIGHTER SHOWS UP, RITSUKA WON'T NEED YOU ANYMORE.
SNERK
IF SO, THEN ...
IT DOESN'T MATTER!!

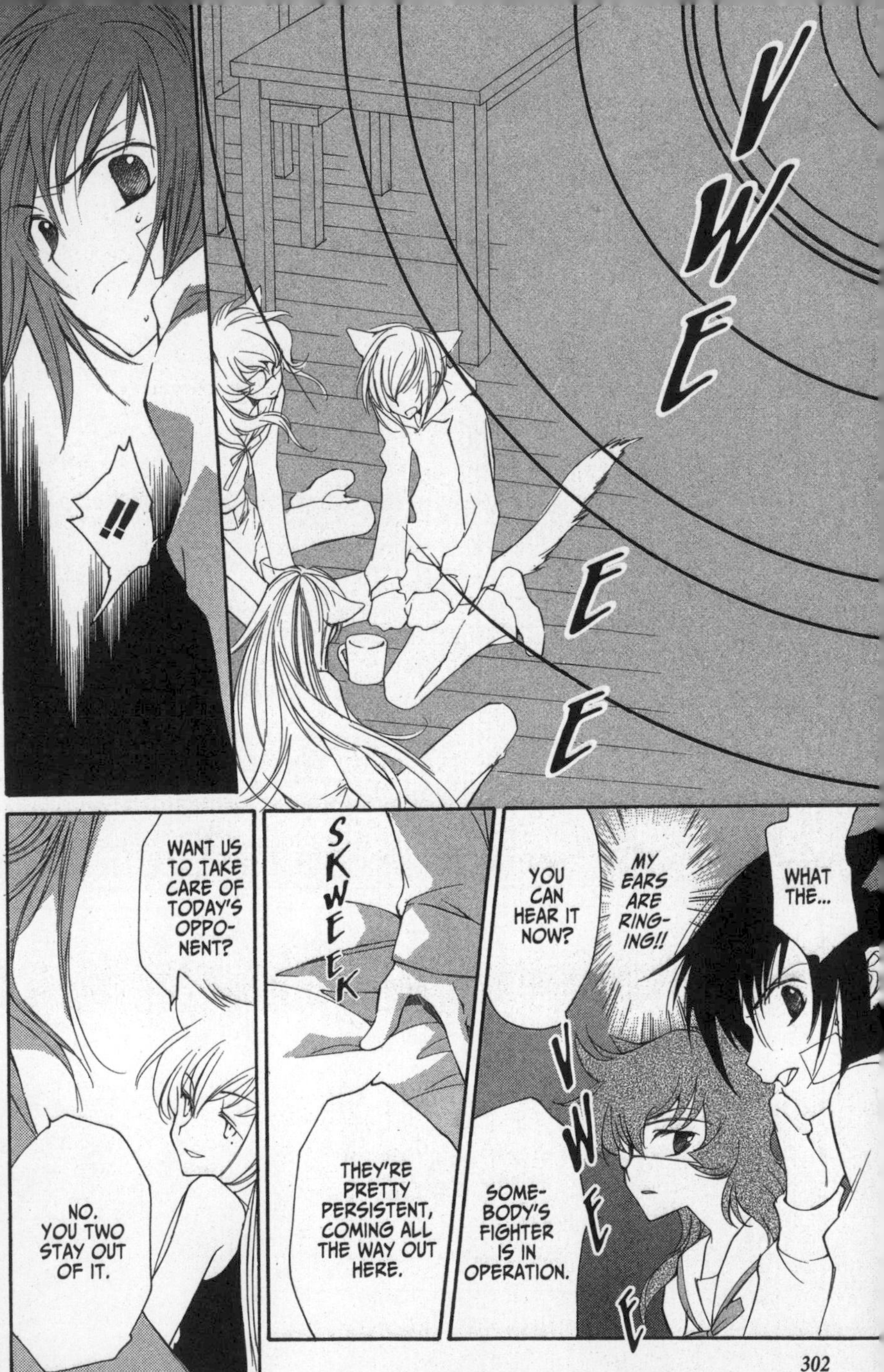
VVWEEEE
!!
WHAT THE...
MY EARS ARE RING-ING!!
YOU CAN HEAR IT NOW?
SOME-BODY'S FIGHTER IS IN OPERATION.
VVWEE
SKWEEK
THEY'RE PRETTY PERSISTENT, COMING ALL THE WAY OUT HERE.
WANT US TO TAKE CARE OF TODAY'S OPPO-NENT?
NO. YOU TWO STAY OUT OF IT.

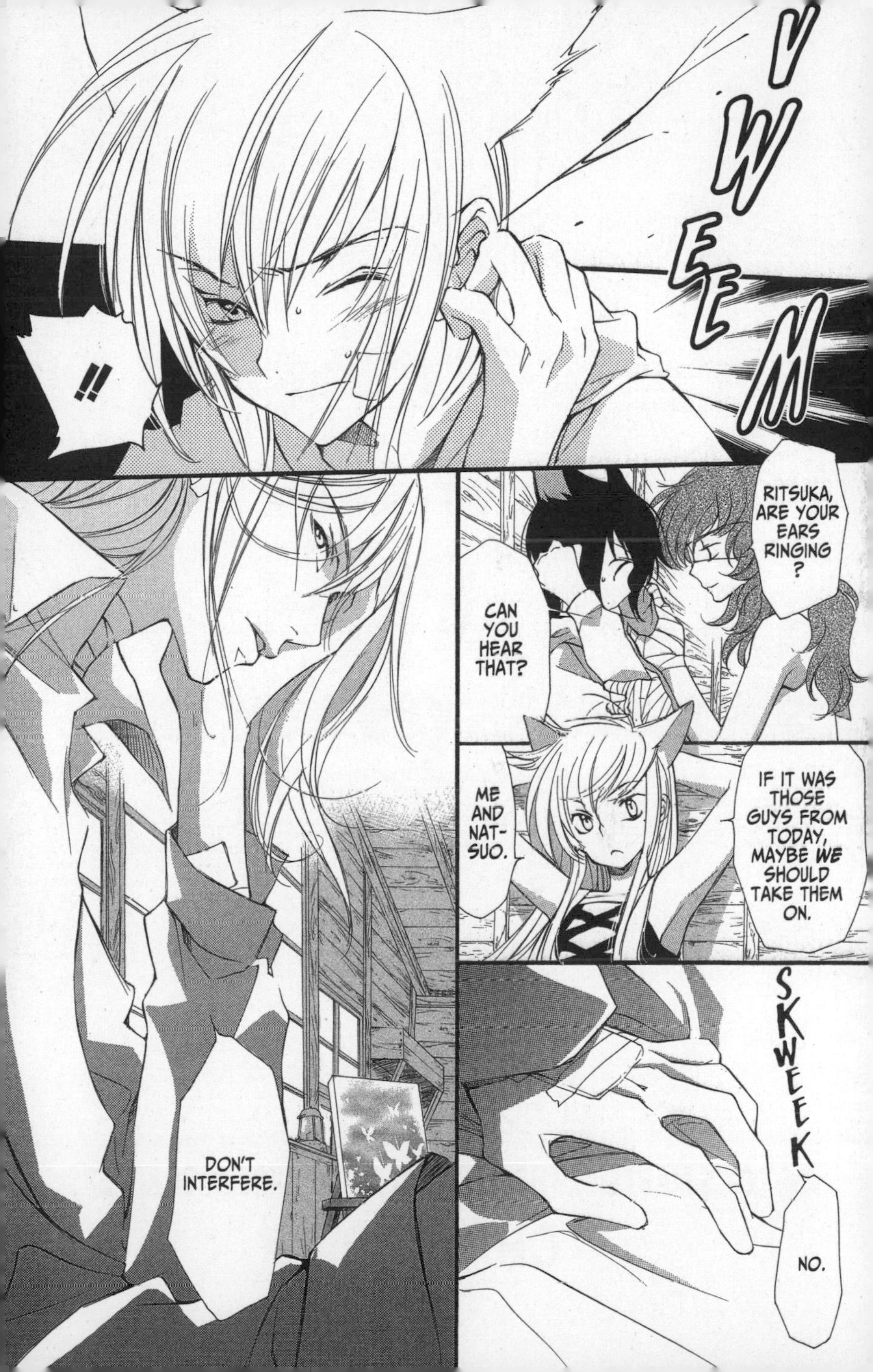
VWEEM
!!
RITSUKA, ARE YOUR EARS RINGING?
CAN YOU HEAR THAT?
IF IT WAS THOSE GUYS FROM TODAY, MAYBE WE SHOULD TAKE THEM ON.
ME AND NAT-SUO.
SKWEEK
NO.
DON'T INTERFERE.

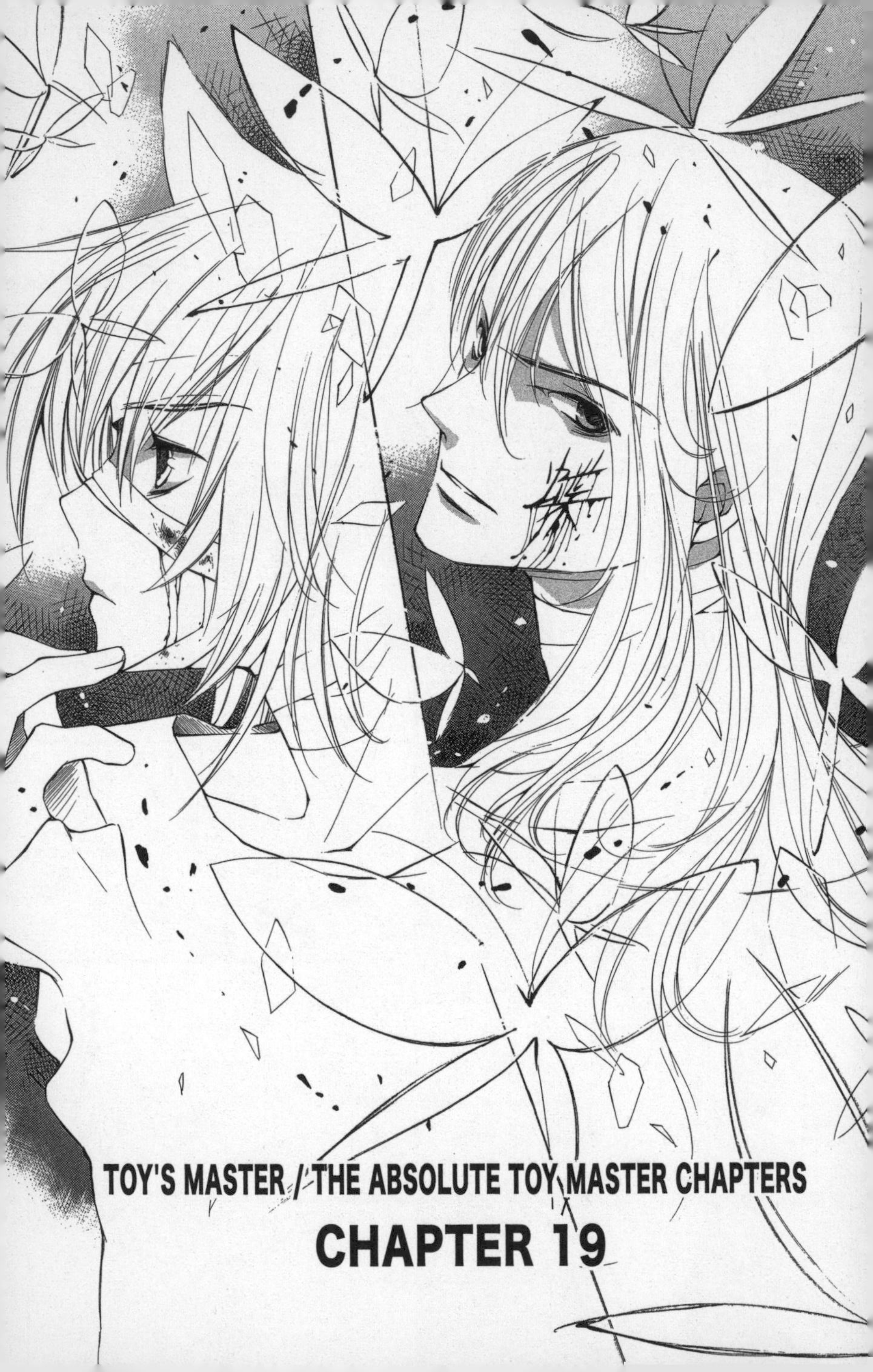
TOY'S MASTER / THE ABSOLUTE TOY MASTER CHAPTERS
CHAPTER 19

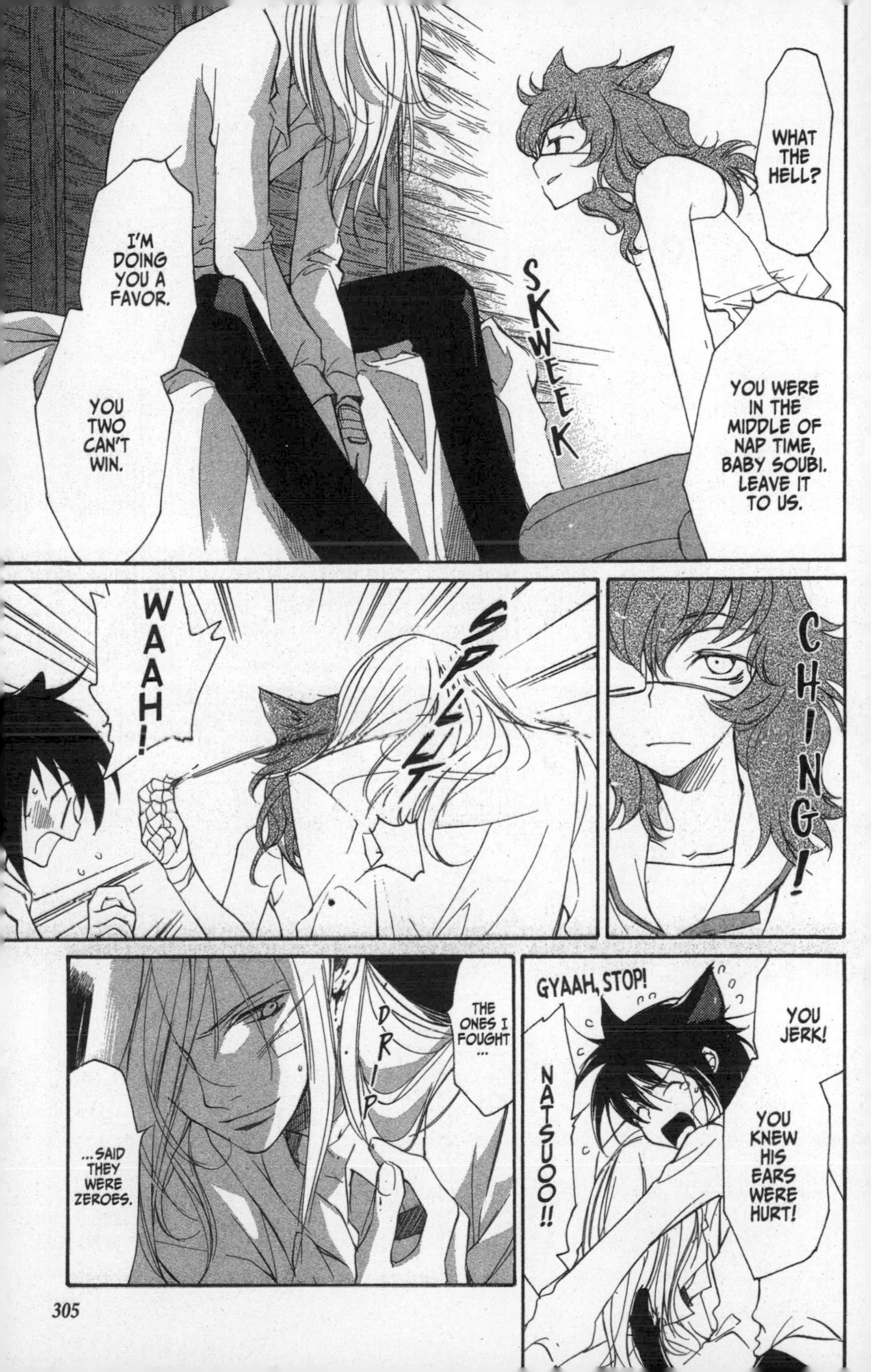
WHAT THE HELL?
YOU WERE IN THE MIDDLE OF NAP TIME, BABY SOUBI. LEAVE IT TO US.
SKWEEK
I'M DOING YOU A FAVOR.
YOU TWO CAN'T WIN.
CHING!
SPLLT
WAAH!
YOU JERK!
YOU KNEW HIS EARS WERE HURT!
GYAAH, STOP!
NATSUOO!!
THE ONES I FOUGHT...
DRIP
...SAID THEY WERE ZEROES.

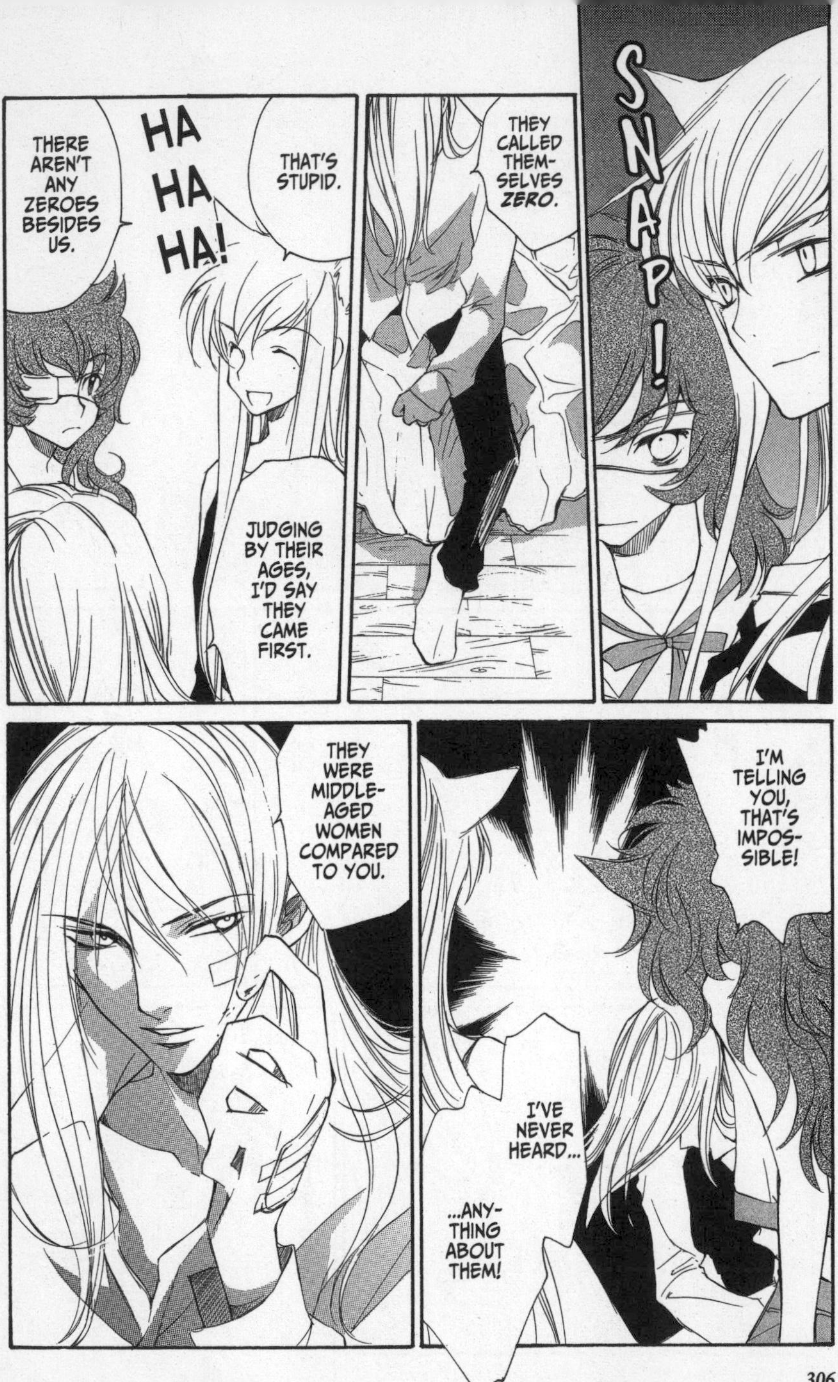
SNAP!
THEY CALLED THEM-SELVES ZERO.
THAT'S STUPID.
HA HA HA!
THERE AREN'T ANY ZEROES BESIDES US.
JUDGING BY THEIR AGES, I'D SAY THEY CAME FIRST.
I'M TELLING YOU, THAT'S IMPOS-SIBLE!
I'VE NEVER HEARD...
...ANY-THING ABOUT THEM!
THEY WERE MIDDLE-AGED WOMEN COMPARED TO YOU.

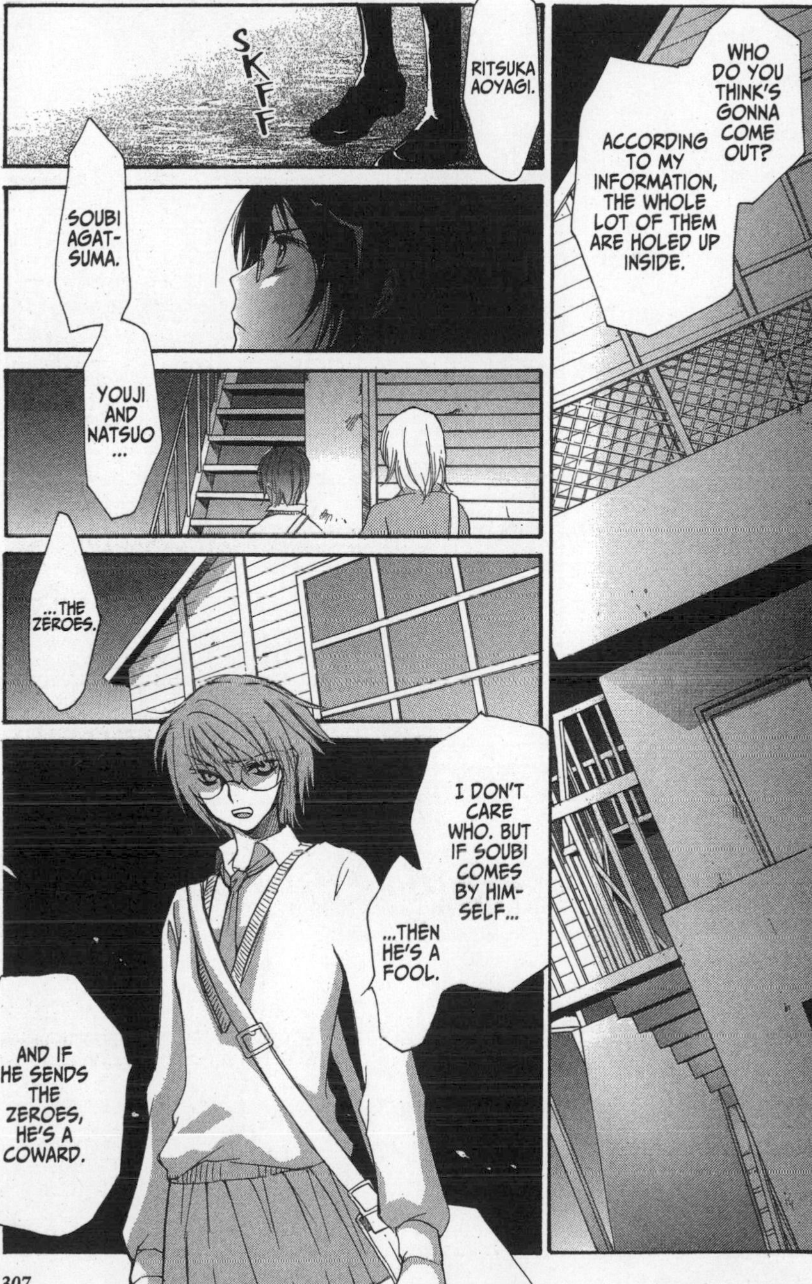
WHO DO YOU THINK'S GONNA COME OUT?
ACCORDING TO MY INFORMATION, THE WHOLE LOT OF THEM ARE HOLED UP INSIDE.
RITSUKA AOYAGI.
SKFF
SOUBI AGATSUMA.
YOUJI AND NATSUO...
...THE ZEROES.
I DON'T CARE WHO. BUT IF SOUBI COMES BY HIMSELF...
...THEN HE'S A FOOL.
AND IF HE SENDS THE ZEROES, HE'S A COWARD.

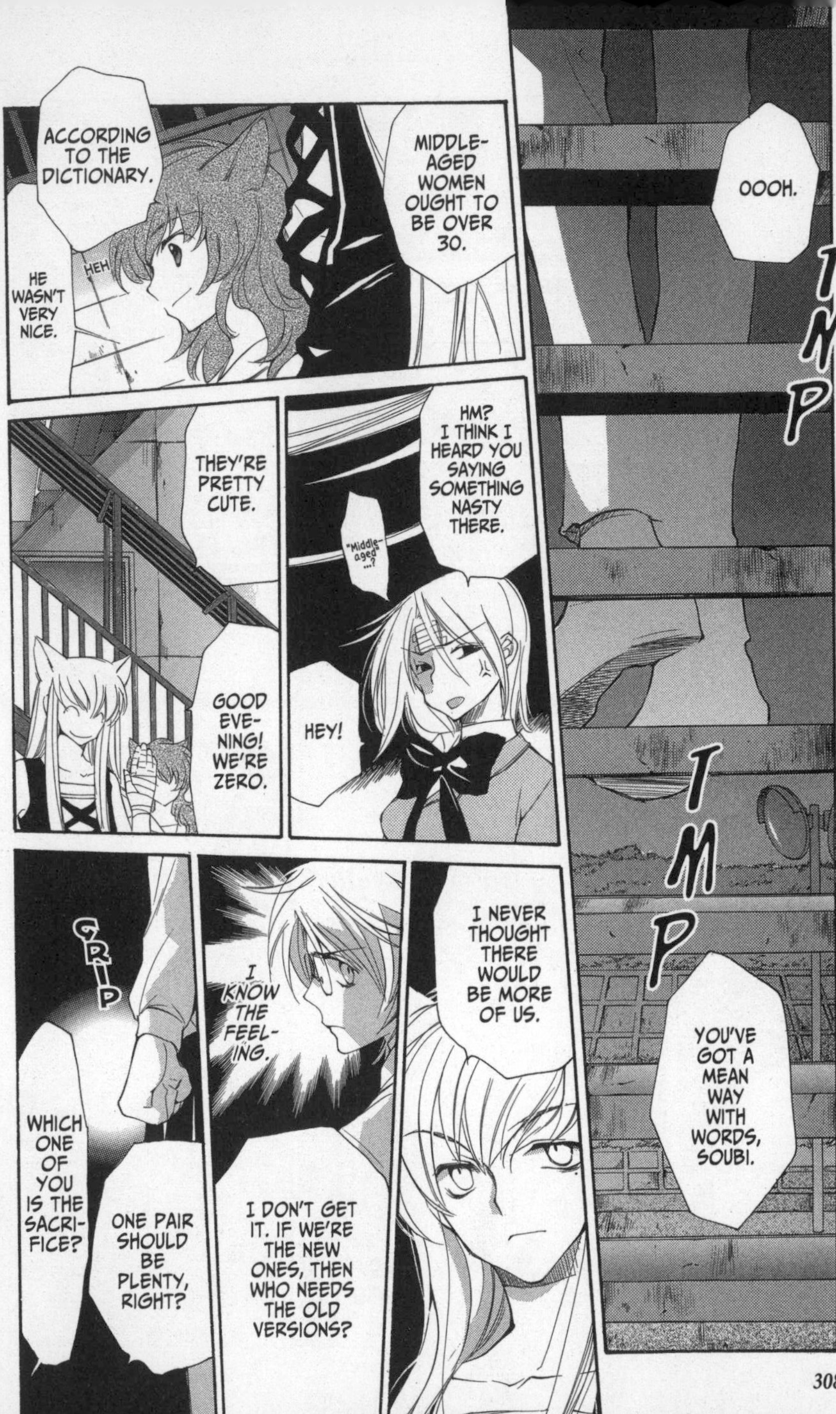
OOOH.
TIMP
TIMP
YOU'VE GOT A MEAN WAY WITH WORDS, SOUBI.
MIDDLE-AGED WOMEN OUGHT TO BE OVER 30.
ACCORDING TO THE DICTIONARY.
HEH
HE WASN'T VERY NICE.
HM? I THINK I HEARD YOU SAYING SOMETHING NASTY THERE.
"Middle-aged"...?
HEY!
THEY'RE PRETTY CUTE.
GOOD EVE-NING! WE'RE ZERO.
I NEVER THOUGHT THERE WOULD BE MORE OF US.
I DON'T GET IT. IF WE'RE THE NEW ONES, THEN WHO NEEDS THE OLD VERSIONS?
I KNOW THE FEEL-ING.
GRIP
ONE PAIR SHOULD BE PLENTY, RIGHT?
WHICH ONE OF YOU IS THE SACRI-FICE?

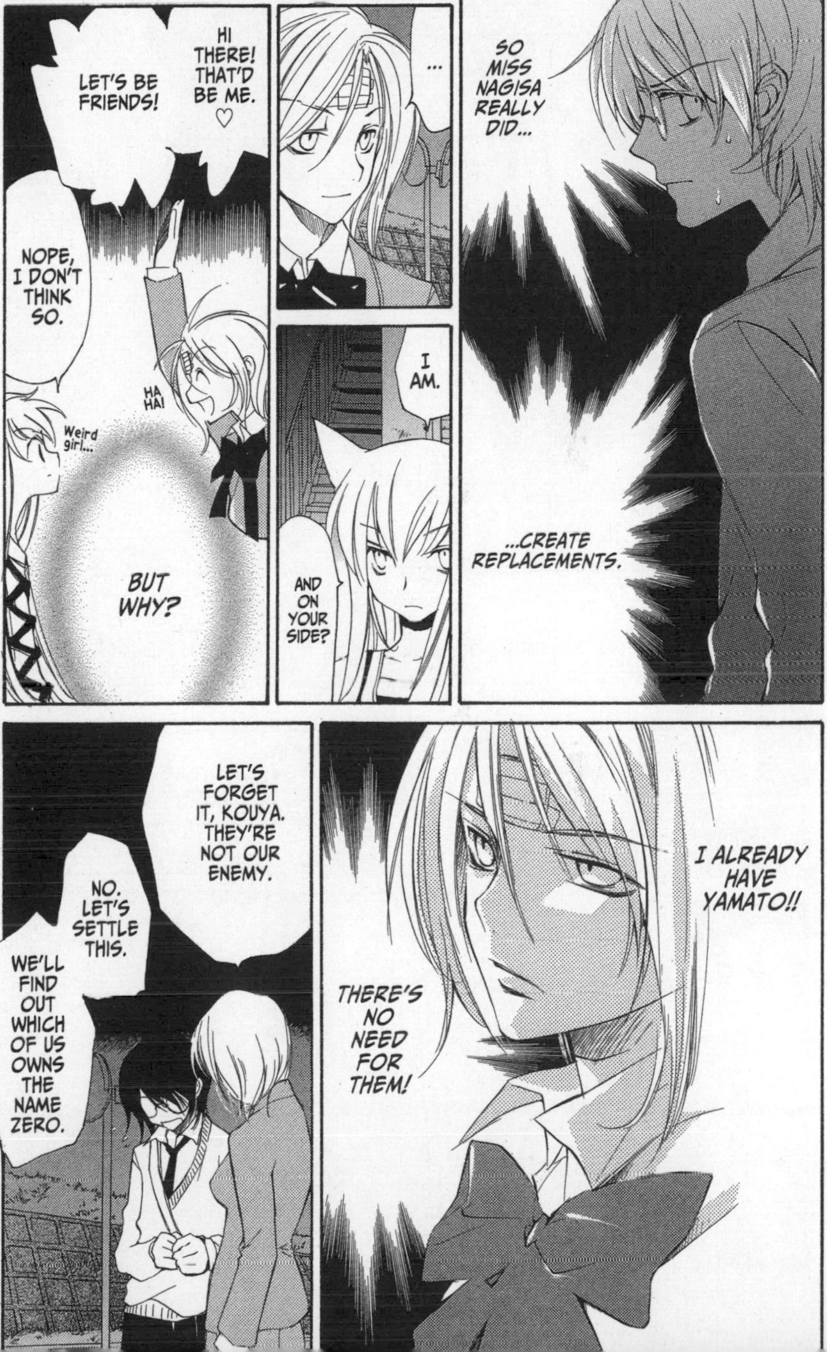
SO MISS NAGISA REALLY DID...
...CREATE REPLACEMENTS.
...
I AM.
AND ON YOUR SIDE?
HI THERE! THAT'D BE ME. ♡
LET'S BE FRIENDS!
NOPE, I DON'T THINK SO.
HA HA!
Weird girl...
BUT WHY?
I ALREADY HAVE YAMATO!!
THERE'S NO NEED FOR THEM!
LET'S FORGET IT, KOUYA. THEY'RE NOT OUR ENEMY.
NO. LET'S SETTLE THIS.
WE'LL FIND OUT WHICH OF US OWNS THE NAME ZERO.

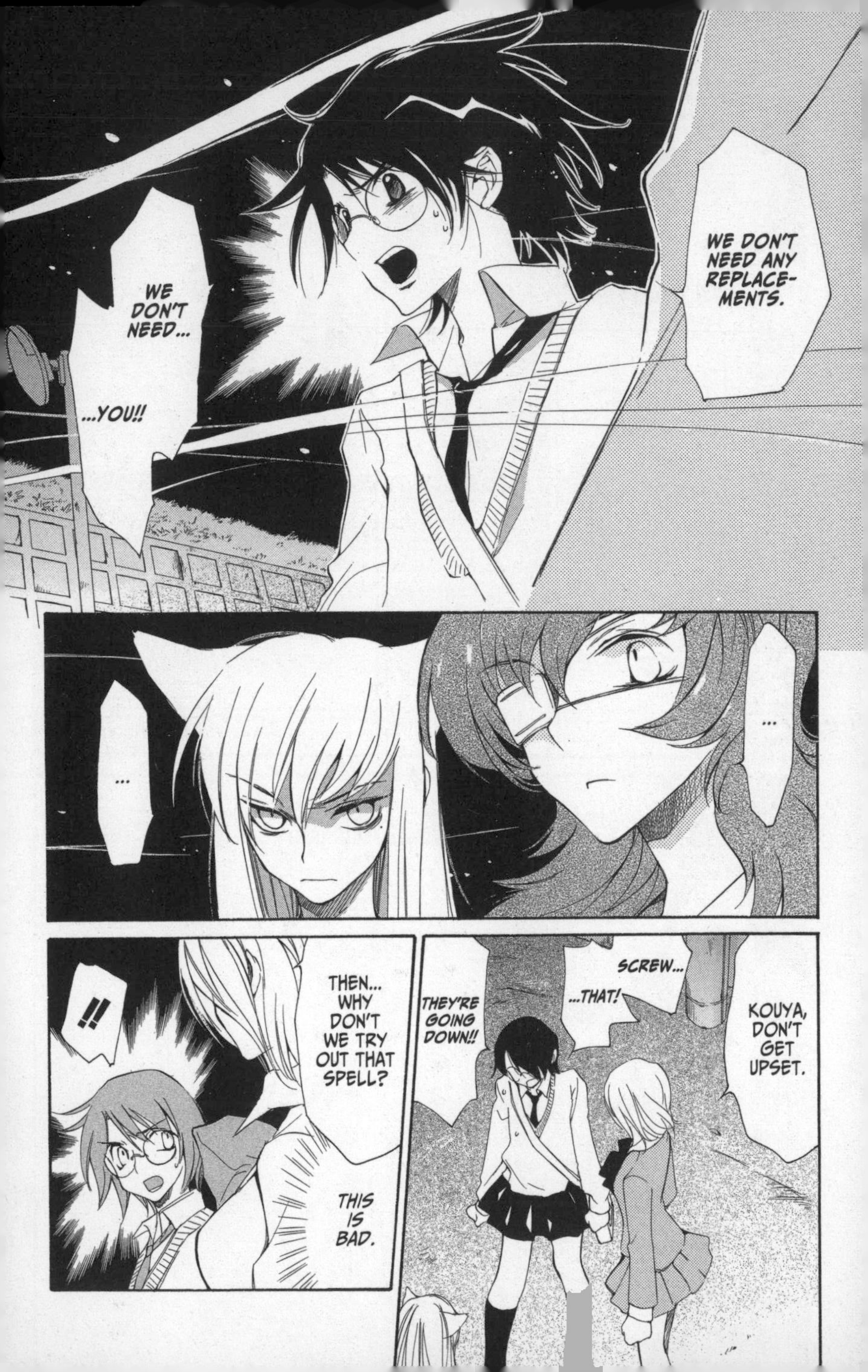
WE DON'T NEED ANY REPLACE-MENTS.
WE DON'T NEED...
...YOU!!
...
...
KOUYA, DON'T GET UPSET.
SCREW...
...THAT!
THEY'RE GOING DOWN!!
THEN... WHY DON'T WE TRY OUT THAT SPELL?
!!
THIS IS BAD.

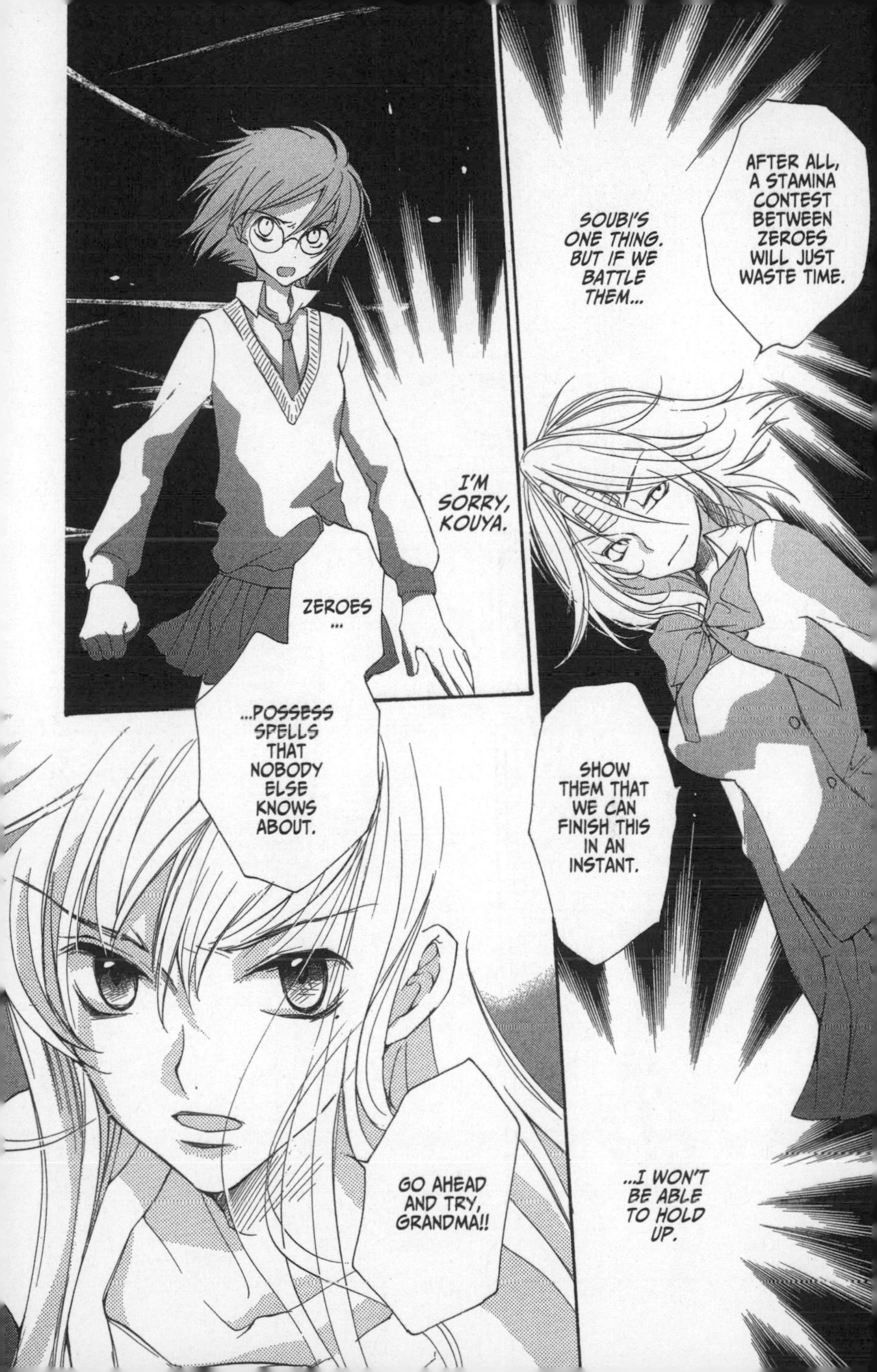
AFTER ALL, A STAMINA CONTEST BETWEEN ZEROES WILL JUST WASTE TIME.
SOUBI'S ONE THING. BUT IF WE BATTLE THEM...
...I WON'T BE ABLE TO HOLD UP.
I'M SORRY, KOUYA.
ZEROES ...
...POSSESS SPELLS THAT NOBODY ELSE KNOWS ABOUT.
SHOW THEM THAT WE CAN FINISH THIS IN AN INSTANT.
GO AHEAD AND TRY, GRANDMA!!

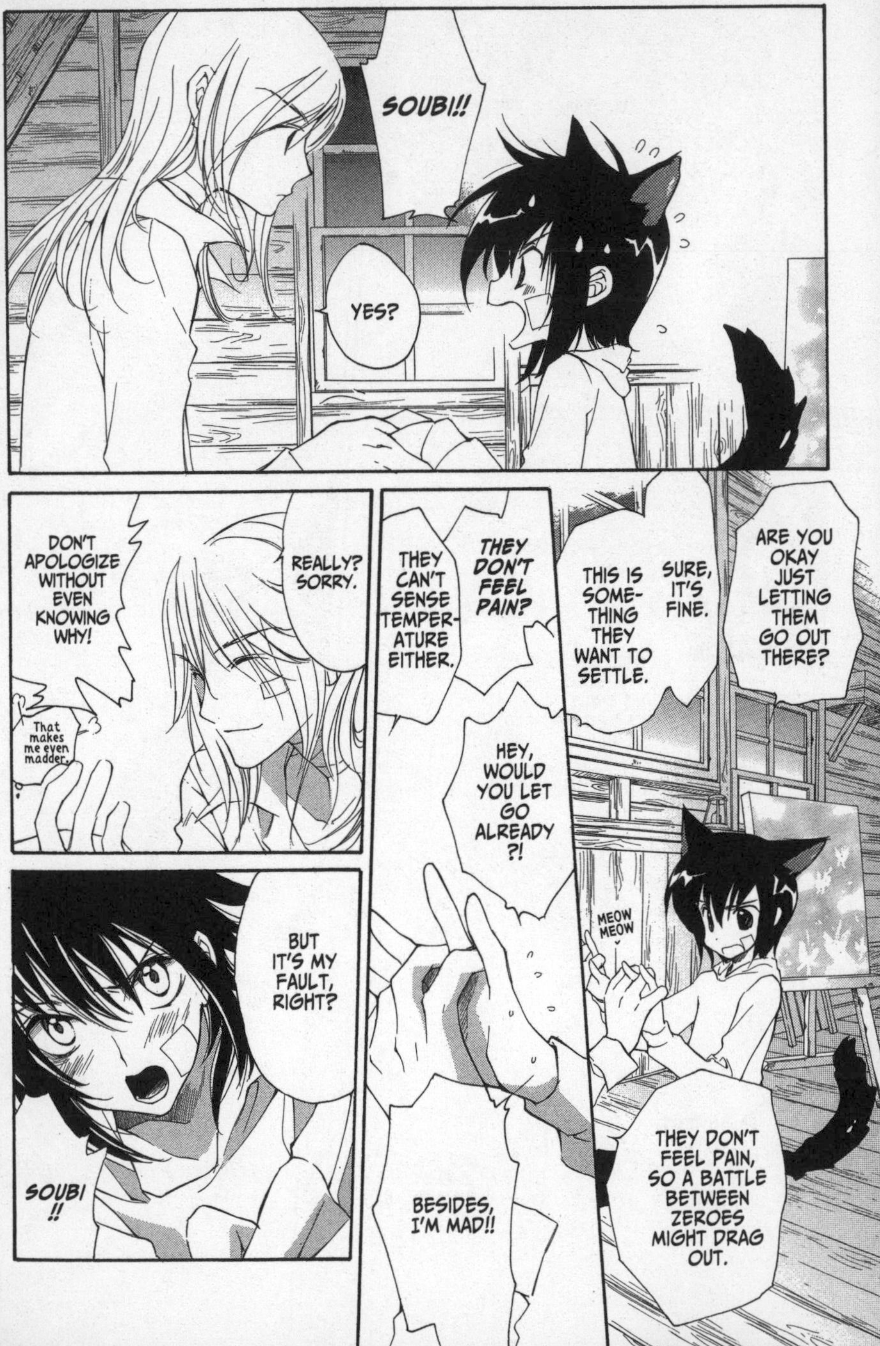
SOUBI!!
YES?
ARE YOU OKAY JUST LETTING THEM GO OUT THERE?
SURE, IT'S FINE.
THIS IS SOME-THING THEY WANT TO SETTLE.
THEY DON'T FEEL PAIN?
THEY CAN'T SENSE TEMPER-ATURE EITHER.
MEOW MEOW
THEY DON'T FEEL PAIN, SO A BATTLE BETWEEN ZEROES MIGHT DRAG OUT.
HEY, WOULD YOU LET GO ALREADY?!
BESIDES, I'M MAD!!
REALLY? SORRY.
DON'T APOLOGIZE WITHOUT EVEN KNOWING WHY!
That makes me even madder.
BUT IT'S MY FAULT, RIGHT?
SOUBI!!

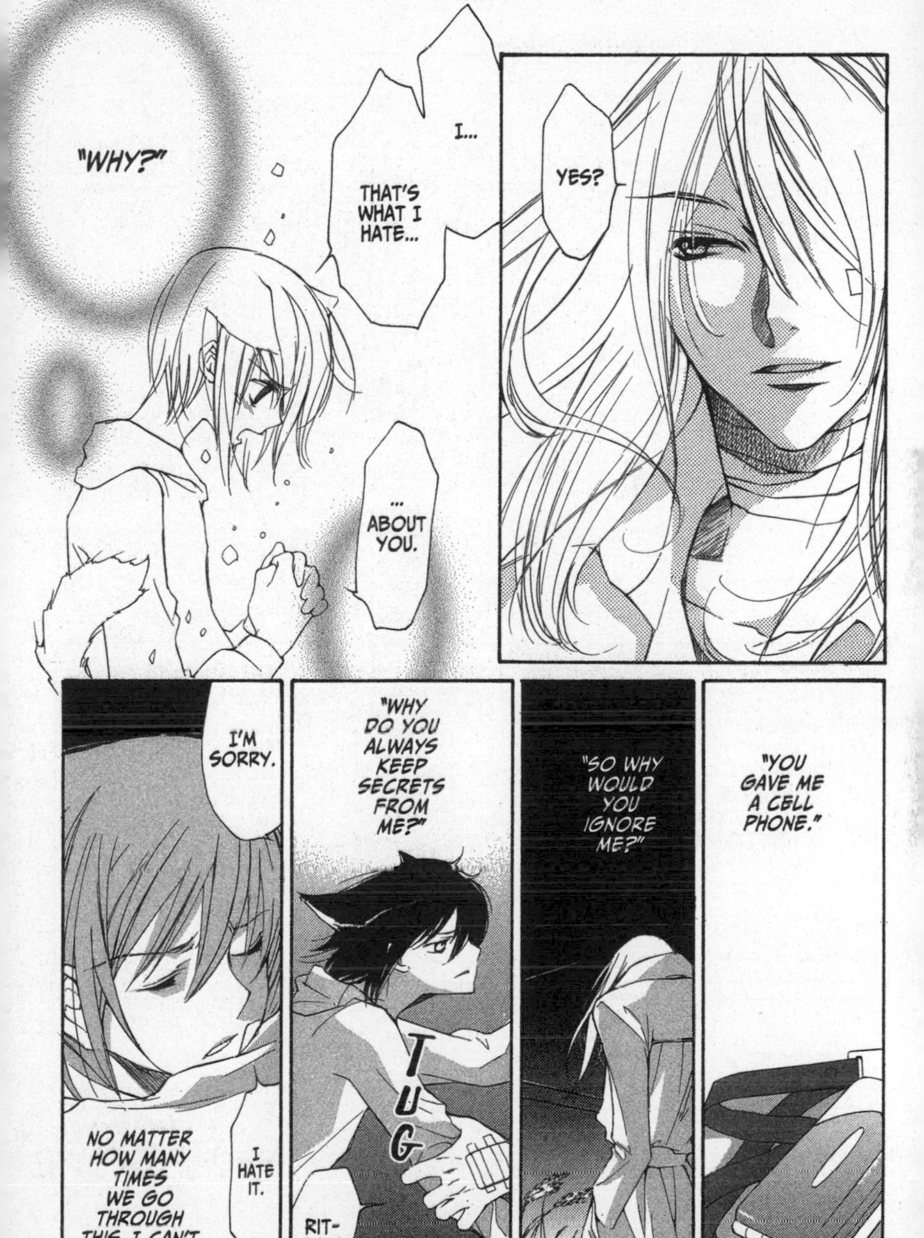
YES?
I...
THAT'S WHAT I HATE...
... ABOUT YOU.
"WHY?"
"YOU GAVE ME A CELL PHONE."
"SO WHY WOULD YOU IGNORE ME?"
"WHY DO YOU ALWAYS KEEP SECRETS FROM ME?"
TUG
RIT-SUKA?
I'M SORRY.
I HATE IT.
NO MATTER HOW MANY TIMES WE GO THROUGH THIS, I CAN'T GET THE WORDS OUT.

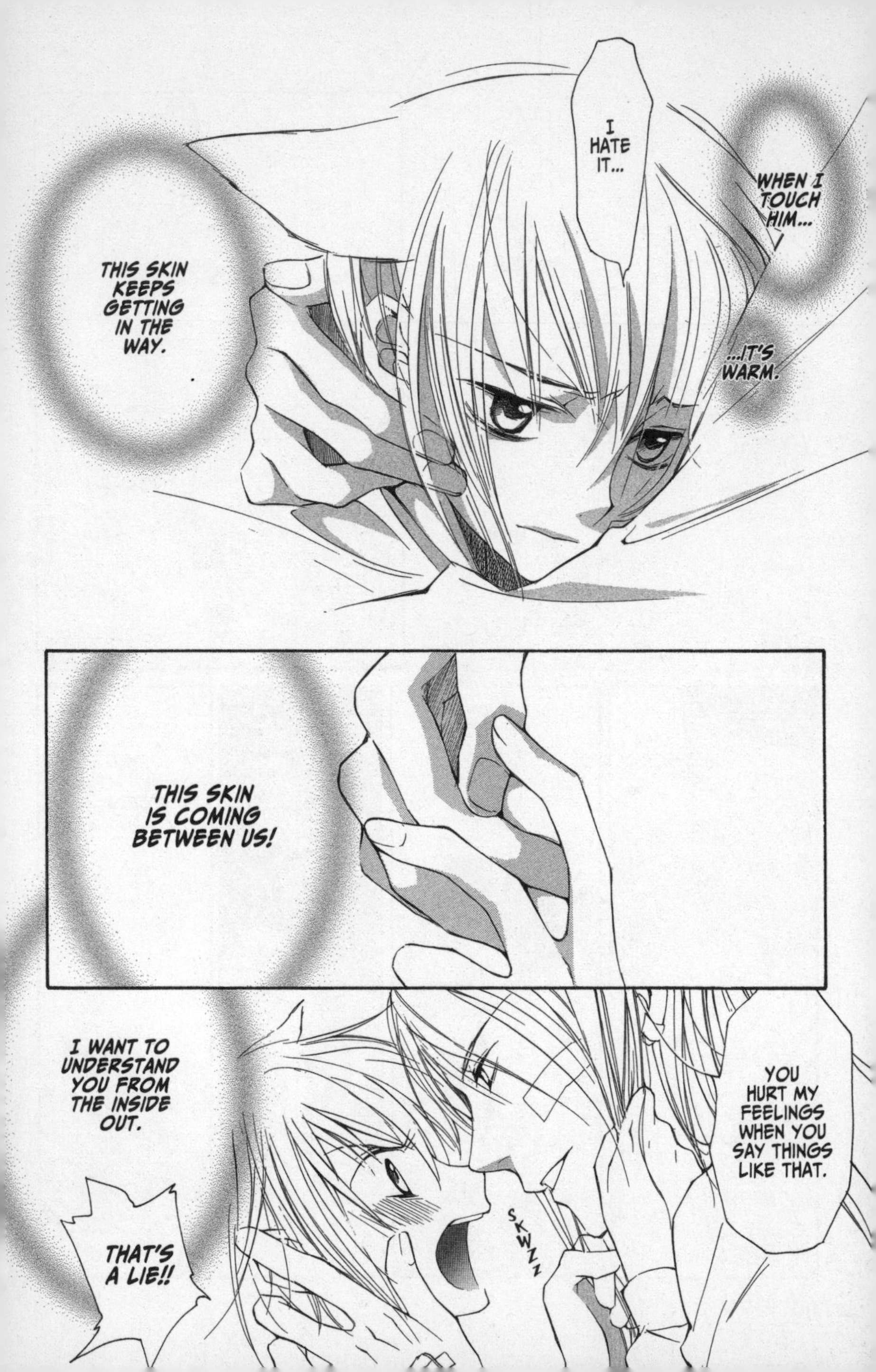
WHEN I TOUCH HIM...
...IT'S WARM.
I HATE IT...
THIS SKIN KEEPS GETTING IN THE WAY.
THIS SKIN IS COMING BETWEEN US!
YOU HURT MY FEELINGS WHEN YOU SAY THINGS LIKE THAT.
SKWZZ
I WANT TO UNDERSTAND YOU FROM THE INSIDE OUT.
THAT'S A LIE!!

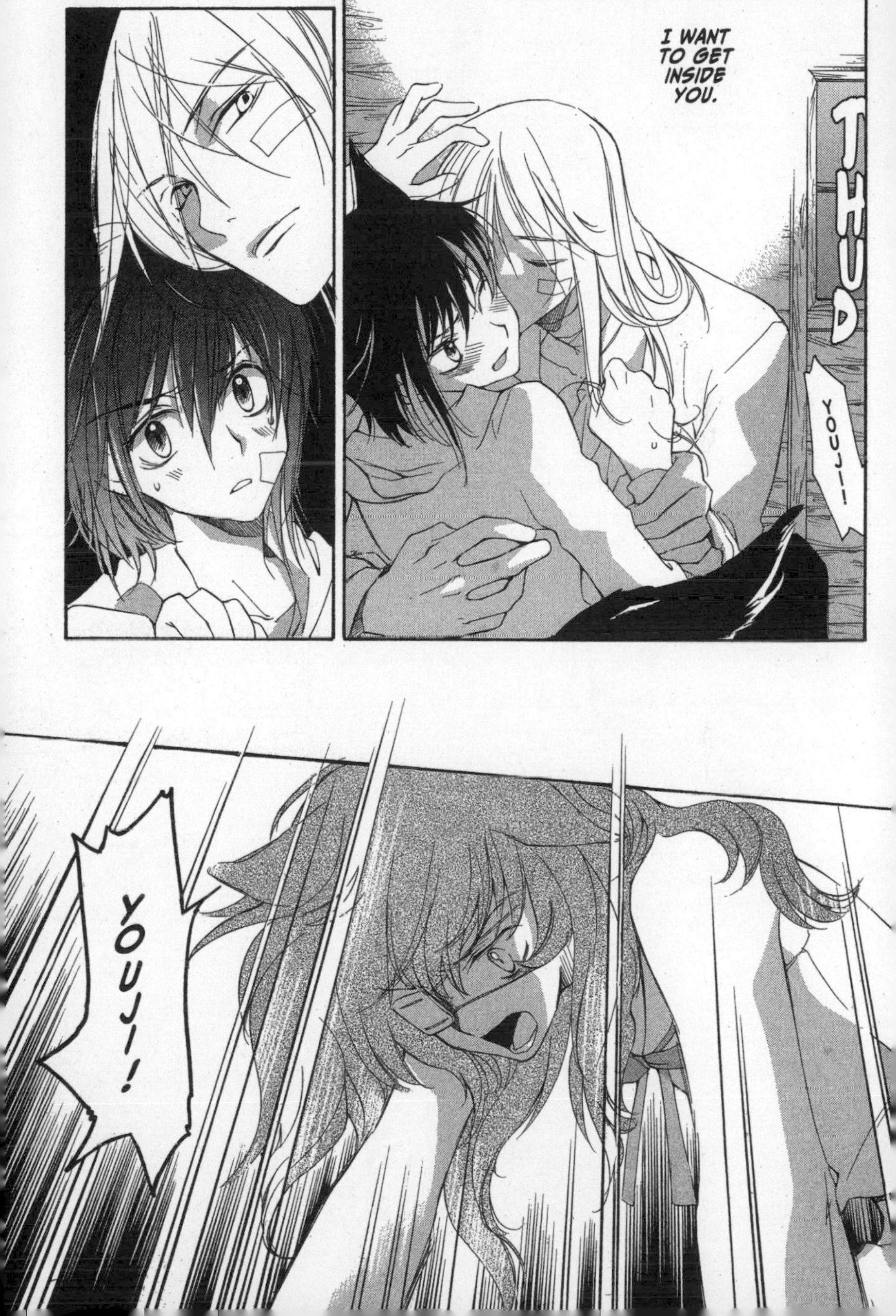
I WANT TO GET INSIDE YOU.
THUD
YOUJI!
YOUJI!!

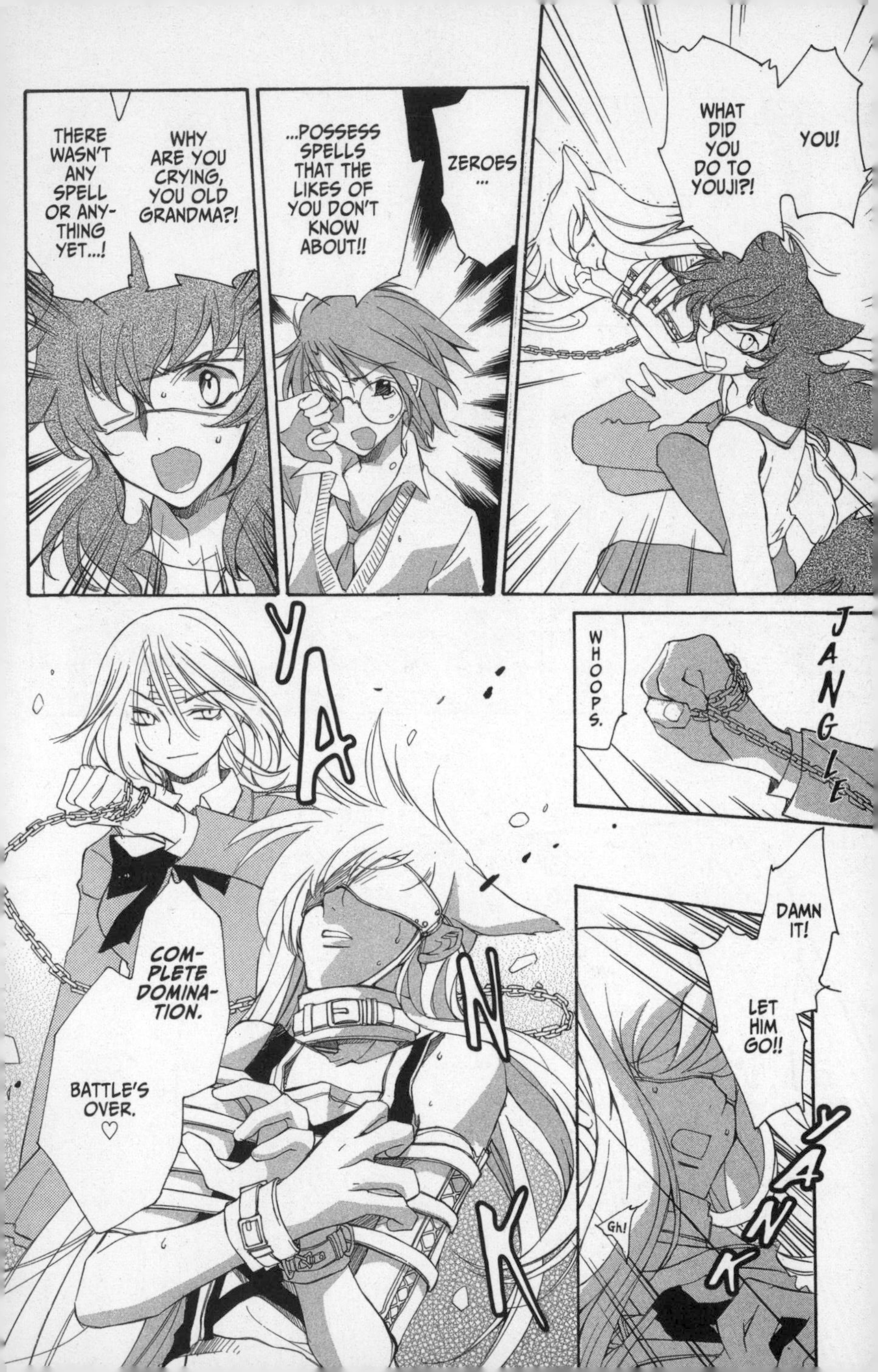
YOU!
WHAT DID YOU DO TO YOUJI?!
ZEROES...
...POSSESS SPELLS THAT THE LIKES OF YOU DON'T KNOW ABOUT!!
WHY ARE YOU CRYING, YOU OLD GRANDMA?!
THERE WASN'T ANY SPELL OR ANY-THING YET...!
JANGLE
WHOOPS.
DAMN IT!
LET HIM GO!!
YANK
Gh!
YANK
COMPLETE DOMINATION.
BATTLE'S OVER. ♡

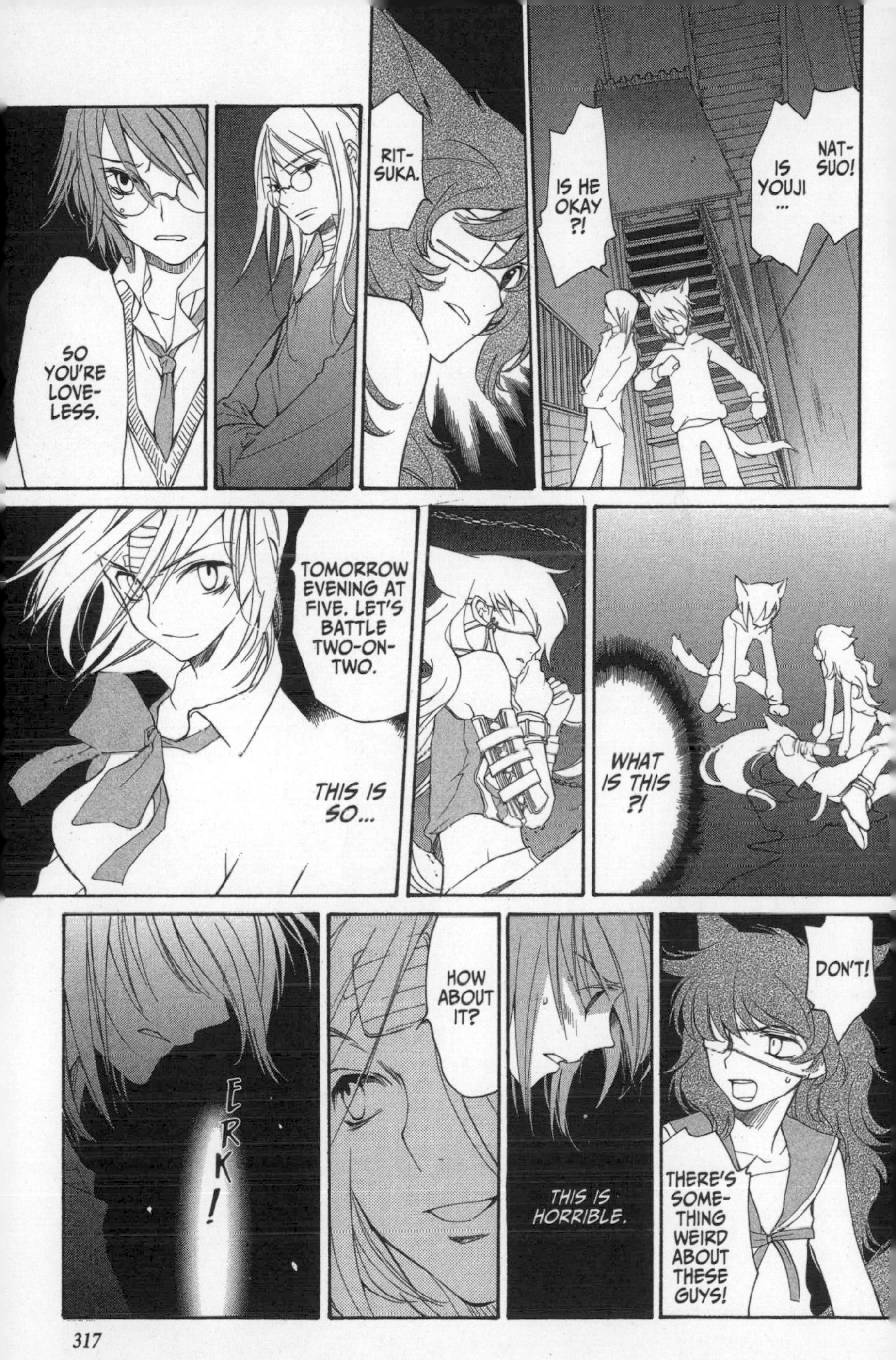
NAT-SUO!
IS YOUJI ...
IS HE OKAY ?!
RIT-SUKA.
SO YOU'RE LOVE-LESS.
WHAT IS THIS ?!
TOMORROW EVENING AT FIVE. LET'S BATTLE TWO-ON-TWO.
THIS IS SO...
DON'T!
THERE'S SOME-THING WEIRD ABOUT THESE GUYS!
THIS IS HORRIBLE.
HOW ABOUT IT?
ERK!

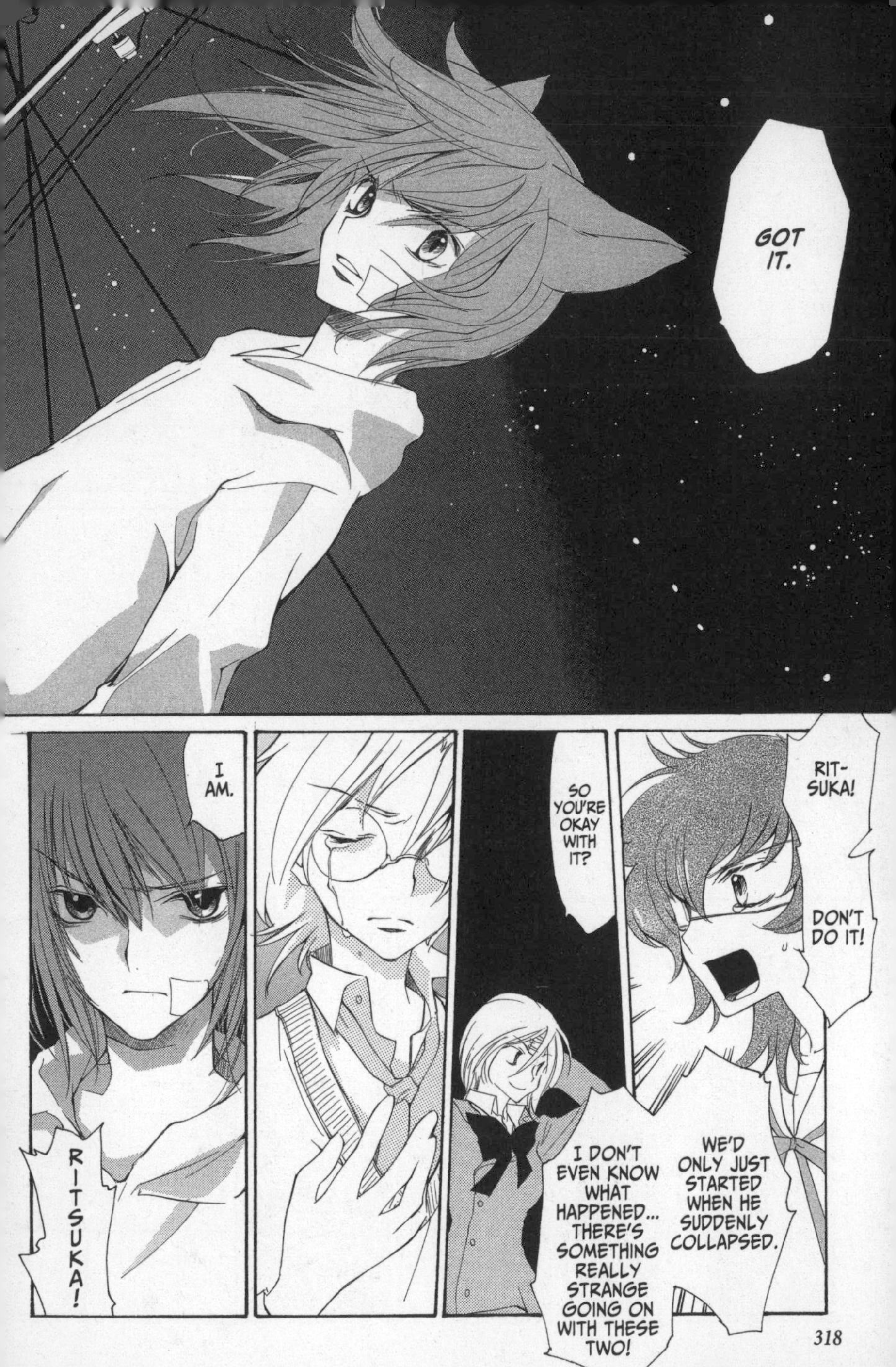
GOT IT.
RIT-SUKA!
DON'T DO IT!
SO YOU'RE OKAY WITH IT?
WE'D ONLY JUST STARTED WHEN HE SUDDENLY COLLAPSED.
I DON'T EVEN KNOW WHAT HAPPENED... THERE'S SOMETHING REALLY STRANGE GOING ON WITH THESE TWO!
I AM.
RITSUKA!

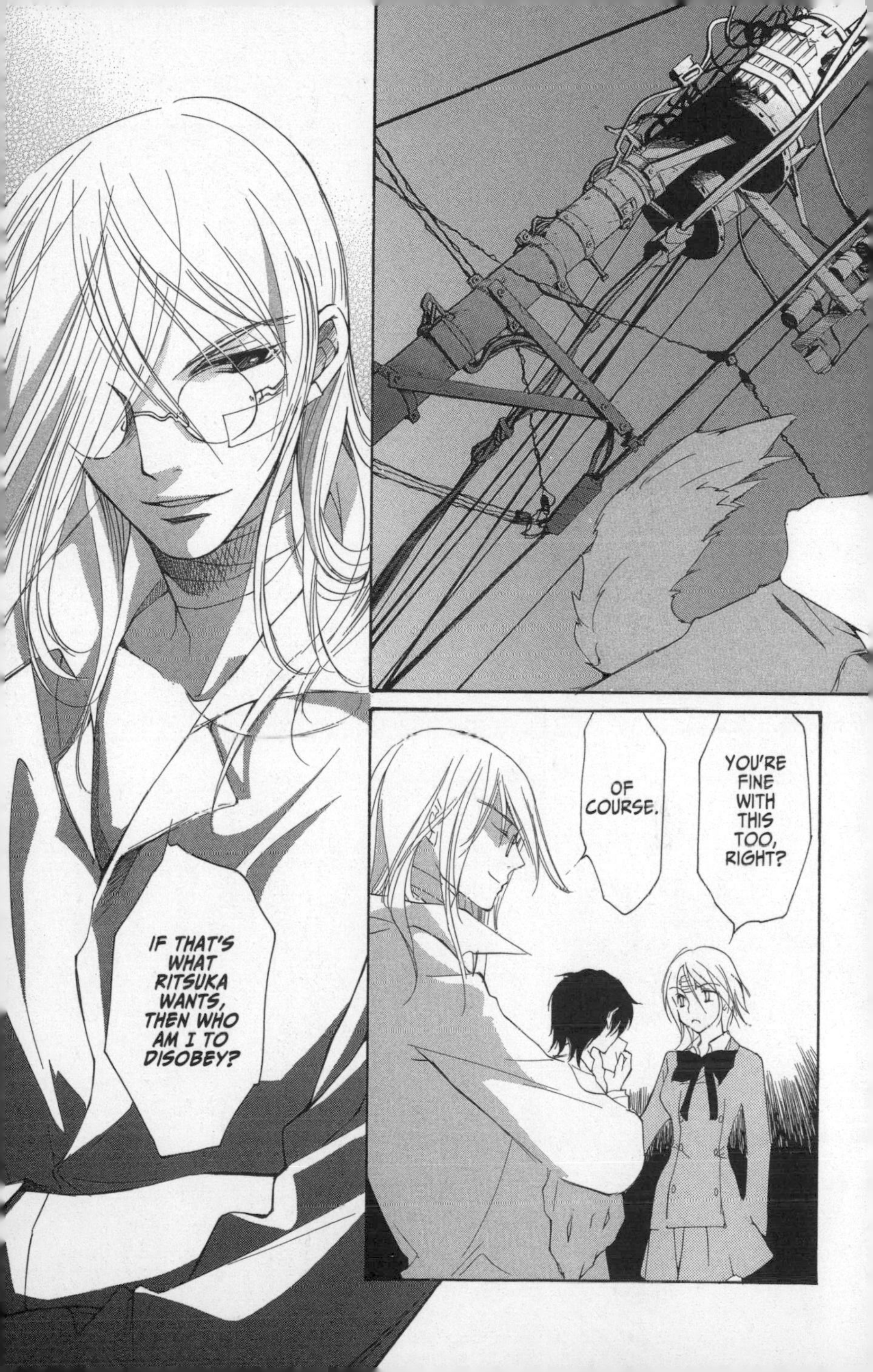
YOU'RE FINE WITH THIS TOO, RIGHT?
OF COURSE.
IF THAT'S WHAT RITSUKA WANTS, THEN WHO AM I TO DISOBEY?

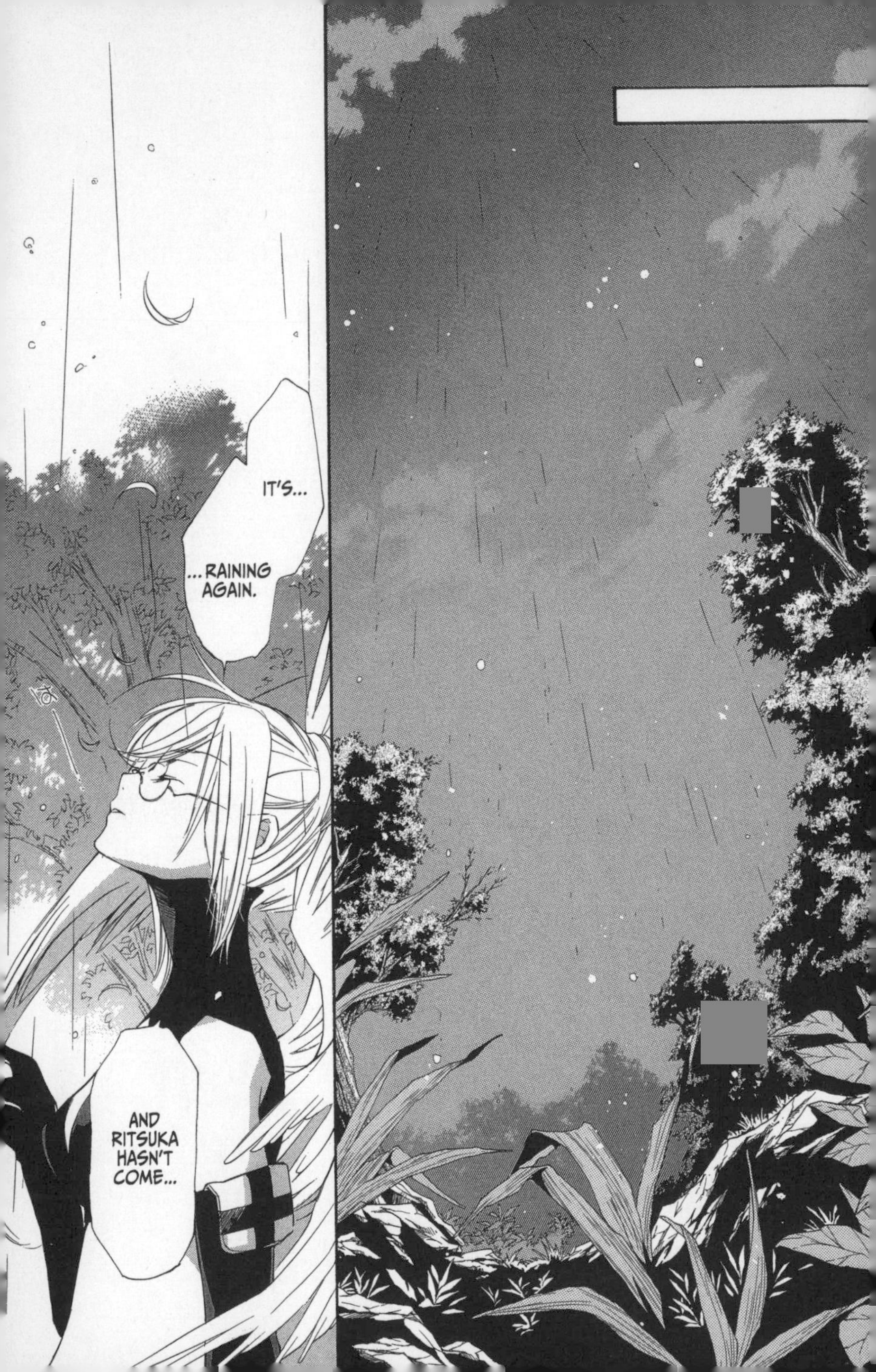
IT'S...
...RAINING AGAIN.
AND RITSUKA HASN'T COME...

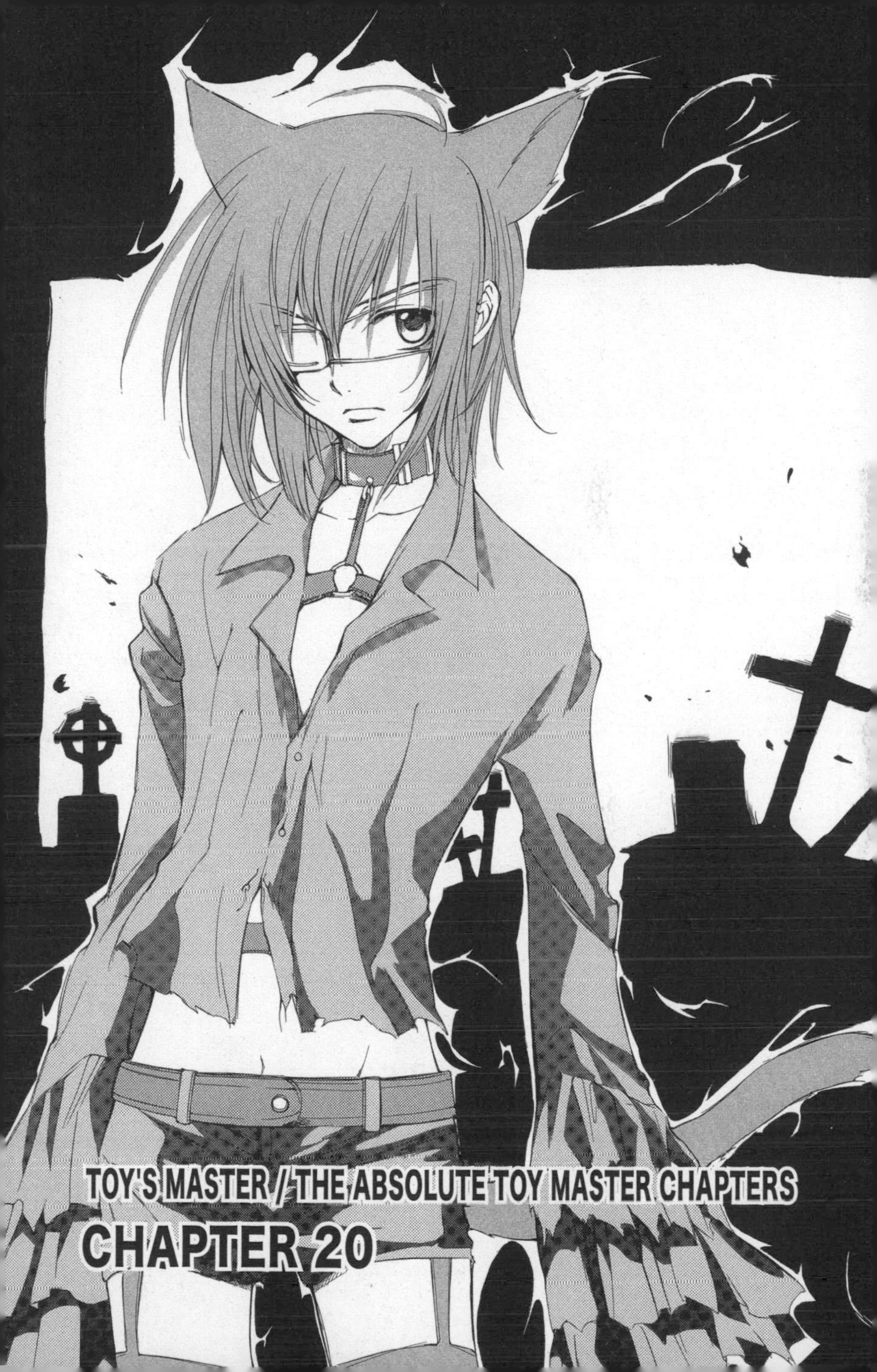
TOY'S MASTER / THE ABSOLUTE TOY MASTER CHAPTERS
CHAPTER 20

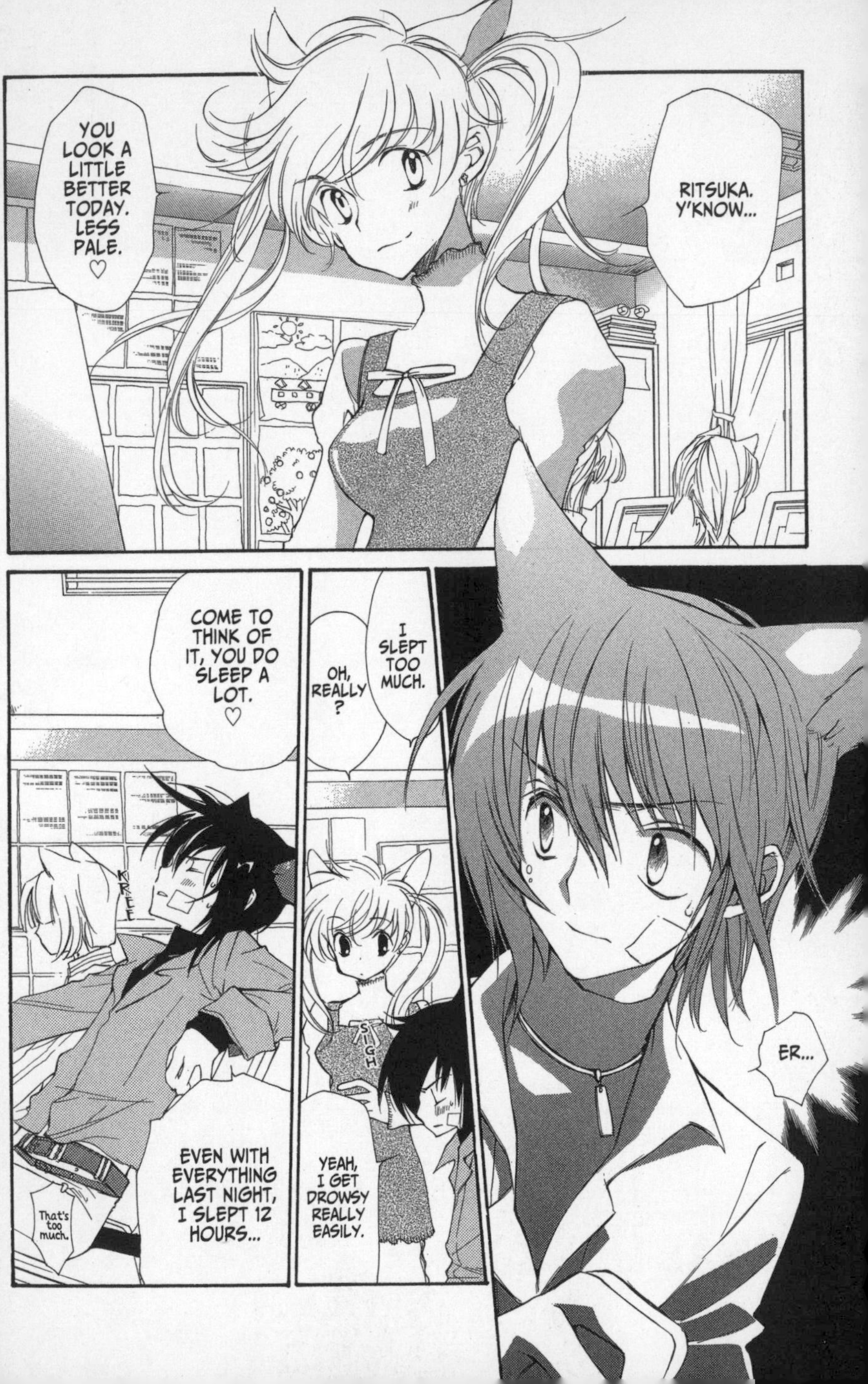
RITSUKA. Y'KNOW...
YOU LOOK A LITTLE BETTER TODAY. LESS PALE. ♡
ER...
I SLEPT TOO MUCH.
OH, REALLY?
SIGH
YEAH, I GET DROWSY REALLY EASILY.
COME TO THINK OF IT, YOU DO SLEEP A LOT. ♡
EVEN WITH EVERYTHING LAST NIGHT, I SLEPT 12 HOURS...
That's too much.

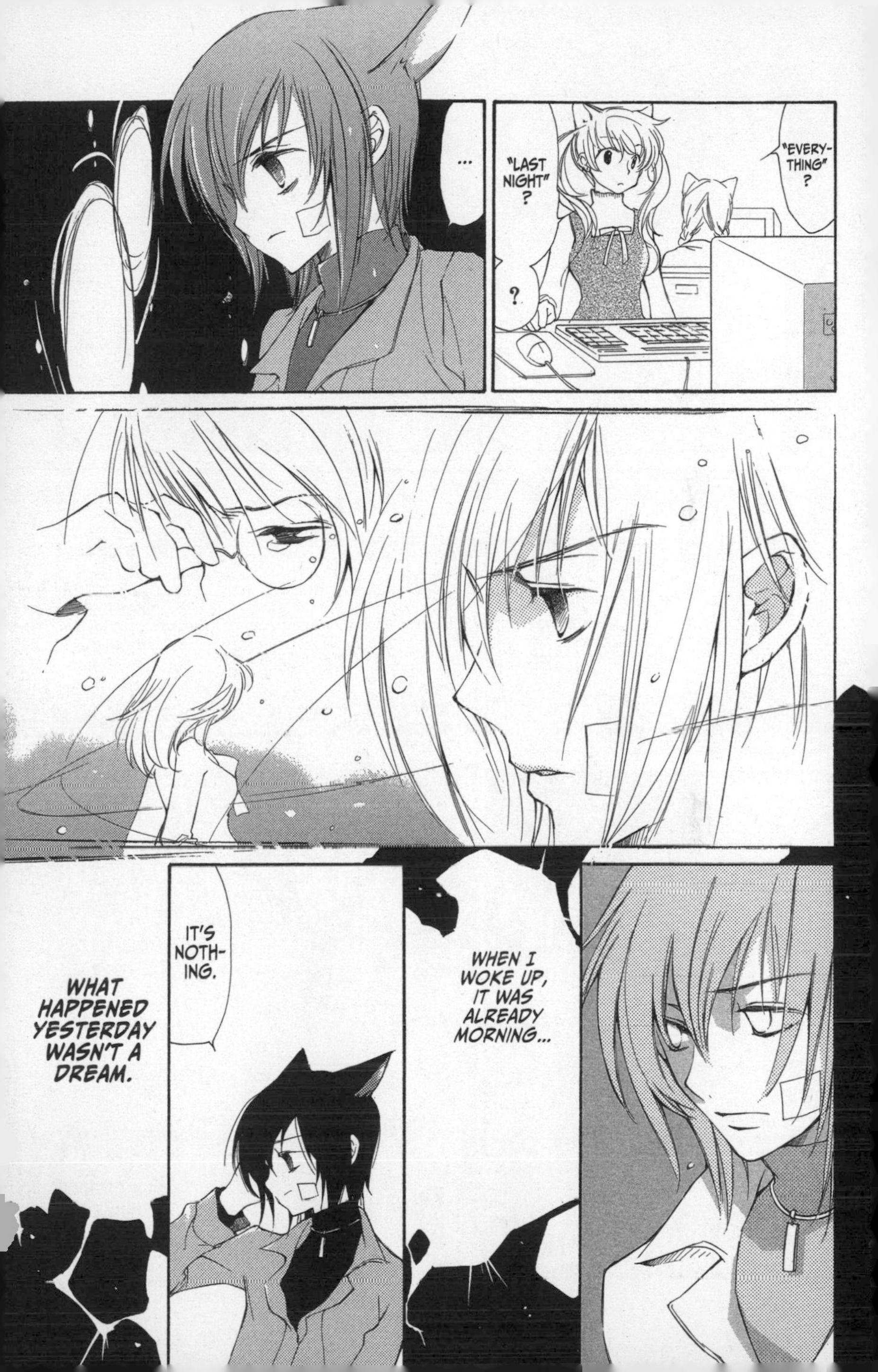
"EVERY-THING" ?
"LAST NIGHT" ?
?
...
WHEN I WOKE UP, IT WAS ALREADY MORNING...
IT'S NOTHING.
WHAT HAPPENED YESTERDAY WASN'T A DREAM.

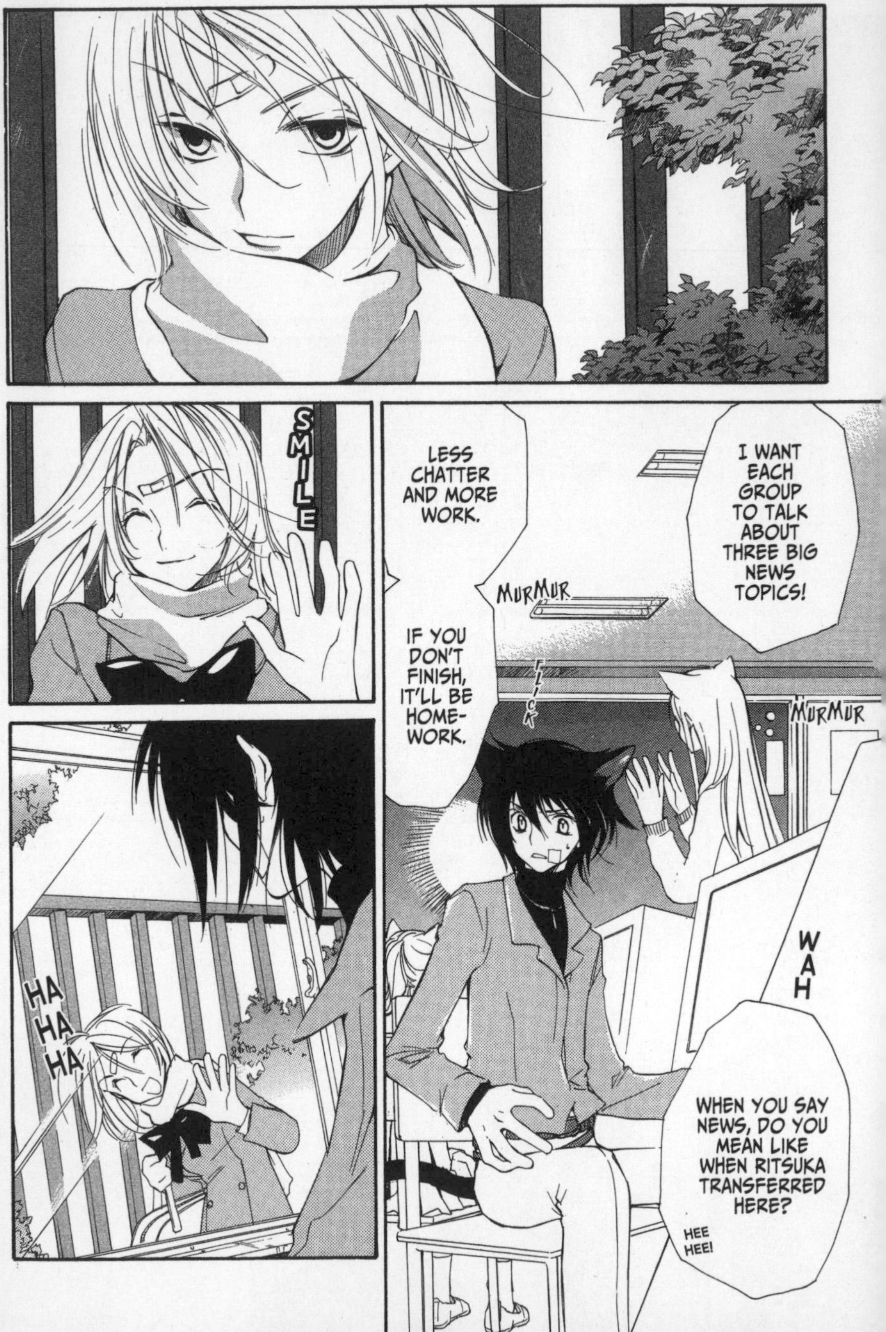
I WANT EACH GROUP TO TALK ABOUT THREE BIG NEWS TOPICS!
LESS CHATTER AND MORE WORK.
MURMUR
IF YOU DON'T FINISH, IT'LL BE HOME-WORK.
FLICK
MURMUR
WAH
WHEN YOU SAY NEWS, DO YOU MEAN LIKE WHEN RITSUKA TRANSFERRED HERE?
HEE HEE!
SMILE
HA HA HA

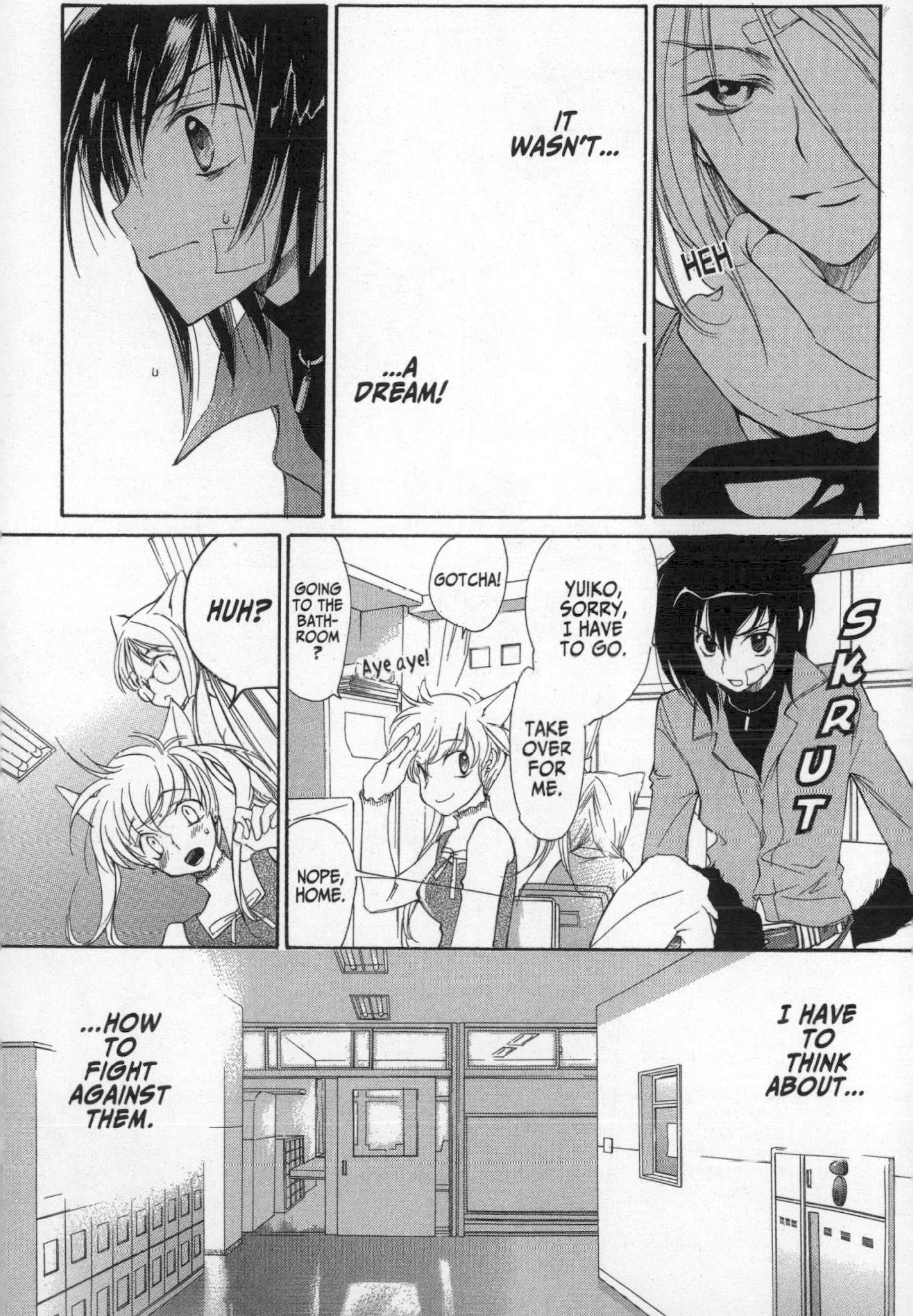
HEH
IT WASN'T...
...A DREAM!
SKRUT
YUIKO, SORRY, I HAVE TO GO.
TAKE OVER FOR ME.
GOTCHA!
Aye aye!
GOING TO THE BATH-ROOM?
NOPE, HOME.
HUH?
I HAVE TO THINK ABOUT...
...HOW TO FIGHT AGAINST THEM.

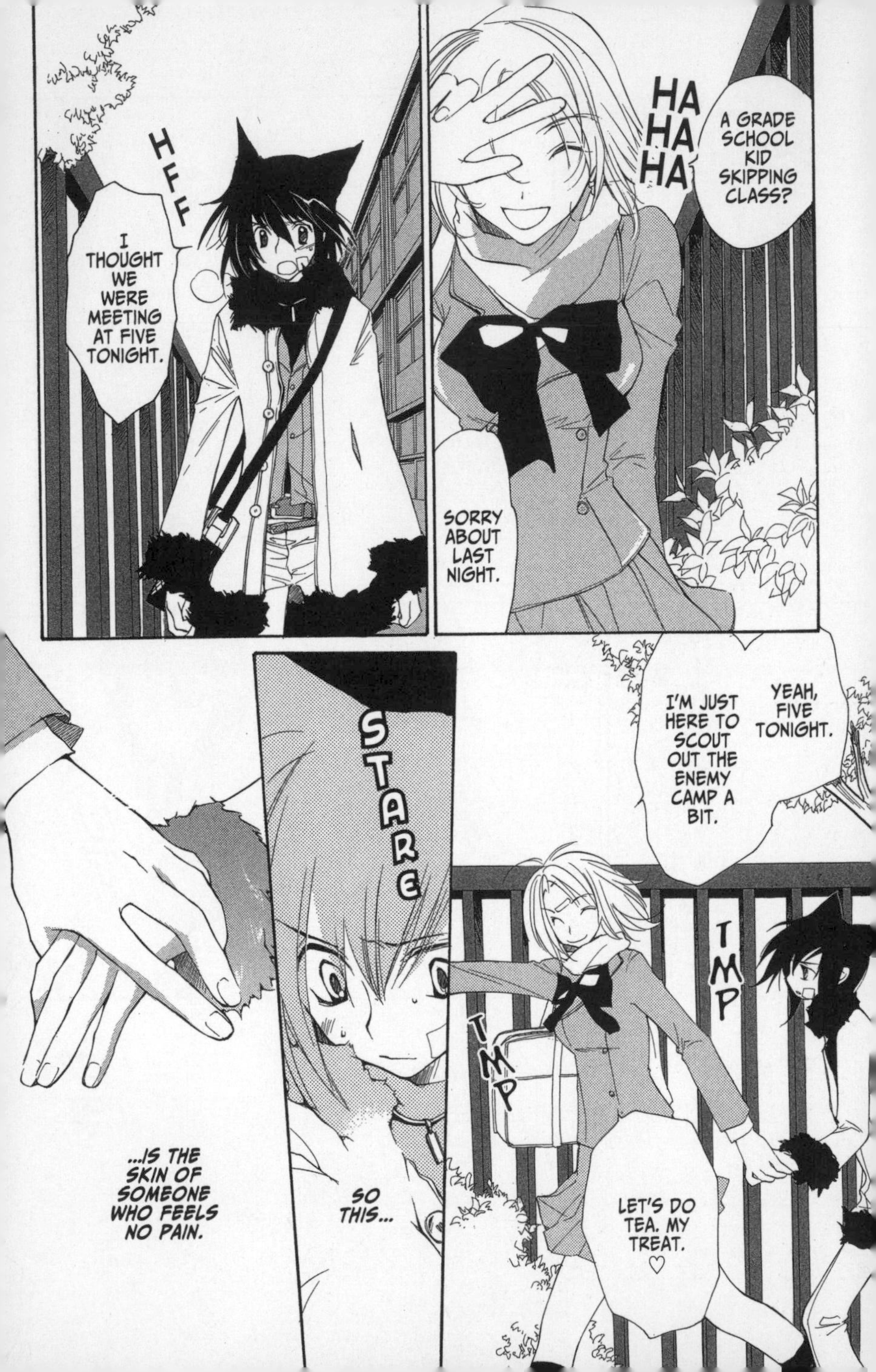
A GRADE SCHOOL KID SKIPPING CLASS?
HA HA HA
SORRY ABOUT LAST NIGHT.
HFF
I THOUGHT WE WERE MEETING AT FIVE TONIGHT.
YEAH, FIVE TONIGHT.
I'M JUST HERE TO SCOUT OUT THE ENEMY CAMP A BIT.
TMP
TMP
LET'S DO TEA. MY TREAT. ♡
STARE
SO THIS...
...IS THE SKIN OF SOMEONE WHO FEELS NO PAIN.

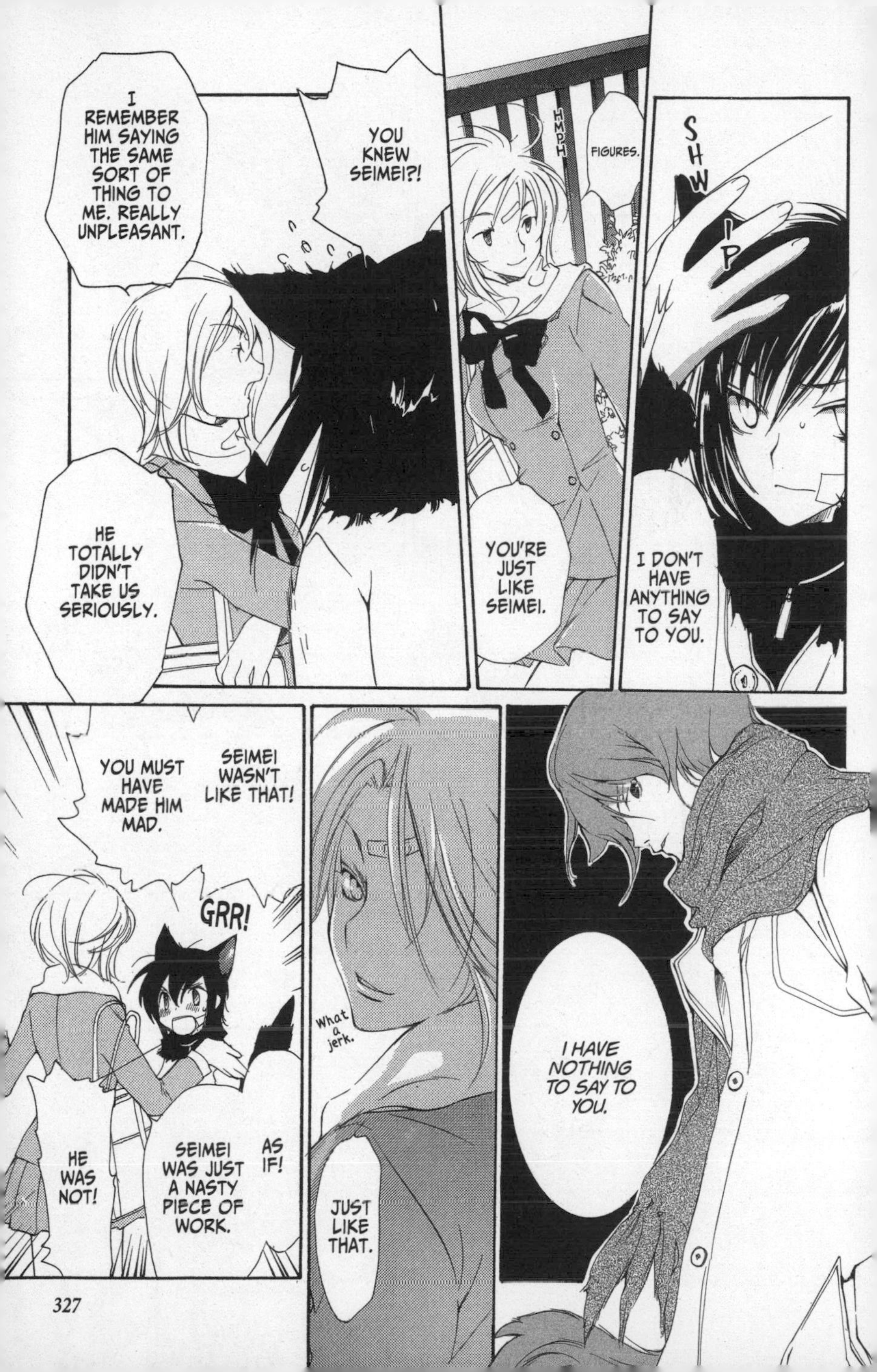
SHWIP
I DON'T HAVE ANYTHING TO SAY TO YOU.
HMPH
FIGURES.
YOU'RE JUST LIKE SEIMEI.
YOU KNEW SEIMEI?!
I REMEMBER HIM SAYING THE SAME SORT OF THING TO ME. REALLY UNPLEASANT.
HE TOTALLY DIDN'T TAKE US SERIOUSLY.
I HAVE NOTHING TO SAY TO YOU.
What a jerk.
JUST LIKE THAT.
SEIMEI WASN'T LIKE THAT!
YOU MUST HAVE MADE HIM MAD.
GRR!
AS IF!
SEIMEI WAS JUST A NASTY PIECE OF WORK.
HE WAS NOT!

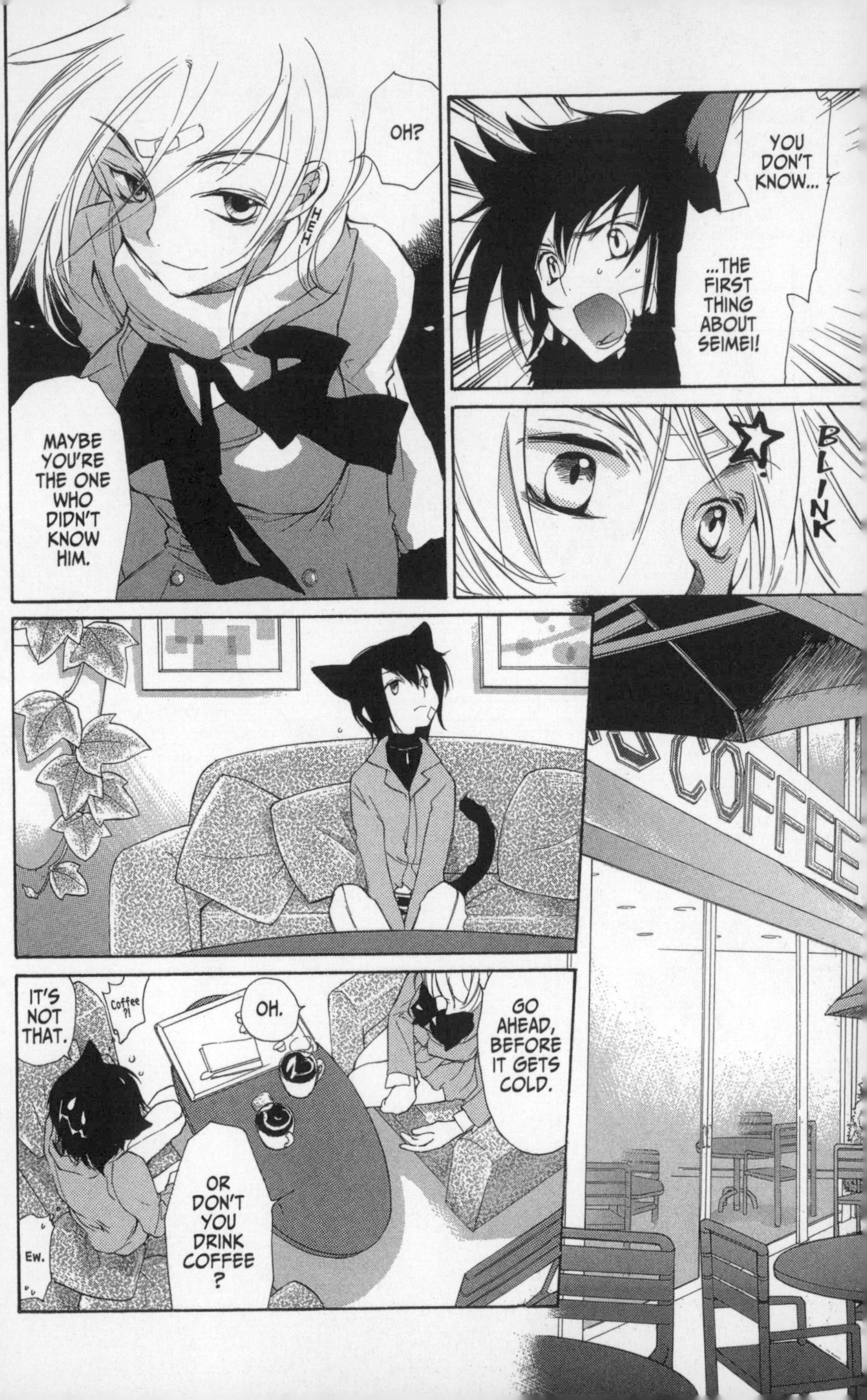
YOU DON'T KNOW...
...THE FIRST THING ABOUT SEIMEI!
BLINK
OH?
HEH
MAYBE YOU'RE THE ONE WHO DIDN'T KNOW HIM.
COFFEE
GO AHEAD, BEFORE IT GETS COLD.
OH.
Coffee?!
IT'S NOT THAT.
OR DON'T YOU DRINK COFFEE?
Ew.

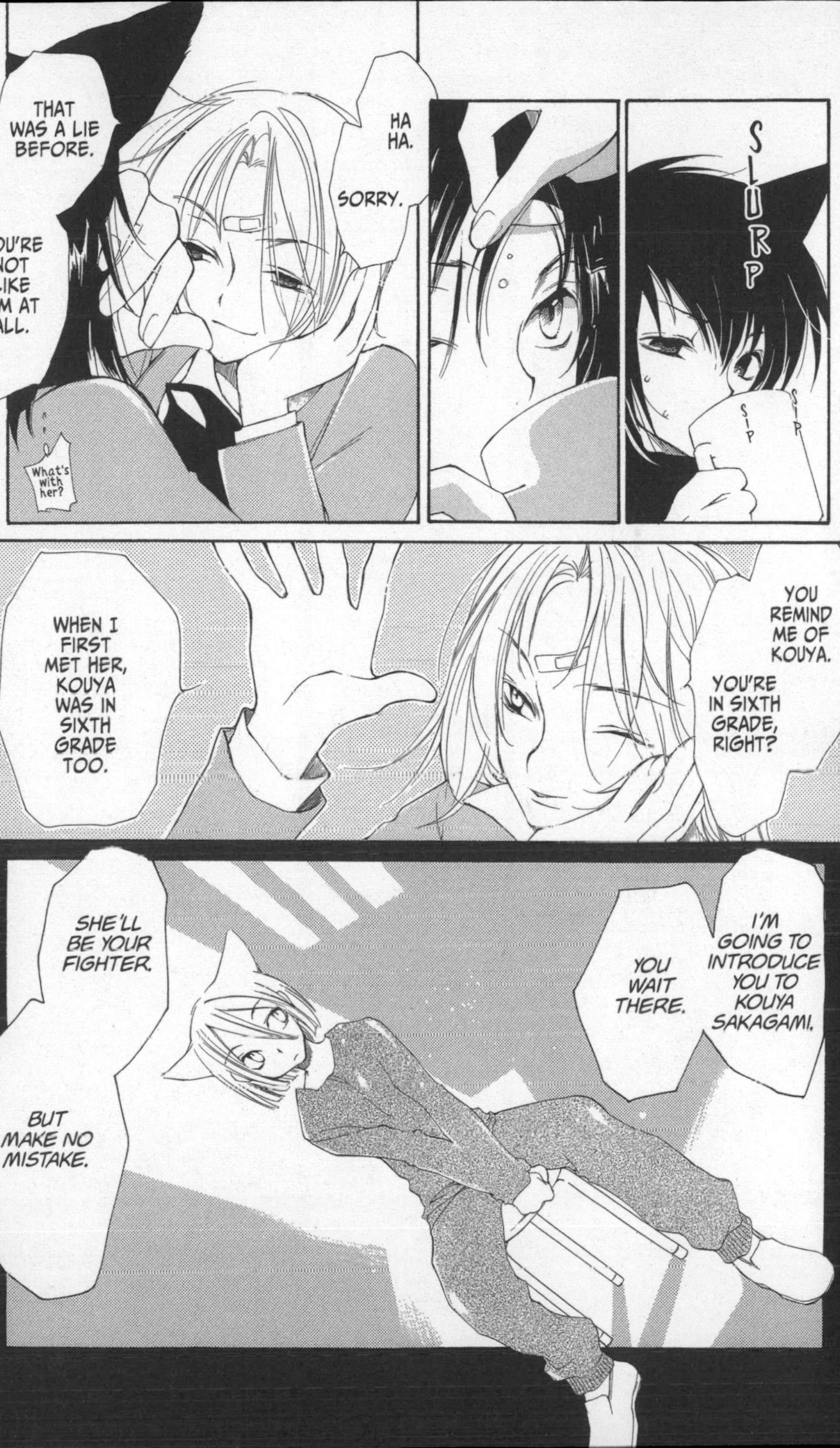
SLURP
SIP SIP
HA HA.
SORRY.
THAT WAS A LIE BEFORE.
YOU'RE NOT LIKE HIM AT ALL.
What's with her?
YOU REMIND ME OF KOUYA.
YOU'RE IN SIXTH GRADE, RIGHT?
WHEN I FIRST MET HER, KOUYA WAS IN SIXTH GRADE TOO.
I'M GOING TO INTRODUCE YOU TO KOUYA SAKAGAMI.
YOU WAIT THERE.
SHE'LL BE YOUR FIGHTER.
BUT MAKE NO MISTAKE.

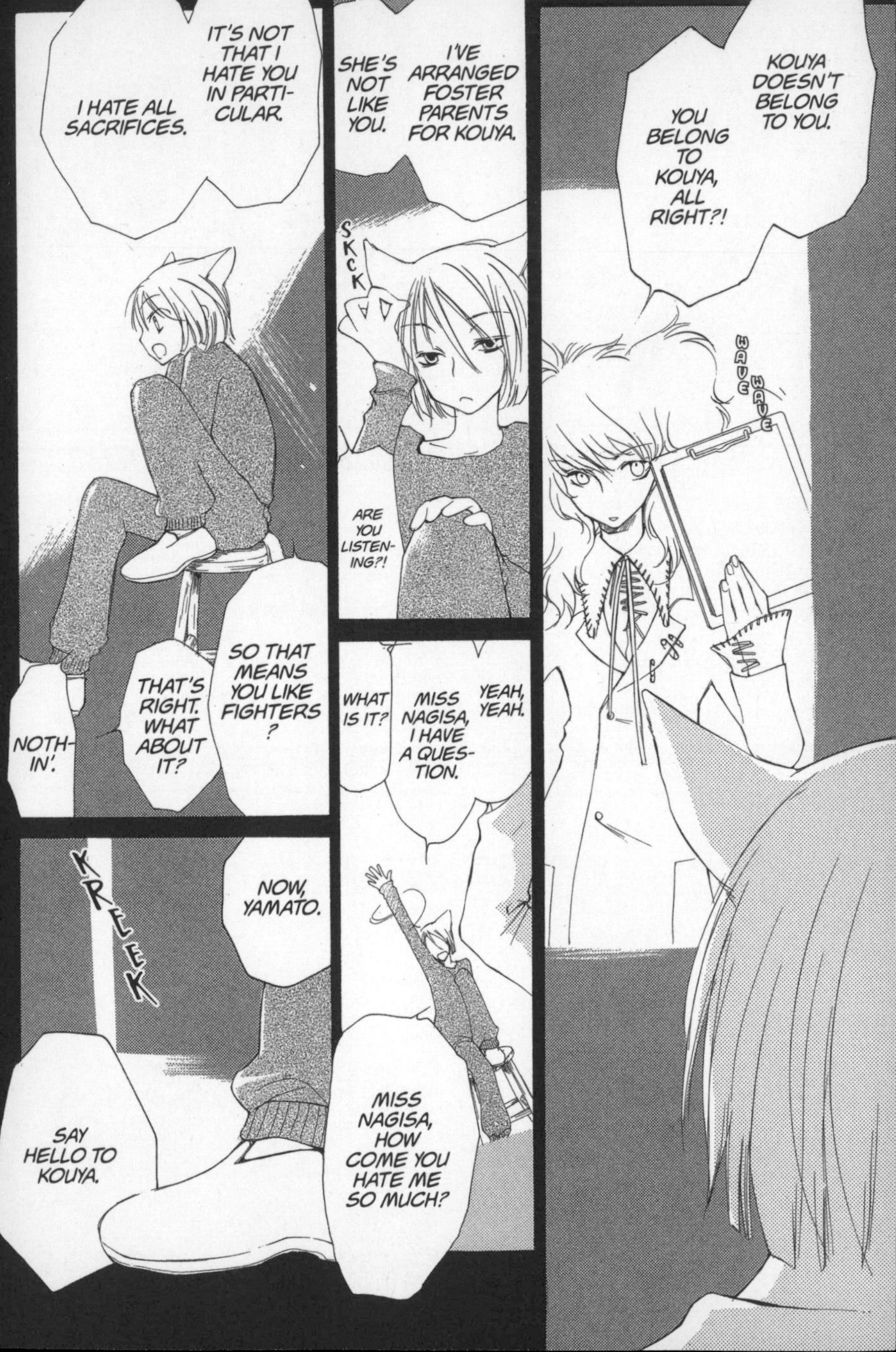
KOUYA DOESN'T BELONG TO YOU.
YOU BELONG TO KOUYA, ALL RIGHT?!
WAVE WAVE
I'VE ARRANGED FOSTER PARENTS FOR KOUYA.
SHE'S NOT LIKE YOU.
SKCK
ARE YOU LISTENING?!
IT'S NOT THAT I HATE YOU IN PARTICULAR.
I HATE ALL SACRIFICES.
SO THAT MEANS YOU LIKE FIGHTERS?
THAT'S RIGHT. WHAT ABOUT IT?
NOTHIN'.
YEAH, YEAH.
MISS NAGISA, I HAVE A QUESTION.
WHAT IS IT?
MISS NAGISA, HOW COME YOU HATE ME SO MUCH?
NOW, YAMATO.
KRELEK
SAY HELLO TO KOUYA.

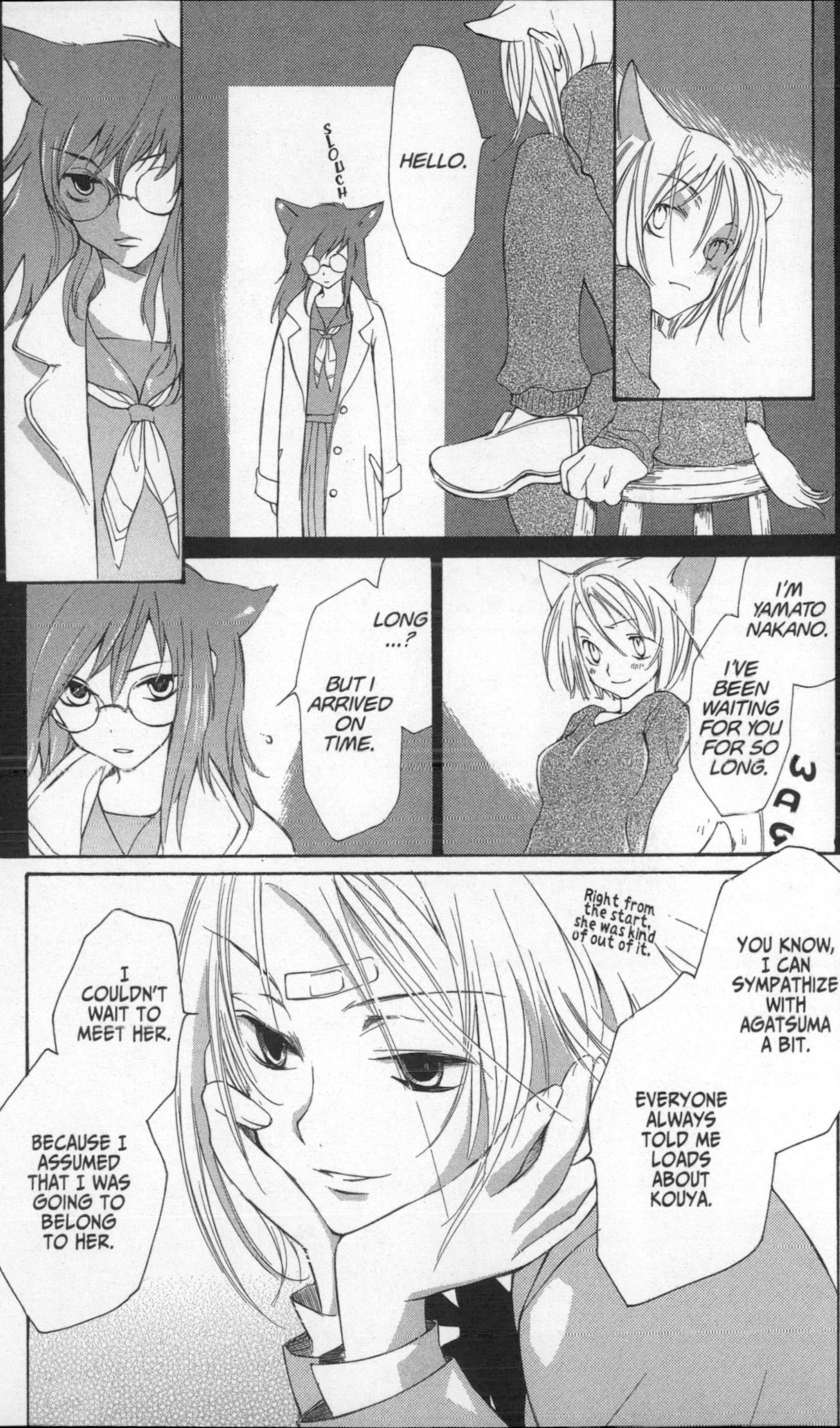
HELLO.
SLOUCH
I'M YAMATO NAKANO.
I'VE BEEN WAITING FOR YOU FOR SO LONG.
WAG
LONG ...?
BUT I ARRIVED ON TIME.
YOU KNOW, I CAN SYMPATHIZE WITH AGATSUMA A BIT.
Right from the start, she was kind of out of it.
EVERYONE ALWAYS TOLD ME LOADS ABOUT KOUYA.
I COULDN'T WAIT TO MEET HER.
BECAUSE I ASSUMED THAT I WAS GOING TO BELONG TO HER.

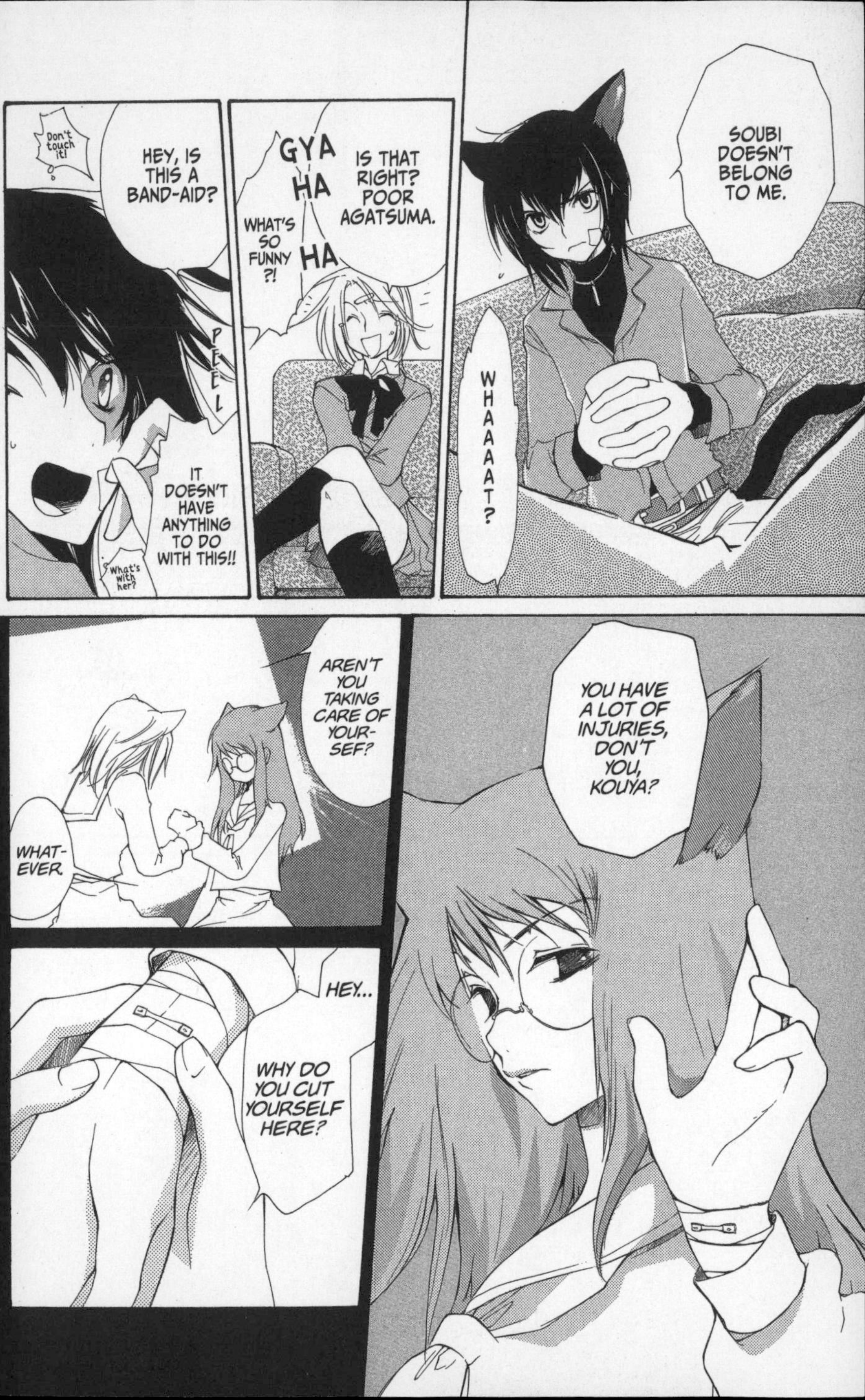
SOUBI DOESN'T BELONG TO ME.
WHAAAAAT?
IS THAT RIGHT? POOR AGATSUMA.
GYA HA HA
WHAT'S SO FUNNY ?!
HEY, IS THIS A BAND-AID?
Don't touch it!
PEEL
IT DOESN'T HAVE ANYTHING TO DO WITH THIS!!
What's with her?
YOU HAVE A LOT OF INJURIES, DON'T YOU, KOUYA?
AREN'T YOU TAKING CARE OF YOUR-SEF?
WHAT-EVER.
HEY...
WHY DO YOU CUT YOURSELF HERE?

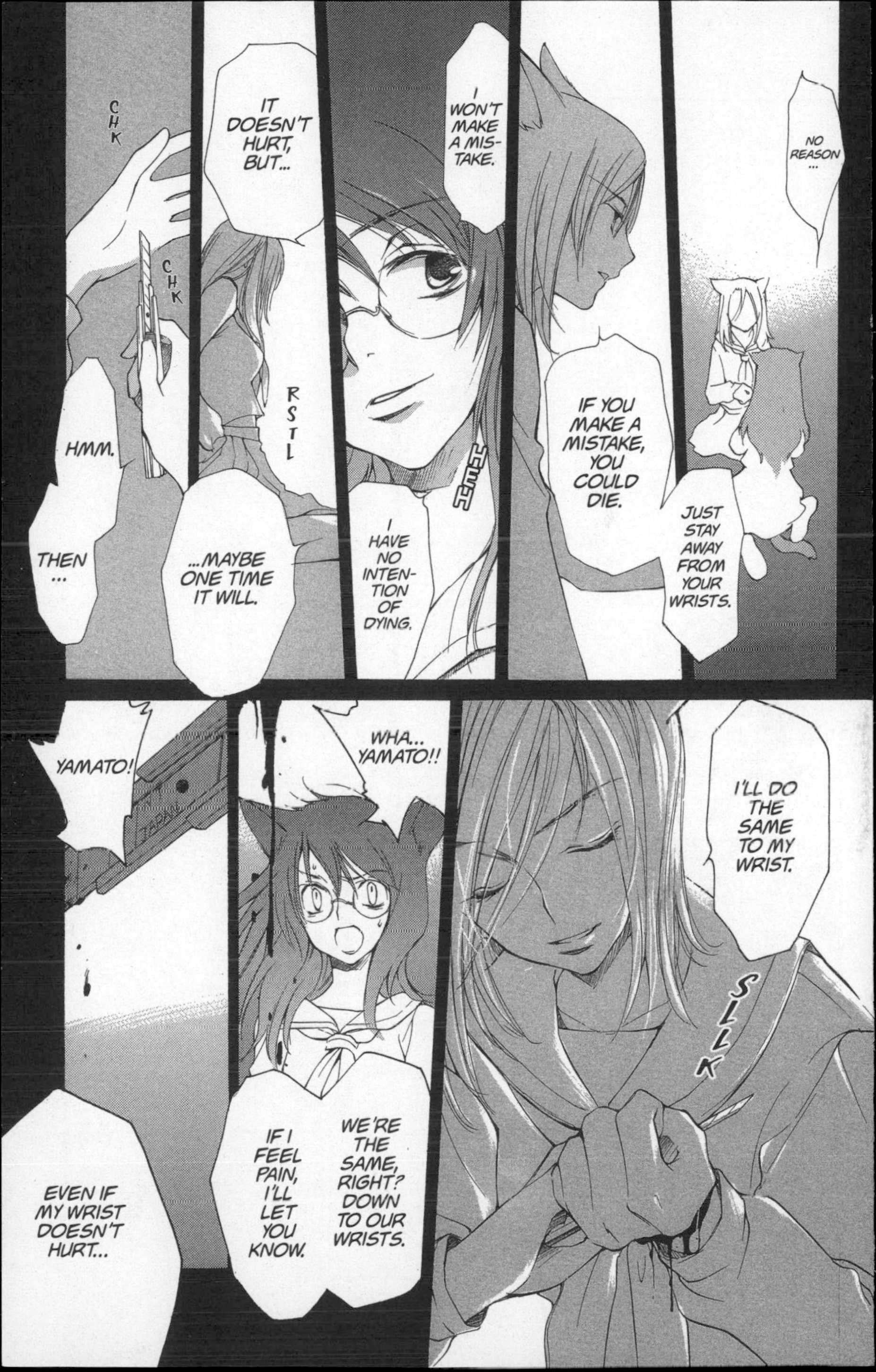
NO REASON ...
JUST STAY AWAY FROM YOUR WRISTS.
IF YOU MAKE A MISTAKE, YOU COULD DIE.
I WON'T MAKE A MIS-TAKE.
HEH
I HAVE NO INTEN-TION OF DYING.
IT DOESN'T HURT, BUT...
RSTL
...MAYBE ONE TIME IT WILL.
CHK
CHK
HMM.
THEN ...
I'LL DO THE SAME TO MY WRIST.
SLLK
WHA... YAMATO!!
WE'RE THE SAME, RIGHT? DOWN TO OUR WRISTS.
IF I FEEL PAIN, I'LL LET YOU KNOW.
YAMATO!
EVEN IF MY WRIST DOESN'T HURT...

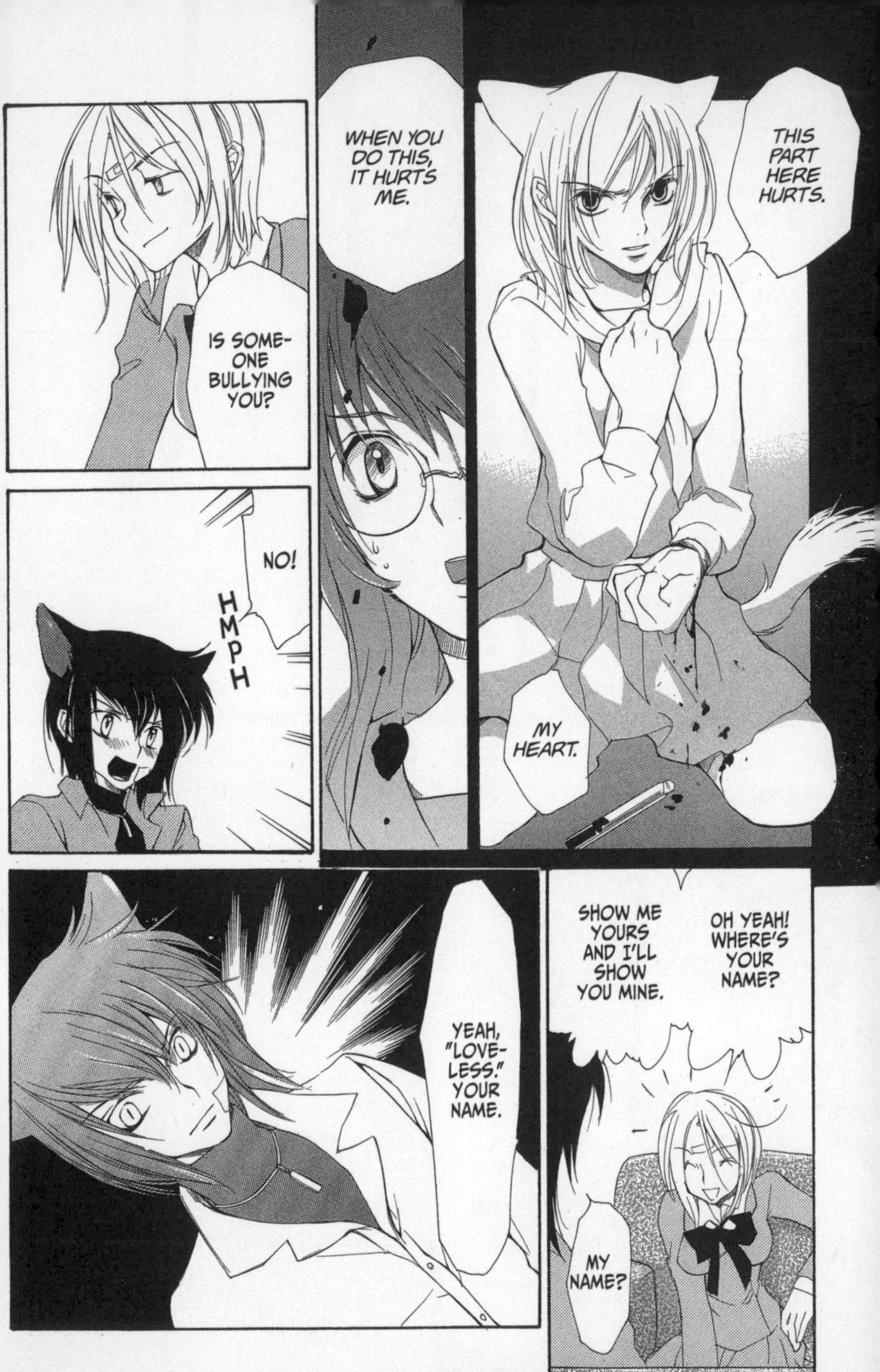
THIS PART HERE HURTS.
MY HEART.
WHEN YOU DO THIS, IT HURTS ME.
IS SOME-ONE BULLYING YOU?
NO!
HMPH
OH YEAH! WHERE'S YOUR NAME?
SHOW ME YOURS AND I'LL SHOW YOU MINE.
MY NAME?
YEAH, "LOVE-LESS." YOUR NAME.

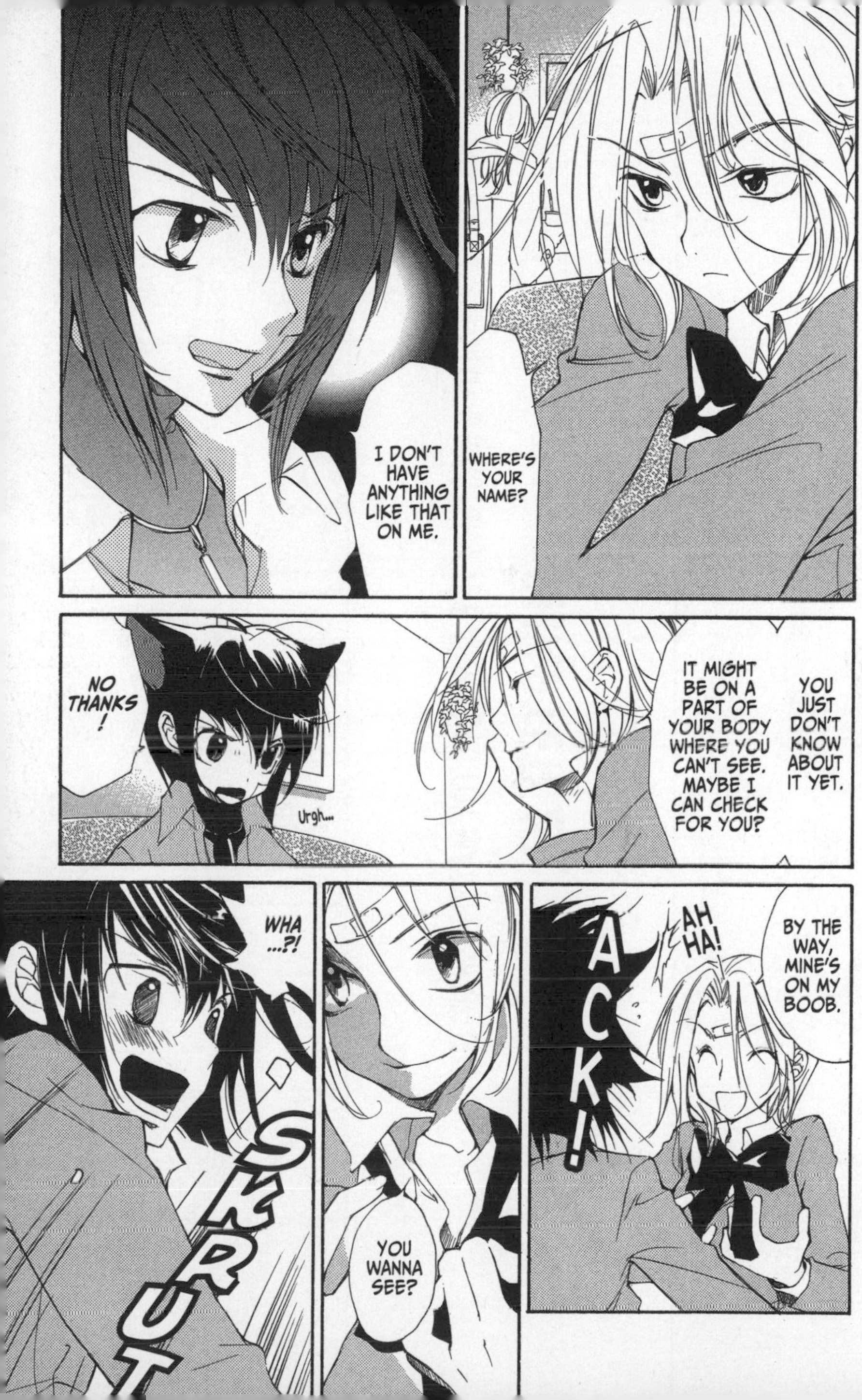
WHERE'S YOUR NAME?
I DON'T HAVE ANYTHING LIKE THAT ON ME.
YOU JUST DON'T KNOW ABOUT IT YET.
IT MIGHT BE ON A PART OF YOUR BODY WHERE YOU CAN'T SEE. MAYBE I CAN CHECK FOR YOU?
Urgh...
NO THANKS!
BY THE WAY, MINE'S ON MY BOOB.
AH HA!
ACK!
YOU WANNA SEE?
WHA...?!
SKRUT

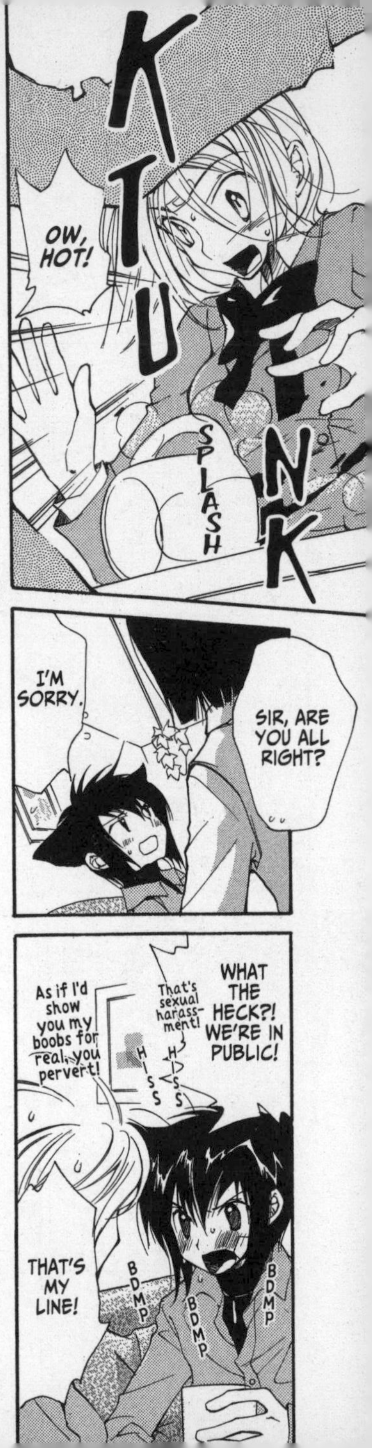
KTUNK
OW, HOT!
SPLASH
SIR, ARE YOU ALL RIGHT?
I'M SORRY.
WHAT THE HECK?! WE'RE IN PUBLIC!
That's sexual harass-ment!
HISS HISS
As if I'd show you my boobs for real, you pervert!
THAT'S MY LINE!
BDMP BDMP BDMP

TOY'S MASTER / THE ABSOLUTE TOY MASTER CHAPTERS

CHAPTER 21

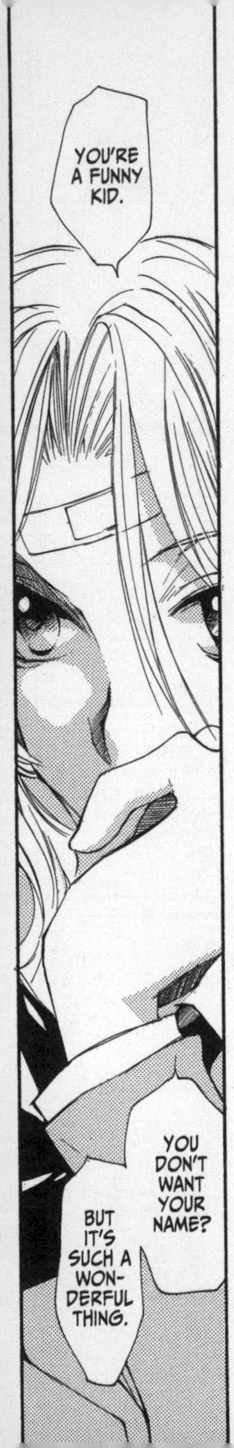
YOU'RE A FUNNY KID.
YOU DON'T WANT YOUR NAME?
BUT IT'S SUCH A WON-DERFUL THING.

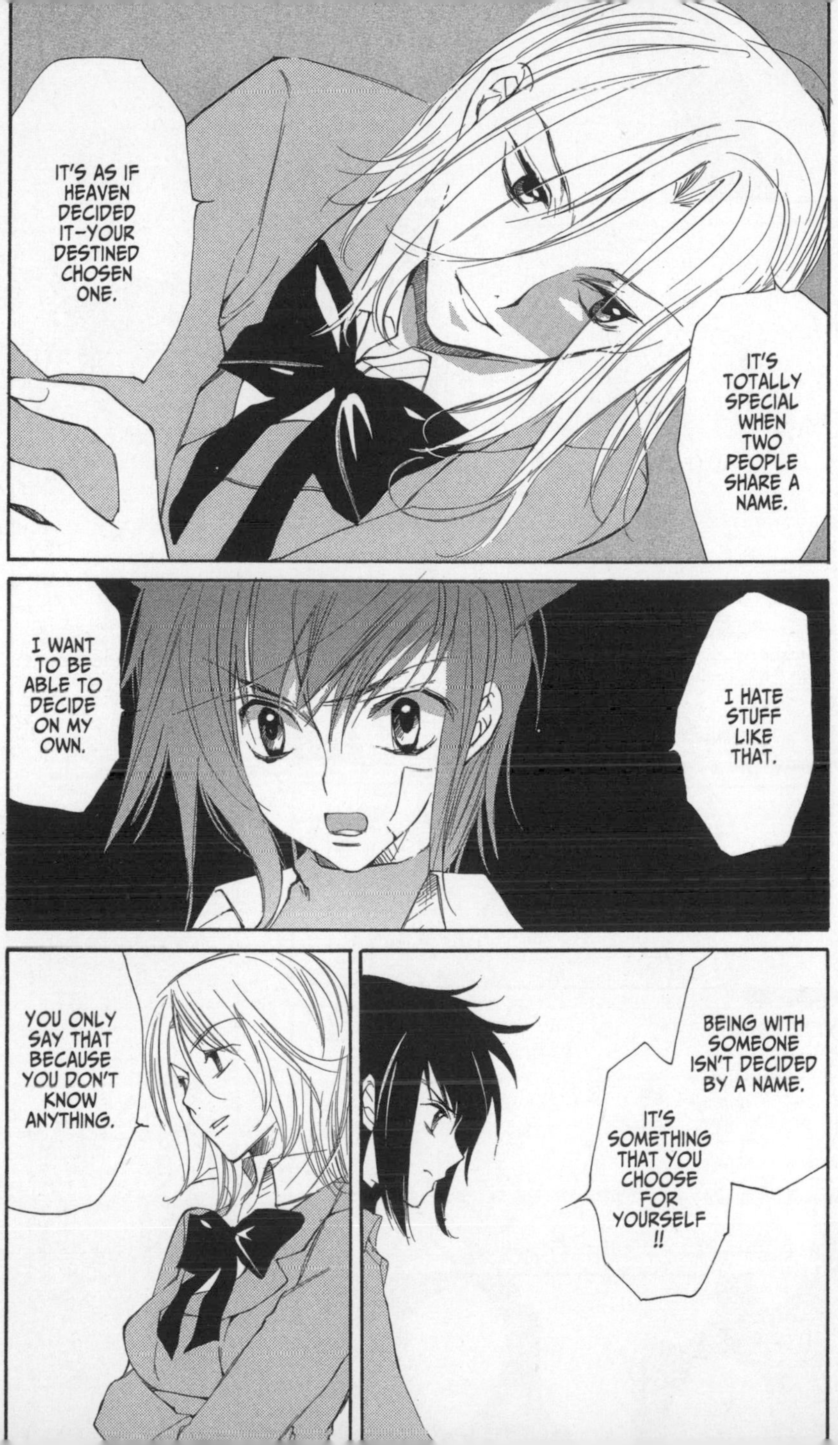
IT'S TOTALLY SPECIAL WHEN TWO PEOPLE SHARE A NAME.
IT'S AS IF HEAVEN DECIDED IT—YOUR DESTINED CHOSEN ONE.
I HATE STUFF LIKE THAT.
I WANT TO BE ABLE TO DECIDE ON MY OWN.
BEING WITH SOMEONE ISN'T DECIDED BY A NAME.
IT'S SOMETHING THAT YOU CHOOSE FOR YOURSELF!!
YOU ONLY SAY THAT BECAUSE YOU DON'T KNOW ANYTHING.

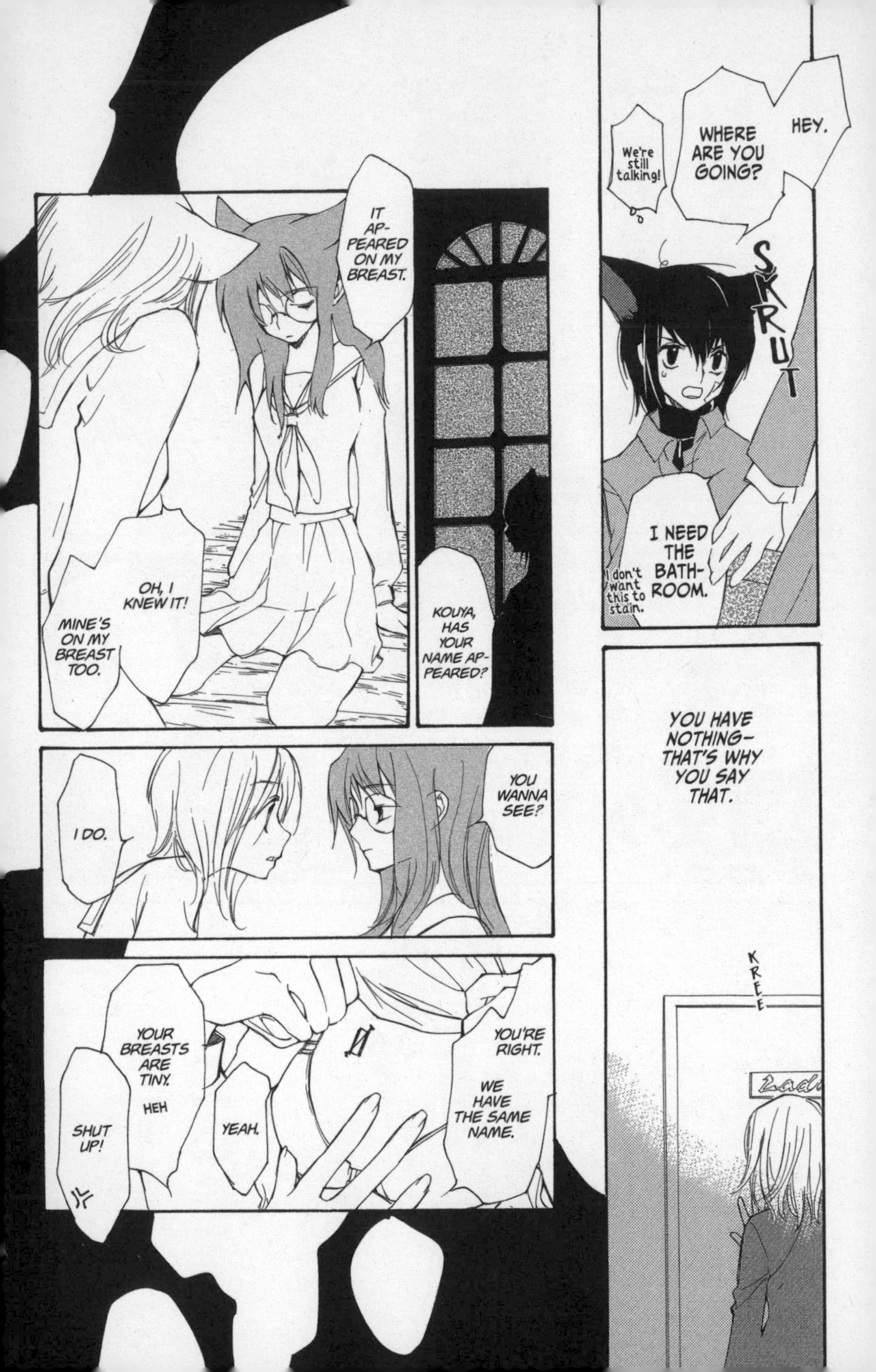
HEY.
WHERE ARE YOU GOING?
We're still talking!
SKRUT
I NEED THE BATHROOM.
I don't want this to stain.
YOU HAVE NOTHING—THAT'S WHY YOU SAY THAT.
KREE
KOUYA, HAS YOUR NAME APPEARED?
IT APPEARED ON MY BREAST.
OH, I KNEW IT!
MINE'S ON MY BREAST TOO.
YOU WANNA SEE?
I DO.
YOU'RE RIGHT.
WE HAVE THE SAME NAME.
YEAH.
YOUR BREASTS ARE TINY.
HEH
SHUT UP!

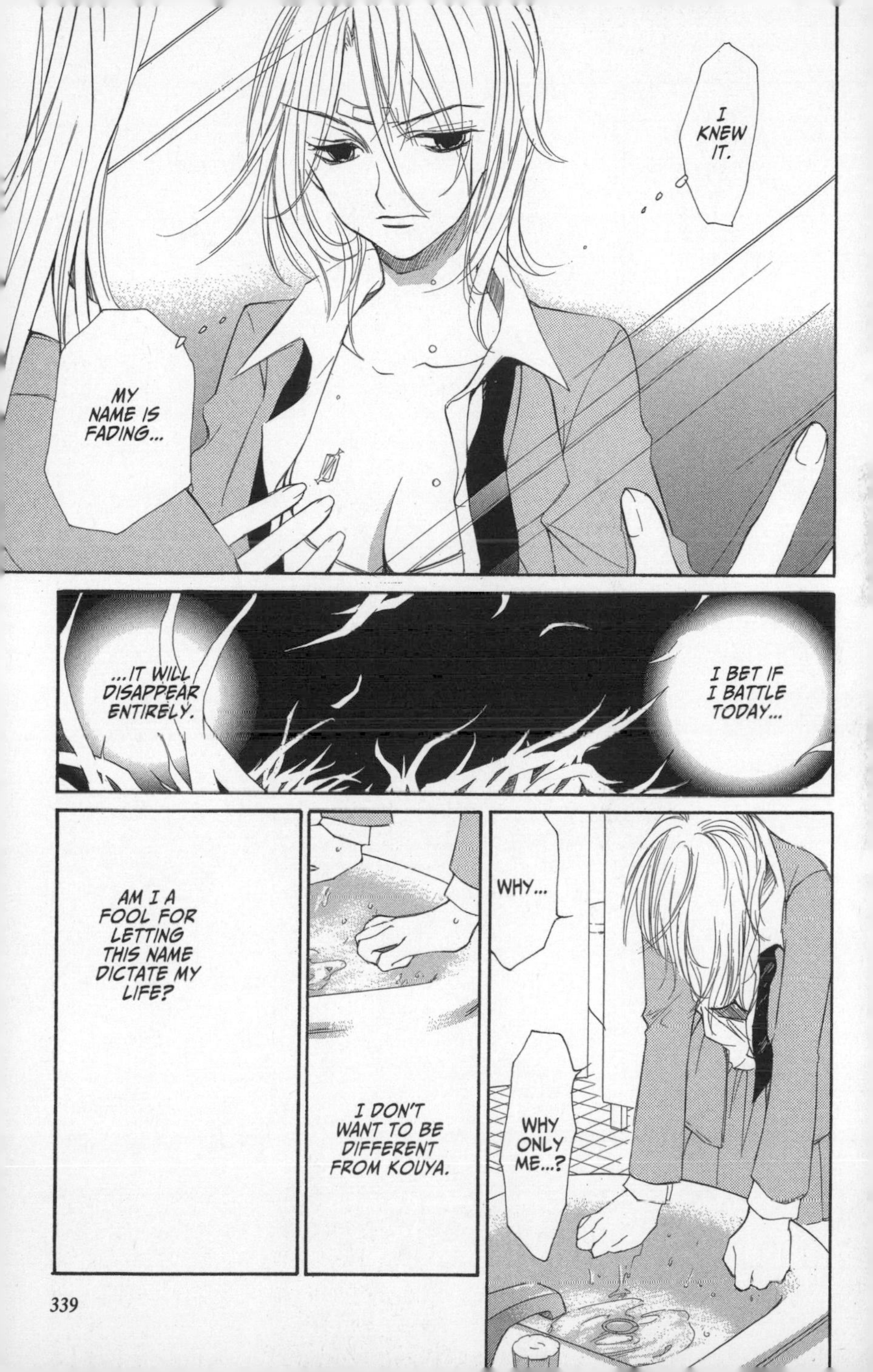
I KNEW IT.
MY NAME IS FADING...
I BET IF I BATTLE TODAY...
...IT WILL DISAPPEAR ENTIRELY.
WHY...
WHY ONLY ME...?
I DON'T WANT TO BE DIFFERENT FROM KOUYA.
AM I A FOOL FOR LETTING THIS NAME DICTATE MY LIFE?

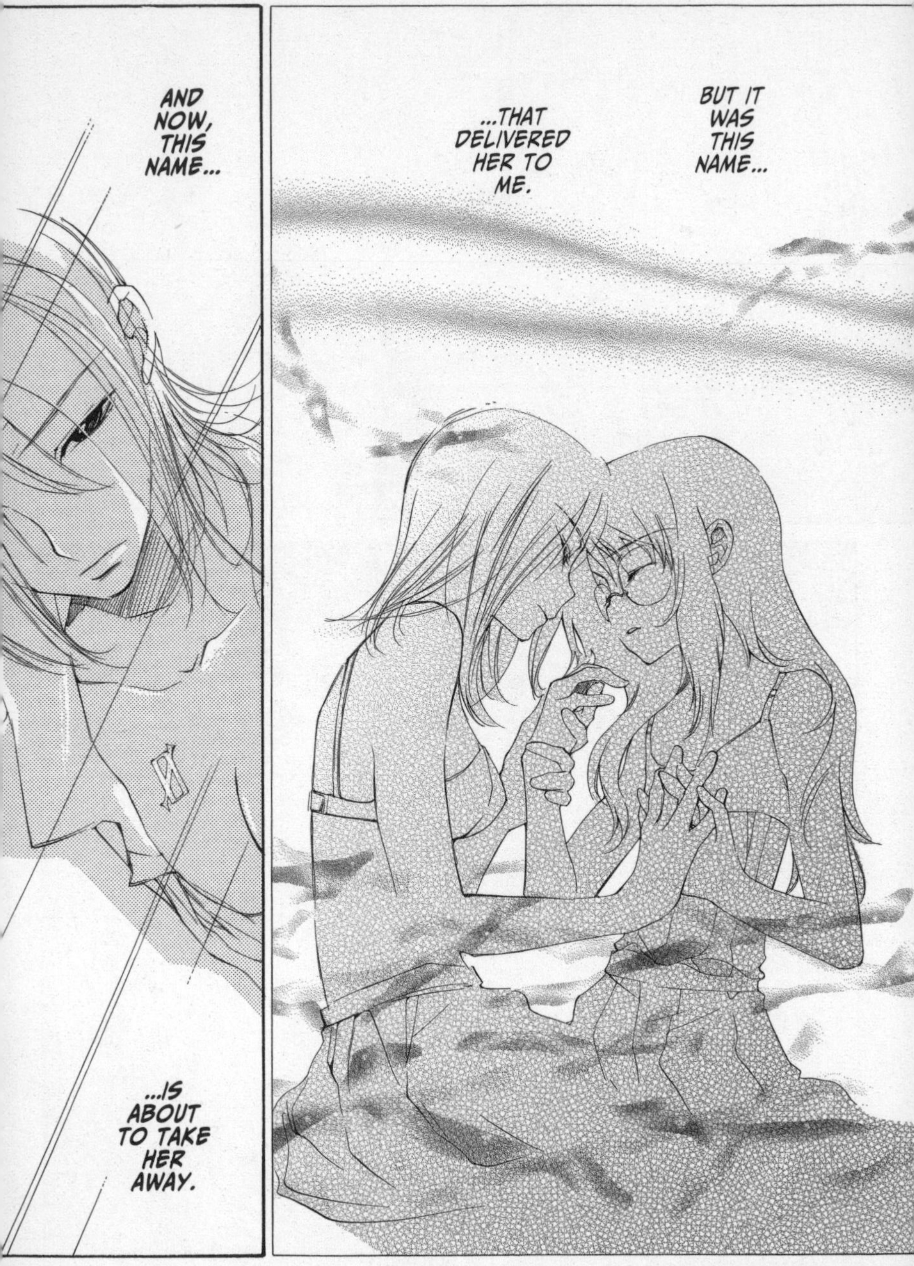
BUT IT WAS THIS NAME...
...THAT DELIVERED HER TO ME.
AND NOW, THIS NAME...
...IS ABOUT TO TAKE HER AWAY.

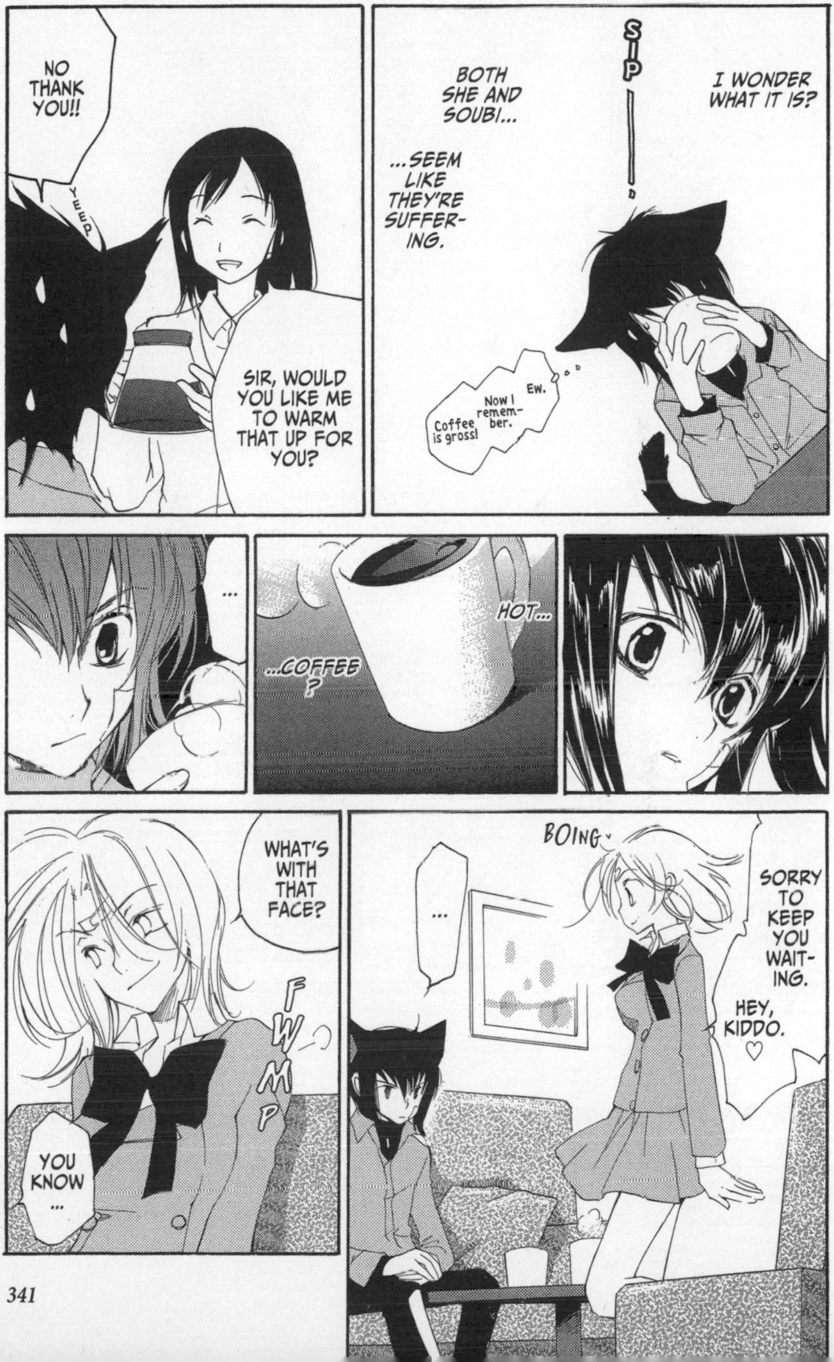
I WONDER WHAT IT IS?
SIP
BOTH SHE AND SOUBI...
...SEEM LIKE THEY'RE SUFFER-ING.
Ew. Now I remem-ber. Coffee is gross!
SIR, WOULD YOU LIKE ME TO WARM THAT UP FOR YOU?
NO THANK YOU!!
YEEP
HOT...
...COFFEE?
...
SORRY TO KEEP YOU WAIT-ING.
HEY, KIDDO. ♡
BOING
...
WHAT'S WITH THAT FACE?
FWMP
YOU KNOW ...

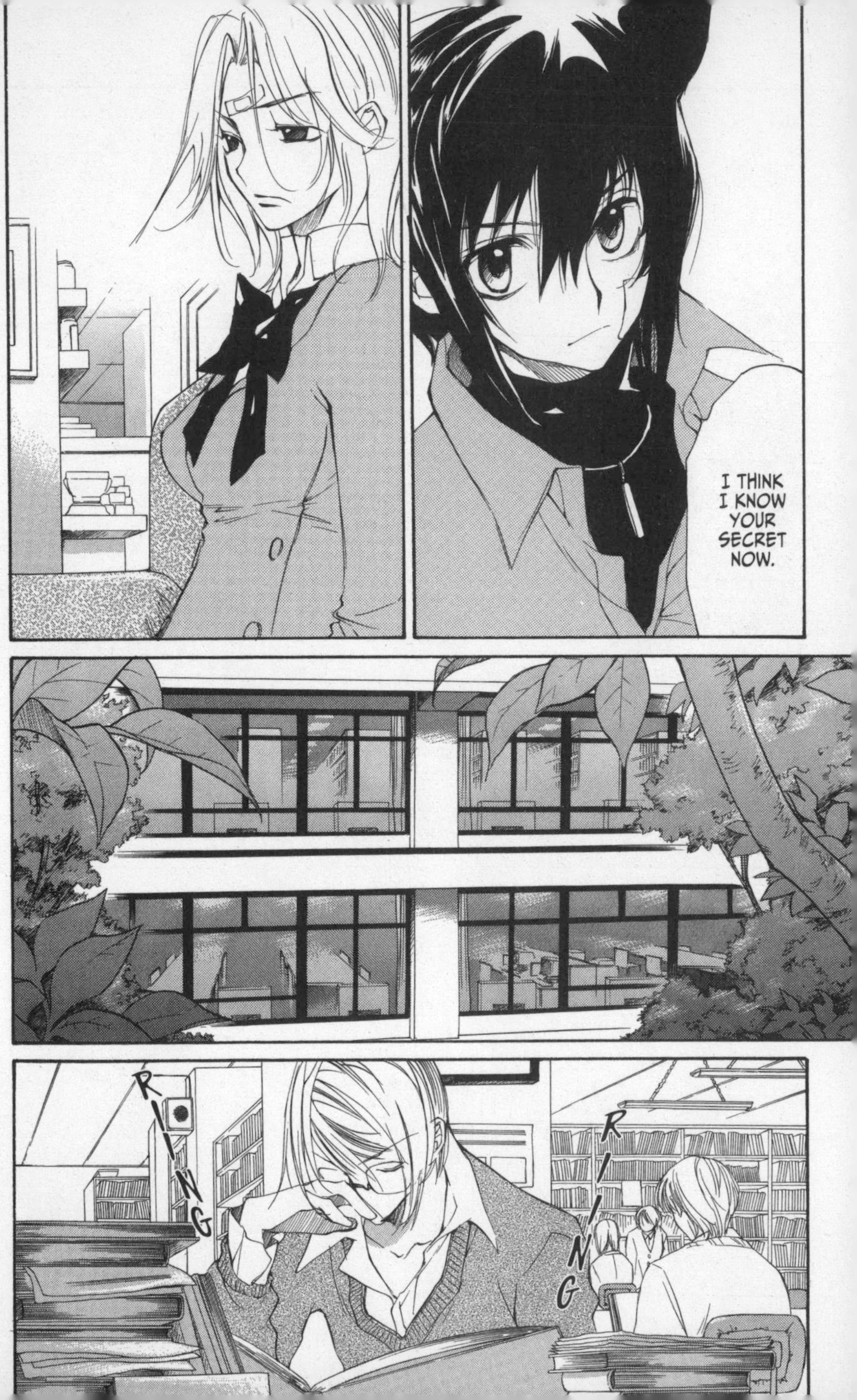
I THINK I KNOW YOUR SECRET NOW.
RIIING
RIIING

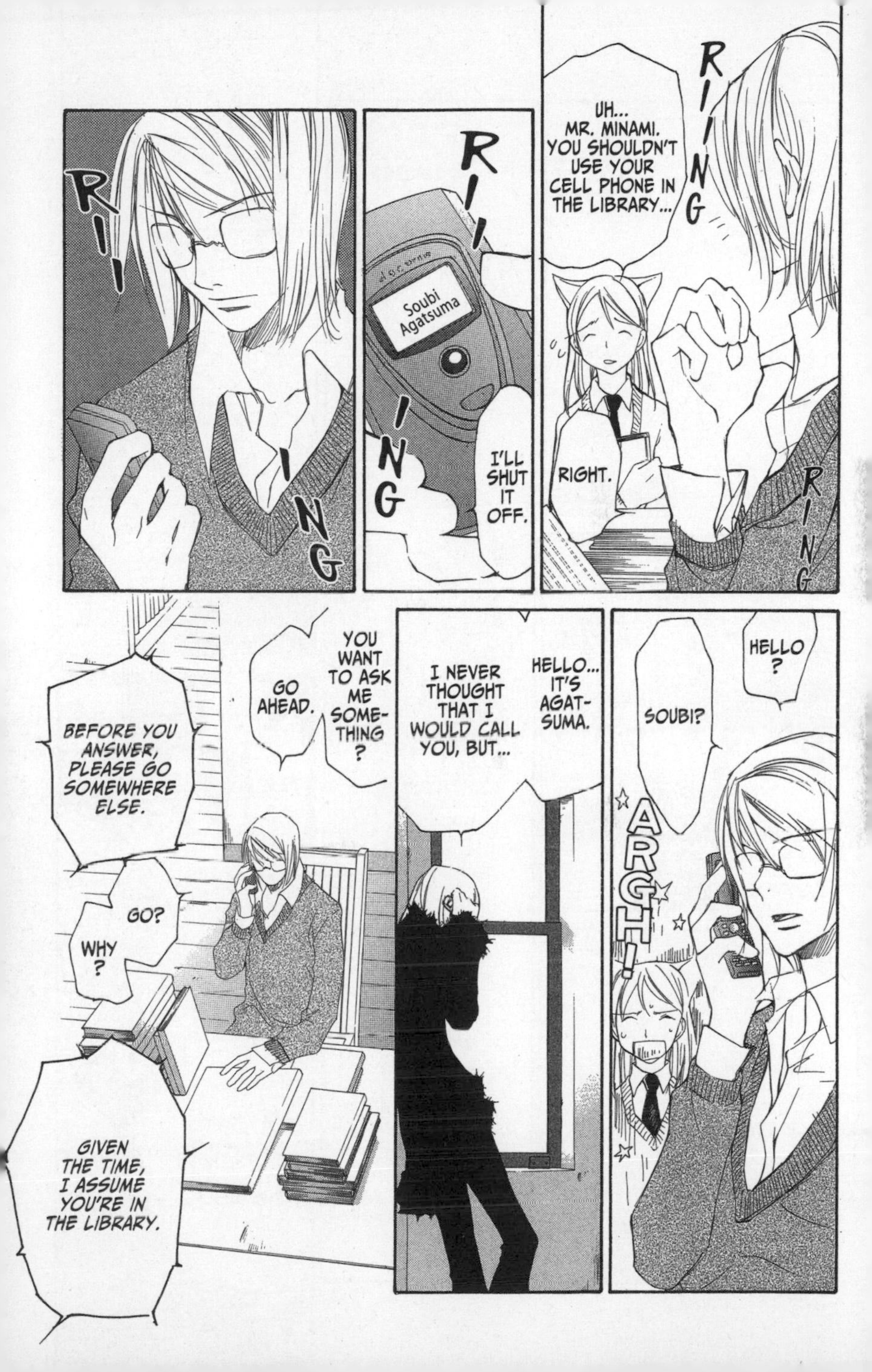
RIING
UH... MR. MINAMI. YOU SHOULDN'T USE YOUR CELL PHONE IN THE LIBRARY...
RIGHT.
RING
RIIING
Soubi Agatsuma
I'LL SHUT IT OFF.
RIIING
HELLO?
SOUBI?
ARGH!
HELLO... IT'S AGATSUMA.
I NEVER THOUGHT THAT I WOULD CALL YOU, BUT...
YOU WANT TO ASK ME SOMETHING?
GO AHEAD.
BEFORE YOU ANSWER, PLEASE GO SOMEWHERE ELSE.
GO?
WHY?
GIVEN THE TIME, I ASSUME YOU'RE IN THE LIBRARY.

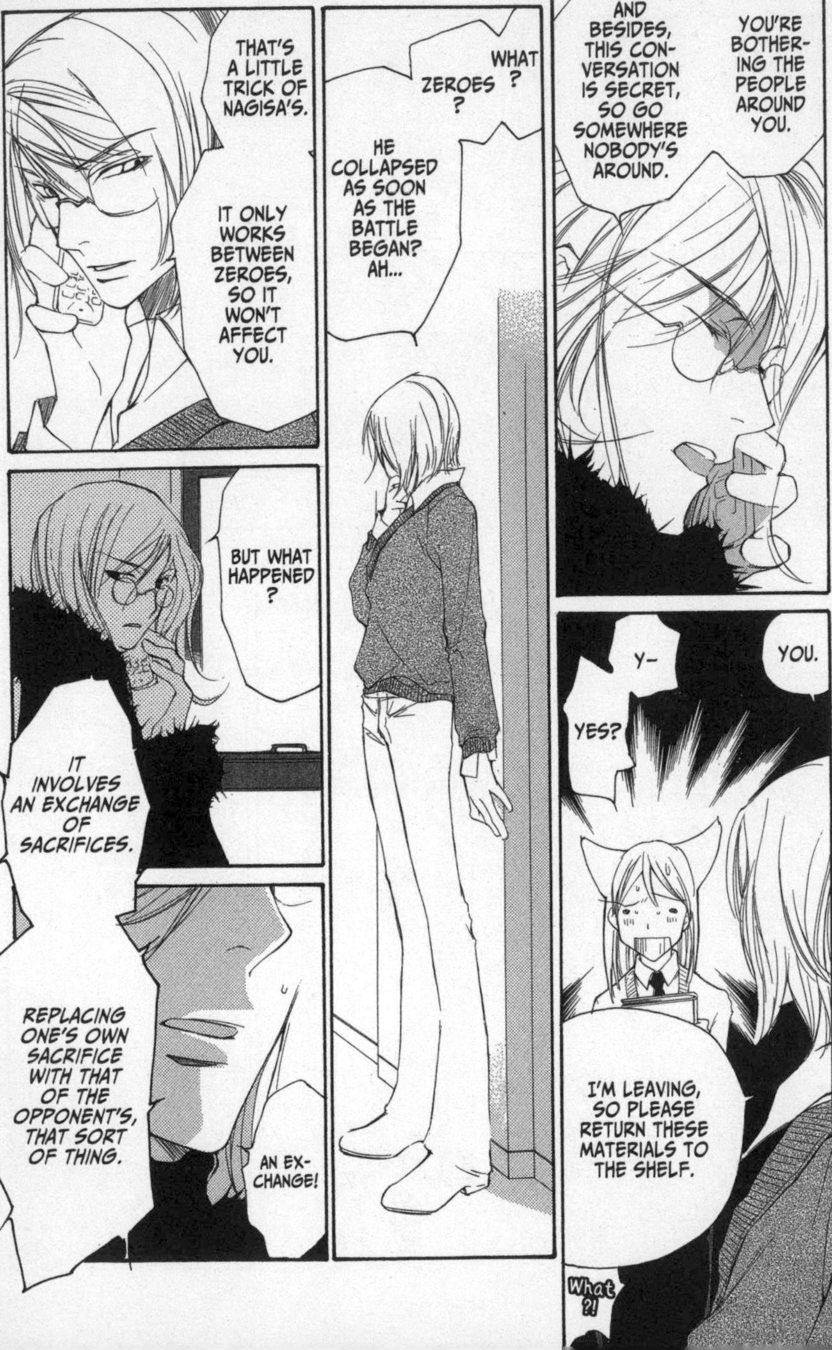
YOU'RE BOTHERING THE PEOPLE AROUND YOU.
AND BESIDES, THIS CONVERSATION IS SECRET, SO GO SOMEWHERE NOBODY'S AROUND.
YOU.
Y-
YES?
I'M LEAVING, SO PLEASE RETURN THESE MATERIALS TO THE SHELF.
What?!
WHAT?
ZEROES?
HE COLLAPSED AS SOON AS THE BATTLE BEGAN? AH...
THAT'S A LITTLE TRICK OF NAGISA'S.
IT ONLY WORKS BETWEEN ZEROES, SO IT WON'T AFFECT YOU.
BUT WHAT HAPPENED?
IT INVOLVES AN EXCHANGE OF SACRIFICES.
REPLACING ONE'S OWN SACRIFICE WITH THAT OF THE OPPONENT'S, THAT SORT OF THING.
AN EXCHANGE!

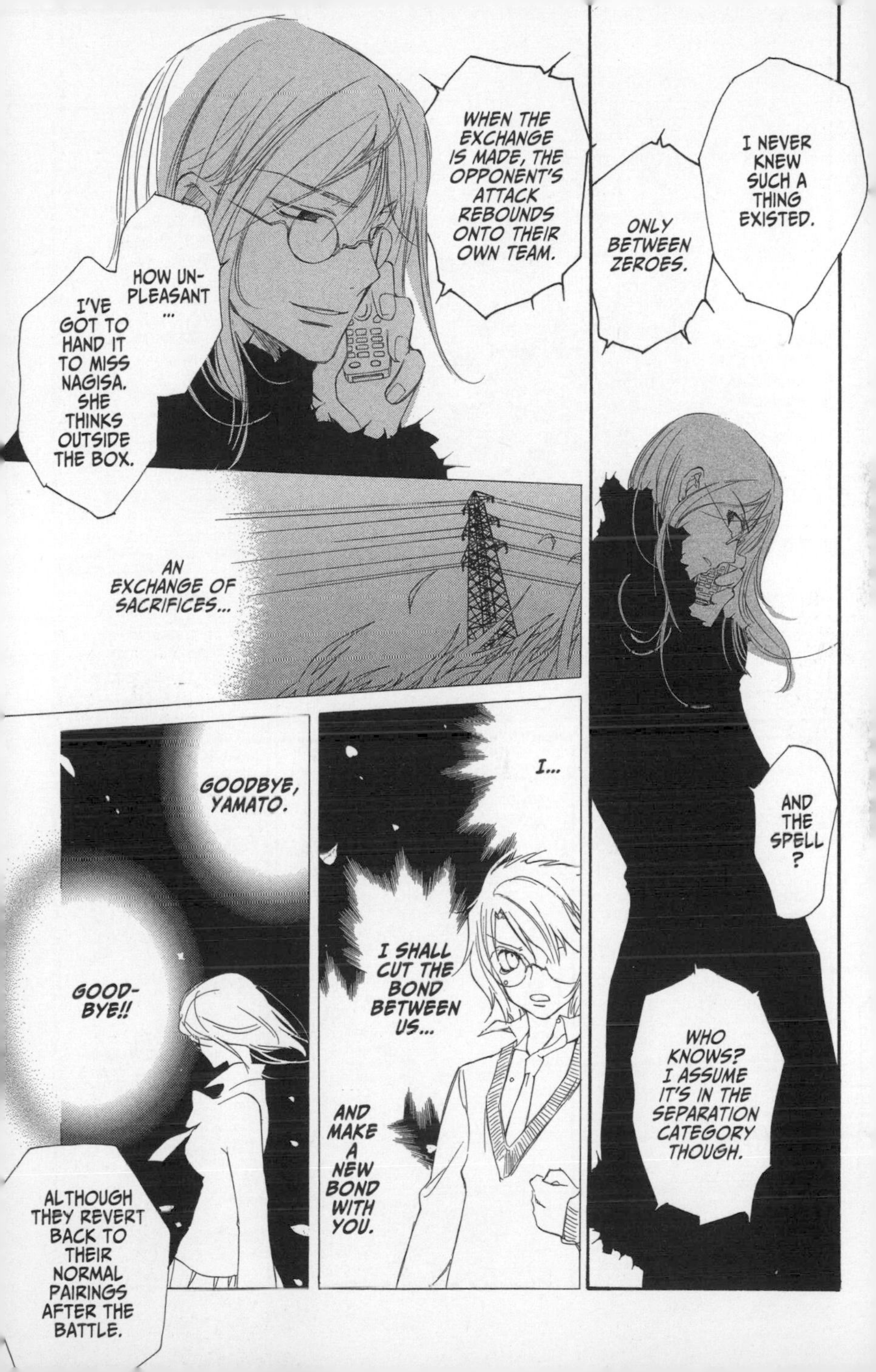
I NEVER KNEW SUCH A THING EXISTED.
ONLY BETWEEN ZEROES.
AND THE SPELL?
WHO KNOWS? I ASSUME IT'S IN THE SEPARATION CATEGORY THOUGH.
WHEN THE EXCHANGE IS MADE, THE OPPONENT'S ATTACK REBOUNDS ONTO THEIR OWN TEAM.
HOW UN-PLEASANT ...
I'VE GOT TO HAND IT TO MISS NAGISA. SHE THINKS OUTSIDE THE BOX.
AN EXCHANGE OF SACRIFICES...
I...
I SHALL CUT THE BOND BETWEEN US...
AND MAKE A NEW BOND WITH YOU.
GOODBYE, YAMATO.
GOOD-BYE!!
ALTHOUGH THEY REVERT BACK TO THEIR NORMAL PAIRINGS AFTER THE BATTLE.

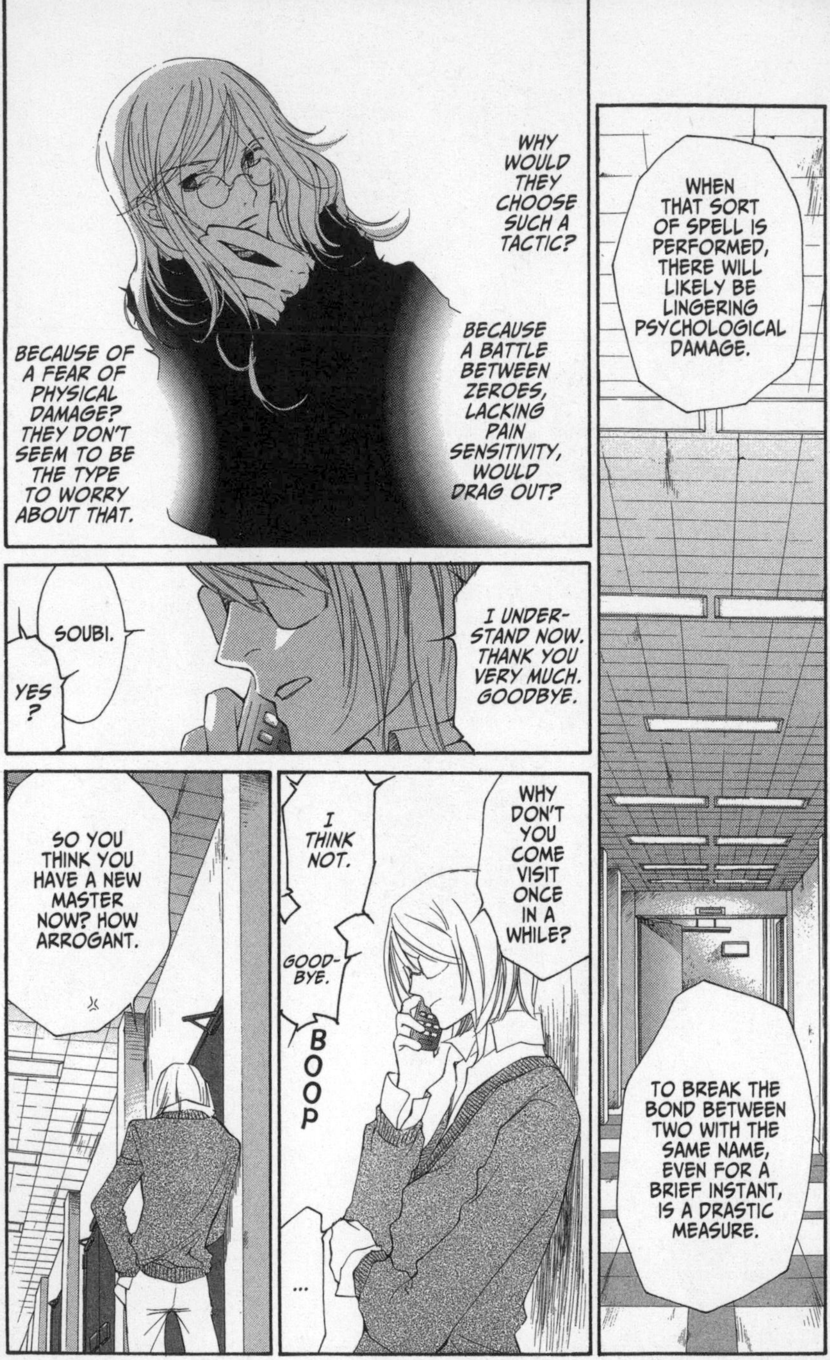
WHEN THAT SORT OF SPELL IS PERFORMED, THERE WILL LIKELY BE LINGERING PSYCHOLOGICAL DAMAGE.
TO BREAK THE BOND BETWEEN TWO WITH THE SAME NAME, EVEN FOR A BRIEF INSTANT, IS A DRASTIC MEASURE.
WHY WOULD THEY CHOOSE SUCH A TACTIC?
BECAUSE A BATTLE BETWEEN ZEROES, LACKING PAIN SENSITIVITY, WOULD DRAG OUT?
BECAUSE OF A FEAR OF PHYSICAL DAMAGE? THEY DON'T SEEM TO BE THE TYPE TO WORRY ABOUT THAT.
I UNDER-STAND NOW. THANK YOU VERY MUCH. GOODBYE.
SOUBI.
YES?
WHY DON'T YOU COME VISIT ONCE IN A WHILE?
I THINK NOT.
GOOD-BYE.
BOOP
...
SO YOU THINK YOU HAVE A NEW MASTER NOW? HOW ARROGANT.

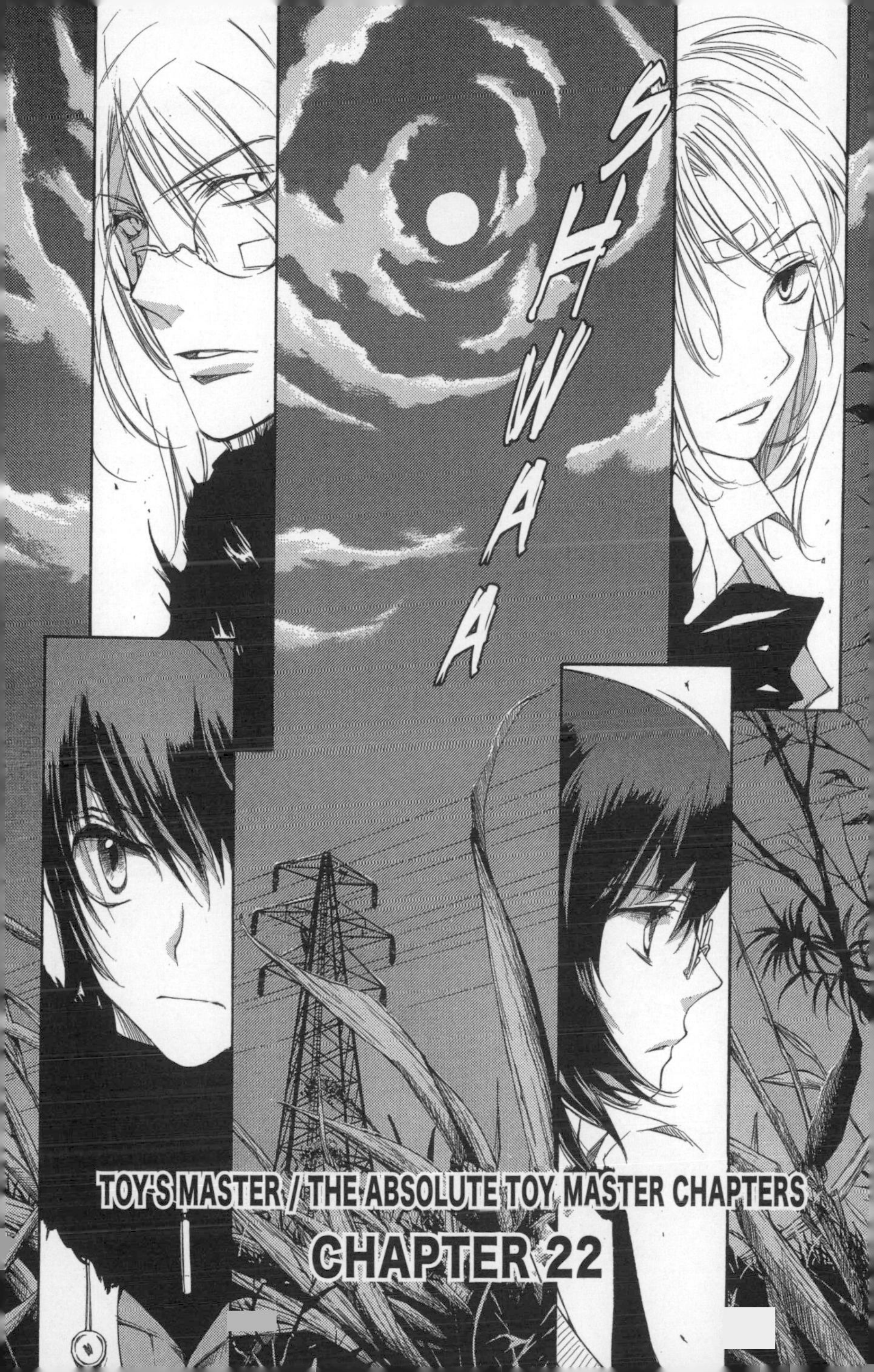
SHWAAA
TOY'S MASTER / THE ABSOLUTE TOY MASTER CHAPTERS
CHAPTER 22

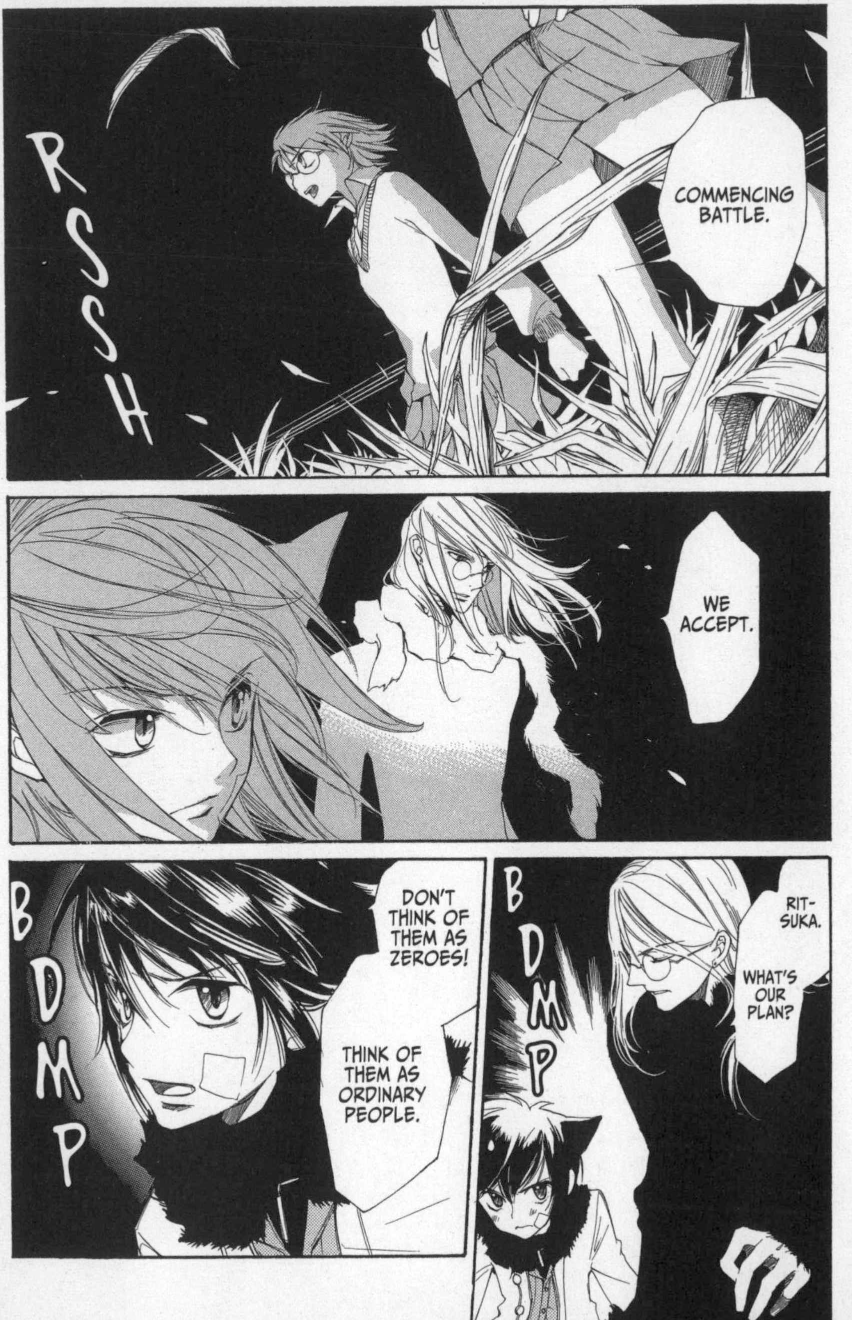
COMMENCING BATTLE.
RSSH
WE ACCEPT.
RIT-SUKA.
WHAT'S OUR PLAN?
BDMP
DON'T THINK OF THEM AS ZEROES!
THINK OF THEM AS ORDINARY PEOPLE.
BDMP

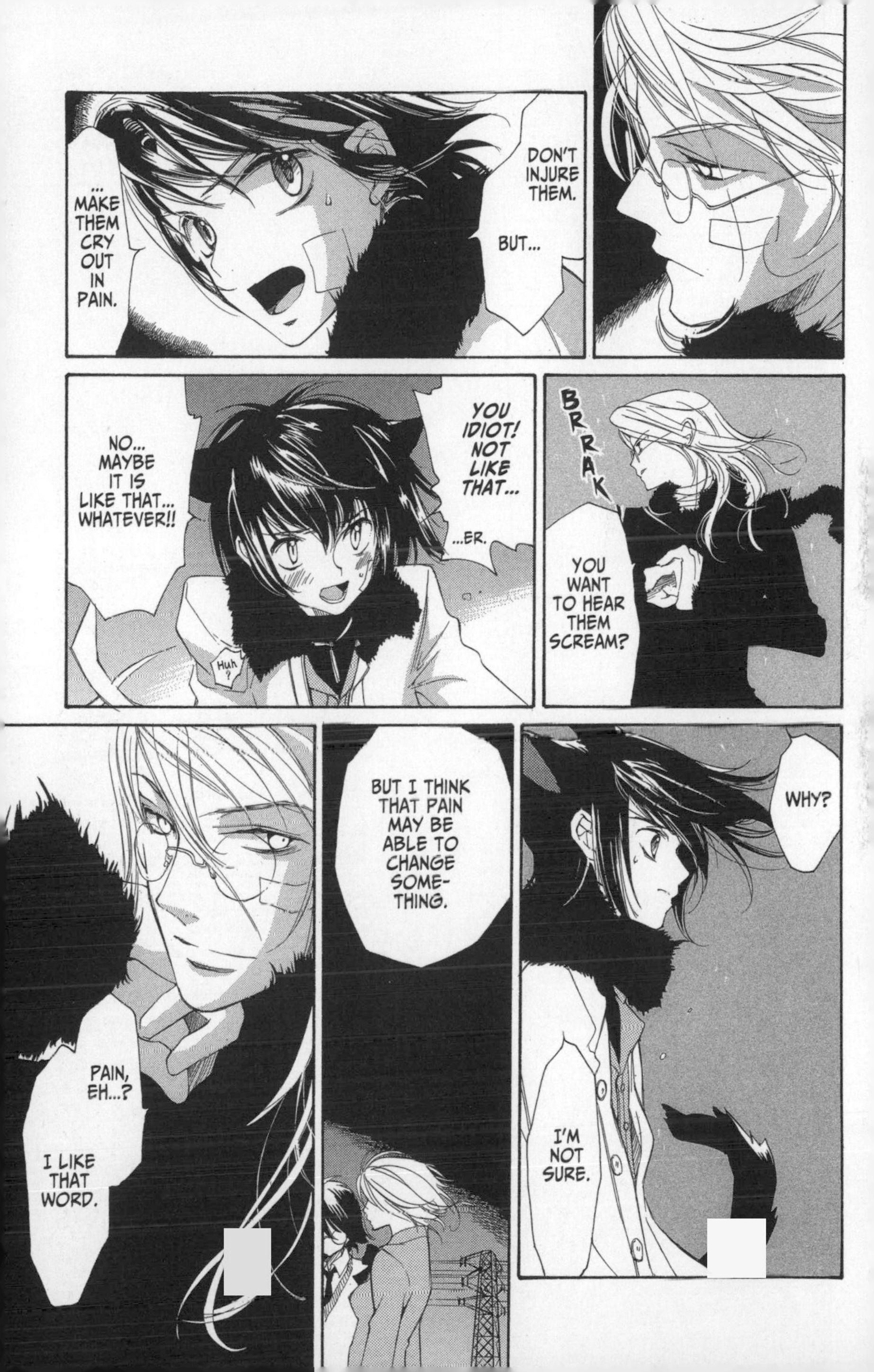
DON'T INJURE THEM.
BUT...
...MAKE THEM CRY OUT IN PAIN.
BRRAK
YOU WANT TO HEAR THEM SCREAM?
YOU IDIOT! NOT LIKE THAT...
...ER.
NO... MAYBE IT IS LIKE THAT... WHATEVER!!
Huh?
WHY?
I'M NOT SURE.
BUT I THINK THAT PAIN MAY BE ABLE TO CHANGE SOMETHING.
PAIN, EH...?
I LIKE THAT WORD.

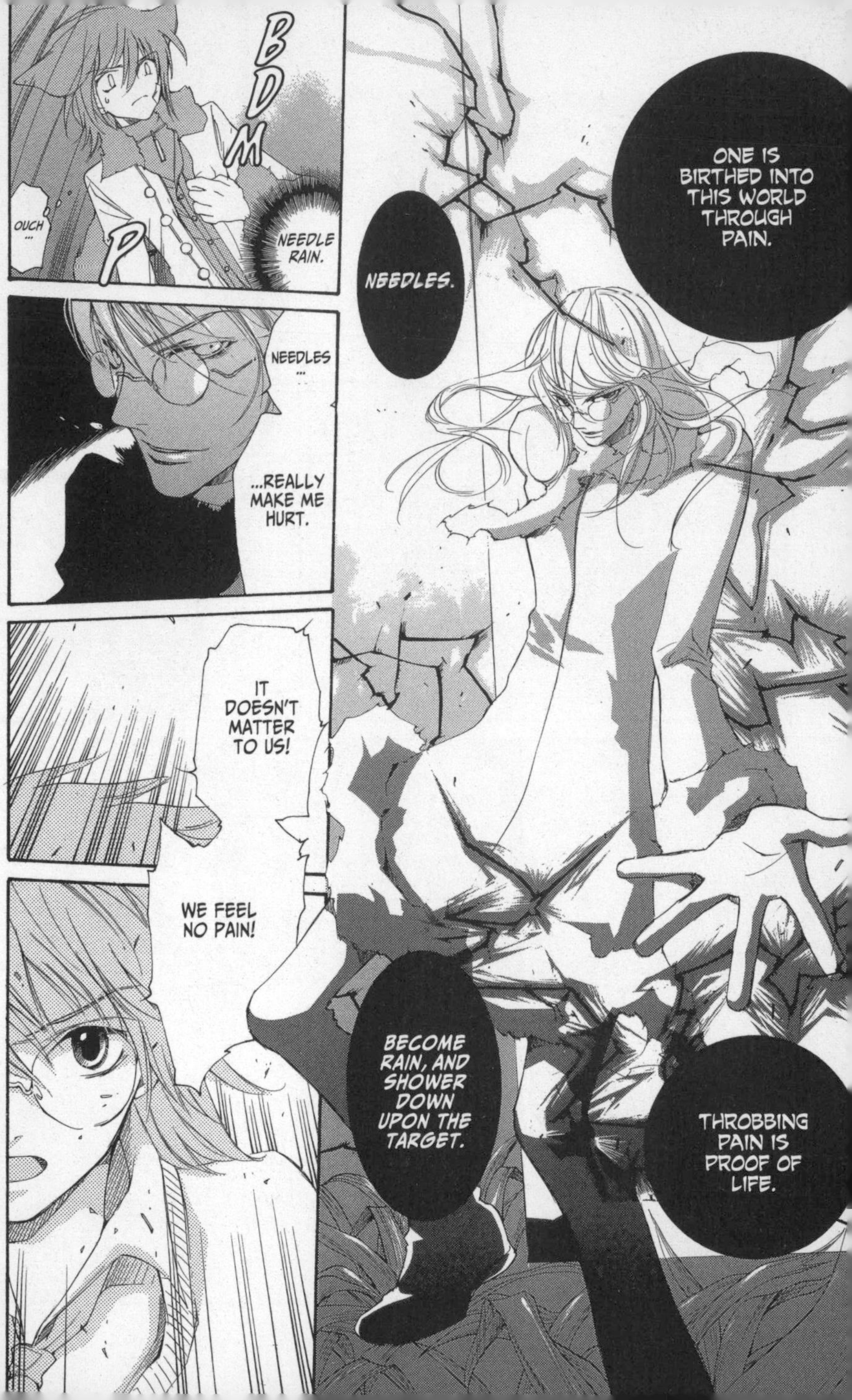
ONE IS BIRTHED INTO THIS WORLD THROUGH PAIN.
NEEDLES.
THROBBING PAIN IS PROOF OF LIFE.
BECOME RAIN, AND SHOWER DOWN UPON THE TARGET.
BDMP
NEEDLE RAIN.
OUCH ...
NEEDLES ...
...REALLY MAKE ME HURT.
IT DOESN'T MATTER TO US!
WE FEEL NO PAIN!

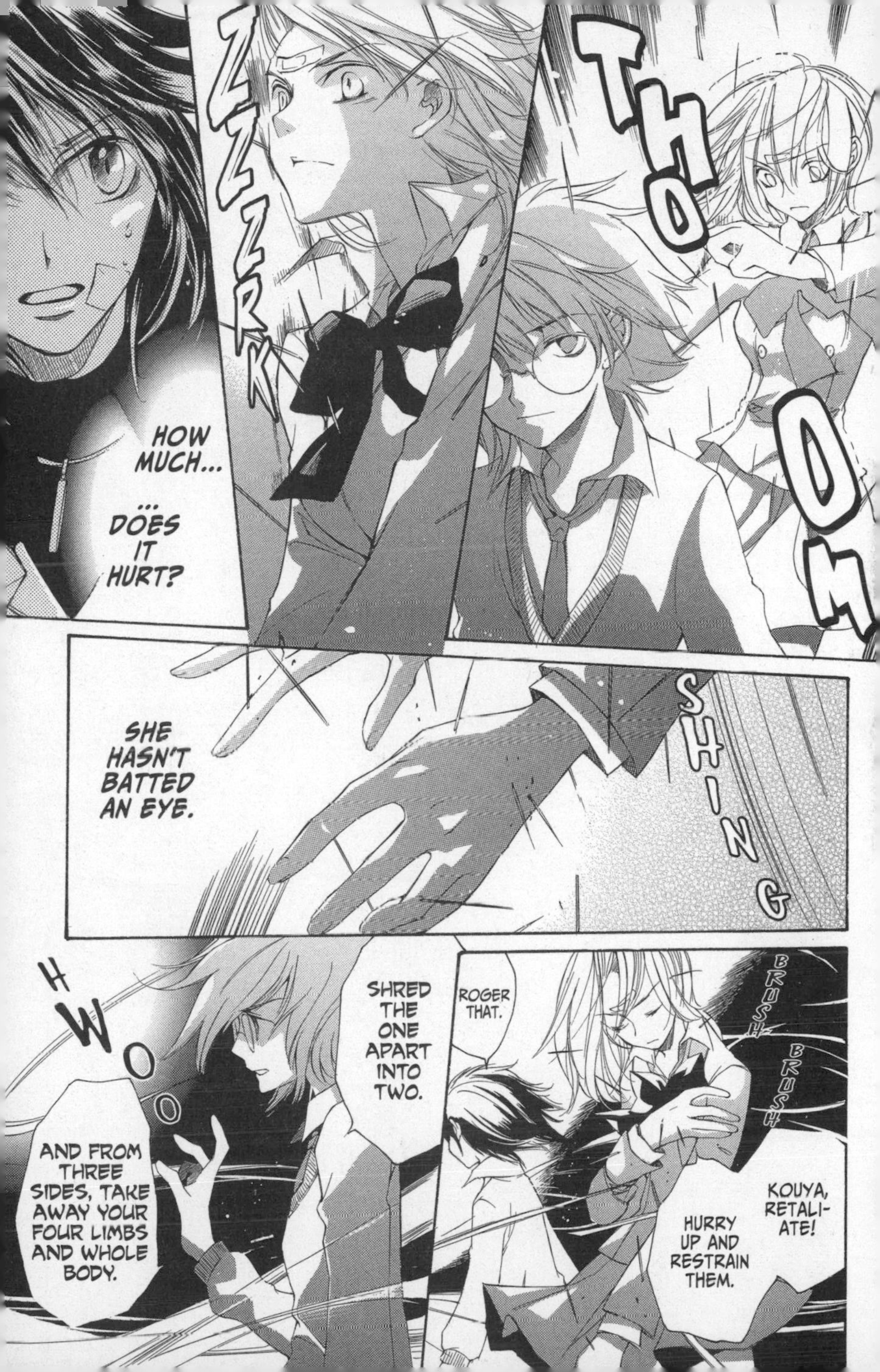
THOOM
ZZZZRK
HOW MUCH...
...DOES IT HURT?
SHING
SHE HASN'T BATTED AN EYE.
BRUSH BRUSH
KOUYA, RETALIATE!
HURRY UP AND RESTRAIN THEM.
ROGER THAT.
SHRED THE ONE APART INTO TWO.
HWOO
AND FROM THREE SIDES, TAKE AWAY YOUR FOUR LIMBS AND WHOLE BODY.

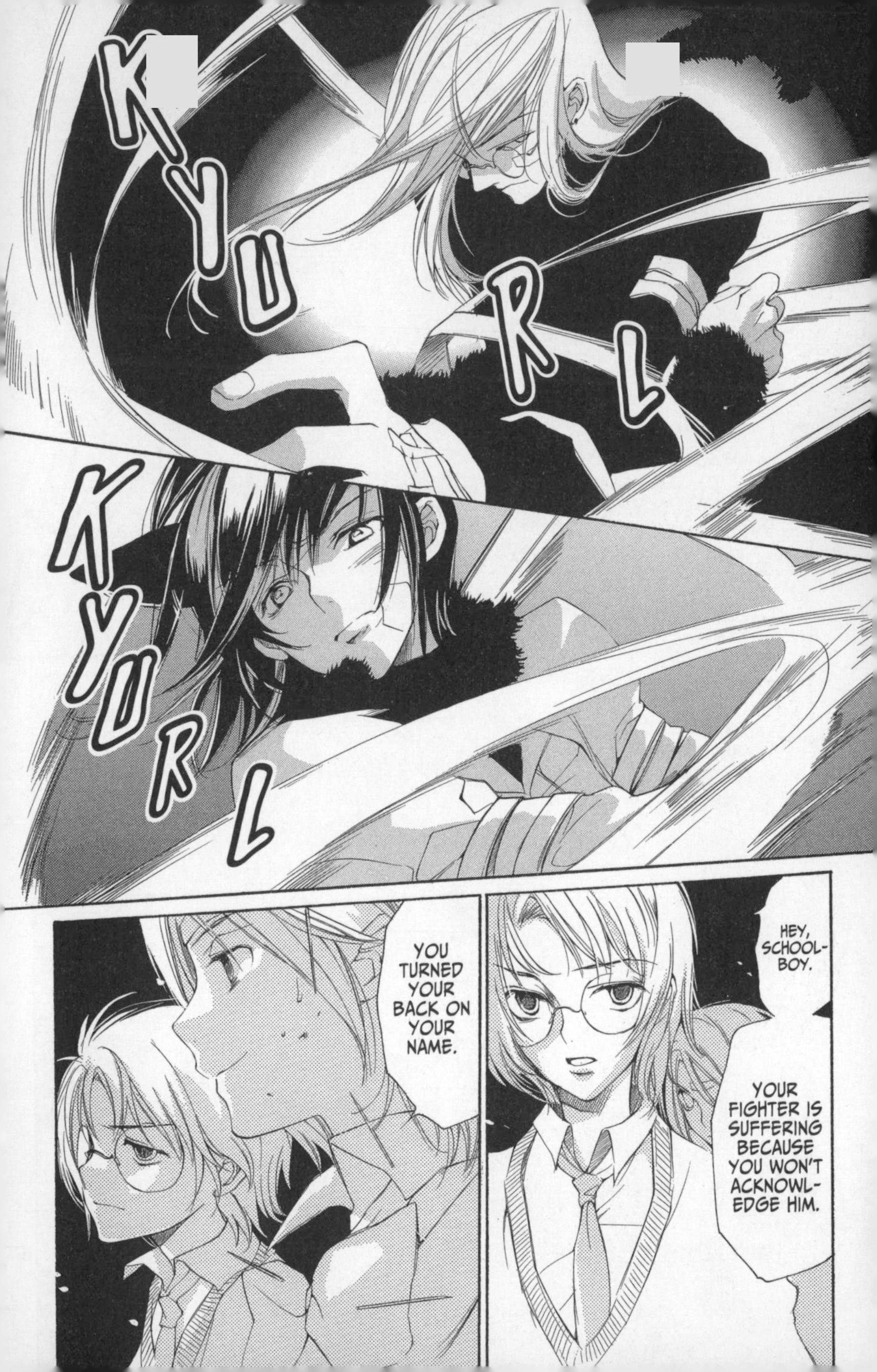
KYURL
KYURL
HEY, SCHOOL-BOY.
YOUR FIGHTER IS SUFFERING BECAUSE YOU WON'T ACKNOWL-EDGE HIM.
YOU TURNED YOUR BACK ON YOUR NAME.

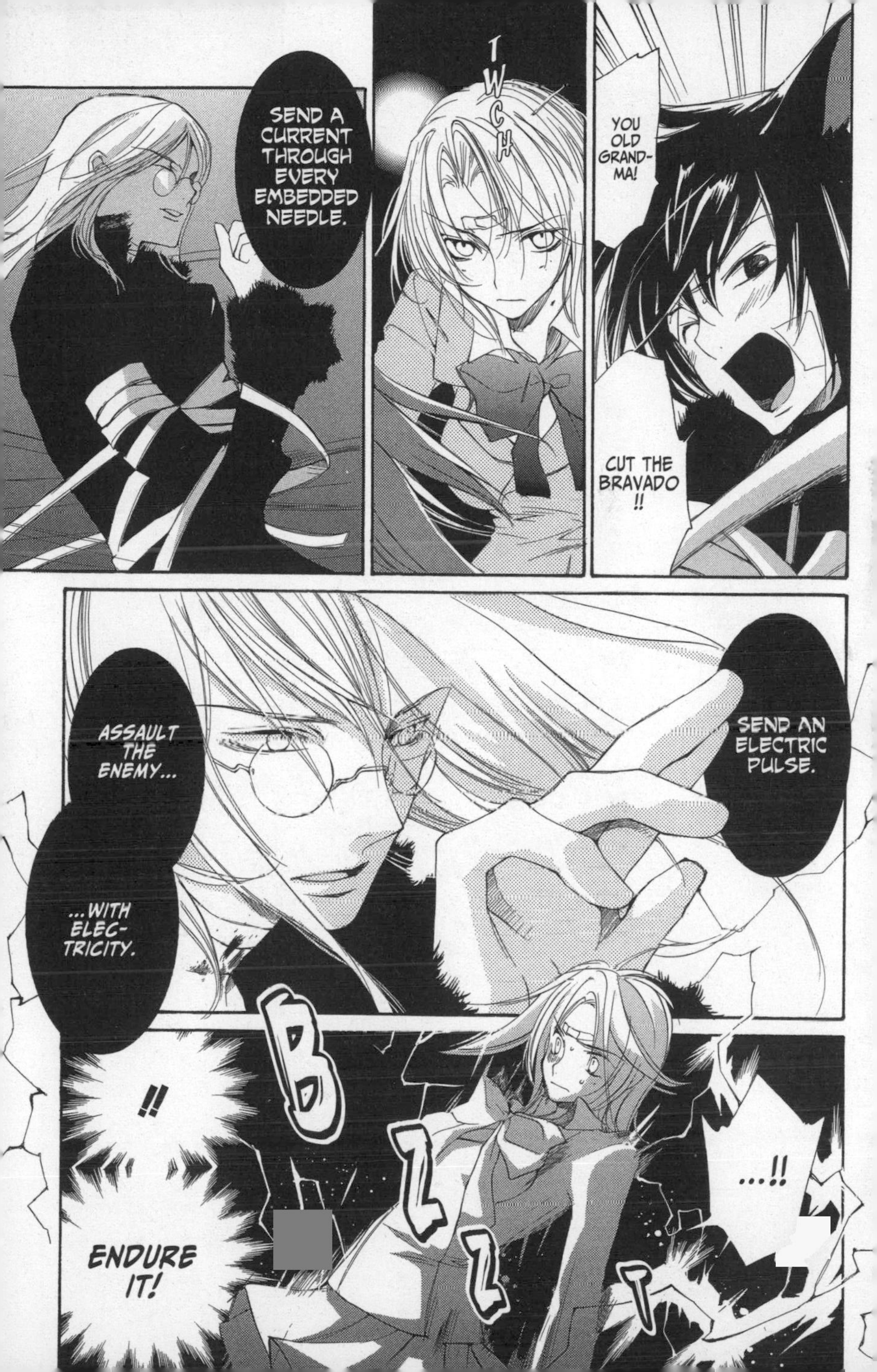
YOU OLD GRAND-MA!
CUT THE BRAVADO !!
TWCH
SEND A CURRENT THROUGH EVERY EMBEDDED NEEDLE.
SEND AN ELECTRIC PULSE.
ASSAULT THE ENEMY...
...WITH ELEC-TRICITY.
...!!
BZZZT
!!
ENDURE IT!

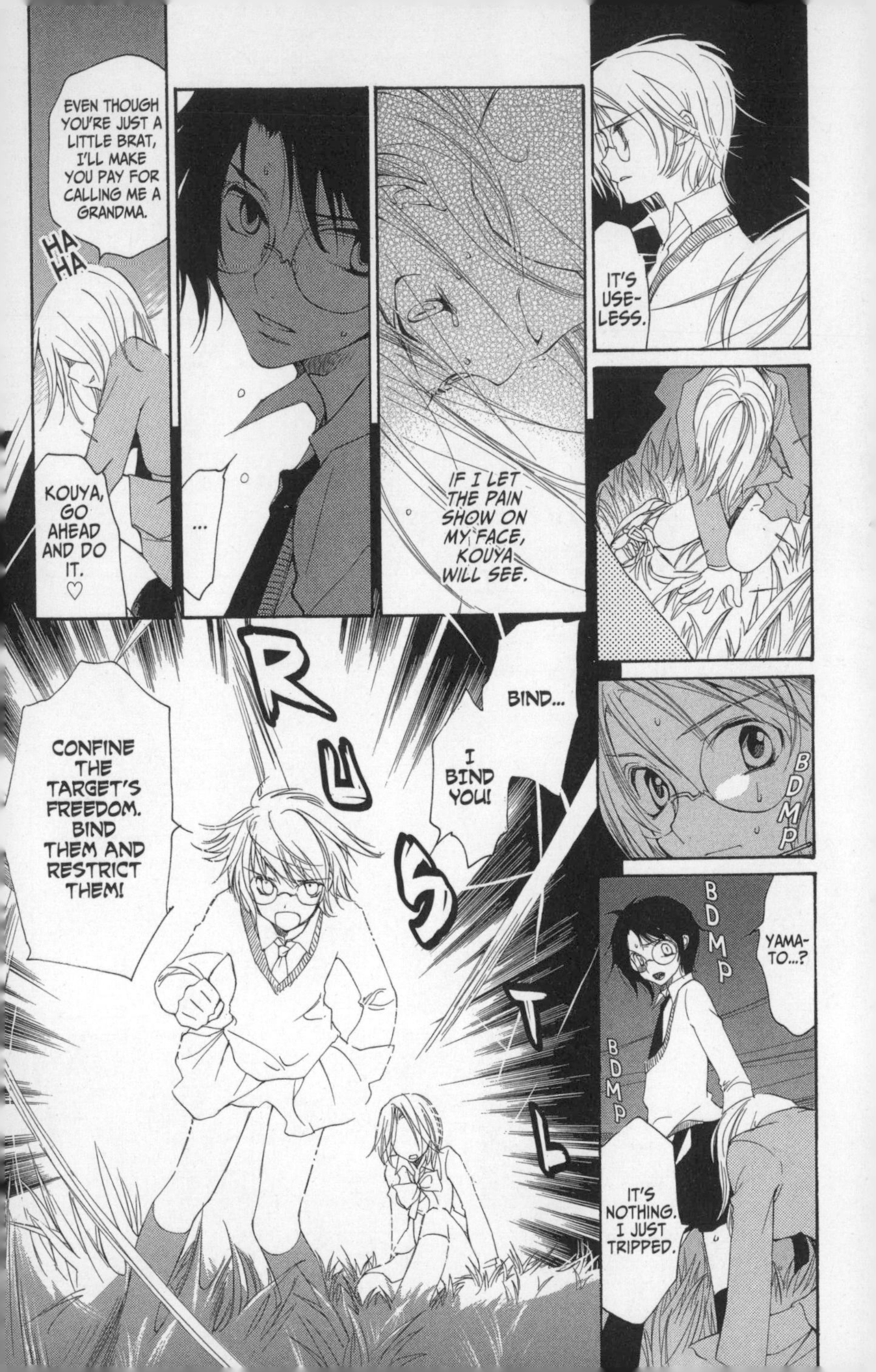
IT'S USELESS.
IF I LET THE PAIN SHOW ON MY FACE, KOUYA WILL SEE.
...
EVEN THOUGH YOU'RE JUST A LITTLE BRAT, I'LL MAKE YOU PAY FOR CALLING ME A GRANDMA.
HA HA
KOUYA, GO AHEAD AND DO IT. ♡
BIND...
I BIND YOU!
RUSTL
CONFINE THE TARGET'S FREEDOM. BIND THEM AND RESTRICT THEM!
BDMP
BDMP
YAMATO...?
BDMP
IT'S NOTHING. I JUST TRIPPED.

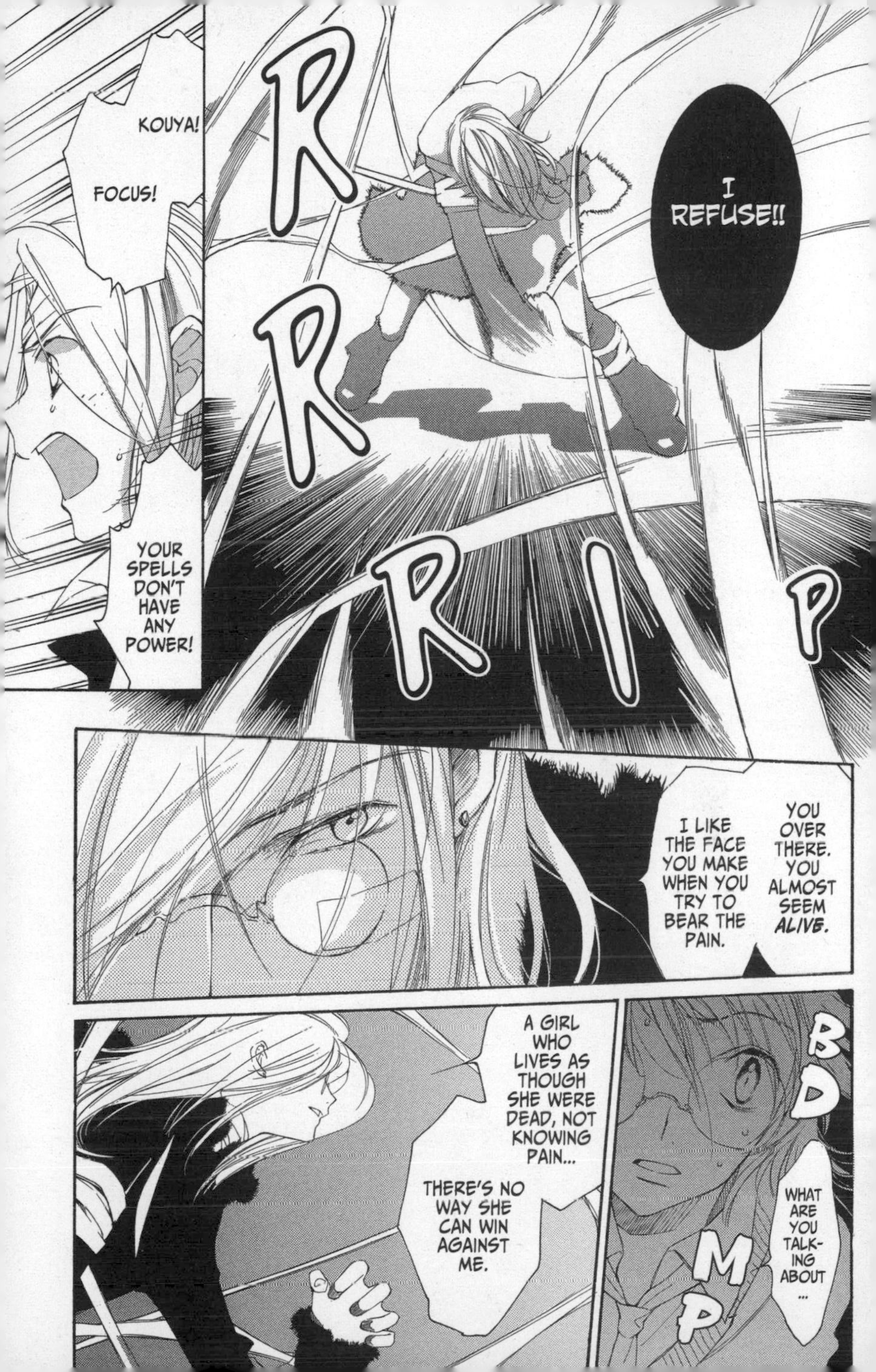
I REFUSE!!
RRRIP
KOUYA!
FOCUS!
YOUR SPELLS DON'T HAVE ANY POWER!
YOU OVER THERE. YOU ALMOST SEEM *ALIVE*.
I LIKE THE FACE YOU MAKE WHEN YOU TRY TO BEAR THE PAIN.
BDMP
WHAT ARE YOU TALKING ABOUT...
A GIRL WHO LIVES AS THOUGH SHE WERE DEAD, NOT KNOWING PAIN...
THERE'S NO WAY SHE CAN WIN AGAINST ME.

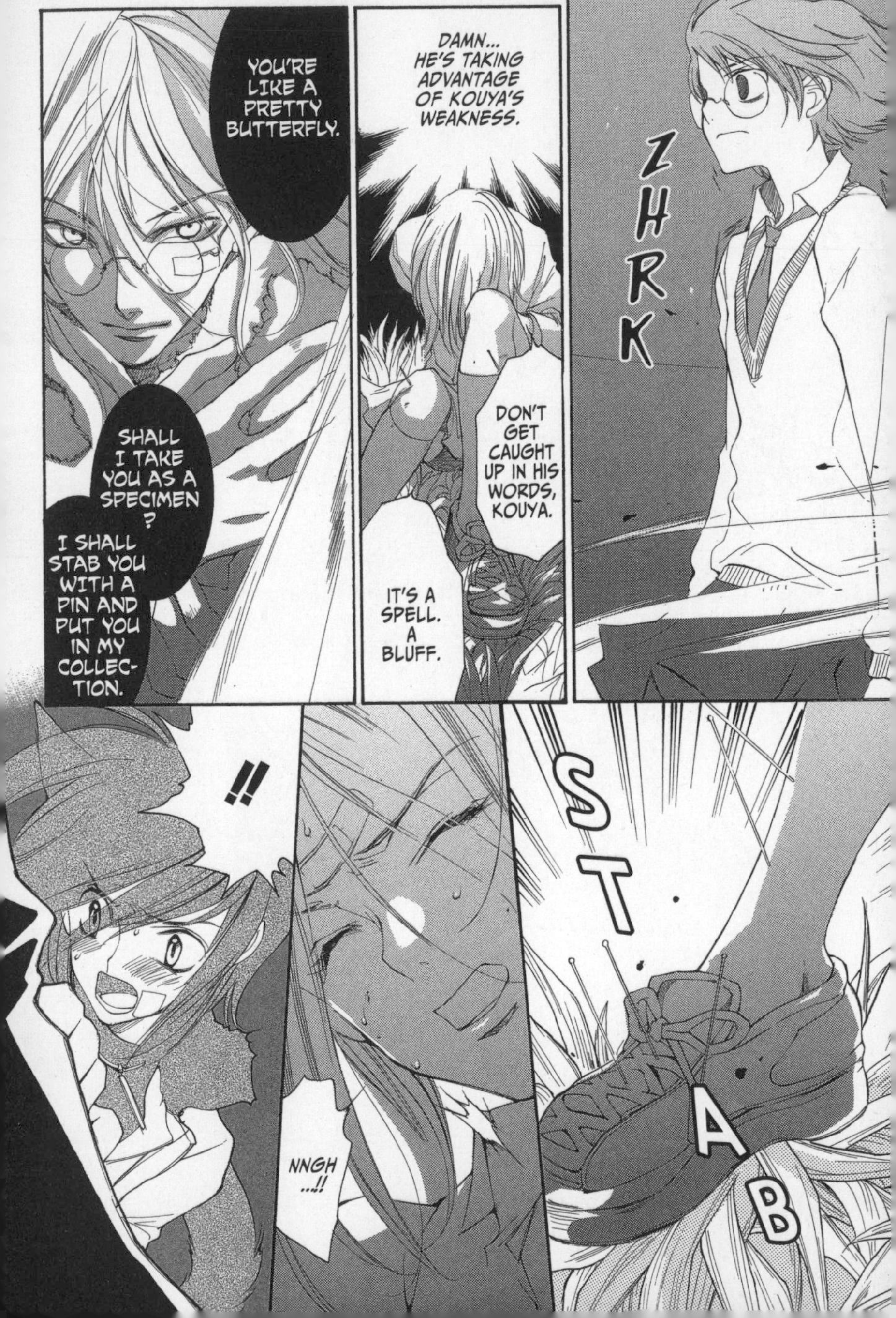
ZHRK
DAMN... HE'S TAKING ADVANTAGE OF KOUYA'S WEAKNESS.
DON'T GET CAUGHT UP IN HIS WORDS, KOUYA.
IT'S A SPELL. A BLUFF.
YOU'RE LIKE A PRETTY BUTTERFLY.
SHALL I TAKE YOU AS A SPECIMEN?
I SHALL STAB YOU WITH A PIN AND PUT YOU IN MY COLLECTION.
STAB
NNGH ...!!
!!

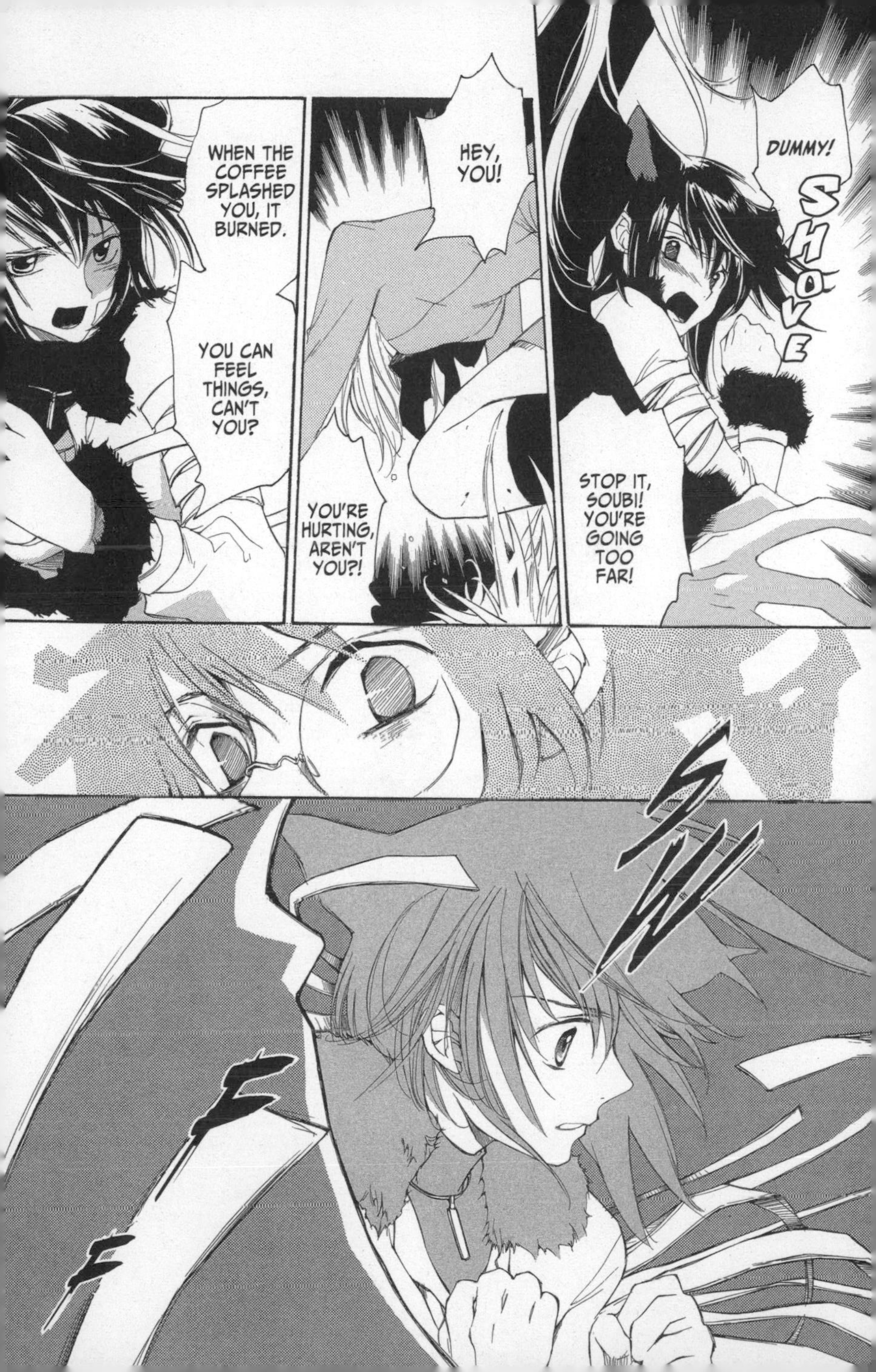
DUMMY!
SHOVE
STOP IT, SOUBI! YOU'RE GOING TOO FAR!
HEY, YOU!
YOU'RE HURTING, AREN'T YOU?!
WHEN THE COFFEE SPLASHED YOU, IT BURNED.
YOU CAN FEEL THINGS, CAN'T YOU?

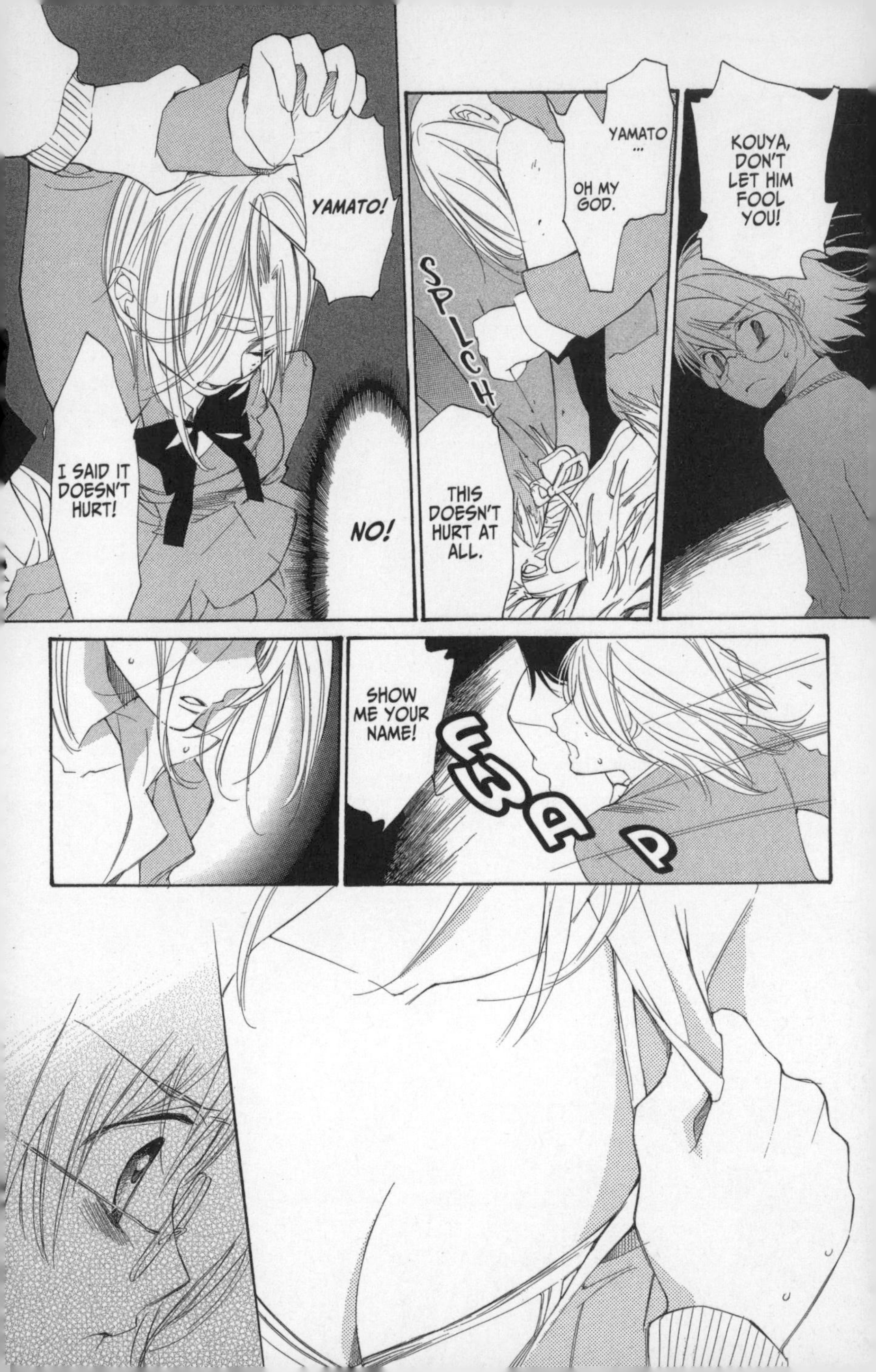

KOUYA, DON'T LET HIM FOOL YOU!
YAMATO ...
OH MY GOD.
SPLICH
THIS DOESN'T HURT AT ALL.
YAMATO!
NO!
I SAID IT DOESN'T HURT!
SHOW ME YOUR NAME!
WHAP

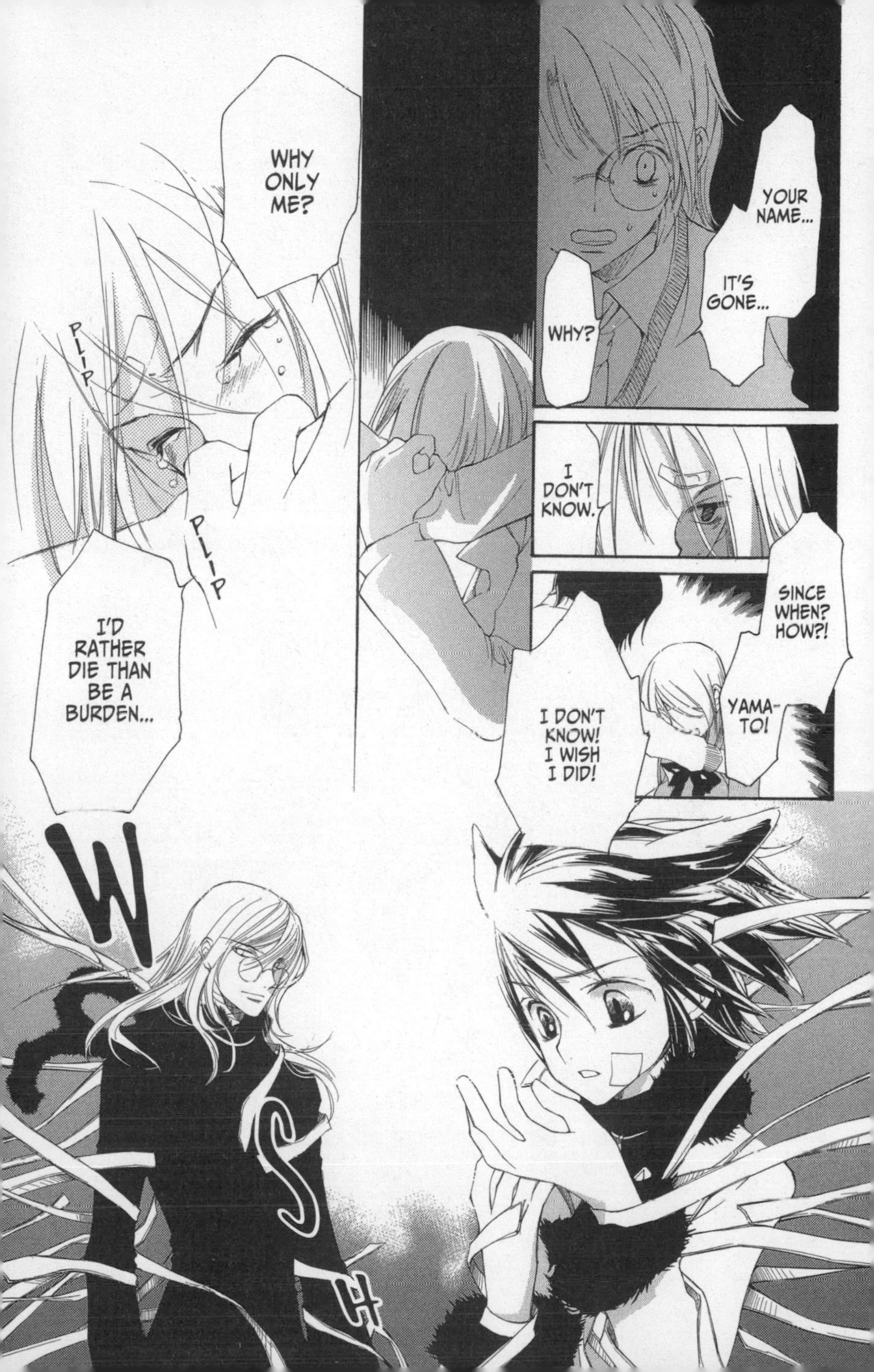
YOUR NAME...
IT'S GONE...
WHY?
I DON'T KNOW.
SINCE WHEN? HOW?!
YAMA-TO!
I DON'T KNOW! I WISH I DID!
WHY ONLY ME?
PLIP
PLIP
I'D RATHER DIE THAN BE A BURDEN...

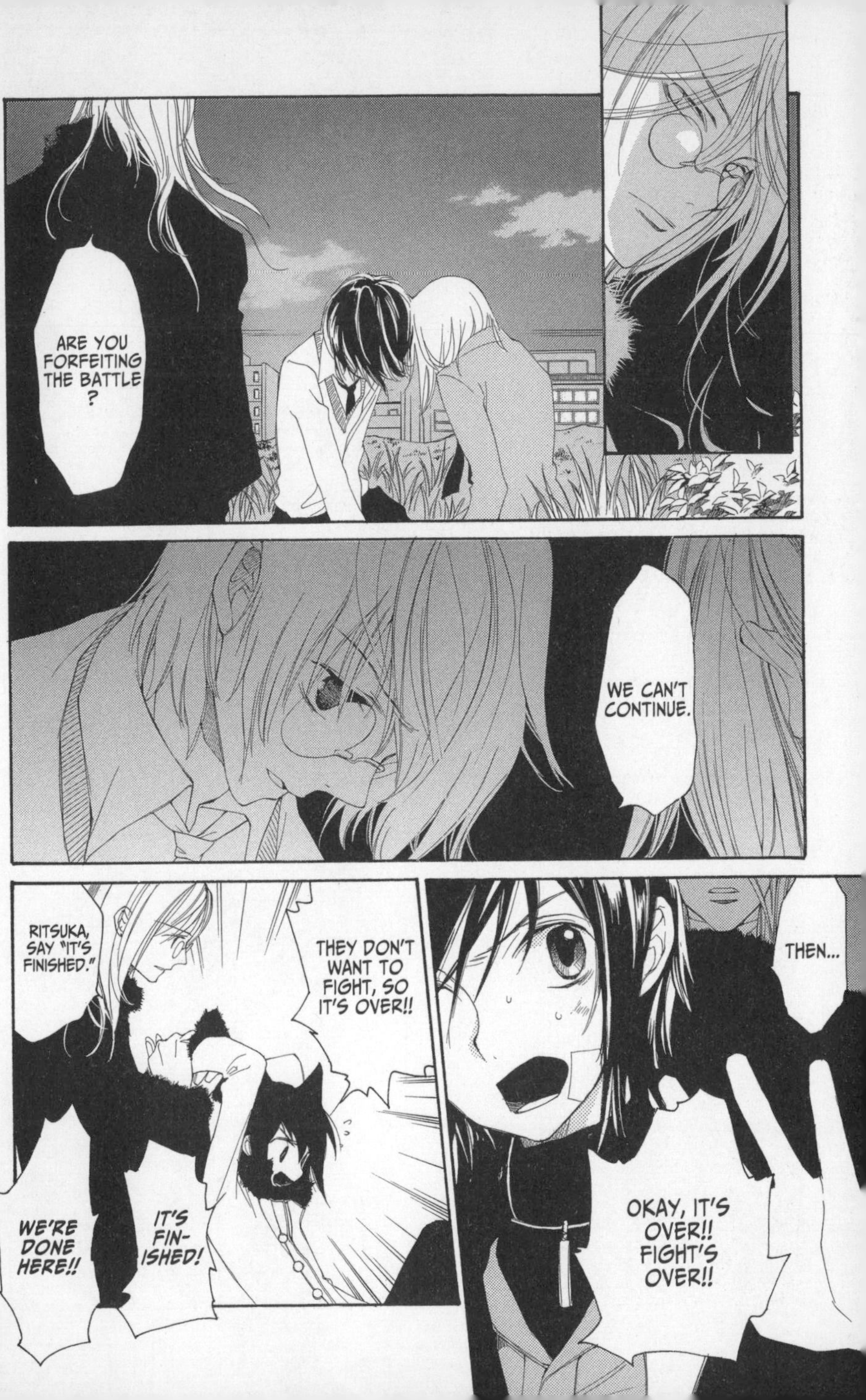
ARE YOU FORFEITING THE BATTLE?
WE CAN'T CONTINUE.
THEN...
OKAY, IT'S OVER!! FIGHT'S OVER!!
THEY DON'T WANT TO FIGHT, SO IT'S OVER!!
RITSUKA, SAY "IT'S FINISHED."
IT'S FIN-ISHED!
WE'RE DONE HERE!!

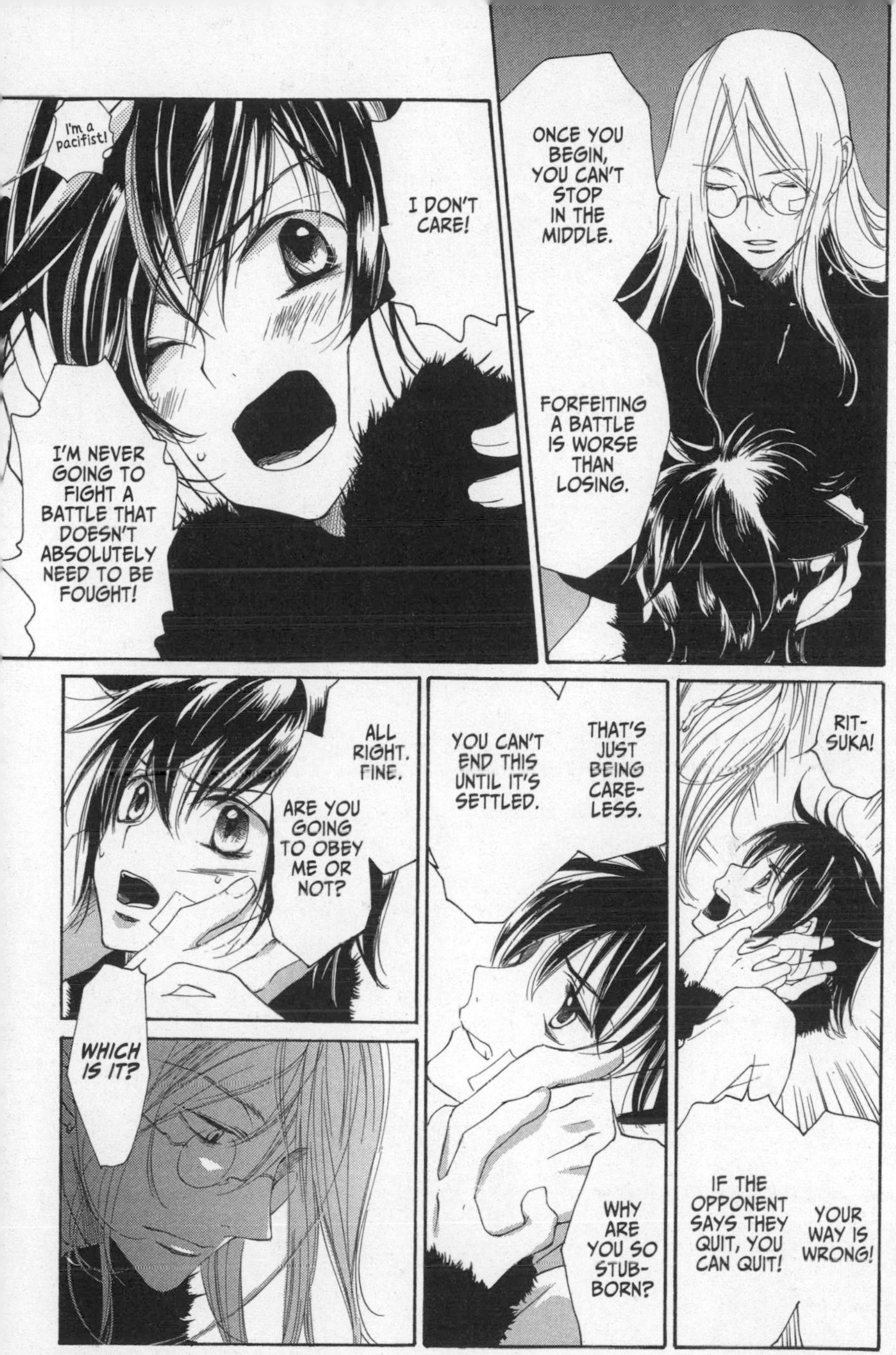
ONCE YOU BEGIN, YOU CAN'T STOP IN THE MIDDLE.
FORFEITING A BATTLE IS WORSE THAN LOSING.
I DON'T CARE!
I'm a pacifist!
I'M NEVER GOING TO FIGHT A BATTLE THAT DOESN'T ABSOLUTELY NEED TO BE FOUGHT!
RIT-SUKA!
YOUR WAY IS WRONG!
IF THE OPPONENT SAYS THEY QUIT, YOU CAN QUIT!
THAT'S JUST BEING CARE-LESS.
YOU CAN'T END THIS UNTIL IT'S SETTLED.
WHY ARE YOU SO STUB-BORN?
ALL RIGHT. FINE.
ARE YOU GOING TO OBEY ME OR NOT?
WHICH IS IT?

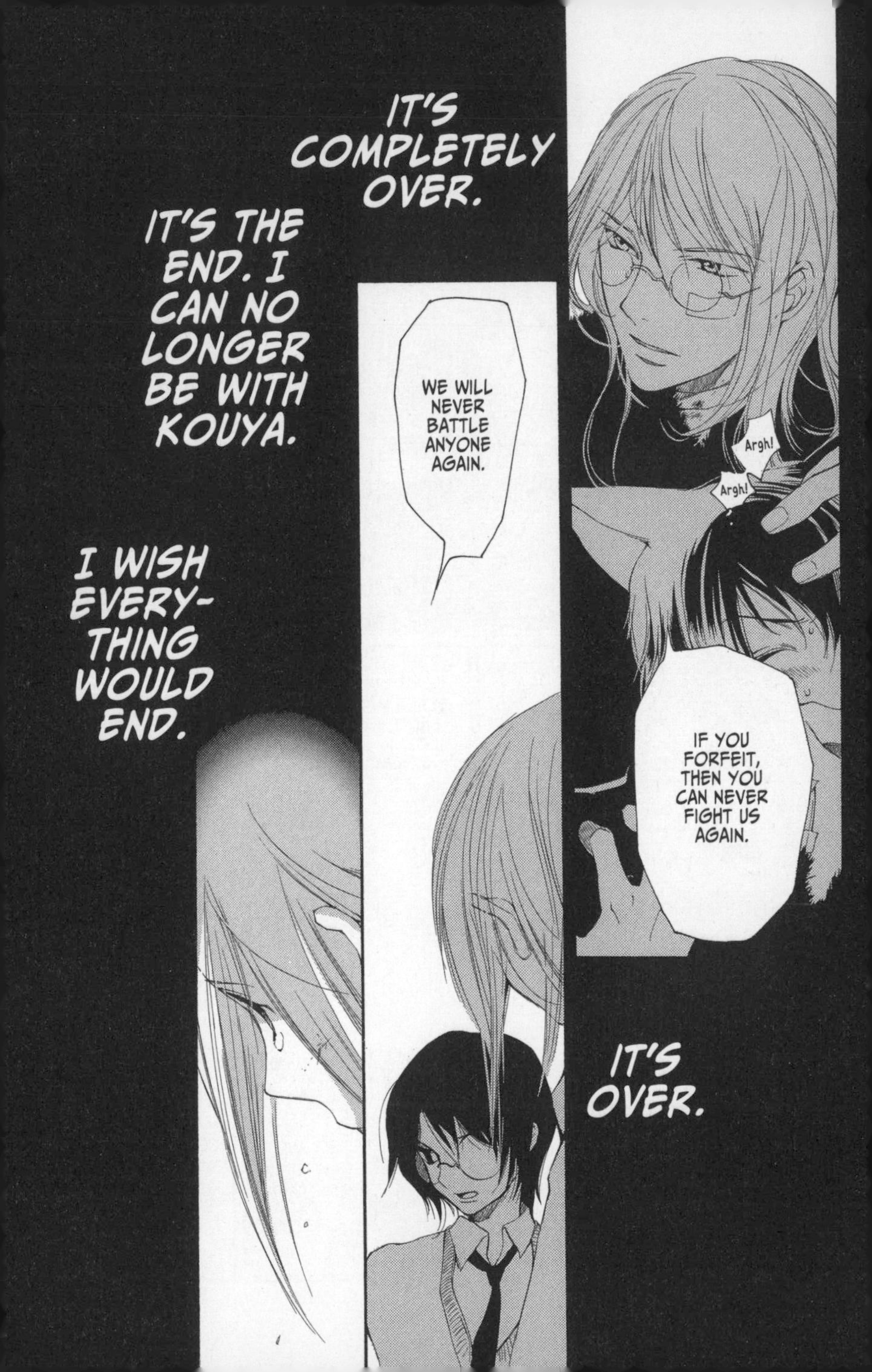
IT'S COMPLETELY OVER.
Argh!
Argh!
IF YOU FORFEIT, THEN YOU CAN NEVER FIGHT US AGAIN.
WE WILL NEVER BATTLE ANYONE AGAIN.
IT'S THE END. I CAN NO LONGER BE WITH KOUYA.
I WISH EVERY-THING WOULD END.
IT'S OVER.

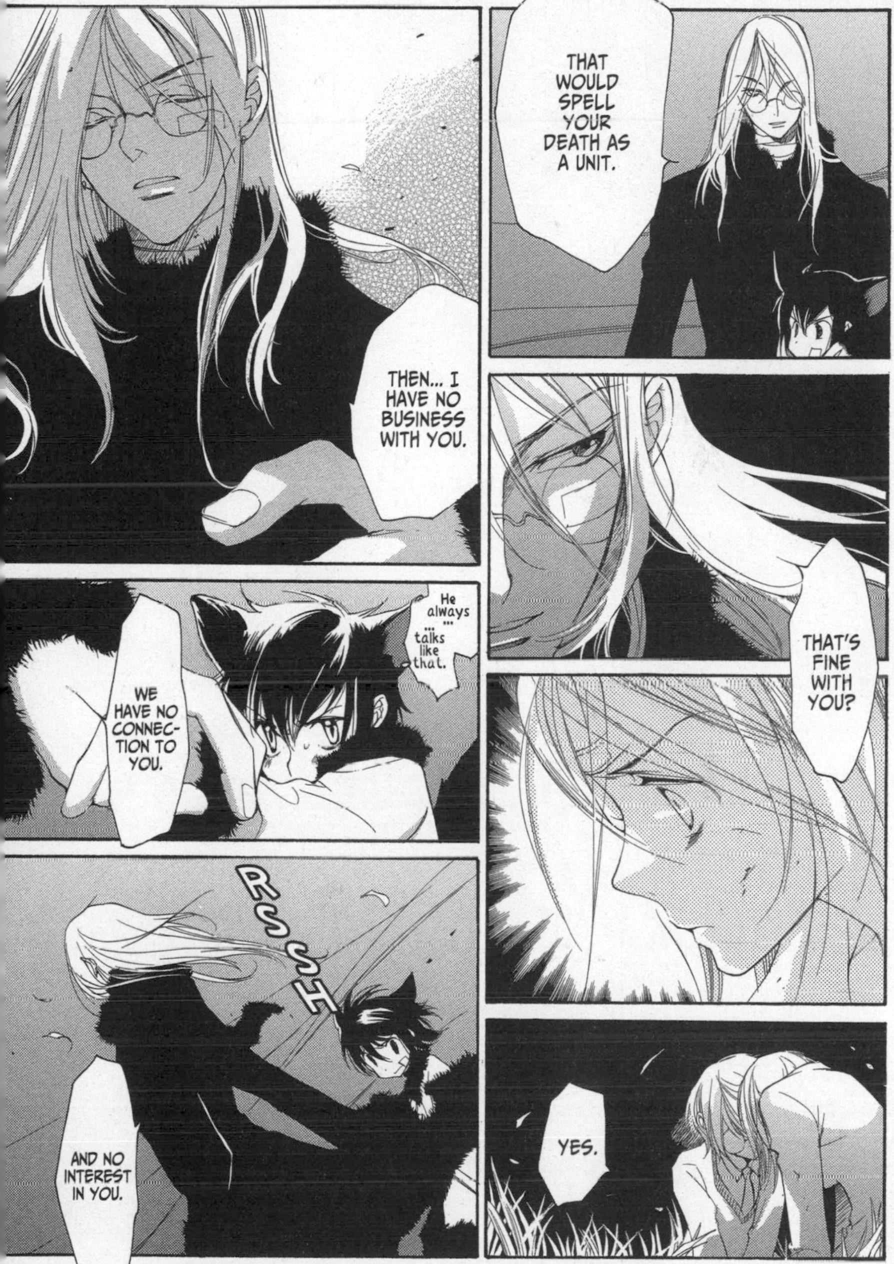
THAT WOULD SPELL YOUR DEATH AS A UNIT.
THEN... I HAVE NO BUSINESS WITH YOU.
WE HAVE NO CONNECTION TO YOU.
He always ... ... talks like that.
RSSH
AND NO INTEREST IN YOU.
THAT'S FINE WITH YOU?
YES.

NO NAME...

KOUYA, I'M SORRY...

WITH THAT GONE, YOU'RE NO LONGER A ZERO.

I TRIED EVERYTHING, BUT COULDN'T STOP MY NAME FROM DISAPPEARING.

...

KISS

IT'S OVER.

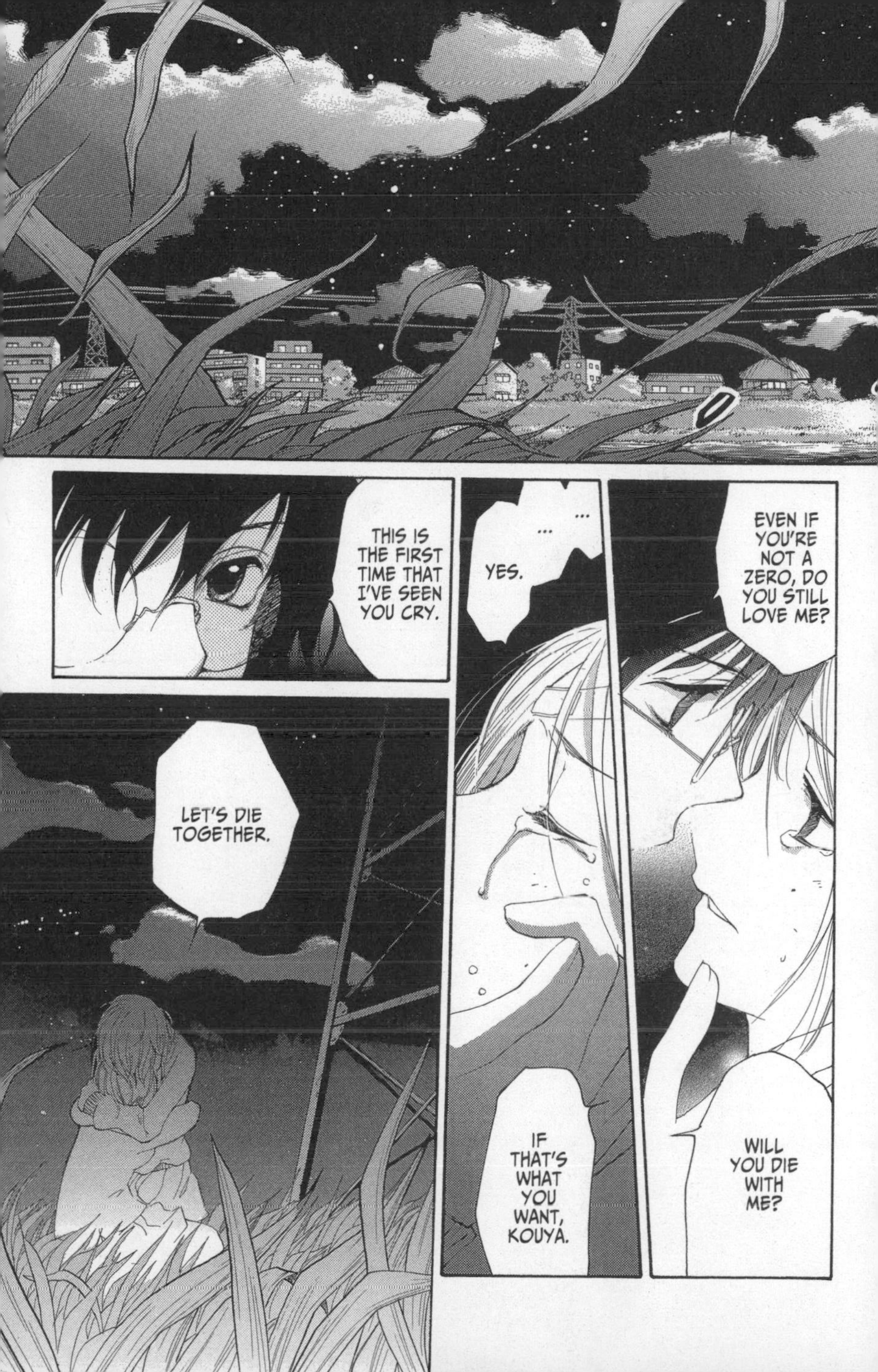
EVEN IF YOU'RE NOT A ZERO, DO YOU STILL LOVE ME?
WILL YOU DIE WITH ME?
... ... YES.
IF THAT'S WHAT YOU WANT, KOUYA.
THIS IS THE FIRST TIME THAT I'VE SEEN YOU CRY.
LET'S DIE TOGETHER.

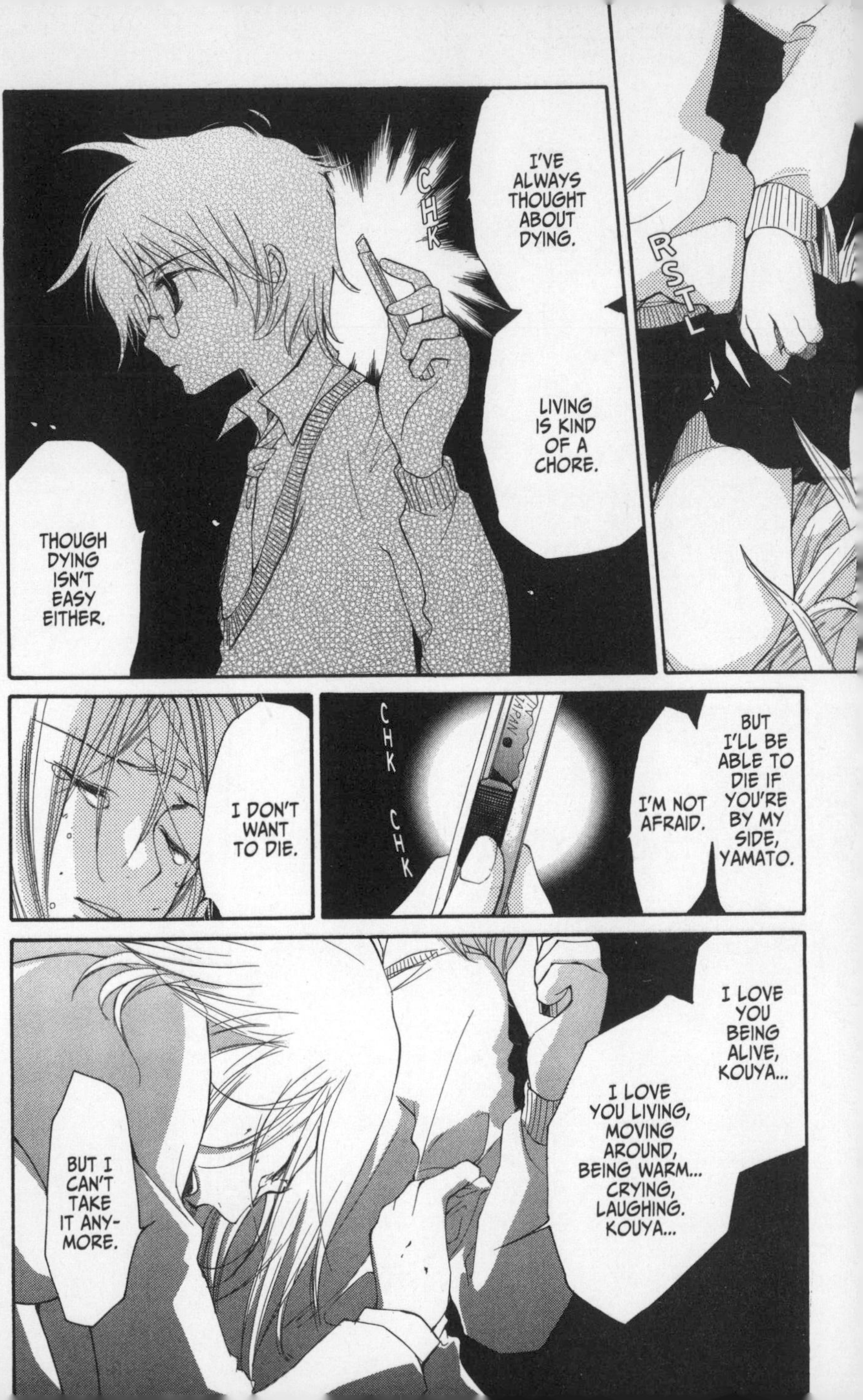
RSTL
I'VE ALWAYS THOUGHT ABOUT DYING.
CHK
LIVING IS KIND OF A CHORE.
THOUGH DYING ISN'T EASY EITHER.
BUT I'LL BE ABLE TO DIE IF YOU'RE BY MY SIDE, YAMATO.
I'M NOT AFRAID.
CHK CHK CHK
I DON'T WANT TO DIE.
I LOVE YOU BEING ALIVE, KOUYA...
I LOVE YOU LIVING, MOVING AROUND, BEING WARM... CRYING, LAUGHING. KOUYA...
BUT I CAN'T TAKE IT ANYMORE.

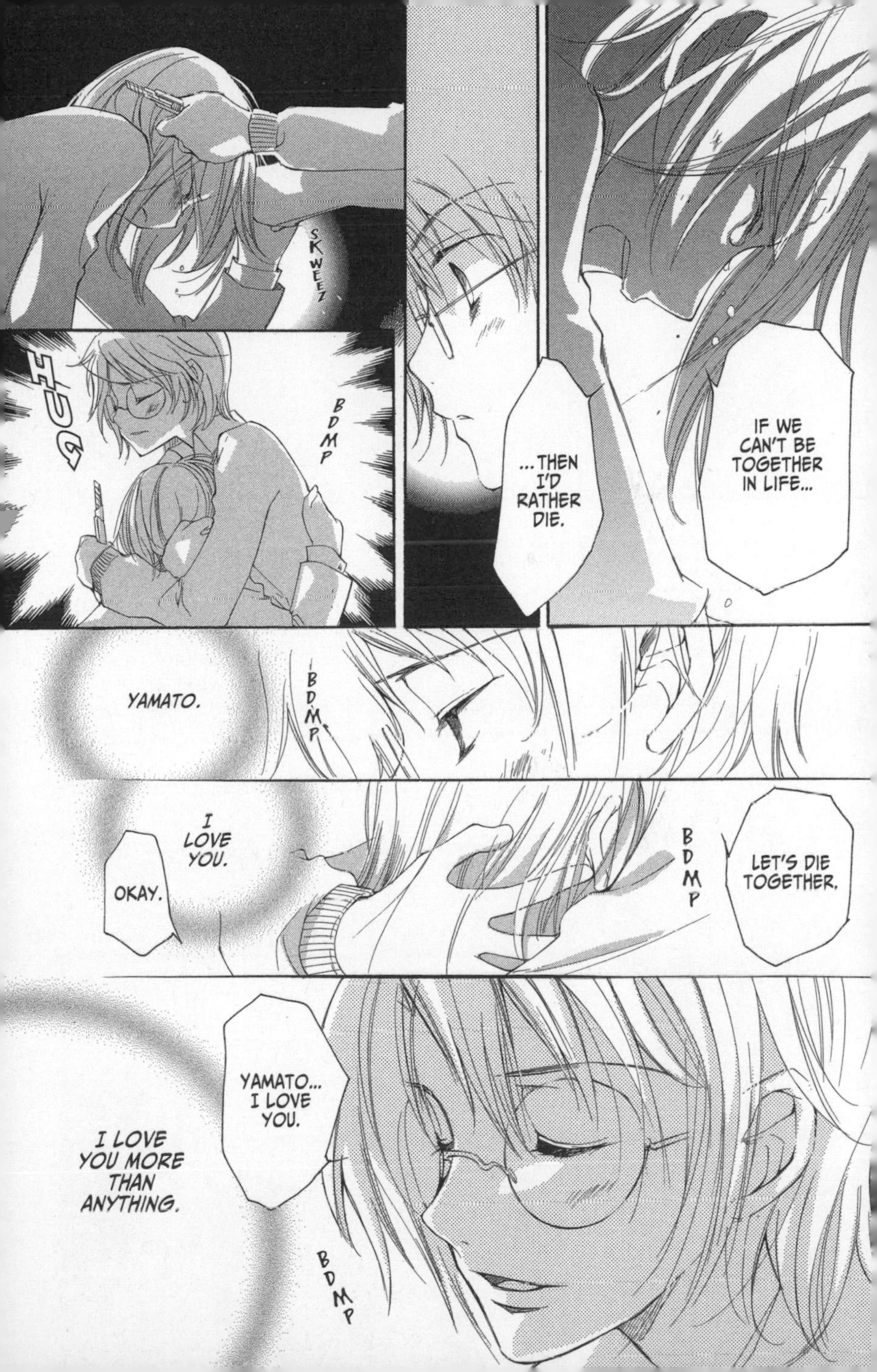
IF WE CAN'T BE TOGETHER IN LIFE...
...THEN I'D RATHER DIE.
SKWEEZ
BDMP
HUG
BDMP
YAMATO.
BDMP
LET'S DIE TOGETHER.
I LOVE YOU.
OKAY.
YAMATO... I LOVE YOU.
I LOVE YOU MORE THAN ANYTHING.
BDMP

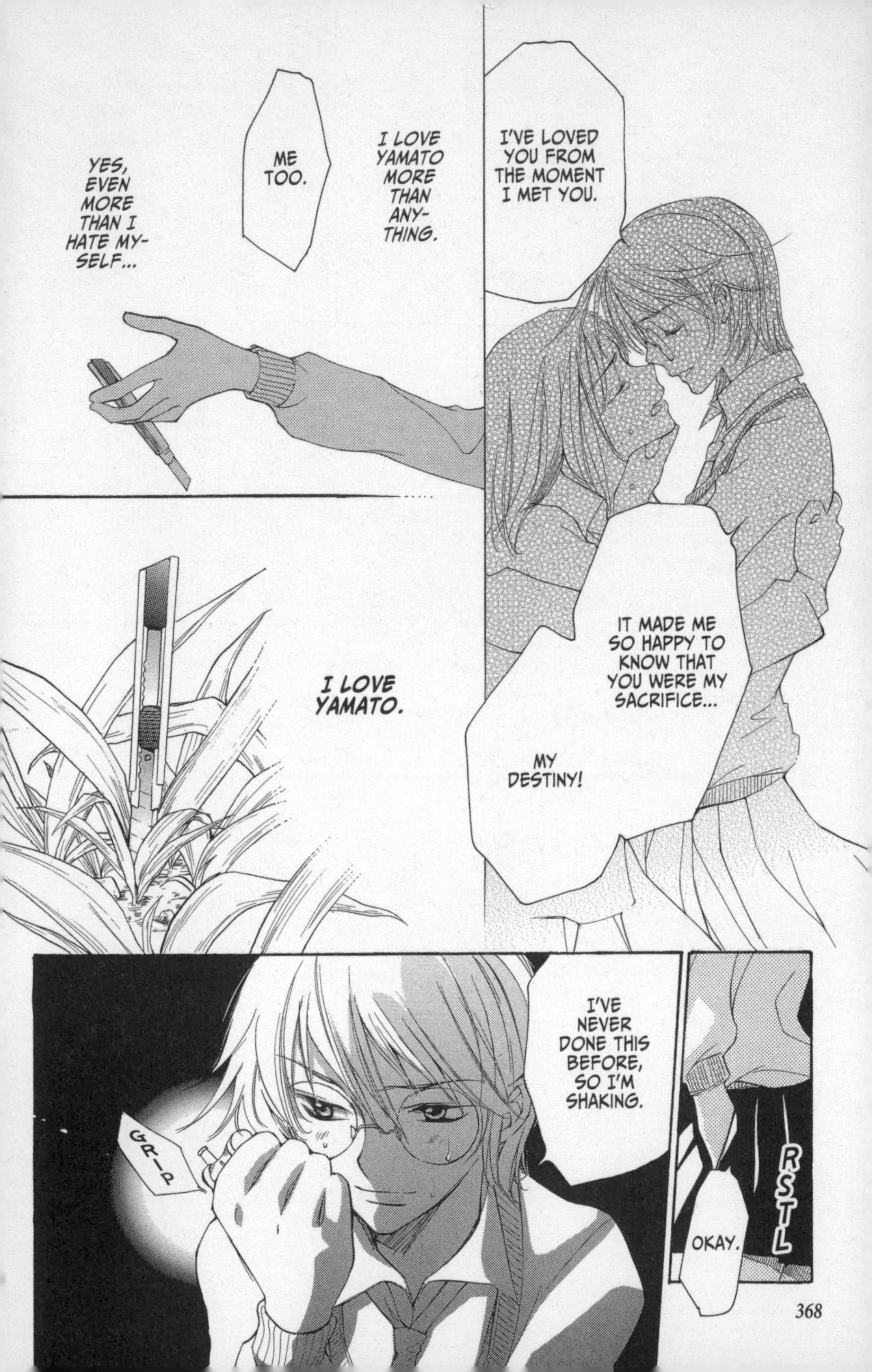
I'VE LOVED YOU FROM THE MOMENT I MET YOU.
IT MADE ME SO HAPPY TO KNOW THAT YOU WERE MY SACRIFICE...
MY DESTINY!
I LOVE YAMATO MORE THAN ANY-THING.
ME TOO.
YES, EVEN MORE THAN I HATE MY-SELF...
I LOVE YAMATO.
RSTL
OKAY.
I'VE NEVER DONE THIS BEFORE, SO I'M SHAKING.
GRIP

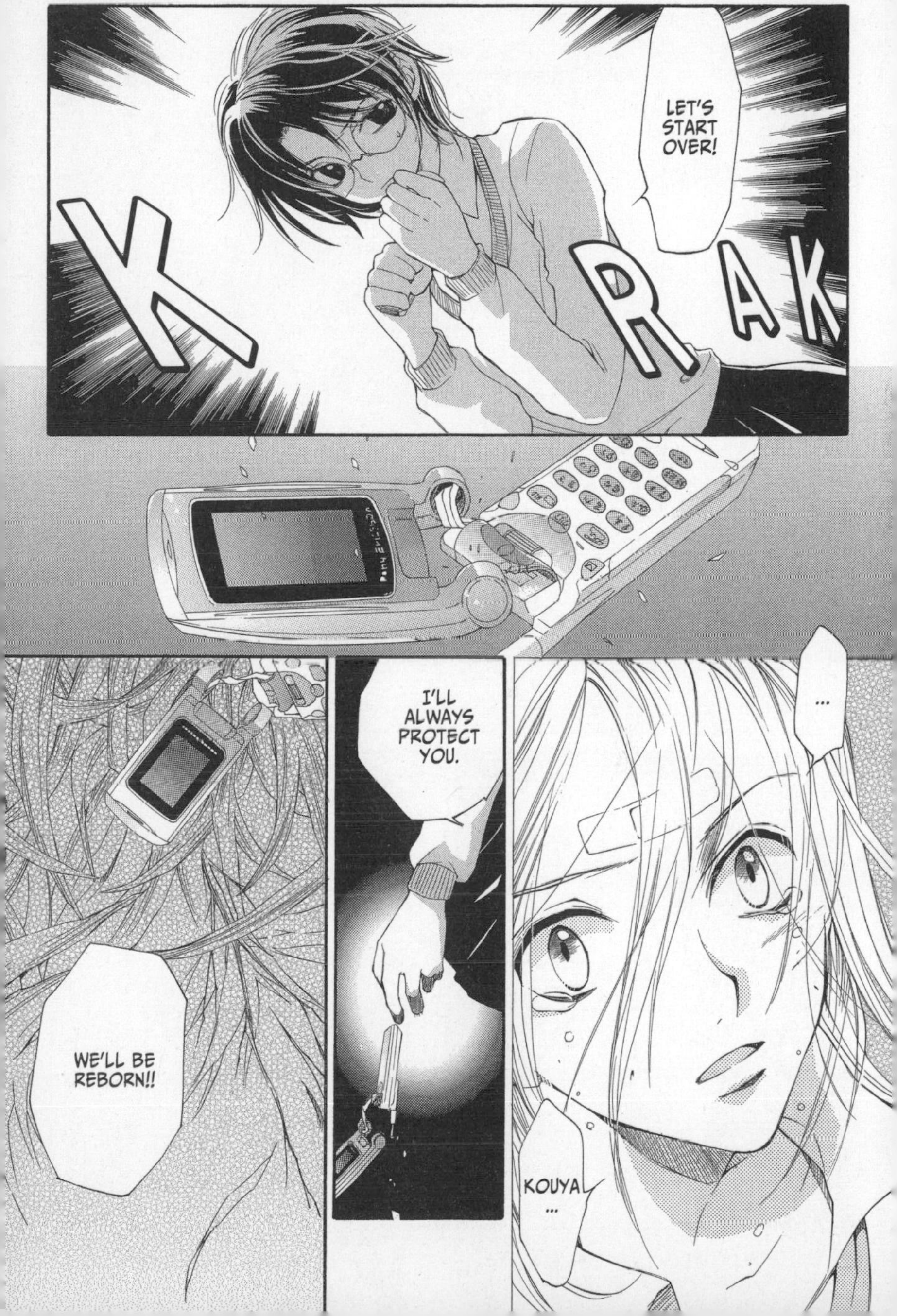
LET'S START OVER!
KRAK
...
KOUYA ...
I'LL ALWAYS PROTECT YOU.
WE'LL BE REBORN!!

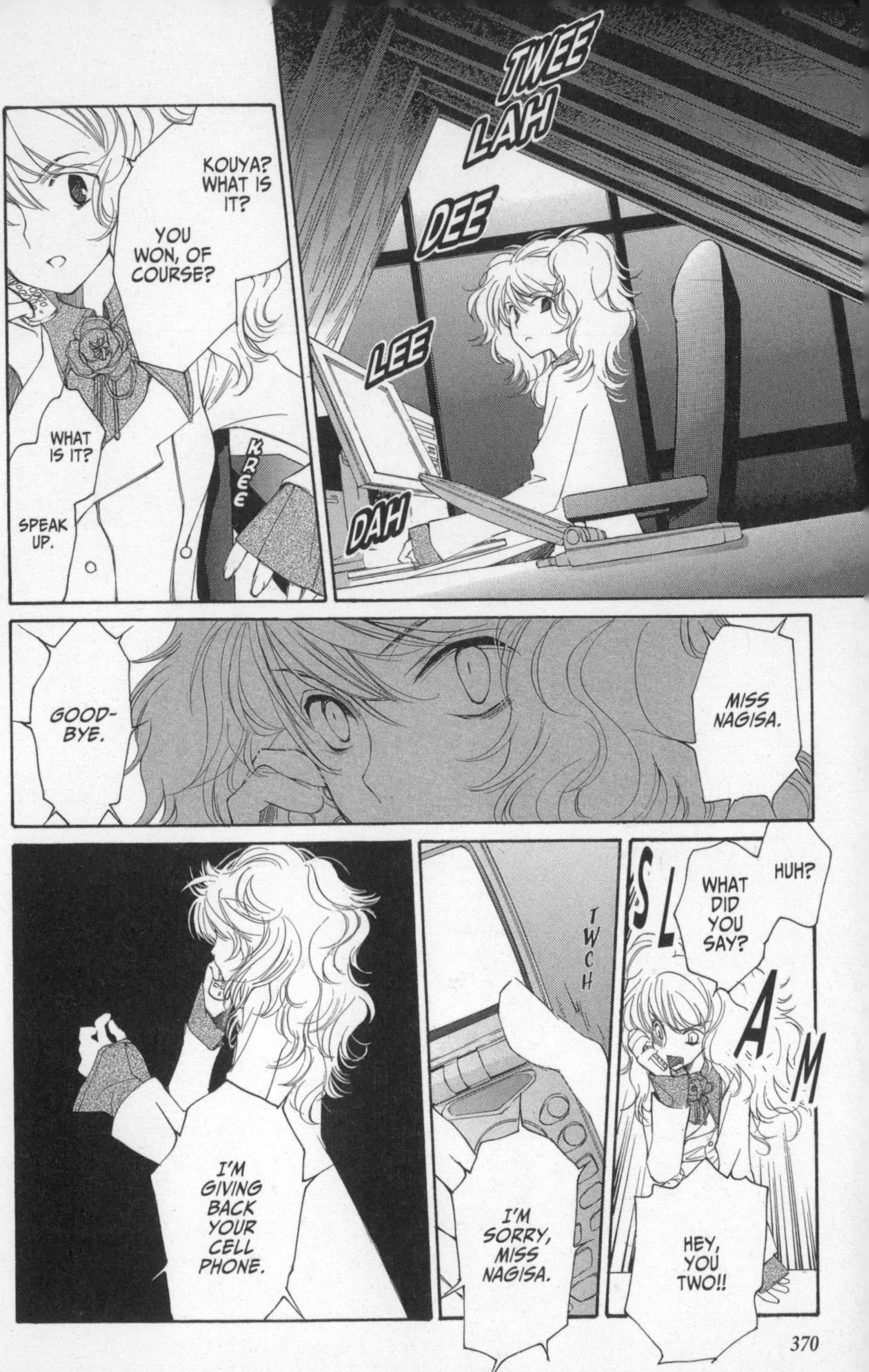
TWEE
LAH
DEE
LEE
DAH
KOUYA? WHAT IS IT?
YOU WON, OF COURSE?
KREE
WHAT IS IT?
SPEAK UP.
MISS NAGISA.
GOOD-BYE.
HUH?
WHAT DID YOU SAY?
SLAM
HEY, YOU TWO!!
TWCH
I'M SORRY, MISS NAGISA.
I'M GIVING BACK YOUR CELL PHONE.

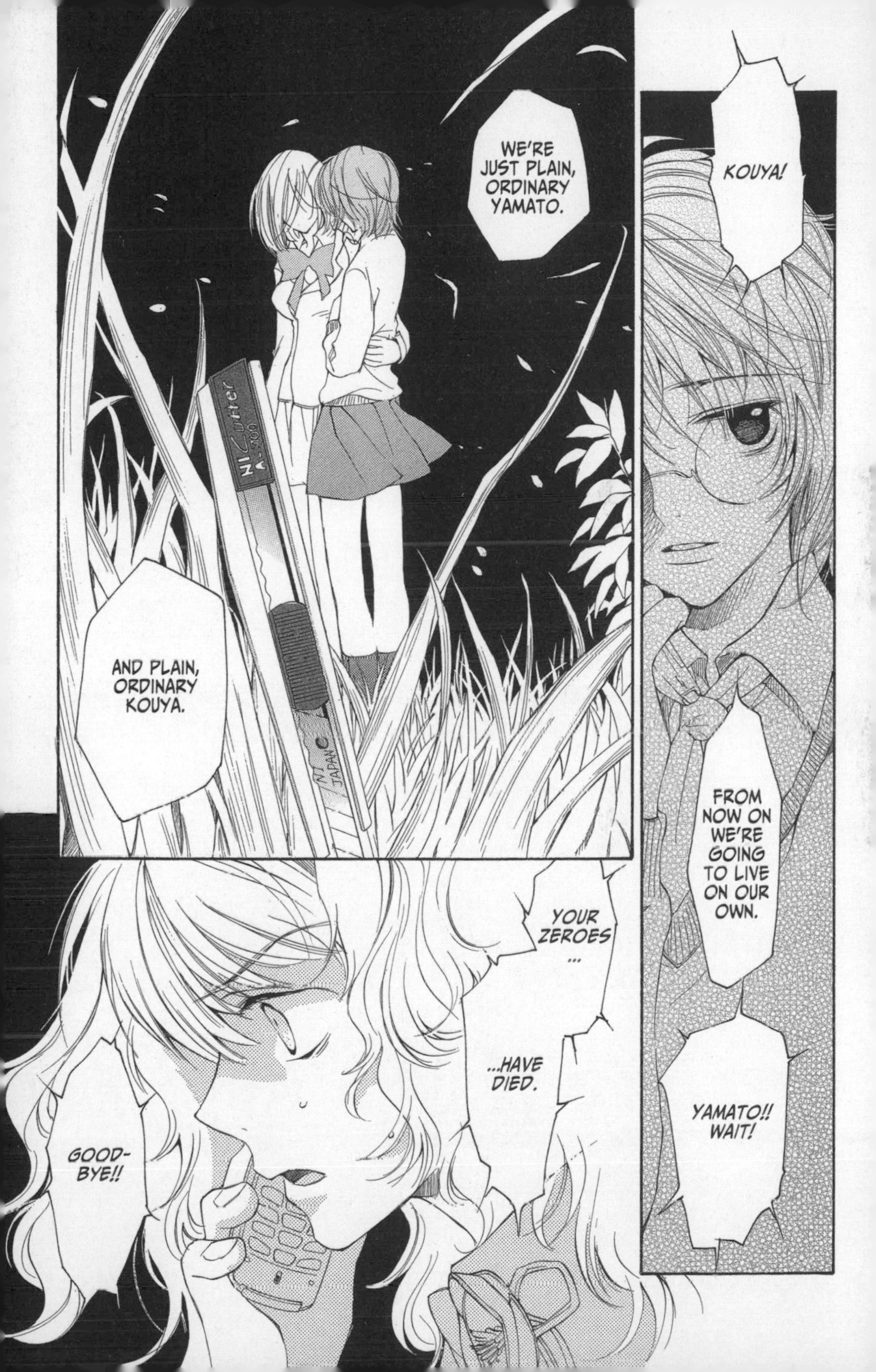
KOUYA!
FROM NOW ON WE'RE GOING TO LIVE ON OUR OWN.
YAMATO!! WAIT!
WE'RE JUST PLAIN, ORDINARY YAMATO.
AND PLAIN, ORDINARY KOUYA.
YOUR ZEROES ...
...HAVE DIED.
GOOD-BYE!!

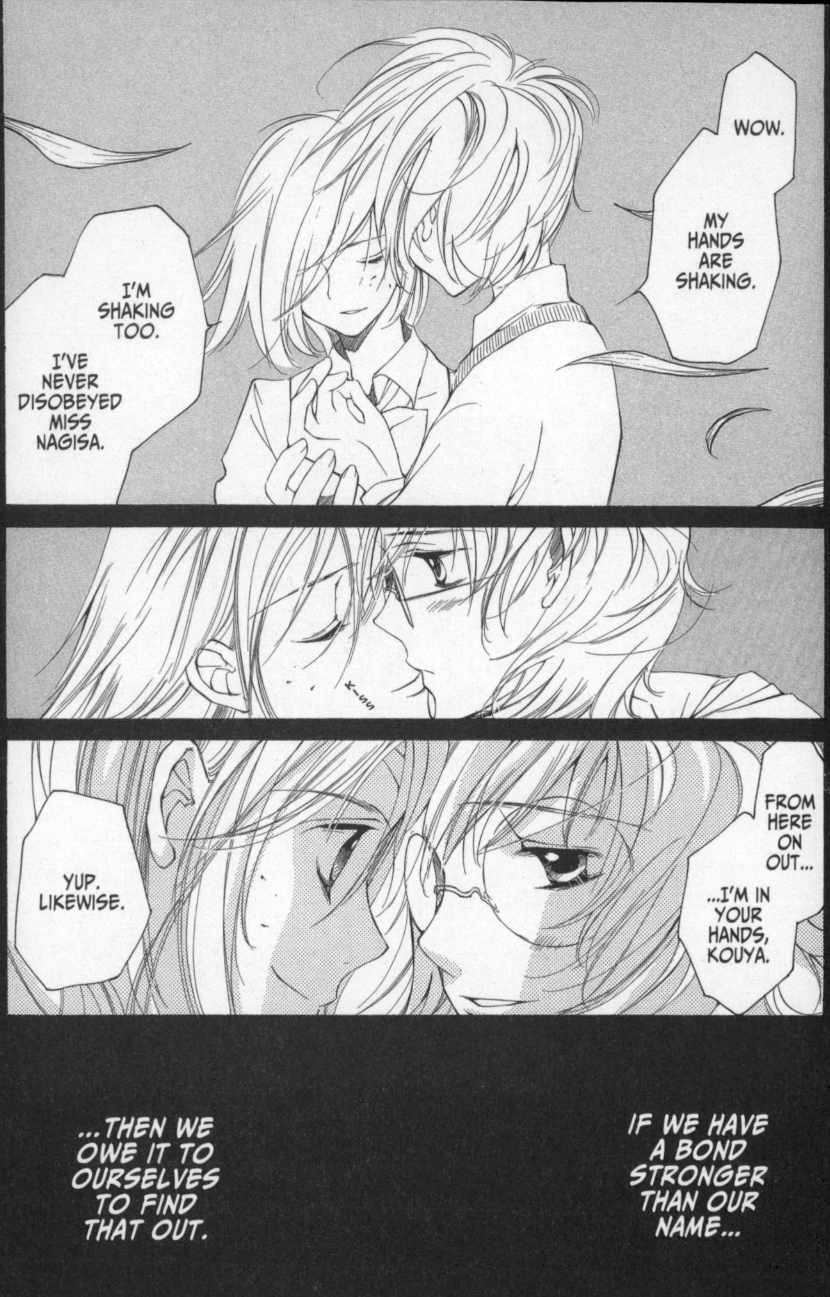
WOW.
MY HANDS ARE SHAKING.
I'M SHAKING TOO.
I'VE NEVER DISOBEYED MISS NAGISA.
FROM HERE ON OUT...
...I'M IN YOUR HANDS, KOUYA.
YUP. LIKEWISE.
IF WE HAVE A BOND STRONGER THAN OUR NAME...
...THEN WE OWE IT TO OURSELVES TO FIND THAT OUT.

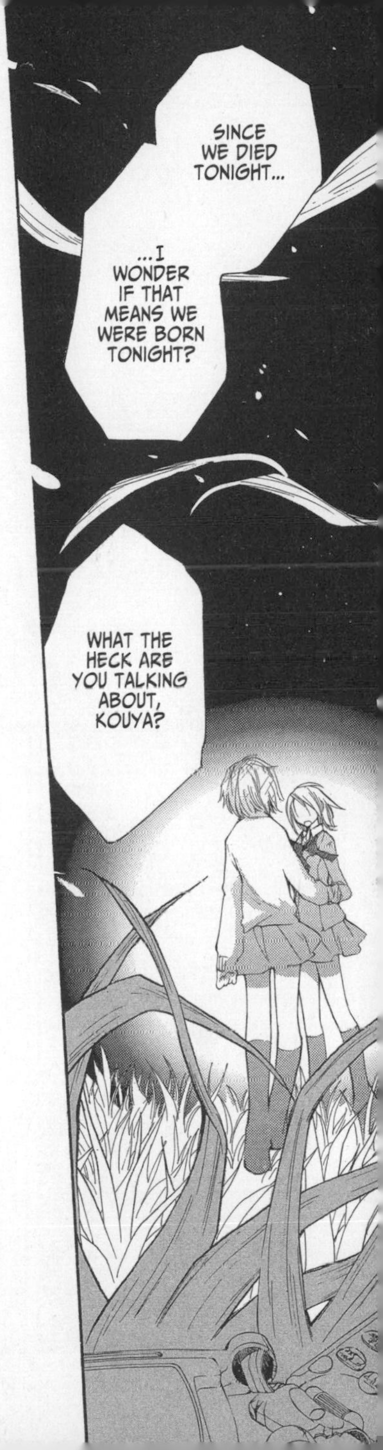
SINCE WE DIED TONIGHT...
...I WONDER IF THAT MEANS WE WERE BORN TONIGHT?
WHAT THE HECK ARE YOU TALKING ABOUT, KOUYA?

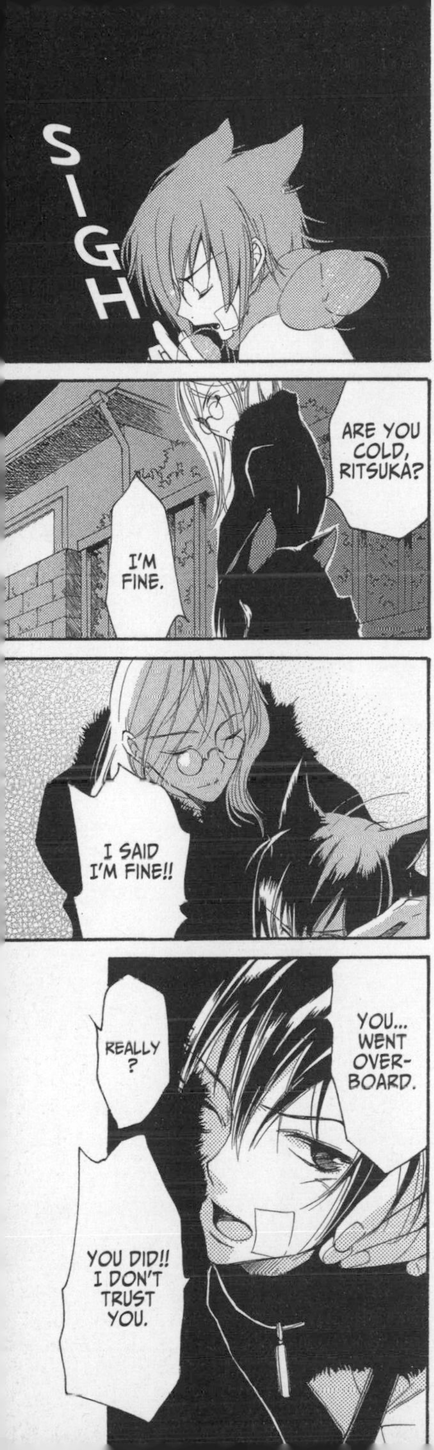
SIGH
ARE YOU COLD, RITSUKA?
I'M FINE.
I SAID I'M FINE!!
YOU... WENT OVER-BOARD.
REALLY?
YOU DID!! I DON'T TRUST YOU.

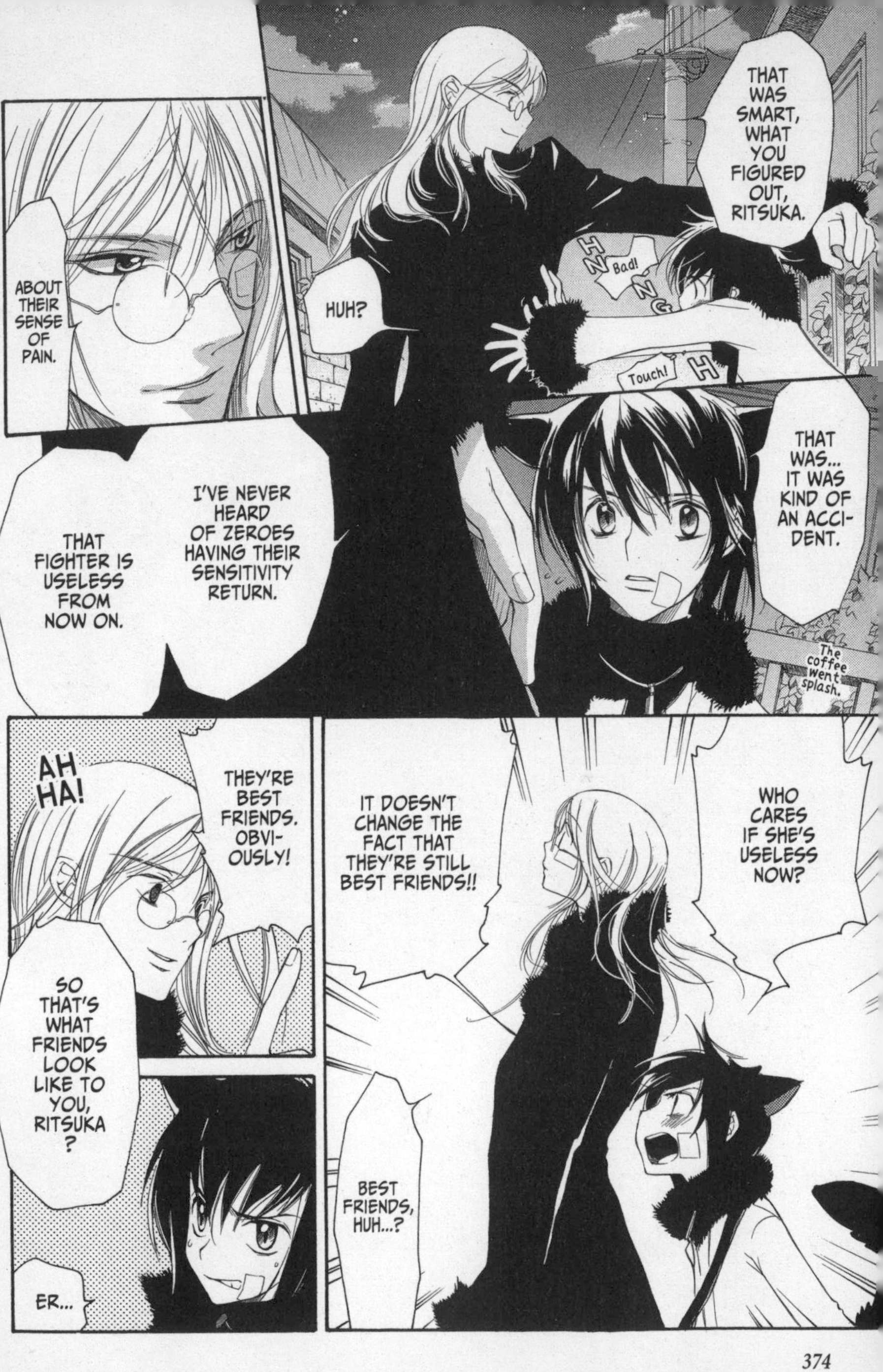
THAT WAS SMART, WHAT YOU FIGURED OUT, RITSUKA.
HUH?
HNNGH
Bad!
Touch!
ABOUT THEIR SENSE OF PAIN.
THAT WAS... IT WAS KIND OF AN ACCI-DENT.
The coffee went splash.
I'VE NEVER HEARD OF ZEROES HAVING THEIR SENSITIVITY RETURN.
THAT FIGHTER IS USELESS FROM NOW ON.
WHO CARES IF SHE'S USELESS NOW?
IT DOESN'T CHANGE THE FACT THAT THEY'RE STILL BEST FRIENDS!!
BEST FRIENDS, HUH...?
AH HA!
THEY'RE BEST FRIENDS. OBVI-OUSLY!
SO THAT'S WHAT FRIENDS LOOK LIKE TO YOU, RITSUKA?
ER...

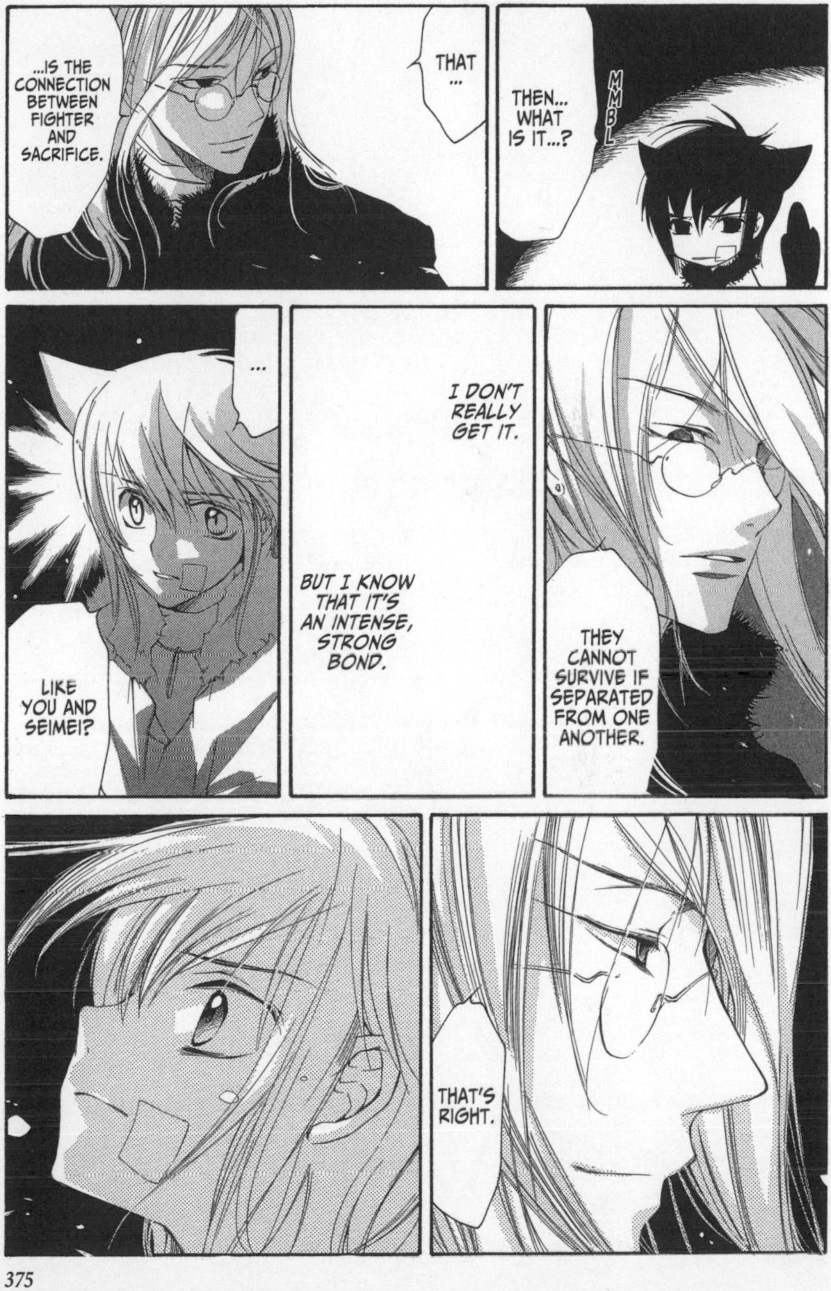
THEN... WHAT IS IT...?
MMBL
THAT ...
...IS THE CONNECTION BETWEEN FIGHTER AND SACRIFICE.
THEY CANNOT SURVIVE IF SEPARATED FROM ONE ANOTHER.
I DON'T REALLY GET IT.
BUT I KNOW THAT IT'S AN INTENSE, STRONG BOND.
...
LIKE YOU AND SEIMEI?
THAT'S RIGHT.

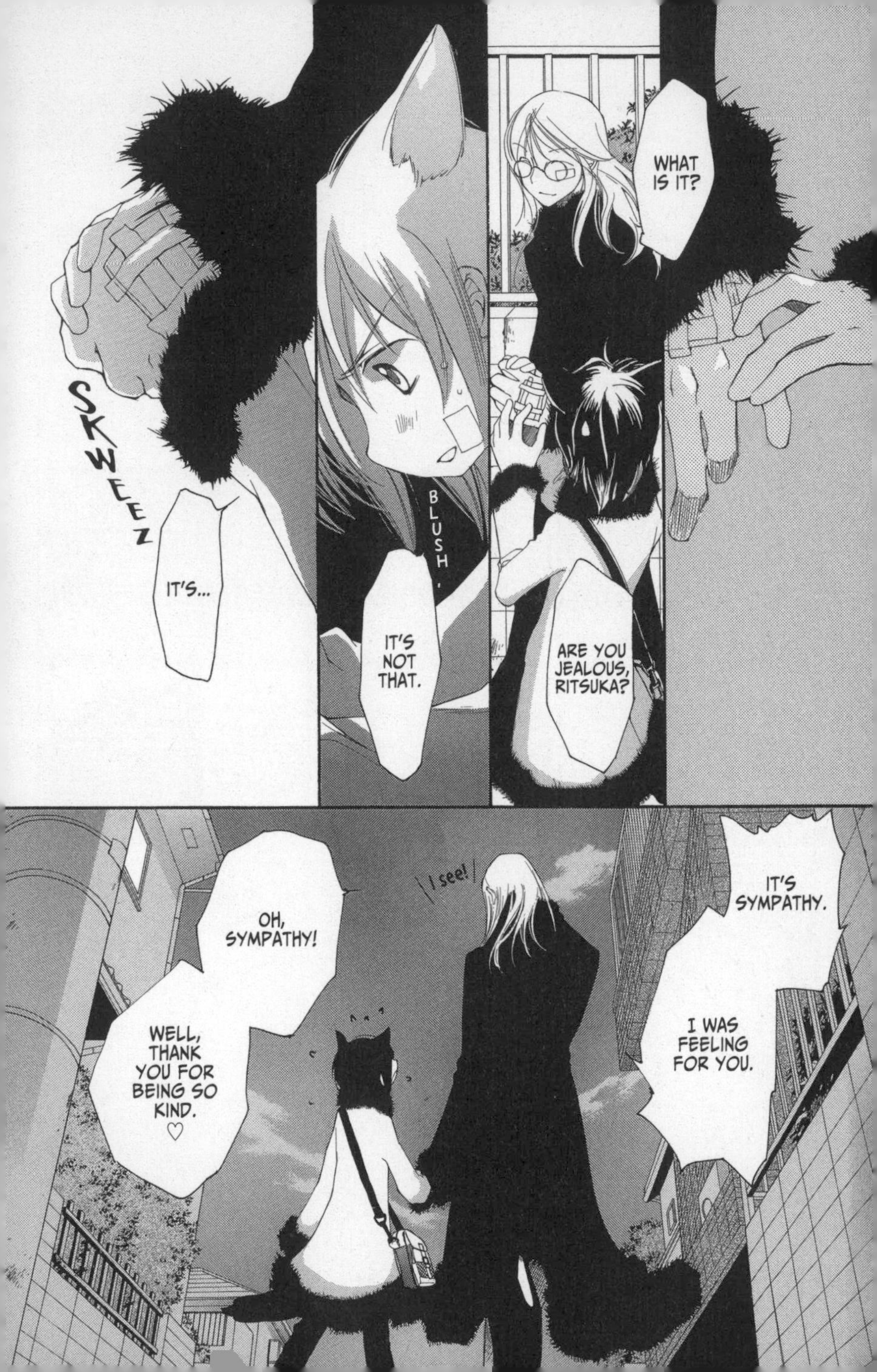
WHAT IS IT?
ARE YOU JEALOUS, RITSUKA?
BLUSH
IT'S NOT THAT.
SKWEEZ
IT'S...
IT'S SYMPATHY.
I WAS FEELING FOR YOU.
I see!
OH, SYMPATHY!
WELL, THANK YOU FOR BEING SO KIND. ♡

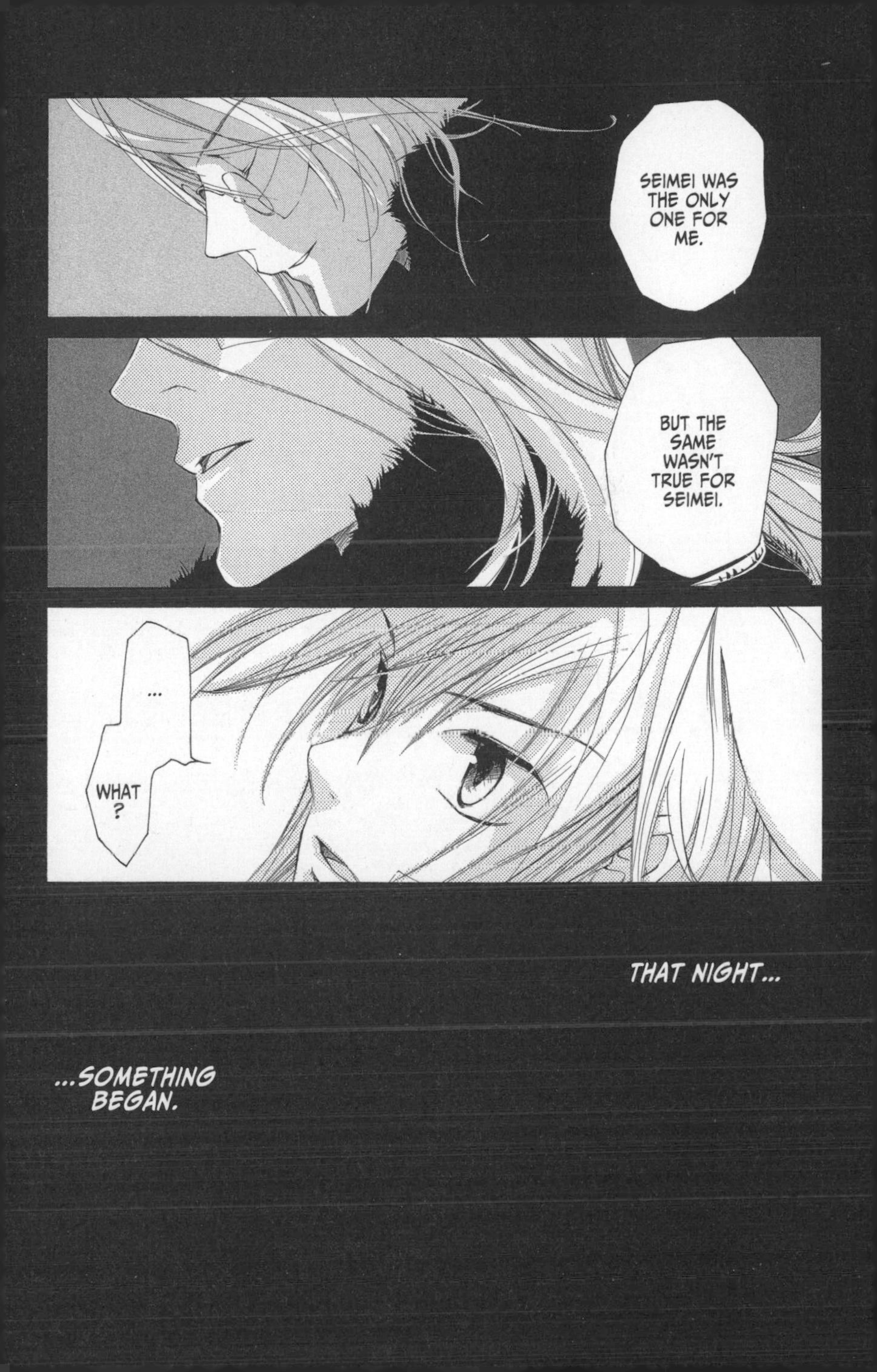
SEIMEI WAS THE ONLY ONE FOR ME.
BUT THE SAME WASN'T TRUE FOR SEIMEI.
... WHAT?
THAT NIGHT...
...SOMETHING BEGAN.

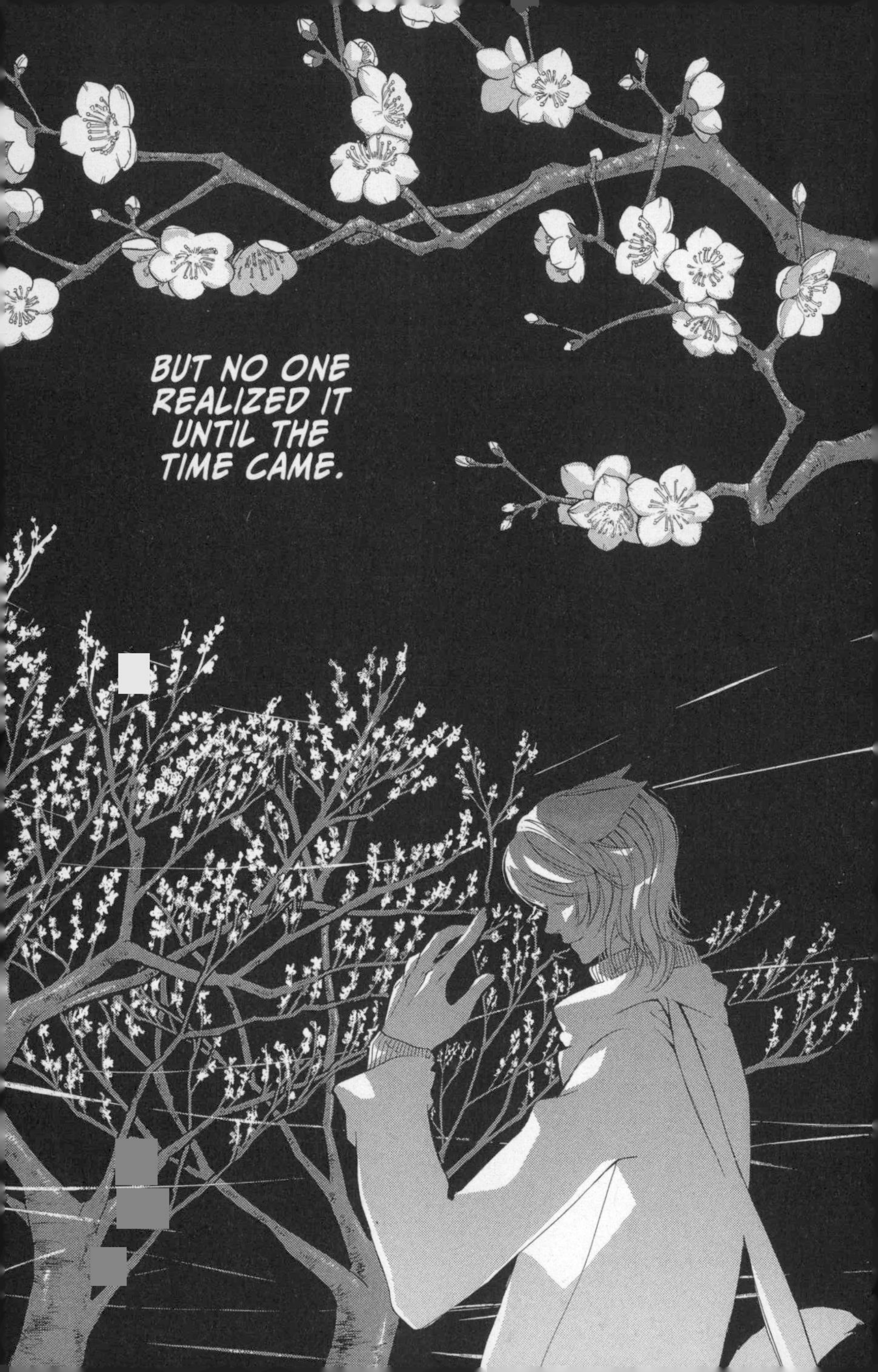
BUT NO ONE REALIZED IT UNTIL THE TIME CAME.

A GIRL NAMED OSAMU

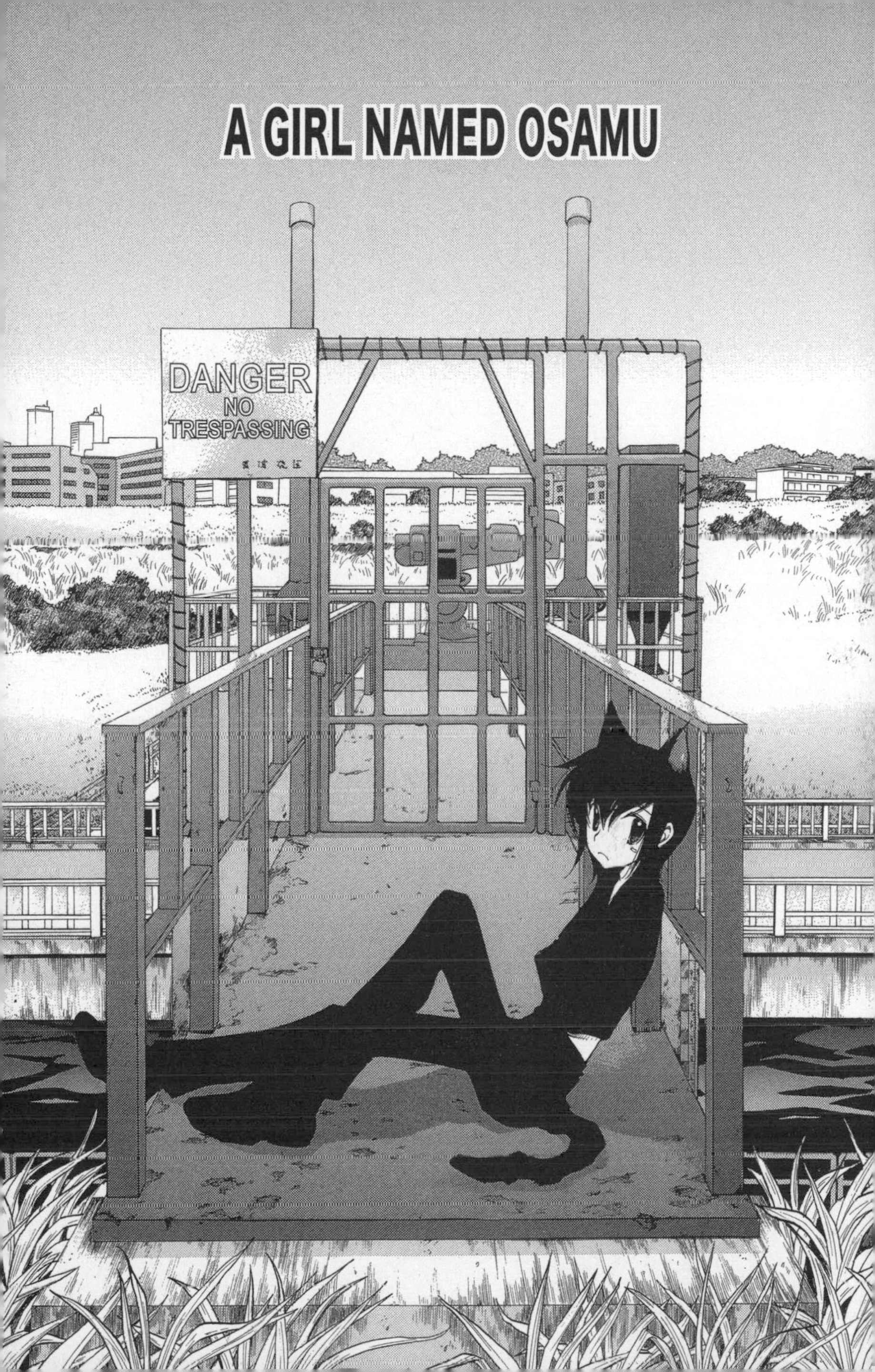
DANGER
NO
TRESPASSING

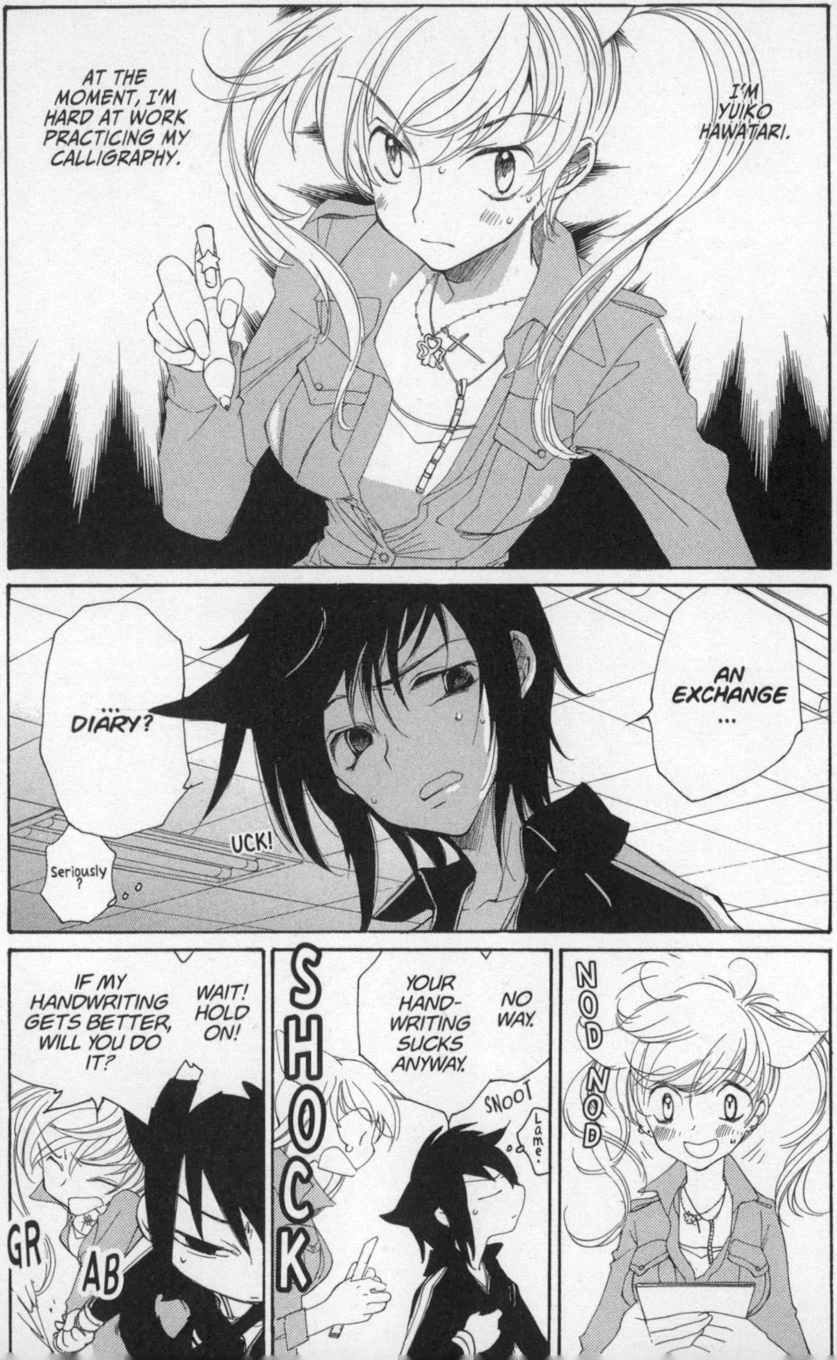
I'M YUIKO HAWATARI.
AT THE MOMENT, I'M HARD AT WORK PRACTICING MY CALLIGRAPHY.
AN EXCHANGE ...
... DIARY?
UCK!
Seriously?
NOD NOD
NO WAY.
YOUR HAND-WRITING SUCKS ANYWAY.
SNOOT
Lame.
SHOCK
WAIT! HOLD ON!
IF MY HANDWRITING GETS BETTER, WILL YOU DO IT?
GRAB

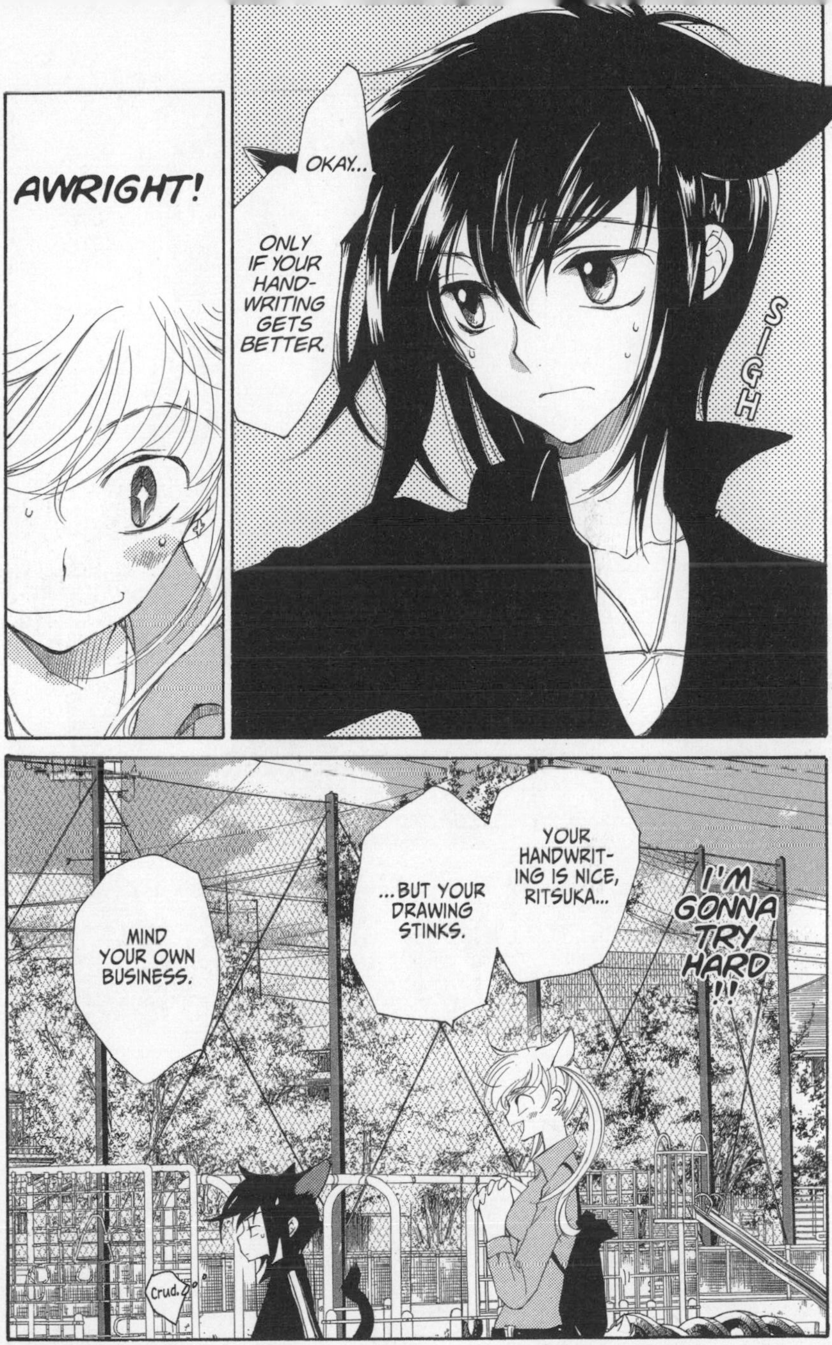
OKAY...
ONLY IF YOUR HAND-WRITING GETS BETTER.
SIGH
AWRIGHT!
I'M GONNA TRY HARD!!
YOUR HANDWRIT-ING IS NICE, RITSUKA...
...BUT YOUR DRAWING STINKS.
MIND YOUR OWN BUSINESS.
Crud.

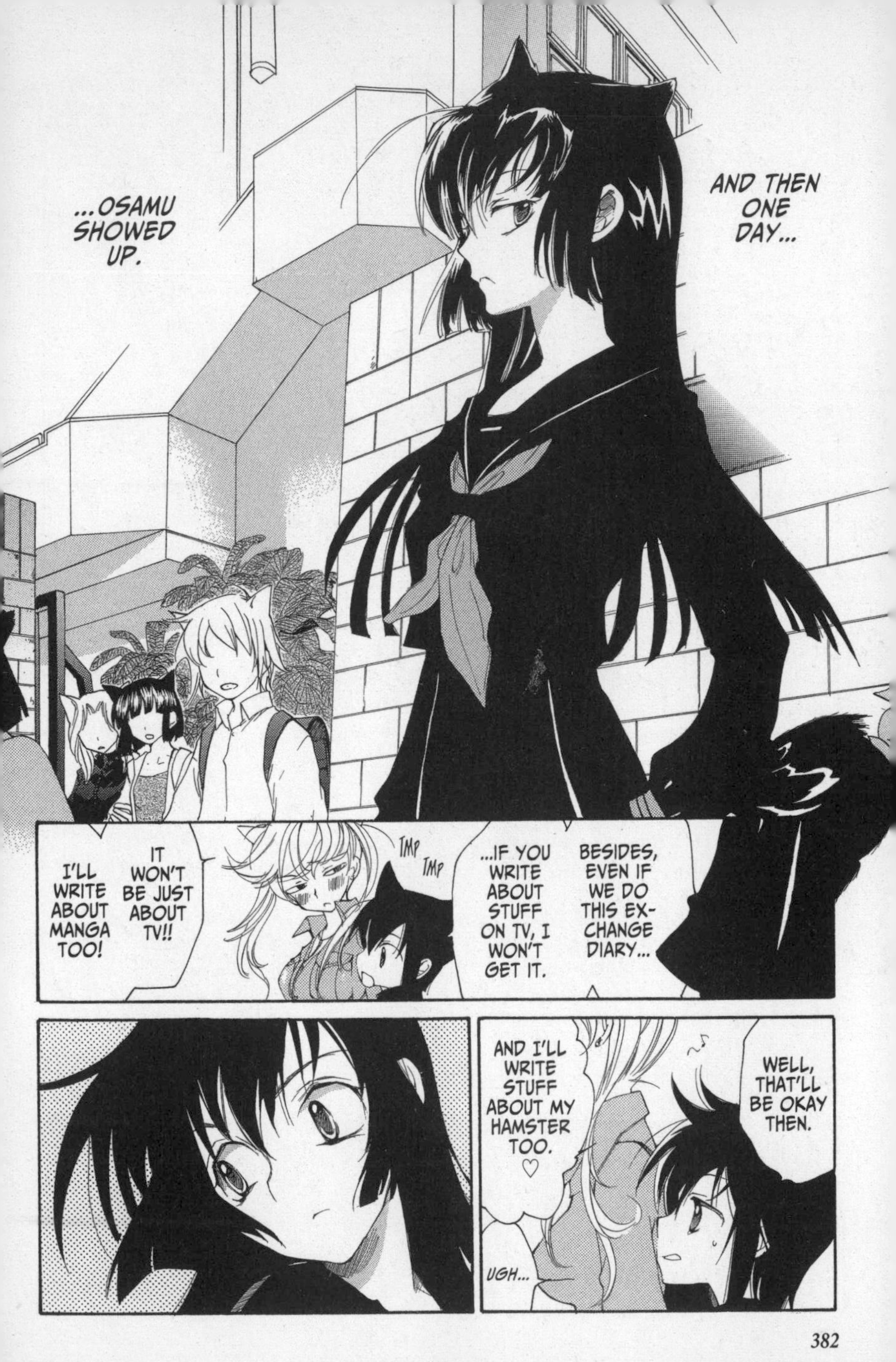
AND THEN ONE DAY...
...OSAMU SHOWED UP.
BESIDES, EVEN IF WE DO THIS EX-CHANGE DIARY...
...IF YOU WRITE ABOUT STUFF ON TV, I WON'T GET IT.
TMP TMP
IT WON'T BE JUST ABOUT TV!!
I'LL WRITE ABOUT MANGA TOO!
WELL, THAT'LL BE OKAY THEN.
AND I'LL WRITE STUFF ABOUT MY HAMSTER TOO. ♡
UGH...

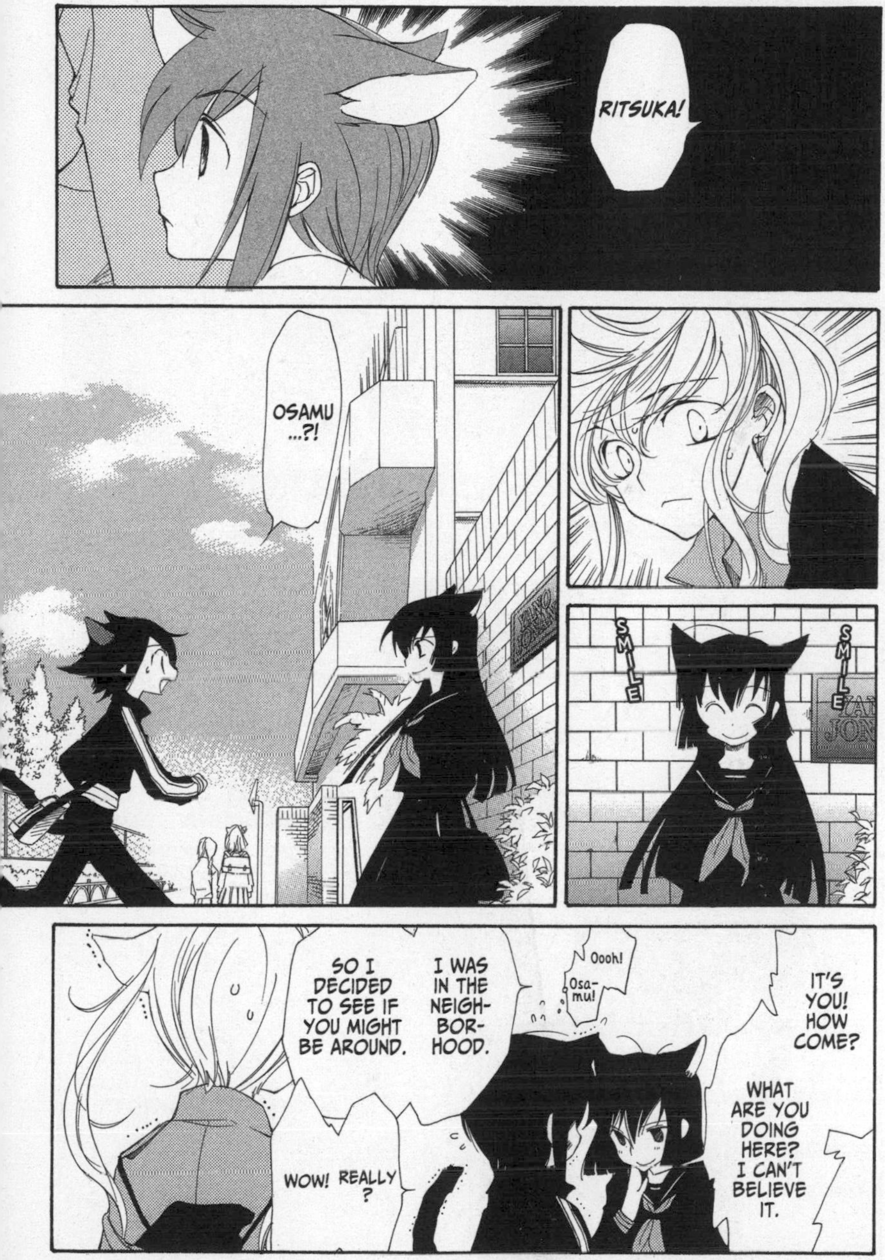
RITSUKA!
SMILE
SMILE
OSAMU ...?!
IT'S YOU! HOW COME?
WHAT ARE YOU DOING HERE? I CAN'T BELIEVE IT.
Oooh!
Osa-mu!
I WAS IN THE NEIGH-BOR-HOOD.
SO I DECIDED TO SEE IF YOU MIGHT BE AROUND.
REALLY?
WOW!

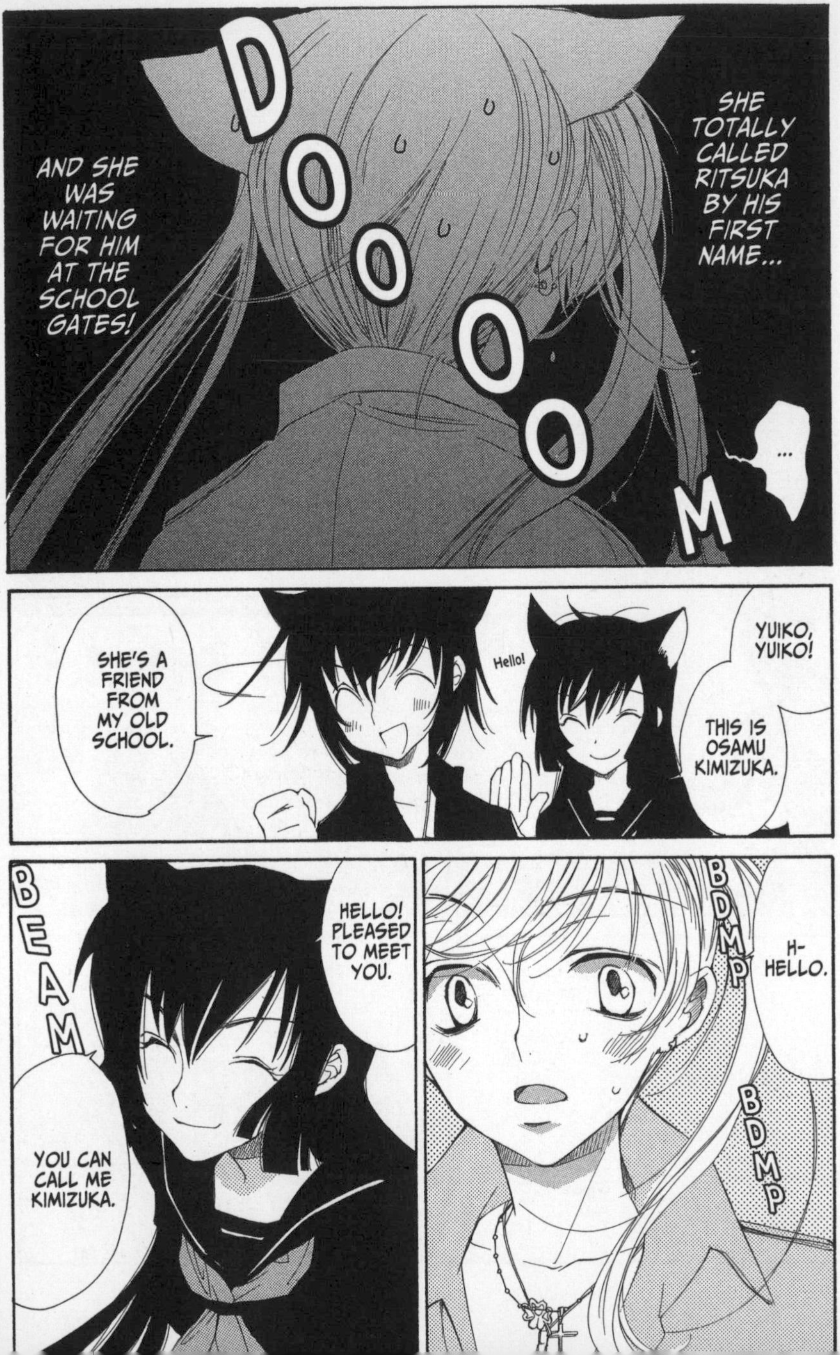
SHE TOTALLY CALLED RITSUKA BY HIS FIRST NAME...
DOOOOOM
AND SHE WAS WAITING FOR HIM AT THE SCHOOL GATES!
...
YUIKO, YUIKO!
THIS IS OSAMU KIMIZUKA.
Hello!
SHE'S A FRIEND FROM MY OLD SCHOOL.
BDMP
H-HELLO.
BDMP
HELLO! PLEASED TO MEET YOU.
BEAM
YOU CAN CALL ME KIMIZUKA.

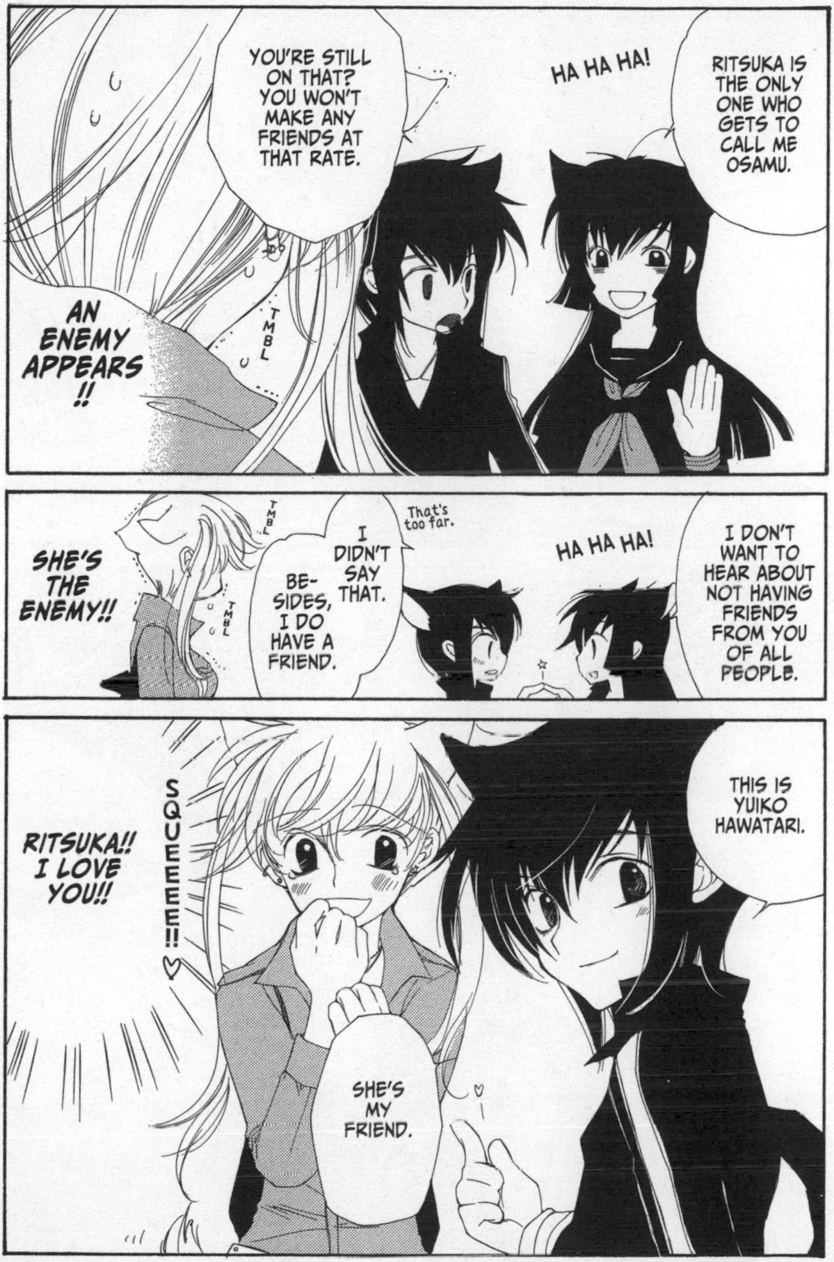
RITSUKA IS THE ONLY ONE WHO GETS TO CALL ME OSAMU.
HA HA HA!
YOU'RE STILL ON THAT? YOU WON'T MAKE ANY FRIENDS AT THAT RATE.
TMBL
AN ENEMY APPEARS!!
I DON'T WANT TO HEAR ABOUT NOT HAVING FRIENDS FROM YOU OF ALL PEOPLE.
HA HA HA!
That's too far.
I DIDN'T SAY THAT.
BE-SIDES, I DO HAVE A FRIEND.
TMBL
TMBL
SHE'S THE ENEMY!!
THIS IS YUIKO HAWATARI.
SHE'S MY FRIEND.
SQUEEEEE!!
RITSUKA!! I LOVE YOU!!

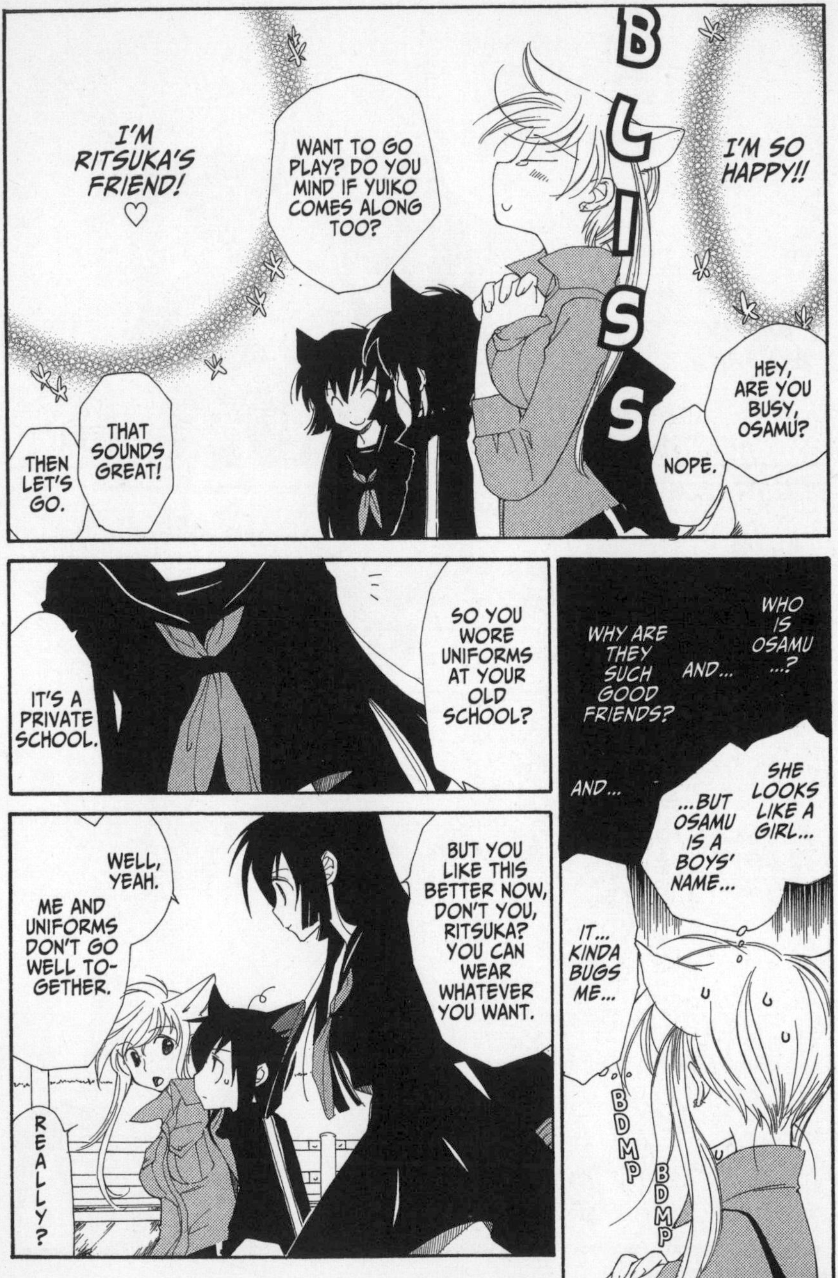
BLISS
I'M SO HAPPY!!
WANT TO GO PLAY? DO YOU MIND IF YUIKO COMES ALONG TOO?
I'M RITSUKA'S FRIEND! ♡
HEY, ARE YOU BUSY, OSAMU?
NOPE.
THAT SOUNDS GREAT!
THEN LET'S GO.
WHO IS OSAMU ...?
AND...
WHY ARE THEY SUCH GOOD FRIENDS?
AND...
SHE LOOKS LIKE A GIRL...
...BUT OSAMU IS A BOYS' NAME...
IT... KINDA BUGS ME...
BDMP
BDMP
SO YOU WORE UNIFORMS AT YOUR OLD SCHOOL?
IT'S A PRIVATE SCHOOL.
BUT YOU LIKE THIS BETTER NOW, DON'T YOU, RITSUKA? YOU CAN WEAR WHATEVER YOU WANT.
WELL, YEAH.
ME AND UNIFORMS DON'T GO WELL TO-GETHER.
REALLY?

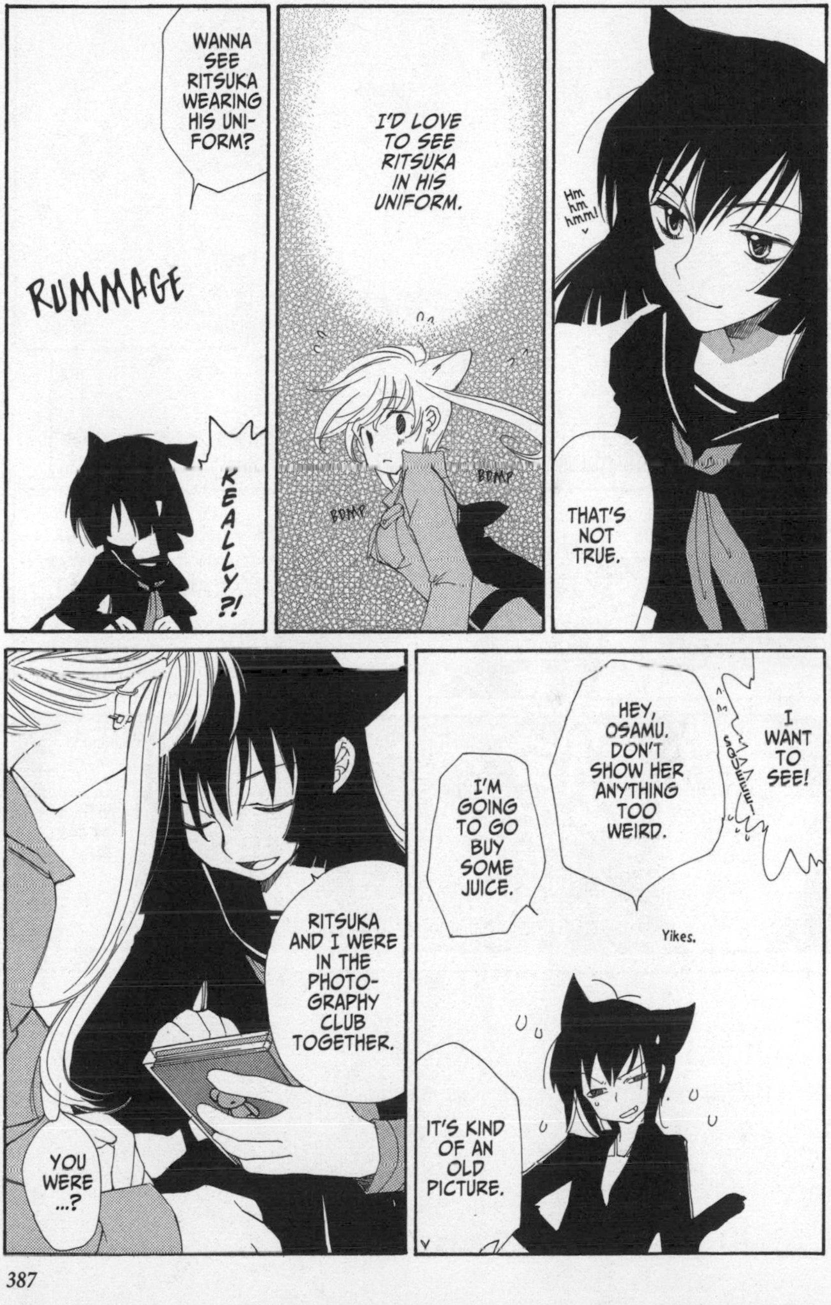
Hm hm hmm!
THAT'S NOT TRUE.
I'D LOVE TO SEE RITSUKA IN HIS UNIFORM.
BOMP
BOMP
WANNA SEE RITSUKA WEARING HIS UNI-FORM?
RUMMAGE
REALLY?!
I WANT TO SEE!
HEY, OSAMU. DON'T SHOW HER ANYTHING TOO WEIRD.
I'M GOING TO GO BUY SOME JUICE.
Yikes.
IT'S KIND OF AN OLD PICTURE.
RITSUKA AND I WERE IN THE PHOTOG-RAPHY CLUB TOGETHER.
YOU WERE ...?

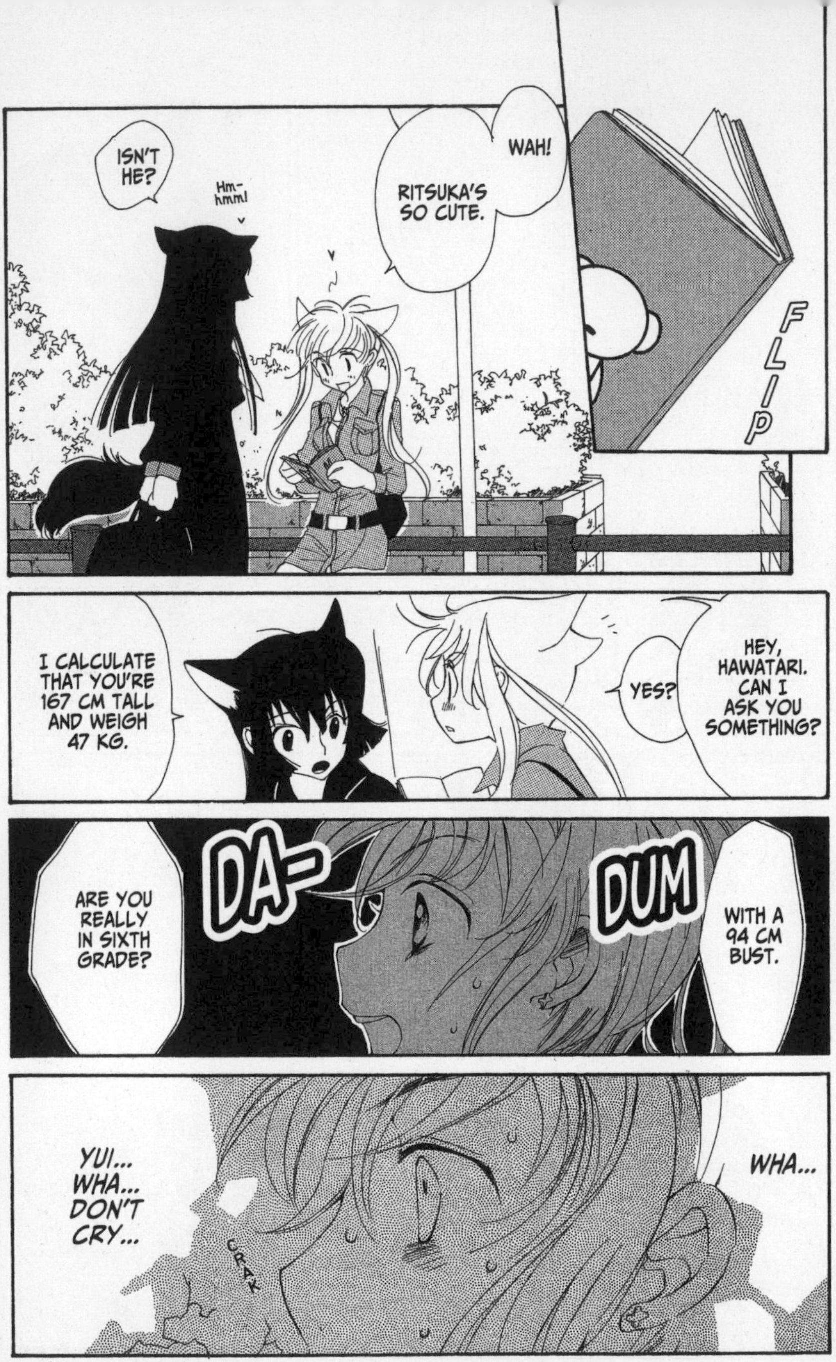
FLIP
WAH!
RITSUKA'S SO CUTE.
ISN'T HE?
Hm-hmm!
HEY, HAWATARI. CAN I ASK YOU SOMETHING?
YES?
I CALCULATE THAT YOU'RE 167 CM TALL AND WEIGH 47 KG.
WITH A 94 CM BUST.
DA-DUM
ARE YOU REALLY IN SIXTH GRADE?
WHA...
CRAK
YUI... WHA... DON'T CRY...

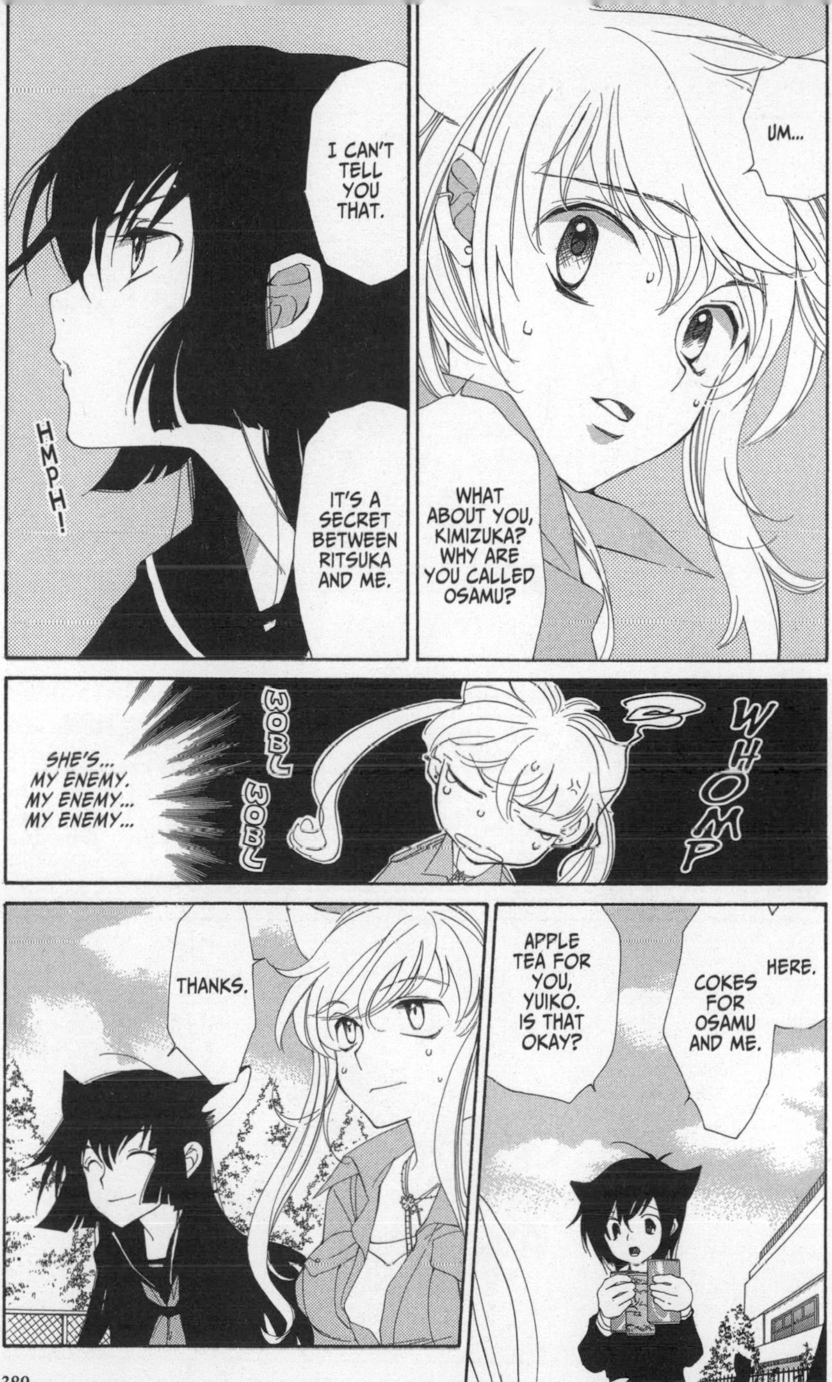
UM...
WHAT ABOUT YOU, KIMIZUKA? WHY ARE YOU CALLED OSAMU?
I CAN'T TELL YOU THAT.
IT'S A SECRET BETWEEN RITSUKA AND ME.
HMPH!
WHOMP
WOBL WOBL
SHE'S... MY ENEMY. MY ENEMY... MY ENEMY...
HERE.
COKES FOR OSAMU AND ME.
APPLE TEA FOR YOU, YUIKO. IS THAT OKAY?
THANKS.

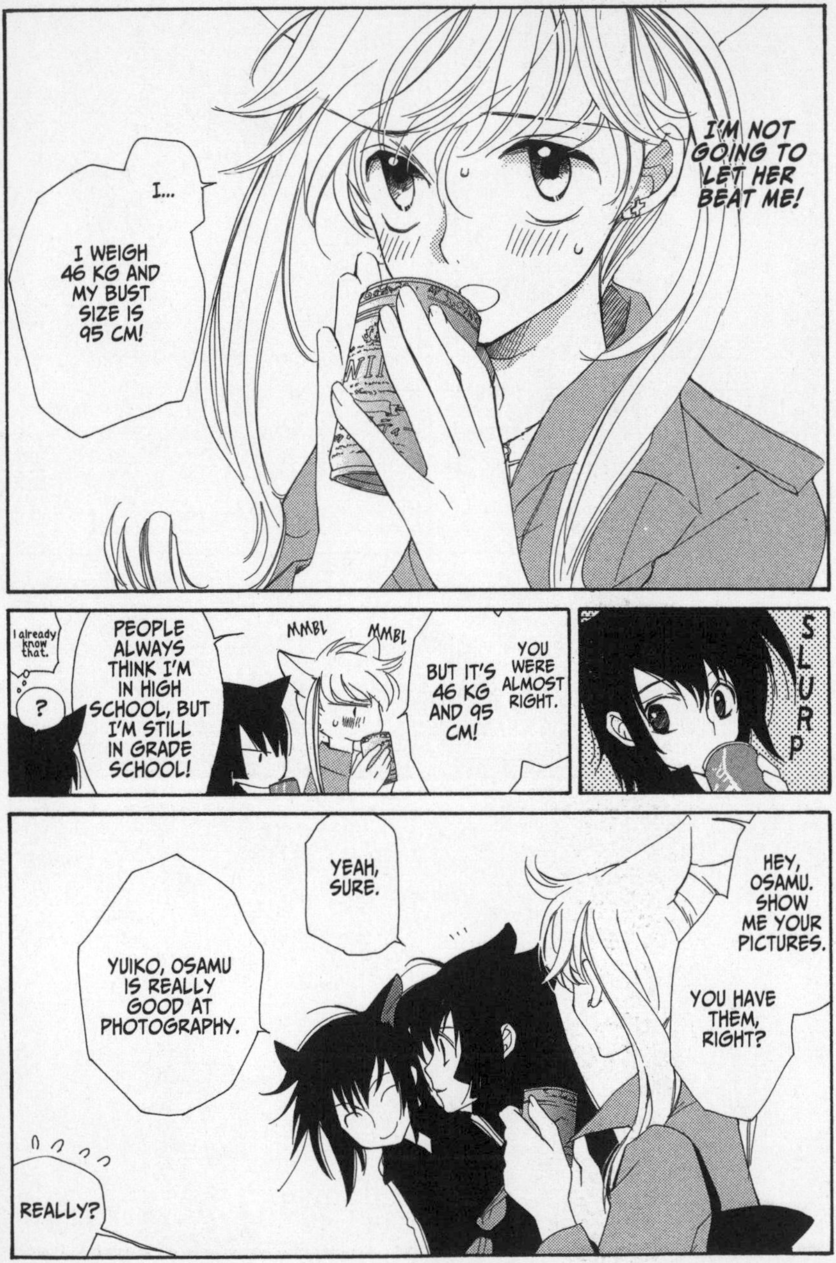
I'M NOT GOING TO LET HER BEAT ME!
I...
I WEIGH 46 KG AND MY BUST SIZE IS 95 CM!
SLURP
YOU WERE ALMOST RIGHT.
BUT IT'S 46 KG AND 95 CM!
MMBL
MMBL
PEOPLE ALWAYS THINK I'M IN HIGH SCHOOL, BUT I'M STILL IN GRADE SCHOOL!
?
I already know that.
HEY, OSAMU. SHOW ME YOUR PICTURES.
YOU HAVE THEM, RIGHT?
YEAH, SURE.
YUIKO, OSAMU IS REALLY GOOD AT PHOTOGRAPHY.
REALLY?

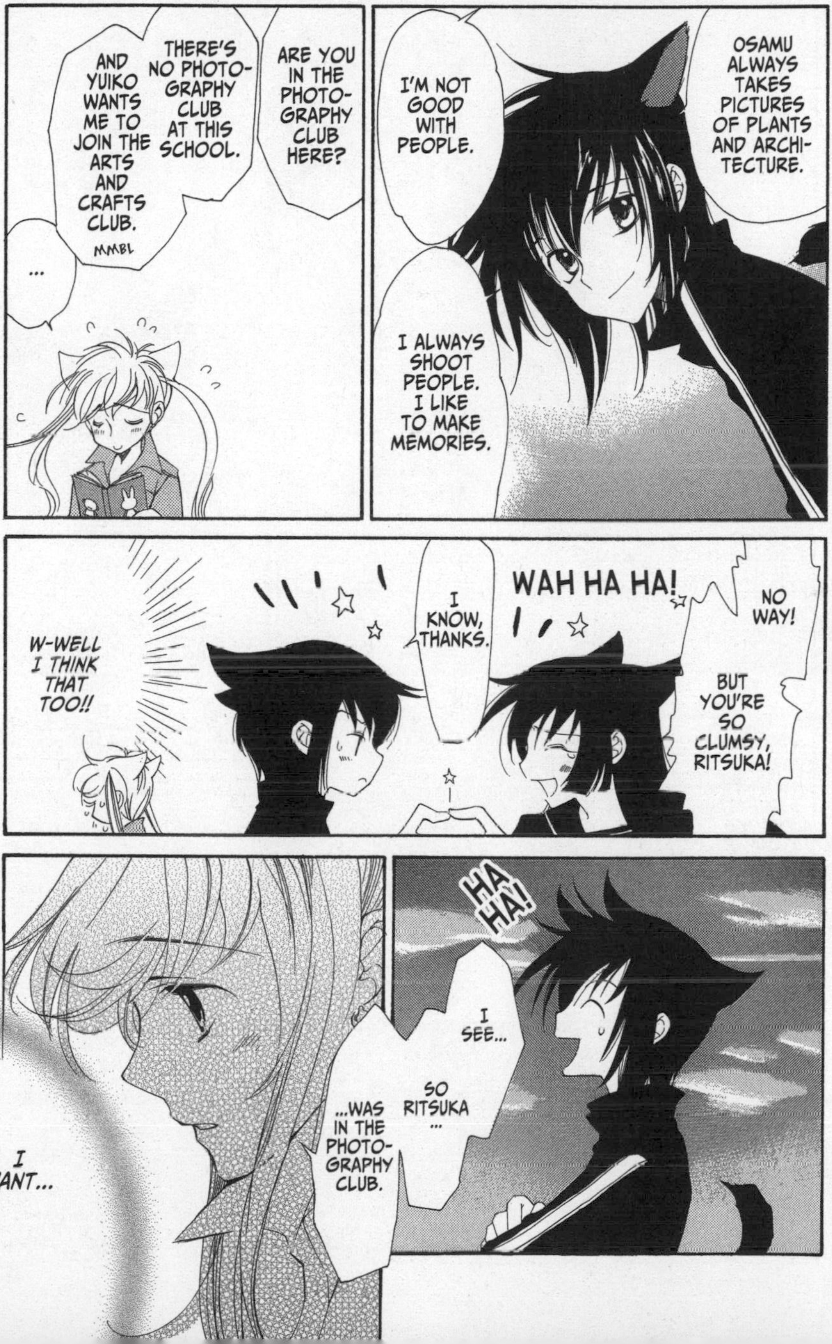
OSAMU ALWAYS TAKES PICTURES OF PLANTS AND ARCHITECTURE.
I'M NOT GOOD WITH PEOPLE.
I ALWAYS SHOOT PEOPLE. I LIKE TO MAKE MEMORIES.
ARE YOU IN THE PHOTOGRAPHY CLUB HERE?
THERE'S NO PHOTOGRAPHY CLUB AT THIS SCHOOL.
AND YUIKO WANTS ME TO JOIN THE ARTS AND CRAFTS CLUB.
MMBL
...
NO WAY!
BUT YOU'RE SO CLUMSY, RITSUKA!
WAH HA HA!
I KNOW, THANKS.
W-WELL I THINK THAT TOO!!
HA HA!
I SEE...
SO RITSUKA ...
...WAS IN THE PHOTOGRAPHY CLUB.
I WANT...

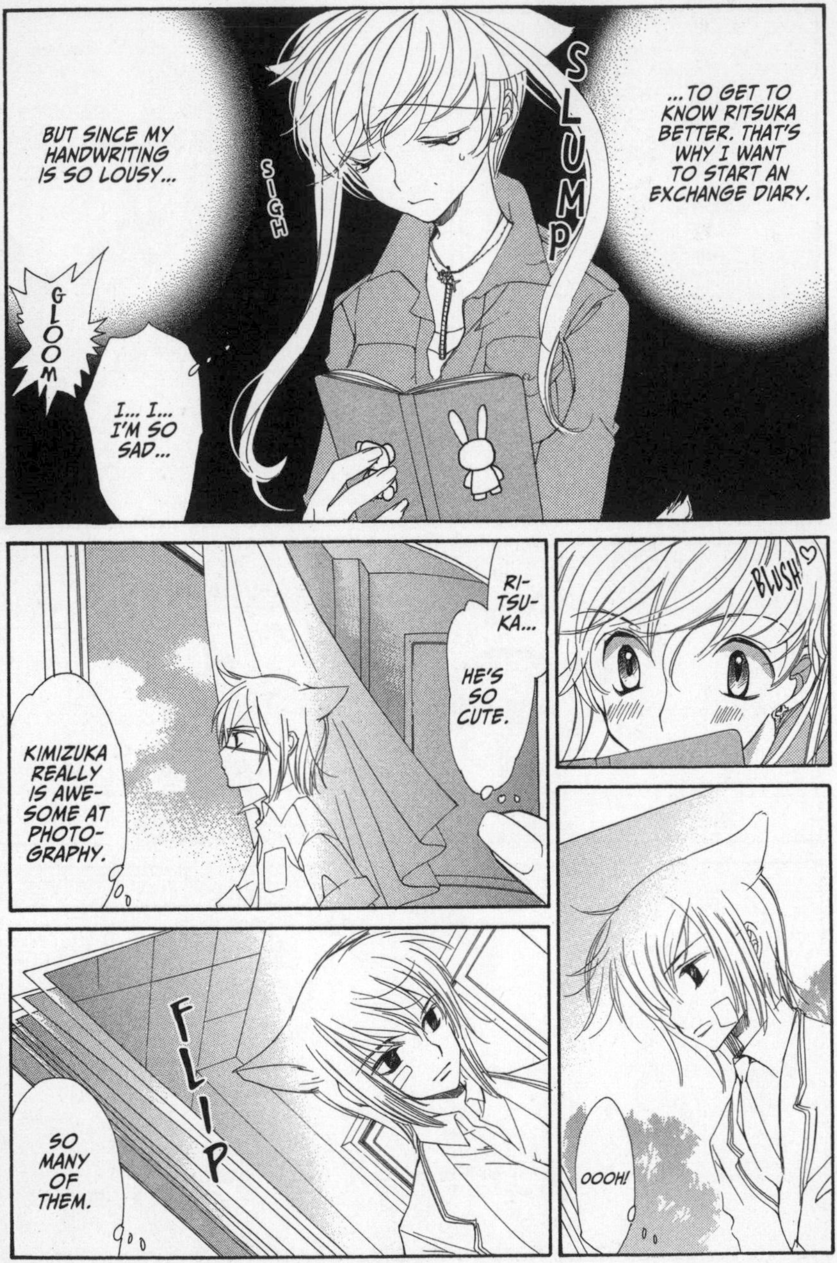
...TO GET TO KNOW RITSUKA BETTER. THAT'S WHY I WANT TO START AN EXCHANGE DIARY.
SLUMP
SIGH
BUT SINCE MY HANDWRITING IS SO LOUSY...
GLOOM
I... I... I'M SO SAD...
BLUSH! ♡
RI-TSU-KA...
HE'S SO CUTE.
KIMIZUKA REALLY IS AWE-SOME AT PHOTO-GRAPHY.
OOOH!
FLIP
SO MANY OF THEM.

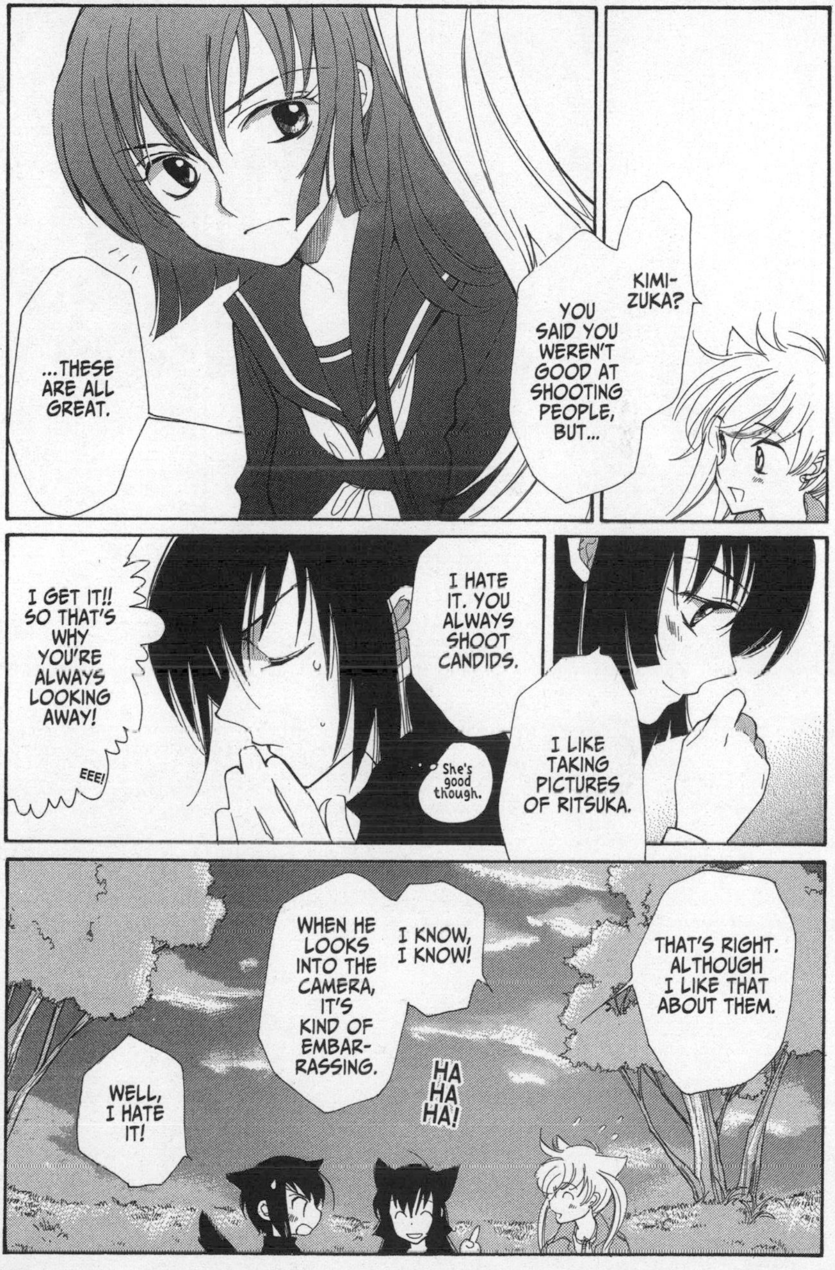
KIMI-ZUKA?
YOU SAID YOU WEREN'T GOOD AT SHOOTING PEOPLE, BUT...
...THESE ARE ALL GREAT.
I LIKE TAKING PICTURES OF RITSUKA.
I HATE IT. YOU ALWAYS SHOOT CANDIDS.
She's good though.
I GET IT!! SO THAT'S WHY YOU'RE ALWAYS LOOKING AWAY!
EEE!
THAT'S RIGHT. ALTHOUGH I LIKE THAT ABOUT THEM.
I KNOW, I KNOW!
WHEN HE LOOKS INTO THE CAMERA, IT'S KIND OF EMBAR-RASSING.
HA HA HA!
WELL, I HATE IT!

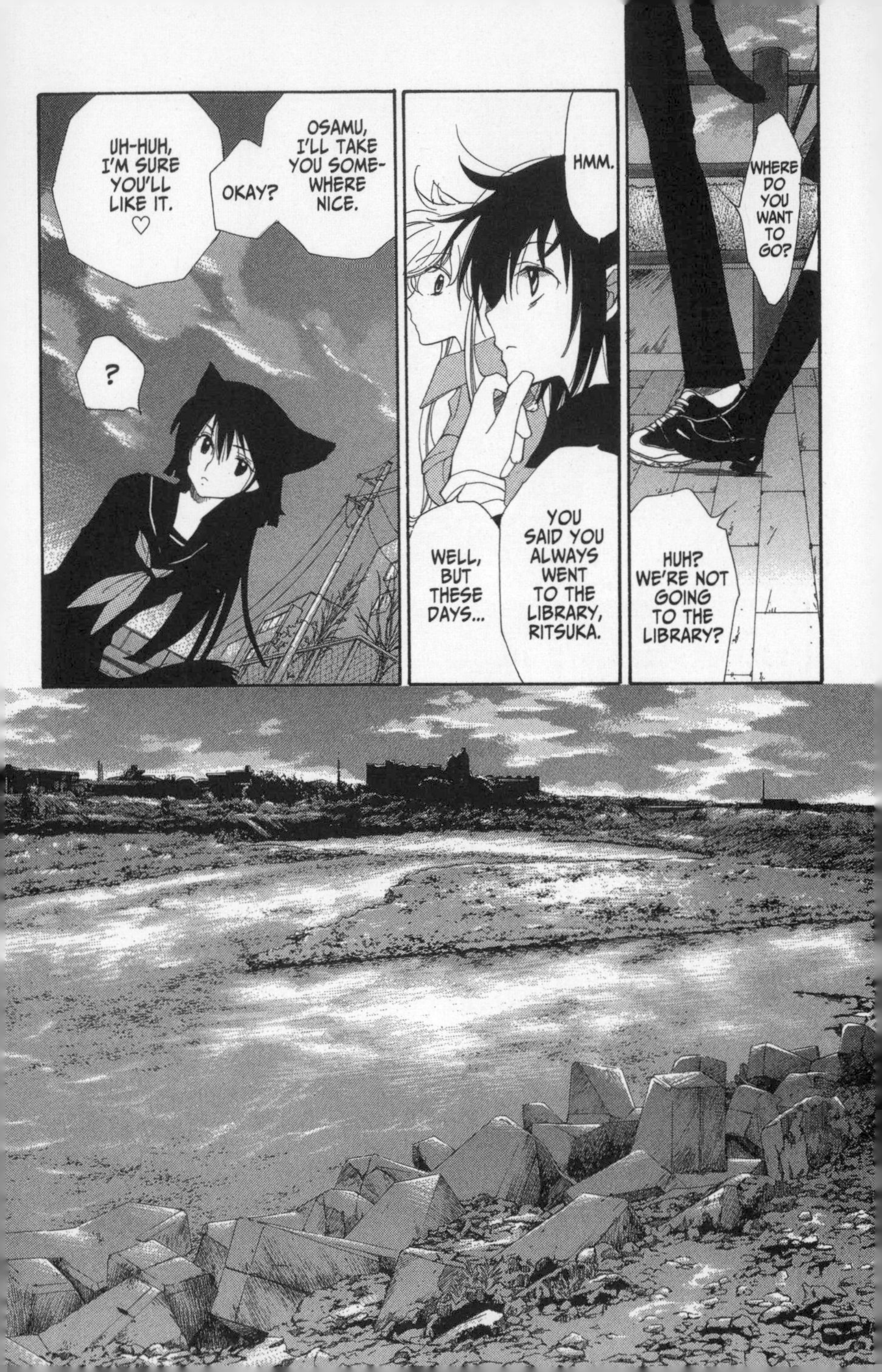
WHERE DO YOU WANT TO GO?
HUH? WE'RE NOT GOING TO THE LIBRARY?
HMM.
YOU SAID YOU ALWAYS WENT TO THE LIBRARY, RITSUKA.
WELL, BUT THESE DAYS...
OSAMU, I'LL TAKE YOU SOME-WHERE NICE.
OKAY?
UH-HUH, I'M SURE YOU'LL LIKE IT. ♡
?

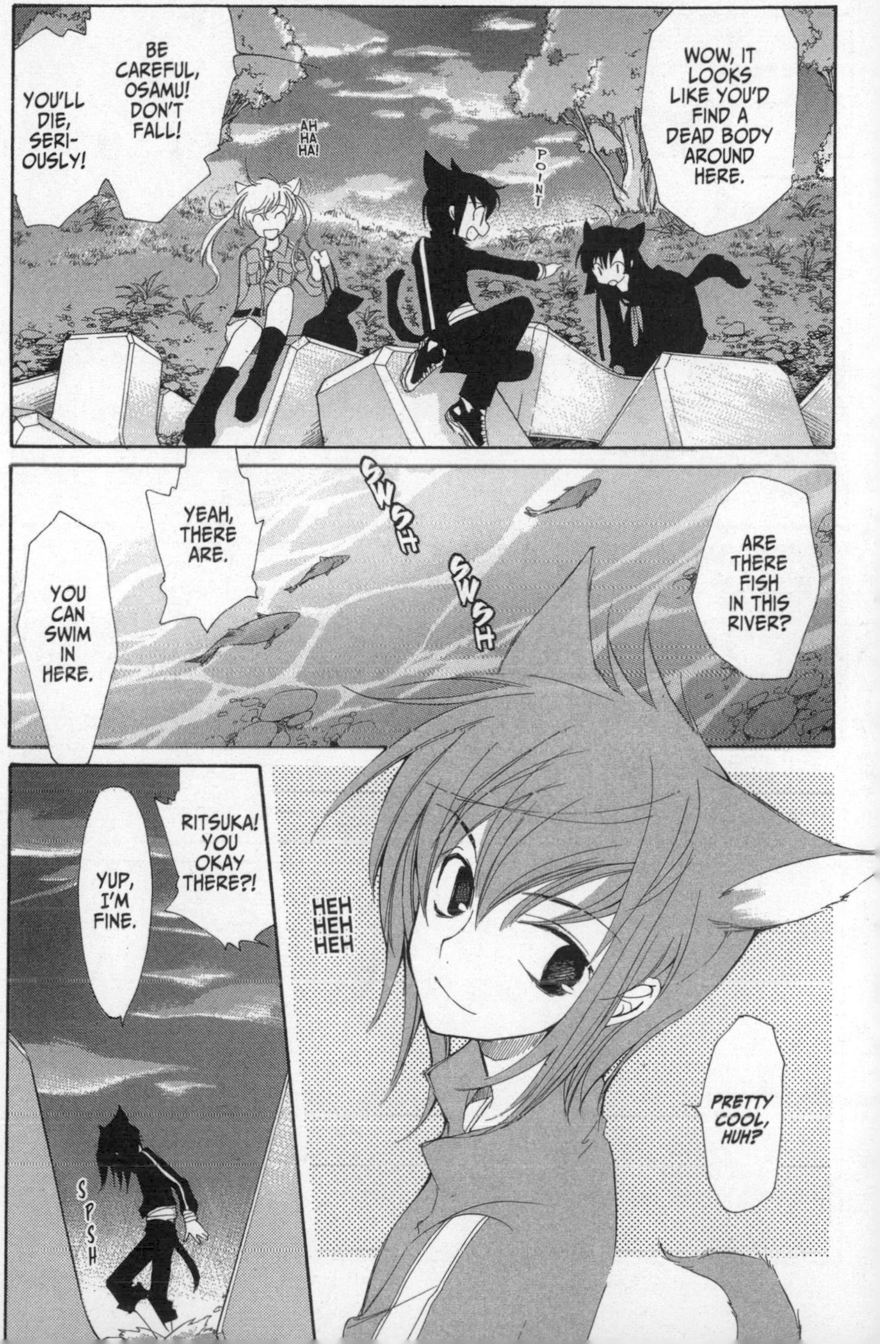
WOW, IT LOOKS LIKE YOU'D FIND A DEAD BODY AROUND HERE.
POINT
AH HA HA!
BE CAREFUL, OSAMU! DON'T FALL!
YOU'LL DIE, SERI-OUSLY!
ARE THERE FISH IN THIS RIVER?
SWSH
SWSH
YEAH, THERE ARE.
YOU CAN SWIM IN HERE.
PRETTY COOL, HUH?
HEH HEH HEH
RITSUKA! YOU OKAY THERE?!
YUP, I'M FINE.
SPSH

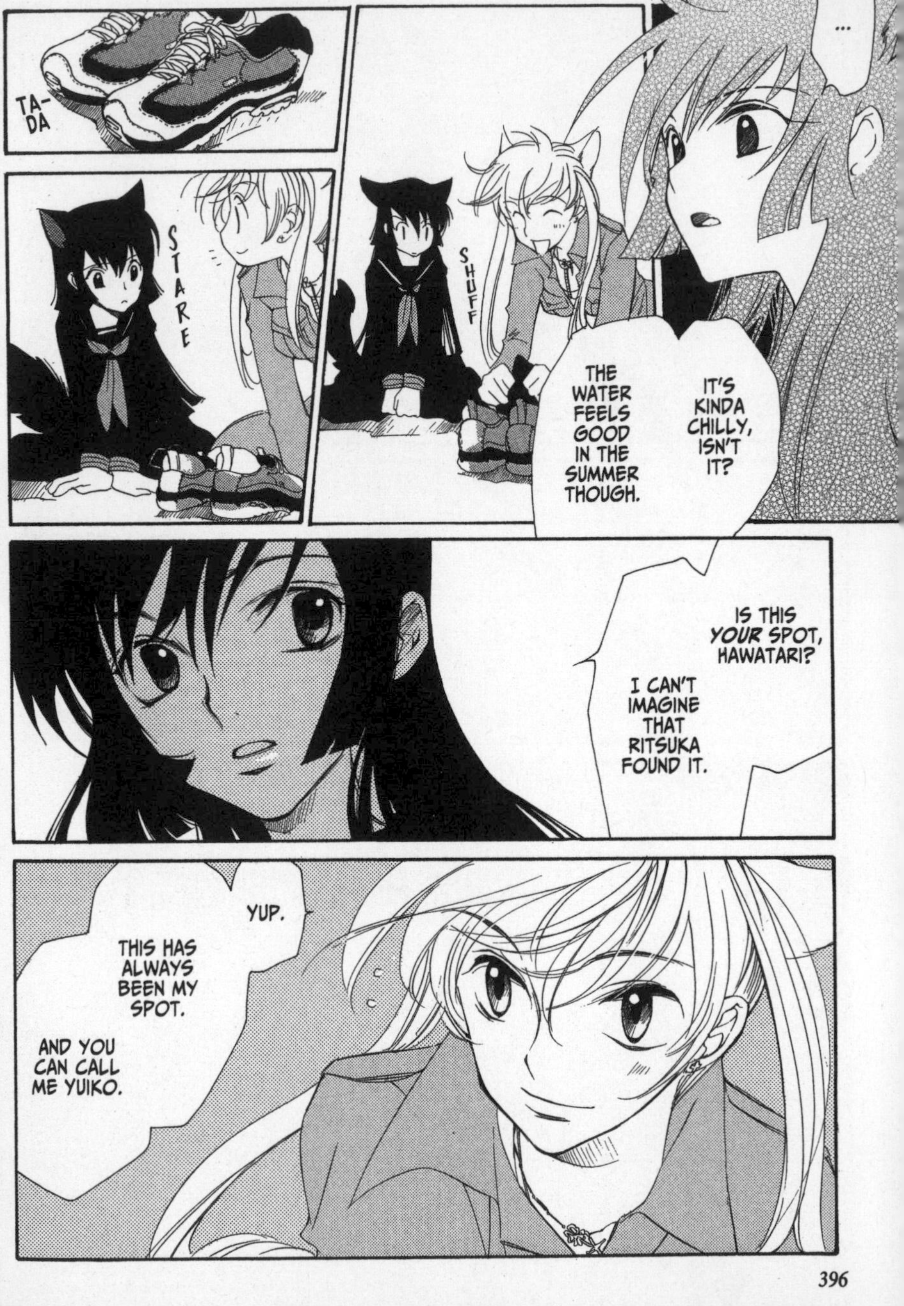
...
IT'S KINDA CHILLY, ISN'T IT?
THE WATER FEELS GOOD IN THE SUMMER THOUGH.
TA-DA
SHUFF
STARE
IS THIS *YOUR* SPOT, HAWATARI?
I CAN'T IMAGINE THAT RITSUKA FOUND IT.
YUP.
THIS HAS ALWAYS BEEN MY SPOT.
AND YOU CAN CALL ME YUIKO.

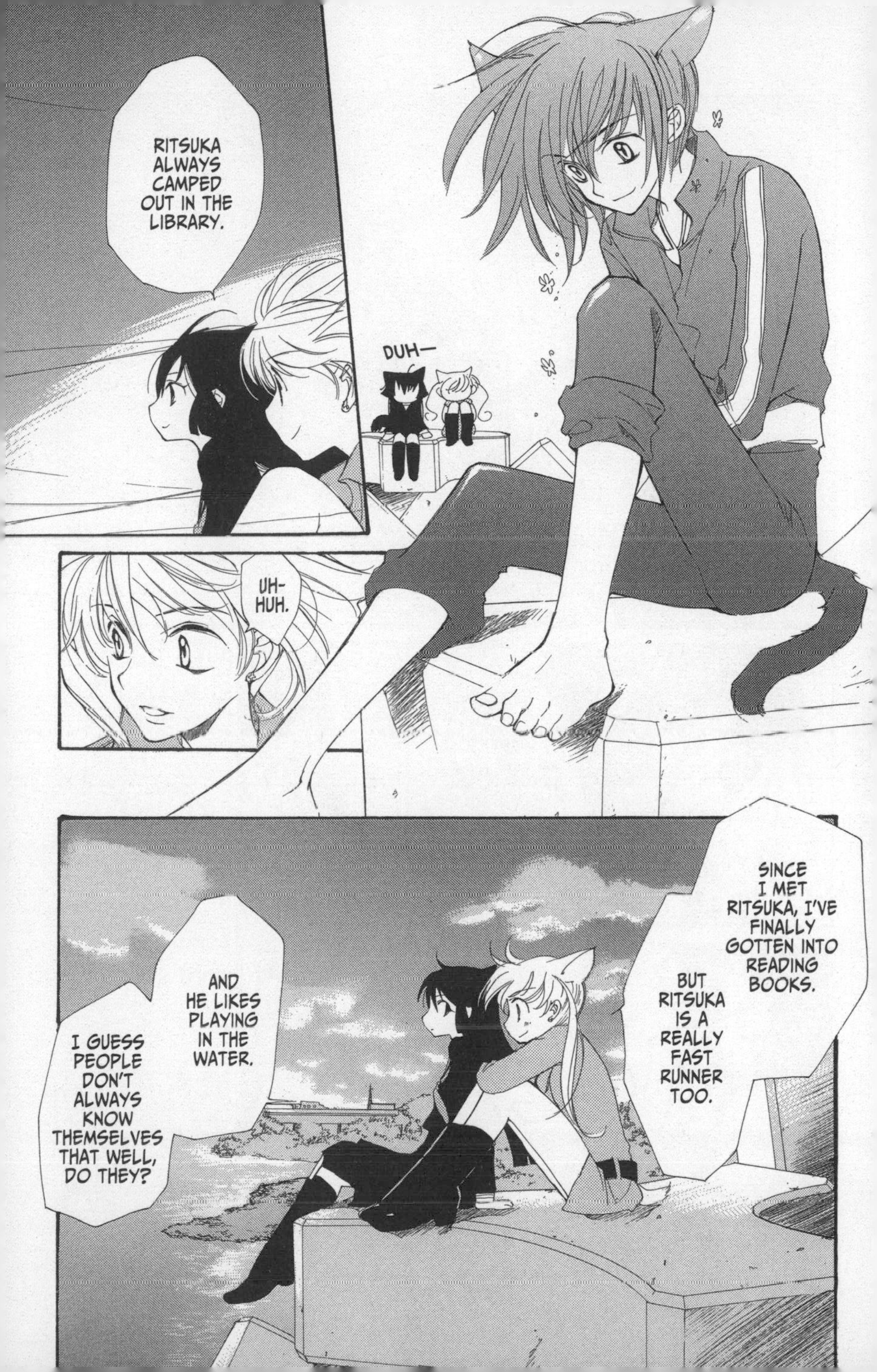
DUH—
RITSUKA ALWAYS CAMPED OUT IN THE LIBRARY.
UH-HUH.
SINCE I MET RITSUKA, I'VE FINALLY GOTTEN INTO READING BOOKS.
BUT RITSUKA IS A REALLY FAST RUNNER TOO.
AND HE LIKES PLAYING IN THE WATER.
I GUESS PEOPLE DON'T ALWAYS KNOW THEMSELVES THAT WELL, DO THEY?

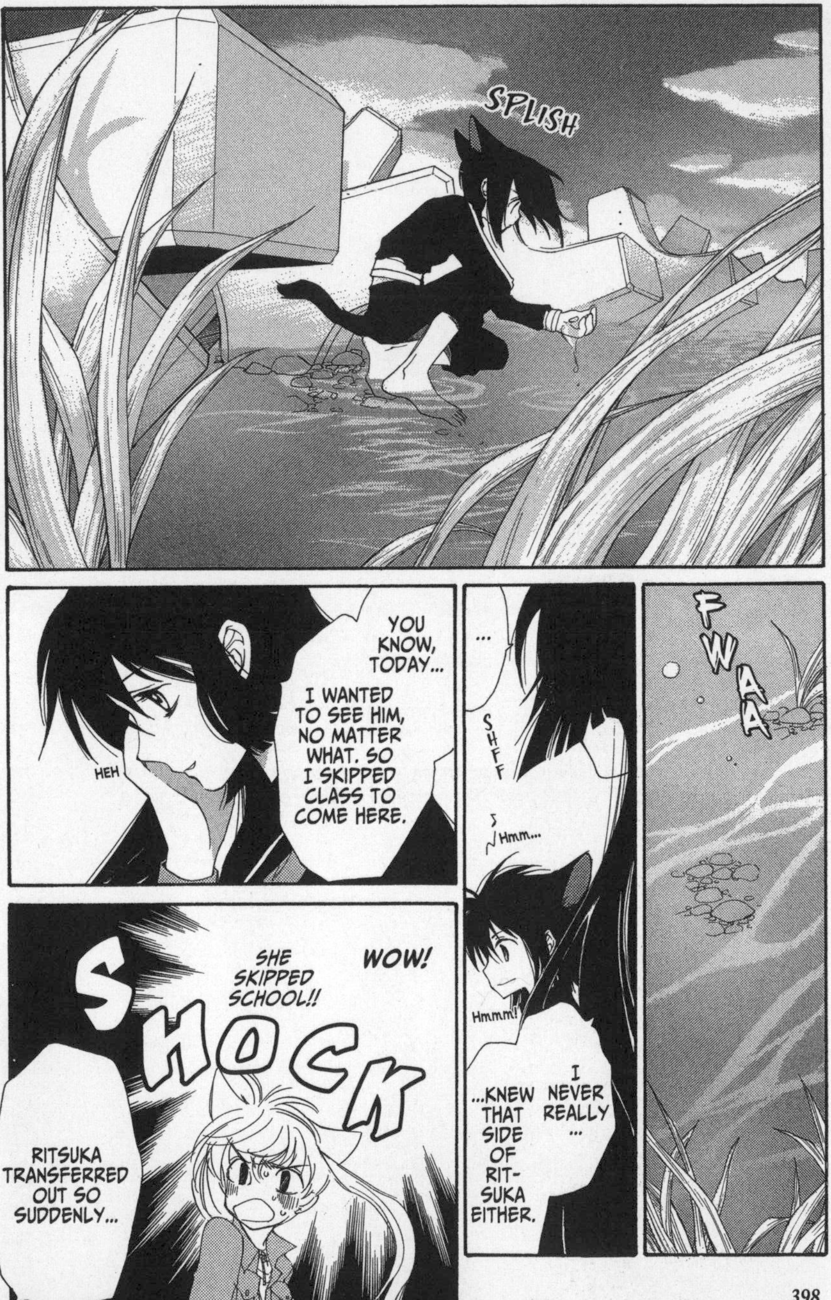
SPLISH
FWAA
...
SHFF
Hmm...
Hmmm!
I NEVER REALLY ...
...KNEW THAT SIDE OF RIT-SUKA EITHER.
YOU KNOW, TODAY...
I WANTED TO SEE HIM, NO MATTER WHAT. SO I SKIPPED CLASS TO COME HERE.
HEH
WOW!
SHE SKIPPED SCHOOL!!
SHOCK
RITSUKA TRANSFERRED OUT SO SUDDENLY...

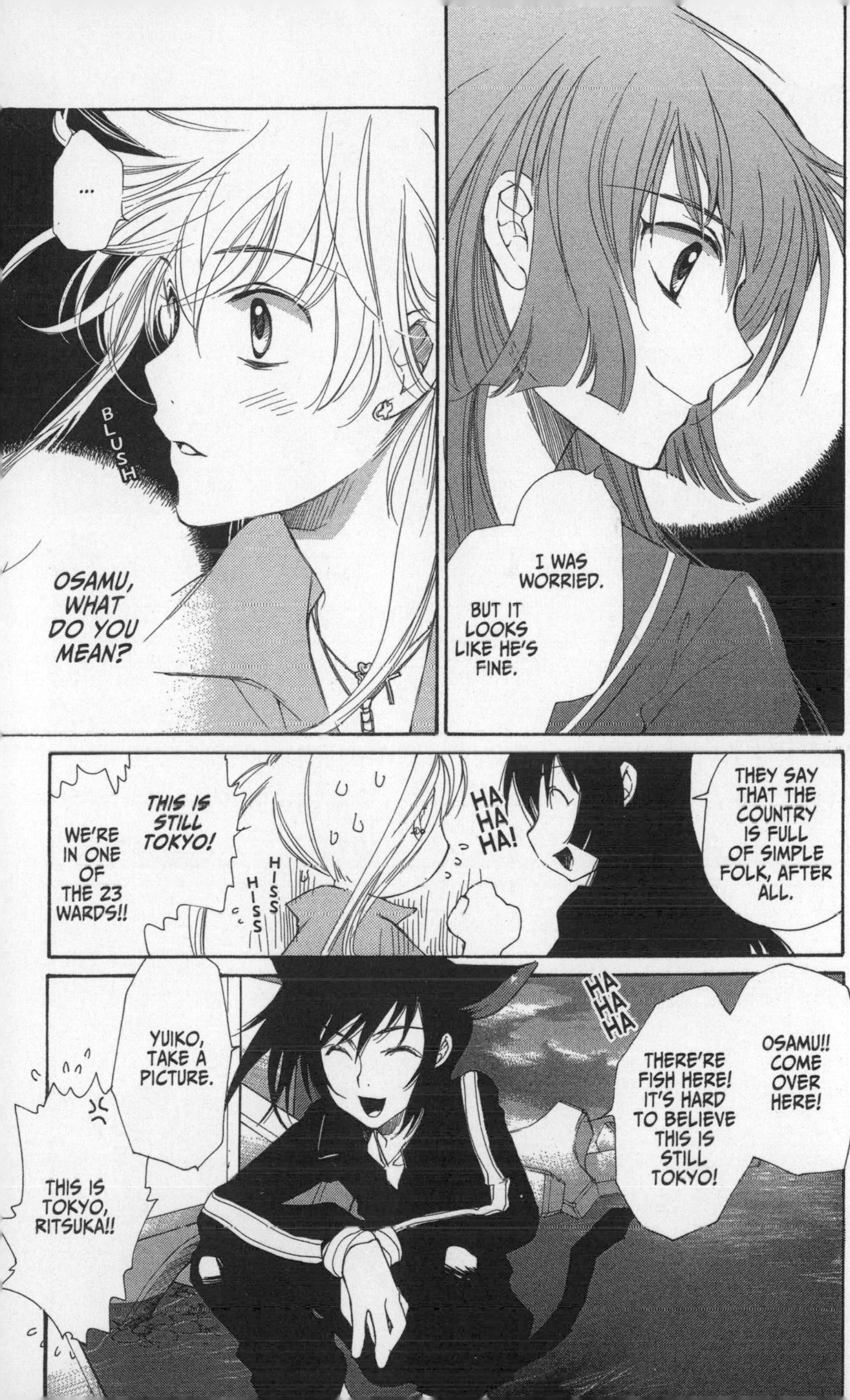
I WAS WORRIED.
BUT IT LOOKS LIKE HE'S FINE.
...
BLUSH
OSAMU, WHAT DO YOU MEAN?
THEY SAY THAT THE COUNTRY IS FULL OF SIMPLE FOLK, AFTER ALL.
HA HA HA!
HISS HISS
THIS IS STILL TOKYO!
WE'RE IN ONE OF THE 23 WARDS!!
OSAMU!! COME OVER HERE!
THERE'RE FISH HERE! IT'S HARD TO BELIEVE THIS IS STILL TOKYO!
HA HA HA
YUIKO, TAKE A PICTURE.
THIS IS TOKYO, RITSUKA!!

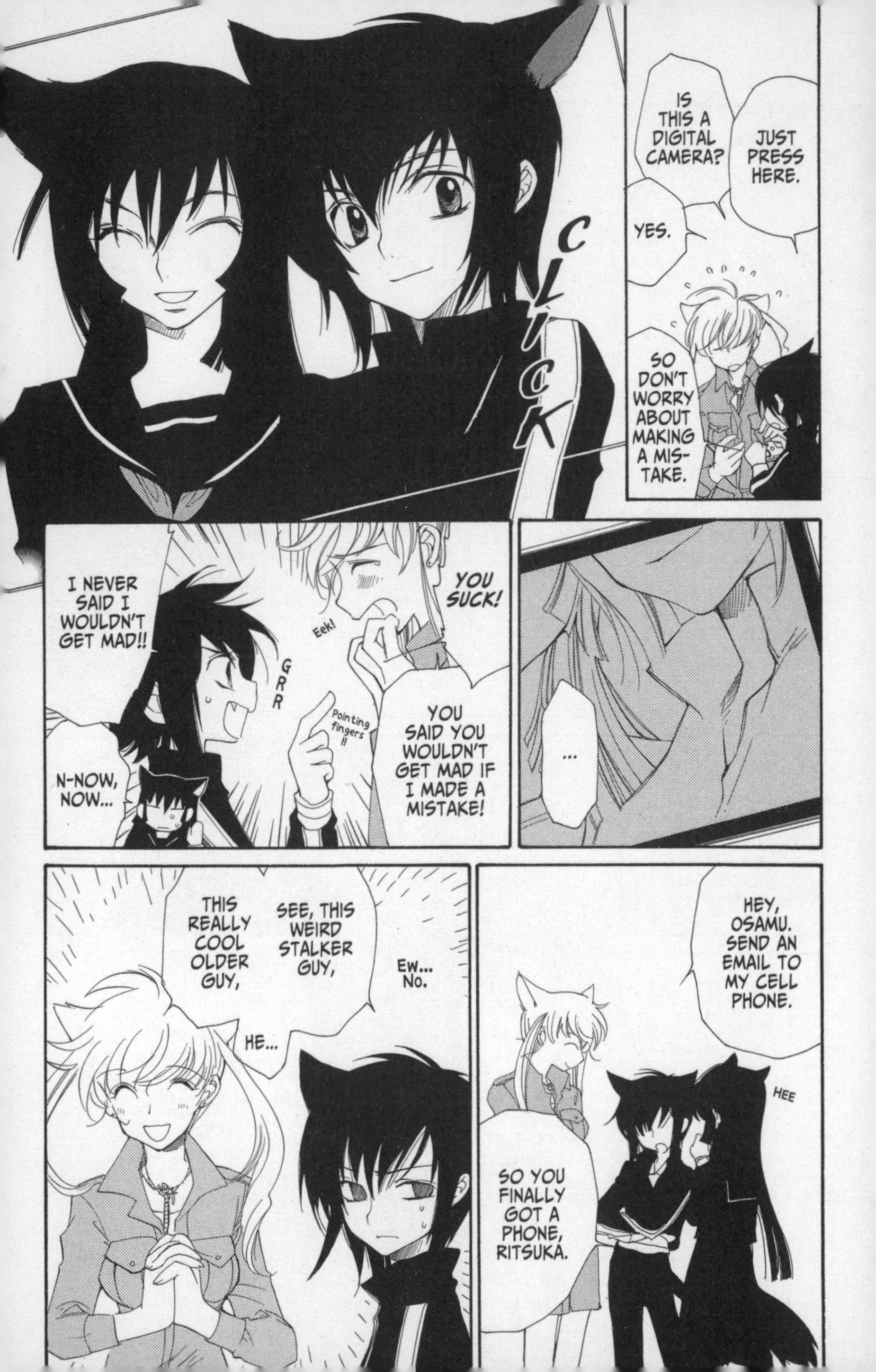
IS THIS A DIGITAL CAMERA?
YES.
JUST PRESS HERE.
SO DON'T WORRY ABOUT MAKING A MIS-TAKE.
CLICK
...
YOU SUCK!
Eek!
YOU SAID YOU WOULDN'T GET MAD IF I MADE A MISTAKE!
I NEVER SAID I WOULDN'T GET MAD!!
GRR
Pointing fingers!!
N-NOW, NOW...
HEY, OSAMU. SEND AN EMAIL TO MY CELL PHONE.
HEE
SO YOU FINALLY GOT A PHONE, RITSUKA.
SEE, THIS WEIRD STALKER GUY,
Ew... No.
THIS REALLY COOL OLDER GUY,
HE...

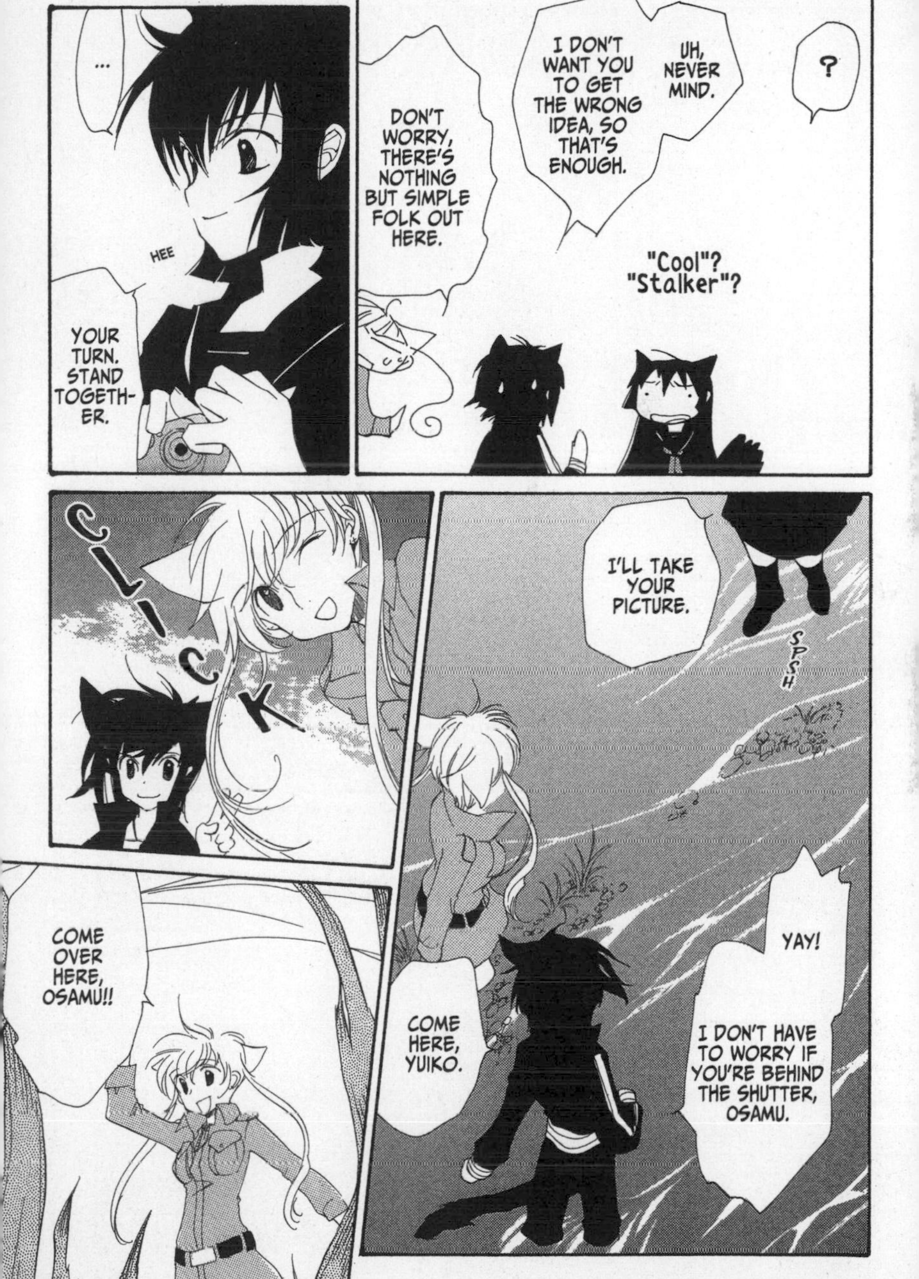
?
UH, NEVER MIND.
I DON'T WANT YOU TO GET THE WRONG IDEA, SO THAT'S ENOUGH.
DON'T WORRY, THERE'S NOTHING BUT SIMPLE FOLK OUT HERE.
"Cool"? "Stalker"?
...
HEE
YOUR TURN. STAND TOGETH-ER.
I'LL TAKE YOUR PICTURE.
SPSH
YAY!
I DON'T HAVE TO WORRY IF YOU'RE BEHIND THE SHUTTER, OSAMU.
COME HERE, YUIKO.
CLICK
COME OVER HERE, OSAMU!!

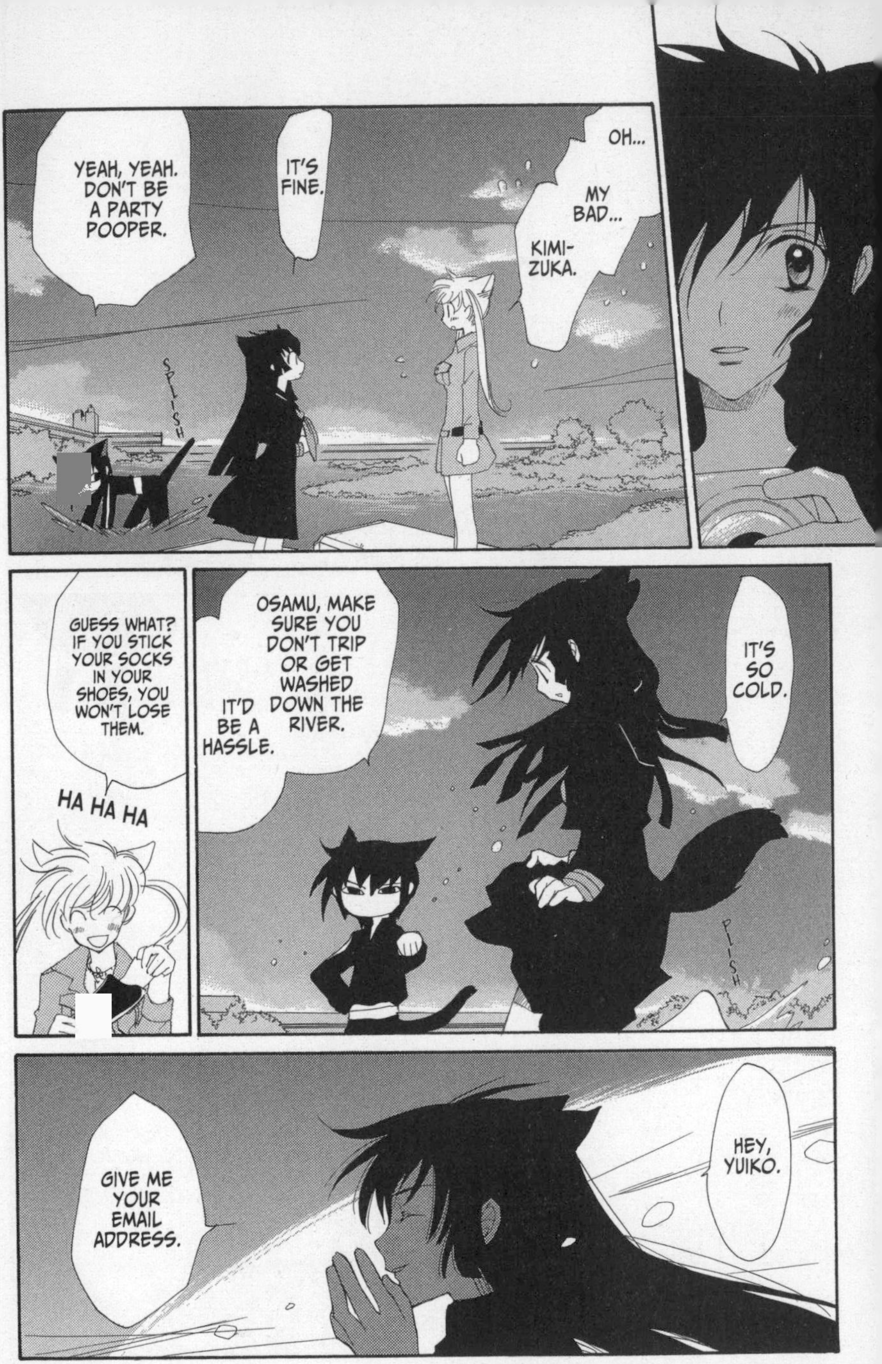
OH...
MY BAD...
KIMI-ZUKA.
IT'S FINE.
YEAH, YEAH. DON'T BE A PARTY POOPER.
SPLISH
IT'S SO COLD.
OSAMU, MAKE SURE YOU DON'T TRIP OR GET WASHED DOWN THE RIVER.
IT'D BE A HASSLE.
PLISH
GUESS WHAT? IF YOU STICK YOUR SOCKS IN YOUR SHOES, YOU WON'T LOSE THEM.
HA HA HA
HEY, YUIKO.
GIVE ME YOUR EMAIL ADDRESS.

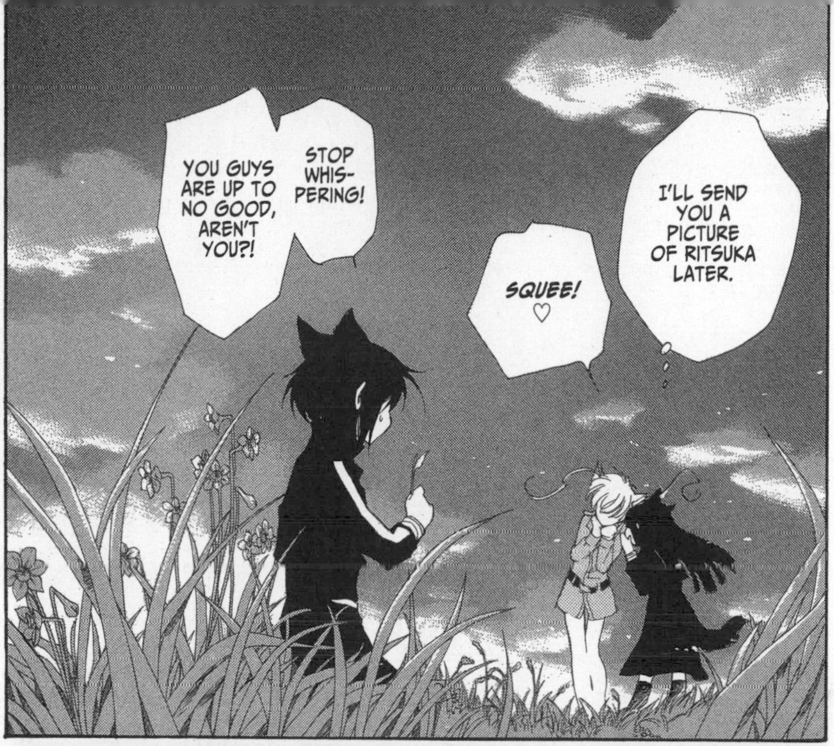
I'LL SEND YOU A PICTURE OF RITSUKA LATER.
SQUEE! ♡
STOP WHIS-PERING!
YOU GUYS ARE UP TO NO GOOD, AREN'T YOU?!

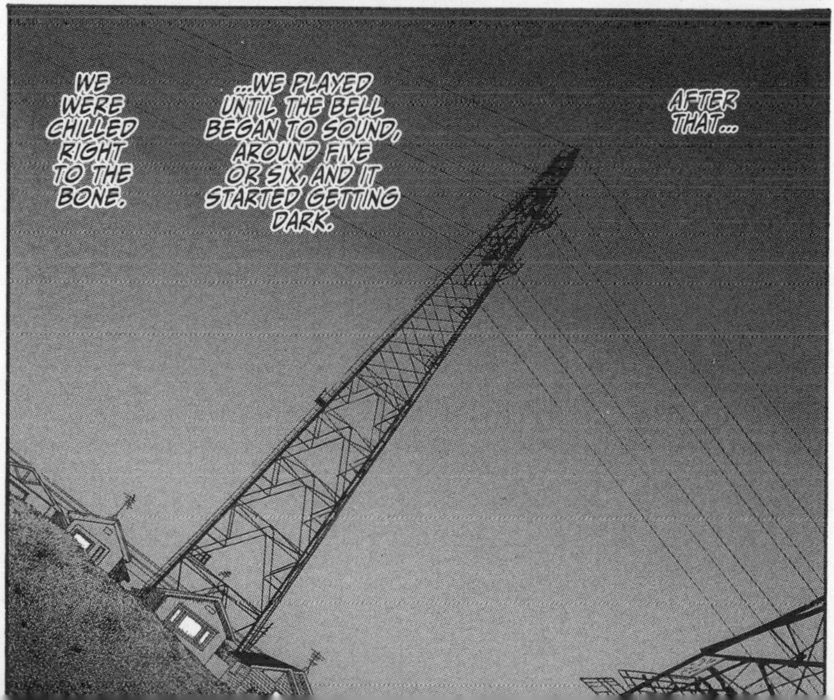
AFTER THAT...
...WE PLAYED UNTIL THE BELL BEGAN TO SOUND, AROUND FIVE OR SIX, AND IT STARTED GETTING DARK.
WE WERE CHILLED RIGHT TO THE BONE.

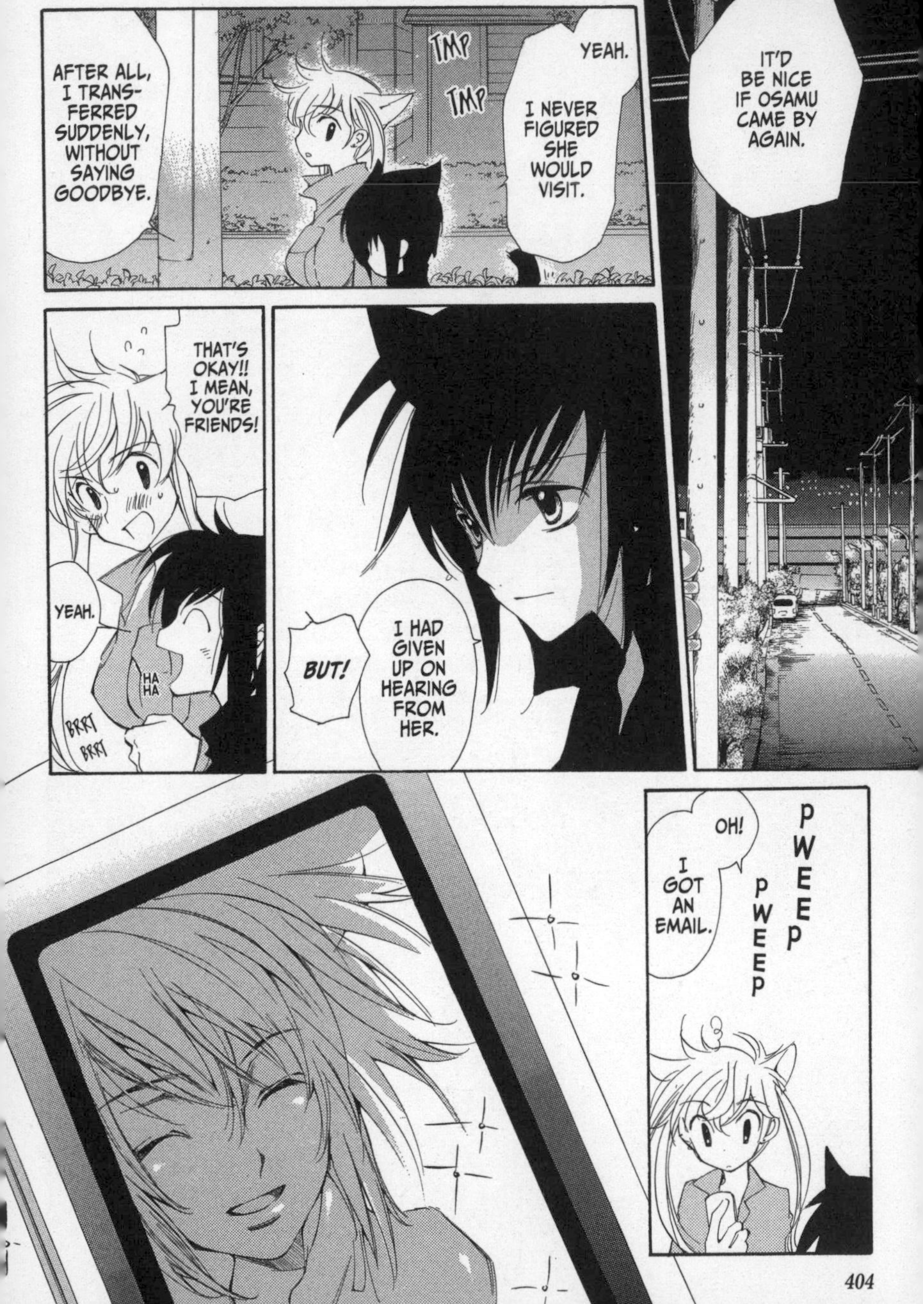
IT'D BE NICE IF OSAMU CAME BY AGAIN.
TMP TMP
YEAH.
I NEVER FIGURED SHE WOULD VISIT.
AFTER ALL, I TRANS-FERRED SUDDENLY, WITHOUT SAYING GOODBYE.
I HAD GIVEN UP ON HEARING FROM HER.
BUT!
THAT'S OKAY!! I MEAN, YOU'RE FRIENDS!
YEAH.
HA HA
BRRT BRRT
OH!
I GOT AN EMAIL.
PWEEP PWEEP

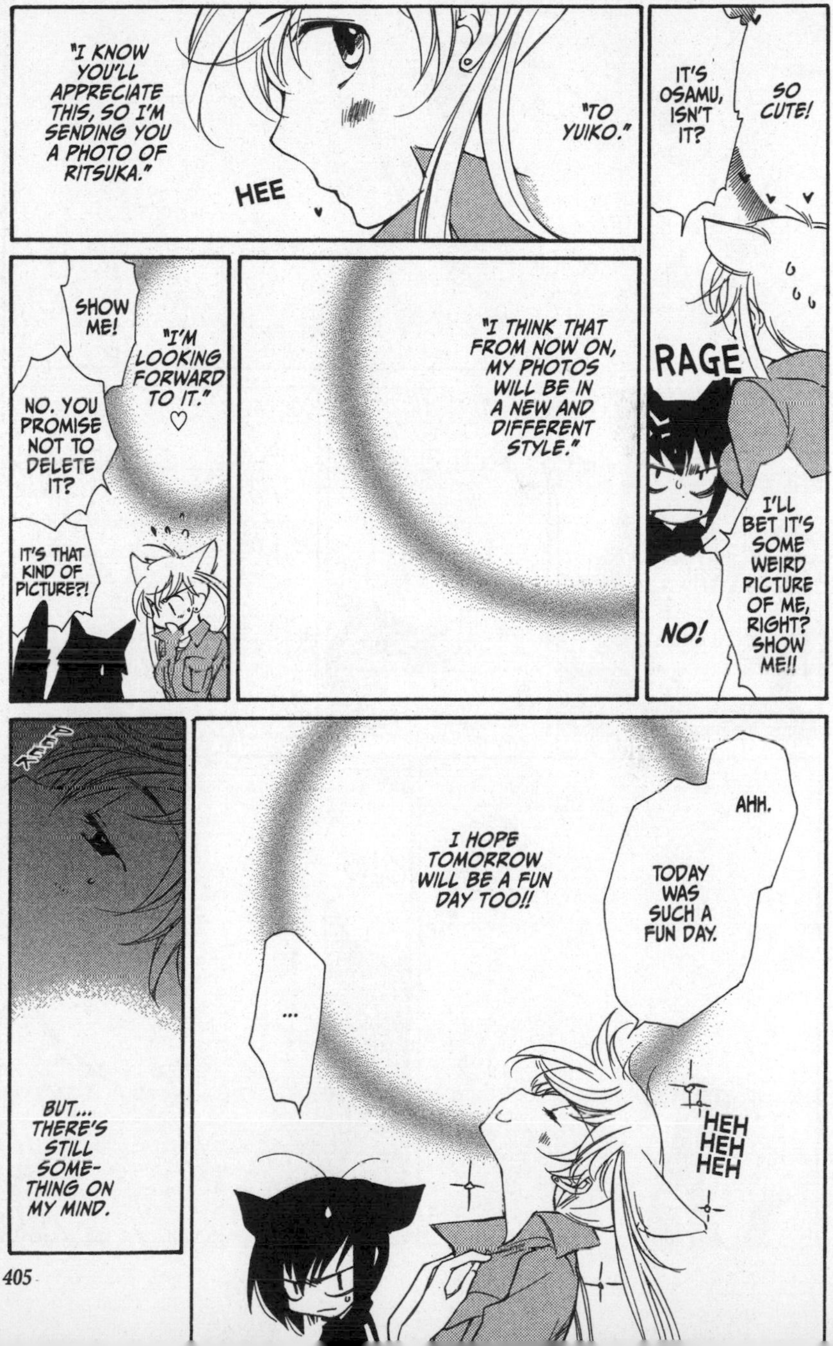
SO CUTE!
IT'S OSAMU, ISN'T IT?
RAGE
I'LL BET IT'S SOME WEIRD PICTURE OF ME, RIGHT? SHOW ME!!
NO!
"TO YUIKO."
"I KNOW YOU'LL APPRECIATE THIS, SO I'M SENDING YOU A PHOTO OF RITSUKA."
HEE
"I THINK THAT FROM NOW ON, MY PHOTOS WILL BE IN A NEW AND DIFFERENT STYLE."
"I'M LOOKING FORWARD TO IT." ♡
SHOW ME!
NO. YOU PROMISE NOT TO DELETE IT?
IT'S THAT KIND OF PICTURE?!
AHH.
TODAY WAS SUCH A FUN DAY.
I HOPE TOMORROW WILL BE A FUN DAY TOO!!
...
HEH HEH HEH
BUT... THERE'S STILL SOME-THING ON MY MIND.

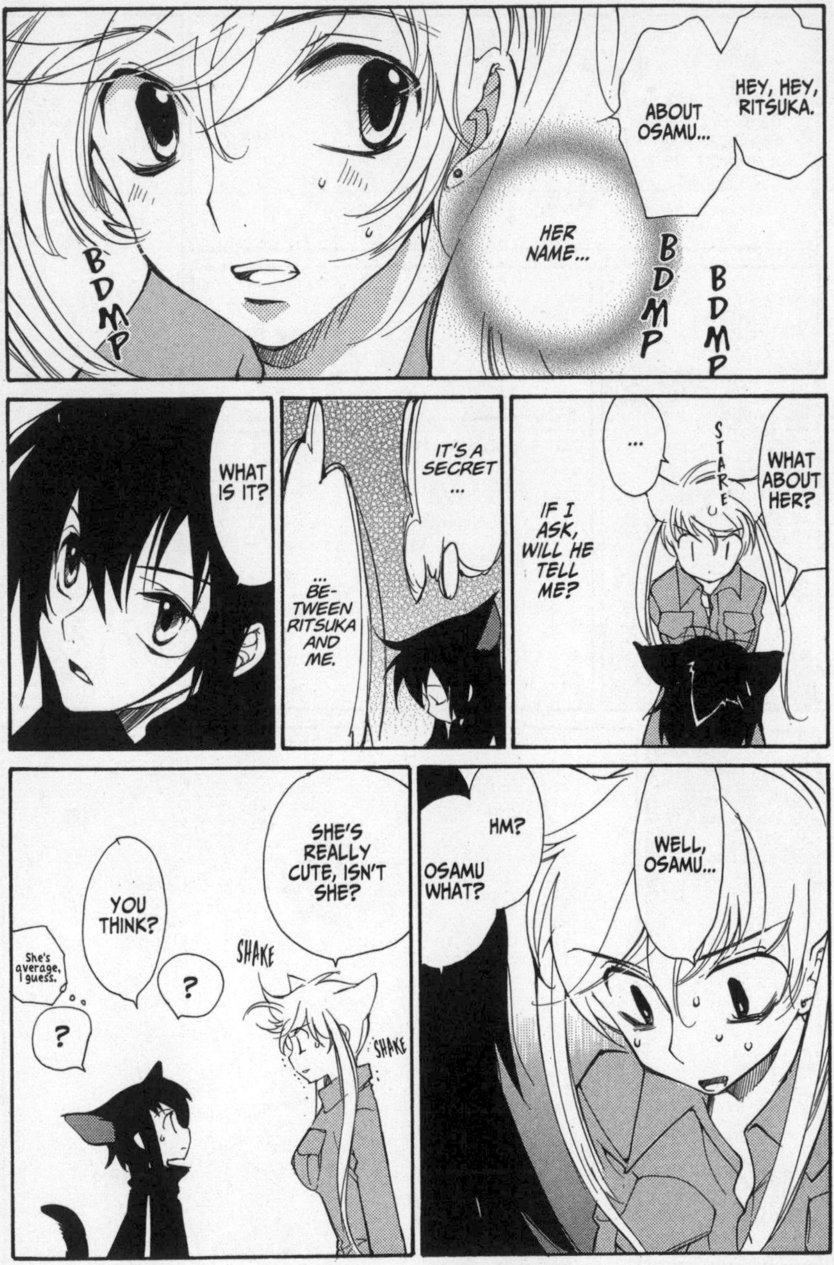
HEY, HEY, RITSUKA.
ABOUT OSAMU...
HER NAME...
BDMP
BDMP
BDMP
WHAT ABOUT HER?
STARE
...
IF I ASK, WILL HE TELL ME?
IT'S A SECRET ...
... BE-TWEEN RITSUKA AND ME.
WHAT IS IT?
WELL, OSAMU...
HM?
OSAMU WHAT?
SHE'S REALLY CUTE, ISN'T SHE?
SHAKE
SHAKE
YOU THINK?
?
She's average, I guess.
?

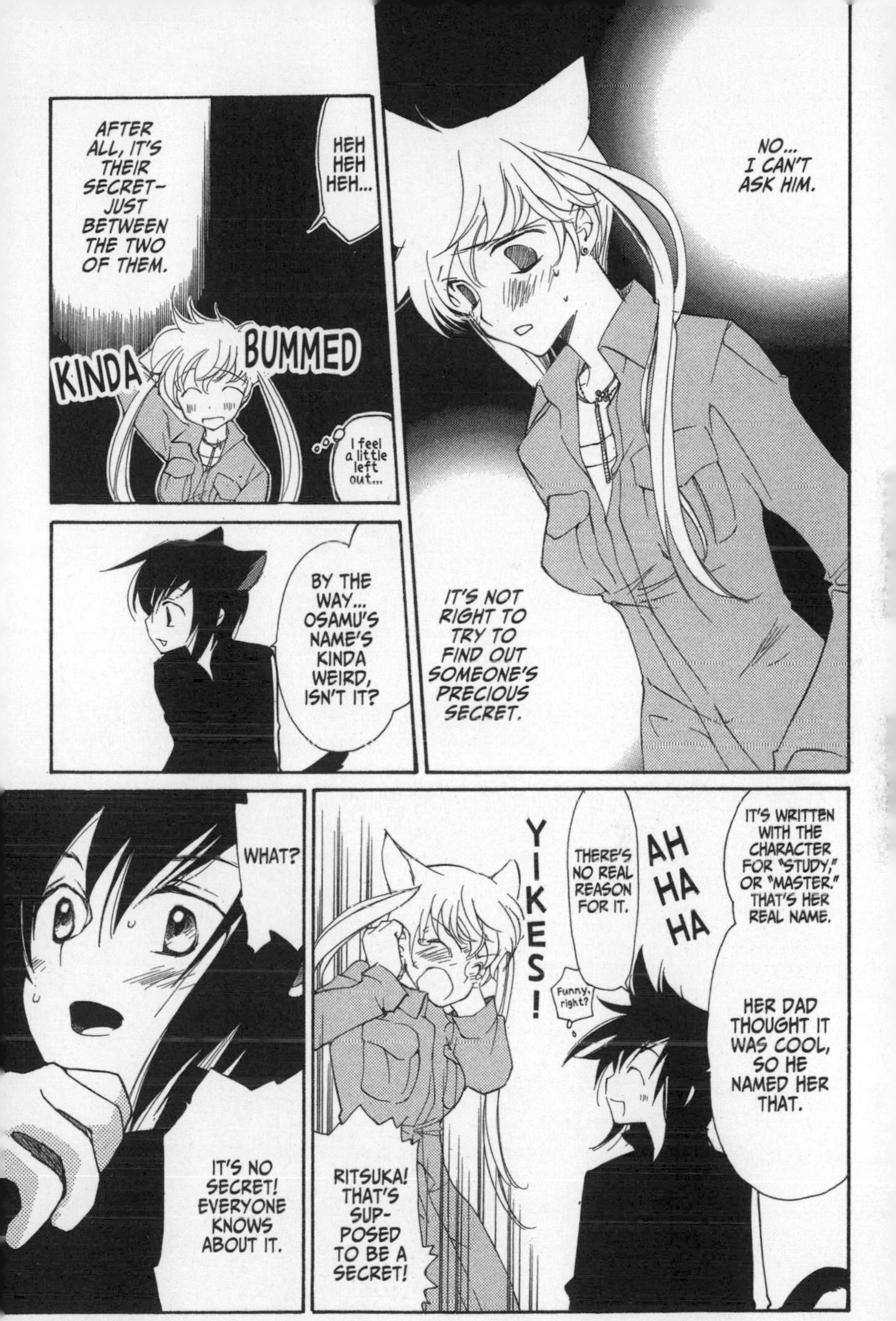
NO... I CAN'T ASK HIM.
IT'S NOT RIGHT TO TRY TO FIND OUT SOMEONE'S PRECIOUS SECRET.
HEH HEH HEH...
AFTER ALL, IT'S THEIR SECRET— JUST BETWEEN THE TWO OF THEM.
KINDA BUMMED
I feel a little left out...
BY THE WAY... OSAMU'S NAME'S KINDA WEIRD, ISN'T IT?
IT'S WRITTEN WITH THE CHARACTER FOR "STUDY," OR "MASTER." THAT'S HER REAL NAME.
AH HA HA
THERE'S NO REAL REASON FOR IT.
HER DAD THOUGHT IT WAS COOL, SO HE NAMED HER THAT.
Funny, right?
YIKES!
RITSUKA! THAT'S SUP-POSED TO BE A SECRET!
WHAT?
IT'S NO SECRET! EVERYONE KNOWS ABOUT IT.

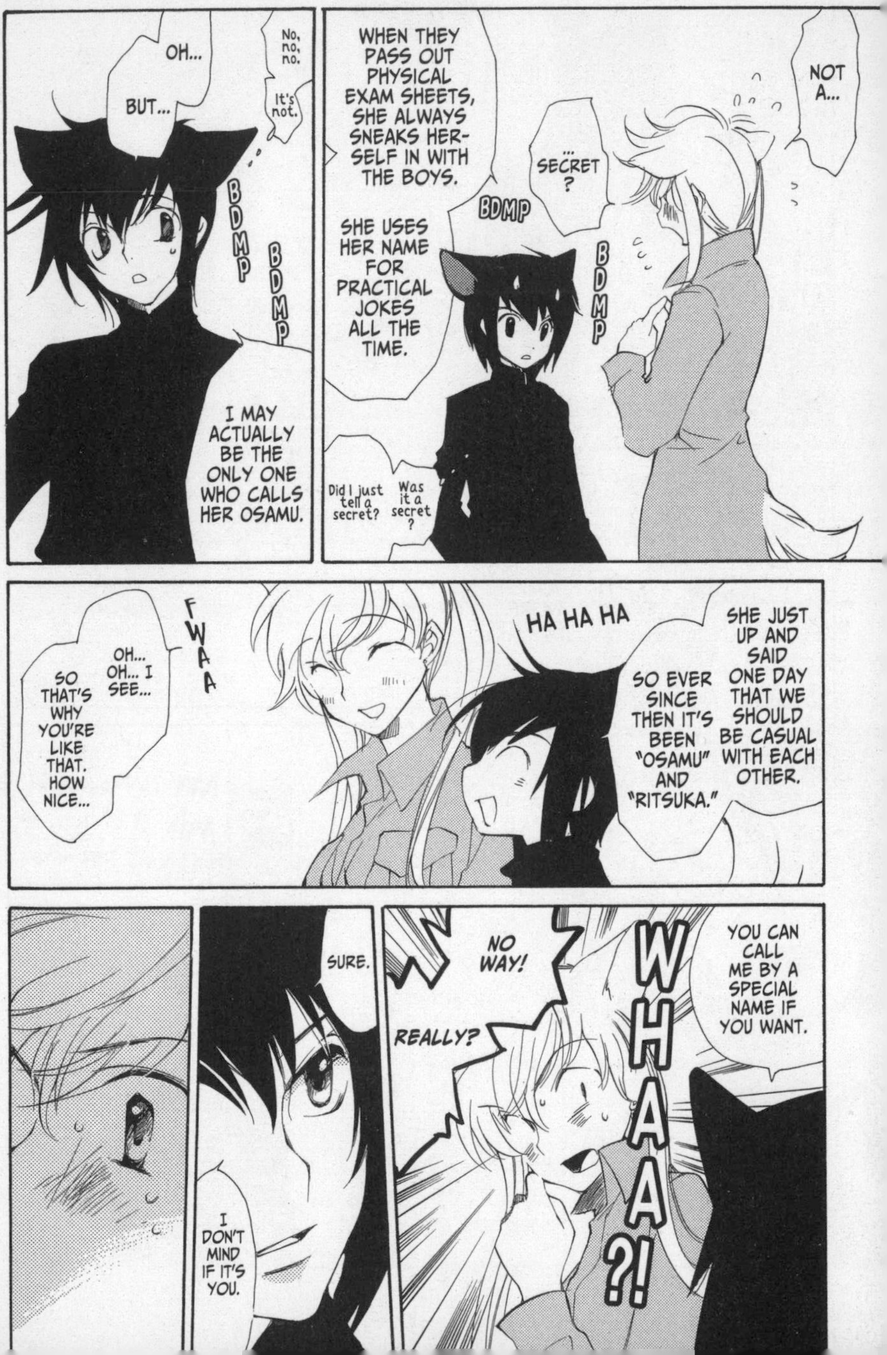
NOT A...
...SECRET?
BDMP
WHEN THEY PASS OUT PHYSICAL EXAM SHEETS, SHE ALWAYS SNEAKS HERSELF IN WITH THE BOYS.
SHE USES HER NAME FOR PRACTICAL JOKES ALL THE TIME.
BDMP
Was it a secret?
Did I just tell a secret?
No, no, no.
It's not.
OH... BUT...
BDMP
BDMP
I MAY ACTUALLY BE THE ONLY ONE WHO CALLS HER OSAMU.
SHE JUST UP AND SAID ONE DAY THAT WE SHOULD BE CASUAL WITH EACH OTHER.
SO EVER SINCE THEN IT'S BEEN "OSAMU" AND "RITSUKA."
HA HA HA
FWAA
OH... OH... I SEE...
SO THAT'S WHY YOU'RE LIKE THAT. HOW NICE...
YOU CAN CALL ME BY A SPECIAL NAME IF YOU WANT.
WHAAA?!
NO WAY!
REALLY?
SURE.
I DON'T MIND IF IT'S YOU.

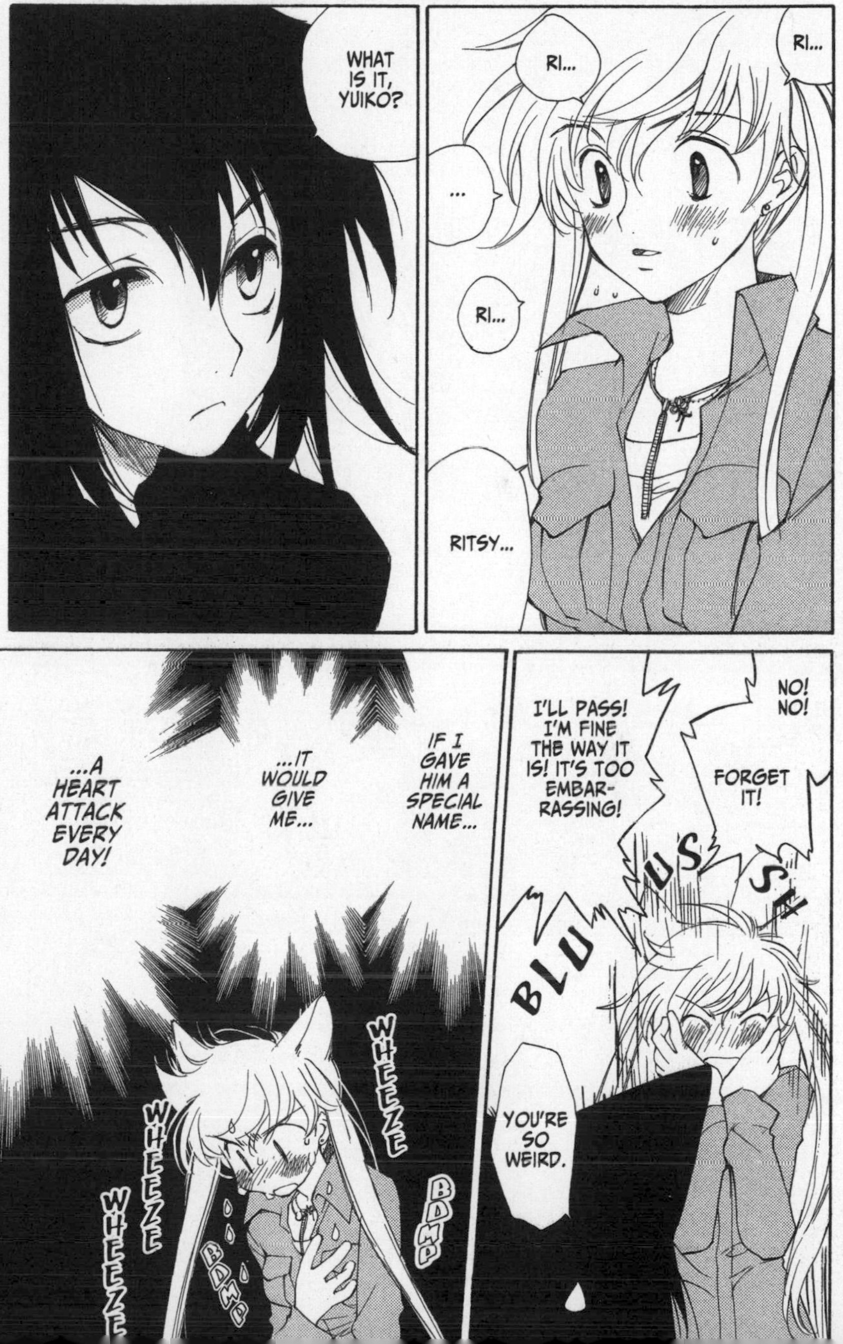
RI...
RI...
...
RI...
RITSY...
WHAT IS IT, YUIKO?
NO! NO!
FORGET IT!
I'LL PASS! I'M FINE THE WAY IT IS! IT'S TOO EMBAR-RASSING!
BLUSSH
YOU'RE SO WEIRD.
IF I GAVE HIM A SPECIAL NAME...
...IT WOULD GIVE ME...
...A HEART ATTACK EVERY DAY!
WHEEZE
BDMP
WHEEZE
WHEEZE
BDMP

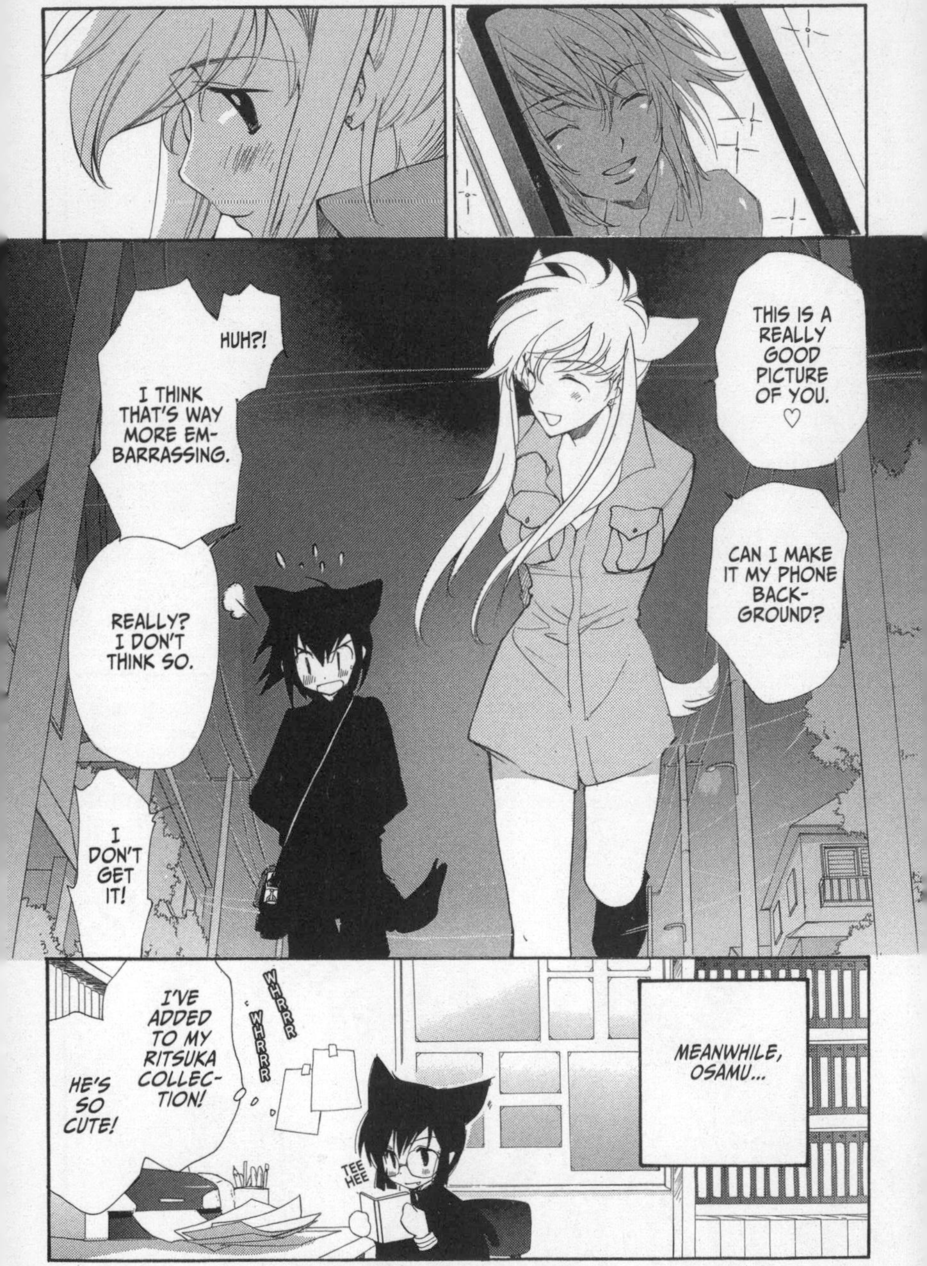
THIS IS A REALLY GOOD PICTURE OF YOU. ♡
CAN I MAKE IT MY PHONE BACKGROUND?
HUH?!
I THINK THAT'S WAY MORE EM-BARRASSING.
REALLY? I DON'T THINK SO.
I DON'T GET IT!
MEANWHILE, OSAMU...
TEE HEE
WHRRR
WHRRR
I'VE ADDED TO MY RITSUKA COLLEC-TION!
HE'S SO CUTE!

LOVELESS 4 / END

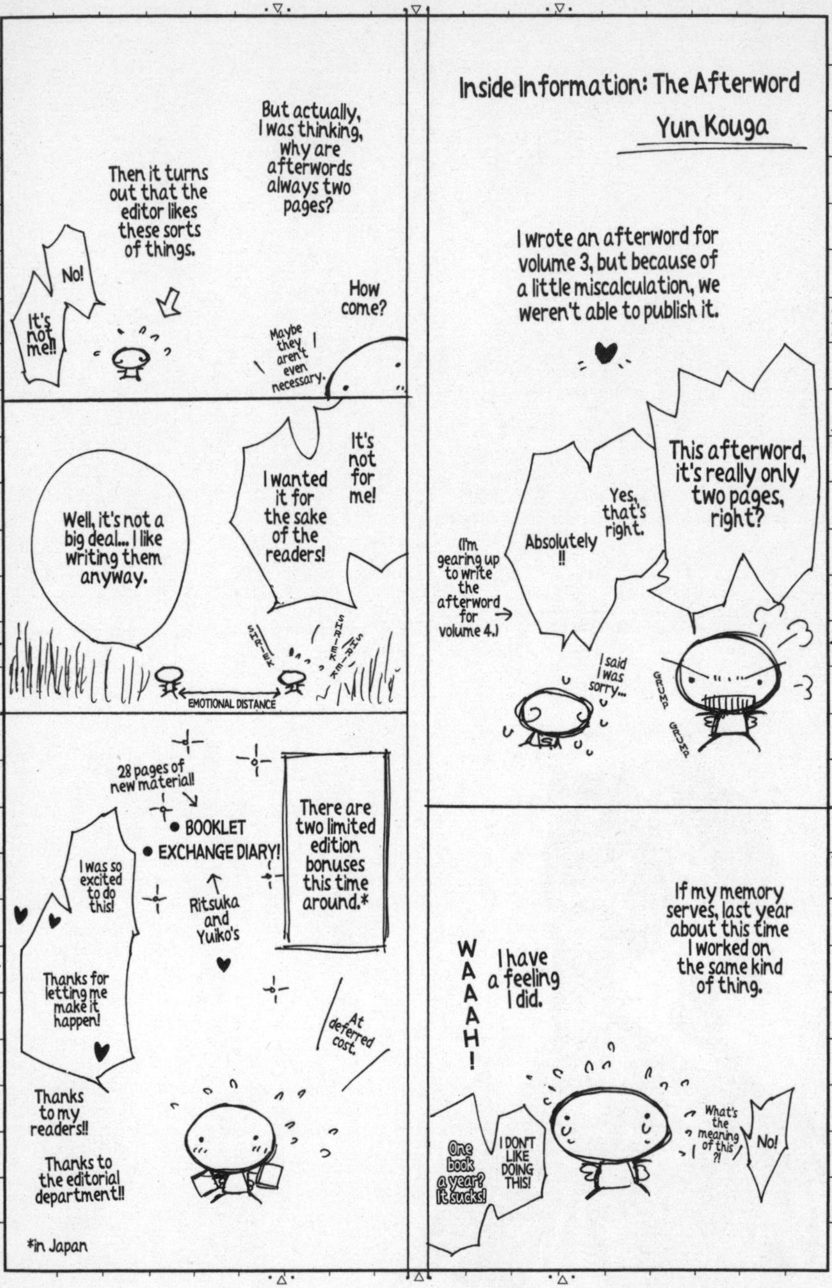
Inside Information: The Afterword
Yun Kouga
I wrote an afterword for volume 3, but because of a little miscalculation, we weren't able to publish it.
This afterword, it's really only two pages, right?
Yes, that's right.
Absolutely!!
(I'm gearing up to write the afterword for volume 4.)
I said I was sorry...
GRUMP
GRUMP
If my memory serves, last year about this time I worked on the same kind of thing.
I have a feeling I did.
WAAAH!
What's the meaning of this?!
No!
I DON'T LIKE DOING THIS!
One book a year? It sucks!
But actually, I was thinking, why are afterwords always two pages?
Then it turns out that the editor likes these sorts of things.
No!
It's not me!!
How come?
Maybe they aren't even necessary.
It's not for me!
I wanted it for the sake of the readers!
Well, it's not a big deal... I like writing them anyway.
SHRIEK
SHRIEK
SHRIEK
EMOTIONAL DISTANCE
There are two limited edition bonuses this time around.*
28 pages of new material!
BOOKLET
EXCHANGE DIARY!
Ritsuka and Yuiko's
I was so excited to do this!
Thanks for letting me make it happen!
At deferred cost.
Thanks to my readers!!
Thanks to the editorial department!!
*in Japan

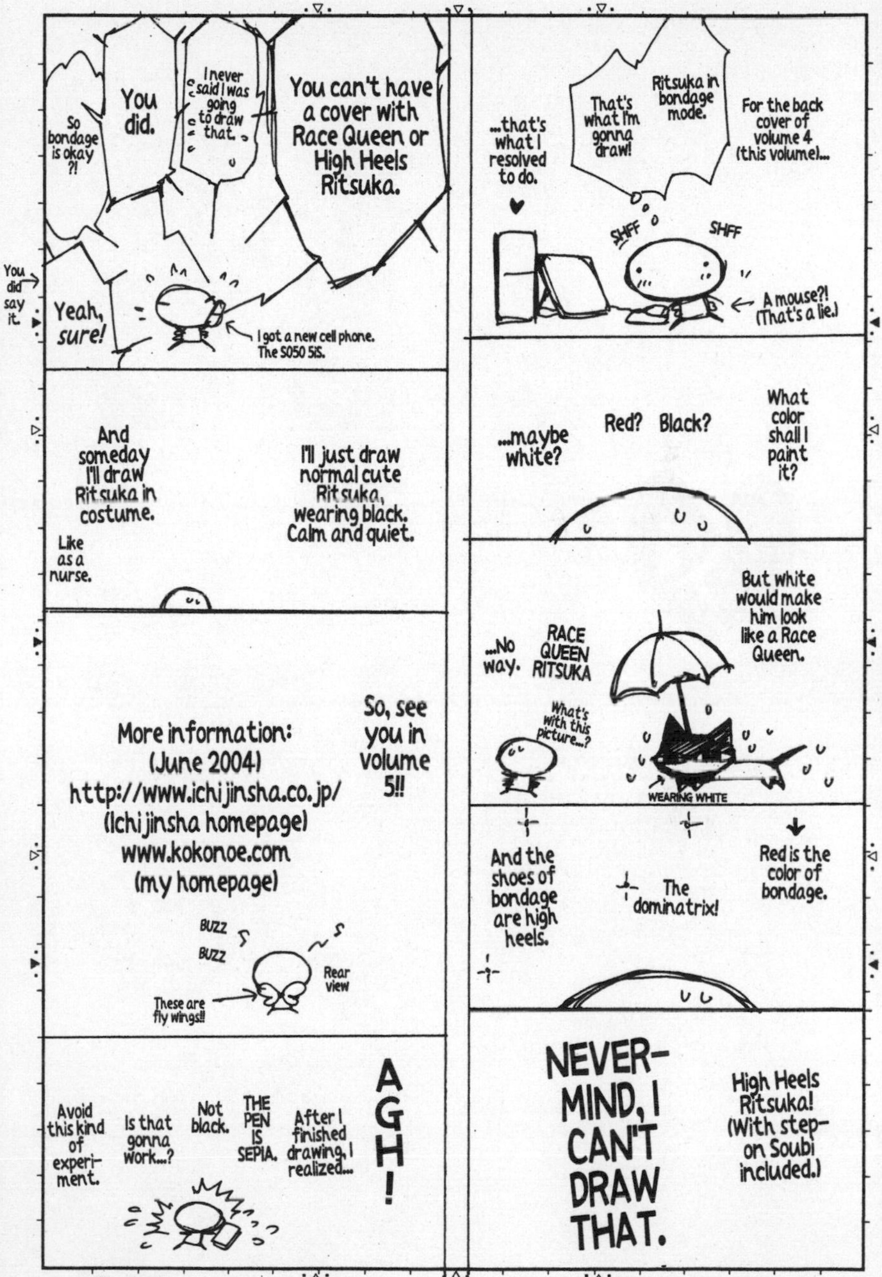
For the back cover of volume 4 (this volume)...
Ritsuka in bondage mode.
That's what I'm gonna draw!
...that's what I resolved to do.
SHFF
SHFF
A mouse?! (That's a lie.)
What color shall I paint it?
Red? Black?
...maybe white?
But white would make him look like a Race Queen.
RACE QUEEN RITSUKA
...No way.
What's with this picture...?
WEARING WHITE
Red is the color of bondage.
The dominatrix!
And the shoes of bondage are high heels.
High Heels Ritsuka! (With step-on Soubi included.)
NEVER-MIND, I CAN'T DRAW THAT.
You can't have a cover with Race Queen or High Heels Ritsuka.
I never said I was going to draw that.
You did.
So bondage is okay?!
Yeah, sure!
You did say it.
I got a new cell phone. The SO50 5iS.
I'll just draw normal cute Ritsuka, wearing black. Calm and quiet.
And someday I'll draw Ritsuka in costume.
Like as a nurse.
So, see you in volume 5!!
More information:
(June 2004)
http://www.ichijinsha.co.jp/
(Ichijinsha homepage)
www.kokonoe.com
(my homepage)
BUZZ
BUZZ
Rear view
These are fly wings!!
AGH!
After I finished drawing, I realized...
THE PEN IS SEPIA.
Not black.
Is that gonna work...?
Avoid this kind of experiment.

The end.

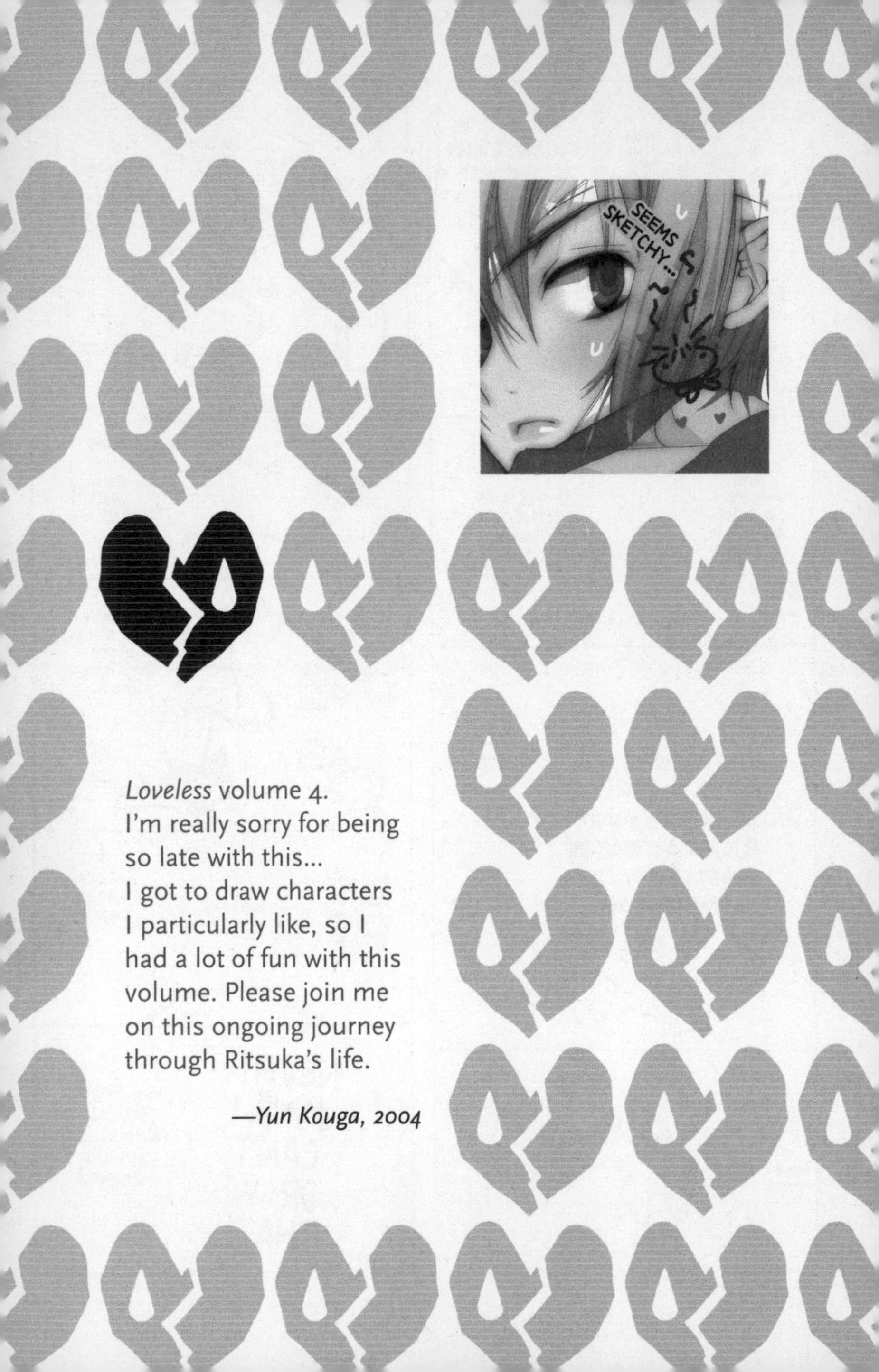
SEEMS SKETCHY...

Loveless volume 4.
I'm really sorry for being so late with this...
I got to draw characters I particularly like, so I had a lot of fun with this volume. Please join me on this ongoing journey through Ritsuka's life.

—*Yun Kouga, 2004*

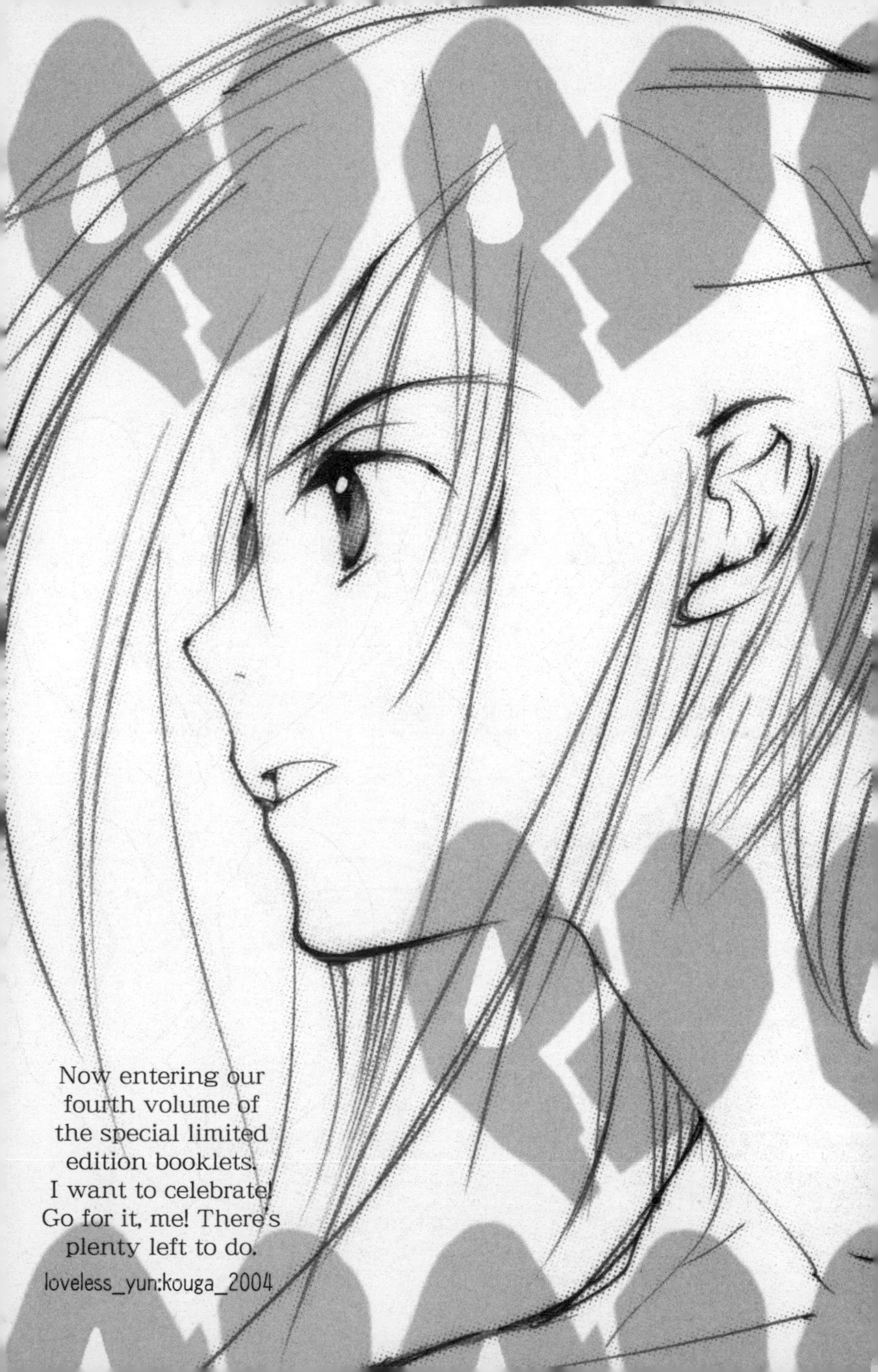
Now entering our
fourth volume of
the special limited
edition booklets.
I want to celebrate!
Go for it, me! There's
plenty left to do.
loveless_yun:kouga_2004

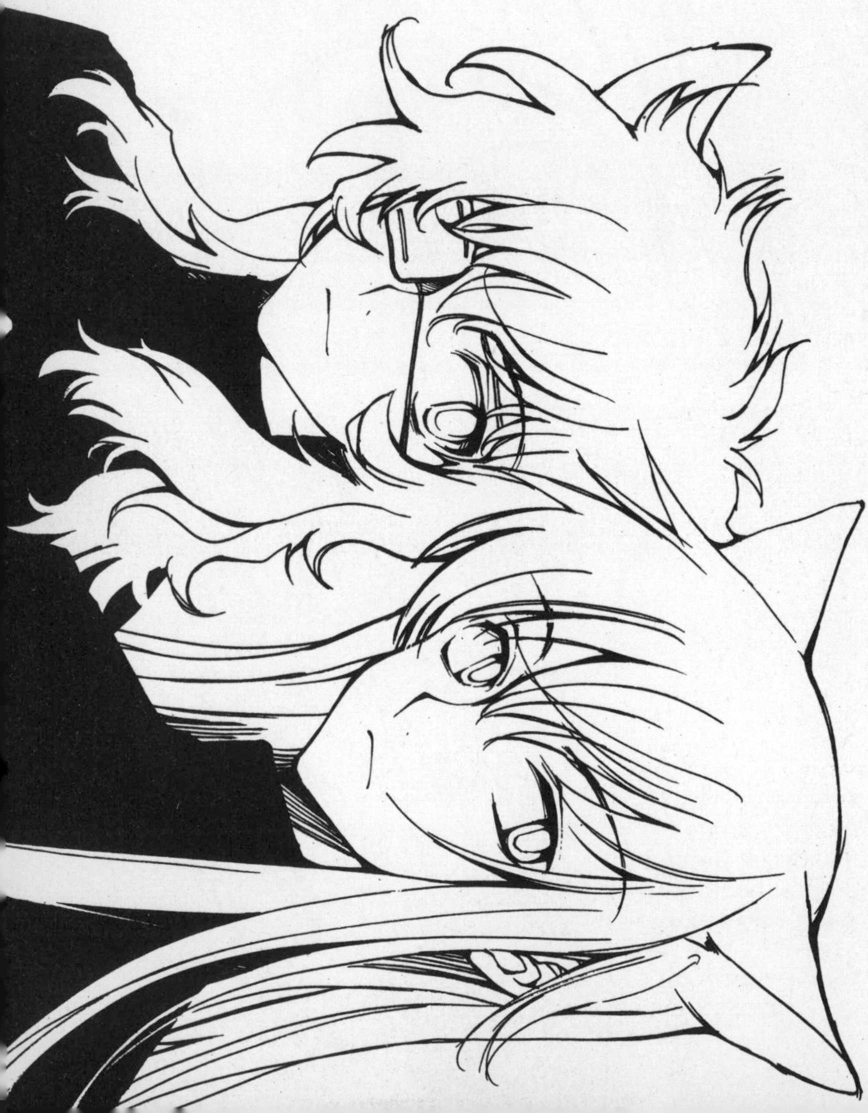

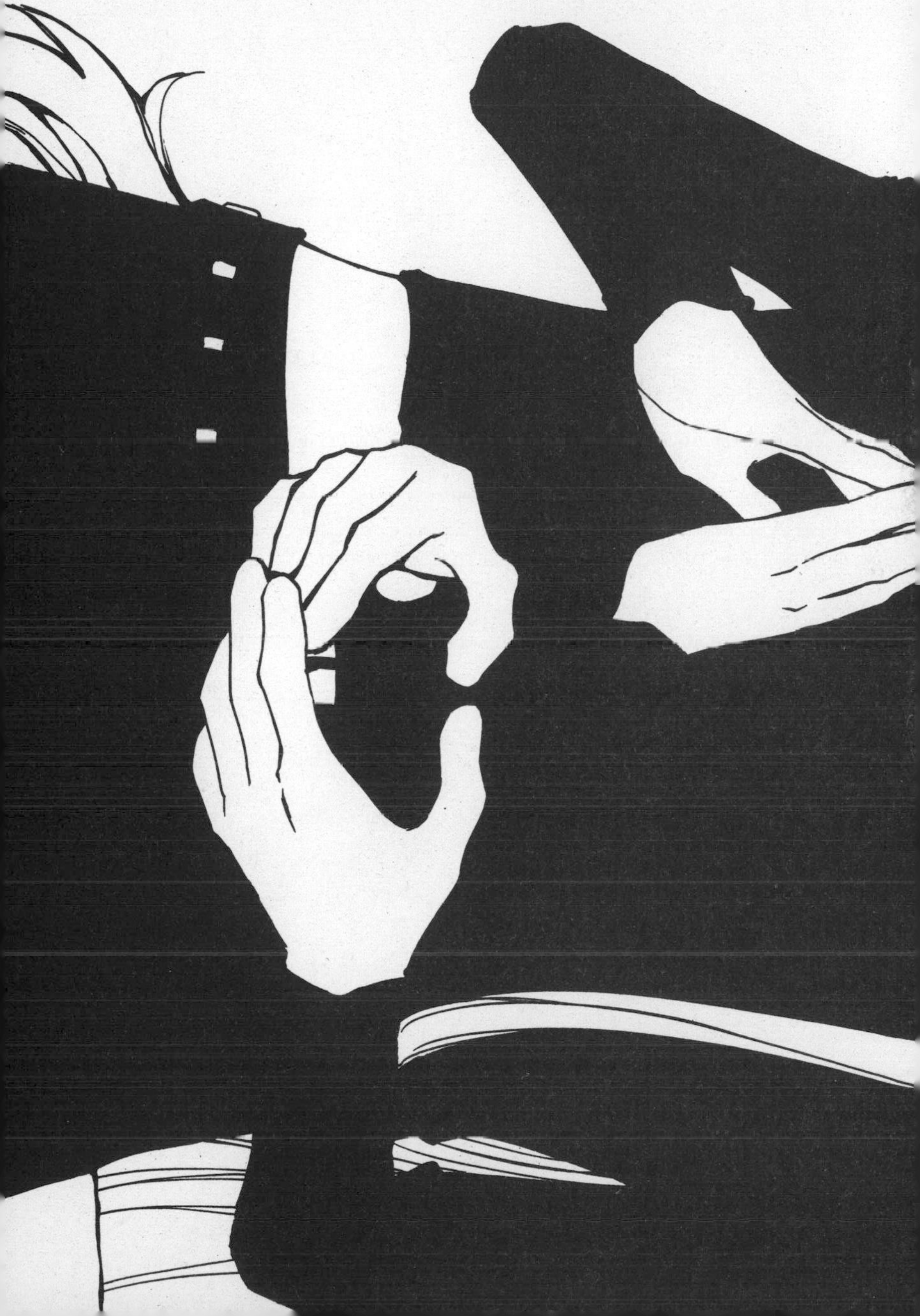

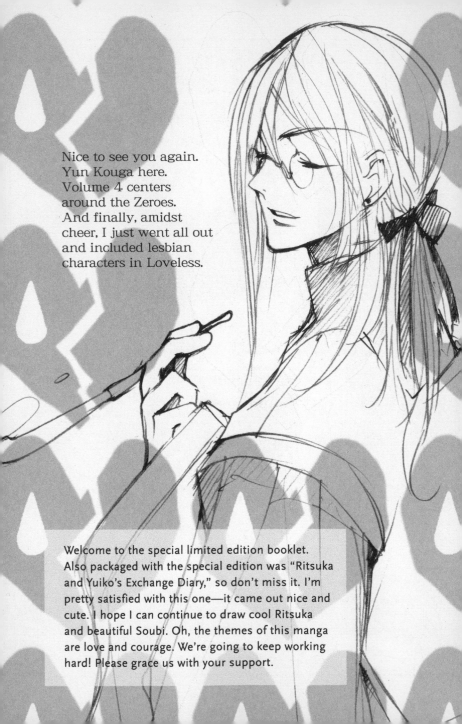

Nice to see you again.
Yun Kouga here.
Volume 4 centers
around the Zeroes.
And finally, amidst
cheer, I just went all out
and included lesbian
characters in Loveless.

Welcome to the special limited edition booklet.
Also packaged with the special edition was "Ritsuka
and Yuiko's Exchange Diary," so don't miss it. I'm
pretty satisfied with this one—it came out nice and
cute. I hope I can continue to draw cool Ritsuka
and beautiful Soubi. Oh, the themes of this manga
are love and courage. We're going to keep working
hard! Please grace us with your support.

THE FIVE RITSUKAS

EVERYONE'S HEART HOLDS FIVE SELVES (OR SO I HEARD).

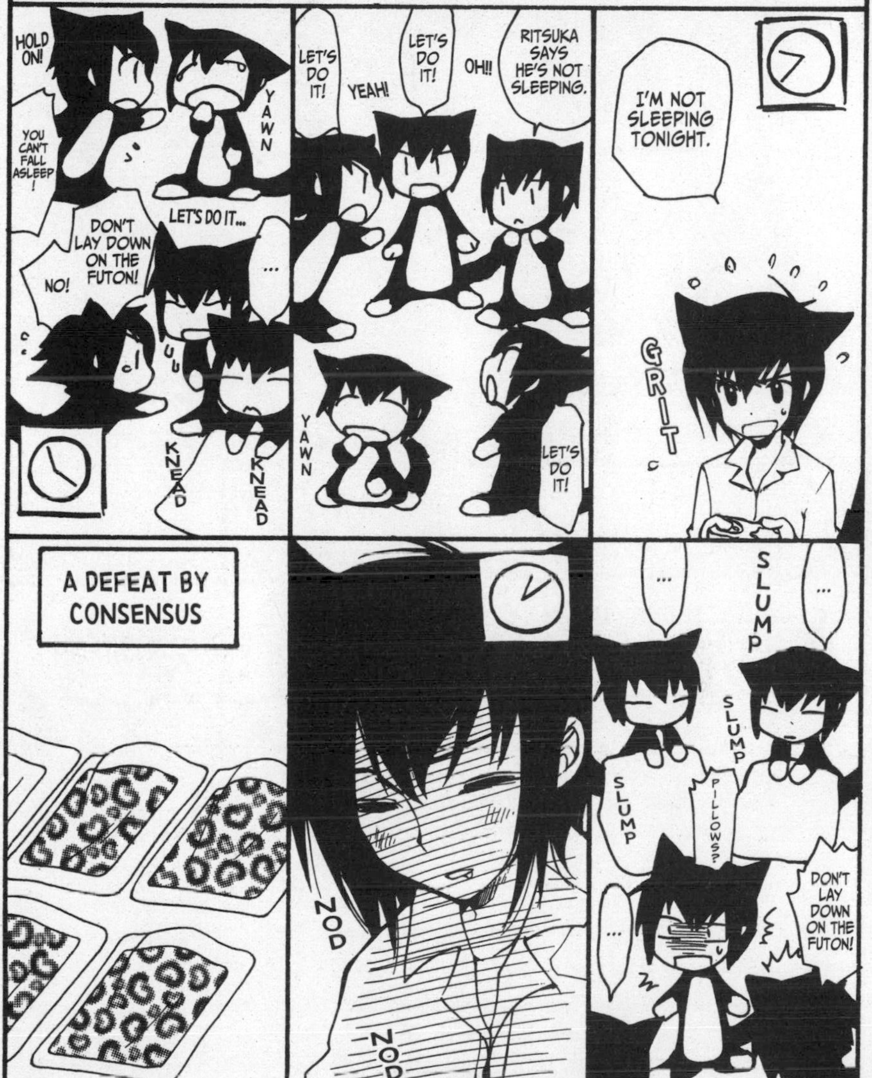
I'M NOT SLEEPING TONIGHT.
GRIT
RITSUKA SAYS HE'S NOT SLEEPING.
OH!!
LET'S DO IT!
YEAH!
LET'S DO IT!
LET'S DO IT!
YAWN
YAWN
HOLD ON!
YOU CAN'T FALL ASLEEP!
LET'S DO IT...
...
DON'T LAY DOWN ON THE FUTON!
NO!
KNEAD
KNEAD
...
SLUMP
...
SLUMP
PILLOWS?
SLUMP
DON'T LAY DOWN ON THE FUTON!
...
NOD
NOD
A DEFEAT BY CONSENSUS

THE FIVE RITSUKAS

FIGHTING IS BAD, EXCEPT WHEN YOU HAVE TO....?

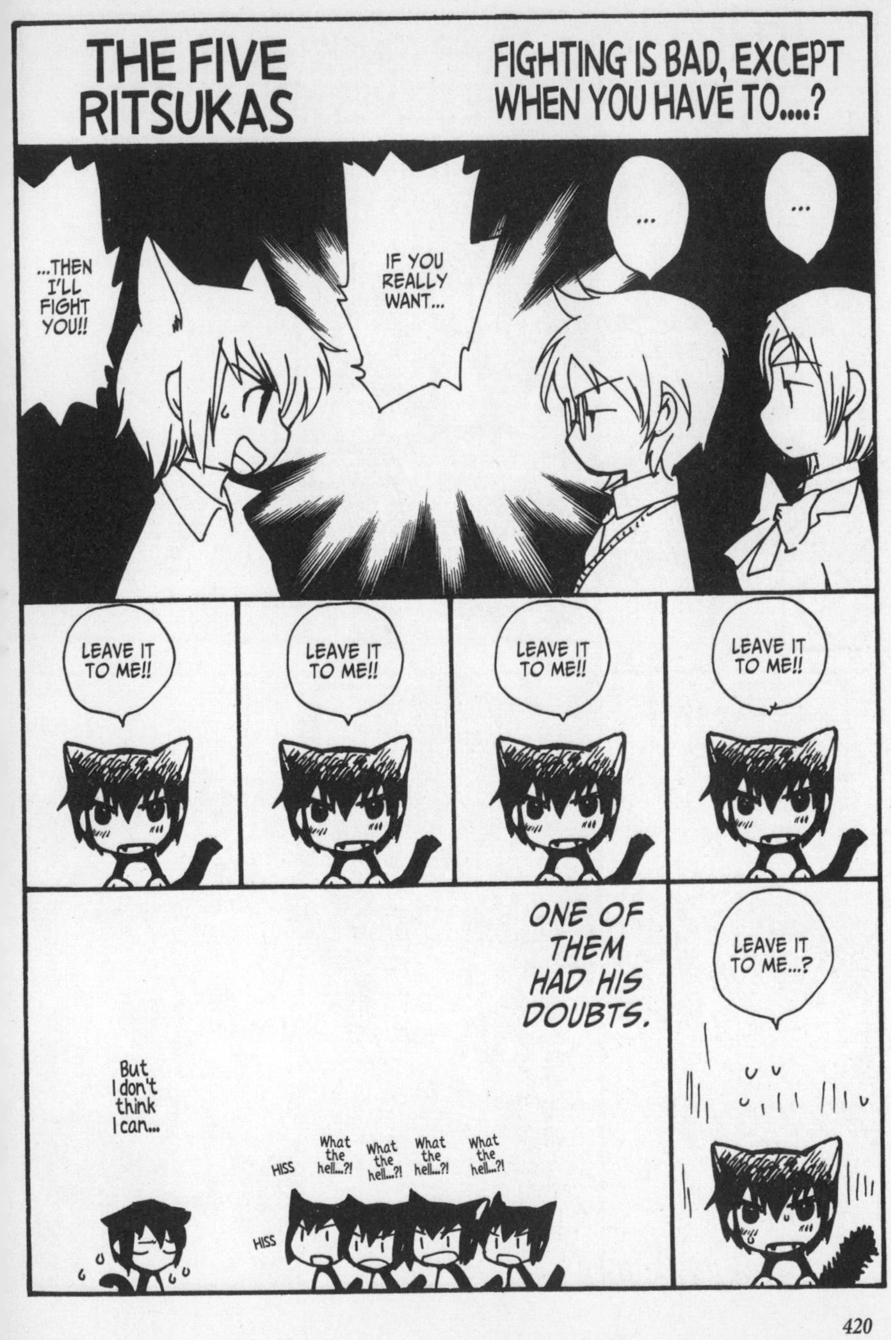
...
...
IF YOU REALLY WANT...
...THEN I'LL FIGHT YOU!!
LEAVE IT TO ME!!
LEAVE IT TO ME!!
LEAVE IT TO ME!!
LEAVE IT TO ME!!
LEAVE IT TO ME...?
ONE OF THEM HAD HIS DOUBTS.
What the hell...?!
What the hell...?!
What the hell...?!
What the hell...?!
HISS
HISS
But I don't think I can...

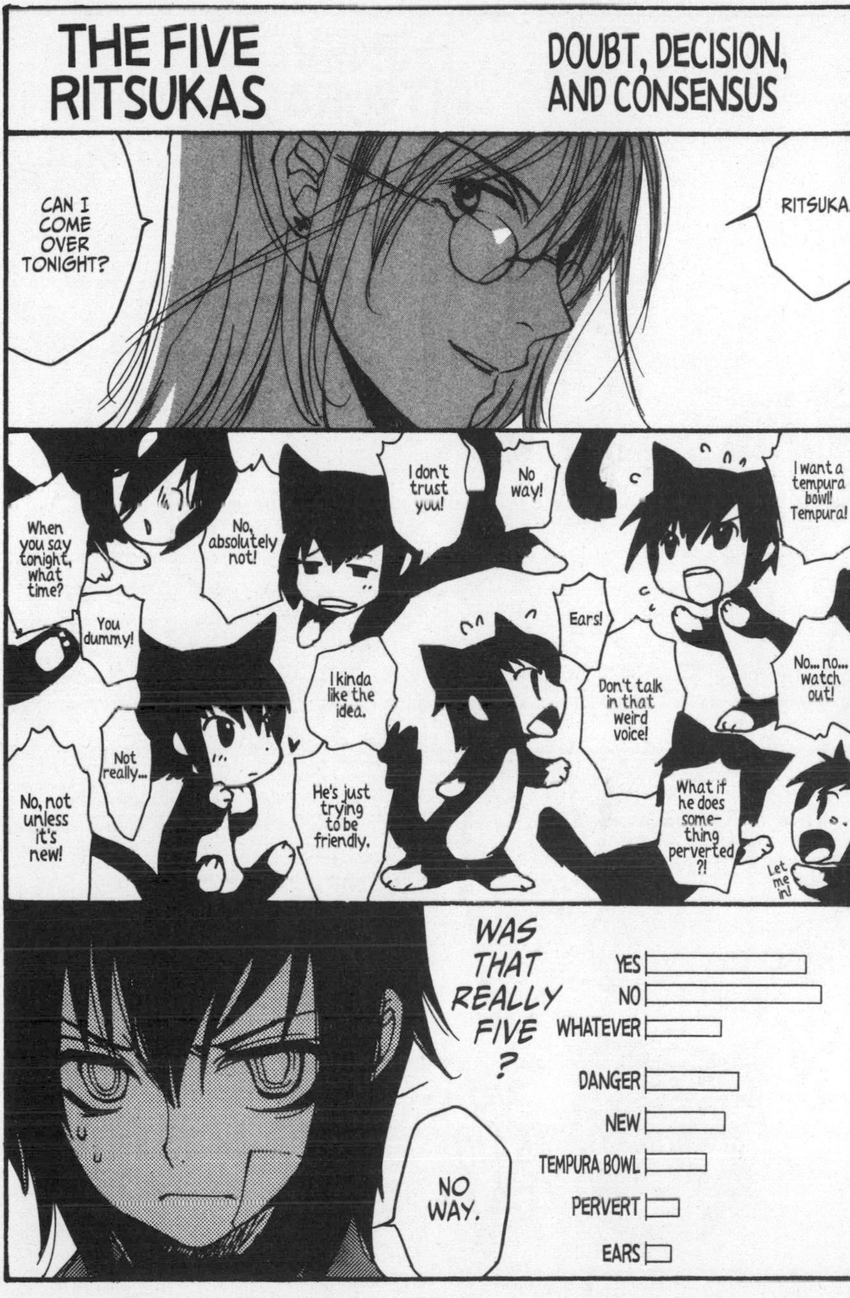
THE FIVE RITSUKAS
DOUBT, DECISION, AND CONSENSUS
RITSUKA.
CAN I COME OVER TONIGHT?
I want a tempura bowl! Tempura!
No way!
I don't trust you!
No, absolutely not!
When you say tonight, what time?
Ears!
No... no... watch out!
Don't talk in that weird voice!
I kinda like the idea.
You dummy!
What if he does some-thing perverted?!
Let me in!
He's just trying to be friendly.
Not really...
No, not unless it's new!
WAS THAT REALLY FIVE?
YES
NO
WHATEVER
DANGER
NEW
TEMPURA BOWL
PERVERT
EARS
NO WAY.

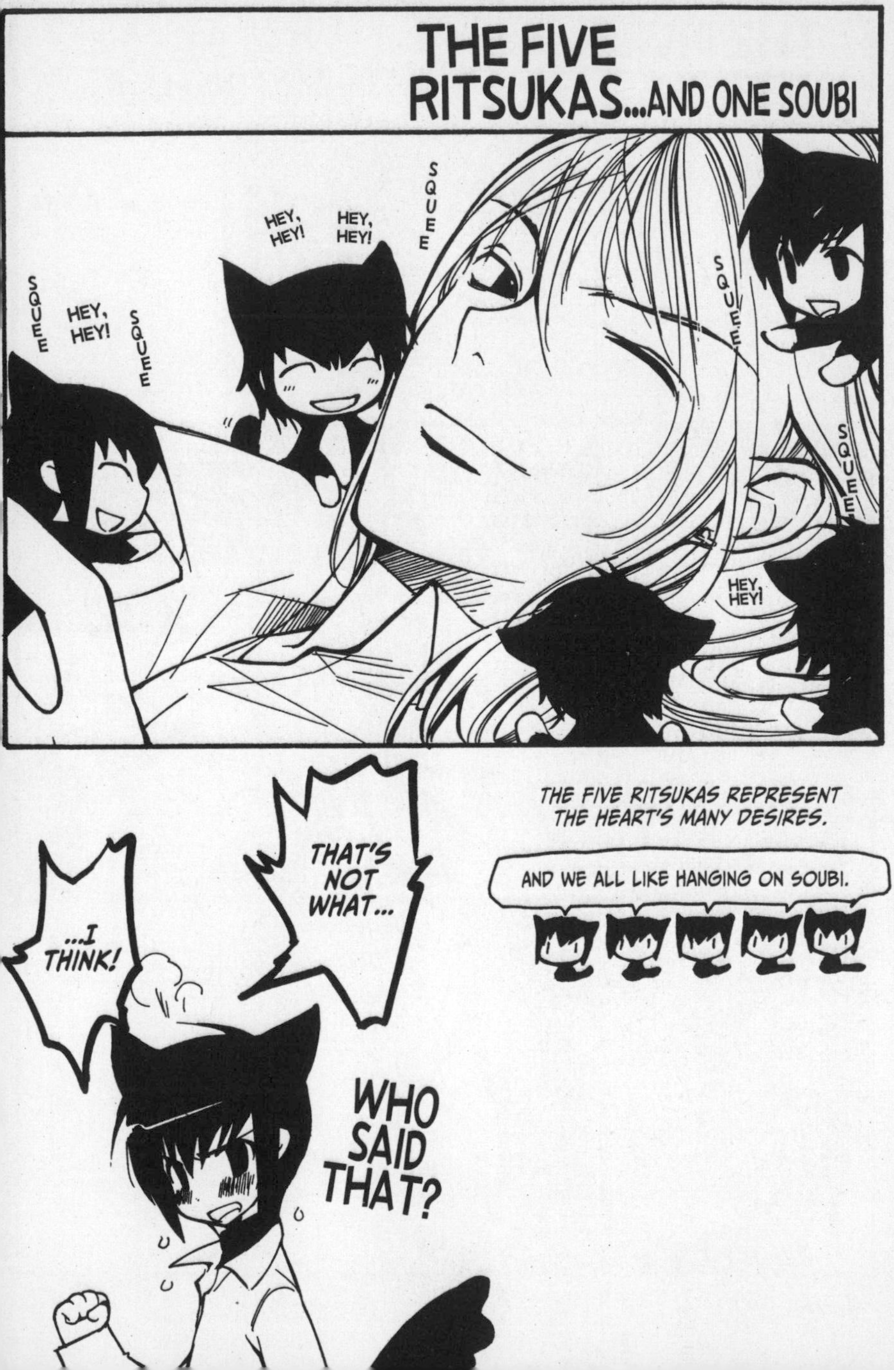
THE FIVE RITSUKAS...AND ONE SOUBI
SQUEE
SQUEE
HEY, HEY!
SQUEE
HEY, HEY!
HEY, HEY!
SQUEE
HEY, HEY!
SQUEE
THE FIVE RITSUKAS REPRESENT THE HEART'S MANY DESIRES.
AND WE ALL LIKE HANGING ON SOUBI.
THAT'S NOT WHAT...
...I THINK!
WHO SAID THAT?

THE FIVE RITSUKAS...AND ONE SOUBI

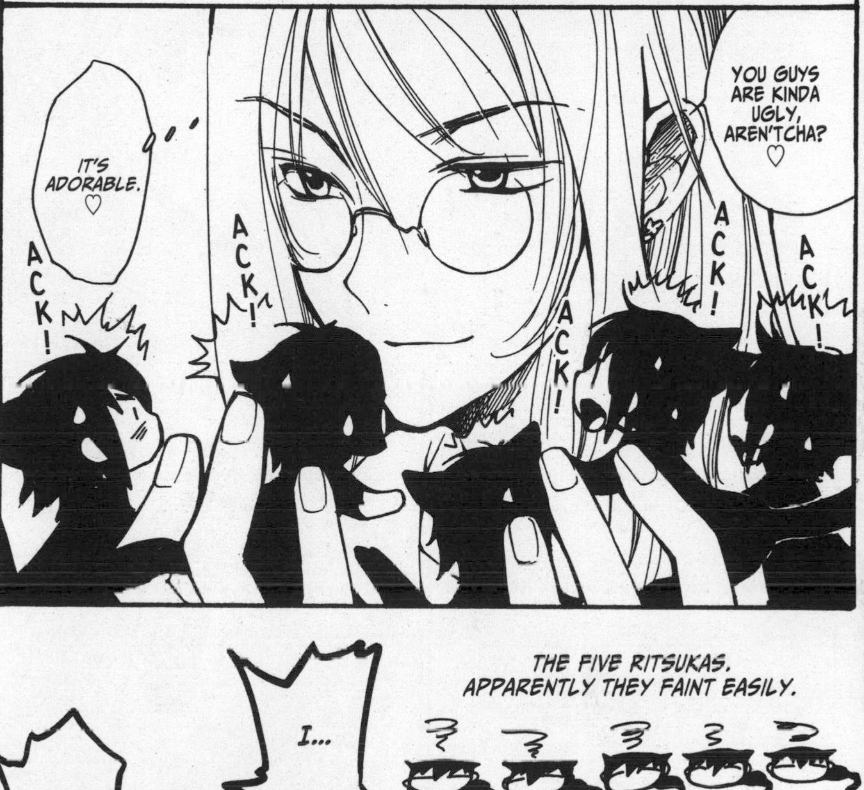
YOU GUYS ARE KINDA UGLY, AREN'TCHA? ♡
ACK!
ACK!
ACK!
ACK!
ACK!
IT'S ADORABLE. ♡

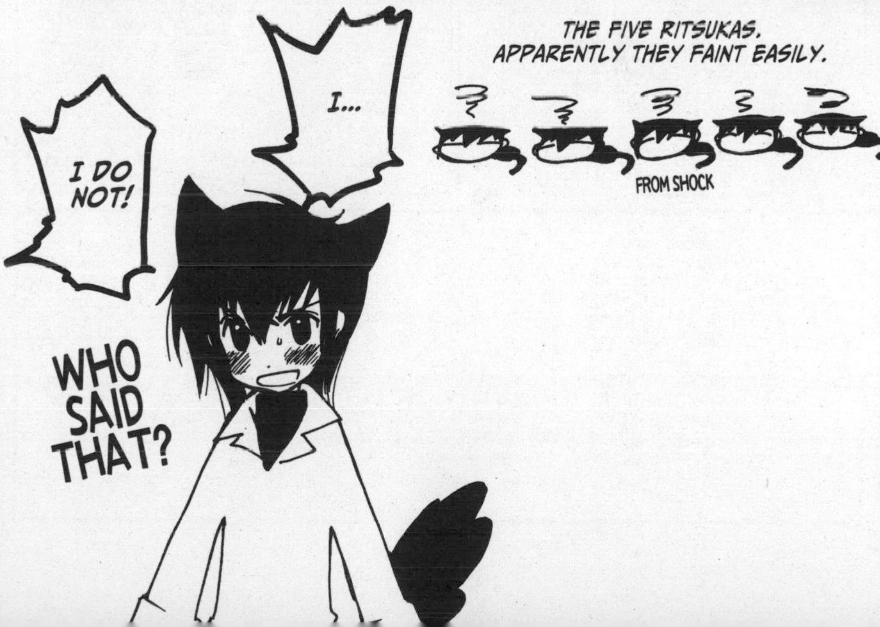
THE FIVE RITSUKAS. APPARENTLY THEY FAINT EASILY.
FROM SHOCK
I...
I DO NOT!
WHO SAID THAT?

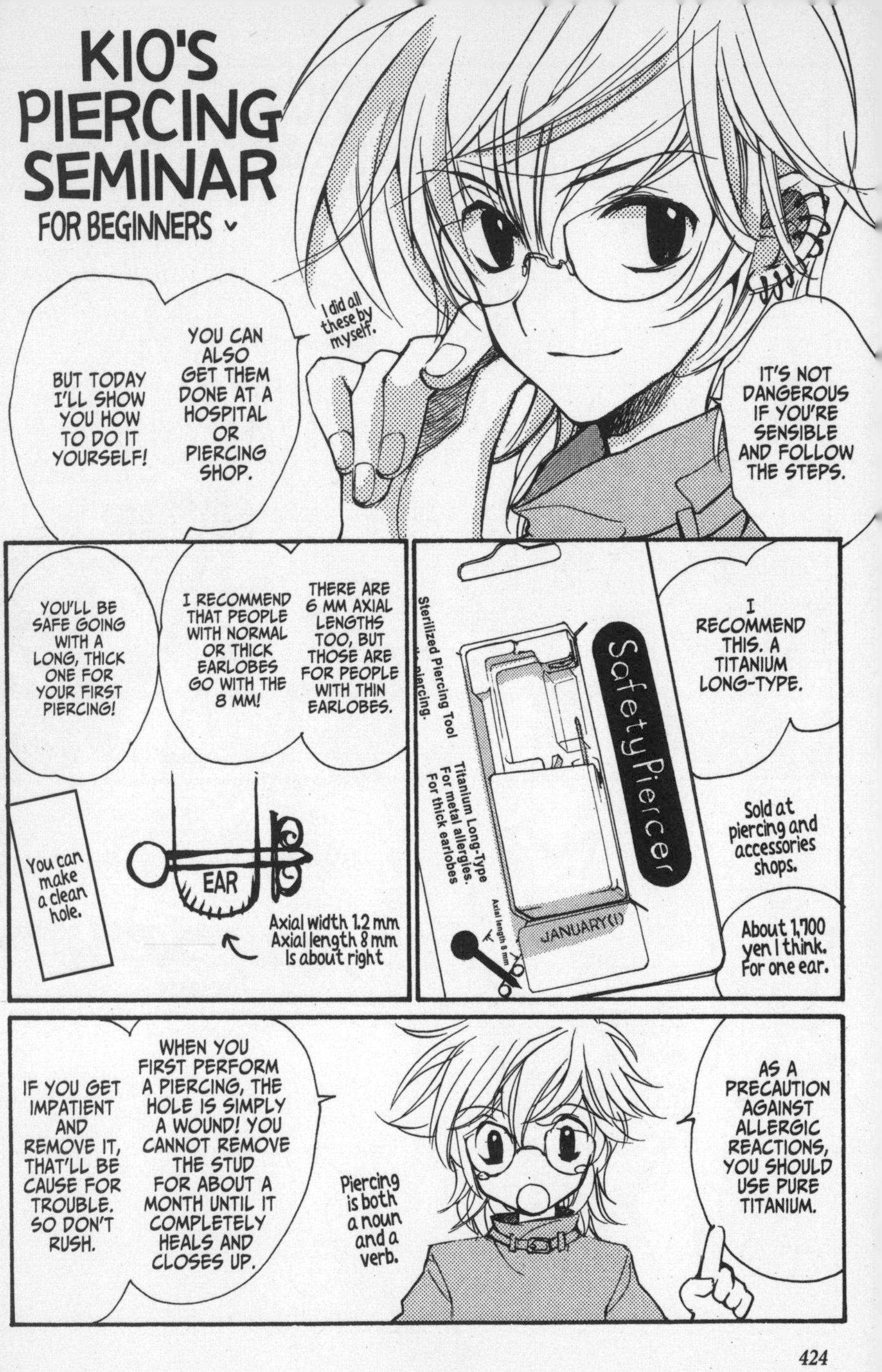
KIO'S PIERCING SEMINAR FOR BEGINNERS
IT'S NOT DANGEROUS IF YOU'RE SENSIBLE AND FOLLOW THE STEPS.
I did all these by myself.
YOU CAN ALSO GET THEM DONE AT A HOSPITAL OR PIERCING SHOP.
BUT TODAY I'LL SHOW YOU HOW TO DO IT YOURSELF!
I RECOMMEND THIS. A TITANIUM LONG-TYPE.
SafetyPiercer
Sterilized Piercing Tool
Titanium Long-Type For metal allergies For thick earlobes
Axial length 8 mm
JANUARY(I)
Sold at piercing and accessories shops.
About 1,700 yen I think. For one ear.
THERE ARE 6 MM AXIAL LENGTHS TOO, BUT THOSE ARE FOR PEOPLE WITH THIN EARLOBES.
I RECOMMEND THAT PEOPLE WITH NORMAL OR THICK EARLOBES GO WITH THE 8 MM!
YOU'LL BE SAFE GOING WITH A LONG, THICK ONE FOR YOUR FIRST PIERCING!
EAR
Axial width 1.2 mm Axial length 8 mm Is about right
You can make a clean hole.
AS A PRECAUTION AGAINST ALLERGIC REACTIONS, YOU SHOULD USE PURE TITANIUM.
Piercing is both a noun and a verb.
WHEN YOU FIRST PERFORM A PIERCING, THE HOLE IS SIMPLY A WOUND! YOU CANNOT REMOVE THE STUD FOR ABOUT A MONTH UNTIL IT COMPLETELY HEALS AND CLOSES UP.
IF YOU GET IMPATIENT AND REMOVE IT, THAT'LL BE CAUSE FOR TROUBLE. SO DON'T RUSH.

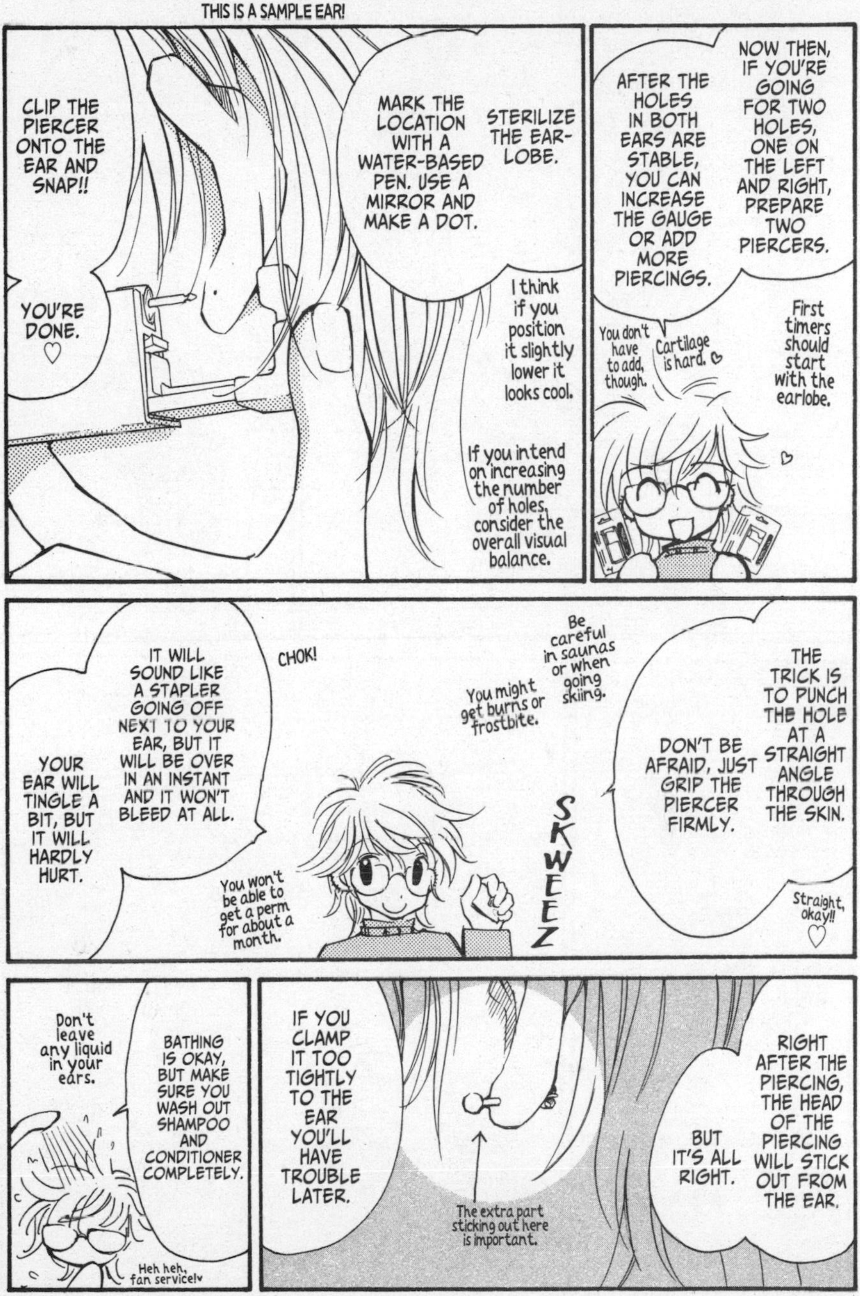
NOW THEN, IF YOU'RE GOING FOR TWO HOLES, ONE ON THE LEFT AND RIGHT, PREPARE TWO PIERCERS.
AFTER THE HOLES IN BOTH EARS ARE STABLE, YOU CAN INCREASE THE GAUGE OR ADD MORE PIERCINGS.
First timers should start with the earlobe. ♡
Cartilage is hard. ♡
You don't have to add, though.
THIS IS A SAMPLE EAR!
STERILIZE THE EARLOBE.
MARK THE LOCATION WITH A WATER-BASED PEN. USE A MIRROR AND MAKE A DOT.
I think if you position it slightly lower it looks cool.
If you intend on increasing the number of holes, consider the overall visual balance.
CLIP THE PIERCER ONTO THE EAR AND SNAP!!
YOU'RE DONE. ♡
THE TRICK IS TO PUNCH THE HOLE AT A STRAIGHT ANGLE THROUGH THE SKIN.
DON'T BE AFRAID, JUST GRIP THE PIERCER FIRMLY.
Straight, okay!! ♡
SKWEEZ
Be careful in saunas or when going skiing.
You might get burns or frostbite.
CHOK!
IT WILL SOUND LIKE A STAPLER GOING OFF NEXT TO YOUR EAR, BUT IT WILL BE OVER IN AN INSTANT AND IT WON'T BLEED AT ALL.
YOUR EAR WILL TINGLE A BIT, BUT IT WILL HARDLY HURT.
You won't be able to get a perm for about a month.
RIGHT AFTER THE PIERCING, THE HEAD OF THE PIERCING WILL STICK OUT FROM THE EAR.
BUT IT'S ALL RIGHT.
IF YOU CLAMP IT TOO TIGHTLY TO THE EAR YOU'LL HAVE TROUBLE LATER.
The extra part sticking out here is important.
BATHING IS OKAY, BUT MAKE SURE YOU WASH OUT SHAMPOO AND CONDITIONER COMPLETELY.
Don't leave any liquid in your ears.
Heh heh, fan service!♥

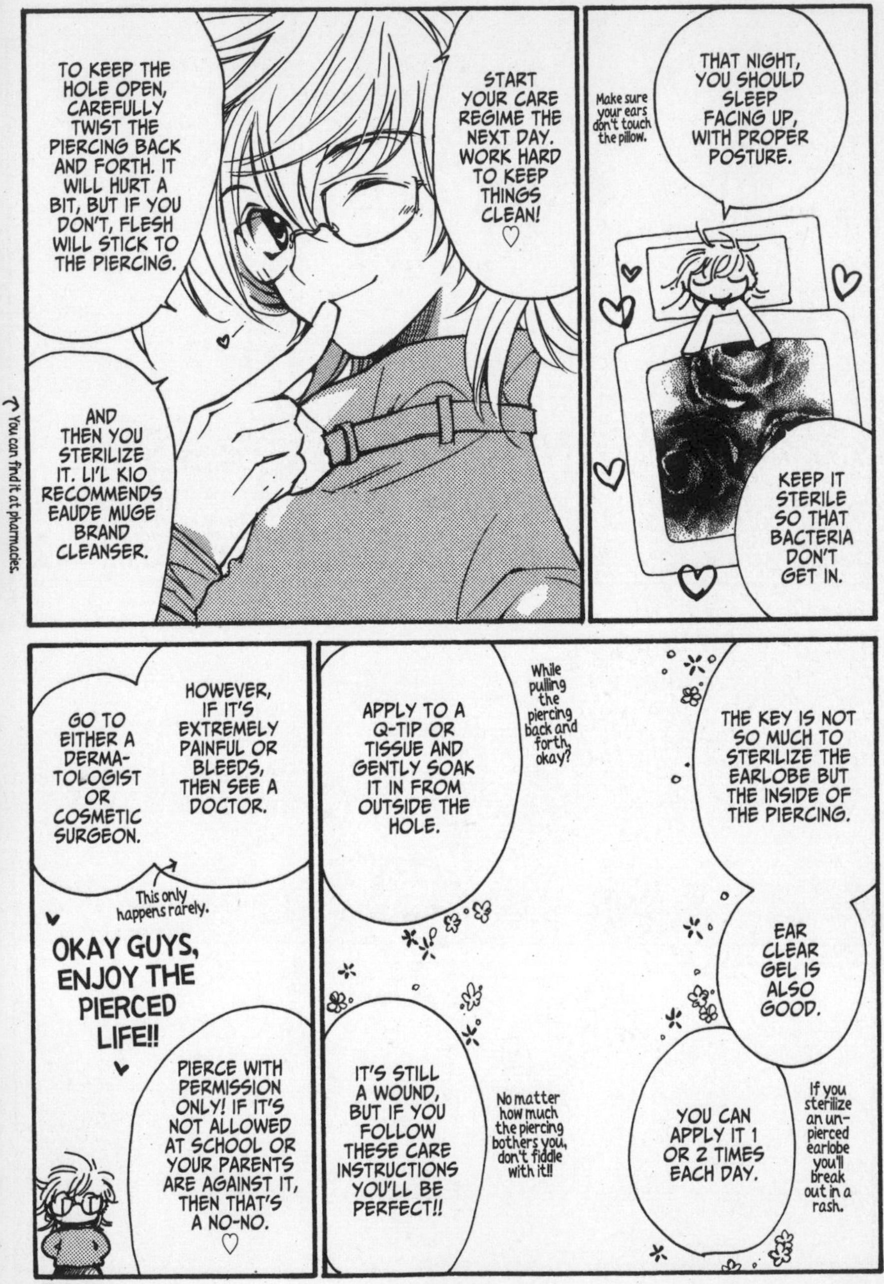
THAT NIGHT, YOU SHOULD SLEEP FACING UP, WITH PROPER POSTURE.
Make sure your ears don't touch the pillow.
KEEP IT STERILE SO THAT BACTERIA DON'T GET IN.
START YOUR CARE REGIME THE NEXT DAY. WORK HARD TO KEEP THINGS CLEAN! ♡
TO KEEP THE HOLE OPEN, CAREFULLY TWIST THE PIERCING BACK AND FORTH. IT WILL HURT A BIT, BUT IF YOU DON'T, FLESH WILL STICK TO THE PIERCING.
AND THEN YOU STERILIZE IT. LI'L KIO RECOMMENDS EAUDE MUGE BRAND CLEANSER.
You can find it at pharmacies.
THE KEY IS NOT SO MUCH TO STERILIZE THE EARLOBE BUT THE INSIDE OF THE PIERCING.
While pulling the piercing back and forth, okay?
APPLY TO A Q-TIP OR TISSUE AND GENTLY SOAK IT IN FROM OUTSIDE THE HOLE.
EAR CLEAR GEL IS ALSO GOOD.
If you sterilize an un-pierced earlobe you'll break out in a rash.
YOU CAN APPLY IT 1 OR 2 TIMES EACH DAY.
No matter how much the piercing bothers you, don't fiddle with it!!
IT'S STILL A WOUND, BUT IF YOU FOLLOW THESE CARE INSTRUCTIONS YOU'LL BE PERFECT!!
HOWEVER, IF IT'S EXTREMELY PAINFUL OR BLEEDS, THEN SEE A DOCTOR.
GO TO EITHER A DERMA-TOLOGIST OR COSMETIC SURGEON.
This only happens rarely.
PIERCE WITH PERMISSION ONLY! IF IT'S NOT ALLOWED AT SCHOOL OR YOUR PARENTS ARE AGAINST IT, THEN THAT'S A NO-NO. ♡
OKAY GUYS, ENJOY THE PIERCED LIFE!!

END

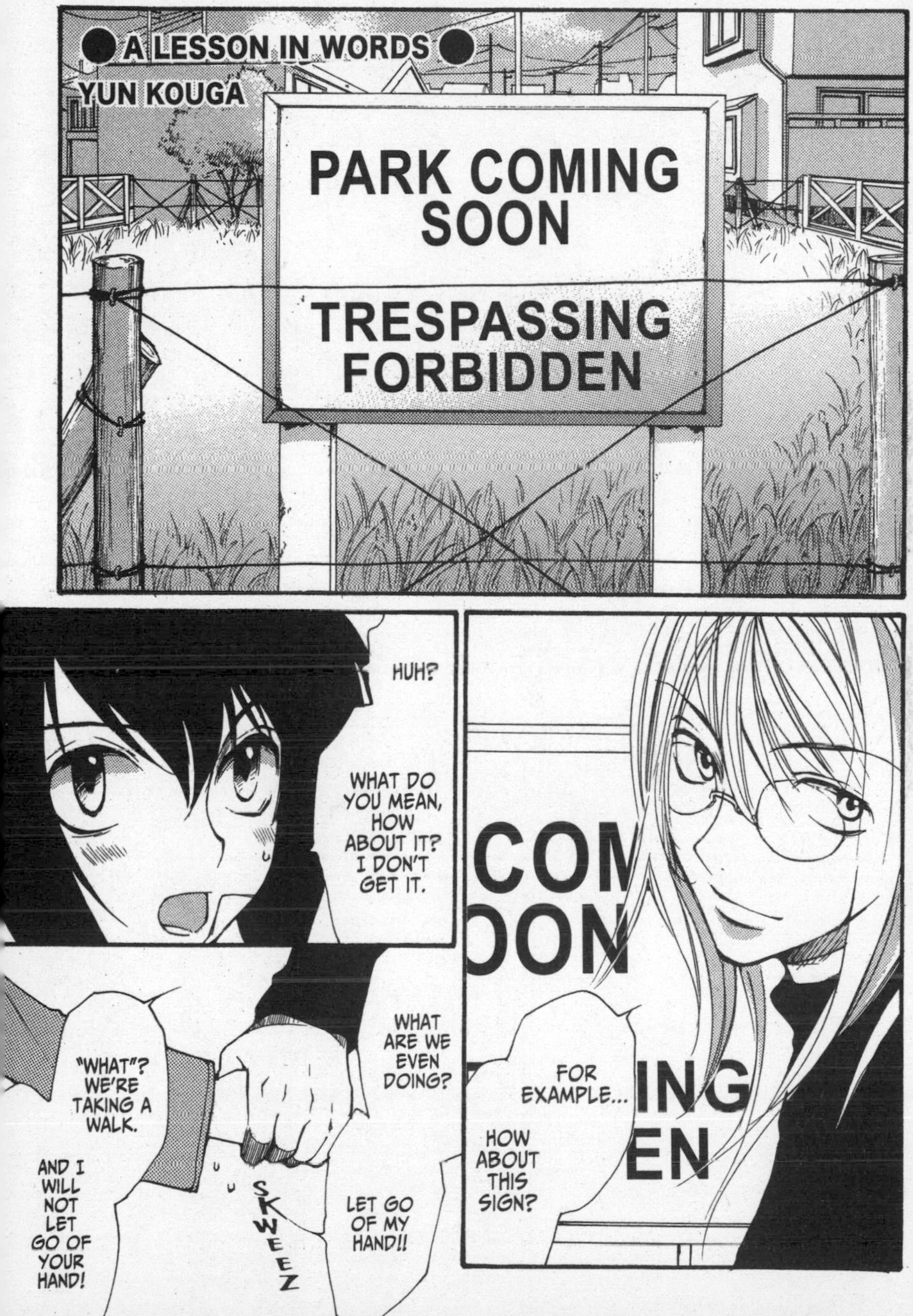
A LESSON IN WORDS
YUN KOUGA
PARK COMING SOON
TRESPASSING FORBIDDEN
FOR EXAMPLE...
HOW ABOUT THIS SIGN?
HUH?
WHAT DO YOU MEAN, HOW ABOUT IT? I DON'T GET IT.
WHAT ARE WE EVEN DOING?
"WHAT"? WE'RE TAKING A WALK.
LET GO OF MY HAND!!
SKWEEZ
AND I WILL NOT LET GO OF YOUR HAND!

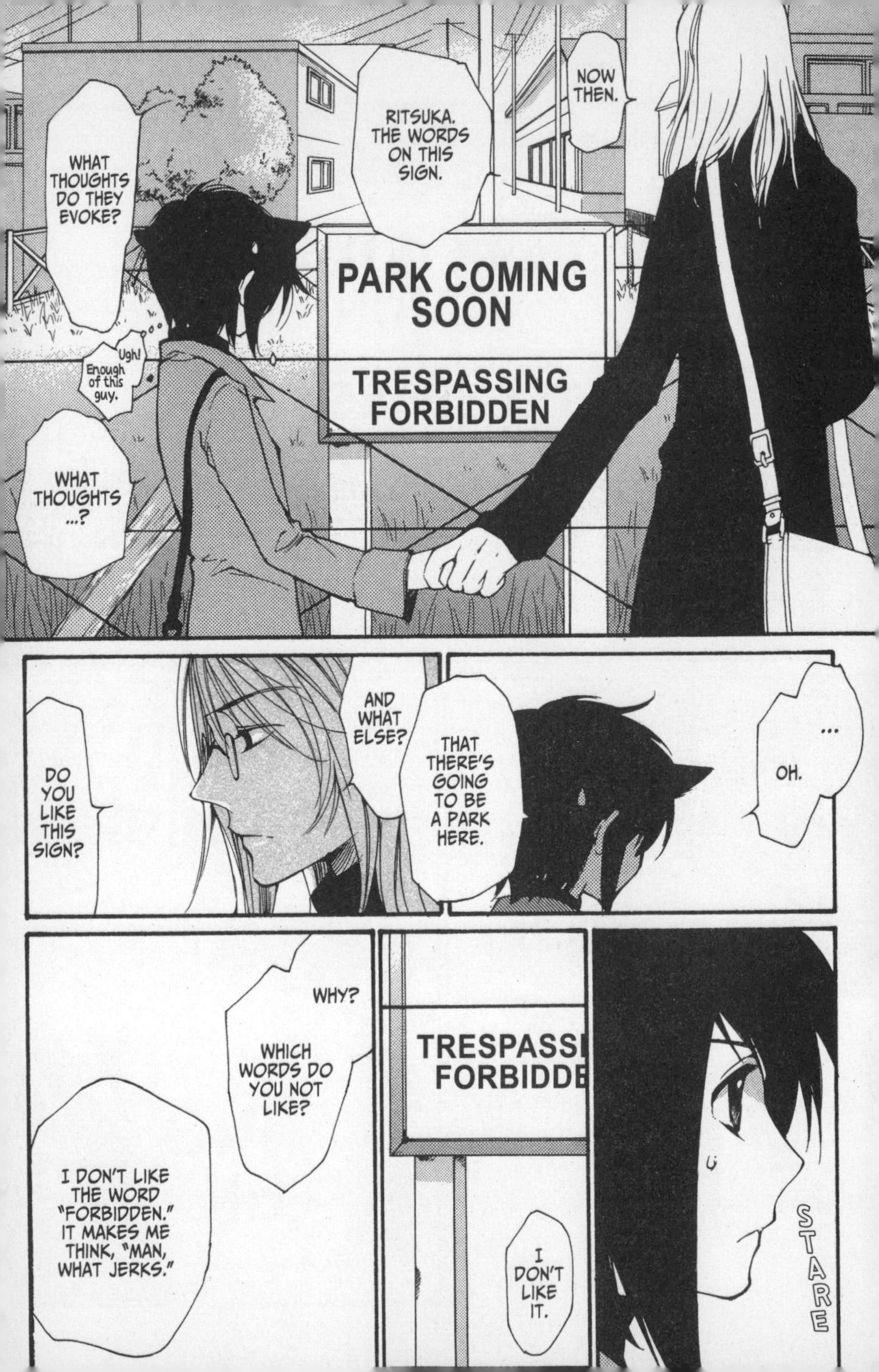
NOW THEN.
RITSUKA. THE WORDS ON THIS SIGN.
PARK COMING SOON
TRESPASSING FORBIDDEN
WHAT THOUGHTS DO THEY EVOKE?
Ugh! Enough of this guy.
WHAT THOUGHTS ...?
... OH.
THAT THERE'S GOING TO BE A PARK HERE.
AND WHAT ELSE?
DO YOU LIKE THIS SIGN?
STARE
TRESPASSI
FORBIDDE
I DON'T LIKE IT.
WHY?
WHICH WORDS DO YOU NOT LIKE?
I DON'T LIKE THE WORD "FORBIDDEN." IT MAKES ME THINK, "MAN, WHAT JERKS."

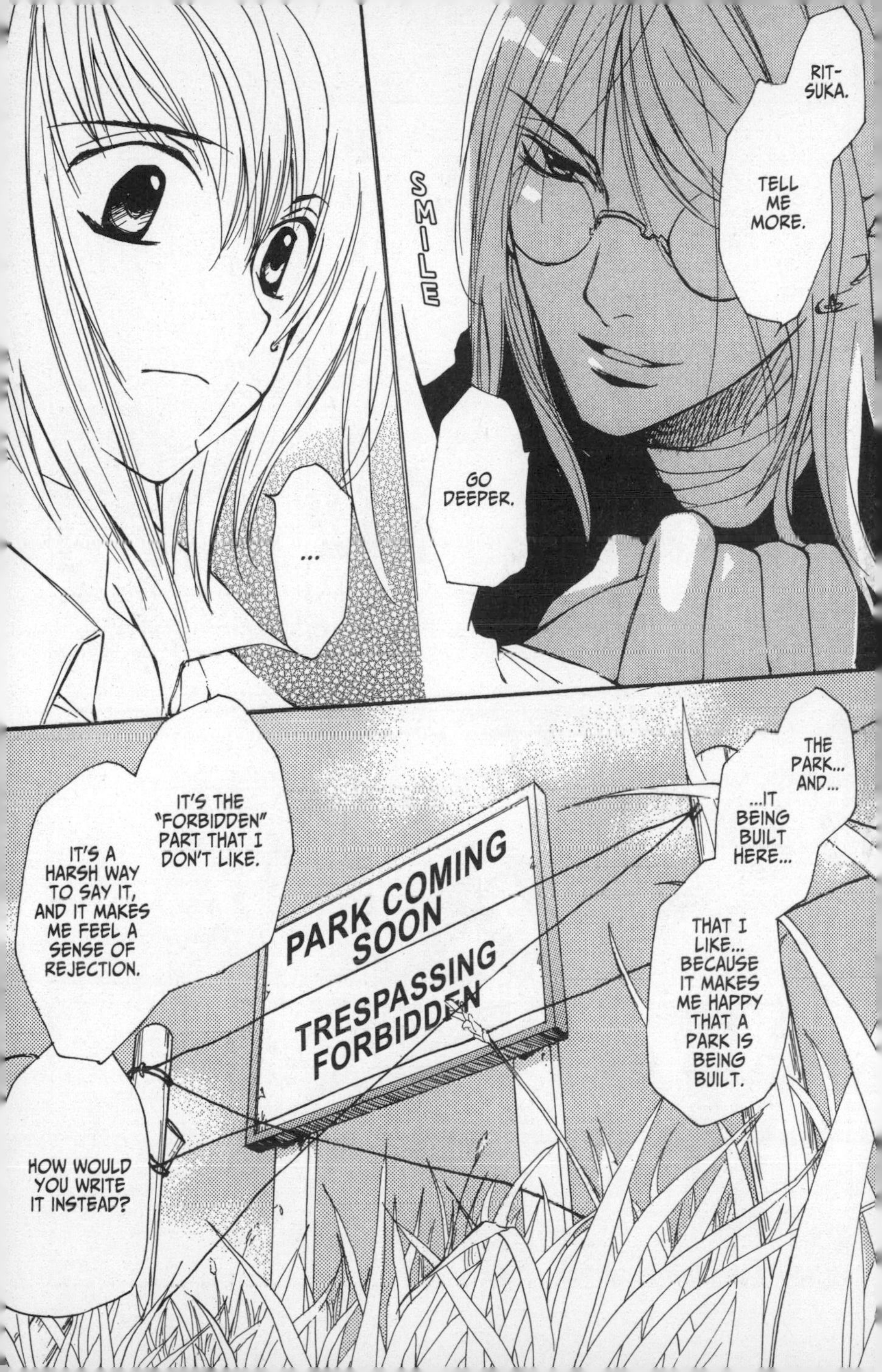
RIT-SUKA.
TELL ME MORE.
SMILE
GO DEEPER.
...
THE PARK... AND...
...IT BEING BUILT HERE...
THAT I LIKE... BECAUSE IT MAKES ME HAPPY THAT A PARK IS BEING BUILT.
PARK COMING SOON
TRESPASSING FORBIDDEN
IT'S THE "FORBIDDEN" PART THAT I DON'T LIKE.
IT'S A HARSH WAY TO SAY IT, AND IT MAKES ME FEEL A SENSE OF REJECTION.
HOW WOULD YOU WRITE IT INSTEAD?

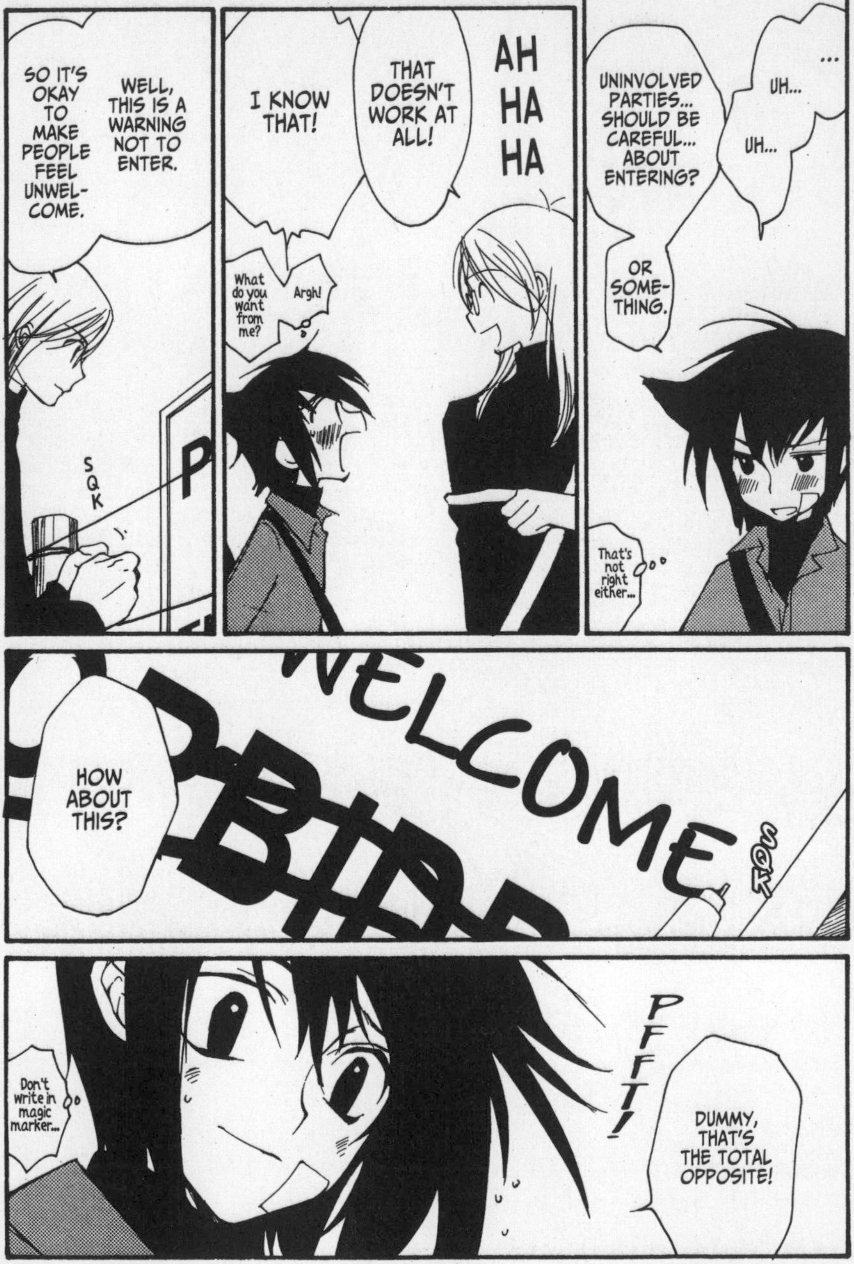
...
UH...
UH...
UNINVOLVED PARTIES... SHOULD BE CAREFUL... ABOUT ENTERING?
OR SOMETHING.
That's not right either...
AH HA HA
THAT DOESN'T WORK AT ALL!
I KNOW THAT!
Argh!
What do you want from me?
WELL, THIS IS A WARNING NOT TO ENTER.
SO IT'S OKAY TO MAKE PEOPLE FEEL UNWELCOME.
SQK
SQK
WELCOME
HOW ABOUT THIS?
PFFT!
DUMMY, THAT'S THE TOTAL OPPOSITE!
Don't write in magic marker...

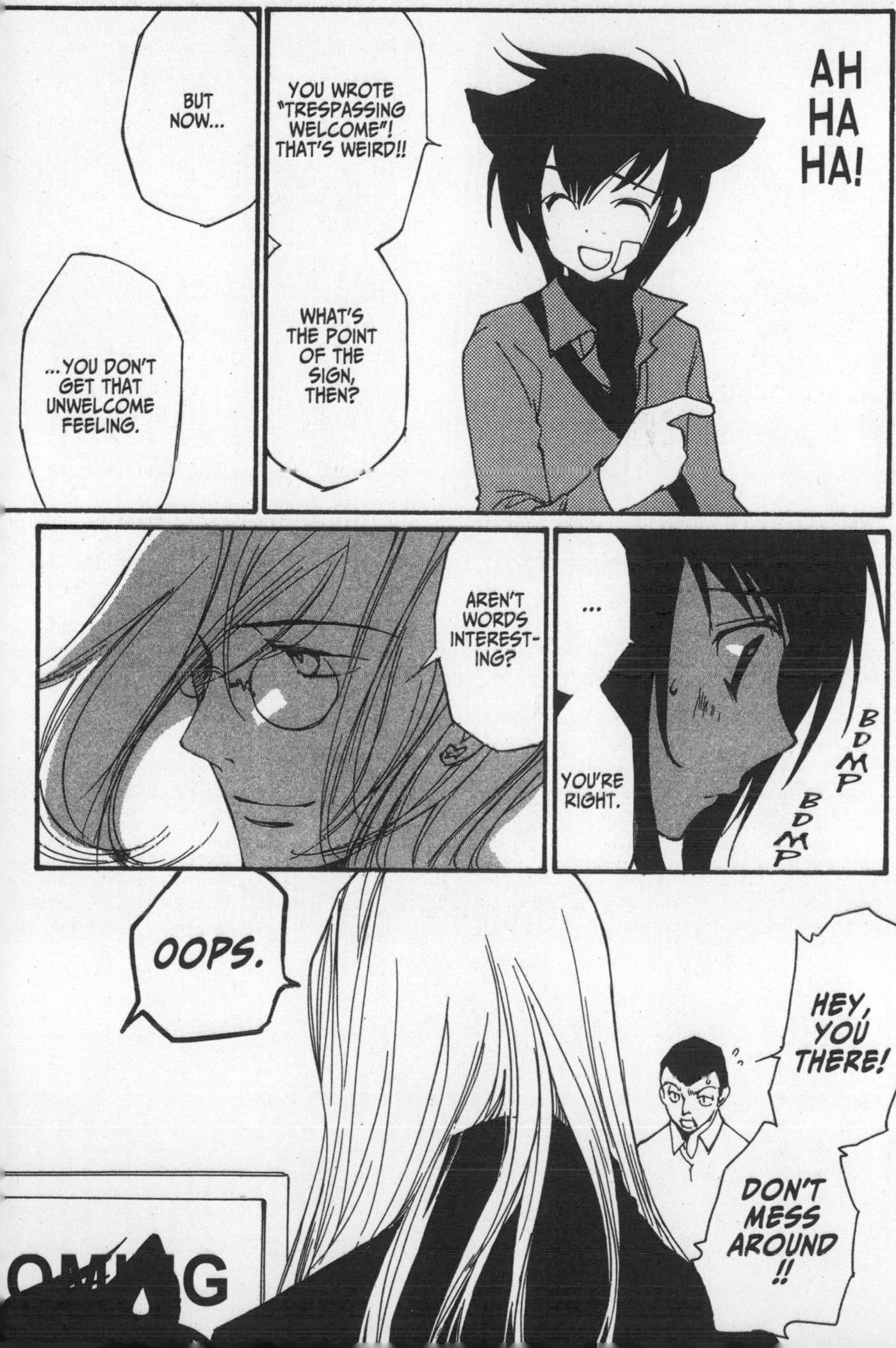
AH HA HA!
YOU WROTE "TRESPASSING WELCOME"! THAT'S WEIRD!!
WHAT'S THE POINT OF THE SIGN, THEN?
BUT NOW...
...YOU DON'T GET THAT UNWELCOME FEELING.
...
YOU'RE RIGHT.
BDMP BDMP
AREN'T WORDS INTERESTING?
HEY, YOU THERE!
DON'T MESS AROUND!!
OOPS.

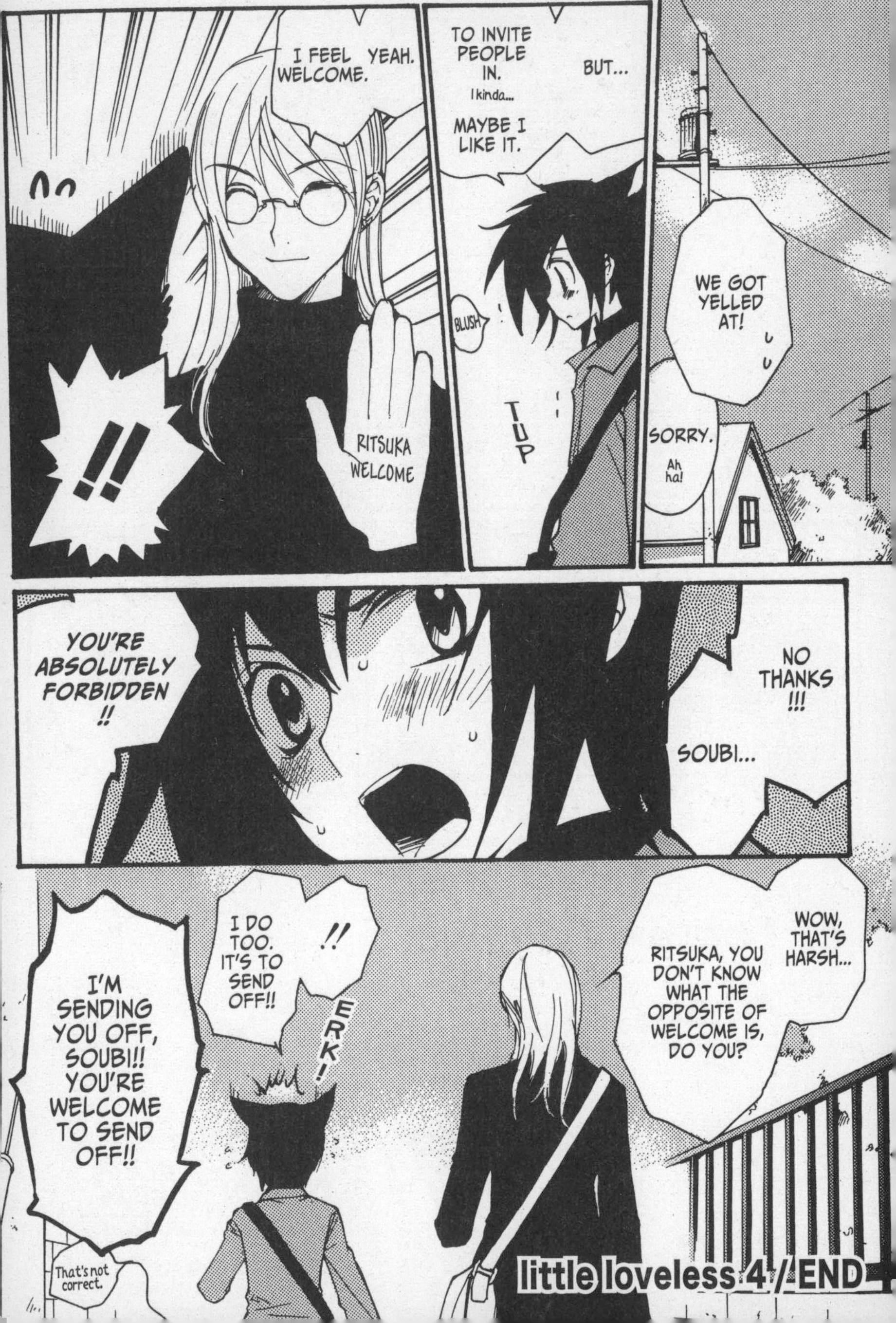
WE GOT YELLED AT!
SORRY.
Ah ha!
BUT...
TO INVITE PEOPLE IN.
I kinda...
MAYBE I LIKE IT.
BLUSH
TUP
YEAH.
I FEEL WELCOME.
RITSUKA WELCOME
!!
NO THANKS!!!
SOUBI...
YOU'RE ABSOLUTELY FORBIDDEN!!
WOW, THAT'S HARSH...
RITSUKA, YOU DON'T KNOW WHAT THE OPPOSITE OF WELCOME IS, DO YOU?
ERK!
!!
I DO TOO. IT'S TO SEND OFF!!
I'M SENDING YOU OFF, SOUBI!! YOU'RE WELCOME TO SEND OFF!!
That's not correct.
little loveless 4 / END

Today, a Conversation at Akasaka Mi~~zuke~~tsuke Where It is Surprisingly Raining

Kouga: The time has arrived again for our conversation. Even if you would rather it not. Kouga here.

Sugino: It has arrived, hasn't it? The last obstacle of these special limited edition booklets. I'm Editor Sugino.

Ⓚ: Thank you for allowing me to create an exchange diary booklet as an additional bonus this time. I'm overworking you, Master Sugi!! *PFFT*

Ⓢ: I'll do anything. I'm looking at this and thinking, "Who's Sugino?" The exchange diary came out really cute, didn't it?

Ⓚ: A lot of work went into it. The cover paper is special... I think Yuiko would like it.

Ⓢ: Yuiko? Don't you mean YOU? Either way, it's been a long road to volume 4, hasn't it?

Ⓚ: Plays girly. *BLUSH* Ngh!! It wasn't long! WAAAAH! That's bullying and it looks bad!!

Ⓢ: It is not bullying. Those are the voices of our readers who eagerly await your work!! But it's finally been published. How are you feeling right now?

Ⓚ: Volume 5!! I'm feeling like volume 5!! I also feel that kuzu fruit is delicious.

Ⓢ: ...I have no idea what you're saying! But kuzu fruit is definitely delicious... Don't you have any thoughts about VOLUME 4?

Ⓚ: I think it came out cute. The contents are...the contents. I'll work hard. I'll make it more fun!! That's what I feel.

Ⓢ: This was a Zero-centric volume, wasn't it? There's still so far to go. I'm impressed. Keep working harder!! There's my two cents.

Ⓚ: Uh-huh. But this time around Ritsuka and Soubi didn't flirt too much, did they? That's not good.

Ⓢ: Flirt...? No, that's okay. But Ms. Shinonome has all but vanished. That's bad.

Ⓚ: It's not bad!!! She makes her usual appearances. Soubi has lovers living in his house. A pair of them!!

Ⓢ: Soubi is involved in child kidnapping. That's bad. I'm going to tell Ms. Shinonome.

Ⓚ: It's not child kidnapping so much as allowing a lover to live with you. But when the legal wife runs into them it's...y'know...

Ⓢ: That's the worst case scenario, isn't it, when the wife and the lover become friends? But no. They're all good kids.

Ⓚ: That's the worst case...? Soubi's okay with it. A lot of people appeared in this volume.

Ⓢ: Is that so. There were a lot of characters, weren't there? So is the story finally going to hit its stride?

Ⓚ: Mm-hmm, sure. The stage is basically set. There's just one more character...

Ⓢ: Let's spice up the conversation! How's your private life these days? Is it bad to change the subject?

Ⓚ: What's the big idea, throwing a curveball like that? It's okay, though!! I'm working out with dumbbells!!

Ⓢ: Are you going for the macho look?

Ⓚ: I sure am!! I'm going for the 3 kg dumbbells!! You should take care of your health too, you know.

Ⓢ: But what if you injure your arms? You've got to be careful. I'm going to go on a diet.

Ⓚ: Lifting dumbbells is part of dieting too. You can lift barbells. 150 kg ones.

Ⓢ: You want me to starting bench pressing? :D Health is precious... Actually, I've started to think that I want to live a long life.

Ⓚ: Why?

Ⓢ: Because it's the survivors who win. The last man standing wins.

Ⓚ: You're greedy.

Ⓢ: That's a lie. You're twice as greedy as the average person. Are you telling me you don't want to live longer than everyone else?

Ⓚ: By the way, over at the next table they were doing sales for copyright control systems. (We are at the Cozy Corner in Akasaka Mitsuke).

Ⓢ: Ignore me, will you? :D That's true. They were these music industry types. I'm against copyright control!

Ⓚ: This is me ignoring you. There are too many industry salesperson types here (at Cozy Corner). But thanks to that, it doesn't matter how long we stay here.

Ⓢ: We're in the manga industry, after all.

Ⓚ: Yes, well... It's pretty rare for us to be in Mitsuke. Manga people prefer Zero-Sum in Shinjuku...

Ⓢ: The most interesting manga in the 21st century comes from Shinjuku 2-chome!! Straight up! :D

Ⓚ: From the 8th floor of the No. 3 Tamaya Building!!

Ⓢ: ... in conclusion... When will volume 5 come out?

Ⓚ: 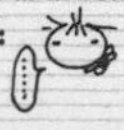 **That's a secret. (...but not too far in the future... *NGH*) A lesson learned from the last time.**

THE END.

Today's Journal by: Kouga Date: Thursday, June 24

TODAY'S NEWS:

TOMORROW AT LAST!!

VOLUME 4 ON SALE!!!

Congratulations!

I'm trudging along on the website too, so come and visit.

www.kokonoe.com

Probably...

TOP 3 THINGS I WANT:

1. A scanner larger than B4 paper

2. Property in Setagaya Ward

3. Scotch tape (I ran out)

TOP 3 FAVORITE:
COUPLES IN VOLUME 4:

1. Yamato and Kouya
   The girl Zeroes

2. Youji and Natsuo
   The baby Zeroes

3. Ritsuka and Soubi
   Our heroes in third place...

TODAY'S REFLECTION

My pages ...

No, I won't say it.

Tomorrow's Journal by:

Sugino

Hello!

...promise you'll write something!

Free Talk:

I've kept you waiting for a long time.
This is volume 4!!
I really hope you enjoy it.
It was a lot of fun for me.
See you again in volume 5.
This has been Yun Kouga.
Signing off.

Today's Journal by: Sugino Date: Friday, June 25

TODAY'S NEWS:

VOLUME 4 ON SALE!!!

...I mean, it is, right?

Because today's the release date!♡

TOP 3 THINGS I WANT:

1. Good **PAGES**
2. A lot of **PAGES**
3. A deadline met for **PAGES**

TOP 3 FAVORITE: DRINKS:

1. Lemorea
   It relaxes me...
2. Oi Ocha
3. Nama Oolong Tea
   CHUG CHUG

TODAY'S REFLECTION

I can't say it. I reflect every day.

WAAAH!!

Tomorrow's Journal by:

Kouga

Hello!

I'm tapped out...

Free Talk:

We're about to reach the main part of Loveless, where things really get good! Look forward to it. I'm going to continue to kick Yun Kouga's butt today and tomorrow.

All the best.

You don't want to see me every day, right? Right?

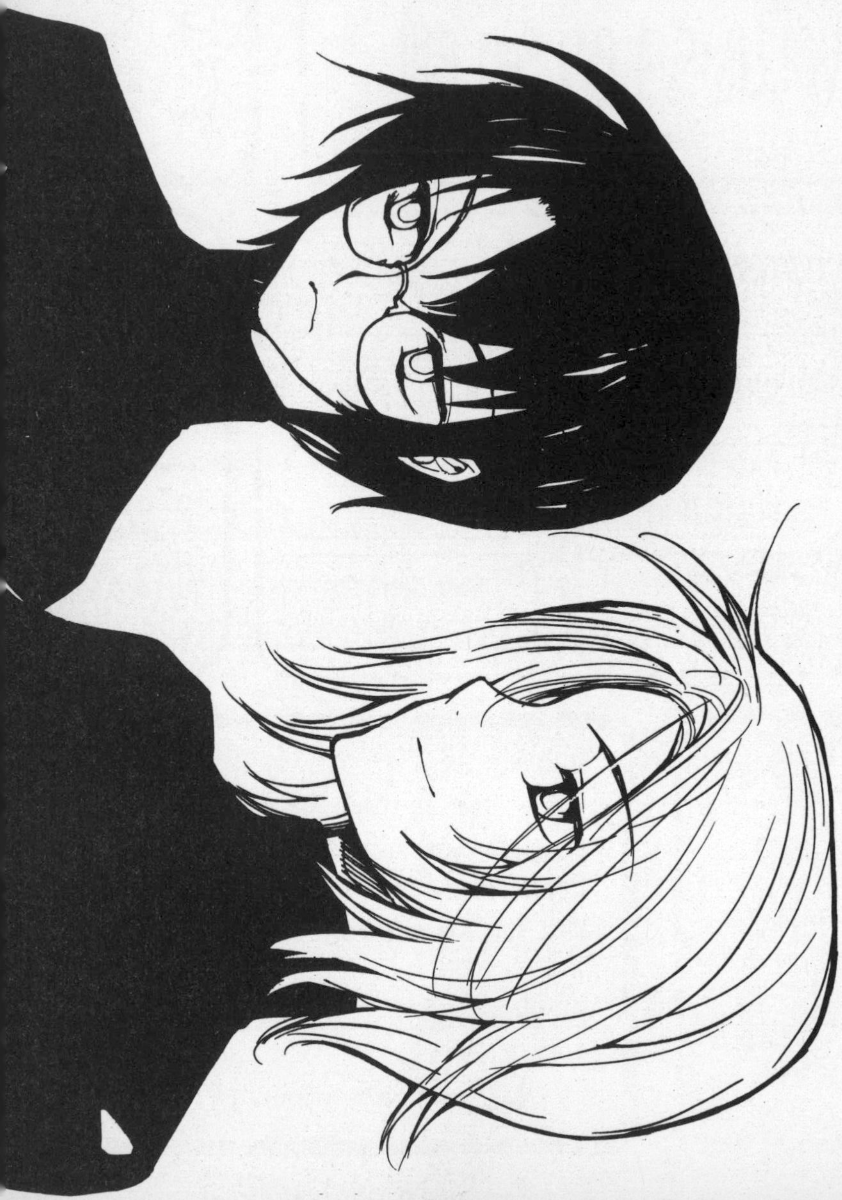

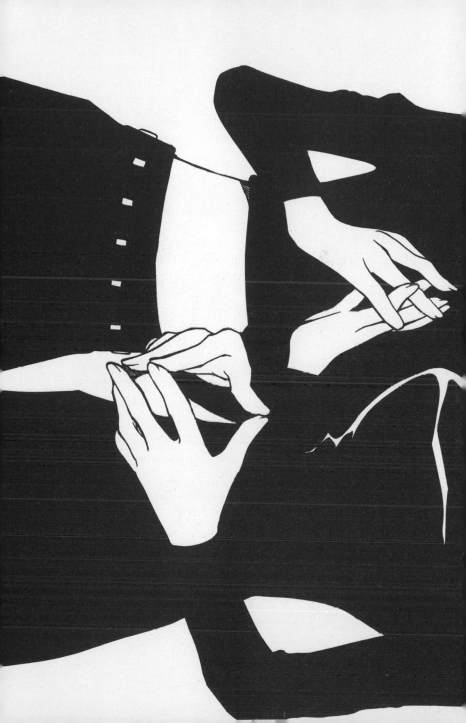

3×4
ENO

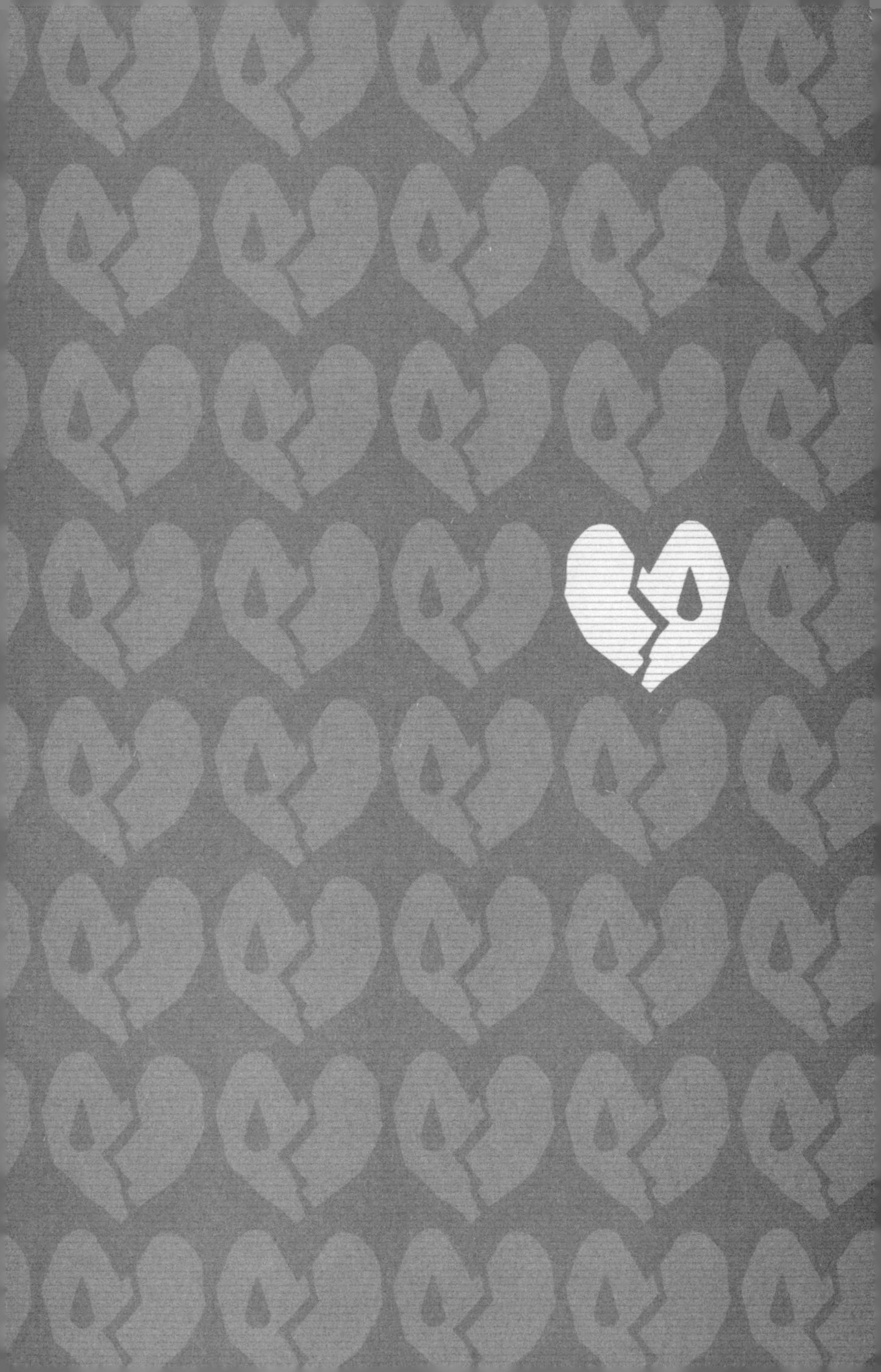

YUN_KOUGA

began her career as a
doujinshi author and
debuted in 1986 with the
original manga *Metal Heart*,
serialized in *Comic VAL*.
She is the creator of the
popular series *Loveless* and
Earthian, along with many
manga and anime projects,
including character design
for *Gundam 00*. Her works
Crown of Love and *Gestalt*
are also published by VIZ.

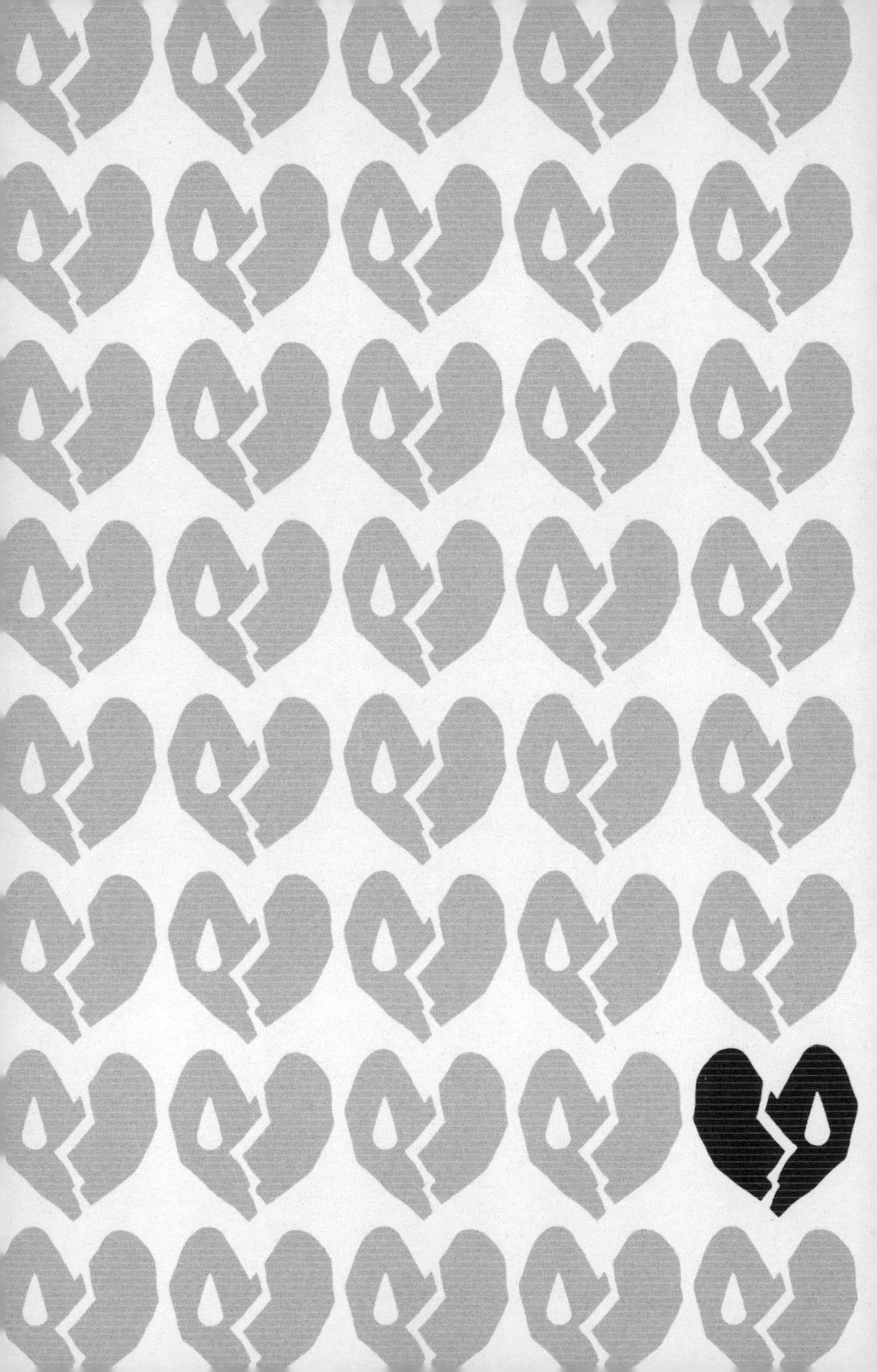

Loveless

Volumes 3 + 4
VIZ Media Edition

Story and Art by YUN KOUGA

Translation // RAY YOSHIMOTO
English Adaptation // LILLIAN DIAZ-PRZYBYL
Touch-Up Art + Lettering // JAMES DASHIELL
Design // FAWN LAU
Editor // HOPE DONOVAN

Original Japanese edition published by ICHIJINSHA, INC., Tokyo.
English translation rights arranged with ICHIJINSHA, INC.

Printed in the U.S.A.

Published by VIZ Media, LLC
P.O. Box 77010
San Francisco, CA 94107

10 9 8 7 6 5 4 3 2
First printing, January 2013
Second printing, August 2015

VIZ media
www.viz.com

RATED T FOR TEEN

PARENTAL ADVISORY
LOVELESS is rated T for Teen and is recommended for ages 13 and up. This volume contains adult situations.
ratings.viz.com

IN THE NEXT VOLUME_5+6

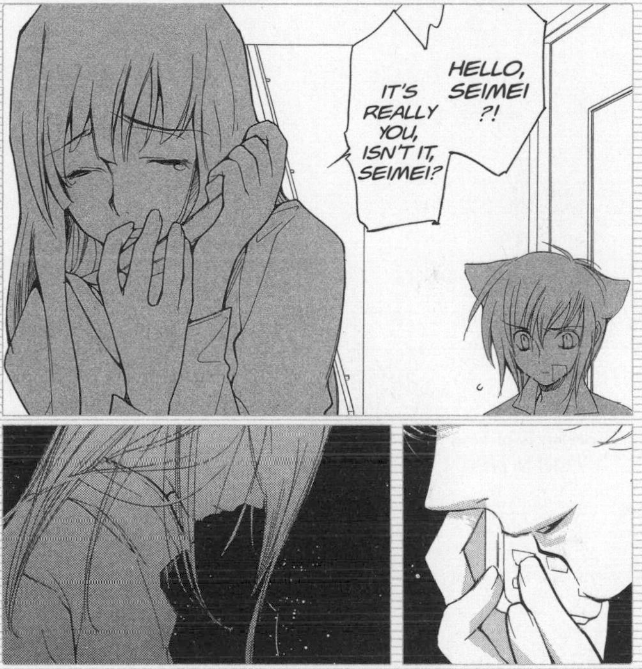
HELLO, SEIMEI?!
IT'S REALLY YOU, ISN'T IT, SEIMEI?

Ritsuka's determination to find answers brings very dire consequences. While Ritsuka is confined at home by his abusive mother, Soubi uncovers a truth about Seimei so shocking that it completely shatters his fragile sense of self.

THIS IS THE END OF THE BOOK.

Loveless is printed from right to left in the original Japanese format
in order to present Yun Kouga's art as it was meant to be seen.